symbolic interaction

Burke, Grammar of
Motives

Symbolic Interaction

a reader in social psychology

2nd edition

JEROME G. MANIS
Western Michigan University

BERNARD N. MELTZER
Central Michigan University

 Allyn and Bacon, Inc., Boston

Contents

PART III. SELF   *229*

PART IV. MIND   *319*

PART V. RESEARCH IMPLICATIONS AND APPLICATIONS *433*

CONCLUSION *575*

Preface
to the second edition

Since the appearance in 1967 of the first edition of this book, we have been gratified by the publication of several other textbooks, monographs, and anthologies with similar orientations.[1] A growing research literature in books and professional journals also attests to the significance and viability of symbolic interactionism, as does the diffusion of this perspective within the disciplines of sociology and social psychology.

Currently, symbolic interactionism can no longer be identified with a few individuals at a few major universities. The articles in this book are representative of the work of a great number of contributors to theory and research. Their efforts, as well as the many more cited in the Selected Bibliography at the close of each Part of the book, are evidence of the widespread prevalence of the symbolic interactionism perspective in American social psychology.

The present edition embodies some important changes from the earlier one. More than a third of the selections are new, and the total number of selections has been increased, along with the total number of pages in the book. We have retained, however, our emphasis on current, significant, and readable materials—both theoretical and empirical. Of greater significance is the inclusion of recent selections from the social psychologies spawned or strongly influenced by symbolic interactionism: ethnomethodology, labeling theory, dramaturgical sociology, and the "sociology of the absurd."[2] These orientations emphasize the active, self-aware nature of human conduct and enjoin those who wish to understand that conduct, whether for scientific or "everyday" reasons, to take the standpoint of the actor. Drawing inspiration from existentialism and phenomenology, as well as from symbolic interactionism, they number among their major progenitors such diverse names as Edmund Husserl and his interpreters,

Alfred Schutz and Maurice Merleau-Ponty; Jean-Paul Sartre and Edward A. Tiryakian; Erving Goffman; and Edwin M. Lemert, along with George Herbert Mead and other classical symbolic interactionists. Representative of the newer orientations are the selections in this book by Arlene Kaplan Daniels (selection 46), Harold Garfinkel (selections 17 and 32), Erving Goffman (selections 20 and 45), George Psathas (selection 9), and Marvin B. Scott and Stanford M. Lyman (selection 36).

The editors herewith acknowledge their special indebtedness to Carl J. Couch, University of Iowa, and John W. Petras, Central Michigan University, who prepared intensive evaluations of the first edition. Their critical comments and suggestions, while as frequently rejected as accepted by us, informed the present edition. We also thank our many other colleagues in the field who appraised the earlier edition for us and who made numerous suggestions for the revised edition. And, finally, we offer our gratitude to Gary L. Folven and Nancy L. Murphy of Allyn and Bacon, Inc., who gave us their painstaking and invaluable assistance in various phases of the production of this book.

J G M

B N M

FOOTNOTES

1. Among these are Herbert Blumer, *Symbolic Interactionism: Perspective and Method* (Englewood Cliffs: Prentice-Hall, Inc., 1969); Alfred R. Lindesmith and Anselm L. Strauss (eds.), *Readings in Social Psychology* (New York: Holt, Rinehart & Winston, Inc., 1969); Peter McHugh, *Defining the Situation: The Organization of Meaning in Social Interaction* (Indianapolis: The Bobbs-Merrill Co., Inc., 1968); Tamotsu Shibutani (ed.), *Human Nature and Collective Behavior: Papers in Honor of Herbert Blumer* (Englewood Cliffs: Prentice-Hall, Inc., 1970); Gregory P. Stone and Harvey A. Farberman (eds.), *Social Psychology Through Symbolic Interaction* (Waltham: Ginn/Blaisdell, 1970).

2. The following books are representative of these approaches: Hans Peter Dreitzel (ed.), *Recent Sociology, No. 2: Patterns of Communicative Behavior* (London: Collier-Macmillan, Ltd., 1970); Jack D. Douglas (ed.), *Understanding Everyday Life: Toward the Reconstruction of Sociological Knowledge* (Chicago: Aldine Publishing Company, 1970); Harold Garfinkel, *Studies in Ethnomethodology* (Englewood Cliffs: Prentice-Hall, Inc., 1967); Erving Goffman, *Interaction Ritual: Essays on Face-to-Face Behavior* (Chicago: Aldine Publishing Company, 1967); Stanford M. Lyman and Marvin B. Scott, *A Sociology of the Absurd* (New York: Appleton-Century-Crofts, 1970); George J. McCall and J. L. Simmons, *Identities and Interactions: An Examination of Human Associations in Everyday Life* (New York: The Free Press, 1966).

Preface

to the first edition

This book is, we believe, the *first* attempt to bring together a sizable number of previously published contributions to symbolic interactionist theory,[1] a theory, or orientation, which has influenced most American sociologists specializing in social psychology.[2]

The historical development of symbolic interactionism has been traced by several writers.[3] Its roots are to be found in the rationalism of John Locke, the foreshadowing of the role-taking process by such "Scottish Moralists" as David Hume and Adam Smith, the idealist epistemology of Kant, and other diverse sources. Its emergence as a distinct perspective in social psychology occurred in the work of John Dewey, Charles Horton Cooley, James Mark Baldwin, William I. Thomas, Florian Znaniecki, and, most notably, George Herbert Mead. Mead, the chief architect of symbolic interactionism, lectured at the University of Chicago between 1893 and 1931, and books based upon lecture-notes taken by students in his classes were published after his death in 1931.[4]

Since then, the two foremost exponents of the orientation have been Herbert G. Blumer and the late Manford H. Kuhn. At the University of Chicago and, currently, the University of California at Berkeley, Blumer has continued to lead what can properly be called the "Chicago school" of symbolic interactionism. Stressing the *processual* character of human behavior and the need for "sympathetic introspection" in the study of human behavior, the school includes most of the writers represented in this book. Kuhn's "self theory," based at the State University of Iowa, has sought to "operationalize" symbolic interactionism by reconceptualizing the self in structural terms, by abandoning such "nonempirical" concepts as Mead's "I," and by developing paper-and-pencil measures of the self.

The organization of the readings in this book is quite simple. Part I introduces the reader to the fundamental concepts, propositions and methods of symbolic interactionism; Parts II, III, and IV organize readings under rubrics corresponding to the words in the title of Mead's vastly influential book. Our transposition of the order of these words more accurately reflects the Meadian emphasis upon the priority of society to the rise of individual selves and minds. Part V gives attention to readings which are less concerned with the explication of concepts than with their applications in exploring a wide range of topics. Following each part is a briefly annotated Selected Bibliography which suggests additional readings for the interested reader.

The introductory comments for each part have been kept brief. By selecting material that would, largely, speak for itself, we have reduced to a minimum the need for editorial comment.

In selecting material for this collection, we were confronted by an embarrassment of riches. Only a small portion of the works we considered worthwhile is included, because of limitations of space. Conspicuous omissions are the writings of Ernst Cassirer, Kurt Riezler, Walter Coutu, and Arnold Rose. What we present to the reader, therefore, aims at representativeness, not comprehensiveness. The criteria guiding our selection of items are several. We have sought a judicious blend of "classics" and more recent works, of speculative and research products. We have given preference to items not readily available to students in multiple copies, to items that would be readable by undergraduate students, and to items by a number of different authors rather than by a few "name" people. In addition, we have tried to avoid fragmentation of selections; articles appear in their entirety, and excerpts from books are self-sufficient units of thought.

A word of explanation is needed about our omission of readings from Mead's works. We considered such readings superfluous for the following reasons: the extensive citations of his thinking in various other selections, the inclusion of a summary of his ideas, and the accessibility of his major ideas in college libraries and bookstores.[5]

This collection is designed, primarily, for use as supplementary reading in courses in social psychology, especially those in which intensive attention is given to symbolic interactionism. Our hopes for the book stress its stimulation, not of doctrinaire devotion, but of critical assessment of that perspective.

We are indebted to the various authors, journals, and publishers out of whose materials we constructed this compilation. In a very real sense, the book is the product of their labors. Both of us also acknowledge the important role played by Herbert Blumer's courses at the University of Chicago in directing our attention and interest to the subject of this book.

FOOTNOTES

1. A book by Rose compiles thirty-four articles written from the standpoint of symbolic interactionism; however, all but nine of these were written specifically for

his book. See Arnold M. Rose (ed.), *Human Behavior and Social Processes* (Boston: Houghton Mifflin Company, 1962).

2. The more widely used social psychology textbooks incorporating symbolic interaction theory have been: E. T. Krueger and Walter C. Reckless, *Social Psychology* (New York: Longmans, Green and Company, 1930); Walter Coutu, *Emergent Human Nature* (New York: Alfred A. Knopf, 1949); Alfred R. Lindesmith and Anselm L. Strauss, *Social Psychology* (New York: The Dryden Press, 1949, revised, 1956); Robert E. L. Faris, *Social Psychology* (New York: The Ronald Press Company, 1952); Hubert Bonner, *Social Psychology* (New York: American Book Company, 1953); Hans Gerth and C. Wright Mills, *Character and Social Structure* (New York: Harcourt, Brace & World, Inc., 1953); Tamotsu Shibutani, *Society and Personality* (Englewood Cliffs: Prentice-Hall, Inc., 1961).

3. See, for example, Fay Berger Karpf, *American Social Psychology* (New York: McGraw-Hill Book Company, 1932), *passim*; Floyd Nelson House, *The Development of Sociology* (McGraw-Hill Book Company, 1936), Chapter 27; Don Martindale, *The Nature and Types of Sociological Theory* (Boston: Houghton Mifflin Company, 1960), Chapter 14.

4. Of most relevance is *Mind, Self and Society* (Chicago: The University of Chicago Press, 1934), edited by Charles W. Morris.

5. Books summarizing Mead's position or including selections from his work abound. See, for example: Grace Chin Lee, *George Herbert Mead* (New York: King's Crown Press, 1945); Paul E. Pfuetze, *The Social Self* (New York: Bookman Associates, 1954); Anselm Strauss (ed.), *George Herbert Mead on Social Psychology* (Chicago: The University of Chicago Press, 1964); Andrew J. Reck (ed.), *Selected Writings: George Herbert Mead* (Indianapolis: The Bobbs-Merrill Co., Inc., 1964).

part I

Theory
& methods

Symbolic interactionism constitutes both a theoretical perspective within social psychology and, in the view of many of its interpreters and critics, a methodological orientation as well. Its concern with the "inner," or phenomenological, aspects of human behavior is considered by them to have both substantive and research-technique implications. The following selections present some of the fundamental concepts and propositions held in common by symbolic interactionists. In addition, they indicate some of the divergent views on how the validity of such theoretical materials can be tested. These views range from a demand for a special methodology that stresses "feeling one's way inside the experience of the actor" to one that coincides with traditional scientific method.

Controversies over theory and method were accentuated during the late nineteenth and early twentieth centuries. During this period, the natural sciences were successful in their efforts to understand, predict, and control the physical world. Such achievements led scholars to examine the distinctiveness of the social world and the applicability of natural-science methods.

Perhaps we can clarify the nature of some of the major ideas at issue by briefly contrasting the antithetical views of George Herbert Mead, exemplar of symbolic interactionism, with those of John B. Watson, founder of the school of behaviorism in psychology. Like Watsonian radical behaviorism, Mead's approach includes the observable actions of individuals; but, unlike the former, it conceives "behavior" in broad enough terms to include *covert* activity. This inclusion is deemed necessary to understanding the distinctive character of human conduct, which Mead considers a qualitatively different emergent from infrahuman behavior. Watson's behaviorism, on the other hand, reduces human behavior to the mechanisms found on the infrahuman level. Thus, while Watson insists upon a strictly "scientific" study of overt behavior, Mead allows for an intuitive, *verstehende* investigation of aspects of behavior excluded from the former's purview.

Today among symbolic interactionists, the debate takes a less extreme form. All agree that the cognitive and affective elements of human conduct must be studied; the point of contention is the extent to which the more "subjective," noncommunicable techniques of study may be used.

A related point of contention concerns the differential importance of social and psychic forces. In its earliest form, this debate centered upon "nature versus nurture"—environment compared to heredity.

This difference in perspective may be illustrated by the polar positions taken by the first two textbooks published, in 1908, under the title *Social Psychology*. Edward A. Ross, a sociologist, viewed the individual as coerced by the social processes of suggestion and imitation. In contrast, William H. McDougall, a psychologist, traced social interaction and institutions to individual "instincts."

While these positions are now considered oversimplified, social psychologists still differ on the relative significance of the individual and society. Symbolic interactionists stress the primacy of society. Yet they are also inclined to consider the individual as an active, creative source of behavior.

Contemporary symbolic interactionists credit Cooley, Dewey, and Mead with the converging interests and contributions responsible for the widespread influence of this perspective. During nearly four decades as a philosopher at the University of Chicago, Mead formulated and taught his developing theory. His approach, which he called "social behaviorism," is summarized in the article by Bernard N. Meltzer. We hope that this resumé of Mead's basic assumptions and concepts will encourage the reader to delve into its major source, *Mind, Self and Society*.

Freud's great contributions to psychiatry, psychology, and sociology permit a valuable benchmark for assessing Mead's work. Guy E. Swanson's comparison reveals some of the similarities and differences in their approaches to social behavior. Even more pertinent to our concern is the critical analysis this comparison generates.

The article by Bernard N. Meltzer and John W. Petras compares and analyzes the divergent perspectives of two leading symbolic interactionists and their students. At the University of Chicago, Herbert Blumer became the "Chicago school's" foremost spokesman, elaborating an interpretive view of human and group phenomena. At the University of Iowa, Manford Kuhn adopted a more positivist position. Both Blumer's and Kuhn's writings are represented in Part I and elsewhere in this book.

Recent developments are the concern of Kuhn's detailed article. The contributions of "self-defined" symbolic interactionists, as well as nonadherents, serve as the basis for his excellent integration of these contemporary achievements.

Although the first four articles focus primarily on substantive theory, the following readings were selected for their methodological emphasis. A central feature of symbolic interactionism is its implication for empirical inquiry. On the premise that "each theory demands a special view of methods," Norman K. Denzin formulates seven methodological principles congruent with the theory.

Blumer's article questions the applicability of conventional methods of variable analysis. His criticisms need to be viewed in conjunction with both his theoretical and broader methodological contributions, such as the leading article in Part II and the first chapter of his recent book, *Symbolic Interaction*. Taken together, the two writings suggest that the nature of man both requires and provides certain essential tools for the study of himself and his society.

Two articles exemplify the research techniques of "Chicago" and "Iowa" researchers: Howard S. Becker and Blanche Geer discuss the distinctive features of participant observation, while Manford H. Kuhn and Thomas S. McPartland introduce the Twenty Statements Test. Later sections, particularly Part V, illustrate the research methods of contemporary symbolic interactionists.

During the 1960s, ethnomethodology has drawn upon and influenced the work of symbolic interactionists. George Psathas compares that perspective with ethnoscience in anthropology and explores the relationship of these ethnomethods to phenomenology. Later articles by Harold Garfinkel, Marvin B. Scott and Stanford M. Lyman, and Arlene Kaplan Daniels illustrate this orientation and its techniques.

Currently, symbolic interactionism can no longer be identified with a few individuals at a few major universities. The articles in this and later sections represent the work of a great number of theorists and researchers. Their efforts, as well as the many more cited in the bibliographies at the close of each part, evidence the widespread prevalence of the symbolic interactionist perspective in American social psychology.

The selections in Part I tend to be of broader scope and higher abstraction than those in other parts of this book, where the selections focus more sharply on explication and empirical testing of important concepts in symbolic interaction theory introduced herein. The reader is advised to refer back to Part I from time to time to place in context various later materials.

1 BERNARD N. MELTZER

Mead's Social Psychology

A. Preliminary Remarks

While Mead's system of Social Psychology is given its fullest exposition in *Mind, Self and Society,* each of three other books(as well as a few articles) rounds out the complete picture.

It should be pointed out at this juncture that Mead himself published no full-length systematic statement of his theory. All four of the books bearing his authorship are posthumously collected and edited works. They comprise a loose accumulation of his lecture notes, fragmentary manuscripts, and tentative drafts of unpublished essays. Since the chief aim of his editors has been completeness—rather than organization—the books consist, in considerable part, of alternative formulations, highly repetitive materials, and sketchily developed ideas.

Nevertheless, a brief description of these volumes is in order, since they constitute the major source-materials concerning Mead's social psychology.

Philosophy of the Present (1932) contains the Paul Carus Foundation lectures delivered by Mead in 1930, a year before his death. These lectures present a philosophy of history from the pragmatist's point of view. Moreover, this volume presents his ideas on the analogous developments of social experience and of scientific hypotheses.

Mind, Self and Society (1934) is chiefly a collection of lectures delivered to his classes in Social Psychology at the University of Chicago.

Movements of Thought in the 19th Century (1936) is largely a collection of lectures delivered to his classes in the History of Ideas.

Philosophy of the Act (1938), according to Paul Schilpp, represents a fairly *systematic* statement of the philosophy of pragmatism. This "systematic" statement I found (as did G. S. Lee) to be made up of essays and miscellaneous fragments, which are technical and repetitious, obscure and difficult.

A final observation regarding the content of these books should be made: Mead's orientation is generally *philosophical*. Rather than marshalling his own empirical evidence, he uses the findings of various sciences and employs frequent apt and insightful illustrations from everyday life. These

Bernard N. Meltzer "Mead's Social Psychology." From *The Social Psychology of George Herbert Mead,* pp. 10–31, 1964, Center for Sociological Research, Western Michigan University.

illustrations usually are not used to provide points, but rather to serve as data to be analyzed in terms of his scheme.

Before launching upon a presentation of Mead's social-psychological theories, it might be wise to explain his designation of his viewpoint as that of "Social Behaviorism." By this term Mead means to refer to the description of behavior at the distinctively human level. Thus, for social behaviorism, the basic datum is the social act. As we shall later see, the study of social acts entails concern with the covert aspects of behavior. Further, the concept of the "social act" implies that human conduct and experience has a fundamental social dimension—that the social context is an inescapable element in distinctively human actions.

Like Watsonian radical behaviorism, Mead's social behaviorism starts with the observable actions of individuals; but *unlike* the former, social behaviorism conceives behavior in broad enough terms to include *covert* activity. This inclusion is deemed necessary to understanding the distinctive character of human conduct, which Mead considers a qualitatively different emergent from infrahuman behavior. Watson's behaviorism, on the other hand, reduces human behavior to the very same mechanisms as are found on the infrahuman level. As a corollary, Watson sees the social dimension of human behavior as merely a sort of external influence upon the individual. Mead, by contrast, views generically human behavior as *social* behavior, human acts as *social* acts. For Mead, both the content and the very existence of distinctively human behavior are accountable only on a social basis. (These distinctions should become more clear in the course of this report.)

It can readily be inferred from this brief explanation of Mead's usage of the term "social behaviorism" that, before we can explore the nature and function of the mind—which Mead considers a uniquely human attribute—supporting theories of society, and of self—another uniquely human attribute—require elaboration. Hence, the natural, logical order of Mead's thinking seems to have been society, self, and mind—rather than "Mind, Self, and Society."

B. *Content of Mead's Social Psychology*

1. SOCIETY

According to Mead, all group life is essentially a matter of cooperative behavior. Mead makes a distinction, however, between infrahuman society and human society. Insects—whose society most closely approximates the complexity of human social life—act together in certain ways because of their biological make-up. Thus, their cooperative behavior is physiologically determined. This is shown by many facts, among which is the fact of the fixity, the stability, of the relationships of insect-society members to one another. Insects, according to the evidence, go on for countless generations without any difference in their patterns of association. This picture of infrahuman society remains essentially valid as one ascends the scale of animal life, until we arrive at the human level.

In the case of human association, the situation is fundamentally different. Human cooperation is not brought about by mere physiological factors. The very diversity of the patterns of human group life makes it quite clear that human cooperative life cannot be explained in the same terms as the cooperative life of insects and the lower animals. The fact that human patterns are not stabilized and cannot be explained in biological terms led Mead to seek another basis of explanation of human association. Such cooperation can only be brought about by some process wherein: (a) each acting individual ascertains the *intention* of the acts of others, and then (b) makes his own response on the basis of that intention. What this means is that, in order for human beings to cooperate, there must be present some sort of mechanism whereby each acting individual: (a) can come to understand the lines of action of others, and (b) can guide his own behavior to fit in with those lines of action. Human behavior is not a matter of responding directly to the activities of others. Rather, it involves responding to the *intentions* of others, *i.e.*, to the future, intended behavior of others— not merely to their present actions.

We can better understand the character of this distinctively human mode of interaction between individuals by contrasting it with the infrahuman "conversation of gestures." For example when a mother hen clucks, her chicks will respond by running to her. This does not imply however, that the hen clucks *in order* to guide the chicks, *i.e.*, with the *intention* of guiding them. Clucking is a natural sign or signal—rather than a significant (meaningful) symbol—as it is not meaningful to the hen. That is, the hen (according to Mead) does not take the role, or viewpoint, of the chicks toward its own gesture and respond to it, in imagination, as they do. The hen does not envision the response of the chicks to her clucking. Thus, hens and chicks do not share the same experience.

Let us take another illustration by Mead: Two hostile dogs, in the pre-fight stage, may go through an elaborate conversation of gestures (snarling, growling, baring fangs, walking stiff-leggedly around one another, etc.). The dogs are adjusting themselves to one another by responding to one another's gestures. (A gesture is that portion of an act which represents the entire act; it is the initial, overt phase of the act, which epitomizes it, *e.g.*, shaking one's fist at someone.) Now, in the case of the dogs the response to a gesture is dictated by pre-established tendencies to respond in certain ways. Each gesture leads to a direct, immediate, automatic, and unreflecting response by the recipient of the gesture (the other dog). Neither dog responds to the *intention* of the gestures. Further, each dog does not make his gestures with the intent of eliciting certain responses in the other dog. Thus, animal interaction is devoid of conscious, deliberate meaning.

To summarize: Gestures, at the non-human or non-linguistic level, do not carry the connotation of conscious meaning or intent, but serve merely as cues for the appropriate responses of others. Gestural communication takes place immediately, without any interruption of the act, without the mediation of a definition or meaning. Each organism adjusts "instinctively" to the other; it does not stop and figure out which response it will give. Its behavior is, largely, a series of direct automatic responses to stimuli.

Human beings, on the other hand, respond to one another on the basis of the intentions or meanings of gestures. This renders the gesture *symbolic*, i.e., the gesture becomes a symbol to be interpreted; it becomes something which, in the imaginations of the participants, stands for the entire act.

Thus, individual A begins to act, i.e., makes a gesture: for example, he draws back an arm. Individual B (who perceives the gesture) completes, or fills in, the act in his imagination; i.e., B imaginatively projects the gesture into the future: "He will strike me." In other words, B perceives what the gesture stands for, thus getting its meaning. In contrast to the direct responses of the chicks and the dogs, the human being inserts an interpretation between the gesture of another and his response to it. Human behavior involves responses to *interpreted* stimuli.[1]

We see, then, that people respond to one another on the basis of imaginative activity. In order to engage in concerted behavior, however, each participating individual must be able to attach the same meaning to the same gesture. Unless interacting individuals interpret gestures similarly, unless they fill out the imagined portion in the same way, there can be no cooperative action. This is another way of saying what has by now become a truism in sociology and social psychology: Human society rests upon a basis of *consensus*, i.e., the sharing of meanings in the form of common understandings and expectations.

In the case of the human being, each person has the ability to respond to his own gestures; and thus, it is possible to have the same meaning for the gestures as other persons. (For example: As I say "chair," I present to myself the same image as to my hearer; moreover, the same image as when someone else says "chair.") This ability to stimulate oneself as one stimu-

---

[1] The foregoing distinctions can also be expressed in terms of the differences between "signs," or "signals," and symbols. A sign stands for something else because of the fact that it is present at approximately the same time and place with that "something else." A symbol, on the other hand, stands for something else because its users have agreed to let it stand for that "something else." Thus, signs are directly and intrinsically linked with present or proximate situations; while symbols, having arbitrary and conventional, rather than intrinsic, meanings, transcend the immediate situation. (We shall return to this important point in our discussion of "mind.") Only symbols, of course, involve interpretation, self-stimulation and shared meaning.

lates another, and to respond to oneself as another does, Mead ascribes largely to man's vocal-auditory mechanism. (The ability to hear oneself implies at least the potentiality for responding to oneself.) When a gesture has a shared, common meaning, when it is—in other words—a *linguistic* element, we can designate it as a "significant symbol." (Take the words, "Open the window": the pattern of action symbolized by these words must be in the mind of the speaker as well as the listener. Each must respond, in imagination, to the words in the same way. The speaker must have an image of the listener responding to his words by opening the window, and the listener must have an image of his opening the window.)

The imaginative completion of an act—which Mead calls "meaning" and which represents mental activity—necessarily takes place through *role-taking*. To complete imaginatively the total act which a gesture stands for, the individual must put himself in the position of the other person, must identify with him. The earliest beginnings of role-taking occur when an already established act of another individual is stopped short of completion, thereby requiring the observing individual to fill in, or complete, the activity imaginatively. (For example, a crying infant may have an image of its mother coming to stop its crying.)

As Mead points out, then, the relation of human beings to one another arises from the developed ability of the human being to respond to his own gestures. This ability enables different human beings to respond in the same way to the same gesture, thereby sharing one another's experience.

This latter point is of great importance. Behavior is viewed as "social" not simply when it is a response to others, but rather when it has incorporated in it the behavior of others. The human being responds to himself as other persons respond to him, and in so doing he imaginatively shares the conduct of others. That is, in imagining their response he shares that response.[2]

2. SELF

To state that the human being can respond to his own gestures necessarily implies that he possesses a *self*. In referring to the human being as having a self, Mead simply means that such an individual may act socially toward himself, just as toward others. He may praise, blame, or encourage himself; he may become disgusted with himself, may seek to punish himself, and so forth. Thus, the human being may become the object of his own actions. The self is formed in the same way as other objects—through the "definitions" made by others.

[2] To anyone who has taken even one course in sociology it is probably superfluous to stress the importance of symbols, particularly language, in the acquisition of all other elements of culture. The process of socialization is essentially a process of symbolic interaction.

The mechanism whereby the individual becomes able to view himself as an object is that of role-taking, involving the process of communication, especially by vocal gestures or speech. (Such communication necessarily involves role-taking.) It is only by taking the role of others that the individual can come to see himself as an object. The standpoint of others provides a platform for getting outside oneself and thus viewing oneself. The development of the self is concurrent with the development of the ability to take roles.

The crucial importance of language in this process must be under-scored. It is through language (significant symbols) that the child acquires the meanings and definitions of those around him. By learning the symbols of his groups, he comes to internalize their definitions of events or things, including their definitions of his own conduct.

It is quite evident that, rather than assuming the existence of selves and explaining society thereby, Mead starts out from the prior existence of society as the context within which selves arise. This view contrasts with the nominalistic position of the Social Contract theorists and of various individualistic psychologies.

Genesis of the Self. The relationship between role-playing and various stages in the development of the self is described below:

1. *Preparatory Stage* (not explicitly named by Mead, but inferable from various fragmentary essays). This stage is one of meaningless imitation by the infant (for example, "reading" the newspaper). The child does certain things that others near it do without any understanding of what he is doing. Such imitation, however, implies that the child is incipiently taking the roles of those around it, *i.e.*, is on the verge of putting itself in the position of others and acting like them.

2. *Play Stage.* In this stage the actual playing of roles occurs. The child plays mother, teacher, storekeeper, postman, streetcar conductor, Mr. Jones, etc. What is of central importance in such play-acting is that it places the child in the position where it is able to act back toward itself in such roles as "mother" or "teacher." In this stage, then, the child first begins to form a self, that is, to direct activity toward itself—and it does so by taking the roles of others. This is clearly indicated by use of the third person in referring to oneself instead of the first person: "John wants . . .," "John is a bad boy."

   However, in this stage the young child's configuration of roles is unstable; the child passes from one role to another in unorganized, inconsistent fashion. He has, as yet, no unitary standpoint from which to view himself, and hence, he has no unified conception of himself. In other words, the child forms a number of separate and discrete objects of itself, depending on the roles in which it acts toward itself.

3. *Game Stage.* This is the "completing" stage of the self. In time, the child finds himself in situations wherein he must take a number of roles simultaneously. That is, he must respond to the expectations of several people at the same time. This sort of situation is exemplified by the game of baseball—to use Mead's own illustration. Each player must visualize the intentions and expectations of several other players. In such situations the child must take the roles of groups of individuals as over against particular roles. The child becomes enabled to do this by abstracting a "composite" role out of the concrete roles of particular persons. In the course of his association with others, then, he builds up a *generalized other*, a generalized role or standpoint from which he views himself and his behavior. This generalized other represents, then, the set of standpoints which are common to the group.

Having achieved this generalized standpoint, the individual can conduct himself in an organized, consistent manner. He can view himself from a consistent standpoint. This means, then, that the individual can transcend the local and present expectations and definitions with which he comes in contact. An illustration of this point would be the Englishman who "dresses for dinner" in the wilds of Africa. Thus, through having a generalized other, the individual becomes emancipated from the pressures of the peculiarities of the immediate situation. He can act with a certain amount of consistency in a variety of situations because he acts in accordance with a generalized set of expectations and definitions that he has internalized.

The "I" and the "Me." The self is essentially a social process within the individual involving two analytically distinguishable phases: The "I" and the "Me."

The "I" is the impulsive tendency of the individual. It is the initial, spontaneous, unorganized aspect of human experience. Thus, it represents the undirected tendencies of the individual.

The "Me" represents the incorporated other within the individual. Thus, it comprises the organized set of attitudes and definitions, understandings and expectations—or simply meanings—common to the group. In any given situation, the "Me" comprises the generalized other and, often, some particular other.

Every act begins in the form of an "I" and usually ends in the form of the "Me." For the "I" represents the initiation of the act prior to its coming under control of the definitions or expectations of others (the "Me"). The "I" thus gives *propulsion* while the "Me" gives *direction* to the act. Human behavior, then, can be viewed as a perpetual series of initiations of acts by the "I" and of acting-back-upon the act (that is, guidance of the act) by the "Me." The act is a resultant of this interplay.

The "I," being spontaneous and propulsive, offers the potentiality for new, creative activity. The "Me," being regulatory, disposes the individual to both goal-directed activity and conformity. In the operation of these aspects of the self, we have the basis for, on the one hand, social control and, on the other, novelty and innovation. We are thus provided with a basis for understanding the mutuality of the relationship between the individual and society.[3]

Implications of Selfhood. Some of the major implications of selfhood in human behavior are as follows:

1. The possession of a self makes of the individual a society in miniature. That is, he may engage in interaction with himself just as two or more different individuals might. In the course of this interaction, he can come to view himself in a new way, thereby bringing about changes in himself.
2. The ability to act toward oneself makes possible an inner experience which need not reach overt expression. That is, the individual, by virtue of having a self, is thereby endowed with the possibility of having a mental life: He can make indications to himself—which constitutes *mind*.
3. The individual with a self is thereby enabled to direct and control his behavior. Instead of being subject to all impulses and stimuli directly playing upon him, the individual can check, guide, and organize his behavior. He is, then, *not* a mere passive agent.

All three of these implications of selfhood may be summarized by the statement that the self and the mind (mental activity) are twin emergents in the social process.

[3] At first glance, Mead's "I" and "Me" may appear to bear a close affinity with Freud's concepts of Id, Ego, and Superego. The resemblance is, for the most part, more apparent than real. While the Superego is held to be harshly frustrating and repressive of the instinctual, libidinous, and aggressive Id, the "Me" is held to provide necessary direction—often of a *gratifying* nature—to the otherwise undirected impulses constituting the "I." Putting the matter in figurative terms: Freud views the Id and the Superego as locked in combat upon the battleground of the Ego; Mead sees the "I" and "Me" engaged in close collaboration. This difference in perspective may derive from different preoccupations: Freud was primarily concerned with tension, anxiety, and "abnormal" behavior; Mead was primarily concerned with behavior generically.

It is true, on the other hand, that the Id, Ego, and Superego—particularly as modified by such neo-Freudians as Karen Horney, Erich Fromm, and H. S. Sullivan—converge at a few points with the "I" and "Me." This is especially evident in the emphasis of both the Superego and "Me" concepts upon the internalization of the norms of significant others through the process of identification, or role-taking.

Incidentally, it should be noted that both sets of concepts refer to processes of behavior, *not* to concrete entities or structures. See, also, the discussion of "mind" which follows.

3. MIND

Development of Mind. As in the instance of his consideration of the self, Mead rejects individualistic psychologies, in which the social process (society, social interaction) is viewed as presupposing, and being a product of, mind. In direct contrast is his view that mind presupposes, and is a product of, the social process. Mind is seen by Mead as developing correlatively with the self, constituting (in a very important sense) the self in action.

Mead's hypothesis regarding mind (as regarding the self) is that the mental emerges out of the organic life of man through communication. The mind is present only at certain points in human behavior, *viz.*, when significant symbols are being used by the individual. This view dispenses with the substantive notion of mind as existing as a box-like container in the head, or as some kind of fixed, ever-present entity. Mind is seen as a *process*, which manifests itself whenever the individual is interacting with himself by using significant symbols.

Mead begins his discussion of the mind with a consideration of the relation of the organism to its environment. He points out that the central principle in all organic behavior is that of continuous adjustment, or adaptation, to an environing field. We cannot regard the environment as having a fixed character for all organisms, as being the same for all organisms. All behavior involves selective attention and perception. The organism accepts certain events in its field, or vicinity, as stimuli and rejects or overlooks certain others as irrelevant to its needs. (For example, an animal battling for life ignores food.) Bombarded constantly by stimuli, the organism selects those stimuli or aspects of its field which pertain to, are functional to, the acts in which the organism is engaged. Thus, the organism has a hand in determining the nature of its environment. What this means, then, is that Mead, along with Dewey, regards all life as ongoing activity, and views stimuli—not as initiators of activity—but as elements selected by the organism in the furtherance of that activity.

Perception is thus an activity that involves selective attention to certain aspects of a situation, rather than a mere matter of something coming into the individual's nervous system and leaving an impression. Visual perception, *e.g.*, is more than a matter of just opening one's eyes and responding to what falls on the retina.

The determination of the environment by the biologic individual (infrahumans and the unsocialized infant) is not a cognitive relationship. It is selective, but does not involve consciousness, in the sense of reflective intelligence. At the distinctively human level, on the other hand, there is a hesitancy, an inhibition of overt conduct, which is *not* involved in the selective attention of animal behavior. In this period of inhibition, mind is present.

For human behavior involves inhibiting an act and trying out the varying approaches in imagination. In contrast, as we have seen, the acts of the biologic individual are relatively immediate, direct, and made up of innate or habitual ways of reacting. In other words, the unsocialized organism lacks consciousness of meaning. This being the case, the organism has no means for the abstract analysis of its field when new situations are met, and hence no means for the reorganization of action-tendencies in the light of that analysis.[4]

Minded behavior (in Mead's sense) arises around problems. It represents, to repeat an important point, a temporary inhibition of action wherein the individual is attempting to prevision the future. It consists of presenting to oneself, tentatively and in advance of overt behavior, the different possibilities or alternatives of future action with reference to a given situation. The future is, thus, present in terms of images of prospective lines of action from which the individual can make a selection. The mental process is, then, one of delaying, organizing, and selecting a response to the stimuli of the environment. This implies that the individual *constructs* his act, rather than responding in predetermined ways. Mind makes it possible for the individual purposively to control and organize his responses. Needless to say, this view contradicts the stimulus-response conception of human behavior.

When the act of an animal is checked, it may engage in overt trial and error or random activity. In the case of blocked human acts, the trial and error may be carried on covertly, implicitly. Consequences can be imaginatively "tried out" in advance. This is what is primarily meant by "mind," "reflective thinking," or "abstract thinking."

What this involves is the ability to indicate elements of the field or situation, abstract them from the situation, and recombine them so that procedures can be considered in advance of their execution. Thus, to quote a well-known example, the intelligence of the detective as over against the intelligence of the bloodhound lies in the capacity of the former to isolate and indicate (to himself and to others) what the particular characters are which will call out the response of apprehending the fugitive criminal.

The mind is social in both origin and function. It arises in the social process of communication. Through association with the members of his groups, the individual comes to internalize the definitions transmitted to him through linguistic symbols, learns to assume the perspectives of others,

---

[4] The reader should recognize here, in a new guise, our earlier distinction between signs and symbols. Signs have "intrinsic" meanings which induce direct reactions; symbols have arbitrary meanings which require interpretations by the actor prior to his response or action. The former, it will be recalled, are "tied to" the immediate situation, while the latter "transcend" the immediate situation. Thus, symbols may refer to past or future events, to hypothetical situations, to nonexistent or imaginary objects, and so forth.

and thereby acquires the ability to think. When the mind has risen in this process, it operates to maintain and adjust the individual in his society; and it enables the society to persist. The persistence of a human society depends, as we have seen, upon consensus; and consensus necessarily entails minded behavior.

The mind is social in function in the sense that the individual continually indicates to himself in the role of others and controls his activity with reference to the definitions provided by others. In order to carry on thought, he must have some standpoint from which to converse with himself. He gets this standpoint by importing into himself the roles of others.

By "taking the role of the other," as I earlier pointed out, we can see ourselves as others see us, and arouse in ourselves the responses that we call out in others. It is this conversation with ourselves, between the representation of the other (in the form of the "Me") and our impulses (in the form of the "I") that constitutes the mind. Thus, what the individual actually does in minded behavior is to carry on an internal conversation. By addressing himself from the standpoint of the generalized other, the individual has a universe of discourse, a system of common symbols and meanings, with which to address himself. These are presupposed as the context for minded behavior.

Mead holds, then, that mental activity is a peculiar type of activity that goes on in the experience of the person. The activity is that of the person responding to himself, of indicating things to himself.

To repeat, mind originates in the social process, in association with others. There is little doubt that human beings lived together in groups before mind ever evolved. But there emerged, because of certain biological developments, the point where human beings were able to respond to their own acts and gestures. It was at this point that mind, or minded behavior, emerged. Similarly, mind comes into existence for the individual at the point where the individual is capable of responding to his own behavior, *i.e.*, where he can designate things to himself.

Summarizing this brief treatment of mind, mental activity, or reflective thinking, we may say that it is a matter of making indications of meanings to oneself as to others. This is another way of saying that mind is the process of using significant symbols. For thinking goes on when an individual uses a symbol to call out in himself the responses which others would make. Mind, then, is symbolic behavior.[5] As such, mind is an emergent

---

[5] A growing number of linguists, semanticists, and students of speech disorders are becoming aware of the central role of symbols in the *content*, as well as the process of thought. Edward Sapir and Benjamin Whorf have formulated "the principle of linguistic relativity," which holds that the structure of a language influences the manner in which the users of the language will perceive, comprehend, and act toward reality. Wendell Johnson, in the field of semantics, and Kurt Goldstein, in the study of aphasia, are representative investigators who have recognized the way in which symbols structure perception and thought. Mead's theory clearly foreshadows these developments.

from non-symbolic behavior and is fundamentally irreducible to the stimulus-response mechanisms which characterize the latter form of behavior.

It should be evident that Mead avoids both the behavioristic fallacy of reduction and the individualistic fallacy of taking for granted the phenomenon that is to be explained.

Objects. Returning to Mead's discussion of the organism-in-environment, we can now give more explicit attention to his treatment of *objects.* As we have seen, we cannot regard the environment as having a fixed character for all organisms. The environment is a function of the animal's own character, being greatly determined by the make-up of the animal. Each animal largely selects its own environment. It selects out the stimuli toward which it acts, its make-up and on-going activity determining the kinds of stimuli it will select. Further, the qualities which are possessed by the objects toward which the animal acts arise from the kind of experiences that the animal has with the objects. (To illustrate, grass is not the same phenomenon for a cat and for a cow.) The environment and its qualities, then, are always functional to the structure of the animal.

As one passes on to the human level, the relation of the individual to the world becomes markedly more complicated. This is so because the human being is capable of forming objects. Animals, lacking symbols, see stimuli, such as patches of color—not objects. An object has to be detached, pointed out, "imaged" to oneself. The human being's environment is constituted largely by objects.

Now, let us look at the relation of the individual to objects. An object represents a plan of action. That is, an object doesn't exist for the individual in some pre-established form. Perception of any object has telescoped in it a series of experiences which one would have if he carried out the plan of action toward that object. The object has no qualities for the individual, aside from those which would result from his carrying out a plan of action. In this respect, the object is constituted by one's activities with reference to it. (For example, chalk is the sum of qualities which are perceived as a result of one's actions: a hard, smooth, white writing implement.)

The objects which constitute the "effective environment," the individual's experienced environment, are established by the individual's activities. To the extent that his activity varies, his environment varies. In other words, objects change as activities toward them change. (Chalk, for instance, may become a missile.)

Objects, which are constituted by the activities of the human individual, are largely *shared* objects. They stand for common patterns of activity of individuals. This is true, Mead points out, by virtue of the fact that objects arise, and are present in experience, only in the process of being indicated to oneself (and, hence, explicitly or implicitly, to others). In other words, the perspective from which one indicates an object implicates definitions by others. Needless to say, these definitions involve language, or significant symbols. The individual acquires a commonality of perspective with others by learning the symbols by which they designate aspects of the world.[6]

4. THE ACT

All human activity other than reflex and habitual action is built up in the process of its execution; *i.e.,* behavior is constructed as it goes along, for decisions must be made at several points. The significance of this fact is that people act—rather than merely react.

For Mead, the unit of study is "the act," which comprises both overt and covert aspects of human action. Within the act, all the separated categories of the traditional, orthodox psychologies find a place. Attention, perception, imagination, reasoning, emotion, and so forth, are seen as parts of the act—rather than as more or less extrinsic influences upon it. Human behavior presents itself in the form of acts, rather than of concatenations of minute responses.

The act, then, encompasses the total process involved in human activity. It is viewed as a complete span of action: Its initial point is an impulse and its terminal point some objective which gives release to the impulse. In between, the individual is in the process of constructing, organizing his behavior. It is during this period that the act undergoes its most significant phase of development. In the case of human behavior, this period is marked by the play of images of possible goals or lines of action upon the impulse, thus directing the activity to its consummation.

In pointing out that the act begins with an impulse, Mead means that organisms experience disturbances of equilibrium. In the case of the lower animals, their biological make-up channelizes the impulse toward appropriate goals. In the case of the human being, the mere presence of an impulse leads to nothing but mere random, unorganized activity. This is most clearly—but definitely not exclusively—seen in the instance of the behavior of infants. Until the defining actions of others set up goals for it, the human infant's behavior is unchannelized. It is the function of images to direct, organize and construct this activity. The presence in behavior of images implies, of course, a process of indicating to oneself, or mind.

The act may have a short span (*e.g.,* attending a particular class

---

[6] The contrast between this view of learning and the neo-behavioristic "learning theory" of Clark Hull and other psychologists should be clearly evident. Basically, learning theorists attempt to reduce human learning to the mechanisms found in infrahuman learning. This is reflected in their tendency to ignore the role of linguistic symbols in human behavior, their conceptualization of human activity in terms of stimulus-response couplets, and their view of learning as equivalent with conditioning. (For an excellent critique of learning theory from the symbolic interactionist standpoint, see: Manford H. Kuhn, "Kinsey's View of Human Behavior," *Social Problems*, 1 (April 1954), pp. 119–125.

meeting, or starting a new page of notes) or may involve the major portion of a person's life (*e.g.*, trying to achieve a successful career). Moreover, acts are parts of an interlacing of previous acts, and are built up, one upon another. This is in contradistinction to the view that behavior is a series of discrete stimulus-response bonds. Conceiving human behavior in terms of acts, we become aware of the necessity for viewing any particular act within its psychosocial context.[7]

Using the concept of the act, Mead sets up classes of acts—the automatic act, the blocked act, the incomplete act, and the retrospective act— and analyzes them in terms of his frame of reference. Space does not permit presentation of these intriguing analyses.

C. Summary

At several points in this report the reader must have been aware of the extremely closely interwoven character of Mead's various concepts. In the discussions of society, of self, and of mind, certain ideas seemed to require frequent (and, perhaps, repetitious) statement. A brief summary of Mead's position may help to reveal more meaningfully the way in which his key concepts interlock and logically imply one another.

The human individual is born into a society characterized by *symbolic interaction*. The use of *significant symbols* by those around him enables him to pass from the conversation of gestures—which involves direct, unmeaningful response to the overt acts of others—to the occasional *taking of the roles* of others. This role-taking enables him to share the perspectives of others. Concurrent with role-taking, the *self* develops, *i.e.*, the capacity to act toward oneself. Action toward oneself comes to take the form of viewing oneself from the standpoint, or perspective, of the *generalized other* (the composite representative of others, of society, within

---

[7] The reader may have noted that this discussion makes no explicit reference to the problem of motivation. Mead had little to say regarding motives. Adherents to his general orientation have tended either to regard motives as implicit in the concept of *object* ("a plan of action") or to consider them "mere" verbal labels offered in supposed explanation of the actions of oneself or of others.

In my judgment, a conception of motivation can be formulated that is both useful and consistent with Mead's theories. Motivation can refer to "a process of defining (symbolically, of course) the goal of an act." Thus, while both human and infrahuman behavior may be viewed as goal-directed, only human behavior would be considered "motivated." Just as "motive" would be restricted to the human level, "drive" might serve a comparable function on the infrahuman level.

This would not imply that motives lie back of, or "cause," human acts. Rather, human acts are in constant process of construction, and the goal-definitions by individuals undergo constant reformulation. I mean to designate by "motive," however, the definition the individual makes, *at any given time*, of the objectives of his own specific acts. Such definitions, obviously, would be socially derived.

the individual), which implies defining one's behavior in terms of the expectations of others. In the process of such viewing of oneself, the individual
must carry on symbolic interaction with himself, involving an internal conversation beween his impulsive aspect (the "I") and the incorporated perspectives of others (the "Me"). The *mind*, or mental activity, is present in
behavior whenever such symbolic interaction goes on—whether the individual is merely "thinking" (in the everyday sense of the word) or is also
interacting with another individual. (In both cases the individual must indicate things to himself.) Mental activity necessarily involves *meanings*,
which usually attach to, and define, *objects*. The meaning of an object or
event is simply an image of the pattern of action which defines the object or
event. That is, the completion in one's imagination of an act, or the mental
picture of the actions and experiences symbolized by an object, defines the
act or the object. In the unit of study that Mead calls "the *act*," all of the
foregoing processes are usually entailed. The concluding point to be made
in this summary is the same as the point with which I began: Mead's concepts intertwine and mutually imply one another. To drive home this important point, I must emphasize that human society (characterized by
symbolic interaction) both precedes the rise of individual selves and minds,
and is maintained by the rise of individual selves and minds. This means,
then, that symbolic interaction is both the medium for the development of
human beings and the process by which human beings associate as human beings.

Finally, it should be clearly evident by now that any distinctively human act necessarily involves: symbolic interaction, role-taking, meaning,
mind, and self. Where one of these concepts is involved, the others are, also,
necessarily involved. Here we see, unmistakably, the organic unity of
Mead's position.

D. Critique

In criticizing Mead's social psychology, it should be borne in mind that he
gave his position no extended systematic write-up; that most of the published material which forms the basis of our knowledge of that position
was not originally intended for publication, at least not in the form in which
it has been printed; and that the various alternative statements of that position that appear in his posthumous works sometimes carry conflicting par-
ticulars. Still, we can evaluate only on the basis of the available, published
materials.

1.   Many of Mead's major concepts are somewhat vague and "fuzzy," ne-
cessitating an "intuitive" grasp of their meaning. This vagueness stems,
I believe, primarily from two sources: (1) the fragmentary and alternative

formulations of his idea; and (2) his emergent view of human conduct, which inescapably entangles him in the necessity of striking a balance between the continuity of infrahuman and human behavior, on the one hand, and the novelty of human behavior, on the other.

(a) For example, the exact nature of "impulses" is not clearly specified. Whether impulses are biological in character, or can also be socially derived, is not clear from Mead's exposition. However, the contexts in which the term sometimes appears suggest that the latter interpretation would be more valid and useful.

(b) Similarly, the intertwined concepts of "meaning" and of "mind" are not consistently employed. At times, these terms are used generically, applying to both infrahuman and human levels of behavior, and at times specifically, applying only at the level of self-conscious human conduct. Fortunately, the context of each usage usually provides a key to Mead's intended meanings.

(c) Coincident with Mead's varying referents of "mind" and of "meaning," we find his vacillation between a restriction of role-taking ability to the human level (in symbolic interaction) and his granting of that ability to infrahuman animals (in the conversation of gestures). Again, we are fortunate in having his distinction between self-conscious role-playing and unwitting role-playing. The reader of Mead must bear in mind that the latter type of "role-playing" is *not* what Mead usually has in mind when he employs the concept.

(d) The concept of the "I," as William Kolb indicates, represents a vaguely-defined residual category. Mead clearly specifies the nature of the "Me," but in effect, labels the "I" as simply the not-Me aspect of the self. As in the case of the very closely related concept of "impulse," Mead does not indicate the limits of the "I." From his discussion, the "I" would seem, however—and this is an inference—to include everything from biological urges to the effects of individual variations in life-history patterns. Still, as Barnes and Becker point out, the "I" serves the very useful purpose of evading a complete collective, or sociological, determinism of human conduct.

The ambiguity of the concept of the "I" also reveals itself in the various discussions in the secondary literature on Mead's treatment of habitual behavior. For some writers, habitual acts represent manifestations of the operation of the "I" alone; for others, of the "Me" alone; and for still others, a fusion of the "I" and the "Me."

(e) The concept of "self" also lacks clear, unambiguous definition in Mead's work. A certain amount of confusion enters the picture when the self is defined in terms of "the individual's viewing himself as an object." This confusion is not at all dissipated by Mead's tendency to vary between, on the one hand, synonymous usages of "self" and "self-consciousness" and on the other hand, slightly different usages of these two terms.

(f) Mead's concept of the "generalized other" needs sharpening. He oversimplifies the concept by assuming, apparently, a single, universal generalized other for the members of each society—rather than a variety of generalized others (even for the same individuals), at different levels of generality.[8] The inadequacy of this concept is clearly shown in his characterization of the criminal as one who "has not taken on the attitude of the generalized other toward property, (and who therefore) lacks a completely developed self." Such a characterization overlooks, of course, the sociogenic elements in crime causation.

(g) A final case of vagueness of conceptualization that we shall consider relates to Mead's usages of "object" and "image." Both of these are described as "telescoped acts," and both are used at times interchangeably and at times slightly differently. It is probably safe to infer that images are the mental representations of objects, *i.e.*, that images are the imaginative projections of the acts which define objects.

Other sources of ambiguity lie in Mead's varying uses of the concepts of "attitude," "gesture," and "symbol"; his vacillation between, on the one hand, ascribing objects and images to the infrahuman level of behavior and, on the other hand, denying them to that level; etc. All of these ambiguities and inconsistencies reflect chiefly the confusion engendered by publication of all the alternative formulations of Mead's ideas—the early formulations along with the later. The thoughtful and assiduous reader of Mead, however, should be able to abstract out some single, fairly consistent statement of Mead's position.

2. A second series of adverse criticisms centers around certain broad substantive omissions in Mead's theory.

(a) Mead's position, as Blumer states, constitutes a purely analytical scheme, which lacks content. That is, he presents an analysis of human conduct in terms of the mechanisms of development of such conduct, but indicates few ingredients of that conduct. In concerning himself wholly with process but not content, with the "how" but not the "why" of conduct, he provides no basis for explaining specific behaviors. For example, he gives no clues as to why one object rather than another will be formed by an individual or group. Thus, his scheme, as it stands, has no explanatory value with reference to such matters as the rise of particular popular heroes, or the high valuation of money, or the myth of Santa Claus.

(b) Related to this "error" of omission is Mead's virtual ignoring of the role of affective elements in the rise of the self and in social interaction

---

[8] Current work on "reference groups" has served to remedy this deficiency. True, several competing definitions of this concept are extant. I have in mind, however, the conception of reference groups as collections of "significant others," that is, of persons with whom a given individual identifies and who, therefore, have a significant influence upon his personality.

generally. The importance of the sentiments and emotions manifested in personal relationships are given no recognition in Mead's position. This lack is supplied—perhaps, oversupplied—in Cooley's work.

(c) Nothing in Mead's theory enables a clear stand on the matter of the nature (or even existence) of the unconscious, or subconscious, and the related mechanisms of adjustment.

3. Mead's position can also be criticized from a third and final general standpoint, that of methodology.

(a) First of all, Mead's theory, for the most part, does not seem to be highly researchable. As yet, little truly significant research has been conducted chiefly in terms of his frame of reference. Recent efforts to measure self-conceptions may help to remedy this deficiency.

(b) Mead, himself, gives no explicit formulation as to how his analytical scheme can be used in research. He makes no specific recommendations as to the techniques appropriate to the study of human behavior.

(c) As I indicated earlier in this report, Mead presents no systematic evidence for his position. Nevertheless, many social psychologists find his theory highly congruent wih the experiences of everyday life—something which cannot be as readily said for a number of competing positions.

E. Positive Contribution

The extent of Mead's contribution to social psychology can be only roughly gauged by reference to the work of other adherents of the Symbolic Interactionist approach. Among the more eminent sociologists and social psychologists influenced by his viewpoint are: Cooley, Thomas, Park, Burgess, E. Faris, and Blumer. Some of the textbooks which incorporate his position are: in sociology, those by Park and Burgess, Dawson and Gettys, Francis Merrill, Kingsley Davis; in social psychology, Lindesmith and Strauss, M. Sherif, T. Newcomb, Walter Coutu, and Hubert Bonner. In addition, the recent interests in "role theory," "reference-group theory," and "self-theory" represent, basically, derivatives of Symbolic Interactionism.

Mead's substantive contribution has converged with, or at least has found some parallels in, certain methodological positions in modern sociology and social psychology. Such positions are those in which study of the inner, subjective part of the act is deemed indispensable. Methodologies of this sort are indicated by (1) Thomas' concept of "definition of the situation," (2) Cooley's "sympathetic introspection," (3) Weber's "*Verstehen*," (4) Znaniecki's "humanistic coefficient," (5) MacIver's "dynamic assessment," (6) Sorokin's "logico-meaningful analysis," and other references to the covert aspects of human conduct.

Mead's more specific contributions can be only briefly listed in this report:

1. He contributed to the increasing acceptance of the view that human conduct is carried on primarily by the defining of situations in which one acts; that is, the view that distinctively human behavior is behavior in terms of what situations *symbolize*. This is the essence of the Symbolic Interactionist viewpoint.
2. Adopting a distinctly sociological perspective, he helped direct attention to the fact that mind and self are not biologically given, but are social emergents.
3. He delineated the way in which language serves as a mechanism for the appearance of mind and self.
4. His concept of the "self" explains how the development, or socialization, of the human being both enmeshes the individual in society and frees him from society. For the individual with a self is not passive, but can employ his self in an interaction which may result in selections divergent from group definitions.
5. An extremely provocative conception of the nature of the human mind is provided by him: He views mind, or the mental, as an importation within the individual of the social process, *i.e.*, of the process of social interaction.
6. His concept of the "act" points out the tendency for individuals to construct their behavior in the course of activity and thus, to "carve out" their objects, their environments. What this means is that human beings are not passive puppets who respond mechanically to stimuli. They are, rather, active participants in a highly organized society, and what they perceive is functional in their ongoing activity. This theoretical position implies the importance of acquired predispositions (interests, values, etc.) and of the social context of behavior. It points to the influential significance of the group settings in which perceptions occur, and also places the meaning of what is perceived in the context of the ongoing activities of persons. This leads directly into the next contribution by Mead.
7. He described how the members of a human group develop and form a common world, *i.e.*, common objects, common understandings and expectations.
8. He illuminated the character of social interaction by showing that human beings *share* one another's behavior instead of merely responding to each other's overt, external behavior as do infrahuman organisms.

As a concluding and overall evaluation of Mead as a contributor to social psychology, I can do no better than to repeat Dewey's oft-quoted appraisal: "His was a seminal mind of the first order."

Mead and Freud:
Their Relevance for Social Psychology[1]

Freud would enjoy and, doubtless, interpret the ambivalence of social psychologists toward George Mead and himself. Their ideas are viewed by many scientists with great deference and grave doubt. Mead and Freud are held to be both indispensible and incompatible. Mead's work is generally considered fundamental but without fruitful implications for research; Freud's as provocative but wrong.

It should be understood that all social psychologists are not deeply ambivalent about Mead and Freud. It is a symptom primarily of those who look to sociology as their intellectual home. The average textbook by a sociological social psychologist cites Mead and Freud more often than any of the other theorists who wrote extensively before 1935. Moreover, these books employ symbolic interactionism and psychoanalytic thinking as their major frameworks.

I want to examine the present and prospective roles of Mead and Freud in the development of a sociological social psychology. My intent is not that of offering an intellectual history. My objective is to clarify some of the potential contributions of Mead and Freud to a sociological social psychology, to locate the essential nature of the incompatibility and convergence between them, and to assess their prospective relations to empirical research. To accomplish this purpose in a limited amount of space, I deal with only some of the topics they treat. Because it seems the more fundamental, my focus is on their treatments of mind as a process rather than on their accounts of the individual's organization as a self or as a personality.

I should say at once that there are certain points which I intend to ignore. I accept as fact, but will pass over, Freud's tendencies toward instinctivism and Lamarckianism, his penchant for fictive histories of doubtful worth, and his lack of knowledge about, or understanding of, the differences between cultures. At the same time, I shall assume that it is consistent with the best evidence to say that Freud was usually correct in believing that his major conceptual distinctions represented important empirical discrimina-

Guy E. Swanson, "Mead and Freud: Their Relevance for Social Psychology," *Sociometry*, vol. 24 (December 1961), pp. 319–339, by permission of the journal and author.
[1] Revision of a paper read at the 1960 meetings of the American Sociological Association.

tions.[2] I have no desire to join in that variety of revisionism which removes most of Freud's empirical observations while amputating instincts and the inheritance of acquired characteristics. I shall, in short, treat Freud, not neo-Freudianism.

Further, I shall not concern myself with the important controversies about the metaphysics and social values of pragmatism, functionalism, and psychoanalysis or with their relation to public affairs.[3] My present interest is an empirical fruitfulness and technical adequacy of these theories for the problems of social psychology. What are those problems?

The Problems of Social Psychology

Social psychology is the study of the relations between human individuals and social organizations. The nature of these relations depends on one's conception of the parties involved. Because social psychologists have no consensus on this matter, the following statements represent only my personal preferences.

By "individuals" I mean not organisms as such, but organisms engaged in selecting from, adapting to, and utilizing their surroundings. These processes are what Dewey and Mead called "mind." The organism's current potential for engaging in such a process is called its "personality."

The organism, as such, is significant for the individual on two accounts. First, its internal processes provide requirements which force it to import resources from the environment and determine the classes of environmental objects which may be so imported. Second, the organism is a self-stabilizing organization or system. This means that its internal processes operate in a manner that admits or rejects elements from the environment according to their likely effects on the system's stability. In this way, each organism's self-stabilizing processes afford a kind of unitary standard against which the environment is evaluated. Thus the sustained internal coherence of the organism provides one ground for the organization and coherence of the individual.

Social relations are the influences that individuals exert on one another. It is customary to say that one individual influences another only because he affects his associate's access to resources. Individuals have relations because they are resources for one another or because they affect the means for obtaining such resources.

Social relations are always orderly and, in that sense, organized. This

---

2 The evidence is surveyed in Blum (5).

3 For a consideration of Mead's relation to these controversies, see Blau (4), Pfuetze (33), and Natanson (25). Important evaluations of Freud in relation to these controversies are found in Bartlett (3), Marcuse (21), Kaplan (19), and Rieff (34).

does not mean, however, that they always are organizations. The terms "social organization" refers to a social relation in which the individuals concerned so behave as to prevent the disruption of their mutual influences by extraneous events. (When this self-stabilizing process occurs with some awareness by the individuals of its existence and function, we speak of their relationship as a "group.")

It is usually said that organisms, individuals, and social organizations are analytically separate from one another. This analytical separation is important primarily because it represents empirical independence. I shall take it as established that organisms, individuals and social organizations are independent in three senses: They are not reducible to one another, they exercise measurable constraints on one another, and, in a given population over any given period of time, the variance in the internal processes of each of these three systems or organizations may show considerable independence from variations in the other two.

This empirical independence is not equivalent to a lack of relationship. It is a potential and, occasionally, actual independence which documents the existence of three different and equally real organizations. Thus, we find that individuals provide resources required by organic systems; social organizations provide resources required by individuals. But, once each of these systems is in being, we can turn the matter around. As an organization or system, each has internal processes which operate to produce stabilization. Thus the requirements of groups for stability impose obligations and limitations on individuals who need to maintain those groups for their own purposes. In their turn, individuals, as systems, impose comparable demands and constraints on the organisms which they serve.[4]

Like the relations between individuals and social organizations, social psychology moves in two primary directions. It seeks, on the one hand, a description of individuals and of their relations to each other's resources that will explain the rise and properties of social organizations. It seeks, conversely, to define the requirements imposed on individuals by participation in social organizations and the consequences for individuals of their imposition.

Among psychological social psychologists, the greater portion have studied individuals and their relations as the source of organizations.[5] A majority of the social psychologists trained in sociology show special interest in the effects of organizations on participating individuals.

Social psychologists have sought to understand the rise of organization among individuals through the study of interpersonal influence, power, communication, symbols, and the media of communication. Their work on

---

[4] Some of the evidence especially relevant to this point is reviewed by Olds (26).

[5] This variety of approach is illustrated in Floyd Allport's early work (1). Perhaps the the most recent survey and synthesis appears in Thibaut and Kelley's book on groups (39).

elementary collective behavior, as well as many laboratory investigations of small groups, illustrates the same concern.

A different set of investigations illustrates efforts to explain the effects of organizations on individuals and to state the conditions under which these occur. Organizations persist if individuals depend on their presence, become responsible adherents to their norms, and contribute to the solution of their problems. The social psychologist's concern with socialization, self-control, and commitment to the group reflects his interest in the effects of organizations on individuals. So also does his effort to explain how values, attitudes, and opinions are acquired and gain some degree of order and stability as indicated by the rise of individualities, identities, and selves. The explanation of individual opposition or indifference to organizational requirements has been of special interest, as has over-conformity to those requirements.

The properties of social organizations play a special role in organizing sociological work in social psychology. It is those properties which distinguish social organizations from everything else in the environment that the social psychologist pursues as conditions that shape the mind. It is those features of mind relevant for explaining these same distinctive organizational properties and their variations that are of concern as he seeks to account for the rise of groups. In short, the defining properties of social organizations, and variations on those properties and on emergents from them, afford the coherence in a sociological social psychology. Among the candidates for inclusion in a list of such properties are social norms,[6] systems of symbols, sentiments conceived after the manner of Cooley, and Bales's "system problems."

The Problems of Mead and Freud

Neither Freud nor Mead set out to develop a social psychology. The philosophical tradition which Mead sought to advance defined its task as that of clarifying the relation between knowing and being—between epistemology and ontology—between the sentient organism and its environment (24). Interest was focused on the conditions of a valid knowledge of being. Valid knowledge was conceived as rational, intelligible, and self-conscious. This conception led, in turn, to a search for the empirical connections among signs, thought, organic action, and the environment, and to a concern with the universality of ideas and the reality of relations. Mead's social behaviorism finds its major problem in accounting for rationality, or, as he liked to call it, "reflective thought." His special contribution is an explana-

---

[6] In the sense employed by Durkheim. His definition and its implications are reviewed with unusual clarity by Peristiany (32).

tion for the varying access which men may have to the covert parts of their own acts and the consequences of such access for the effectiveness of man's relation to the environment. Mead locates the foundations of rationality in symbolic responses which people provide for the covert aspects of each other's behavior. If those responses are absent, men cannot think reflectively.

Like Mead, Freud wanted to account for rationality. Whereas Mead was concerned with the irrationality which appears because the environment does not respond properly to the individual's inner life, Freud sought to understand the irrationality produced by subjective conditions which prevent the individual from properly interpreting the world around him. The personalities of his patients prevented their experiencing gratification.

Because Mead finds the locus of irrationality in the absence of certain environmental events, his major focus is on the peripheral processes of behavior—on perception, the selection of stimuli, the character of the reinforcement provided by stimuli, the reformulation of instrumental acts, and the release of blocked impulse into the environment. Freud, on the other hand, wants to change the balance of forces internal to the individual with the aim of removing subjective conditions which block a correct appraisal of the environment. This leads to a conceptualization of the principal components of personality and of the distortions which their relations impose upon the individual's contacts with the environment.[7]

It is evident that Mead and Freud had quite different aspects of behavior at the center of their attention. The wide difference in their interest is a major reason why each of them retains a special claim on our attention.

Mead, Freud, and Social Psychology

We have seen that the development of a social psychology involves certain steps. Organism, mind, and social organization must be differentiated from one another and their relations identified. Minded organisms—individuals— must be so described that their relevance for organizations, whether as creators or as objects, is readily exposed.

Neither Mead nor Freud has much to offer us in the way of a description of social organization. Neither presents any detailed technical treatment of the rise of organization out of interaction. Both do something to distinguish and characterize organisms and minds. Both say a great deal about the impact of organizations on individuals. What of value does each

---

[7] There is some justice in the charge that Freud was mechanistic in his treatment of impulses, attitudes, and the like. On the other hand, this treatment does much to capture the perseverating and inflexible character of his patients' behavior. For discussions of Freud's mechanistic tendencies, see Allport (2), Bartlett (3), and Osborn (27).

have to offer us and how does each compare with the other? Let us begin with Mead.

MEAD

From the beginning of their acquaintance with Mead's work, many sociological social psychologists valued two of its features. The first was its sophisticated presentation of a functionalist psychology. The second was its bold extension of functionalism to explain certain of the individual's inner processes, certain of the covert aspects of acts.

a. Functionalism. Since its inception, functionalism[8] has been the perennial American psychology. Many of its principles became so well accepted as to be unquestioned. Heidbreder (15) said in 1933:

> . . . functionalism does not, at present, stand out in American psychology as a distinct school and system. It did so only in its beginnings, when it had the conspicuousness of a new movement—in particular, of a movement opposed to structuralism. . . .
>
> . . . in functionalism, American psychology passed through a phase of its development in which it brought together and organized many tendencies already in existence, utilizing them so successfully that they passed into general practice. To treat of mental activities as well as contents, to think in terms of adaptations and adjustments, to observe psychological processes in relation to their setting, to regard man as a biological organism adapting itself to its environment—all these procedures have been so widely accepted in psychology that they no longer attract special attention.

If anything, functionalist views are even more firmly rooted in academic psychology today. Perhaps the most dramatic evidence for this is the steady revision in functionalist directions of Hullian learning theory, the closest lineal descendent of Watson's behaviorism (16, 23).

Functionalism was a psychology well adapted to the requirements of sociologists and social psychologists. It fitted both their data and their theoretical tastes. More than this, it had survived the rigorous test of explaining the same phenomena treated by competing schemes while avoiding their errors.

Functionalism was not rooted in elementarist or mechanical premises. The relations among men or attitudes or particles were just as valid in ontological status as the men, attitudes, or particles themselves. Moreover, the individual element, seen from the standpoint of the organization or system in which it participated, had meaning as a part of that system—had a role in the system. This role was a condition of being, equal in validity to the element's role as one of the ingredients from which the system first arose. Here, then, was a sophisticated philosophy that agreed with the sociologist's social realism.

---

8 Functionalism's origins are traced in Blau (4), Hook (17) and White (40).

By granting ontological independence to relations among elements and by seeing the nature of elements as transformed by their involvement in such relations, functionalism made tenable the position that general ideas could possess empirical independence and validity. This conclusion supported those who wanted to take seriously, and treat as independently variable, the special class of general ideas designated by terms like symbols, social norms, and culture. Faris (10) and others quickly understood that here was an outlook which credited with full reality and potency "all that is noble in us as well as the ignoble" and enabled one to treat "the emergence within the actions of men of what we know as distinctly human."

The functionalists also provided conceptions of behavior itself that were congenial to sociology. Of particular importance was their description of the relation between body and mind.

Sociologists had already been impressed with the variability of behavior between cultures and between different periods in the development of given cultures. Any psychology congruent with these observations must allow for considerable malleability in behavior. Functionalism did just that.

It pictured the human organism coming out upon the world's stage equipped with a certain range of sensory capacity and with that vague impulsive quality which signalizes life. The living organism, by virtue of being alive, must have some intercourse with the environment. It is not self-sufficient and must engage in a constant interchange of energy with the environment. The organism moves ceaselessly; but only those features of the environment which it is equipped to perceive and which, additionally, impede its passage are of interest for the psychologist. Only toward these does mind arise. The psychologist's task, as Mead and other functionalists saw it, was to assume life and to explain how it comes to take one direction rather than another. Direction is movement toward or away from impediments. Life so directed is mind.

This vision of man pictures him as originally innocent of all knowledge concerning his world. It describes conditions that require sustained relations with that world, and provides the environment with a significant role in determining what those relations will be. But it does more.[9]

[9] It would probably be correct to say that the topics of special interest to sociologists in the 1920s and 1930s enhanced their enthusiasm for Mead. Their concern with urbanism as a way of life and with social marginality turned attention to the conditions under which man could be a problem to himself, to discussions of identity and individuality. Mead provided terms and principles for this discussion. The same interests in urbanism stressed the difference between ecological and normative relations—between interaction not mediated by common rules and symbols and interaction in which these media were present. Mead stressed this same distinction and provided an explanation of its consequences. Again, the twenties and thirties were years in which, like other American intellectuals, sociologists sought to find a place in scientific explanations for morality and religion, truth and honor, ideas and affect, history and aesthetics. This place had to be one which did not reduce these entities to epiphenomena. Mead, like Dewey, James, Pierce, and Cooley, sought to provide such a place.

It describes some of those relations as instrumental. We must remember, in this connection, that the functionalists were providing an account of mind, not of behavior. An instrumental relation—mind—connects the organism and the environment. If we consider the individual seeking to establish a viable relation of this kind, he is, by definition, rational. By this I mean that he is, by definition, seeking means fitted for his ends. Means which are not fitting, in this sense, will be rejected. Mind, so conceived, is indeed a malleable affair.

This malleability is further enhanced by another feature of the functionalist's conception. Mind, as they liked to say, lies between organism and environment. Many features of the environment change regardless of the organism's stability. Therefore, whether the individual recognizes it or not, mind also changes.

It is worth remembering that this malleability granted to mind follows inexorably from the way it is defined. The functionalists were saying: If individuals seek those relations to the environment which permit the release of a given impulse, the relations chosen will be those known and available alternatives that suffice. The organism is presumed to be ready and willing. The environment determines what ends can be realized and under what conditions. The functionalists simply did not treat the problem of the intra-individual conditions that determined whether and when the individual would take the first steps to establish instrumental relations.

From this same definition of mind there follows the characteristic functionalist attitude toward the conceptualization of "reinforcement." The typical learning psychologist conceives the environment's reinforcements as rewards or deprivations, and describes them in such terms as recency, frequency, regularity, and amount. The classical functionalist did not find this description wrong. It was incomplete. These bare categories are inadequate for describing the variable relations between impulses and environment of which mind consists. They do not enable one to differentiate between love and lust, between fear and hate, between an aesthetic judgment and an ethical decision. From a functionalist view, the concepts conventional in learning psychology inform us only of the degree of fit between some impulse and the environment, and the probability that this fit will recur. Such information is necessary, but insufficient for a description or explanation, however general, of mind and its variations. It is quite clear that two instrumental relations can be identical with respect to these learning variables and very different in all other respects.

An adequate conceptualization of the dimensions of mind is still lacking. We can understand the social psychologist's flirtations with Kenneth Burke's dramaturgical vocabulary or with Lewin's properties of the life space or with Parsons' categories of action as efforts to construct appropriate conceptions.

What all of these efforts have in common is the description of the distinguishing features of an instrumental relationship—what Dewey and Mead would have called the description of the "whole meaning." The sociological social psychologist is likely to believe that humans learn about social relations, not by fitting together bits and pieces of experience, but by grasping the general character of roles and norms. If roles and norms are instances of mind, there is no need to seek in neural associations for the process by which they are constructed. Instead, the association among their elements is interpreted as instrumental, not neural, in character. Functionalism shows how this can be so.

I have said that sociologists found malleability and "whole meanings" in behavior and appreciated functionalism as a psychology which took them into account. Functionalism was suited for many other purposes as well.

Sociologists often conceived of social relations and organizations as instruments that enabled individuals to obtain what they would have lacked without sustained help from other people. Functionalism was the psychology of instrumental relations. Sociologists were impressed with the importance of the cultural inheritance in determining man's view of his environment. Functionalism, as an instrumental psychology, dictated that the environment played a part in conduct only if it was relevant for the organism's requirements, including those requirements it had gained through living with other people and learning from them.

It has sometimes been charged that functionalist social psychology advances two incompatible pictures of mind. On the one hand, it sees mind as easily changed, on the other as locked forever in its own internal functioning, prevented by its definitions from encountering the outer world.

What this criticism refers to as incompatible visions of mind actually represents earlier and later stages of action. The organism is conceived as attending only to those objects that are relevant for the release of impulse. However, once the organism constitutes some object in the environment as a stimulus, once, that is to say, it perceives some object in the framework of its impulses or motives and describes its instrumental relevance, the properties of that object play a part in conduct. They either validate or invalidate the organism's instrumental hypotheses. A line of action persists as long as it continues to be validated by the environment. It stops when the environment provides no reinforcement or negative reinforcement. Organisms that perceive the same environment in the same fashion will receive the same reinforcement from it.

Mead's account opposes the view that conduct is determined solely by the organism or by the environment. It is not opposed, in principle, to a deterministic view of behavior. Organic necessities and past experience determine the hypotheses which the organism advances in the early stages of action. Once stimuli are constituted, they write their responses to the organism's proposals in a firm, round, determining hand.

We find, then, that functionalism has multiple appeals for sociological social psychologists. It readily enables the treatment of social relations as instrumental. It affords a significant role both to a determining environment and a selecting individual. It provides a clear distinction between mind and body. It agrees with the sociological disposition to take relations as ontologically valid and to search for whole meanings in order to understand and predict.

b. Functionalism and Intra-Psychic Events. It is with functionalism's treatment of intra-psychic events—of the covert stages of action—that we come to Mead's special contributions to social psychology. Because functionalism views mind as a relation between organism and environment, all special aspects of mind are also such relationships. These include perceiving, attending, evaluating, and responding. These processes become intrapsychic events in the form of expectations about the world which are acquired from participating in it and learning about it.

When Mead took this general functionalist approach to mind and applied it to reflective thought, he was forced to locate instrumental relations between organism and environment that might provide the special instances of mind represented by self-conscious problem solving. The grounds on which he concluded that only human interaction mediated by the standardized symbols of language could provide such relations are too well known to require review. They indicate one significant method by which the *dynamics* of social relations, as well as their elements, become a part of mind. We shall return to this point in discussing Freud.

FREUD

Like Dewey and Mead, Freud appreciated the importance of the mind-body problem (18). Like them, he evolved a position which provides a significant place both for human biology and for the environment in the determination of behavior. Freud, like the functionalists, pictures the adaptive behaviors of the organism flowing from motives, with stimuli being constituted, as such, by the perspective which motives afford.

There are further similarities. Both Freud and the functionalists conceive of each act as the product of a total situation, not of isolated stimuli or single impulses. Both believe that behaviors persist only because they contribute to the organism's survival. Both, though with somewhat different emphases, deny the validity of introspection as a tool for investigating conduct. Both distinguish sharply between the original nature provided by human biology and the human nature produced by man's experience with his fellows. Finally, Freud comes closer than is often appreciated to the functionalist position concerning the indeterminate character of the newborn's psychic life (5). Mead and Dewey stress the formless nature of original impulsivity. Freud separates libido as a kind of unorganized and impressionable impulsivity from those tissue states like hunger and thirst in which a periodicity of appearance is determined more by biology than experience and for which the range of suitable environmental reinforcements is quite narrow. By contrast, the organism's libido or sexuality is a generalized propensity to act, gaining structure and differentiation by virtue of its history in the environment. As Sartre (35) observes, "The libido is nothing besides its concrete fixations, save for a permanent possibility of fixing anything whatsoever upon anything whatsoever."[10]

We must turn once more to the problems of central concern for Mead and Freud to understand the essential differences between them. Mead sought the conditions of valid knowledge and defined such knowledge as the appropriate alignments of means and ends, the alignment of the act in its covert and overt aspects with the objective environment.

As we have seen, Freud's concern was with gratification. Now gratification is not a property of mind. Instead, it refers to the net balance of the organism's profits and losses resulting from his transactions with the environment. Mind is a means from which this balance emerges. Mead takes it as objectively problematic that acts and objects can be well aligned, but assumes that gratification will follow if they are. Freud assumes that such alignment is possible, but finds alignment, as such, insufficient to assure gratification.

Mead tells us how impulses, once aroused, become related to objects with which they can effect an interchange of energy. But Freud must explain why some individuals seem unable to express impulses and why others cannot modify their conduct as a result of encounters with objects. Freud would agree that, once an impulsive process is involved in becoming related instrumentally to objects, the character of the objects does much to determine the nature of the relationship that emerges and the likelihood that this impulse will arise again or in its present form.[11] Mind, as defined by Mead would be recognized by Freud as changeable. But Freud was provoked by those conditions before and after mind which prevented it from arising; which produced, not instrumental relations, but other behavioral processes. Those processes, separated from experience, are not readily changed by it.

To pursue his objectives, Freud moved in several directions. He sought, first, to characterize impulsivity prior to its shaping by contacts with the environment. He tried, second, to explain why some parts of the body were found more often than others to be centrally involved in the organism's gratification. He worked, third, to characterize the environment in terms of its potentialities for limiting the full expression of impulse. Fourth, he described certain common relations among impulse, erogenous zones, and

[10] McDougall (22), who welcomed Freud to the ranks of hormic psychologists, was especially critical of this indeterminate character of many Freudian "instincts."

[11] See, for example, Freud's (13) treatment of ego, the reality principle, and secondary process. A convenient review appears in Fenichel (11).

environmental limitations. (Seen as stable patterns in a state of equilibrium, these relations are the Freudian types of character—orality, anality and the others. Considered as a self-stabilizing arrangement restoring equilibrium after its disruption by impulse or environment, these relationships are the mechanisms of defense—projection, denial, reaction formation, and the rest.) Finally, Freud developed a theory concerning the conditions sufficient to permit the individual to experience the available gratifications—a theory of therapy.

What were Freud's conclusions from these explorations of the psychology of gratification? What is their relevance for a social psychology?

In Freud's description of impulse, we find a first condition that prevents perfect gratification. Original impulsivity knows no limits. Its source is in the internal requirements of the organism. The environment cannot provide for the full satisfaction of those limitless requirements or offer adequate compensatory satisfactions for those it denies. Given the nature of impulse, not just civilization, but any environment, is a source of discontents.

Other things being equal, such discontents are likely to become associated with the orifices of the body because these zones provide individuals with maximal pleasure. Instrumental relations with the environment have these zones as their primary foci because pleasure and pain are greatest there.

Although of lesser importance as sources of pleasure, other parts of the body have some potentialities of the same order. The eyes, ears, fingers, and limbs are relatively important. Presumably the ear lobes and the small of the back, lacking as they are in receptive sensitivity and instrumental relevance, are among the least significant sources of pleasure.

The body's zones differ not only in the degree of their erogenous potential, but in the *mode* by which each affords gratifications from contact with objects. These modes are instrumental relations shaped by the physiological properties of the several zones. Thus gratification by way of the mouth and lips involves sucking, chewing, licking, tasting, and incorporation. Gratification by way of the genitals involves insertion or reception.

Freud understood perfectly well that the organism, as a totality including its acquired skills, and not just these special zones, was the source of many gratifications. For the weight-lifter, the muscular development of the small of the back may be greatly prized; for the Kulya woman, her earlobes, grossly distended by bronze rings, are of great significance. For the intellectual, the quick mind and the apt phrase are matters of pride. But, Freud insisted, these sources of pleasure are added to those that biology originally provides, and the acquired sources become available much later in life. The socialization of the erogenous zones, coming first, establishes, as it were, a set of premises with which later socialization must contend. First, unless the individual is adequately gratified from these original sources, it is unlikely that he will have the energy available to venture a search for gratification from less immediate and less concrete sources. Second, if the mode of gratification from a later and more abstract source has features common to the mode built into some erogenous zone, some association is likely to arise between them. This association is illustrated in the famous formula (14) by which a child is proposed as the equivalent of a penis, which is shown to be equivalent to feces. It is not a matter of the individual confusing these objects with one another in perceptual or cognitive terms. Were that to occur, it would indicate grave pathology. What Freud does say is that these three objects come to be equivalent with respect to the mode through which they give pleasure to anal women.

Freud was more convinced than most of us are likely to be of the potency of the original erogenous modes for determining the nature of all later gratification. It is difficult, however, to dismiss the existence of many associations between these earlier modes and those which come later. Common figures of speech, verified interpretations of projective symbols, and clinical records provide countless illustrations of such associations (12).

In any case, one must add such associations to the inherent insatiability of impulse as sources which frustrate gratification. According to the best evidence available to Freud or to us, such associations would emerge from the phasing of neural activity. Unlike associations that arise in instrumental relations between impulse and objects, these associations between attitudes are not an aspect of mind. They are not governed by instrumental laws and utility functions, and their occurrence interferes with the operation of such laws and functions.

Consider, next, Freud's description of the environment. It is given in terms of that environment's limitations to pleasure. If those limitations make it dangerous for the individual to indicate that he has a given impulse, whether he expresses it or not, they have the quality of superego. If the limitations merely qualify the timing and means of impulse expression, they have the quality of ego. Now we are back in the realm of mind—of instrumental relations, but these relations are classified from a perspective not considered by Mead, and, what is more important, Freud's categories raise novel problems for mind's future expression.

Like Mead, Freud observed that only other people respond to our impulses as distinguished from the overt phases of our acts. Consequently, only other people will provide limitations with superego qualities.

A distinctive consequence of superego limitations is that, once they are accepted, the process we call mind vanishes, but the impulse need not. It is not merely unimplemented, it is defined in principle as unimplementable. The further associations it develops with other impulses and attitudes and the transformations it undergoes seem to owe little to instrumental associations and much to the internal self-stabilizing processes of the organisms.

Looking back over this sketch of impulse, body zones, and modes, and superego, we see that each involves considerations that fall outside the scope of a concept of mind as presented in functionalism. Yet none requires the assumption of instincts—of instrumental action established solely through biological inheritance. In a variety of ways, each of these three impediments to gratification calls our attention to non-instrumental, intraorganic events that precede, follow, or accompany mind, relating to it but having a significant degree of independent variance. We are reminded once more that Mead and Freud supplement each other's work by examining somewhat different phases of behavior. Because Freud wrote on such matters, we can be certain that he would have agreed with the functionalists concerning many of the properties of mind.[12] He would, however, have seen those properties as insufficient to account for psychopathology.

The varieties of character and the mechanisms of defense are the final result of Freud's work. Here all the ingredients previously sketched become organized in a systematic fashion. Freud, as Frenkel-Brunswik said (12):

> . . . tends to view character structure from a defensive point of view, and social influences as a series of traumata which bring to a halt or discontinue instinctual gratification and expression.
> . . . This view does not do justice to all the satisfactions gained from moving along constructive social avenues.

A number of somewhat independent observers have come to a similar view of the types of character. Erikson (9), Fromm (15), and Parsons (29, 30), for example, propose that these types represent residues of the major stages of socialization.[13] Only Parsons offers a coherent account of the appearance of these particular types of character and of the order in which they arise. In essence he suggests that each type of character represents the skills required to perform adequately in one of the four major roles embodied in social systems. These roles—these organizational facts—provide the key theoretical apparatus for explaining the rise of these types of character. We may note, first, that we are now confronted by a truly social psychological account and, second, that this account pictures these particular types of character not merely as relevant for participating in some organizations but as descriptions of skills essential for participation in all organizations. One version of this approach may suffice to indicate its general character.[14]

In interactional terms, dependency is the central fact of orality as a stage of development or as a type of character. From the standpoint of its parents, the infant is functionally dependent upon adults for its survival, but

---

[12] Freud's discussion appears in (13).

[13] The interpretation that follows was developed originally in Swanson (38).

[14] For another characterization of the interactional significance of these stages, see Swanson (36).

is unaware of its need for social support. It gradually learns that it is dependent. If the infant does not learn to be dependent, there is no foundation for the remaining stages and they will not appear.

The central interactional fact of anality is responsibility. Once the young child is committed to depend on others, they can and do make demands on him which facilitate their living together. The child must accept some responsibility for his own conduct, must exercise self-surveillance, or stable, continued interdependence is an intolerable burden to his elders. There is general agreement that most children find these responsibilities difficult to accept, and come only gradually to feel comfortable in living with them.

Observers are also in agreement in believing that the requirement for a child's assumption of stable participation with peers and others outside his family forces the generalization of dependent and responsible relations to these additional groups. Parsons has given us an especially sensitive and detailed picture of the way in which the structural demands of the family as an organization, the ultimate requirements of the total society for more mature forms of social participation, and the child's current interpersonal skills all interact to produce first the oedipal crisis and, if that is resolved successfully, the golden years of latency which take us from the fourth or fifth year to the brink of adolescence. It is plausible to regard such a sequence as common in all cultures with, perhaps some variations in timing. It is important to understand that the basic anal character, dependent and responsible, is retained throughout these stages. It is simply extended in the social relations to which it applies.

It is toward the end of childhood that another ingredient is added to this anal pattern, the ingredient of independence, or, more suggestively, of competent performance. This is the particular sign of the phallic character. We may believe that relations with peers and others outside the family are of special importance in this development.

By independence, I mean that the child is expected to be able to show sufficient self-confidence to enter easily upon new tasks and new social relations without looking to his family for constant guidance and nurturance. This is not primarily a matter of possessing appropriate intellectual and motor skills, although these are necessary. The focus of the phallic period is the demonstration that one can establish new social relations as the occasion demands and participate responsibly in them. These abilities are the fruit of latency and the foundation for the final step—the emergence of the genital character.

The genital character is dependent, responsible, and competent. In addition, he makes positive contributions to the development and maintenance of the groups to which he belongs. The description and explanation of genitality are the least developed in existing discussions of Freud's typology. Fromm catches the spirit of the matter in speaking of genitality as "the productive orientation (15)." I take this to mean that the individual feels obligated not merely to obey some limited set of rules, but to enhance and add to the lives of his fellows. He is no longer only a beneficiary of society, but one of its fully responsible operators, his welfare bound inextricably with the welfare of the whole organization.

I have been describing the normative and desirable aspects of these four types of character. Each has, of course, its deviant forms. But, in desired form or otherwise, the great sweep of Freud's typology is from dependence to contribution, from rudimentary commitment to social relations with one's parents to commitment to ever-larger groups, from conformity to set demands to an obligation for the performance of whatever services may be necessary for social growth and survival. From the individual's perspective, these stages look somewhat different. Freud was always alert to the competition between individual needs and social demands. As sociological social psychologists, however, we may view the sequence from the organizational standpoint, seeing in it the growth of the individual's social commitments.

This social, and, we may note, functionalist, account of Freud's characterology helps us to identify its powers and limitations. It touches on only a small part of the phenomena of development and socialization. That part, however, is of central importance for sociology. Whatever else we may say of them, social roles represent positions in a pattern of influence among actors, and influence, in its turn, rests on dependence. More than this, moral, stable, and continued influence requires responsibility, competence, and contribution. Freud's typology enables us to describe significantly different readinesses with which individuals characteristically engage in such relations (36). When, as often happens, we find individuals who seek roles that are unusual in the general character of the influence which their holders exercise or receive, we can have some assurance that Freud's types will allow us to characterize those individuals in a fashion that complements our description of their roles. It was Lasswell (20) who seems first to have recognized and employed this special affinity of the psychosexual character levels for describing personality in terms compatible with essential features of all social roles.[15]

The several mechanisms of defense—turning against the self, projection, reaction formation, and the rest—are closely tied to the psychosexual stages. Each can be shown to represent an instrumental relation to one's self and others which reconciles some socially deviant desire with the particular type of dependency and obligation associated with one of the stages of socialization, I have described these connections elsewhere, and wish only to call attention to the fact that the defenses, like the types of char-

---

[15] Early usage of psychoanalytic ideas by sociologists is surveyed in Burgess (6) and Eliot (7).

acter, are built upon the fundamental nature and basic vicissitudes of social commitments (37).

The defenses are, however, of special interest in a comparison of Mead and Freud. Each is a special instance of social control being imported as self-control. Each first exists as a relation between persons, becoming internalized in the course of learning to participate in such relations. In each case, the whole relationship, which includes the influences that actors exert on one another, is imported. Thus what are often called the "dynamics" of the relationship are internalized along with the actors concerned. We need not infer, as Freud often does, that these dynamics are somehow supplied by the central nervous system. The relations involved are instrumental, not neural, in character.

If we are right in saying that the defenses represent one set of fundamental varieties of self-control, they must, in Mead's theory, represent a fundamental categorization of the varieties of self-awareness. It is true that the defenses constitute only one such categorization, but it is one of special relevance for the study of social organization and social control. It provides a set of problems of description and explanation in which the joint powers of Meadian and Freudian thinking can be exploited.

Conclusion

I began this paper by observing that social psychologists often considered Mead to be theoretically fundamental but empirically unfruitful; Freud as empirically provocative but theoretically wrong. What does our survey of their work suggest concerning these judgments?

I believe there are three reasons for the current view of Mead. First, he provides a way of formulating important aspects of almost any problem we touch in social psychology, but does not suggest many problems for investigation. Second, certain of his most relevant premises are untestable. Third, many of these features of his scheme which are testable do not fall within the social psychologist's purview.

Every problem of interest in social psychology requires that we make some judgments about the relation of mind to body and social organization. Unless this relation is one that sees these three as independent but interacting, our problem is destroyed before it is answered. Mead's version of functionalist psychology provides what we require, and does so more admirably than do other available schemes.

But, as Mead left it, his functionalism does little to specify systematic relations among body, mind, and social organization and the various forms of each. In short, he left us a general approach for the formulation of our problems, but did not suggest a wealth of problems at which we should look.

Second, Mead is peculiarly unfortunate in having proposed as a major social psychological premise a dictum that seems untestable, whatever its heuristic value. I have in mind his judgment that self-awareness and reflective thought are products of social interaction mediated by language signs and products of it alone. The only relevant test of this notion would require a population of biologically normal human adults who had managed, without undue trauma, to become knowledgeable about a differentiated environment, who had learned to employ certain common vocal gestures instrumentally but not reflexively, and who lacked all human contacts from birth to maturity. I believe it is time to label as irrelevant for Mead's premise all of the materials on feral men, infra-human primates, aphasics, schizophrenics, and children. None of these provides a reasonable test of Mead's ideas. The accounts of ferals are of doubtful validity. The chimpanzees and gorillas lack human biology as well as symbols. It is as plausible to explain the aphasic's difficulty from the damage to his brain as from his conceptual disorders. Schizophrenia seems more a result of traumatic rearing than of miseducation in symbol usage. The very young child is biologically and experientially immature as well as unskilled in language.

Although I am disposed to believe that Mead's premise is sound, I am also disposed to believe that it cannot be demonstrated to be so. I would propose that whatever use we may make of Mead should not depend on the truth of this particular premise, and that we stop fruitless debate about its validity.

I suggested, third, that many of the testable features of Mead's scheme do not fall within the purview of social psychology. Such matters as the exploratory and impulsive character of the organism (41), the existence and nature of choices which are not guided self-consciously yet not distorted by repression (8), and the nature and growth of motives (26) are under intensive investigation by experimental psychologists. In each case, the evidence strongly supports a functionalist interpretation. In no case, however, are variations in social organization, as such, of crucial theoretical importance. The problems addressed are those of psychology proper, not of social psychology.

Freud's present status in social psychology is almost the exact complement of Mead's. In its original form, Freud's theory of mind was unacceptable. Once we separate out its instinctive and Lamarckian features, however, we find two remaining clusters of ideas, each of which continues to be useful, each being supported by considerable evidence (26). The first cluster is not a theory of mind, it is a theory of neural and organic functioning without consideration for the organism's instrumental relations with its environment. This theory is of the source of conditions that precede, accompany, and follow the presence of mind and provide limits to gratification.

The second cluster of ideas consists of features of instrumental relations, of mind, especially significant for understanding the way in which the social environment limits gratification. These include superego, the types of character, the methods of defense, and the process of therapy. Each has proven surprisingly easy to rationalize by means of a functionalist approach, and each fits readily into our growing social psychological treatment of socialization and social control (28, 31, 42).

Freud was wrong because he failed to distinguish clearly between mind and intra-organic functioning and because he overgeneralized the values and experiences of his patients. Freud is provocative because he provides a rich set of differentiations readily interpretable as variations in mind which, in turn, are particularly significant consequences of social organization's impact on individuals.

We should not conclude, however, that Freud and Mead have left us a psychology completely adequate for our needs. There are many current developments that extend or modify their work. Parsons' categories of action, devised to bring greater coherence to our burgeoning knowledge, represent just an elaboration of an instrumental view of mind. So also do the rapidly growing studies of identity, of socialization, of semantic principles, and of interaction process. The explanation of social change is pressing hard upon functionalism's scant treatment of reinforcement and of the processes by which images are selected to guide the release of blocked impulses. The interpretation of personality adjustment in old age is demanding a more adequate picture of the limits to the place of mind in the total pattern of behavior. Investigators have been forced to develop the causal and functional laws so scarce in psychoanalysis. Given these developments, and many others, it is unlikely that the ideas of Mead or Freud will soon be only curiosities in the museums of our discipline.

References

1. Allport, F. H., *Social Psychology*, Boston: Houghton Mifflin Co., 1924.
2. Allport, G. W., "Dewey's Individual and Social Psychology," in P. A. Schilpp (ed.), *The Philosophy of John Dewey*, Evanston: Northwestern University, 1939, 263–290.
3. Bartlett, F. H., *Sigmund Freud, A Marxian Essay*, London: Victor Gollancz, Ltd., 1938.
4. Blau, J. L., *Men and Movements in American Philosophy*, New York: Prentice-Hall, Inc., 1952.
5. Blum, G. S., *Psychoanalytic Theories of Personality*, New York: McGraw-Hill Book Co., Inc., 1953.
6. Burgess, E. W., "The Influence of Sigmund Freud upon Sociology in the United States," *The American Journal of Sociology*, 1939, 45, 356–374.
7. Eliot, T. D., "Interactions of Psychiatric and Social Theory Prior to 1940," in A. M. Rose (ed.), *Mental Health and Mental Disorder, A Sociological Approach*, New York: W. W. Norton and Co., Inc., 1955, 18–41.
8. Eriksen, C. W., "Subception: Fact or Artifact?" *The Psychological Review*, 1956, 63, 74–80.

9. Erikson, E. H., *Childhood and Society*, New York: W. W. Norton and Co., Inc., 1950.
10. Faris, E., "The Social Psychology of George Mead," *The American Journal of Sociology*, 1937, 43, 396.
11. Fenichel, O., *The Psychoanalytic Theory of Neurosis*, New York: W. W. Norton and Co., Inc., 1945.
12. Frenkel-Brunswik, E., "Psychoanalysis and the Unity of Science," *Proceedings of the American Academy of Arts and Sciences*, 1954, 80, 297–299.
13. Freud, S., *The Ego and the Id*, London: Hogarth Press, 1927.
14. Freud, S., "On the Transformation of Instincts with Special Reference to Anal Eroticism," *Collected Papers*, vol. 2, London: Hogarth Press, 1948, 164–171.
15. Fromm, E., *Man for Himself, An Inquiry into the Psychology of Ethics*, New York: Rinehart and Co., Inc., 1947, 50–117.
16. Hilgard, E. R., *Theories of Learning*, New York: Appleton-Century-Crofts, Inc., 1956, Chapter 14.
17. Hook, S., *John Dewey, An Intellectual Portrait*, New York: The John Day Co., 1939.
18. Jones, E., *The Life and Work of Sigmund Freud*, vol. 1, New York: Basic Books, Inc., 1953, 367–379.
19. Kaplan, A., "Freud and Modern Philosophy," in B. Nelson (ed.), *Freud and the Twentieth Century*, New York: Meridian Books, Inc., 1957, 209–229.
20. Lasswell, H. D., *Psychopathology and Politics*, Chicago: The University of Chicago Press, 1930.
21. Marcuse, H., *Eros and Civilization*, Boston: Beacon Press, 1955.
22. McDougall, W., *Psycho-Analysis and Social Psychology*, London: Methuen and Co., Ltd., 1936.
23. Miller, N. E., "Liberalization of Basic S-R Concepts: Extensions to Conflict Behavior, Motivation and Social Learning," in S. Koch (ed.), *Psychology: A Study of a Science. Study I: Conceptual and Systematic*, vol. 2, New York: McGraw-Hill Book Co., Inc., 1959, 196–292.
24. Morris, C., "Pierce, Mead, and Pragmatism," *The Philosophical Review*, 1938, 47, 100–127.
25. Natanson, M., *The Social Dynamics of George H. Mead*, Washington, D.C.: Public Affairs Press, 1956.
26. Olds, J., *The Growth and Structure of Motives*, Glencoe, Ill.: The Free Press, 1956, 60–63.
27. Osborn, R., *Freud and Marx, A Dialectical Study*, London: Victor Gollancz, Ltd., 1937.
28. Parsons, T., "An Approach to Psychological Theory in Terms of the Theory of Action," in S. Koch (ed.), *Psychology: A Study of a Science, Study I: Conceptual and Systematic*, vol. 3, New York: McGraw-Hill Book Co., Inc., 1959, 612–711.
29. Parsons, T., "Family Structure and the Socialization of the Child," in T. Parsons and R. F. Bales (eds.), *Family, Socialization and Interaction Process*, Glencoe, Ill.: The Free Press, 1955, 35–131.
30. Parsons, T., "The Organization of Personality as a System of Action," in T. Parsons and R. F. Bales (eds.), *Family, Socialization and Interaction Process*, Glencoe, Ill.: The Free Press, 1955, 133–186.
31. Parsons, T., "Psychology and Sociology," in J. Gillin (ed.), *For a Science of Social Man*, New York: The Macmillan Co., 1954, 67–101.
32. Peristiany, J. G., "Introduction," in E. Durkheim, *Sociology and Philosophy*, Glencoe, Ill.: The Free Press, 1953, vii–xxxii.
33. Pfuetze, P. E., *The Social Self*, New York: Bookman Associates, 1954.
34. Rieff, P., *Freud: The Mind of the Moralist*, New York: The Viking Press, 1959.
35. Sartre, J. P., *Existential Psychoanalysis*, New York: Philosophical Library, 1953, 74.
36. Swanson, G. E., "Agitation in Face-to-Face Contacts: A Study of the Personalities of Orators," *The Public Opinion Quarterly*, 1957, 21, 288–294.
37. Swanson, G. E., "Determinants of the Individual's Defenses Against Inner Conflict: Review and Reformation," in J. Glidewell (ed.), *Parental Attitudes and Child Behavior*, Springfield, Ill.: Charles C. Thomas, 1961, 5–41.

38. Swanson, G. E., "Individual Development as the Learning of a Sequence of Social Roles," Technical Paper P-5, Detroit Area Study of the University of Michigan, 1952.
39. Thibaut, J. W. and H. H. Kelley, The Social Psychology of Groups, New York: John Wiley and Sons, Inc., 1959.
40. White, M. G., The Origin of Dewey's Instrumentalism, New York: Columbia University Press, 1943.
41. White, R. W., "Motivation Reconsidered: The Concept of Competence," The Psychological Review, 1959, 66, 297–333.
42. Wilson, A. T. M., E. L. Trist, and A. Curle, "Transitional Communities and Social Reconnection . . .," in G. E. Swanson and Others (eds.), Readings in Social Psychology, New York: Henry Holt and Co., 1952, 561–579.

3   BERNARD N. MELTZER & JOHN W. PETRAS

The Chicago and Iowa Schools of Symbolic Interactionism

Although the nature of symbolic interaction theory has been explored and analyzed as a substantive school in itself, there have been no analyses of the variations that exist within the approach. Our purpose in this paper is to explore the differences between two major variations within the interactionist orientation: the Chicago school and the Iowa school. Although the major theoretical issues dividing these two orientations have been the subject of debate since the dissemination of the ideas of George Herbert Mead into the general population of American sociologists, it is only within the last fifteen to twenty years that these differences have crystallized into two distinctive approaches.

If Charles H. Cooley, John Dewey, George Herbert Mead, and William I. Thomas are considered to be the most influential of the early interactionists, one can single out several shared characteristics within their works. All conceptualized the individual and society as inseparable and interdependent units. Individuals, living together in society, were viewed as reflective and interacting beings possessing selves. In the words of Herbert Blumer, it was taken as a point of logical necessity that the study of human

Bernard N. Meltzer and John W. Petras, "The Chicago and Iowa Schools of Symbolic Interactionism" in Tamotsu Shibutani, Ed., Human Nature and Collective Behavior: Papers in Honor of Herbert Blumer, © 1970. Reprinted by permission of Prentice-Hall, Inc., Englewood Cliffs, N.J.

behavior begin with the fact of human association.[1] While common today, this position represented a departure from the tradition of Lester Ward and the mainstream of early American sociology, in which the individual and society were viewed as discrete and, therefore, separable units. It was as a reaction against this orientation in American sociology that the early interactionists developed the notion of interaction and unity between the individual and society. In response to individualistic perspectives on motivation, they often emphasized the positive role of the social group in its influence upon behavior. The nature of this reaction leads directly into the second characteristic of the early interactionists: a concern with the social development of the self and personality, coupled, however, with the recognition that such a theory had to account adequately for the role of biological factors in human behavior.[2]

Lester Ward and the early American sociologists had pictured the individual as the ultimate source of behavior; e.g., Ward traced motivation to innate tendencies that were manifested in fear of pain and desire for pleasure. The resulting social psychology stressed an inherent dualism in the individual and society relationship. The early interactionists, however, used the term "impulse" to refer to innate biological tendencies that could be satisfied only *within* the social group. Impulse, as opposed to instinct, entailed undifferentiated tension-states. The end result of this approach was a unique combination of the biological and social natures of man in which innate tendencies, in the form of diffuse tensions, had the ends of satisfaction defined by the social order. Group membership was a prerequisite for individual satisfaction, for only through group membership did the ends of satisfaction become defined for the individual members.[3]

The third characteristic of early interactionism concerns the meaning of symbolic behavior. Today, there is a tendency to equate language with the symbolic component. In actuality, the early interactionists utilized language as the principal symbolic form only in certain specific aspects of their theories, e.g., Mead's discussion of self-reflexiveness. As far as the early interactionists were concerned, the point to be emphasized was not *how* men communicated, but the fact that they were influenced *by* their communications in interaction. The fabric of society developed out of shared meanings, and it was here that the significance of the symbolic element rested.

---

[1] Herbert Blumer, "Psychological Import of the Human Group," *Group Relations at the Crossroads,* ed. Muzafer Sherif and M. O. Wilson (New York: Harper & Row, Publishers, 1953), p. 193.

[2] Cf. Roscoe C. Hinkle, "Antecedents of the Action Orientation in American Sociology Before 1935," *American Sociological Review,* XXVIII (1963), 712.

[3] Cf. Kimball Young and Linton Freeman, "Social Psychology and Sociology," *Modern Sociological Theory,* ed. Howard Becker and A. Boskoff (New York: The Dryden Press, 1957), p. 564.

As a final characteristic of early interactionism, one can point to the nature of the research that it generated in American sociology. The guiding methodological principle of the early interactionists was that individuals could never be understood apart from the social situations in which they were participating selves. The basic assumption was not that situational characteristics explain all behavior, but that knowing the individual's own interpretation of those situational characteristics was indispensable for understanding his behavior. The influence of this assumption was to lead to a reevaluation of an established methodological technique, interviewing, and to aid in the establishment of a developing technique, case histories. Information gathered in the interview was no longer seen as merely data for reconstructing the individual's situation, but also as a reflection of behavioral processes leading up to the interpretation he communicated in the interview. What had once been the simple recording of behavior as recounted to the interviewer was now seen as a microcosm of the processes characteristic of society as a whole. Implicit was the idea, especially associated with Mead, of taking the role of the other, along with its complementary notion of mutual influence between the self and the other. While not expanded upon within the interview context, interaction along the lines of the self-other relationship was explored in several early research studies.

It was not until much later in the development of American sociology that the original assumptions of the early interactionists began to be tested empirically. The vast majority of these later studies was directed at the particular concepts of identity, role, and self. The Iowa school was formed out of these later studies, aided by the convergence of three developments in American sociology: the rise of social psychology, the growth of role theory, and the introduction of the concept *reference group* with its associated empirical research.

The Two Schools

THE PROGENITORS

During the past generation, the two foremost exponents of the symbolic interactionist orientation have been Herbert Blumer and the late Manford H. Kuhn. At the University of Chicago and, later, at the University of California at Berkeley, Blumer has led some of his students in what can properly be called the "Chicago school" of interactionism, which continues the classical Meadian tradition. Kuhn's Self-Theory, based at the State University of Iowa, constitutes a major variant of this tradition, which we shall call the "Iowa school." This latter school is sustained almost exclusively by Kuhn's students, largely through articles published in *The Sociological*

Quarterly. Important substantive and methodological differences distinguish these schools. An examination of the writings of the chief protagonist of each school enables a delineation and illustration of these differences.

A few words about Kuhn's intellectual background may be helpful in understanding his modifications of symbolic interactionism. In the course of earning both his master's and doctor's degrees at the University of Wisconsin (in 1934 and 1941, respectively), Kuhn was introduced to the Meadian perspective by Kimball Young, an eclectic proponent of that perspective. After brief stints of teaching at the University of Wisconsin (1937–42), Whittier College (1942–43), and Mount Holyoke College (1943–46), in 1946 Kuhn settled down at the State University of Iowa, where he remained until his death in 1963. While holding this post, he encountered graduate students who were being exposed to Gustav Bergman's logical positivism and to Kenneth Spence's positivistic contributions to the disciplines of psychology and the philosophy of science. The impact of the influences so briefly sketched here is readily apparent in Kuhn's works.

METHODOLOGICAL DIFFERENCES

The most fundamental point of divergence between the Chicago and Iowa schools of symbolic interactionism is, probably, that of methodology. Just as in the various disciplines concerned with human behavior, we find here the interminable opposition between humanistic and scientific viewpoints. Blumer tends to argue the case for a distinctive methodology in the study of man, while Kuhn stresses the commonality of method in all scientific disciplines. As in the nineteenth-century *Geisteswissenschaften–Naturwissenschaften* debate, one position implies an idiographic (or nongeneralizing) function of the behavior disciplines, and the other a nomothetic (or generalizing) function. Thus, Blumer seeks simply "to make modern society intelligible," while Kuhn seeks universal predictions of social conduct. The specific features of this methodological divergence can be presented in terms of three intimately related topics: (1) the relative merits of phenomenological and operational approaches, (2) the appropriate techniques of observation, and (3) the nature of the concepts to be used in the analysis of human behavior.

Blumer's demand for a special methodology lays stress upon the need for "feeling one's way inside the experience of the actor." The student of human behavior, he holds, must get inside the actor's world and must see the world as the actor sees it, for the actor's behavior takes place on the basis of his own particular meanings. Through sympathetic introspection, the student takes the standpoint of the acting unit whose behavior he is studying and attempts to use each actor's own categories in capturing his world of meaning. This intuitive, *verstehende* approach seeks intimate understanding rather than intersubjective agreement among investigators.

In a posthumously published article, Kuhn describes as "perhaps the most significant contribution of the Iowa research" its demonstration "that the key ideas of symbolic interactionism could be operationalized and utilized successfully in empirical research.[4] In the same article, he refers to self theory as an effort to develop a set of generalizations tested by empirical research—in contrast with the earlier "body of conjectural and deductive orientations" constituting symbolic interactionism. With this effort in mind, Kuhn sought to "empiricize" Mead's ideas by reconceptualizing or abandoning those he deemed "nonempirical" and by developing techniques of observation that were consistent with this aim. Repeatedly, his writings called for the operational definition of concepts, for methods that would meet "the usual scientific criteria," and for a "standardized, objective, and dependable process of measurement . . . of significant variables."[5] It should be understood, however, that Kuhn and the Iowa school do not reject the study of the covert aspects of the act. Rather, they urge the use of objective overt-behavioral indices (chiefly verbalizations by the actor) of the covert aspects.

Given Blumer's insistence upon sympathetic introspection, it is not surprising to find him advocating the use of such techniques of observation as life histories, autobiographies, case studies, diaries, letters, interviews (especially of the nondirective type), and, most important, participant observation. Only through close association with those who are being studied, he maintains, can the investigator come to know their inner world. His basic criticism of the experimental, instrumental, and quantitative approach, in the form of questionnaires, schedules, tests, and detached observation "from the outside," is that it fails to catch the "meanings" which crucially mediate and determine the ways in which individuals respond to objects and situations. He appears to be troubled but little by critics of the "soft science" techniques. Among the strictures most frequently directed at such techniques are the following: These techniques are subjective and, hence, unsuited to the development of scientific knowledge; information gathered through their use is too variable and unique for comparison and generalization; they tend to be too time-consuming for convenient use; it is not known how we can teach the skills required in their use; and they do not, typically, receive use in the testing of explicitly formulated theories by procedures subject to independent validation.

One would almost be justified in equating Kuhn's methodology with the technique of the Twenty Statements Test (TST), as Tucker does.[6] This

---

[4] Manford H. Kuhn, "Major Trends in Symbolic Interaction Theory in the Past Twenty-five Years," *The Sociological Quarterly*, V (1964), 61–84.

[5] C. Addison Hickman and Manford H. Kuhn, *Individuals, Groups, and Economic Behavior* (New York: Dryden Press, 1956), pp. 224–25.

[6] Charles W. Tucker, "Some Methodological Problems of Kuhn's Self Theory," *The Sociological Quarterly*, VII (1966), 345–58.

test, known also as the "Who Am I" Test, was developed by Kuhn in 1950 as part of his effort to transform the concepts of symbolic interactionism into variables that might be employed to test empirical propositions. Concerned with the construction of an instrument for eliciting self-attitudes, Kuhn explicitly rejected as unfeasible all attempts to "get inside the individual and observe these interior plans of action directly" or to infer them from overt behavior. He concluded, rather, that such procedures as questionnaires and attitude scales could be adapted to identify and measure self-attitudes. The resultant TST, based upon an open-response model, requires a content analysis of the responses and lends itself to Guttman-scale analysis. Today, the TST is the most widely used instrument in the study of self-conceptions. A section (entitled "Iowa Studies of Self-Attitudes") of the 1958 meetings of the American Sociological Association was devoted to it. The TST has been involved in over 100 reported researches, and it achieved a degree of national popular attention when it was administered to the early astronauts.

In studying "the natural social world of our experience"—a phrase that recurs in Blumer's writings—he urges the employment of "sensitizing concepts." As Gideon Sjoberg and Roger Nett point out, "That Blumer objects to operational definitions of concepts and advocates the use of 'sensitizing concepts' is consistent with his image of social reality."[7] This image includes both societal fluidity and the actor's ability to reshape his environment. Contrasting conventional scientific concepts ("definitive concepts") with sensitizing concepts, Blumer maintains that the former provide prescriptions of what to see, while the latter merely suggest directions along which to look. The concept should, he adds, sensitize one to the task of "working with and through the distinctive nature of the empirical instance, instead of casting this unique nature aside. . . ."[8] In Blumer's view, the student of human conduct moves from the concept to the concrete distinctiveness of the instance, for he has to use the distinctive expression in order to detect the common. Putting it more fully:

> Because of the varying nature of the concrete expression from instance to instance we have to rely, apparently, on general guides and not on fixed objective traits or modes of expression. To invert the matter, since what we infer does not express itself in the same fixed way, we are not able to rely on fixed objective expressions to make the inference.[9]

We can be quite brief in presenting the viewpoint of Kuhn and the Iowa school on the nature and function of concepts. In his endeavor to con-

[7] Gideon Sjoberg and Roger Nett, *A Methodology for Social Research* (New York: Harper & Row, 1968), p. 59.
[8] Herbert Blumer, "What Is Wrong with Social Theory?" *American Sociological Review*, XIX (1954), 8.
[9] *Ibid.*

vert imprecise Meadian concepts into research variables, Kuhn formulated explicitly operational definitions of "self," "social act," "social object," "reference group," and other concepts. One instructive example is the following portion of his discussion of the self: "Operationally the self may be defined . . . as answers which an individual gives to the question which he directs to himself, 'Who am I?' or to the question another directs to him, such as 'What kind of a person are you?', 'Who are you?', etc."[10] The first of these proposed questions, of course, is the basis of the TST.

A final comment on the methodological divergences between the two schools relates to Blumer's well-known attack on the utilization in social inquiry of variables—with their implications of a static, stimulus-response image of human behavior. Despite Kuhn's rejection of psychological behaviorism, his quest for variables commits him to some of its favored methodological orientations. Thus, it is clear that our two protagonists assign different priorities to relevance and precision of understanding, as well as to the discovery and the testing of ideas. One could plausibly argue, moreover, that, while Blumer's image of man led him to a particular methodology, Kuhn's methodological predilections led him to a particular image of man. To these somewhat contrasting images we now turn.

INDETERMINACY OR DETERMINACY

A second salient difference between the two schools raises the ancient question of the degree to which man's behavior is free or determined. Viewing human behavior in terms of the interplay between the spontaneous and the socially-determined aspects of the self, Blumer builds into such behavior an unpredictable, indeterminate dimension. For him, this interplay is the fundamental source of innovation in society. Proponents of the Iowa school, by contrast, reject both indeterminism in human conduct and the explanation of social innovation based on the emergent, creative element in human action. The place of impulse in conduct constitutes the key issue.

In order to facilitate understanding of this issue, it may be useful to review certain widely known ideas. Following Mead's treatment quite closely, Blumer sees the self as involving two analytically distinguishable phases, the I and the Me. The first of these, the I, is the impulsive tendency of the individual. It is the initial, spontaneous, unorganized aspect of human experience. Thus, it represents the undisciplined, unrestrained, and undirected tendencies of the individual, which usually take the form of diffuse and undifferentiated activity. The Me, on the other hand, represents the incorporated other within the individual. Hence, it comprises the organized set of attitudes and definitions common to the group. In any given situation,

---

[10] From "Lectures on the Self" by Manford Kuhn, mimeographed, n.d., p. 4.

the Me comprises the generalized other and, often, some particular other. Every act begins in the form of an I and, generally, ends in the form of a Me. The I represents the initiation of the act prior to its coming under the control of the definitions or expectations of others (the Me). The I thus gives *propulsion*, while the Me gives *direction* to the act. Human behavior, then, is viewed as an ongoing series of initiations by impulses (the I) and of guidance of the act by the Me. The act is a result of this interplay and "cannot be accounted for by factors which precede the act."[11]

It is not entirely clear from Blumer's work whether the indeterminacy that marks human conduct is merely the product of the exploratory, improvising, and impulsive I or is an emergent from the interaction between the I and the Me. Contrasting the symbolic-interactionist view with stimulus-response approaches and other conventional views, he points out that the former is interested in *action*, and the latter in *reaction*. More specifically, he indicates that activity begins with an inner impulse rather than with an external stimulus, and that this activity may undergo a significant course of development before coming to overt expression. This development may bring the emergence of new definitions and new arrangements of definitions. In any case, Blumer exhibits skepticism of social science theories purporting to present determinate, precisely predictive propositions.

Kuhn's self theory takes no explicit cognizance of either impulses or the I-Me components of the self. For him, behavior is determined—as in conventional role theory—by the actor's definitions, including self-definitions. Thus, the self becomes solely a Me, and conduct is held to be wholly predictable (in principle) on the basis of internalized expectations. If we know the actor's reference groups, according to Kuhn, we can predict his self-attitudes; and, if we know his self-attitudes, we can predict his behavior. In short, antecedent conditions determine the person's self; and the self determines his conduct. This view, of course, conveniently disposes of such nonempirical conceptions as the I and impulses. At the same time, it preserves a premise that many deem essential to the scientific enterprise, that of determinism. In so doing, however, it ignores the processual character of the self, a point to which we shall devote a part of the next section.

If the foregoing discussion were exhaustive of the determinacy-indeterminacy controversy as it is manifested in the two schools, the controversy might be relatively easy to resolve. Either or both standpoints might compromise simply by operating within a *probabilistic* frame of reference for human behavior. As the next section will show, however, the controversy has important implications for other substantive elements in the viewpoints of the two schools.

---

[11] Herbert Blumer, "Society as Symbolic Interaction," *Human Behavior and Social Processes*, ed. Arnold M. Rose (Boston: Houghton Mifflin Company, 1962), p. 183.

PROCESS VERSUS STRUCTURE

In the course of the preceding discussion, passing reference was made to related fundamental divergences in imagery. We now turn our attention to a more explicit and fuller presentation of these divergences, placing them in the context of a process-structure distinction. The Chicagoans have tended to conceive of both self and society in processual terms, while the Iowans have stressed structural conceptions of both phenomena. These divergent views are more clearly discernible in two very closely related topics: (1) images of behavior as "constructed" or "released," and (2) images of role performance as "role-making" or "role-playing."

Blumer states his predilection for a processual image of human conduct and his repudiation of the structuralist image in the following terms:

> . . . the likening of human group life to the operation of a mechanical structure, or to the functioning of an organism, or to a system seeking equilibrium, seems to me to face grave difficulties in view of the formative and explorative character of interaction as the participants judge each other and guide their own acts by that judgment.[12]

Similarly, as previously noted, he refers to the self as a process of interaction between the I and the Me, and not merely a summation of the two aspects nor an organization of attitudes. This reflexive process is one in which the actor makes indications to himself, that is to say, notes things and determines their import for his line of action. Thus, action is seen to be built up, or constructed, in the course of its execution, rather than "merely being released from a preexisting psychological structure by factors playing on the structure."[13] The conditions that account for the action are not present at its beginning—"with the mechanism of self-interaction the human being ceases to be a responding organism whose behavior is a product of what plays upon him from the outside, the inside, or both."[14] Rather, he rehearses his behavior, summoning up plans of action, assessing them, changing them, and forming new ones, while indicating to himself what his action will be. This tentative, exploratory process gives rise, we have seen, to the possibility of novelty in behavior.

Kuhn has maintained that "the individual is not merely a passive agent automatically responding to the group-assigned meanings of objects."[15] Nevertheless, he and his adherents are led by their methodological and deterministic commitments slightly away from this disavowal. They

---

[12] Blumer, "Psychological Import of the Human Group," *op. cit.*, p. 199.

[13] Herbert Blumer, "Sociological Implications of the Thought of George Herbert Mead," *American Journal of Sociology*, LXXI (1966), 536.

[14] *Ibid.*, p. 535.

[15] Hickman and Kuhn, *op. cit.*, p. 26.

view the self as a structure of attitudes derived from the individual's internalized statuses and roles and assign causal significance in behavior to these
somewhat fixed characteristics. That these elements are considered stable
"traits" during a given time period is reflected in the use of the TST as a
predictor of behavior without specification of the situation in which the test
is administered or to which the predictions will be applied.[16] This same
assumption of relative stability is found in Kuhn's implied notion of a
"core" self, as expressed in his view that "Central to an individual's conception of himself is his identity, that is, his generalized position in society. . . ."[17] By omitting the I, impulses, or the spontaneous component
of the self from consideration, Kuhn is constrained to ignore the process
of interplay between the different aspects of the self.

Implied in the foregoing discussion are divergent conceptions of
the nature of role-behavior. These conceptions can be summarized as "role-
making," which designates a tentative, dynamic, and creative process, and
"role-playing" (sometimes termed "role-taking" by some writers), which
designates responses to the role-expectations of others. Both Dennis Wrong
and Ralph Turner have referred to the changing character of role theory.
Originally such theory depicted an exploratory and creative interaction
process, one marked by fluidity and, often, by some measure of innovation.
This theory, however, has increasingly come to be employed as a refinement
of conformity, or social control, theory. Resisting this trend toward a collective determinism, Blumer describes human group life as a process of formative transaction. He sees cultural norms, status positions, and role
relationships as merely the frameworks within which social action takes
place and not as the crucial determinants of that action. Together with
other members of the Chicago school, he conceives of man as creating or re-
making his environment, as "carving out" his world of objects in the
course of action—rather than simply responding to normative prescriptions.

In sharp contrast, Kuhn, as we have seen, conceives of personality as
an organization of attitudes which are, in effect, the internalization of the
individual's role recipes. The individual's roles are described as the norms
by which he structures objects and situations. Putting the matter quite
clearly, Kuhn writes:

> As self theory views the individual, he derives his plans of action from the
> roles he plays and the statuses he occupies in the groups with which he
> feels identified—his reference groups. His attitudes toward himself as an
> object are the best indexes to these plans of action, and hence to the action

---

[16] Cf. Tucker, *op. cit.*, pp. 354–55. Tucker also points out that the TST requires the
investigator to impose his own meanings on the subject's responses, which contradicts
the purported theoretical assumptions of the test.
[17] From "Lectures on the Self" by Manford Kuhn, *op. cit.*, p. 6.

itself, in that they are the anchoring points from which self-evaluations and other-evaluations are made.[18]

To anyone familiar with the TST, in which the conformity assumption is implicit, the above explicit statement comes as no surprise. This assumption is foreshadowed, also, in an early (pre-TST) essay by Kuhn in which he writes, "Social and cultural factors become determinants of personality factors only as the individual comes to internalize the roles he plays and the statuses he occupies. He asks 'Who am I?' and can answer this question of identity only in terms of his social position. . . ."[19] For Kuhn, even idiosyncratic elements in role-performance are fully explainable in terms of the role-expectations held by the actor's reference groups.

We see, then, that Blumer and Kuhn ascribe different qualities to the self. Blumer contends that the self is a process of internal conversation, in the course of which the actor can come to view himself in a new way, thereby bringing about changes in himself. Moreover, in his transactions with others, there occurs a flowing sequence of interpretation of the conduct of others, during which the actor may subject his attributes to highly variable use—or disuse. As Blumer writes, "The vital dependency of the attitude on the nature of the ongoing interaction suggests how fallacious it is to use the attitude to construct the scheme of that interaction."[20] Kuhn, on the other hand, describes both the self and human interaction as structures. The organized set of self-attitudes serves as a system of preestablished plans of action. And human association takes the form of fairly stable, ready-made patterns of role and counter-role prescriptions. Thus, for him behavior-prescriptions and behavior-predictions tend to coincide.

ONE OR TWO LEVELS OF INTERACTION

The two schools also differ on many relatively minor points. In this brief section we shall deal only with one of these points, one we consider more noteworthy than the rest.

Following Mead, Blumer refers to two kinds, or levels, of human interaction: symbolic interaction (which is uniquely human), and non-symbolic interaction (which is shared with infrahumans). The latter is a conversation of gestures, essentially of a stimulus-response character, in which each organism responds to the perceived actions, or gestures, of the other and makes no effort to ascertain the viewpoint of the other. An example is the vague feelings of uneasiness two persons may experience in

---

[18] Hickman and Kuhn, *op. cit.*, p. 45.

[19] Manford H. Kuhn, "Factors in Personality: Socio-Cultural Determinants As Seen Through the Amish," *Aspects of Culture and Personality*, ed. Francis L. K. Hsu (New York: Abelard-Schuman Limited, 1954), p. 60.

[20] Blumer, "Psychological Import of the Human Group," *op. cit.*, p. 199.

one another's presence, a feeling that may spiral in intensity even in the absence of symbolic behavior. Such interaction may involve either unwitting and unintended responses or responses to unindicated aspects of the other.

True, this level of interaction has received little theoretical attention and even less research attention from members of the Chicago school. But it appears to have been ignored completely by the Iowa school. Focusing its concern upon the interaction of socialized persons and viewing such interaction as responsive only to internalized meanings, the latter school leaves no room for nonsymbolic behavior. This omission is to be expected, of course, in view of this school's negation of the I concept. What emerges, then, is a conception of human interaction as a highly cognitive, non-affective phenomenon.

A SUMMARY OF THE DIFFERENCES

A close examination of the foregoing differentiation between the Chicago and Iowa schools of symbolic interactionism reveals the indicated differences to have an organic, systematic character. It is useful, in making this point, to recall an argument presented earlier: While Blumer's image of man dictates his methodology, Kuhn's methodology dictates his image of man. Thus, Blumer begins with a depiction of man's behavior as entailing a dialogue between impulses and social definitions, in the course of which acts are constructed. He proceeds to recognize a level of interaction devoid of social definitions and reflecting sheerly spontaneous behavior. Holding the two preceding ideas, he questions the extent to which human behavior is predictable. And finally, in the light of all of the foregoing imagery components, he must urge a methodology that combines scientific and humanistic elements.

Oppositely, Kuhn starts from a scientistic concern. This, although joined with his symbolic-interactionist orientation, brings him to an acceptance of a basically deterministic image of behavior. In the service of both scientism and determinism, he denies to the I any role in conduct, thereby dismissing the possibilities of both emergence and nonsymbolic interaction. Recognizing the magnitude of these modifications of symbolic interactionism, he relinquishes the conventional name of that orientation in favor of "self theory."

Prospects for Reconvergence

While our primary task in this paper has been to demonstrate major differences between the Chicago and Iowa schools of symbolic interaction theory, we shall conclude by examining the possibilities for reconvergence of the two approaches. Although it may be too early to state whether or not symbolic interaction theory will experience a reconciliation of the two schools, the likelihood that this will occur can be examined within the context of trends in American sociology as a whole.

One of the most notable developments in American sociology during the past several years has been the continually increasing interest in a sociology of sociology, reflected in the number of articles published on this subject, as well as in the time and space, both official and unofficial, allotted the subject at recent meetings of state, regional, and national sociological associations. As a consequence of this interest there has been a reconsideration of the origins of many of the established schools within sociology. We can expect that, as individuals involved in the various aspects of symbolic interaction theory experience a revived interest in their own intellectual antecedents, the differences among them will lessen, bringing a greater appreciation of the similarities due to a common intellectual heritage.

A second trend within American sociology that could prove influential in effecting a reconvergence of the Chicago and Iowa schools is the growth of interest in studies of adult socialization. Corresponding to this growth is the rapid increase of studies interested in the concepts of identity and self at the adult level. The very notion of "adult socialization" serves to incorporate work from both schools. The "adult" aspect is generally measured through some form of self test, and the TST is the most widely used self-inventory test. On the other hand, the "socialization" element has led to a renewed interest in and usage of some of the basic principles that were developed by members of the Chicago school.

Perhaps the most widespread development in American sociology, and one which involves the contributions of both the Chicago and Iowa schools, has been in the interrelated areas of reference group theory and role theory. Recent publications that question the various definitions of reference group, as well as the applicability of the concept to various types of research situations, have forced a reexamination of some of the basic principles underlying this approach.[21] Also, attempts that have been made to delineate clearly what is meant by role theory and the wealth of studies classifying themselves by this label have drawn attention to the major conceptualizations of role, as used in both the Chicago and Iowa schools.[22]

A fourth development concerns the revitalization of an interest in the biological elements in behavior. Recent interest in this area differs from earlier interest in the following manner: In their earliest sociological applica-

---

[21] Cf. Maureen E. Cain, "Suggested Developments for Role and Reference Group Analysis," *British Journal of Sociology*, XIX (1968), 191–205; Nicholas P. Pollis, "Reference Group Re-Examined," *British Journal of Sociology*, XIX (1968), 300–307; and Herbert Hyman and Eleanor Singer, eds., *Readings in Reference Group Theory and Research* (New York: The Free Press of Glencoe, Inc., 1968).

[22] Cf. Bruce J. Biddle and Edwin J. Thomas, eds., *Role Theory: Concepts and Research* (New York: John Wiley & Sons, Inc., 1966); Theodore R. Sarbin and Vernon L. Allen, "Role Theory," *The Handbook of Social Psychology*, ed. Gardner Lindzey and Eliot Aronson (Cambridge: Addison-Wesley Publishing Co., Inc., 1968), Vol. I, pp. 488–567.

tion, biological factors were often treated as the most fundamental determinants of action. After the decline of instinct theories of motivation in American sociology there ensued a long period during which sociological explanations incorporating biological factors were regarded as unfashionable or unscientific. However, recent sociological works involving genetic factors in behavior give considerable weight to the social factor, so that biological and social elements are seen as co-determinants. The work in this area is presently restricted to a small minority of sociologists. A widening of interest, however, would very likely begin in symbolic interaction theory, which, as pointed out earlier in this paper, has been one of the few schools of thought to retain the notion that biological factors must be considered in any complete explanation of behavior.[23]

Finally, we might look at a matter which, paradoxically, members of the Iowa school took as their major point of departure from the Chicago tradition: the interest in, and emphasis upon, the operationalization of the key concepts of symbolic interaction theory. Blumer has consistently emphasized the need for conceptual clarity as a prerequisite to operationalization. It seems that the major differences on this point center less on the problem of operationalization itself than on the type of operationalization that is possible, given a particular definition of the key concepts, e.g., "self." As in the Blumer-Bales debate, the real issue involves such matters as the twofold, processual conceptualization of the self.

Of course, there are other avenues open to the two schools for a possible reconvergence. In our limited amount of space, we have presented what we consider to be the most important ones. We should also like to point out that several developments can work in the opposite direction, i.e., against a reconvergence. For example, we may soon see the specification of role theory as something independent of the two schools of symbolic interaction theory rather than as a subspecialty within the general area. In effect, this has already occurred with the dramaturgical school, which, as popularized through the works of Erving Goffman, was originally closely related to the Chicago school. However, Hugh D. Duncan recently has developed the idea that the advancement of sociology is in part dependent upon the creation of a sociological model of communication to be tested in propositional form.[24] Thus a reconvergence could take the form of many of the original differences between the two schools becoming assimilated into the mainstream of American sociology, dulling the distinctiveness of each.

There remains, of course, still another possibility. As in the past and present, the two schools may continue the pattern of taking little

[23] Cf. Bruce K. Eckland, "Genetics and Sociology: A Reconsideration," *American Sociological Review*, XXXII (1967), 173–94.

[24] Hugh D. Duncan, *Symbols in Society* (New York: Oxford University Press, Inc., 1968).

cognizance of one another and of going their separate ways. This pattern is evidenced by the fact that representatives of each school rarely cite the works of the other school. This type of parochialism is fostered by the fundamental and perhaps irreconcilable divergence of the schools on the methodological level.

4   MANFORD H. KUHN

Major Trends in Symbolic Interaction Theory in the Past Twenty-Five Years

The year 1937 lies virtually in the middle of a four-year period which saw the publication of *Mind, Self, and Society, Movements of Thought in the Nineteenth Century*, and *The Philosophy of the Act*.[1] It would represent the greatest naiveté to suggest that thus the year 1937 represented the introduction of symbolic interactionism. We are all aware of the long development: from James, Baldwin, and Cooley to Thomas, Faris, Dewey, Blumer, and Young. Even the Tardean imitation and suggestion which underlay Ross's *Social Psychology*[2] contributed a good deal ordinarily not credited to him in the development of interaction theory. Nor is it the fact that Mead represents the fullest development of the orientation that makes so significant the posthumous publication of his works (for which we may conveniently take 1937 as an anchoring point). Mead's ideas had been known for a very long time. He had taught University of Chicago students from 1893 to 1931. His notions were bruited about in classes and seminars wherever there were professors conducting them who had

Manford H. Kuhn, "Major Trends in Symbolic Interaction Theory in the Past Twenty-five Years," *The Sociological Quarterly*, vol. 5 (Winter 1964), pp. 61–84. Reprinted by permission.

Paper read before the Midwest Sociological Society at its twenty-fifth anniversary meetings, Des Moines, Iowa, April 12–14, 1962. (The paper was prepared for oral presentation. Footnotes have been added. Where additional information is given which was not implied or suggested in the original text, this has been clearly indicated—The Editor.)

[1] George H. Mead, *Mind, Self and Society*, ed. with an Introduction by Charles W. Morris (Chicago: Univ. of Chicago Press, 1934); *Movements of Thought in the Nineteenth Century*, ed. by Merritt H. Moore (Chicago: Univ. of Chicago Press, 1936); *The Philosophy of the Act*, ed. by Charles W. Morris (Chicago: Univ. of Chicago Press, 1938).

[2] Edward Alsworth Ross, *Social Psychology* (New York, 1908).

studied at the University of Chicago—not least in the great heartland included in the Midwest of our society. Some of Mead's students had published their versions of his ideas or quotations from some of his philosophical papers—Kimball Young's *Source Book in Social Psychology* of a decade earlier contained a paper by Mead, and his *Social Psychology* bore the strong imprint of Meadian interactionism.[3]

No, the significance of the publication of Mead's books is that it ended what must be termed the long era of the "oral tradition," the era in which most of the germinating ideas had been passed about by word of mouth. (It should be noted parenthetically that Mead had published earlier a considerable number of papers, but they were mainly in journals devoted to philosophy and ethics, journals not likely to be read by sociologists or social psychologists. His only paper in a sociological journal—of which I am aware—was his assessment of Cooley's theories.)[4]

The oral tradition, it must be noted, has some generic peculiarities which are evidenced equally by primitive myth and by unpublished intellectual orientation: there tends to be much (almost ritual) repetition; there is a strain to "get it right," that is, to be correct; there is much debate over orthodoxy, and whatever intellectual powers there may be, are more devoted to casuistry and criticism than to inquiry and creativity. The mnemic effort freed from its task of remembering "how it goes" is somehow transformed into energy for imagination on the one hand and for the drudgery of testing and justification on the other. This is what was made possible by the belated publication of the three books by Mead.

Mead had not been the only one of the symbolic interactionists who had failed to publish. The year 1937 was the one in which some of the papers of Ellsworth Faris appeared under the title, *The Nature of Human Nature.*[5] Here, too, was a belated publication which, in its sprinkling and scatter, speaks more for what Faris never published—a rounded theoretical conception of his social psychology. Thomas' *theoretical* formulations were similarly scarce, scattered and incomplete—however influential. While Dewey published voluminously, his chief formulation of symbolic interaction theory is, in my view, his *Experience and Nature* which did

---

[3] George H. Mead, "Thought, Symbols, and Language," in Kimball Young (ed.), *Source Book for Social Psychology* (New York: Alfred A. Knopf, 1928), pp. 341–46, reprinted from "The Behavioristic Account of the Significant Symbol," *Journal of Philosophy*, 19: 159–63 (1922). Kimball Young, *Social Psychology: An Analysis of Social Behavior* (New York: F. S. Crofts, 1930).

[4] [Kuhn is referring to George H. Mead, "Cooley's Contribution to American Social Thought," *American Journal of Sociology*, 35:693–706 (Mar., 1930). The same journal did in fact publish two earlier papers by Mead: "The Working Hypothesis in Social Reform," *American Journal of Sociology*, 5:367–71 (Nov., 1899); "The Psychology of Primitive Justice," *ibid.*, 23:577–602 (Mar. 1918).—The Editor.]

[5] Ellsworth Faris, *The Nature of Human Nature and Other Essays in Social Psychology* (New York and London: McGraw-Hill, 1937).

not appear until late and which is written in such a forbidding Germanic version of the English language that many sociologists and social psychologists have not read it even yet.[6] Blumer, the young and promising heir apparent, has published relatively little and has nowhere gathered together a rounded version of his point of view.

But even though the oral tradition has some tendency to continue in symbolic interactionism, the past twenty-five years have seen a marked increase in all kinds of activity involving the published symbol: three textbooks on "our side of the social psychological fence"—that by R. E. L. Faris, that by Lindesmith and Strauss (now in its second edition) and the very recent one by Shibutani;[7] a sizable fraction of Newcomb's text[8] and lesser amounts of others on the "other side"; a considerable number of monographs, and into the hundreds of journal articles.

Basically the past twenty-five years have constituted, in contrast to the preceding era, the *age of inquiry* in symbolic interactionism.

But while it has been an era of inquiry, the inquiry has been directed at the testing and developing of what amounts almost to a welter of sub-theories going by a variety of names other than symbolic interactionism. This spawning of smaller, less inclusive theories has been due, in my opinion, neither to the propensity of scholars to attempt to make names for themselves by renaming what has already been proposed, nor to their having modified or augmented symbolic interaction in significant measure. This development of sub- or related orientations has stemmed from the essential ambiguities and contradictions in the Meadian statement—ambiguities and contradictions which were generally interpreted to be dark, inscrutable complexities too difficult to understand as long as the orientation remained largely in the oral tradition. Much of this confusion and contradiction may be summed up—but only in a vastly oversimplifying way and for purposes limited to immediate ones I hope here to expound—as a contradiction between [determinacy] and [indeterminacy] in Mead's overall point of view.

It is apparent that Mead took the view that the individual is initially dependent on the antecedent existence of a social system, specifically as it exists in the ongoing process of a functioning language, for the means wherewith to engage in experience or to take any kind of self-conscious and self-directed action. This internalization of language and the concomitant internalization of the role of the other has, in the Meadian description,

[6] John Dewey, *Experience and Nature* (Chicago: Open Court Publishing Company, 1925).

[7] Robert E. L. Faris, *Social Psychology* (New York: The Ronald Press, 1953); Alfred R. Lindesmith and Anselm L. Strauss, *Social Psychology* (New York: The Dryden Press, 1949: rev. ed., 1956); Tamotsu Shibutani, *Society and Personality: An Interactionist Approach to Social Psychology* (Englewood Cliffs, N.J.: Prentice-Hall, 1961).

[8] Theodore M. Newcomb, *Social Psychology* (New York: The Dryden Press, 1950).

nothing in it inconsistent with strict regularity or determinism.[9] Yet, as Mead proposed the *I* and the *Me* as the internal conversationalists constituting in their conversation the self, he indicated that the *I* is impulsive and essentially unpredictable—and furthermore that the *I* is the initiating, acting aspect of the self. It is never completely clear whether he meant only that the *I* is *subjectively* unpredictable or that it is indeterminate in a scientific sense.

Furthermore, it seems apparent that there was a basic initiative attributed to the self in the whole process of role-taking, at any rate after the early learning of language and probably even during that process as well. Mead, after all, insisted that the self constitutes its own environment, its own reality. Furthermore, there is the implicit possibility of indeterminacy in the whole conversation between the *I* and the *Me*. And, finally, it is possible to see in Mead's notion of the self such an antithesis to structure, such a dynamically volatile process of shifting self-indications that, whatever the *theoretical* view of determinacy vs. indeterminacy in any of the attributes of the self, the whole matter is so evanescent and shifting that it is obviously a practical impossibility to obtain access to any—possibly determinate—antecedents in time to make usable or testable predictions.

We may sum up this set of ambiguities about determinism as follows: The notion that the *I* is indeterminate but the *Me's* are determinate; the notion that both the *I* and the *Me's* are indeterminate; the notion that whereas both the *I* and *Me's* are determinate results of identifiable events, the interaction (conversation) between the two is somehow itself indeterminate or emergent.

But this is a preliminary view and does not cover the varieties of ways in which symbolic interactionism may be structured and, for that matter, has been structured by those proposing inquiry under its aegis. The two most frequently complicating considerations are: (1) the question whether the self is conceived, for research purposes, as the antecedent variable with criterion events (especially behaviors) as consequent variables, or conversely whether antecedent variables (ascribed identities, affiliations, associations, or communication variables and other events) are conceived to predict—that is, to exist in regularity with—consequent self variations; and (2) the question whether the relevant antecedent variables are conceived to be *immediate* or *remote* in time with respect to the events thought of as consequent.

This set of questions and ambiguities in symbolic interaction theory has led to a variety of answers. One answer structures human behavior deterministically by conceiving antecedent, causal variables to be con-

[9] "Mead's account of conduct . . . is not opposed, in principle, to a deterministic view of behavior."—Guy E. Swanson, "Mead and Freud, Their Relevance for Social Psychology." *Sociometry* 24:327 (Dec., 1961).

temporaneous social ones with the consequent ones having to do with the nature or structure of the self (either as a whole or of the elements seen to constitute the whole).

A second answer conceives the antecedent variables to be historical or developmental, thus possibly quite temporally remote from the consequent variables which are, as in the first answer, taken to be the nature or structure of the self, either holistically or elementally constituted.

A third answer conceives the antecedent variables to be the self, either as a whole or elementally, and the consequent variables to be those of overt behavior.

A fourth answer conceives the antecedent variables to be self variables which among themselves produce consequent, novel, but determinate self-attributes.

A similar variety of *indeterminate* answers has been given to the questions raised by ambiguities and inconsistencies in symbolic interaction orientation.

One answer appears to see virtually all significant attributes of behavior to be internal choices and other self-indications, all of which are conceived to be emergent, with no observable, regular antecedent.

Another is similar to this view but sees antecedents to these internal events in experiences lost, or partially lost, in the antiquity of the individual's early biography, and without too close a dependence on, or regularity with, such early happenings.

A third sees the significant variables as external behaviors which are either unrelated to the self, or deviously related, or only loosely related to the self. Such is often the kind of orientation held by those who see a sharp disjunction between public and private selves, where the private self is the true self with unresearchable antecedents, and where the public self is the social self, both in that it relates to observable behaviors and in that it has social antecedents.

A fourth conceives external events to be shaped more or less unpredictably by self-activities which in turn are "self-developed," *i.e.*, indeterminate in any testable way.

If one were to arrogate to oneself the privilege of deciding these issues and others raised essentially by the ambiguities in symbolic interaction orientation, one could narrow sharply the task of surveying the major trends in this theory in the past twenty-five years. This, however, I deem to be neither proper nor useful. Similarly, if symbolic interactionists had their own professional organization, their own journal or journals, their own pontifical leader or tight-knit little clique of leaders clearly assigned the role of determining the "correct" view among competing doctrinal differences, the survey of the fruits of orthodoxy might be simple. Instead, however, we have none of these things, and for the most part we wish none of them. But the consequences are that there is a welter of partial orientations which bear varying relationships to the general point of view.

There is, for example, *role theory*. Role theory has many intellectual antecedents other than those in Cooley, Dewey, Thomas, Faris, and Mead. There are debts, for instance, to Linton, to Moreno, to Parsons; there are often overtones of one or another of the learning theories. These are but a few of the strands of thought in role theory. Yet role theory is not sharply distinguishable—if at all—from symbolic interactionism. The *emphasis* in role theory is on overt role playing and on the researchable relation between role expectations and role performances; the emphasis is either less, or altogether lacking, on role-taking, on the interior processes of the self, and what Shibutani calls the sentiments are often ignored. Thus role theory tends toward what Turner wishes to call the processes of conformity.[10]

Yet I must underscore the word *emphasis*, for in Sarbin's useful chapter in the *Handbook of Social Psychology*, there is no ignoring of self nor of empathy, nor is there in his own research (of which there is a fine example indicating a positive relation between role-taking ability on the one hand and degree of malleability of self-conception on the other).[11] But on the whole, role theory has implied [determinacy] of Type I.

Among the important contributions of the quarter-century under the general aegis of role theory have been the preliminary systematization provided in the early part of Gross, Mason, and McEachern's *Explorations in Role Analysis*, and Turner's paper in Rose's *Human Behavior and Social Processes*, in which issues of determinacy vs. indeterminacy of the sort here proposed for all of symbolic interactionism are made with respect specifically to role theory.[12] Role theory has engendered a great deal of research; in fact, it is as much to role theory as to any other development that I point when I have designated this period under scrutiny as the era of inquiry. This is no place in which to attempt to summarize this research. By and large we can say it has underscored Thomas' dictum that "people tend to play the roles assigned to them." There is by no means any strong evidence that there is a completely determinate relation between role expec-

[10] [Cp. Shibutani, *op. cit.*, pp. 323 ff., 548 ff. *et passim*; Ralph H. Turner, "Role-Taking: Process Versus Conformity," in *Human Behavior and Social Processes: An Interactionist Approach*, Arnold M. Rose, ed. (Boston: Houghton Mifflin, 1962), pp. 20–40.— The Editor].

[11] Theodore R. Sarbin, "Role Theory," in *Handbook of Social Psychology*, ed. by Gardner Lindzey (Cambridge, Mass.: Addison-Wesley Publishing Company, 1954), 1:223–58. [The example of Sarbin's own research that Kuhn probably had in mind is Theodore R. Sarbin and Norman L. Farberow, "Contributions to Role-Taking Theory: A Clinical Study of Self and Role," *Journal of Abnormal and Social Psychology*, 47: 117–25 (Jan., 1952).–The Editor.]

[12] Neal Gross, Ward S. Mason, and Alexander W. McEachern, *Explorations in Role Analysis: Studies of the School Superintendency Role* (New York: John Wiley, 1958); Ralph H. Turner, "Role-Taking: Process Versus Conformity," *op. cit.*

tations or recipes on the one hand and role performance on the other. On the other hand, there is a growing mountain of evidence that with "known" or public role recipes in hand we can make very useful probabilistic predictions with respect to subsequent behaviors, not alone those representing the answering role performances but even those which are but logically related and ancillary behaviors.

Much of the utility of role theory has been demonstrated thus far in the study of internalized role conflicts and contradictions. This study has ranged from the imaginative employment of personal documents and interviews by Mirra Komarovsky in her study of the conflicts surrounding the role of young women in college[13] to the construction of fairly precise and rigorous scales in the measure of such role conflict in the work of Stouffer and Toby. Even in such studies which imply internalization and thus the interposition of intermediate or intervening variables into our Type I determinacy pattern, such intervening variables are basically unnecessary even in the operations by Komarovsky; for although they involved reports of subjective valuations, these reports could have been replaced by direct observations of communications applying the opposing pressures—it was simply inconvenient to do so.

Another equally salient development has been that of *reference group* theory, so-named, of course, by Hyman[14] but getting much of the attention it has received from the concept of relative deprivation as employed by Stouffer in *The American Soldier* and as reworked in the well-known chapter on reference group theory by Merton and Kitt.[15] There have been a number of useful theoretical critiques as well as creative employments of reference group theory, notable among them those of Kelley, Shibutani, Turner, Newcomb, and Sherif. The notion of reference group is obviously closely related to the whole problem of the other as dealt with by Mead and Sullivan on the one hand, and to that of the primary group as described by Cooley and Faris on the other. Much of the employment of this new theory has been so far to provide *ex post* or circular explanation (explanation by naming). Controversy abounds, to be sure, over the meaning of the term *reference group* itself—whether it refers to a normative or to an evaluative function; whether it must point to groups, to categories or both; whether it may best refer to relationships, as Rose suggests, or whether we may

---

[13] Mirra Komarovsky, *Women in the Modern World: Their Education and Their Dilemmas* (Boston: Little, Brown, 1953).

[14] H. Hyman, *The Psychology of Status* (Archives of Psychology, Vol. 38, no. 269, June, 1942).

[15] Robert K. Merton and Alice S. Kitt, "Contributions to the Theory of Reference Group Behavior," in *Continuities in Social Research: Studies in the Scope and Method of "The American Soldier,"* ed. by Robert K. Merton and Paul F. Lazarsfeld (Glencoe, Illinois: The Free Press, 1950): reprinted in Robert K. Merton, *Social Theory and Social Structure,* revised and enlarged edition (Glencoe, Ill.: Free Press, 1957), pp. 225–80.

better use it to refer to derivative orientations, as Shibutani indicates. May we use the term to refer to empirically identifiable attitudes, expectations, and norms of existent *others*, or must we limit ourselves to such matters only after they have been transmuted to the images in the imagination of the *actors* themselves, to which Cooley referred as the "solid facts" of social life?

The classification of reference group theory is difficult, for in the theoretical statements of it, indeterminate model 7 fits, but in the actual application of the theory, determinate models 1 through 4 have been variously employed. The contradictions between theoretical statements and operational implications in reference group theory are one of the most unhappy aspects of symbolic interactionism today, in this author's opinion.

Next consider the related development of points of view known as *social perception* and *person perception*. If we regard the ancient dicta: "We see things not as they are but as we are," and "We do not first see and then define; we define first and then see," as intimately involved in the point of view of symbolic interactionism, we may properly claim at least a strong interest in the development of these interrelated schools. The researches contained in the volume edited by Petrullo and Tagiuri, for example, bear in many instances on hypotheses generated by symbolic interactionism.[16] On the other hand, this research movement is led by men relatively unacquainted with "our" literature. Consequently our own reaction to any one piece of research such as is contained in Petrullo and Tagiuri's volume is that it is in one or more respects naive: in its lack of sophistication about the function of language in interaction, in its failure to employ a concept equivalent to social act or social object or significant other, etc., etc.

Jerome Bruner, whose own experimental work on the differential perception of the size of coins by subjects of different income levels is a classic study in the field of social perception, has admirably stated in summary form the general position of these schools in "Social Psychology and Perception," in the third edition of *Readings in Social Psychology* edited by Maccoby, Newcomb, and Hartley.[17] His summary is such that the symbolic interactionist can easily deduce for himself the common ground this position shares with symbolic interaction theory; I am therefore spared this task by citing this article. I would only object that the Bruner paper misleads somewhat in failing to indicate the degree to which "perceptual set" as a key concept central to this school has come to serve as umbrella for Freudian rather than symbolic interaction variables, and for implying,

---

[16] *Person Perception and Interpersonal Behavior*, ed. by Renato Tagiuri and Luigi Petrullo (Stanford, Calif.: Stanford University Press, 1958).

[17] Jerome Bruner, "Social Psychology and Perception," in *Readings in Social Psychology*, 3rd ed., Editorial Committee: Eleanor E. Maccoby, Theodore M. Newcomb, Eugene L. Hartley (New York: Henry Holt, 1958), pp. 85–94.

on the other hand, that social perception treats what people are doing as central to the nature of what they perceive (for this is not borne out by their experimental designs).

Types of Symbolic Interaction Theory

Presupposing Determinacy	*Presupposing Indeterminacy*

(1) Soc A_1 ⎯⎯⎯►Beh C

(6)   A   Ch*
          Ind

(2) Soc A_1 ⎯⎯⎯►Self C

(7) A_2 ⎯ ⎯ ⎯*⎯►Ch*
                    Ind

(3) Soc A_2⎯⎯⎯►Self C

(8) $Self_{pr}$ A ⎯ ⎯*⎯ ⎯►$Self_{pub}$*

(4) Self A ⎯⎯⎯►Beh C

(9) $Self_{pr}$ A* ⎯ ⎯ ⎯*⎯►Beh C

(5) Self A ⎯⎯⎯►Self C

Where Soc refers to social variable
    Self refers to self variable, either holistic or elementalistic
    $Self_{pr}$ refers to "private self"
    $Self_{pub}$ refers to "public self"
    A indicates antecedent variable
    A_1 indicates immediately antecedent variable
    A_2 indicates antecedent but temporarily distal variable
    C indicates consequent variable
    Beh indicates overt behavioral variable
    Ch indicates internal choice-making
    Ind indicates internal (self) indications
    Em indicates an emergent (I or Me)
    Det indicates a determinate (I or Me)
    Solid arrow indicates a determinate, causal process
    Broken arrow indicates an indeterminate, emergent process
    Asterisk (*) indicates the locus of indeterminacy; this may lie in the nexus between antecedent and consequent variables as well as in any of the following internal aspects of the self:

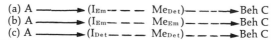

      (a) A ⎯⎯⎯► (I_{Em}⎯ ⎯ ⎯ Me_{Det})⎯ ⎯ ⎯►Beh C
      (b) A ⎯⎯⎯► (I_{Em}⎯ ⎯ ⎯ Me_{Em})⎯ ⎯ ⎯►Beh C
      (c) A ⎯⎯⎯►(I_{Det}⎯ ⎯ ⎯ Me_{Det})⎯ ⎯ ⎯►Beh C

    The models on which social and person perception theory rests appear to be types 1 and 4. That is, they are determinate and tend to designate either immediate or temporally distal antecedent social variables and consequent behavioral variables. Had symbolic interactionists initiated the exploration of this field, they would have emphasized the ways in which the individual conceives himself as antecedent and the manner he perceives other objects including persons as consequent, with probably some attention to designs in which these types of variables are reversed in time.

    So far, we have dealt with subtheories which have had very ambiguous boundaries. The same thing is certainly true of *self* theory with which I have identified my own research activities. It was my intention in 1946 or

1947 to employ a term which would not so much differentiate an emerging point of view from the more or less orthodox ideas of symbolic interaction as it would enable, on the other hand, a distinction between a body of conjectural and deductive orientation—as represented by Cooley, Dewey, and Mead—and a derivative but developing set of generalizations, tested by empirical research. I found later that, at about the same time, Carl Rogers had also termed as self theory his notions in clinical psychology having to do with the varying discrepancies between the actual or perceived self and the ideal self. Since then the term has been variously employed, often as an umbrella word, to cover several or all of the subtheories here under consideration.

The work undertaken by students of symbolic interaction at the State University of Iowa followed in several respects the programmatic proposals of the summary monograph on social psychology in the 1930s by Leonard Cottrell and Ruth Gallagher and of Cottrell's later presidential address before the American Sociological Society; that is to say, there has been considerable attention to the self itself and to role-taking.[18] McPartland[19] pioneered in his study relating differential nexi-to-social-structure to the differential characteristics of the self. Later he has studied the relations among self, social strata, and the differential syndromes of mental-emotional disturbance. Fred Waisanen[20] explored relations between self characteristics and prejudice. Stewart[21] demonstrated the often alleged relation of the self to a system of objects, as did Carl Waisanen[22] and Wynona Garretson[23] in other ways. Maranell[24] studied relations between self and role-taking and began the exploration of transparency, the obverse of empathy. Rogler[25] established that there is a direct relation between role-

[18] Leonard S. Cottrell, Jr., and Ruth Gallagher, *Developments in Social Psychology, 1930–1940* (New York: Beacon Press, 1941); Leonard S. Cottrell, Jr., "Some Neglected Problems in Social Psychology," *American Sociological Review*, 15:705–12 (Dec., 1950).

[19] Thomas S. McPartland, "The Self and Social Structure," unpublished doctoral dissertation, State University of Iowa, 1953; "Self Conception, Social Class, and Mental Health," *Human Organization*, 17:24–29 (1958); T. S. McPartland, John H. Cumming and Wynona S. Garretson, "Self Conception and Ward Behavior in Two Psychiatric Hospitals," *Sociometry*, 24:11–24 (June, 1961).

[20] F. B. Waisanen, "The Prejudice Variable: A Social Psychological and Methodological Study," unpublished doctoral dissertation, State University of Iowa, 1954.

[21] Robert L. Stewart, "The Self and Other Objects: Their Measurement and Interrelationship," unpublished doctoral dissertation, State University of Iowa, 1955.

[22] Carl E. Waisanen, "Preference Aspects of Self-Attitudes," unpublished doctoral dissertation, State University of Iowa, 1957.

[23] Wynona Smutz Garretson, "College as Social Object: A Study in Consensus," unpublished doctoral dissertation, State University of Iowa, 1961; "The Consensual Definition of Social Objects," *Sociological Quarterly*, 3:107–13 (Apr., 1962).

[24] Gary M. Maranell, "Role-Taking: Empathy and Transparency," unpublished doctoral dissertation, State University of Iowa, 1959.

[25] Lloyd H. Rogler, "An Experimental Study of the Relationship between Structured Behavior Patterns and Accuracy of Social Sensitivity," unpublished doctoral dissertation, State University of Iowa, 1957.

taking and access to a communication system. The validation and extension of symbolic interaction ideas represented in these researches is for the most part preliminary and one must assess it as modest. Perhaps the most significant contribution of the Iowa research is simply that in which it joins the research of Miyamoto and Dornbusch, Deutsch and Solomon, Dick, Dinitz and Mangus, McKee and Sheriffs, Stryker, Videbeck and Bates, and many others in demonstrating to some degree at least that the key ideas of symbolic interactionism could be operationalized and utilized successfully in empirical research.[26]

Self theory of this variety has implied one or another of the five determinate models in our diagram, although this point is implicit rather than explicit, and never a salient issue. The general attempt rests on the notion that there is among the several important matters a process considered nomothetic or genotypical by the symbolic interaction orientation.

Among the subtheories that seem to imply indeterminacy—phenomenological theory, the study of careers, language, and culture of Sapir and Whorf, the interpersonal theory of H. S. Sullivan, the self-constancy and self-actualizing theories of such men as Stegner and Maslow—one seems to stand out as just a shade more radical and eye-catching than the rest: the *dramaturgical* school of Kenneth Burke, Erving Goffman, and possibly Nelson Foote and Gregory Stone. The most significant alteration made by this school is the general transmutation of the social act from what in traditional symbolic interactionism had continued to be paradoxically an individual model (triggered by organic tensions and impulses and following through the course of the action with reference to the single—almost feral—man to equilibrium, restitution of tensionlessness in the organism) to the team-of-players model which implies that social agenda rather than tissue conditions serve to initiate the act and to cue its end as well. This, of course, is but one of the extremely provocative aspects of dramaturgical theory, especially as initiated by Burke and developed by Goffman.

The difficulties with this subtheory are, in the main, those of deriving from it any testable generalizations. One must be tentative about this, it seems to me, for this was exactly the complaint lodged against the whole of symbolic interaction orientation in its early years. It may well be that ingenious solutions will be found to the problems of operationalizing the basic conceptions of this orientation.

Of the models we suggest diagrammatically, numbers 8 and 9 seem to be the ones most frequently implied in dramaturgical theory, although the team characteristics of Goffman's units appear to imply models indicating team rather than individual conduct.

The longitudinal study of socialization and especially of career trajectories, best indicated in the work of E. C. Hughes and Howard S. Becker,

---

[26] See the appended bibliography.

seems also to lie on the indeterminacy side. The work of these two men is virtually as imaginative and as creative as that of Burke and of Goffman. There is, in the literature, no more insightful account of the relation of the actor to a social object through the processes of communication and of self-definition, than Becker's account of becoming a marijuana user.[27] Hughes's sensitivity to lingual indicators of status is wonderfully revealed in his well-known and fundamental essay, "Work and the Self."[28] In it he presents a modern-age social psychological interpretation of "what the social classes owe to each other."

Again, the difficulties with this approach seem to lie in operationalization. It is most difficult to establish generalizations valid for human behavior without methods wherewith to make precise checks on intersubjective perceptions of events such as are involved in witnessing transitional stages in a socialization process or rites of passage in the trajectory of a career.

The indeterminate model on which this approach seems to rest is our type no. 7; that is, the antecedent variables, temporarily distal, are loosely (indeterminately) related to the processes of choice and self-indication which constitute the self.

The *interpersonal theory* of psychiatry proposed by Harry Stack Sullivan was constructed early in this quarter-century period.[29] It has been almost ubiquitously incorporated into the general body of symbolic interaction orientation, or perhaps the verb should be "reincorporated" since Sullivan had been well introduced to Meadian theory in the 1920s and had built the interpersonal theory in significant part out of elements provided by Mead on the one hand and by Freud on the other. The theory is distinctive for the unique way in which it manages a synthesis of Meadian and Freudian viewpoints without admitting any of the Freudian nonsense about phylogenetic inheritance of unconscious sense of guilt, the early Oedipus notion, the nature of man pitted against society, etc., while utilizing to the full the power of Freudian explanation of interpersonal rivalry and of distortions in communication—down to the utilization of the concept of self-derogation and self-rejection and repression (the not-me)—concepts hinging on interpersonal relations (reflected appraisals by others) rather than on thwarted instincts and biological drives as Freud had it.

Unfortunately the Sullivan interpersonal theory is quite disjoined from ideas of culture and of formal social organization. This has led Shibutani to set up disjunctive self components: Those derived from conventional role-playing and those derived as sentiments from the kinds

---

[27] Howard S. Becker, "Becoming a Marihuana User," *American Journal of Sociology* 59:235–42 (Nov., 1953) [reprinted in Part V of this book—The Editor]. [Cp. Howard S. Becker, *Outsiders: Studies in the Sociology of Deviance* (New York: Free Press of Glencoe, 1963)–The Editor.]

[28] Everett C. Hughes, "Work and the Self," in *Social Psychology at the Crossroads: The University of Oklahoma Lectures in Social Psychology,* ed. by John H. Rohrer and Muzafer Sherif (New York: Harper and Brothers, 1951), pp. 313–23.

[29] See the appended bibliography.

of interpersonal processes Sullivan described, completely divorced from culture and organized systems. It is also unfortunate that the interpersonal theory suffers from the same difficulties as the other indeterminate theories: inability to apply the usual scientific methods in order to build increasingly supported, dependable generalizations. The Sullivan model appears to rest on a combination of models, 7, 8, and 9, thus indicating looseness between antecedent, intervening and consequent variables, plus the possibility for further emergence in the interior processes of the self. The specific, temporally distal, antecedent variables, on which the theory rests are those having to do with what Sullivan calls the *parataxic* and *prototaxic* stages in what is essentially the preverbal period. In these, there is no real opportunity conceived for direct empirical observation, and thus there is further indeterminacy beyond the posited looseness between these stages and later self-attributes.

One more indeterminate subtheory is the Sapir-Whorf-Cassirer *language and culture orientation*.[30] This is truly a theory behind a theory, for it tends to be presumed by symbolic interactionists as being preliminary even to a consideration of the basic assumptions of the theory under review. The language and culture point of view is surely so familiar as not to need much description. It points to the basic proposition that a language consists of a very finite and limited number of concepts out of an unlimited set of possibilities. Furthermore it underscores the fact that even the ultimate and basic concepts—which we in our society think of as those dealing with time, motion, matter and space—are themselves lingually variable and relative. And, perhaps even more important, it takes the position that the very grammar of a language is based on an unspoken, taken-for-granted logic which determines how people in that society think about anything. Thus it must follow that the categorization of one's self and his attributes, as well as of his others, and of the significant nonhuman objects in his system of objects is entirely dependent on the language of his group. He cannot think of himself or his experiences, or of his relationships, except in the arbitrary conceptualizations provided him in his language.

This is an indeterminate theory in so far as the individual person's behavior is concerned, for the language only sets the basic framework for his thought and the outer limits, beyond which he cannot conceive of things. Within these limits, and around this framework, there is a looseness of connection. No determinate statements are suggested. However, attached as a preliminary set of assumptions to any of the previously examined determinate subtheories, this point of view removes it from determinacy only in the sense that, as is pointed out posthumously in the

---

[30] [See, *e.g.* Edward Sapir, *Language: An Introduction to the Study of Speech* (New York: Harcourt, Brace, 1921): Benjamin L. Whorf, *Language, Thought and Reality: Selected Writings* edited by John B. Carroll (Technology Press of Massachusetts Institute of Technology, 1956); Ernest Cassirer, *The Philosophy of Symbolic Forms*, 2 vols. (New Haven: Yale Univ. Press, 1953–1955)–The Editor.]

American Anthropologist by the late Clyde Kluckhohn, the Whorf-Sapir-Cassirer notions are basically untestable.[31]

There are a number of other subtheories which have had their development during these past twenty-five years and which are related in one or several respects to symbolic interactionism, and which serve, if nothing else, to suggest extensions or amendments to the orientation. These include such points of view as cognitive theory, field theory, phenomenology, the developmental notions of Piaget, the current scrutiny of identity which bears strong overtones of ego psychology, the self-constancy theory of Stager and others, and the self-actualizing theory of Maslow, in addition to which there is the self theory of Carl Rogers, already mentioned. Many of those theories were developed by students in the field of psychology. Few indicate acquaintance with the intellectual stream to which symbolic interactionism belongs. The line I have drawn, excluding these from consideration but including the ones I have discussed, is highly arbitrary and may not be defensible in any other sense than that time places limitations even upon the most condensed of discussions.

Applications

So far we have considered the development of amplifications, subtheories, and operationalizations of symbolic interaction theory. We cannot conclude without considering the promising starts made in applying the orientation to problem areas. There is the much neglected book by Lemert, *Social Pathology*,[32] which should have been called *A Social Psychology of Deviants*, in which the author makes the interesting proposal that a fundamental distinction exists in the behaviors of those whose deviation is accompanied by no corresponding self-definition and those whose deviation is so accompanied—he refers to the difference as secondary differentiation.

Much of the application of symbolic interaction theory has been made by students of crime and delinquency—notably Crossey, Glaser and Reckless. Of the Iowa students, Nardini in the field of the criminal,[33] Mulford in the area of the alcoholic,[34] Hurlburt in the area of family adjustment,[35]

[31] Clyde Kluckhohn, "Notes on Some Anthropological Aspects of Communication," *American Anthropologist* 63:895–910 (Oct., 1961).

[32] Edwin M. Lemert, *Social Pathology: Approach to the Theory of Sociopathic Behavior* (New York: McGraw-Hill, 1951).

[33] William Nardini, "Criminal Self-Conceptions in the Penal Community: An Empirical Study," unpublished doctoral dissertation, State University of Iowa, 1959.

[34] Harold A. Mulford, Jr., "Toward an Instrument to Identify and Measure the Self, Significant Others, and Alcohol in the Symbolic Environment: An Empirical Study," unpublished doctoral dissertation, State University of Iowa, 1955.

[35] Julia Knaff Hurlburt, "Role Expectations and the Self: An Empirical Study of Their Relationship to Marital Adjustment," unpublished doctoral dissertation, State University of Iowa, 1960.

and Nass in the field of driver safety records,[36] have made application of self-dimensions as antecedent variables in promising endeavors to understand consequent variable behavior in problem fields. The new compilation edited by Rose already referred to, *Human Behavior and Social Processes*, contains as its third and final section a set of papers on the relation of interaction theory to social problem areas. Notable is Rose's own paper presenting his social-psychological theory of neurosis, which has a number of parallels with Sullivan's theory, but is distinctive in most respects for its general application of the symbolic interaction orientation.[37]

Neglected Problems

I cannot leave the consideration of the development of symbolic interactionism in the past twenty-five years without reconsidering the title of Cottrell's presidential address—the question of "neglected problems." Many of the problems which he found to be neglected are still neglected, while others—such as role-taking, on which his own student, R. F. Dymond, made such a notable start[38]—are beginning to be studied with more and more sophistication.

There is no time here to make a thorough canvass of neglected problems, but I should like to mention two. One is the failure to make appropriate conceptualization of the varieties of functional relations that regularly occur between self and other. At present we appear to be in that rather foolish and useless situation in which we debate what a reference group really is. Most of the suggestions point to varieties of functional relations between self and groups or categories of others. The question ought not to be which of these is really a reference group, but rather, what special term shall we agree to use for each particular relation?[39] Having reached a consensus on a constructed vocabulary with which to refer to these

[36] Gilbert D. Nass, "A Study of the Teen-Age Driver, His Self-Definition, and Definition of the Driving Situation," unpublished Master's thesis, State University of Iowa, 1958.

[37] Arnold M. Rose, "A Systematic Summary of Symbolic Interaction Theory," in *Human Behavior and Social Processes.*

[38] [See Rosalind F. Dymond, "A Preliminary Investigation of the Relation of Insight and Empathy," *Journal of Consulting Psychology*, 12:228–33 (1948); "A Scale for the Measurement of Empathic Ability," *Journal of Consulting Psychology*, 13:127–33 (1949), reprinted in *Small Groups: Studies in Social Interaction*, ed. by A. Paul Hare, Edgar F. Borgatta, and Robert F. Bales (New York: Alfred A. Knopf, 1955), pp. 226–35. See also Rosalind F. Dymond, Anne S. Hughes, and Virginia L. Raabe, "Measurable Changes in Empathy with Age," *Journal of Consulting Psychology*, 16:202–6 (1952); Rosalind Dymond Cartwright, Julius Seeman, and Donald L. Grummon, "Patterns of Perceived Interpersonal Relations," *Sociometry* 19:166–77 (Sept., 1956)—The Editor.]

[39] [Cp. Manford H. Kuhn, "The Reference Group Reconsidered" (in this issue of *The Sociological Quarterly*), which was written shortly after the present essay.—The Editor.]

functional relationships between self and other, we need then to consider the serious questions of operationalization. What kinds of questions must be asked to discover the nature of the particular relationship under inquiry?

A second pressing question implied in much of this paper has to do with the process by which self-conceptions change. Some theorists, notably those who lean toward the indeterminate side, discuss self-change as if it were most volatile and evanescent; the self shifts with each new indication one makes to himself, and these indications are the constant accompaniments of experience. Others see in the self the more or less stable, continuous, organizing principle for the personality, offering the only constant, non-shifting anchorage for the perception of other objects. We have arrived at the point in sharpening of the tools by which we may identify self-attributes and measure them and compare them with those of others, where we may treat this issue as a researchable question. As we attempt to measure the relative stability of the self, we need to study the concomitants of self-attitude change. It may be argued that the self, like any attitude, may be usefully treated as an hypothesis which the individual holds about himself, and with respect to which he holds certain notions about testing for validity. We need to study in short what correlates of self-attitude stability are phenomenal and which are non-conscious and outside self-directed control.

If I may be permitted a brief look at the crystal ball, I would see in it for the next twenty-five years of symbolic interaction theory an accelerated development of research techniques on the one hand, and a coalescing of most of the separate subtheories under consideration in this paper on the other. I have a basic confidence that symbolic interactionism will hold its own and gain against the competition of such major theories as psychoanalysis, the learning theories, and field theory. The reason I am confident is that I believe that of these major theories only symbolic interactionism is logically consistent with the basic propositions of the social sciences: the psychic unity of man (Boas); the extreme cultural variability of man; the creativity of man; the continual socializability and modifiability of man; the ability of man to feed back complex correctives to his behavior without engaging in trial and error, or conditioning, learning.

Bibliography

Apple, D. "Learning Theory and Socialization," *American Sociological Review*, 16:23–27 (Feb., 1951). Comment by J. Gillin, *American Sociological Review*, 16:384 (June, 1951).
Argyris, C. "The Fusion of an Individual with the Organization," *American Sociological Review*, 19:267–72 (June, 1954).
Becker, Ernest. "Socialization, Command of Performance, and Mental Illness," *American Journal of Sociology*, 67:484–501 (Mar., 1962).
Becker, Howard S. "Problems of Inference and Proof in Participant Observation," *American Sociological Review*, 23:652–60 (Dec., 1958).

Becker, Howard S., and Carper, James. "The Elements of Identification with an Occupation," *American Sociological Review*, 21:341–48 (June, 1956).

Becker, Howard S., and Geer, Blanche. "The Fate of Idealism in Medical School," *American Sociological Review*, 23:50–56 (Feb., 1958).

Blau, Zena Smith. "Changes in Status and Age Identification," *American Sociological Review*, 21:198–203 (Apr., 1956).

Blumer, Herbert. "Sociological Analysis and the Variable," *American Sociological Review*, 21:683–90 (Dec., 1956).

Boogs, Stephen T. "An Interactional Study of Ojibwa Socialization," *American Sociological Review*, 21:191–98 (Apr., 1956).

Bordua, David J. "Authoritarianism and Intolerance of Nonconformists," *Sociometry*, 24:198–216 (June, 1961).

Brim, Orville J., Jr. "Family Structure and Sex Role Learning by Children: A Further Analysis of Helen Koch's Data," *Sociometry*, 21:1–16 (Mar., 1958).

Brown, J. C. "An Experiment in Role-Taking," *American Sociological Review*, 17:587–97 (Oct., 1952).

Bucher, Rue, and Strauss, Anselm. "Professions in Process," *American Journal of Sociology*, 66:325–34 (Jan., 1961).

Burke, Kenneth. *A Grammar of Motives*. New York: Prentice-Hall, 1945.

———. *A Rhetoric of Motives*. New York: Prentice-Hall, 1950.

Cameron, Norman. *The Psychology of Behavior Disorders*. Boston: Houghton Mifflin Co., 1947.

Cartwright, Rosalind Dymond, Seeman, Julius, and Grummon, Donald L. "Patterns of Perceived Interpersonal Relations," *Sociometry*, 19:166–77 (Sept., 1956).

Clark, John P. "Measuring Alienation Within a Social System," *American Sociological Review*, 24:849–52 (Dec., 1959).

Coates, Chas. H., and Pellegrin, Roland J. "Executives and Supervisors: Contrasting Self-Conceptions and Conceptions of Each Other," *American Sociological Review*, 22:217–20 (Apr., 1957).

Corwin, Ronald G. "A Study of Identity in Nursing," *Sociological Quarterly*, 2:69–86 (Apr., 1961).

Couch, Carl J. "Self-Attitudes and Degree of Agreement with Immediate Others," *American Journal of Sociology*, 63:491–96 (Mar., 1958).

———. "Family Role Specialization and Self-Attitudes in Children," *Sociological Quarterly*, 3:115–21 (Apr., 1962).

Cottrell, L. A., Jr. "The Adjustment of the Individual to His Age and Sex Roles," *American Sociological Review*, 7:617–20 (Oct., 1942).

———. "The Analysis of Situational Fields in Social Psychology," *American Sociological Review*, 7:370–82 (June, 1942).

———. "Some Neglected Problems in Social Psychology," *American Sociological Review*, 15:705–12 (Dec., 1950).

Coutu, Walter, *Emergent Human Nature*. New York: Knopf, 1949.

———. "Role-Playing *vs.* Role-Taking: An Appeal for Clarification," *American Sociological Review*, 16:180–87 (Apr., 1951). Comment by J. L. Moreno, *ibid.*, 16:550–51 (Aug., 1951).

Dai, B. "A Socio-Psychiatric Approach to Personality Organization," *American Sociological Review*, 17:44–49 (Feb., 1952).

———. "Personality Problems in Chinese Culture," *American Sociological Review*, 6:688–96 (Oct., 1941).

Davis, James A. "A Formal Interpretation of the Theory of Relative Deprivation," *Sociometry*, 22:280–96 (Dec., 1959).

Deutsch, Morton, and Solomon, Leonard. "Reactions to Evaluations by Others as Influenced by Self-Evaluations," *Sociometry*, 22:93–112 (June, 1959).

Dick, Harry R. "The Office Worker: Attitudes toward Self, Labor and Management," *Sociological Quarterly*, 3:45–56 (Jan., 1962).

Dinitz, Simon, Mangus, A. R., and Passamanick, Benjamin. "Integration and Conflict in Self-Other Conceptions as Factors in Mental Illness," *Sociometry*, 22:44–55 (Mar., 1959).

Faris, R. E. L. Social Psychology. New York: Ronald Press, 1952.
———. "Sociological Causes of Genius," American Sociological Review, 5:689–99 (Oct., 1940).
Foote, Nelson N. "Anachronism and Synchronism in Sociology," Sociometry, 21:17–29 (Mar., 1958).
———. "Identification as a Basis for a Theory of Motivation," American Sociological Review, 16:14–21 (Feb., 1951). Comment by R. Bendix, ibid., 16:22 (Feb., 1951).
Garretson, Wynona Smutz. "The Consensual Definition of Social Objects," Sociological Quarterly, 3:107–13 (Apr., 1962).
Gerth, Hans, and Mills, C. Wright. Character and Social Structure. New York: Harcourt Brace and Co., 1953.
Getzels, J. W., and Guba, E. G. "Role, Role Conflict and Effectiveness: An Empirical Study," American Sociological Review, 19:164–75 (Apr., 1954).
Glaser, Daniel. "Criminality Theories and Behavioral Images," American Journal of Sociology, 61:433–44 (Mar., 1956).
Goffman, Erving. The Presentation of Self in Everyday Life. Garden City, N.Y.: Doubleday Anchor, 1959.
Goldhamer, H. "Recent Developments in Personality Studies," American Sociological Review, 13:555–65 (Oct., 1948).
Gough, H. G. "A New Dimension of Status: I. Development of a Personality Scale," American Sociological Review, 13:401–9 (Aug., 1948).
Gross, Neal, Mason, Ward S., and McEachern, Alexander W. Explorations in Role Analysis: Studies of the School Superintendent Role. New York: Wiley, 1958.
Halbwachs, M. "Individual Psychology and Collective Psychology," American Sociological Review, 3:615–23 (Oct., 1938).
Heider, Fritz. The Psychology of Interpersonal Relations. New York: Wiley, 1958.
Hyman, H. The Psychology of Status (Archives of Psychology, vol. 38. no. 269, 1942).
Ichheiser, G. "Structure and Dynamics of Interpersonal Relations," American Sociological Review, 8:302–5 (June, 1943).
Jackson, Jay. "Reference Group Processes in a Formal Organization," Sociometry, 22:307–27 (Dec., 1959).
Kohn, Melvin L. "Social Class and the Exercise of Parental Authority," American Sociological Review, 24:352–66 (June, 1959).
Kohn, A. Robert, and Fiedler, Fred E. "Age and Sex Differences in the Perceptions of Persons," Sociometry, 24:157–64 (June, 1961).
Kuenzli, Alfred E. (ed.) The Phenomenological Problem. New York: Harper, 1959. Papers by Combs, Snygg, McLeod, Brewster Smith, Jessor, et al.
Lemert, Edwin M. Social Psychology. New York: McGraw Hill, 1951.
Lindesmith, A. R. "The Drug Addict as a Psychopath," American Sociological Review, 5:914–20 (Dec., 1940).
Littman, Richard A., Moore, Robert C. A., and Jones, John Pierce. "Social Class Differences in Child Rearing: A Third Community for Comparison with Chicago and Newton," American Sociological Review, 22:694–704 (Dec., 1957).
Lundy, Richard M. "Self Perceptions and Descriptions of Opposite Sex Sociometric Choices," Sociometry, 19:272–77 (Dec., 1956).
———. "Self Perceptions Regarding M–F and Descriptions Same and Opposite Sex Sociometric Choices," Sociometry, 21:238–46 (Sept., 1958).
McKee, John P., and Sherriffs, Alex C. "Men's and Women's Beliefs, Ideals, and Self-Concepts," American Journal of Sociology, 64:356–63 (Jan., 1959).
McPartland, T. S., Cumming, John H., and Garretson, Wynona S. "Self-Conception and Ward Behavior in Two Psychiatric Hospitals," Sociometry, 24:111–24 (June, 1961).
Mead, George Herbert. Mind, Self, and Society. Chicago: University of Chicago Press, 1934.
———. Movements of Thought in the Nineteenth Century. Chicago: University of Chicago Press, 1936.
———. The Philosophy of the Act. Chicago: University of Chicago Press, 1938.
Merrill, Francis, "Stendhal and the Self: A Study in the Sociology of Literature," American Journal of Sociology, 66:446–53 (Mar., 1961).

Merton, Robert K., and Kitt, Alice S. "Contributions to the Theory of Reference Group Behavior," in R. K. Merton and P. F. Lazarsfeld (eds.), *Continuities in Social Research: Studies in the Scope and Method of "The American Soldier."* Glencoe, Ill.: Free Press, 1950.

Mills, C. Wright. "Language, Logic and Culture," *American Sociological Review,* 4:670–80 (Oct., 1939).

———. "Situated Actions and Vocabularies of Motive," *American Sociological Review,* 5:904–13 (Dec., 1940).

Miyamoto, S. Frank, and Dornbusch, Sanford M. "A Test of Interactionist Hypotheses of Self-Conception," *American Journal of Sociology,* 61:399–403 (Mar., 1956).

Motz, A. B. "The Role Conception Inventory: A Tool for Research in Social Psychology," *American Sociological Review,* 17:465–71 (Aug., 1952).

Mullahy, Patrick. *The Contributions of Harry Stack Sullivan.* New York: Hermitage House, 1952.

Nathanson, Maurice. *The Social Dynamics of George H. Mead.* Washington, D.C.: Public Affairs Press, 1956.

Pfuetze, Paul E. *The Social Self.* New York: Bookman Associates, 1954.

Phillips, Bernard S. "A Role Theory Approach to Adjustment in Old Age," *American Sociological Review,* 22:212–17 (Apr., 1957).

Reckless, Walter C., Dinitz, Simon, and Murray, Ellen. "Self Concept as an Insulator Against Delinquency," *American Sociological Review,* 21:744–46 (Dec., 1956).

Reckless, Walter C., Dinitz, Simon, and Kay, Barbara. "The Self Component in Potential Delinquency and Potential Non-Delinquency," *American Sociological Review,* 22:566–70 (Oct., 1957).

Rose, Arnold (ed.) *Human Behavior and Social Processes.* Boston: Houghton Mifflin Co., 1962.

Rosengren, William R. "The Self in the Emotionally Disturbed," *American Journal of Sociology,* 66:454–62 (Mar., 1961).

Sarbin, Theodore, "Role Theory," in Gardner Lindzey (ed.), *Handbook of Social Psychology* (Cambridge, Mass.: Addison-Wesley Publ. Co., 1945), vol. 1, ch. 6, pp. 223–58.

Schuessler, K. F., and Strauss, A. "A Study of Concept Learning by Scale Analysis," *American Sociological Review,* 15:752–62 (Dec., 1950).

Shibutani, Tamotsu. *Society and Personality.* Englewood Cliffs, N.J.: Prentice-Hall, 1961.

Simpson, Richard L., and Simpson, Ida Harper. "The Psychiatric Attendant: Development of an Occupational Self-Image in a Low-Status Occupation," *American Sociological Review,* 24:389–92 (June, 1959).

Slater, Philip E. "Parental Role Differentiation," *American Journal of Sociology,* 67:296–311 (Nov., 1961).

Strauss, Anselm. *Mirrors and Masks: The Search for Identity.* Glencoe, Ill.: The Free Press, 1959.

Stryker, Sheldon. "Role-Taking Accuracy and Adjustment," *Sociometry,* 20:286–96 (Dec., 1957).

Sullivan, Harry Stack. "A Note on the Implications of Psychiatry. The Study of Interpersonal Relations for Investigations in the Social Sciences," *American Journal of Sociology,* 42:846–61 (May, 1937).

———. "Conceptions of Modern Psychiatry," *Psychiatry,* 3:1–117 (1940).

———. *Conceptions of Modern Psychiatry.* Washington: Wm. A. White Psychiatric Foundation, 1947.

———. *The Interpersonal Theory of Psychiatry.* New York: Norton, 1953.

Swanson, Guy E. "Mead and Freud: Their Relevance for Social Psychology," *Sociometry,* 24:319–39 (Dec., 1961).

Tagiuri, Renato, and Petrullo, Luigi (eds.) *Person Perception and Interpersonal Behavior.* Stanford, Calif.: Stanford University Press, 1958.

Tremmel, Wm. C. *The Social Concepts of George Herbert Mead.* Emporia State Research Studies, Kansas State Teachers College, vol. 5, no. 4 (June, 1957).

Troyer, W. L. "Mead's Social and Functional Theory of Mind," *American Sociological Review*, 11:198–202 (Apr., 1946).

Turner, R. H. "Moral Judgment: A Study in Roles," *American Sociological Review*, 17:70–77 (Feb., 1952).

―――. "Self and Other in Moral Judgment," *American Sociological Review*, 19:249–59 (June, 1954).

Videbeck, Richard. "Self-Conception and the Reactions of Others," *Sociometry*, 23:351–59 (Dec., 1960).

Videbeck, Richard, and Bates, Alan P. "An Experimental Study of Conformity to Role Expectations," *Sociometry*, 22:1–11 (Mar., 1959).

Watson, Jeanne. "A Formal Analysis of Sociable Interaction," *Sociometry*, 21:269–80 (Dec., 1958).

White, L. A. "Culturological vs. Psychological Interpretations of Human Behavior," *American Sociological Review*, 12:686–98 (Dec., 1947).

Whorf, Benjamin Lee. *Language, Thought and Reality*. New York: Wiley and the Technology Press of MIT, 1956.

Wylie, Ruth. *The Self Concept: A Critical Survey of Pertinent Research Literature*. Lincoln: University of Nebraska Press, 1961.

5   NORMAN K. DENZIN

The Research Act

The Interrelationship of Theory and Method

The sociological enterprise may be said to rest on these elements: theory, methodology, research activity, and the sociological imagination. The function of *theory*, which I define as an integrated body of propositions, the derivation of which leads to explanation of some social phenomenon, is to give order and insight to research activities. *Methodology*, on the other hand, represents the principal ways the sociologist acts on his environment; his methods, be they experiments, surveys, or life histories, lead to different features of this reality, and it is through his methods that he makes his research public and reproducible by others. As the sociologist moves from his theories to the selection of methods, the emergence of that vague process called *research activity* can be seen. In this process the personal preferences of a scientist for one theory or method emerge. Furthermore, his selection of a given problem area (e.g., delinquency, the family, etc.) often represents a highly personal decision.

Order is given to theory, methodology, and research activity through the use of what Mills termed the *sociological imagination*.

The sociological imagination, I remind you, in considerable part consists of the capacity to shift from one perspective to another, and in the process to build up an adequate view of a total society and its components. It is this imagination, of course, that sets off the social scientist from the mere technician. Adequate technicians can be trained in a few years. The sociological imagination can also be cultivated; certainly it seldom occurs without a great deal of routine work. Yet there is an unexpected quality about it. . . . There is a playfulness of mind back of such combining as well as a truly fierce drive to make sense of the world, which the technician as such usually lacks. Perhaps he is too well trained, too precisely trained. Since one can be *trained* only in what is already known, training sometimes incapacitates one from learning new ways; it makes one rebel against what is bound to be at first loose and even sloppy. But you cling to such vague images and notions, if they are yours, and you must work them out. For it is in such forms that original ideas, if any, almost always first appear [1959, pp. 211–12].

The sociological imagination demands variability in the research process. The processes by which sociology is done should not be made too rigorous; an open mind is required. What some regard as doctrinaire will be challenged by others and, therefore, methodological and theoretical principles must always be evaluated in terms of the sociological imagination. Rather than applying just a set of methodological principles to research strategies—which leads to an even greater gap between theory and method—I combine a theoretical perspective with a series of methodological rules, with symbolic interactionism as the theoretical framework and taking certain key principles from the scientific method and applying them to both theory and method. My aim is first to show that each method takes on a different meaning when analyzed in the interactionist framework—and hence can be shown to have different relevance for that theory—and second, by employing notions from the scientific method, I indicate how these methods can best be put to use to fit the demands of interaction theory. Third, and returning to the central thesis, I will suggest that methods are not atheoretical tools, but rather means of acting on the environment and making that environment meaningful. This point of view will, I hope, permit sociologists to overcome what I view as errors of the past, and reduce the gap that presently exists between theory and method. It should also lead sociologists to cease using methods in rote and ritualistic fashion, and enable us to move away from middle-range and small-scope theories to what I will term formal theory (see Simmel, 1950). Finally, I hope that this perspective will assist sociology toward the goal of a mature science of human interaction.

The Interactionist Perspective

The interactionist's conception of human behavior assumes that behavior is self-directed and observable at two distinct levels—the symbolic and the interactional (or behavioral). By "self-directed," I mean that humans can act toward themselves as they would toward any other object. As Blumer (1966) says, the human may "perceive himself, have conceptions of himself, communicate with himself, and act toward himself [p. 535]." This behavior, which Blumer calls "self-interaction," permits humans to plan and to align their actions with others. Integral to this position is the proposition that man's social world is not constituted of objects that have intrinsic meaning, but that the meaning of objects lies in man's plans of action. Human experience is such that the process of defining objects is ever changing, subject to redefinitions, relocations, and realignments, and for conduct toward any object to be meaningful, the definition of the object must be consensual. That is, if I cannot persuade another sociologist to accept my definition of what a particular research method means, I shall be incapable of discussing my actions with him.

The interactionist assumes that humans are able to act because they have agreed on the meanings they will attach to the relevant objects in their environment. But before such consensus can occur, common symbolic languages must be present, and in sociology it is mandatory that agreement over basic terms be established before serious activity can begin. Consequently it will be necessary to give precise definitions to the terms *theory, method, experiment, social survey, participant observation* and *validity*. The interactionist additionally assumes that man learns his basic symbols, his conceptions of self, and the definitions he attaches to his social objects through interaction with others. Man simultaneously carries on conversations with himself and with his significant others.

Methodological Consideration from Interaction Theory

Given these basics of the interactionist perspective, I can now propose a series of principles that this perspective demands of its methodologies. If human behavior is observable at two levels—the symbolic and the behavioral—then central to understanding such behavior are the range and variety of symbols and symbolic meanings shared, communicated, and manipulated by interacting selves in social situations. Society contributes two essential elements that reflect directly on concrete interactions: the symbols, or various languages provided and communicated through the socialization process; and the concrete behavioral settings in which behavior occurs.

An interactionist assumes that a complete analysis of human conduct will capture the symbolic meanings that emerge over time in interaction. But the sociologist must also capture variations in ongoing patterns of behavior that reflect these symbols, images, and conceptions of self. These symbols are manifold and complex, verbal and nonverbal, intended and unintended. Verbal utterance, nonverbal gesture, mode and style of dress, and manner of speech all provide clues to the symbolic meanings that become translated into and emerge out of interaction.

The *first methodological principle* is that symbols and interaction must be brought together before an investigation is complete. To focus only on symbols, as an attitude questionnaire might, fails to record the emergent and novel relationships these symbols have with observable behavior. If I am studying the relationship between marijuana use and the strategies of concealing the drug in the presence of nonusers I will want to show that a marijuana user's attitude toward outsiders is reflected in his behavior in their presence. It would be insufficient to document only the fact that users do not like to get "high" when an outsider is present. Committed to the interactionist position, I must go further and demonstrate how this attitude is influenced by contact with nonusers.

Becker (1953, 1955, 1962) has provided such an analysis. In his interviews (1962, p. 597) it was discovered that among nonregular smokers fear of discovery took two forms: that nonusers would discover marijuana in one's possession; and that one would "be unable to hide the effects of the drug when he is 'high' with nonusers." This type of user adopts deliberate strategies to conceal the effects and presence of marijuana; he may even smoke infrequently because he cannot find a "safe" setting. Among regular users such fears are not present, although Becker indicated that as their interactional contacts change regular users may find it necessary to revert to only occasional use. One regular user who had married a nonuser eventually turned to irregular use. The following excerpt from Becker describes this pattern and demonstrates how the meanings attached to the social object (marijuana) actually emerged in patterns of interaction:

(This man had used marihuana quite intensively but his wife objected to it.) Of course, largely the reason I cut off was my wife. There were a few times when I'd feel like . . . didn't actually crave for it but would just like to have had some. (He was unable to continue using the drug except irregularly on those occasions when he was away from his wife's presence and control [1962, p. 598].)

A *second methodological principle* suggests that because symbols, meanings, and definitions are forged into self-definitions and attitudes, the reflective nature of selfhood must be captured. That is, the investigator must indicate how shifting definitions of self are reflected in ongoing patterns of behavior. He must, therefore, view human conduct from the point of view of those he is studying—"take the role of the acting other in concrete situations"—and this may range from learning the other's language to capturing his salient views of self. Returning to the example of the marijuana user, it would be necessary to learn the language of marijuana subcultures, which, as Becker shows, includes special words for getting "high" and has various categorizations for "outsiders."

Taking the role of the acting other permits the sociologist to escape the *fallacy of objectivism;* that is, the substitution of his own perspective for that of those he is studying. Too often the sociologist enters the field with preconceptions that prevent him from allowing those studies to tell it "as they see it." A student of marijuana use, for example, may incorrectly generalize from his own experiences with it to the group of users he is studying. Often the investigator will find that the meanings he has learned to attach to an object have no relevance for the people he is observing. This error occurs frequently in areas of conduct undergoing rapid change; studies of racial interaction, political activity, fads and fashions, and even analyses of stratification hierarchies in bureaucracies may provide cases where the definitions of the sociologist bear only slight resemblances to the actual situation.

Everyday and Scientific Conceptions of Reality

I wish to maintain a distinction between the sociologist's conceptions of his subject's behavior and the motives and definitions that subjects ascribe to their own conduct. The way a subject explains his behavior is likely to differ from the way a sociologist would. Marijuana users, for example, do not employ such terms as "morality," "rationalization," "collusion," "social control," "subculture," "socialization," or "role behavior." Commenting on this fact Becker notes that the sociological view of the world is "abstract, relativistic and generalizing [1964, p. 273]." On the other hand, the everyday conception of reality that guides our subject's conduct is specific, tends not to be generalizing, and is based on special concepts that often lack any scientific validity.

These points suggest that it is insufficient merely to state that the sociologist must take the role of the acting other in his investigations, and that a distinction must be made between everyday conceptions of reality and scientific conceptions of that reality. An adherence to my second principle suggests that the sociologist first learns the everyday conceptions of this reality and then interprets that reality from the stance of his sociological theory. This is the strategy Becker employed in his analysis of the marijuana user. He began with a symbolic interactionist conception of human conduct, and applied it to behavior in the marijuana subculture. His concepts were shaped by the meanings given them by the user, but he retained their sociological meaning. The sociologist must operate between two worlds when he engages in research—the everyday world of his subjects and the world of his own sociological perspective. Sociological explanations ultimately given for a set of behaviors are not likely to be completely understood by those studied; even if they prove understandable, subjects may not agree with or accept them, perhaps because they have been placed in a category they do not like or because elements of their behavior they prefer hidden have been made public. An irreducible conflict will always exist between the sociological perspective and the perspective of everyday life (Becker, 1964). This is a fact the sociologist must recognize. I raise this problem at this point to indicate that a commitment to my second principle goes further than merely taking the role of the other; sociologists must also place their interpretations within a sociological perspective.

Taking the role of the acting other leads to the *third methodological principle:* The investigator must simultaneously link man's symbols and conceptions of self with the social circles and relationships that furnish him with those symbols and conceptions. Too frequently failure to achieve this link leaves studies of human conduct at an individualistic level, and as a consequence the impact of broader social structures on subjects' conduct can be only indirectly inferred. This principle is not unique to the interactionist perspective, but derives ultimately from a conception of sociology that holds that the impact of social structure on groups and individuals must be examined.

Applying this principle to the study of marijuana use suggests that the investigator must demonstrate how an individual user's definitions of the object are related to his group's conceptions. The following excerpt from Becker's interview with a regular user satisfies this principle.

(You don't dig [like] alcohol then?) No, I don't dig it at all. (Why not?) I don't know. I just don't. Well, see, here's the thing. Before I was at the age where kids start drinking I was already getting on (using marihuana) and I saw the advantages of getting on, you know, I mean there was no sickness and it was much cheaper. That was one of the first things I learned, man. Why do you want to drink? Drinking is dumb, you know. It's so much cheaper to get on and you don't get sick, and it's not sloppy and takes less time. And it just grew to be the thing you know. So I got on before I drank, you know. . . .

(What do you mean that's one of the first things you learned?) Well, I mean, as I say, I was just starting to play jobs as a musician when I got on and I was also in a position to drink on the jobs, you know. And these guys just told me it was silly to drink. They didn't drink either [1962, p. 603].

This interview offers an excellent instance of how a person's attitude toward a social object represents a combination of his own attitudes and those of his social groups. My third principle is satisfied when personal and social perspectives are blended in a fashion similar to Becker's analysis. In Chapters 7 through 11 I show that the major methods of the sociologist meet this requirement in different ways.

The *fourth methodological principle* derives from the statement that any society provides its members with a variety of behavior settings within which interaction can occur. Research methods must therefore consider the "situated aspects" of human conduct—that is, whenever sociologists engage in observation, they must record the dynamics of their specific observational situations. Situations vary widely in terms of the norms governing conduct within them, and participants in any behavioral setting both create and interpret the rules that influence normal conduct within that situation. Recording the situationality of human interaction would be less important if it were not that symbols, meanings, conceptions of self, and actions toward social objects all vary because of the situation. As shown by Becker's study of marijuana users, in "safe" situations among regular users, the marijuana smoker is likely to get "high" and feel no restraints in discussing the effects of the object on his conduct; in "unsafe" situations he will go to extremes of secrecy and concealment.

"Situating" an observation or a respondent may require no more than asking the respondent to answer questions in terms of the situations where he normally engages in the behavior under study. Stone (1954) achieved this goal in his study of female shoppers in a large urban locale; he explicitly situated his respondents by symbolically placing them within their favored shopping locale, thus permitting a designation and description of relevant activities on that basis.

Social selves, I am suggesting, are situated objects that reflect ongoing definitions of social situations. For this reason both the meanings attached to these situations and the types of selves and interactions that emerge within them must be examined. Stone's investigation treats the meanings attached to shopping situations and indirectly infers the types of selves that flow from them. Becker's study achieves both goals: the meaning or definitions of the situation and the self-attitudes of marijuana users in varying situations.

Implicit thus far has been the assumption that the forms and processes of interaction must be reflected in sociological methodologies. Since the emergent relationship between self-conceptions, definitions of social objects, and ongoing patterns of interaction must be recorded, analyzed, and explained, the *fifth methodological principle* is that research methods must be capable of reflecting both stable and processual behavioral forms. Speaking of models of causation, Becker makes the following argument for processual analyses of human behavior.

All causes do not operate at the same time, and we need a model which takes into account the fact that patterns of behavior *develop* in orderly sequence. In accounting for an individual's use of marijuana, as we shall see later, we must deal with a sequence of steps, of changes in the individual's behavior and perspectives, in order to understand the phenomenon. Each step requires explanation, and what may operate as a cause at one step in the sequence may be of negligible importance at another step. We need, for example, one kind of explanation of how a person comes to be in a situation where marijuana is easily available to him, and another kind of explanation of why, given the fact of its availability, he is willing to experiment with it in the first place. And we need still another explanation of why, having experimented with it, he continues to use it. In a sense, each explanation constitutes a necessary cause of the behavior. That is, no one could become a confirmed marijuana user without going through each step. He must have the drug available, experiment with it, and continue to use it. The explanation of each step is thus part of the explanation of the resulting behavior [1963, p. 23].

As I turn to the individual methods of the sociologist it will become apparent that some are better suited than others for the above kinds of analyses, that surveys better measure static and stable forms of behavior while life histories and participant observation more adequately lend themselves to processual analyses.

The Role of Methods

The *sixth methodological principle* necessarily becomes more abstract and reflects directly on the role of methods in the entire sociological enterprise. It states that the very act of engaging in social research must be seen as a process of symbolic interaction, that being a scientist reflects a continual attempt to lift one's own idiosyncratic experiences to the level of the consensual and the shared meaning. It is in this context that the research method becomes the major means of acting on the symbolic environment and making those actions consensual in the broader community of sociologists.

When a sociologist adopts the surveys as a method of research he does so with the belief that when he reports his results other investigators will understand how he proceeded to gather his observations. The word *survey* designates a social object that has some degree of consensus among other sociologists. But more than this the word implies a vast variety of actions in which one will engage after he has adopted the method. Persons will be sampled, questionnaires will be constructed, responses will be coded, computers will be employed, and some form of statistical analysis will be presented. If, on the other hand, participant observation is chosen as a method, smaller samples will be selected, documents will be collected, informants will be selected, unstructured interviewing will be done, and descriptive statistical analyses will be presented.

If a situation can be imagined in which two sociologists adopt different methods of study, the impact of symbolic interaction on their conduct can be vividly seen. Suppose that the same empirical situation is selected—for example, a mental hospital. The first investigator adopts the survey as his method; the second, participant observation. Each will make different kinds of observations, engage in different analyses, ask different questions, and—as a result—may reach different conclusions. (Of course the fact that they adopted different methods is not the only reason they will reach different conclusions. Their personalities, their values, and their choices of different theories will also contribute to this result.)

Ultimately the sociologist's actions on the empirical world are achieved by the adoption of specific methodologies. His actions are translated into specific methods through lines of action that reflect his definitions of those methods. At the heart of this interaction is the concept. The concept, in conjunction with the research method, enables the sociologist to carry on an interaction with his environment. Observers indicate to themselves what a concept and a method mean and symbolically act toward the designation of those meanings. Sociologists are continually reassessing their imputed object meanings—assessing them against their relationships to theories, their ability to be observed by others, and their ability to generate understanding and explanation of empirical reality.

This point can be illustrated by again turning to Becker's study of the marijuana user. Beginning with an interactionist conception of human conduct, Becker applied the generic principles from that perspective to the problem of how occupancy of a role in a subculture shapes a person's perceptions and activities. His theory suggested that an intimate knowledge of the subject's perspective must be learned, and to this end he adopted the open-ended interview and participant observation as methodological strategies. Beginning with this conception, Becker's main line of action was to approach marijuana users and to have them present their experiences as they saw them. The final result of his analysis was a series of research findings that modified a role theory and subcultural theory of deviant behavior. In formulating his research observations and conclusions, Becker continually assessed his findings against his conceptual framework; his methods and concepts continuously interacted with observations and theory —that is, symbolic interaction guided the process of his research and theory construction.

The scientist, then, designates units of reality to act upon, formulates definitions of those objects, adopts research methods to implement these lines of action, and assesses the fruitfulness of his activity by his ability to develop, test, or modify existing social theory. Thus, both his concept and his research methodology act as empirical *sensitizers* of scientific observation. Concepts and methods open new realms of observation, but concomitantly close others. Two important consequences follow: If each method leads to different features of empirical reality, then no single method can ever completely capture all the relevant features of that reality; consequently, sociologists must learn to employ multiple methods in the analysis of the same empirical events.

It can of course be argued that all research methods stand in an instrumental relationship to the scientific process. Methods become plans of action employed as sociologists move from theory to reality. They are the major means of organizing creative energy and operational activities toward concepts and theories and, as such, they at once release and direct activity, the success of which is assessed by the ability to satisfy the normal criteria of validity while establishing fruitful ties with theory.

Research methods serve to provide the scientist with data that later may be placed in deductive schemes of thought. By observing several discrete instances of a concept or a series of concepts, scientists are able to move above the single instance to the more common problems that transcend immediate perceptions and observations. A failure to move beyond particularistic observations leaves the sociologist at the level of descriptive empiricism. He must establish articulations between his observations and some variety of theory. To the extent that Becker's investigation was related to a theoretical framework, he satisfied this demand. I can now claim another important role for methods in the scientific process: Methods are one of the major ways by which sociologists gather observations to test, modify, and develop theory.

In this sense, methods go hand in hand with the following less rigorous techniques of theory-work. It is reasonable to argue, I believe, that methods do not do all the relevant work for the sociologist. As stated earlier, underlying the use of methods must be a sociological imagination. It is necessary to recognize that such techniques as introspection, the use of imagined experiments, and the playful combination of contradictory concepts also serve as aids in the development of theory. Methods, because of their more public nature are too frequently given greater attention than these other techniques that are of equal relevance. (In Chapter 2 I will develop further the use of introspection and imagined experiments in the construction of social theory.)

The *seventh methodological principle* indicates that from the interactionist's perspective the proper use of concepts is at first sensitizing and only later operational; further, the proper theory becomes formal; and last, the proper causal proposition becomes universal and not statistical. By *sensitizing concepts* I refer to concepts that are not transformed immediately into *operational definitions* through an attitude scale or check list. An operational definition defines a concept by stating how it will be observed. Thus if I offer an *operational definition* for "intelligence," I might state that intelligence is the score received on an I.Q. test. But if I choose a *sensitizing approach* to measuring intelligence, I will leave it nonoperationalized until I enter the field and learn the processes representing it and the specific meanings attached to it by the persons observed. It might be found, for example, that in some settings intelligence is not measured by scores on a test but rather by knowledge and skills pertaining to important processes in the group under analysis. Among marijuana users intelligence might well be represented by an ability to conceal the effects of the drug in the presence of nonusers. Once I have established the meanings of a concept, I can then employ multiple research methods to measure its characteristics. Thus, closed-ended questions, direct participation in the group being studied, and analysis of written documents might be the main strategies of operationalizing a concept. Ultimately, all concepts must be operationalized—must be measured and observed. The sensitizing approach merely delays the point at which operationalization occurs.

Goffman's treatment of stigma provides an excellent example of what I mean by "sensitizing a concept." He began with a rather vague and loose definition of stigma that he claimed was "an attribute that is deeply discrediting." Three types of this attribute were designated: abominations of the body or physical deformities, blemishes on character (mental disorder, homosexuality, addiction, alcoholism), and last, tribal stigma of race, nation, and religion. Moving beyond classification, he analyzed data collected in such traditional sociological specialties as social problems, ethnic relations, social disorganization, criminology, and deviance. From these areas, relevant commonalities were organized around the stigma theme. In summarizing this analysis he states:

> I have argued that stigmatized persons have enough of their situations in life in common to warrant classifying all these persons together for purposes of analysis. An extraction has thus been made from the traditional fields of social problems. . . . These commonalities can be organized on the basis of a very few assumptions regarding human nature. What remains in each one of the traditional fields could then be reexamined for whatever is really special to it, thereby bringing analytical coherence to what is now purely historic and fortuitous unity. Knowing what fields like race relations, aging and mental health share, one could then go on to see, analytically, how they differ. Perhaps in each case the choice would be to retain the old substantive areas, but at least it would be clear that each is merely an area to which one should apply several perspectives, and that the development of any one of these coherent analytic perspectives is not likely to come from those who restrict their interest exclusively to one substantive area [1963, pp. 146–47].

Sensitizing a concept permits the sociologist to discover what is unique about each empirical instance of the concept while he uncovers what it displays in common across many different settings. Such a conception allows, indeed forces, the sociologist to pursue his interactionist view of reality to the empirical extreme.

The notion of formal as opposed to other types of theory will be further developed in chapters 2 and 3. At this point it is only necessary to indicate that such a stance relates directly to the assumption that universal explanations of human behavior can be developed. With Simmel (1950, pp. 3–25), I argue that human conduct presents itself in behavioral forms that differ only in content. The job of sociology is to discover the forms that universally display themselves in slightly different contexts. Simmel termed this the strategy of "formal sociology," an attempt to abstract from generically different phenomenon commonalities or similarities. The synthesis of these common threads into a coherent theoretical framework represents the development of "formal theory."

Society, for Simmel, existed only in forms of interaction:

> More specifically, the interactions we have in mind when we talk of "society" are crystallized as definable, consistent structures such as the state and the family, the guild and the church, social classes and organizations based on common interests.
>
> But in addition to these, there exists an immeasurable number of less conscious forms of relationship and kinds of interaction. Taken singly, they may appear negligible. But since in actuality they are inserted into the comprehensive and, as it were, official social formations, they alone produce society as we know it. . . . Without the interspersed effects of countless minor syntheses, society would break up into a multitude of discontinuous systems. Sociation continuously emerges and ceases, emerges again. . . . That people look at one another and are jealous of one another; that they exchange letters or dine together; that irrespective of all tangible interests they strike one another as pleasant or unpleasant; that gratitude for altruistic acts makes for inseparable union; that one asks another man after a certain street, and that people dress and adorn themselves for one another —the whole gamut of relations that play from one person to another and that may be momentary or permanent, conscious or unconscious, ephemeral or of grave consequence (and from which these illustrations are quite causally drawn), all these incessantly tie men together. Here are the interactions among the atoms of society [1950, pp. 9–10].

The sociological task, for Simmel, became the isolation of these forms of interaction.

> In its very generality, this method is apt to form a common basis for problem areas that previously, in the absence of their mutual contact, lacked a certain clarity. The universality of sociation, which makes for the reciprocal shaping of the individuals, has its correspondence in the singleness of the sociological way of cognition. The sociological approach yields possibilities of solution or of deeper study which may be derived from fields of knowledge continually quite different (perhaps) from the field of particular problem under investigation [1950, p. 14].

As examples of this strategy Simmel suggests that the student of mass crimes might profitably investigate the psychology of theater audiences. Similarly, the student of religion might examine labor unions for what they reveal about religious devotion, the student of political history, the history of art. The argument, I believe, is clear: A series of concepts and propositions from the interactionist perspective are thought to be sufficient to explain the wide ranges of human behavior—whatever the social or cultural context.

More contemporary spokesmen of this position include Goffman and Homans. Goffman proposes a "formal sociological" stance for the analysis of face-to-face interaction.

> Throughout this paper it has been implied that underneath their differences in culture, people everywhere are the same. If persons have a universal human nature, they themselves are not to be looked to for an explanation of it. One must look rather to the fact that societies everywhere, if they are to be societies, must mobilize their members as self-regulating participants in social encounters. One way of mobilizing the individual for this purpose is through ritual; he is taught to be perceptive, to have feelings attached to self and a self expressed through face, to have pride, honor and dignity, to have considerateness, to have tact and a certain amount of poise. . . . If a particular person or group or society seems to have a unique character of its own, it is because its standard set of human-nature elements is pitched and combined in a particular way. Instead of much pride, there may be little. Instead of abiding by rules, there may be much effort to break them safely. But if an encounter or undertaking is to be sustained as a viable system of interaction organized on ritual practices, then these variations must be held within certain bounds and nicely counterbalanced by corresponding modifications in some of the other rules and understandings. Similarly, the human nature of a particular set of persons may be specially designed for the special kind of undertakings in which they participate, but still each of these persons must have within him something of the balance of characteristics required of a usable participant in any ritually organized system of social activity [1967, pp. 44–45].

While the reader need not accept Goffman's theoretical perspective, its thrust is apparent—a small set of very abstract and general principles can explain all human behavior. Statements similar to Goffman's have been made by Homans, who has suggested that principles from economics and behavioral psychology can be employed to explain all of human conduct.

> I believe that, in view of the deficiencies of functional theory, the only type of theory in sociology that stands any chance of becoming a general one is a psychological theory, in the sense that the deductive systems by which we explain social behavior would, if completed, contain among their highest-order propositions one or more of those I call psychological. The time may come when they will lose their place at the top, when they in turn will be shown to be derivable from still more general propositions such as those of

physiology. But the time has not come yet, and psychological propositions remain our most general ones [1964, p. 968].

In the statements of Simmel, Goffman, and Homans there is an explicit commitment to formal sociological theory. Homans' theory would be based on propositions from psychology, Goffman's from functional theory and certain portions of symbolic interaction. In this context I can now *define* formal theory as any set of interrelated propositions based on a small set of concepts. Furthermore, these concepts will be ordered in such a way that some are more specific than others and hence capable of being derived from higher-order statements. Once this feature is achieved, *explanation* of the behavior indicated by those propositions shall be said to have occurred. A last feature of the formal theory, which distinguishes it from other types of theory, is the fact that it explicitly rests on empirical referents. Goffman's formulations are based on the observation that wherever face to face interaction occurs, participants will be observed employing strategies of tact, pride, defense, honor, and dignity. His highest-order proposition holds that all societies train their member-participants in the rituals of face-to-work because to do otherwise would leave that society without participants who could routinely engage in interaction. His lower-order propositions then include predictions concerning the balance between various types of rituals and their enactment in daily encounters.

While I have not extensively quoted from Homans, his highest-order proposition holds that "The more rewarding men find the results of an action, the more likely they are to take this action" [1964, p. 968]. It is Homans' belief that variations on this proposition will explain historical revolutions, daily interactions in work groups, and conduct within social organizations.

The work of these two spokesmen illustrates the use of formal theory as I have defined it. Contrast their perspective with that of Merton (1967, pp. 39–72), who believes that sociologists should develop middle-range theories of specific problem areas. Merton's formulation is too restrictive for our purposes; it leads to the endless proliferation of small-scope theories. (I shall develop this point in greater detail in the next chapter.) Grand theory represents the other alternative; it suggests that one very abstract and general theory can be developed to explain all of human behavior. Unfortunately, as it is currently practiced, grand theory has few, empirical referents. Formal theory, empirically grounded at all points, is preferable to a grand theory with a few empirical referents, or a series of middle-range theories, each of which have their own methods and specific domains.

Basic to formal theory will be universal interactive propositions that are assumed to apply to all instances of the phenomenon studied—at least until a negative case is discovered. By stating that these propositions will be interactive, I suggest that they will describe interrelationships between processes that mutually influence one another. In Becker's analysis of the marijuana user, an explicit reliance on interactive propositions of universal relevance can be seen.

> The analysis is based on fifty intensive interviews with marijuana users from a variety of social backgrounds and present positions in society. The interviews focused on the history of the person's experience with the drug, seeking major changes in his attitude toward it and in his actual use of it and the reasons for these changes. Generalizations stating necessary conditions for the maintenance of use at each level were developed in initial interviews, and tested and revised in the light of each succeeding one. The stated conclusions hold true for all the cases collected and may tentatively be considered as true of all marijuana users in this society, at least until further evidence forces their revisions [1962, p. 592].

Becker's generalizations rest on the assumption that they apply to all persons who have ever used marijuana. More abstractly, his formulations bear a relationship to a formal theory concerning symbolic interaction and the development of self-attitudes in a group setting. The earlier quoted passage describing the marijuana user who altered his using patterns after marrying a nonuser represents a description of an instance of interaction. The user's attitudes toward the object shifted and changed as he was forced to interact daily with a person who did not hold his definitions.

If the fact of human behavior is interaction, then sociological propositions must take an interactional form. In this sense Becker's analysis fits the criterion. The seventh principle, to summarize, is that methods must be constructed so that they contribute to formal theory while at the same time permitting sensitizing concept analysis and the discovery and verification of universal interactive propositions.

The Interactionist Principles in Review

I have shown that interaction theory suggests seven principles against which methods and sociological activity may be evaluated. These principles state:

1. Symbols and interactions must be combined before an investigation is complete.
2. The investigator must take the perspective or "role of the acting other" and view the world from his subjects' point of view—but in so doing he must maintain the distinction between everyday and scientific conceptions of reality.
3. The investigator must link his subjects' symbols and definitions with the social relationships and groups that provide those conceptions.
4. The behavior settings of interaction and scientific observation must be recorded.

5. Research methods must be capable of reflecting process or change as well as static behavioral forms.
6. Conducting research and being a sociologist is best viewed as an act of symbolic interaction. The personal preferences of the sociologist (e.g., his definitions of methods, his values and ideologies, etc.) serve to shape fundamentally his activity as an investigator, and the major way in which he acts on his environment is through his research methods.
7. The proper use of concepts becomes sensitizing and not operational; the proper theory becomes formal and not grand or middle-range; and the causal proposition more properly becomes interactional and universal in application.

References

Becker, Howard S., 1953. "Becoming a Marihuana User." *American Journal of Sociology* 59 (November): 235–42.

———, 1955. "Marihuana Use and Social Control." *Social Problems* 3 (July): 35–44. Reprinted in *Human Behavior and Social Processes*, Arnold M. Rose, ed., pp. 589–607. Boston: Houghton Mifflin.

———, 1963. *Outsiders: Studies in the Sociology of Deviance.* New York: Free Press.

———, 1964. "Problems in the Publication of Field Studies." In *Reflections on Community Studies*, Arthur J. Vidich, Joseph Bensman, Maurice R. Stein, eds. pp. 267–84. New York: John Wiley.

Blumer, Herbert, 1966. "Sociological Implications of the Thought of George Herbert Mead." *American Journal of Sociology* 71(March): 535–44.

Goffman, Erving, 1963. *Stigma.* Englewood Cliffs, New Jersey: Prentice-Hall.

———, 1967. *Interaction Ritual.* Chicago: Aldine Publishing Company.

Homans, George Caspar, 1964. "Contemporary Theory in Sociology." In *Handbook of Modern Sociology*, R. E. L. Faris, ed., pp. 951–77. Chicago: Rand McNally.

Merton, Robert K., 1967. *On Theoretical Sociology.* New York: The Free Press.

Mills, C. Wright, 1959. *The Sociological Imagination.* New York: Oxford University Press.

Simmel, Georg, 1950. *The Sociology of Georg Simmel*, Kurt Wolff, tran. New York: Free Press.

Stone, Gregory P., 1954. "City Shoppers and Urban Identification: Observations of the Social Psychology of City Life." *American Journal of Sociology* 60 (July): 36–45.

Sociological Analysis and the "Variable"

My aim in this paper is to examine critically the scheme of sociological analysis which seeks to reduce human group life to variables and their relations. I shall refer to this scheme, henceforth, as "variable analysis." This scheme is widespread and is growing in acceptance. It seems to be becoming the norm of proper sociological analysis. Its sophisticated forms are becoming the model of correct research procedure. Because of the influence which it is exercising in our discipline, I think that it is desirable to note the more serious of its shortcomings in actual use and to consider certain limits to its effective application. The first part of my paper will deal with the current shortcomings that I have in mind and the second part with the more serious question of the limits to its adequacy.

Shortcomings in Contemporary Variable Analysis

The first shortcoming I wish to note in current variable analysis in our field is the rather chaotic condition that prevails in the selection of variables. There seems to be little limit to what may be chosen or designated as a variable. One may select something as simple as a sex distribution or as complex as depression; something as specific as a birth rate or as vague as social cohesion; something as evident as residential change or as imputed as a collective unconscious; something as generally recognized as hatred or as doctrinaire as the Oedipus complex: something as immediately given as a rate of newspaper circulation to something as elaborately fabricated as an index of anomie. Variables may be selected on the basis of a specious impression of what is important, on the basis of conventional usage, on the basis of what can be secured through a given instrument or technique, on the basis of the demands of some doctrine, or on the basis of an imaginative ingenuity in devising a new term.

Obviously the study of human group life calls for a wide range of variables. However, there is a conspicuous absence of rules, guides, limitations and prohibitions to govern the choice of variables. Relevant rules are not provided even in the thoughtful regulations that accompany sophisti-

Herbert Blumer, "Sociological Analysis and the 'Variable,'" *American Sociological Review*, vol. 21 (December 1956), pp. 683–690. Reprinted by permission.
    Presidential address read at the annual meeting of the American Sociological Society, September 1956.

cated schemes of variable analysis. For example, the rule that variables should be quantitative does not help, because with ingenuity one can impart a quantitative dimension to almost any qualitative item. One can usually construct some kind of a measure or index of it or develop a rating scheme for judges. The proper insistence that a variable have a quantitative dimension does little to lessen the range or variety of items that may be set up as variables. In a comparable manner, the use of experimental design does not seemingly exercise much restriction on the number and kind of variables which may be brought within the framework of the design. Nor, finally, does careful work with variables, such as establishing tests of reliability, or inserting "test variables," exercise much restraint on what may be put into the pool of sociological variables.

In short, there is a great deal of laxity in choosing variables in our field. This laxity is due chiefly to a neglect of the careful reduction of problems that should properly precede the application of the techniques of variable analysis. This prior task requires thorough and careful reflection on the problem to make reasonably sure that one has identified its genuine parts. It requires intensive and extensive familiarity with the empirical area to which the problem refers. It requires a careful and thoughtful assessment of the theoretical schemes that might apply to the problem. Current variable analysis in our field is inclined to slight these requirements both in practice and in the training of students for that practice. The scheme of variable analysis has become for too many just a handy tool to be put to immediate use.

A second shortcoming in variable analysis in our field is the disconcerting absence of generic variables, that is, variables that stand for abstract categories. Generic variables are essential, of course, to an empirical science —they become the key points of its analytical structure. Without generic variables, variable analysis yields only separate and disconnected findings.

There are three kinds of variables in our discipline which are generally regarded as generic variables. None of them, in my judgment, is generic. The first kind is the typical and frequent variable which stands for a class of objects that is tied down to a given historical and cultural situation. Convenient examples are: attitudes toward the Supreme Court, intention to vote Republican, interest in the United Nations, a college education, army draftees and factory unemployment. Each of these variables, even though a class term, has substance only in a given historical context. The variables do not stand directly for items of abstract human group life; their application to human groups around the world, to human groups in the past, and to conceivable human groups in the future is definitely restricted. While their use may yield propositions that hold in given culture settings, they do not yield the abstract knowledge that is the core of an empirical science.

The second apparent kind of generic variable in current use in our discipline is represented by unquestionably abstract sociological categories, such as "social cohesion," "social integration," "assimilation," "authority," and "group morale." In actual use these do not turn out to be the generic variables that their labels would suggest. The difficulty is that such terms, as I sought to point out in an earlier article on sensitizing concepts,[1] have no fixed or uniform indicators. Instead, indicators are constructed to fit the particular problem on which one is working. Thus, certain features are chosen to represent the social integration of cities, but other features are used to represent the social integration of boys' gangs. The indicators chosen to represent morale in a small group of school children are very different from those used to stand for morale in a labor movement. The indicators used in studying attitudes of prejudice show a wide range of variation. It seems clear that indicators are tailored and used to meet the peculiar character of the local problem under study. In my judgment, the abstract categories used as variables in our work turn out with rare exception to be something other than generic categories. They are localized in terms of their content. Some measure of support is given to this assertion by the fact that the use of such abstract categories in variable research adds little to generic knowledge of them. The thousands of "variable" studies of attitudes, for instance, have not contributed to our knowledge of the abstract nature of an attitude; in a similar way the studies of "social cohesion," "social integration," "authority," or "group morale" have done nothing, so far as I can detect, to clarify or augment generic knowledge of these categories.

The third form of apparent generic variable in our work is represented by a special set of class terms like "sex," "age," "birth rate," and "time period." These would seem to be unquestionably generic. Each can be applied universally to human group life; each has the same clear and common meaning in its application. Yet, it appears that in their use in our field they do not function as generic variables. Each has a content that is given by its particular instance of application, e.g., the birth rate in Ceylon, or the sex distribution in the State of Nebraska, or the age distribution in the City of St. Louis. The kind of variable relations that result from their use will be found to be localized and non-generic.

These observations on these three specious kinds of generic variables point, of course, to the fact that variables in sociological research are predominantly disparate and localized in nature. Rarely do they refer satisfactorily to a dimension or property of abstract human group life. With little exception they are bound temporally, spatially, and culturally and are inadequately cast to serve as clear instances of generic sociological categories. Many would contend that this is because variable research and analysis are in a beginning state in our discipline. They believe that with the

---

[1] "What Is Wrong with Social Theory?" *American Sociological Review*, 19 (February 1954), pp. 3–10.

benefit of wider coverage, replication, and the co-ordination of separate studies disparate variable relations may be welded into generic relations. So far there has been little achievement along these lines. Although we already have appreciable accumulations of findings from variable studies, little has been done to convert the findings into generic relations. Such conversion is not an easy task. The difficulty should serve both as a challenge to the effort and an occasion to reflect on the use and limitations of variable analyses.

As a background for noting a third major shortcoming I wish to dwell on the fact that current variable analysis in our field is operating predominantly with disparate and not generic variables and yielding predominantly disparate and not generic relations. With little exception its data and its findings are "here and now," wherever the "here" be located and whenever the "now" be timed. Its analyses, accordingly, are of localized and concrete matters. Yet, as I think logicians would agree, to understand adequately a "here and now" relation it is necessary to understand the "here and now" context. This latter understanding is not provided by variable analysis. The variable relation is a single relation, necessarily stripped bare of the complex of things that sustain it in a "here and now" context. Accordingly, our understanding of it as a "here and now" matter suffers. Let me give one example. A variable relation states that reasonably staunch Erie County Republicans become confirmed in their attachment to their candidate as a result of listening to the campaign materials of the rival party. This bare and interesting finding gives us no picture of them as human beings in their particular world. We do not know the run of their experiences which induced an organization of their sentiments and views, nor do we know what this organization is; we do not know the social atmosphere or codes in their social circles; we do not know the reinforcements and rationalizations that come from their fellows; we do not know the defining process in their circles; we do not know the pressures, the incitants, and the models that came from their niches in the social structure; we do not know how their ethical sensitivities are organized and so what they would tolerate in the way of shocking behavior on the part of their candidate. In short, we do not have the picture to size up and understand what their confirmed attachment to a political candidate means in terms of their experience and their social context. This fuller picture of the "here and now" context is not given by variable relations. This, I believe, is a major shortcoming in variable analysis, insofar as variable analysis seeks to explain meaningfully the disparate and local situations with which it seems to be primarily concerned.

The three shortcomings which I have noted in current variable research in our field are serious but perhaps not crucial. With increasing experience and maturity they will probably be successfully overcome. They suggest, however, the advisability of inquiring more deeply into the interesting and important question of how well variable analysis is suited to the study of human group life in its fuller dimensions.

Limits of Variable Analysis

In my judgment, the crucial limit to the successful application of variable analysis to human group life is set by the process of interpretation or definition that goes on in human groups. This process, which I believe to be the core of human action, gives a character to human group life that seems to be at variance with the logical premises of variable analysis. I wish to explain at some length what I have in mind.

All sociologists—unless I presume too much—recognize that human group activity is carried on, in the main, through a process of interpretation or definition. As human beings we act singly, collectively, and societally on the basis of the meanings which things have for us. Our world consists of innumerable objects—home, church, job, college education, a political election, a friend, an enemy nation, a tooth brush, or what not—each of which has a meaning on the basis of which we act toward it. In our activities we wend our way by recognizing an object to be such and such, by defining the situations with which we are presented, by attaching a meaning to this or that event, and where need be, by devising a new meaning to cover something new or different. This is done by the individual in his personal action, it is done by a group of individuals acting together in concert, it is done in each of the manifold activities which together constitute an institution in operation, and it is done in each of the diversified acts which fit into and make up the patterned activity of a social structure or a society. We can and, I think, must look upon human group life as chiefly a vast interpretative process in which people, singly and collectively, guide themselves by defining the objects, events, and situations which they encounter. Regularized activity inside this process results from the application of stabilized definitions. Thus, an institution carries on its complicated activity through an articulated complex of such stabilized meanings. In the face of new situations or new experiences individuals, groups, institutions and societies find it necessary to form new definitions. These new definitions may enter into the repertoire of stable meanings. This seems to be the characteristic way in which new activities, new relations, and new social structures are formed. The process of interpretation may be viewed as a vast digestive process through which the confrontations of experience are transformed into activity. While the process of interpretation does not embrace everything that leads to the formation of human group activity and structure, it is, I think, the chief means through which human group life goes on and takes shape.

Any scheme designed to analyze human group life in its general character has to fit this process of interpretation. This is the test that I propose to apply to variable analysis. The variables which designate matters which either directly or indirectly confront people and thus enter into human group life would have to operate through this process of interpretation. The variables which designate the results or effects of the happenings which play upon the experience of people would be the outcome of the process of interpretation. Present-day variable analysis in our field is dealing predominantly with such kinds of variables.

There can be no doubt that, when current variable analysis deals with matters or areas of human group life which involve the process of interpretation, it is markedly disposed to ignore the process. The conventional procedure is to identify something which is presumed to operate on group life and treat it as an independent variable, and then to select some form of group activity as the dependent variable. The independent variable is put at the beginning part of the process of interpretation and the dependent variable at the terminal part of the process. The intervening process is ignored or, what amounts to the same thing, taken for granted as something that need not be considered. Let me cite a few typical examples: the presentation of political programs on the radio and the resulting expression of intention to vote; the entrance of Negro residents into a white neighborhood and the resulting attitudes of the white inhabitants toward Negroes; the occurrence of a business depression and the resulting rate of divorce. In such instances—so common to variable analysis in our field—one's concern is with the two variables and not with what lies between them. If one has neutralized other factors which are regarded as possibly exercising influence on the dependent variable, one is content with the conclusion that the observed change in the dependent variable is the necessary result of the independent variable.

This idea that in such areas of group life the independent variable automatically exercises its influence on the dependent variable is, it seems to me, a basic fallacy. There is a process of definition intervening between the events of experience presupposed by the independent variable and the formed behavior represented by the dependent variable. The political programs on the radio are interpreted by the listeners; the Negro invasion into the white neighborhood must be defined by the whites to have any effect on their attitudes; the many events and happenings which together constitute the business depression must be interpreted at their many points by husbands and wives to have any influence on marital relations. This intervening interpretation is essential to the outcome. It gives the meaning to the presentation that sets the response. Because of the integral position of the defining process between the two variables, it becomes necessary, it seems to me, to incorporate the process in the account of the relationship. Little effort is made in variable analysis to do this. Usually the process is completely ignored. Where the process is recognized, its study is regarded as a problem that is independent of the relation between the variables.

The indifference of variable analysis to the process of interpretation is based apparently on the tacit assumption that the independent variable predetermines its interpretation. This assumption has no foundation. The interpretation is not predetermined by the variable as if the variable emanated its own meaning. If there is anything we do know, it is that an object, event or situation in human experience does not carry its own meaning; the meaning is conferred on it.

Now, it is true that in many instances the interpretation of the object, event or situation may be fixed, since the person or people may have an already constructed meaning which is immediately applied to the item. Where such stabilized interpretation occurs and recurs, variable analysis would have no need to consider the interpretation. One could merely say that as a matter of fact under given conditions the independent variable is followed by such and such a change in the dependent variable. The only necessary precaution would be not to assume that the stated relation between the variables was necessarily intrinsic and universal. Since anything that is defined may be redefined, the relation has no intrinsic fixity.

Alongside the instances where interpretation is made by merely applying stabilized meanings there are the many instances where the interpretation has to be constructed. These instances are obviously increasing in our changing society. It is imperative in the case of such instances for variable analysis to include the act of interpretation in its analytic scheme. As far as I can see, variable analysis shuns such inclusion.

Now the question arises, how can variable analysis include the process of interpretation? Presumably the answer would be to treat the act of interpretation as an "intervening variable." But, what does this mean? If it means that interpretation is merely an intervening neutral medium through which the independent variable exercises its influence, then, of course, this would be no answer. Interpretation is a formative or creative process in its own right. It constructs meanings which, as I have said, are not predetermined or determined by the independent variable.

If one accepts this fact and proposes to treat the act of interpretation as a formative process, then the question arises how one is to characterize it as a variable. What quality is one to assign to it, what property or set of properties? One cannot, with any sense, characterize this act of interpretation in terms of the interpretation which it constructs; one cannot take the product to stand for the process. Nor can one characterize the act of interpretation in terms of what enters into it—the objects perceived, the evaluations and assessments made of them, the cues that are suggested, the possible definitions proposed by oneself or by others. These vary from one instance of interpretation to another and, further, shift from point to point in the development of the act. This varying and shifting content offers no basis for making the act of interpretation into a variable.

Nor, it seems to me, is the problem met by proposing to reduce the act of interpretation into component parts and work with these parts as variables. These parts would presumably have to be processual parts—such as perception, cognition, analysis, evaluation, and decision-making in the individual; and discussion, definition of one another's responses and other forms of social interaction in the group. The same difficulty exists in making any of the processual parts into variables that exists in the case of the complete act of interpretation.

The question of how the act of interpretation can be given the qualitative constancy that is logically required in a variable has so far not been answered. While one can devise some kind of a "more or less" dimension for it, the need is to catch it as a variable, or set of variables, in a manner which reflects its functioning in transforming experience into activity. This is the problem, indeed dilemma, which confronts variable analysis in our field. I see no answer to it inside the logical framework of variable analysis. The process of interpretation is not inconsequential or pedantic. It operates too centrally in group and individual experience to be put aside as being of incidental interest.

In addition to the by-passing of the process of interpretation there is, in my judgment, another profound deficiency in variable analysis as a scheme for analyzing human group life. The deficiency stems from the inevitable tendency to work with truncated factors and, as a result, to conceal or misrepresent the actual operations in human group life. The deficiency stems from the logical need of variable analysis to work with discrete, clean-cut and unitary variables. Let me spell this out.

As a working procedure variable analysis seeks necessarily to achieve a clean identification of the relation between two variables. Irrespective of how one may subsequently combine a number of such identified relations—in an additive manner, a clustering, a chain-like arrangement, or a "feedback" scheme—the objective of variable research is initially to isolate a simple and fixed relation between two variables. For this to be done each of the two variables must be set up as a distinct item with a unitary qualitative make-up. This is accomplished first by giving each variable, where needed, a simple quality or dimension, and second by separating the variable from its connection with other variables through their exclusion or neutralization.

A difficulty with this scheme is that the empirical reference of a true sociological variable is not unitary or distinct. When caught in its actual social character, it turns out to be an intricate and inner-moving complex. To illustrate, let me take what seems ostensibly to be a fairly clean-cut variable relation, namely between a birth control program and the birth rate of a given people. Each of these two variables—the program of birth control and the birth rate—can be given a simple discrete and unitary character. For the program of birth control one may choose merely its time period, or select some reasonable measure such as the number of people visiting birth control clinics. For the birth rate, one merely takes it as it is. Apparently, these indications are sufficient to enable the investigator to ascertain the relations between the two variables.

Yet, a scrutiny of what the two variables stand for in the life of the group gives us a different picture. Thus, viewing the program of birth control in terms of *how it enters into the lives of the people,* we need to note many things such as the literacy of the people, the clarity of the printed information, the manner and extent of its distribution, the social position of the directors of the program and of the personnel, how the personnel act, the character of their instructional talks, the way in which people define attendance at birth control clinics, the expressed views of influential personages with reference to the program, how such personages are regarded, and the nature of the discussions among people with regard to the clinics. These are only a few of the matters which relate to how the birth control program might enter into the experience of the people. The number is sufficient, however, to show the complex and inner-moving character of what otherwise might seem to be a simple variable.

A similar picture is given in the case of the other variable—the birth rate. A birth rate of a people seems to be a very simple and unitary matter. Yet, in terms of what it expresses and stands for in group activity it is exceedingly complex and diversified. We need consider only the variety of social factors that impinge on and affect the sex act, even though the sex act is only one of the activities that set the birth rate. The self-conceptions held by men and by women, the conceptions of family life, the values placed on children, accessibility of men and women to each other, physical arrangements in the home, the sanctions given by established institutions, the code of manliness, the pressures from relatives and neighbors, and ideas of what is proper, convenient and tolerable in the sex act—these are a few of the operating factors in the experience of the group that play upon the sex act. They suffice to indicate something of the complex body of actual experience and practice that is represented in and expressed by the birth rate of a human group.

I think it will be found that, when converted into the actual group activity for which it stands, a sociological variable turns out to be an intricate and inner-moving complex. There are, of course, wide ranges of difference between sociological variables in terms of the extent of such complexity. Still, I believe one will generally find that the discrete and unitary character which the labeling of the variable suggests vanishes.

The failure to recognize this is a source of trouble. In variable analysis one is likely to accept the two variables as the simple and unitary items that they seem to be, and to believe that the relation found between them is a realistic analysis of the given area of group life. Actually, in group life the relation is far more likely to be between complex, diversified and moving bodies of activity. The operation of one of these complexes on the other, or the interaction between them, is both concealed and misrepresented by the statement of the relation between the two variables. The statement of the variable relation merely asserts a connection between abbreviated terms of reference. It leaves out the actual complexes of activity and the actual processes of interaction in which human group life has its being. We are here faced, it seems to me, by the fact that the very features which give variable analysis its high merit—the qualitative constancy of the variables, their clean-cut simplicity, their ease of manipulation as a sort of free counter, their ability to be brought into decisive relation—are the features that lead variable analysis to gloss over the character of the real operating factors in group life, and the real interaction and relations between such factors.

The two major difficulties faced by variable analysis point clearly to the need for a markedly different scheme of sociological analysis for the areas in which these difficulties arise. This is not the occasion to spell out the nature of this scheme. I shall merely mention a few of its rudiments to suggest how its character differs fundamentally from that of variable analysis. The scheme would be based on the premise that the chief means through which human group life operates and is formed is a vast, diversified process of definition. The scheme respects the empirical existence of this process. It devotes itself to the analysis of the operation and formation of human group life as these occur through this process. In doing so it seeks to trace the lines of defining experience through which ways of living, patterns of relations, and social forms are developed, rather than to relate these formations to a set of selected items. It views items of social life as articulated inside moving structures and believes that they have to be understood in terms of this articulation. Thus, it handles these items not as discrete things disengaged from their connections but instead, as signs of a supporting context which gives them their social character. In its effort to ferret out lines of definition and networks of moving relation, it relies on a distinctive form of procedure. This procedure is to approach the study of group activity through the eyes and experience of the people who have developed the activity. Hence, it necessarily requires an intimate familiarity with this experience and with the scenes of its operation. It uses broad and interlacing observations and not narrow and disjunctive observations. And, may I add, that like variable analysis, it yields empirical findings and "here-and-now" propositions, although in a different form. Finally, it is no worse off than variable analysis in developing generic knowledge out of its findings and propositions.

In closing, I express a hope that my critical remarks about variable analysis are not misinterpreted to mean that variable analysis is useless or makes no contribution to sociological analysis. The contrary is true. Variable analysis is a fit procedure for those areas of social life and formation that are not mediated by an interpretative process. Such areas exist and are important. Further, in the area of interpretative life variable analysis can be an effective means of unearthing stabilized patterns of interpretation which are not likely to be detected through the direct study of the experience of people. Knowledge of such patterns, or rather of the relations between variables which reflect such patterns, is of great value for understanding group life in its "here-and-now" character and indeed may have significant practical value. All of these appropriate uses give variable analysis a worthy status in our field.

In view, however, of the current tendency of variable analysis to become the norm and model for sociological analysis, I believe it important to recognize its shortcomings and its limitations.

7   HOWARD S. BECKER & BLANCHE GEER

Participant Observation and Interviewing: A Comparison

The most complete form of the sociological datum, after all, is the form in which the participant observer gathers it: an observation of some social event, the events which precede and follow it, and explanations of its meaning by participants and spectators, before, during, and after its occurrence. Such a datum gives us more information about the event under study than data gathered by any other sociological method. Participant observation can thus provide us with a yardstick against which to measure the completeness of data gathered in other ways, a model which can serve to let us know what orders of information escape us when we use other methods.[1]

By participant observation we mean that method in which the observer participates in the daily life of the people under study, either openly in the role of researcher or covertly in some disguised role, observing things that happen, listening to what is said, and questioning people, over some length of time.[2] We want, in this paper, to compare the results of such

Howard S. Becker and Blanche Geer, "Participant Observation and Interviewing: A Comparison," *Human Organization*, vol. 16, no. 3 (Fall 1957), pp. 28–32. Reprinted by permission.

[1] We wish to thank R. Richard Wohl and Thomas S. McPartland for their critical reading of an earlier version of this paper.

[2] Cf. Florence R. Kluckhohn, "The Participant Observer Technique in Small Communities," *American Journal of Sociology*, 45 (Nov., 1940), 331–43; Arthur Vidich, "Participant Observation and the Collection and Interpretation of Data," *ibid.*, 60 (Jan., 1955), 354–60; William Foote Whyte, "Observational Field-Work Methods," in

intensive field work with what might be regarded as the first step in the other direction along this continuum: the detailed and conversational interview (often referred to as the unstructured or undirected interview).[3] In this kind of interview, the interviewer explores many facets of his interviewee's concerns, treating subjects as they come up in conversation, pursuing interesting leads, allowing his imagination and ingenuity full rein as he tries to develop new hypotheses and test them in the course of the interview.

In the course of our current participant observation among medical students,[4] we have thought a good deal about the kinds of things we were discovering which might ordinarily be missed or misunderstood in such an interview. We have no intention of denigrating the interview or even such less precise modes of data gathering as the questionnaire, for there can always be good reasons of practicality, economy, or research design for their use. We simply wish to make explicit the difference in data gathered by one or the other method and to suggest the differing uses to which they can legitimately be put. In general, the shortcomings we attribute to the interview exist when it is used as a source of information about events that have occurred elsewhere and are described to us by informants. Our criticisms are not relevant when analysis is restricted to interpretation of the interviewee's conduct *during the interview,* in which case the researcher has in fact observed the behavior he is talking about.[5]

The differences we consider between the two methods involve two interacting factors: the kinds of words and acts of the people under study that the researcher has access to, and the kind of sensitivity to problems and data produced in him. Our comparison may prove useful by suggesting areas in which interviewing (the more widely used method at present and likely to continue so) can improve its accuracy by taking account of suggestions made from the perspective of the participant observer. We begin by considering some concrete problems: learning the native language, or the problem of the degree to which the interviewer really understands what is said to him; matters interviewees are unable or unwilling to talk about; and

Marie Jahoda, Morton Deutsch, and Stuart W. Cook (eds.), *Research Methods in the Social Sciences* (New York: Dryden Press, 1951), II, 393–514, and *Street Corner Society* (Enlarged Edition) (Chicago: University of Chicago Press, 1955), 279–358.

[3] Two provisos are in order. In the first place, we assume in our comparison that the hypothetical interviewer and participant observer we discuss are equally skilled and sensitive. We assume further that both began their research with equally well formulated problems, so that they are indeed looking for equivalent kinds of data.

[4] This study is sponsored by Community Studies., Inc., of Kansas City, Missouri, and is being carried out at the University of Kansas Medical Center, to whose dean and staff we are indebted for their wholehearted cooperation. Professor Everett C. Hughes of the University of Chicago is director of the project.

[5] For discussion of this point, see Thomas S. McPartland, *Formal Education and the Process of Professionalization: A Study of Student Nurses* (Kansas City, Missouri: Community Studies, Inc., 1957), 2–3.

getting information on matters people see through distorting lenses. We then consider some more general differences between the two methods.

Learning the Native Language

Any social group, to the extent that it is a distinctive unit, will have to some degree a culture differing from that of other groups, a somewhat different set of common understandings around which action is organized, and these differences will find expression in a language whose nuances are peculiar to that group and fully understood only by its members. Members of churches speak differently from members of informal tavern groups; more importantly, members of any particular church or tavern group have cultures, and languages in which they are expressed, which differ somewhat from those of other groups of the same general type. So, although we speak one language and share in many ways in one culture, we cannot assume that we understand precisely what another person, speaking as a member of such a group, means by any particular word. In interviewing members of groups other than our own, then, we are in somewhat the same position as the anthropologist who must learn a primitive language,[6] with the important difference that, as Icheiser has put it, we often do not understand that we do not understand and are thus likely to make errors in interpreting what is said to us. In the case of gross misunderstandings the give and take of conversation may quickly reveal our mistakes, so that the interviewee can correct us; this presumably is one of the chief mechanisms through which the anthropologist acquires a new tongue. But in speaking American English with an interviewee who is, after all, much like us, we may mistakenly assume that we have understood him and the error be small enough that it will not disrupt communication to the point where a correction will be in order.

The interview provides little opportunity of rectifying errors of this kind where they go unrecognized. In contrast, participant observation provides a situation in which the meaning of words can be learned with great precision through study of their use in context, exploration through continuous interviewing of their implications and nuances, and the use of them oneself under the scrutiny of capable speakers of the language. Beyond simply clarifying matters so that the researcher my understand better what people say to each other and to him, such a linguistic exercise may provide research hypotheses of great usefulness. The way in whch one of us learned the meaning of the word "crock," as medical students use it, illustrates these points.

[6] See the discussion in Bronislaw Malinowski, *Magic, Science, and Religion and Other Essays* (Glencoe: The Free Press, 1948), 232–8.

I first heard the word "crock" applied to a patient shortly after I began my field work. The patient in question, a fat, middle-aged woman, complained bitterly of pains in a number of widely separated locations. When I asked the student who had so described her what the word meant, he said that it was used to refer to any patient who had psychosomatic complaints. I asked if that meant that Mr. X——, a young man on the ward whose stomach ulcer had been discussed by a staff physician as typically psychosomatic, was a crock. The student said that that would not be correct usage, but was not able to say why.

Over a period of several weeks, through discussion of many cases seen during morning rounds with the students, I finally arrived at an understanding of the term, realizing that it referred to a patient who complained of many symptoms but had no discoverable organic pathology. I had noticed from the beginning that the term was used in a derogatory way and had also been inquiring into this, asking students why they disliked having crocks assigned to them for examination and diagnosis. At first students denied the derogatory connotations, but repeated observations of their disgust with such assignments soon made such denials unrealistic. Several students eventually explained their dislike in ways of which the following example is typical: "The true crock is a person who you do a great big workup for and who has all of these vague symptoms, and *you really can't find anything the matter with them.*"

Further discussion made it clear that the students regarded patients primarily as objects from which they could learn those aspects of clinical medicine not easily acquired from textbooks and lectures; the crock took a great deal of their time, of which they felt they had little enough, and did not exhibit any interesting disease state from which something might be learned, so that the time invested was wasted. This discovery in turn suggested that I might profitably investigate the general perspective toward medical school which led to such a basis for judgment of patients, and also suggested hypotheses regarding the value system of the hospital hierarchy at whose bottom the student stood.

At the risk of being repetitious, let us point out in this example both the errors avoided and the advantages gained because of the use of participant observation. The term might never have been used by students in an ordinary interview; if it had, the interviewer might easily have assumed that the scatological term from which it in fact is descended provided a complete definition. Because the observer saw students on their daily rounds and heard them discussing everyday problems, he heard the word and was able to pursue it until he arrived at a meaningful definition. Moreover, the knowledge so gained led to further and more general discoveries about the group under study.

This is not to say that all of these things might not be discovered by a program of skillful interviewing, for this might well be possible. But we do suggest that an interviewer may misunderstand common English words when interviewees use them in some more or less esoteric way and not know that he is misunderstanding them, because there will be little chance to check his understanding against either further examples of their use in conversation or instances of the object to which they are applied. This leaves him open to errors of misinterpretation and errors of failing to see connections between items of information he has available, and may prevent him from seeing and exploring important research leads. In dealing with interview data, then, experience with participant observation indicates that both care and imagination must be used in making sure of meanings, for the cultural esoterica of a group may hide behind ordinary language used in special ways.

Matters Interviewees Are Unable or Unwilling to Talk About

Frequently, people do not tell an interviewer all the things he might want to know. This may be because they do not want to, feeling that to speak of some particular subject would be impolitic, impolite, or insensitive, because they do not think to and because the interviewer does not have enough information to inquire into the matter, or because they are not able to. The first case—the problem of "resistance"—is well known and a considerable lore has developed about how to cope with it.[7] It is more difficult to deal with the last two possibilities for the interviewee is not likely to reveal, or the interviewer to become aware, that significant omissions are being made. Many events occur in the life of a social group and the experience of an individual so regularly and uninterruptedly, or so quietly and unnoticed, that people are hardly aware of them, and do not think to comment on them to an interviewer; or they may never have become aware of them at all and be unable to answer even direct questions. Other events may be so unfamiliar that people find it difficult to put into words their vague feelings about what has happened. If an interviewee, for any of these reasons, cannot or will not discuss a certain topic, the researcher will find gaps in his information on matters about which he wants to know and will perhaps fail to become aware of other problems and areas of interest that such discussion might have opened up for him.

This is much less likely to happen when the researcher spends much time with the people he studies as they go about their daily activities, for he can see the very things which might not be reported in an interview. Further, should he desire to question people about matters they cannot or prefer not to talk about, he is able to point to specific incidents which either force them to face the issue (in the case of resistance) or make clear what he means (in

---

[7] See, for example, Arnold M. Rose, "A Research Note on Interviewing," *American Journal of Sociology*, 51 (Sept., 1945), 143–4; and Howard S. Becker, "A Note on Interviewing Tactics," *Human Organization*, 12:4 (Winter, 1954), 31–2.

the case of unfamiliarity). Finally, he can become aware of the full meaning of such hints as are given on subjects people are unwilling to speak openly about and of such inarticulate statements as people are able to make about subjects they cannot clearly formulate, because he frequently knows of these things through his observation and can connect his knowledge with these half-communications.

Researchers working with interview materials, while they are often conscious of these problems, cannot cope with them so well. If they are to deal with matters of this kind it must be by inference. They can only make an educated guess about the things which go unspoken in the interview; it may be very good guess, but it must be a guess. They can employ various tactics to explore for material they feel is there but unspoken, but even when these are fruitful they do not create sensitivity to those problems of which even the interviewer is not aware. The following example indicates how participant observation aids the researcher in getting material, and making the most of the little he gets, on topics lying within this range of restricted communication.

> A few months after the beginning of school, I went to dinner at one of the freshman medical fraternities. It was the night nonresident members came, married ones with their wives. An unmarried student who lived in the house looked around at the visitors and said to me, "We are so much in transition. I have never been in this situation before of meeting fellows and their wives."
>
> This was just the sort of thing we were looking for—change in student relationships arising from group interaction—but I failed in every attempt to make the student describe the "transition" more clearly.
>
> From previous observation, though, I knew there were differences (other than marriage) between the nonresidents and their hosts. The former had all been elected to the fraternity recently, after house officers had gotten to know them through working together (usually on the same cadaver in anatomy lab). They were older than the average original member; instead of coming directly from college, several had had jobs or Army experience before medical school. As a group they were somewhat lower in social position.
>
> These points indicated that the fraternity was bringing together in relative intimacy students different from each other in background and experience. They suggested a search for other instances in which dissimilar groups of students were joining forces, and pointed to a need for hypotheses as to what was behind this process of drawing together on the part of the freshman and its significance for their medical education.

An interviewer, hearing this statement about "transition," would know that the interviewee felt himself in the midst of some kind of change but might not be able to discover anything further about the nature of that change. The participant observer cannot find out, any more than the interviewer can, what the student had in mind, presumably because the student had nothing more in mind than this vague feeling of change. (Interviewees are not sociologists and we ought not to assume that their fumbling statements are attempts, crippled by their lack of technical vocabulary, to express what a sociologist might put in more formal analytic terms.) But he can search for those things in the interviewee's situation which might lead to such a feeling of transition.

While the participant observer can make immediate use of such vague statements as clues to an objective situation, the interviewer is often bothered by the question of whether an interviewee is not simply referring to quite private experiences. As a result, the interviewer will place less reliance on whatever inferences about the facts of the situation he makes, and is less likely to be sure enough of his ground to use them as a basis for further hypotheses. Immediate observation of the scene itself and data from previous observation enable the participant observer to make direct use of whatever hints the informant supplies.

Things People See Through Distorting Lenses

In many of the social relationships we observe, the parties to the relation will have differing ideas as to what ought to go on in it, and frequently as to what does in fact go on in it. These differences in perception will naturally affect what they report in an interview. A man in a subordinate position in an organization in which subordinates believe that their superiors are "out to get them" will interpret many incidents in this light, though the incidents themselves may not seem, either to the other party in the interaction or to the observer, to indicate such malevolence. Any such mythology will distort people's view of events to such a degree that they will report as fact things which have not occurred, but which seem to them to have occurred. Students, for example, frequently invent sets of rules to govern their relations with teachers, and, although the teacher may never have heard of such rules, regard the teachers as malicious when they "disobey" them. The point is that things may be reported in an interview through such a distorting lens, and the interviewer may have no way of knowing what is fact and what is distortion of this kind; participant observation makes it possible to check such points. The following is a particularly clear example.

> Much of the daily teaching was done, and practical work of medical students supervised, in a particular department of the hospital, by the house residents. A great deal of animosity had grown up between the particular group of students I was with at the time and these residents, the students believing that the residents would, for various malicious reasons, subordinate them and embarrass them at every opportunity. Before I joined the group, several of the students told me that the residents were "mean," "nasty," "bitchy," and so on, and had backed these characterizations up with evidence of particular actions.

After I began participating daily with the students on this service, a number of incidents made it clear that the situation was not quite like this. Finally, the matter came completely into the open. I was present when one of the residents suggested a technique that might have prevented a minor relapse in a patient assigned to one of the students; he made it clear that he did not think the relapse in any way the student's fault, but rather that he was simply passing on what he felt to be a good tip. Shortly afterward, this student reported to several other students that the resident had "chewed him out" for failing to use this technique: "What the hell business has he got chewing me out about that for? No one ever told me I was supposed to do it that way." I interrupted to say, "He didn't really chew you out. I thought he was pretty decent about it." Another student said, "Any time they say anything at all to us I consider it a chewing out. Any time they say anything about how we did things, they are chewing us out, no matter how God damn nice they are about it."

In short, participant observation makes it possible to check description against fact and, noting discrepancies, become aware of systematic distortions made by the person under study; such distortions are less likely to be discovered by interviewing alone. This point, let us repeat, is only relevant when the interview is used as a source of information about situations and events the researcher himself has not seen. It is not relevant when it is the person's behavior in the interview itself that is under analysis.

Inference, Process and Context

We have seen, in the previous sections of this paper, some of the ways in which even very good interviews may go astray, at least from the perspective of the field observer. We turn now to a consideration of the more general areas of difference between the two methods, suggesting basic ways in which the gathering and handling of data in each differ.

Since we tend to talk in our analyses about much the same order of thing whether we work from interviews or from participant-observational materials, and to draw conclusions about social relations and the interaction that goes on within them whether we have actually seen these things or only been told about them, it should be clear that in working with interviews we must necessarily infer a great many things we could have observed had we only been in a position to do so. The kinds of errors we have discussed above are primarily errors of inference, errors which arise from the necessity of making assumptions about the relation of interview statements to actual events which may or may not be true; for what we have solid observable evidence on in the first case we have only secondhand reports and indices of in the second, and the gap must be bridged by inference. We must assume, when faced with an account or transcription of an interview, that we understand the meaning of the everyday words used, that the interviewee is able to talk about the things we are interested in, and that his account will be more or less accurate. The examples detailed above suggest that these assumptions do not always hold and that the process of inference involved in interpreting interviews should always be made explicit and checked, where possible, against what can be discovered through observation. Where, as is often the case, this is not possible, conclusions should be limited to those matters the data directly describe.

Let us be quite specific, and return to the earlier example of resident-student hostility. In describing this relationship from interviews with the students alone we might have assumed their description to be accurate and made the inference that the residents were in fact "mean." Observation proved that this inference would have been incorrect, but this does not destroy the analytic usefulness of the original statements made to the field-worker in an informal interview. It does shift the area in which we can make deductions from this datum, however, for we can see that such statements, while incorrect factually, are perfectly good statements of the perspective from which these students interpreted the events in which they were involved. We could not know without observation whether their descriptions were true or false; with the aid of observation we know that the facts of the matter are sometimes quite different, and that the students' perspective is strong enough to override such variant facts. But from the interview alone we could know, not what actually happened in such cases, but what the students thought happened and how they felt about it, and this is the kind of inference we should make. We add to the accuracy of our data when we substitute observable fact for inference. More important, we open the way for the discovery of new hypotheses for the fact we observe may not be the fact we expected to observe. When this happens we face a new problem requiring new hypothetical explanations which can then be further tested in the field.

Substitution of an inference about something for an observation of that thing occurs most frequently in discussions of social process and change, an area in which the advantages of observation over an extended period of time are particularly great. Much sociological writing is concerned, openly or otherwise, with problems of process: The analysis of shifts in group structure, individual self-conception and similar matters. But studies of such phenomena in natural social contexts are typically based on data that tell only part of the story. The analysis may be made from a person's retrospective account, in a single interview, of changes that have taken place; or, more rarely, it is based on a series of interviews, the differences between successive interviews providing the bench marks of change. In either case, many crucial steps in the process and important mechanisms of change must be arrived at through inferences which can be no more than educated guesses.

The difficulties in analyzing change and process on the basis of interview material are particularly important because it is precisely in discussing changes in themselves and their surroundings that interviewees are least likely or able to give an accurate account of events. Changes in the social environment and in the self inevitably produce transformations of perspective, and it is characteristic of such transformations that the person finds it difficult or impossible to remember his former actions, outlook, or feelings. Reinterpreting things from his new perspective, he cannot give an accurate account of the past, for the concepts in which he thinks about it have changed and with them his perceptions and memories.[8] Similarly, a person in the midst of such change may find it difficult to describe what is happening, for he has not developed a perspective or concepts which would allow him to think and talk about these things coherently; the earlier discussion of changes in medical school fraternity life is a case in point.

Participant observation does not have so many difficulties of this sort. One can observe actual changes in behavior over a period of time and note the events which precede and follow them. Similarly, one can carry on a conversation running over weeks and months with the people he is studying and thus become aware of shifts in perspective as they occur. In short, attention can be focused both on what has happened and on what the person says about what has happened. Some inference as to actual steps in the process or mechanisms involved is still required, but the amount of inference necessary is considerably reduced. Again, accuracy is increased and the possibility of new discoveries being made is likewise increased, as the observer becomes aware of more phenomena requiring explanation.

The participant observer is both more aware of these problems of inference and more equipped to deal with them because he operates, when gathering data, in a social context rich in cues and information of all kinds. Because he sees and hears the people he studies in many situations of the kind that normally occur for them, rather than just in an isolated and formal interview, he builds an evergrowing fund of impressions, many of them at the subliminal level, which give him an extensive base for the interpretation and analytic use of any particular datum. This wealth of information and impression sensitizes him to subtleties which might pass unnoticed in an interview and forces him to raise continually new and different questions, which he brings to and tries to answer in succeeding observations.

The biggest difference in the two methods, then, may be not so much that participant observation provides the opportunity for avoiding the errors we have discussed, but that it does this by providing a rich experiential context which causes him to become aware of incongruous or unexplained facts, makes him sensitive to their possible implications and

---

[8] Anselm L. Strauss, "The Development and Transformation of Monetary Meanings in the Child," *American Sociological Review*, 17 (June, 1952), 275–86, and *An Essay on Identity* (unpublished manuscript), *passim*.

connections with other observed facts, and thus pushes him continually to revise and adapt his theoretical orientation and specific problems in the direction of greater relevance to the phenomena under study. Though this kind of context and its attendant benefits cannot be reproduced in interviewing (and the same degree of sensitivity and sense of problem produced in the interviewer), interviewers can profit from an awareness of those limitations of their method suggested by this comparison and perhaps improve their batting average by taking account of them.[9]

[9] We are aware that participant observation raises as many technical problems as it solves. (See, for instance, the discussions in Morris S. Schwartz and Charlotte Green Schwartz, "Problems in Participant Observation," *American Journal of Sociology,* 60 (Jan., 1955), 343–53, and Vidich, *op. cit.*) We feel, however, that there is considerable value in using the strong points of one method to illuminate the shortcomings of another.

8   MANFORD H. KUHN & THOMAS S. McPARTLAND

An Empirical Investigation of Self-Attitudes

Although the self has long been the central concept in the symbolic interaction approach to social psychology, little if anything has been done to employ it directly in empirical research. There are several reasons for this, one of the most important of which is that there has been no consensus regarding the class of phenomena to which the self ought to be operationally ordered. The self has been called an image, a conception, a concept, a feeling, an internalization, a self looking at oneself, and most commonly simply the self (with perhaps the most ambiguous implications of all). One of these many designations of the self has been as *attitudes.* We do not have space here to discuss the theoretical clarification which results from the conscious conceptualization of the self as a set of attitudes[1] except to point out that this conceptualization is most consistent with Mead's view of the self as an object which is in most respects like all other objects, and with his further view that an object is a plan of action (an attitude).

Manford H. Kuhn and Thomas S. McPartland, "An Empirical Investigation of Self-Attitude," *American Sociological Review,* vol. 19 (February 1954), pp. 68–76, by permission of the authors and journal.

The investigation on which this paper is based was made possible by a grant from the Graduate College of the State University of Iowa. The paper is a part of an extended examination of self-theory given before the social psychology section of the Midwest Sociological Society at Omaha, April 25, 1953.

[1] A paper dealing with this view is being prepared by the present authors for publication elsewhere.

If, as we suppose, human behavior is *organized* and *directed*, and if, as we further suppose, the organization and direction are supplied by the individual's *attitudes toward himself*, it ought to be of crucial significance to social psychology to be able to identify and measure self-attitudes. This paper is intended to provide an initial demonstration of the advantages to empirical research from thus treating the self as attitudes.

Problems in the Development of a Self-Attitudes Test

The obvious first step in the application of self-theory to empirical research is the construction and standardization of a test which will identify and measure self-attitudes.

The initial consideration in designing such a test is the question of accessibility. Would people give to investigators the statements which are operative in identifying themselves and therefore in organizing and directing their behavior? Or would they be inclined to hide their significant self-attitudes behind innocuous and conventional fronts? Those following symbolic interaction orientation have apparently guessed the latter to be the case for they have seldom if ever asked direct questions regarding self-attitudes, and have tended to assemble self-attitudes of those they were studying from diverse kinds of statements and behavior through the use of long and dubious chains of inference.

One of the present authors, in an earlier attempt to identify and measure self-attitudes among groups of Amish, Mennonite and Gentile school children,[2] made the assumption that self-attitudes might be studied in a fairly direct manner by collecting statements of role preference and role avoidance, role expectations, models for the self, and the like. While this investigation yielded results which corresponded to the cultural differences involved, it was clear that the self-statements which the children gave were specific to the role situations asked for and that therefore *general* self-attitudes still had to be (somewhat tenuously) inferred from them.

Subsequent pilot studies were made comparing the contents of extended autobiographies of university students with paragraphs written in answer to the question "Who are you?" These paragraphs contained virtually all the items which were yielded by rough content analyses of the self-attitudes in their corresponding autobiographies. This applied to painful and self-derogatory materials as well as to self-enhancing materials. Thus we

---

[2] Manford H. Kuhn, "Family Impact upon Personality," Chapter Five of *Problems in Social Psychology: An Interdisciplinary Inquiry*, edited by J. E. Hulett, Jr., and Ross Stagner, Urbana: University of Illinois Press, 1953, esp. pp. 50–52. A more comprehensive report of this study is to be included in a symposium on culture and personality, edited by Francis L. K. Hsu, to be published in the spring of 1954.

concluded that it might be profitable to construct a test which was aimed directly at self-attitudes.[3]

The device which we then used, and upon the use of which this research report is in major part based, consisted of a single sheet of paper headed by these instructions:

> "There are twenty numbered blanks on the page below. Please write twenty answers to the simple question 'Who am I?' in the blanks. Just give twenty different answers to this question. Answer as if you were giving the answers to yourself, not to somebody else. Write the answers in the order that they occur to you. Don't worry about logic or 'importance.' Go along fairly fast, for time is limited."

Application of the "Twenty-Statements" Test

This test was given to 288 undergraduate students at the State University of Iowa. It was administered during regular class meetings of introductory courses given in the Department of Sociology and Anthropology at various times during the spring of 1952. In a few classes the instructions were presented orally rather than in writing. In every instance students were given twelve minutes in which to complete the test. The students were naïve in the sense that they had not received instruction in the area to which this research was directed.

The number of responses per respondent evoked by these instructions varied from the twenty requested to one or two (with the median being seventeen responses). The responses took the general form "I am. . . ." Frequently "I am" was omitted, the responses consisting of phrases (*e.g.,* "a student," "an athlete," "a blonde") or of single words (*e.g.,* "girl," "married," "religious").

The responses were dealt with by a form of content analysis. They were categorized dichotomously either as *consensual* references or as *subconsensual* references.[4] These content categories distinguish between state-

---

[3] The social scientist, unlike the Freudian, assumes that most human behavior is organized and directed by internalized but consciously held role recipes. See, for example, Theodore Newcomb, *Social Psychology,* New York: Dryden, 1950, for his excellent discussion of the relation of attitudes and symbols to the *direction* of behavior (pp. 77–78, 82), and his discussion of the *directive* (versus the expressive) organization of behavior (pp. 343–344). Those absorbed in the present fashion of projective testing would seem to have the cart before the horse, for relatively few of their subjects have been studied in terms of their directive and overt attitudes. It would seem much more reasonable to run out the implications of findings from tests of such attitudes before attempting to uncover deeplying, unconscious or guarded attitudes. We have concluded that much time is wasted debating *in advance* to what extent people will hide their "true attitudes," whether they be self-attitudes or attitudes toward other objects or states of affairs.

[4] The precise working definitions of the two categories are given in detail in Thomas S. McPartland, *The Self and Social Structure: An Empirical Approach,* Iowa City: State University of Iowa Library, 1953, p. 147, Ph.D. Dissertation, microfilm.

ments which refer to groups and classes whose limits and conditions of membership are matters of common knowledge, *i.e., consensual;* and those which refer to groups, classes, attributes, traits, or any other matters which would require interpretation by the respondent to be precise or to place him relative to other people, *i.e., subconsensual.* Examples of the consensual variety are "student," "girl," "husband," "Baptist," "from Chicago," "pre-med," "daughter," "oldest child," "studying engineering"; that is, statements referring to consensually defined statuses and classes. Examples of the subconsensual category are "happy," "bored," "pretty good student," "too heavy," "good wife," "interesting"; that is, statements without positional reference, or with references to consensual classes obscured by ambiguous modifiers.

The assignment of responses to these dichotomous content categories was highly reliable between different analysts, differences in categorization between two judges occurring less than three times in one hundred responses.

When the content was dichotomized in this way several interesting and useful features emerged:

First, from the ordering of responses on the page it was evident that *respondents tended to exhaust all of the consensual references they would make before they made (if at all) any subconsensual ones;* that is, having once begun to make subconsensual references they tended to make no more consensual references (if indeed they had made any at all). This ordering of responses held whether a respondent made as many as nineteen consensual references or as few as one.

Second, the number of consensual references made by respondents varied from twenty to none. Similarly the number of subconsensual references made by respondents varied from twenty to none. However, the number of consensual and subconsensual references made by any given respondent did not stand in a simple arithmetic relation (such as the number of consensual references plus the number of subconsensual references equals twenty). This resulted from the fact that many respondents made fewer than twenty statements. For example, a respondent might make ten consensual statements and then leave the remaining ten spaces blank, while another might make two consensual references, twelve subconsensual references, and then leave the last six spaces blank.[5] In the analysis on which this report is based, all consensual references are on one side of the dichotomy, while "no-responses" are combined with subconsensual references on the

[5] The variables which result from these characteristics of responses to the "Twenty-Statements" Test are presently being utilized in further research with special reference to clinical use. There are some interesting indications that those with few if any *consensual* statements to make have symptoms of emotional disturbance, while those having few statements *of any kind* to make are of Riesman's "radar" type, taking their cues from each specific situation, and (in the phrase of John Gould) "taking their 'immediate others' to be their 'significant others.' "

other. An individual's "locus score" is simply the number of consensual references he makes on the "Twenty-Statements" Test.

These characteristics of the responses to the "Twenty-Statements" Test satisfy the definition of a Guttman scale. "The scalogram hypothesis is that the items have an order such that, ideally, *persons who answer a given question favorably all have higher ranks on the scale than persons who answer the same question unfavorably.*"[6] In applying this criterion it is necessary to keep in mind that "a given question" refers in this case to a specified one (by order) of the twenty statements, and that a "favorable response" would refer to a statement with a consensual reference—one that places the individual in a social system.

"The items used in a scalogram analysis must have a special *cumulative property.*"[7] Again it must be kept in mind that "the items" must in this case be interpreted in terms of the content analysis and not in terms of the raw responses to the open-ended question. Since a person who, let us say, makes a consensual statement as his seventh has also (in more than ninety percent of the instances) made consensual statements in his first six, and since "consensuality" or "locus" refers to anchorage or self-identification in a social system, a variable which is numerically cumulative, we may regard the criterion of cumulativeness as being satisfied in this test. Guttman states, "A third equivalent definition of a scale is the one upon which our practical scalogram analysis procedures are directly based. It requires that each person's responses should be reproducible from the rank alone. A more technical statement of the condition is that each item shall be a simple function of the persons' ranks."[8] This is true for the test under consideration.

Scores can therefore be assigned which indicate not only *how many* consensual references were made by each respondent, but *which* of his responses fell into the consensual category. The coefficient of reproducibility for this scale, based on 151 respondents, is .903. The test-retest reliability of the scale scores is approximately +.85.

Both for convenience and because consensual references are references to subjective identification by social position we have called the consensual-subconsensual variable the *locus* variable. Table I is a summary of the "scale of locus," and shows among other things the number of respondents approximating each scale type. For example, the first row in Table 1 indicates that 19 respondents most closely approximated Scale Type 20, *i.e.*, making twenty statements of the consensual reference variety. Of their 380 re-

---

[6] S. A. Stouffer, L. Guttman, E. A. Suchman, P. F. Lazarsfeld, S. A. Star, and J. A. Clausen, *Studies in Social Psychology in World War II, Volume IV: Measurement and Prediction*, Princeton: Princeton University Press, 1950, p. 9.

[7] *Ibid.*, p. 10.

[8] *Ibid.*, p. 62.

TABLE 1. The scale of locus, showing scale-types, frequency, total responses[1] in each scale type and the coefficient of reproducibility for each scale type

Scale Type	Frequency	Total Response	Errors	C.R.
20	19	380	41	.892
19	5	100	13	.870
18	1	20	1	.950
17	4	80	7	.913
16	1	20	3	.850
15	6	120	24	.800
14	8	160	9	.937
13	8	160	19	.875
12	4	80	10	.875
11	13	260	21	.915
10	7	140	15	.893
9	9	180	19	.895
8	9	180	15	.912
7	7	140	9	.936
6	10	200	15	.925
5	11	220	24	.891
4	8	160	11	.932
3	12	240	24	.900
2	2	40	5	.875
1	4	80	8	.900
0	3	60	0	1.000
	151	3020	293	.903

[1] Includes failure to respond to a blank as a response.

sponses there were 41 errors (that is, randomly distributed nonconsensual statements), giving a coefficient of reproducibility of .892 for this scale type. At the other end of the scale there were three respondents who belonged in Scale Type O, which is that of making no consensual statements, thus giving a perfect coefficient of reproducibility, 1.00.

Validity of the Test

The problem of validity of a test in a hitherto uninvestigated area is a difficult one. There are generally recognized to be two related but distinct methods of assessing validity. One is by examining the logical relatedness of the test with the body of theory on which it rests. This subsumes the test of validity by correlating test results with the criterion behavior indicated by the theory. The other method is through correlation of the results of the test with other (already standardized) tests of the problem under investigation. When—as in this case—an area has not been previously investigated by inductive research there are no other tests to use as correlational checks. We need not be held up unduly by this consideration, however, for this is apparently a very much misused method of assessing validity in the field of personality research.[9]

There are two kinds of demonstration required to deal properly with the problem of the consistency of the test with its antecedent body of orientational theory. One is that of making explicit the chains of logic which went into the designing of the test, the test operations and the manipulations of the data obtained through its application. The other is that of showing that the test results correlate in some consistent patterns with the kinds of behavior which the orientation asserts are related.

With respect to the first kind of demonstration we need indicate only that the question "Who am I?" is one which might logically be expected to elicit statements about *one's identity;* that is, his social statuses, and the attributes which are in his view relevant to these. To ask him to give these statements "as if to himself" is an endeavor to obtain from him *general* self-attitudes rather than simply ones which might be idiosyncratic to the test situation or those which might be uniquely held toward himself in his relation to the test administrator. The request in the test for as many as twenty statements of self-identity stems from a recognition by the investigators of the *complex* and *multifarious* nature of an individual's statuses, their curiosity regarding the question of whether the *ordering of responses* correlates with the individual's particular anchoring in society, and their interest in exploring the *range* of self-attitudes.

The manipulation of the responses by assigning them to dichotomous categories, that of consensual reference and that of subconsensual reference, rests on the self-theory view that the self is an interiorization of one's positions in social systems. One may assume from this orientation that variations in such self-identifications are equivalents of variations in the ways in which the individuals in a society such as ours have cast their lot within the range of possible reference groups.

---

[9] There has been a considerable tendency to validate each new personality test by correlating its results with those obtained by the already existent ones, without inquiring into *their* validity. See Leonard W. Ferguson, *Personality Measurement*, New York: McGraw-Hill, 1952. Ferguson points out (p. 178) that the Bernreuter Personality Inventory was validated by correlating its scales with scores on the Allport Ascendance-Submission scale, the Bernreuter Self-Sufficiency Scale, the Laird Introversion-Extroversion Schedule and the Thurstone Personality Inventory. The correlations were high. But the Laird and Thurstone tests had been through *no validation process whatsoever*, and the other two were unsatisfactorily validated! He points out, later, that the Bell Adjustment Inventory was validated against the Allport, Thurstone and Bernreuter tests (p. 232), thus pyramiding still another validation on the original shaky base. And so it goes until people have completely forgotten all details of the construction of the earliest tests on whose validity the whole series rests as far as this variety of validation is concerned.

We should note parenthetically that we were not interested in validating this test operation of ours against any of the existent personality tests not alone for the reasons involved in the argument above, but more basically because these other tests were designed from orientations quite foreign to ours. One has only to check the items on any current personality test to see how seldom is there any logical relation to self-theory.

There is an alternative hypothetical mechanism which might be advanced to explain the salience of the consensual reference statement. It is this: Our society requires such a volume of census information from its citizens that the salience of consensual references in the replies to the "Twenty-Statements" Test is according to this hypothesis, simply a superficial carry-over from other questionnaires and forms. On this view those responses which are treated in our investigation as subconsensual are "deeper" self-attitudes, and hence those which lie closer to the "authentic individual."

We do not agree with this view. It is our belief that the ordering of responses is a reflection of the make-up of the self-conception.[10] The fact that the volume of consensual responses (corresponding to social anchorings) varies greatly from respondent to respondent is taken to give indirect confirmation of our position. Another and more direct empirical confirmation is to be found in the fact that three- and four-year-old children when asked "Who are you?" give, in addition to their names, their sex and occasionally their ages; in their instances one cannot allege a carry-over from the giving of census data. Of course only the pragmatic success or failure of the technique here under consideration will give a dependable answer, and the latter part of this report is devoted to an account of one such pragmatic test. This pragmatic test of the usefulness of the scale scores of the "locus" component of self-attitudes may serve also as the second kind of demonstration of the validity of the instrument.

Variations in Self-Attitudes by "Known Groups"

The behavior which we tested for correlation with locus scores derived from our self-attitudes test is that of differential religious affiliation. It is simply one of a multitude of possible investigations which now need to be undertaken to answer the larger question "What values of this variable (locus)

[10] In the ordering of responses we are dealing essentially with the dimension of *salience* of self-attitudes. Theodore Newcomb (in his *Social Psychology*, New York: Dryden, 1950, p. 151) says of salience that it "refers to a person's readiness to respond in a certain way. The more salient a person's attitude the more readily will it be expressed with a minimum of outer stimulation. It seems reasonable to assume that a very salient attitude—one expressed with great spontaneity—has more importance for the person expressing it than does an attitude which he expresses only after a good deal of prodding or questioning. The weakness of direct questions is that they provide no way of measuring the salience of an attitude; we never know whether the attitude would have been expressed at all, or in the same way, apart from the direct question." Thus when a respondent, in reply to the "Who am I?" question on the "Twenty-Statements" Test, writes "I am a man," "I am a student," "I am a football player," it is reasonable to believe that we have far more solid knowledge of the attitudes which organize and direct his behavior than if, on a checklist and among other questions, we had asked "Do you think of yourself as a man?" "Do you think of yourself as a student?" and "Do you think of yourself as an athlete?"

are related to what kinds of behavior and to what trains of social experience?"

Our orientation indicates that the self-conception should vary with differential social anchorage in (a) large, conventional, "respectable," accepted and influential groups; (b) small, weak or different, ambivalently viewed, marginal or dissident groups; or (c) no groups at all (in institutional areas in which a large fraction of the society's membership belongs and is identified by status in one or another of the existent groups). Religious groups and corresponding affiliation by our respondents fitted this model admirably so that we might check differentials in their self-attitudes against differentials in their religious group affiliations. Some religious groups in our society are "majority groups," while others are groups whose subcultures contain norms which set their members at odds with the norms of the larger society. Then, too, a large fraction of the population either has no religious reference group or no religious group membership.

Reports of membership in religious groups in our sample were collected by means of the direct question: "What is your religious affiliation or preference?" The numbers of each variety of affiliation are given in the column under the heading "N" in Table 2. The mean locus scale scores were computed for each of these religious groups and are given in the next column. The mean scale scores ranged from 11.89 (for Catholics) to 5.75 (for

TABLE 2. Variations in self-attitudes by religious affiliation: the significance of observed differences between locus scores of affiliates of various religious denominations

Denomination	N^1	Denominational Mean	Significance of Difference^2	Significance of Difference^3
Roman Catholic	38	11.89	. .	P < .001
"Small Sects"^{4}	20	11.00	not sig.	P < .01
"Protestant"	21	10.47	not sig.	P < .01
Congregationalist	13	10.30	not sig.	P < .01
Lutheran	33	10.09	not sig.	P < .01
"Christian"	11	9.81	not sig.	P < .02
Jewish	19	9.57	not sig.	P < .05
Methodist	73	8.94	P < .02	not sig.
Presbyterian	32	8.18	P < .01	not sig.
"None"	28	5.75	P < .001*	. .

[1] The total N is 288. These 288 include the 151 on whom the locus scale, reported in Table 1, was established, plus 137 cases obtained subsequently.

[2] Computed from the Roman Catholic group mean as the base.

[3] Computed from the group means of "Nones" as the base.

[4] Includes Baptists, Episcopalians, Evangelicals, Mennonites, Nazarenes, Reorganized Latter Day Saints, Unitarians.

* While this and the other measures of statistical significance of difference are such as to give great confidence that the differences are not due to chance, it will only be through repeated correlations of locus scores with other behavior with respect to representative samples that we will be able to discover the theoretical import of the *magnitude* of the difference.

"nones"). These scale scores are simply the mean number of consensual reference statements made by respondents in each of the religious groups.

Analysis of variance revealed a relation between religious affiliation and scale scores significant beyond the one percent level. The differences between group means of Roman Catholics on the one hand and Methodists, Presbyterians, and persons reporting no affiliation on the other, were significant beyond the two percent level. Taking the group reporting no affiliation as the base, we found significant differences between this group-mean and the group-means of Roman Catholics, "small sects," "Protestants," Congregationalists, Lutherans, Christians, and Jews. Although the N's were relatively large, Methodists and Presbyterians did not differ significantly from "nones" at any usually accepted level of statistical significance. The results of this analysis appear in the last two columns in Table 2.

These results indicate clear differences in the relative strength of the more directly socially anchored component of the self-conception among affiliates of certain religious subcultures, but leave open the question of the antecedent correlates of these differences. If one postulates that Roman Catholics have in common with members of small Protestant denominations, Lutherans and Jews the characteristic that religious affiliation is picked out as "important" and differentiating; and that Methodists, Presbyterians, and "indifferentists" have in common the characteristic that religious affiliation is not "important" or that it is taken for granted, then the two clusters of denominations by scale scores make sense.

If this postulate is sound, then Roman Catholics, Jews, and members of small sects should carry religious references more saliently in the self-conception. The "Twenty-Statements" Test provides data on this point.[11]

The salience of a self-reference may be understood as the relative spontaneity with which a particular reference will be used as an orientation in the organization of behavior.[12] In this research, salience of religious reference in the self-conception was measured by the rank of religious reference (if any was made) on the page of twenty statements, mention of religious affiliation in the first place being scored 20, mention in last place scoring 1, and omission of reference to religious affiliation arbitrarily scored zero.

The mean salience of religious references on the "Twenty-Statements" Test ranged from 7.4 for Roman Catholics to 1.82 for "Christians." Analysis of variance of religious references showed salience scores to be related to religious affiliation beyond the one per cent level. The analysis of the significance of the difference between group means appears in Table 3.

---

[11] This, obviously, is a use of data from the "Twenty-Statements" Test in an altogether different way than through the use of them to obtain locus scores. There are, in fact, almost unlimited numbers of ways in which these self-statements may be treated, but each would constitute essentially a new test.

[12] The comments and quotation in footnote 10 above apply equally here.

TABLE 3. Differential self-anchorage in religious groups: the significance of observed differences between mean salience scores of religious references among affiliates of various religious denominations

Denomination	Denominational Mean	Significance of Difference[1]
Roman Catholic	7.39	. .
Lutheran	7.09	not significant
"Small Sects"	7.04	not significant
Jewish	6.68	not significant
Congregationalist	5.54	not significant
Presbyterian	4.47	$P < .01$
Methodist	3.22	$P < .01$
"Christian"	1.82	$P < .01$

[1] Computed from the Roman Catholic group mean as a base.

A completely independent operation was conducted to test this finding of the relation between the social "importance" of group affiliation and "importance" in the self-conception; 116 undergraduates, whose religious affiliations were known, were asked to answer one of two alternative "reference-group" questions: "With what groups do you feel most closely identified?" or "I am proudest of my membership in ———." When respondents were cross-classified (a) by religious affiliation and (b) by their giving or not giving religious affiliation references in response to these direct questions, Table 4 resulted. Since we had obtained, from the self-attitudes research done previously, an empirically derived gradient of "differentism," we used this to make a finer subdivision of these responses, which yielded Table 5.

These independently-derived data support the hypothesized relation between salience in the self-conception and socially defined importance of group membership at high levels of statistical significance.

TABLE 4. Reference group evidence: the dichotomous division of 116 respondents on the basis of religious affiliation and identification with religious groups

	Religious Reference Present	Religious Reference Absent	
Catholics and Jews	13 (5.5)	7 (14.5)	20
All others	19 (26.5)	77 (69.5)	96
Total	32	84	116

Chi Square: 17.03
Q: .875
P less than .0001

TABLE 5. Reference group evidence on the gradient of differentism: the dichotomous division of respondents by religious identification against a trichotomous division by religious affiliation

	Religious Reference Present	Religious Reference Absent	
Catholics and Jews	13 (6.2)	7 (13.8)	20
"Small Sects"	9 (6.2)	11 (13.8)	20
"Large Denominations"	10 (19.6)	53 (43.4)	63
Total	32	71	103

Chi Square: 19.45
T: .37
P less than   .0001

Conclusions

The evidence provided by the "Twenty-Statements" Self-Attitudes Test and by its application to "known groups," in this case religious groups, gives support to the following empirically grounded inferences which have, in our view, rather large theoretical implications:

(1) The consensual (more directly socially anchored) component of the self-conception is the more salient component. Stated differently, consensually supported self-attitudes are at the top of the hierarchy of self-attitudes.

(2) Persons vary over a rather wide range in the relative volume of consensual and subconsensual components in their self-conceptions. It is in this finding that our empirical investigation has given the greatest advance over the purely deductive and more or less literary formulations of George Herbert Mead. Stated in terms of the language of this test, people have locus scores which range from 0 to 20. The variable involved here is one which we can correlate with a wide variety of other attitudes and behavior.

(3) The variation indicated in (1) and (2) can be established and measured by the empirical techniques of attitude research—specifically, the Guttman scaling technique. This gives a dual advantage in that it furthers the presumption that the locus variable is a unitary one and also in that it facilitates the further manipulation of values of the variable with respect to other quantitative problems.

(4) Locus scores vary with religious affiliation, as our initial validation test shows, members of the "differentistic" religious groups having signifi-

cantly higher locus scores than do members of the "conventional" religious groups (using an independent source of information to establish the fact of membership in religious groups).

(5) Religious affiliation references are significantly more salient among the self-attitudes of members of "differentistic" religious groups than among members of "majority" or conventional religious groups.

(6) Corroboratively, the religious group as a reference group appears far more frequently as an answer to a direct, reference-group type of question among those made by members of "differentistic" religious groups.

This is a first (and only partially completed) effort to build a personality test consistent with the assumptions and findings of social science. The social science view is that people organize and direct their behavior in terms of their subjectively defined identifications. These in turn are seen as internalizations of the objective social statuses they occupy, but for prediction we need to have the *subjective* definitions of identity, in view of the looseness between the social systems and the individual occupants of statuses in them in a society such as ours, characterized by alternatives, change, and collective behavior—in short, a society toward the secular end of the scale. Our test elicits these self-definitions.

To complete a comprehensive personality test on this basis we will need to know, in addition to the subjects' subjective identifications in terms of statuses, their roles, role preferences and avoidances and role expectations, their areas of self-threat and vulnerability, their self-enhancing evaluations, their patterns of reference-group election (their "negative others" as well as their "positive others"), and probably their self-dissociated attitudes. Questions such as "What do you do?" "Who do you wish you were?" "What do you intend to do?" "What do you take the most pride in?" "As a member of what groups or categories would you like to count yourself?" are a few of the indicated types in the directions suggested of building a soundly grounded approach to a science of personality and culture.

Ethnomethods and Phenomenology

There are two approaches in the social sciences which have developed in recent years, one in anthropology called ethnoscience, the other in sociology called ethnomethodology. Both have the potential for making a great impact on research in anthropology and sociology. In this paper, I would like to examine these approaches, show some of the similarities and differences between them, comment on their significance, and indicate their relation to phenomenological approaches.

Ethnoscience

Ethnoscience has been defined by Sturtevant[1] as "the system of knowledge and cognition typical of a given culture." He says that, from this point of view, "a culture amounts to the sum of a given society's folk classifications, all of that society's ethnoscience, its particular ways of classifying its material and social universe."

Following this approach, the task of the social scientist is to discover how members of a culture perceive, define and classify, how they actually perform their activities and what meanings they assign to acts occurring in the context of their culture.

Despite the fact that ethnoscience has been called the New Ethnography,[2] there is much in it that is old. Malinowski, some years ago, stated that the aim of the ethnographer is "to grasp the native's point of view, his relation to life, to realize his vision of the world."[3] Anthropologists would

George Psathas, "Ethnomethods and Phenomenology," *Social Research*, vol. 35, no. 3 (September 1968), pp. 500–520, by permission of the journal and author. The author is a member of the Department of Sociology, Boston University.

Author's Note—This paper was presented at the meetings of the American Sociological Association, San Francisco, 1967. I am grateful to Marvin Cummins, Lindsey Churchill, Murray L. Wax and William J. Chambliss for their critical comments on an earlier draft of this paper, and to Martin Kozloff for the many discussions we have had as it has been successively revised. I also wish to express my gratitude to Herbert Spiegelberg for the opportunity to present it to his Workshop on Phenomenology at Washington University, June, 1967.

[1] W. C. Sturtevant, "Studies in Ethnoscience," *American Anthropologist*, Special Publication, 66, Part 2; Romney, A. K., and D'Andrade, R. G. (eds.), "Transcultural Studies in Cognition," Report of a Conference sponsored by the Social Sciences Research Council, 1964.

[2] Sturtevant, *ibid.*, p. 99.

[3] B. Malinowski, *Argonauts of the Western Pacific*, New York: E. P. Dutton and Company, 1950, p. 396.

agree that this has been a central task of anthropology. Ethnoscience may simply be providing a more recent statement of that aim within a framework of new methodology and research techniques.

With reference to the method for determining what the native has "in mind," Malinowski stated:

> . . . we cannot expect to obtain a definite, precise and abstract statement from a philosopher, belonging to the community itself. The native takes his fundamental assumptions for granted, and if he reasons or inquires into matters of belief, it would be always in regard to details and concrete applications. Any attempts on the part of the ethnographer to induce his informant to formulate such a general statement would have to be in the form of leading questions of the worst type because in these leading questions he would have to introduce words and concepts essentially foreign to the native. Once the informant grasped their meaning, his outlook would be warped by our own ideas having been poured into it. Thus, the ethnographer must draw the generalizations for himself, must formulate the abstract statement without the direct help of a native informant.[4]

The ethnoscientist would agree that the phrasing of questions must be carefully done so as not to introduce ideas to the native which were not part of *his* cognitive system. Borrowing from methods in linguistics, he would attempt more systematic (and possibly replicable) questioning procedures to elicit data adequate to the development of a more complete analysis of that aspect of the culture which he is studying. Frake[5] offers examples of question frames for accomplishing such purposes. However, critics of ethnoscience have noted that little attention has been given to the determination of how the questioning process and the relation between the researcher and his native informant affect the responses given. Marvin Harris[6] has also noted that there is little indication of the range or variety of responses given but rather that most reports are phrased in terms of "usually" or "rarely" whenever any indication of frequency is made. (I think this matter needs attention though in my estimation it is not a statistical problem but rather one of determining typifications and, more broadly, essences.)

Goodenough, in a more recent statement of the aim of the New Ethnography, repeats that the aim is to grasp the native's view:

> A society's culture consists of whatever it is one has to *know* or believe in order to operate in a manner acceptable to its members, and to do so in

---

[4] *Ibid.*, p. 396.

[5] C. A. Frake, "Notes on Queries in Ethnography," *American Anthropologist*, 66, Part 2, 1964, pp. 132–145. Of added significance is the fact that Frake undertakes a self-conscious analysis of methodological issues in data collection by anthropologists. The work of the ethnoscientists has stimulated attention to methodological issues, sometimes lacking in anthropology, in contrast to sociology (where sometimes there is more method than data).

[6] M. Harris, "Emics, Etics and the New Ethnography," unpublished paper.

any role that they accept for any one of themselves. . . . It is the forms of things that people have in mind, their models for perceiving, and otherwise interpreting them . . . Ethnographic description, then, requires methods of processing observed phenomena such that we can inductively construct a theory of how our informants have organized the same phenomena. It is the theory, not the phenomena alone, which ethnographic descriptions aim to present.[7]

As this last quotation indicates, the task of the ethnographer is not merely to describe events as he might see them from his observer's perspective, but also to get "inside" those events to see what kind of theory it is that the natives themselves inductively use to organize phenomena in their daily lives. In terms used in phenomenology, the task is to discover how natives "constitute" the phenomena which exist for them in their lives. From a slightly different perspective, the task of the social scientist is to construct a theory of natives' theories, or as Schutz has put it, "a typification of their typifications." (I think that Goodenough's use of the term "theory" can be interpreted in the sense of Schutz's notion of typification.)

Developments in ethnoscience are not being influenced to any great extent by phenomenology. The mainstream of contemporary influence in ethnoscience is coming from linguistics. The influence of linguistics can be seen particularly in research involving the method of componential analysis. This method is stimulating considerable discussion and controversy among anthropologists.[8] Componential analysis is concerned with the relation between the categories of language and objects, concepts or events in the real world, i.e., the "things." The components or conceptual principles which underlie the process by which a name is used to classify things are sought by the investigator. If these principles are discovered, the investigator can then reproduce culturally appropriate behavior since he will have grasped the native's perspective. He will also have discovered what components are significant or relevant to members of the culture being studied.[9]

Typically, componential analyses are made of cognitive systems, i.e., phenomena, which are related to one another categorically, e.g., color systems, kinship systems, botanical taxonomies, etc. Opposed to the cognitive side of the semantic or sign-object relationship is the terminological system of the spoken language. In essence, the relationship between the terminological system (the way he talks about his world) and the cognitive

---

[7] W. Goodenough, "Cultural Anthropology and Linguistics," in Garvin, P. L. (ed.), *Monograph Series on Languages and Linguistics* No. 9, Institute of Languages and Linguistics, Washington: Georgetown University, 1957, pp. 167–173.

[8] For example, see the critical comment by Burling and the rejoinder by Hymes (R. Burling, "Cognition and Componential Analysis: God's Truth or Hocus Pocus," *American Anthropologist*, 66, 1964, pp. 20–28. D. H. Hymes, "Discussion of Burling's Paper," *American Anthropologist*, 66, 1964, pp. 116–119).

[9] I am grateful to Martin Kozloff for the following summary of the method of componential analysis.

system (the way he experiences it) is studied by having the informant make discriminations between a variety of stimuli presented to him and having him name the "things" that he has discriminated, thus presenting the investigator with evidence of how the informant interprets and classifies the world around him. The first phase of an analysis consists of *generating* the terminological system by presenting native informants with a "substitution frame" which can be filled by many possible rsponses, e.g., "the color of this is called ——," at the same time that the informants are presented with a stimulus, e.g., a color sample. In this phase, a list is obtained of names used by the informant in categorizing the stimuli presented to him.

The next phase consists of *classifying* the names into a taxonomy of sub-categories. Taxonomies are composed of "segregates" and "contrast sets." A segregate is a terminologically distinguished array of objects and a contrast set is a series of terminologically contrasted segregates. For example, any color name such as "light red" or "reddish orange" is a segregate because each is a category which can include several particular "light reds" or "reddish oranges." The contrast sets, however, may be named red, green, blue, etc., with each containing a series of segregates composed of particular color stimuli that are named and responded to in the same way. The taxonomy is also generated by substitution frames. One useful frame is a question that asks directly about inclusive relationships, e.g., "is X a kind of Y?", "is reddish-orange a kind of orange?"

The final and most difficult phase involves determining the components or rules that informants use in placing different stimuli within particular segregates or contrast sets. Since not only taxonomies but components differ between cultures, it is necessary that the components be ascertained from the subject's perspective, especially because it is the aim of the method to discover the informant's experience and not to impose or prescribe any schema which the investigator may have.

An example of components drawn from an analysis of the use of English personal pronouns reveals gender, person, number and grammatical function in the components used to generate personal pronouns. From such rules accurate predictions can be made of the word that native speakers will use, e.g., when "I" rather than "me" will be used. The analysis is not considered complete until rules can be formulated that can predict almost any naming response in the cognitive system.[10]

One criticism which can be made of componential analysis is the fact that it narrows the focus of research to the study of classification systems and the use of terms, or linguistic categories, by native speakers. If research focuses only on problems that can be studied with available

---

[10] Frake, "The Ethnographic Study of Cognitive Systems" in T. Gladwin and W. C. Sturtevant (eds.) *Anthropology and Human Behavior*, Washington: The Anthropological Society of Washington, 1962.

methods, then significance may be sacrificed for precision and there exists a danger that techniques will determine the selection of problems for study. For example, much work has been and is being done using componential analysis for the analysis of kinship terms.[11] The kinship system continues, thus, to remain the anthropologists' "white rat," a handy little "subject" that he can study in a variety of ways.

There is a danger that componential analysis will be regarded as *the* method of ethnoscience. Sturtevant notes that "ethnoscientific work has thus far concentrated on the sorts of cognitive structure involved in selection classes: the interrelations of categories considered as sets of possible alternatives under varying environmental conditions. Little attention has yet been paid to the methods required for the investigation of the sort of structures involved in rules of combination, the temporal or spatial ordering of co-occurring categories from different selection classes."[12] There is an obvious need for ethnoscientific work to range more broadly and to develop methods which permit the study of larger structures. The necessity for apprehending essential relationships among the elements of the phenomena being analyzed,[13] as phenomenologists have termed it, remains important. It is not enough to discover and describe the components; rules regarding their possible combinations must also be defined. Further, the analysis of the combinations of "categories from different selection classes," as Sturtevant has put it, will allow for the determination of essential relationships among such elements as they combine to form new phenomena, e.g., sentences, or broader conceptual categories.

In contrast to the work traditionally done in anthropological linguistics, workers in ethnoscience are more willing to enter into semantic analysis, to try to discover the meanings of terms. Further, the meanings they are concerned with are the meanings-in-use, i.e., the everyday meanings used in the present situation, rather than dictionary meanings or etymologically analyzed meanings. In this sense, they have adopted one important attitude or perspective found in phenomenology, namely, that man's cognitive world is "shot through with meaning,"[14] and that it is these meanings which must be understood in order to grasp the life-world of particular others.

The application of componential analysis to native classification sys-

---

[11] A. F. C. Wallace and J. Atkins, "The Meaning of Kinship Terms," *American Anthropologist*, 62, 1960, pp. 58–80.

[12] Sturtevant, *op. cit.*, p. 124. For an exception in which combinations of terms used to refer to different environmental conditions are analyzed, see G. Psathas and J. Henslin, "Dispatched Orders and the Cab Driver: A Study of Locating Activities," *Social Problems*, 14, 1967, pp. 424–443. In this study, radio dispatched messages instructing the cab driver as to the location of a passenger are analyzed.

[13] H. Spiegelberg, *The Phenomenological Movement*, II, The Hague: Martinus Nijhoff, 1965, ch. 14, p. 680.

[14] Spiegelberg, *ibid.*, p. 695.

tems and the discovery of the components which underlie the native speaker's use, i.e., the criteria he uses in assigning a term to an object or event,[15] seem to me to lead to an outcome which phenomenology also seeks, namely, how "things" are constituted. The components are the criteria used by the native speaker to constitute, in an active manner, the phenomena. By discovering the irreducible components which natives use, it is possible to arrive at a complete account which then enables the investigator to generate the constituted phenomena in a form of appearance which is recognizable to the native. This is stated in terms of "accurate prediction of naming responses" by ethnoscientists. In my opinion, it represents an aspect of phenomenological method not explicitly recognized by workers in ethnoscience.

For those more interested in longer utterances or interaction sequences than in particular terms, componential analysis seems cumbersome and perhaps even inappropriate. At least, it has not yet been applied to data of this kind. Because of this lack, it is not yet possible to determine to what extent the method has a built-in limitation. If this limitation exists, then it should be clearly pointed out so that the problems and data will not be "forced" into the framework required by the methodology.

Here is one contrast between the work being done in ethnoscience and that being done in ethnomethodology. The ethnomethodologists, since they are interested in discovering the units of meaning that are operational in the on-going social world, are willing to study more complex social phenomena and not limit themselves to cognitive structures for which linguistic terms exist.[16]

At this point several critical remarks must be made. It is I who have interpreted some aspects of the ethnoscientists' orientation in terms of phenomenology. There is, as yet, no explicit recognition of phenomenology in the work of ethnoscientists. Their work, furthermore, is so heavily influenced by linguistics that they "equate semantic features with cognitive distinctions."[17] Too much of man's behavior is assigned to the cognitive mode and too little to emotions. There is an implicit disdain for the emotional aspect of man's behavior and a tendency to equate the "experience of the world" with the cognitive categories used to describe it.

[15] Whether this analysis is getting at the criteria actually used by the native ("psychological reality") in contrast to the imposition of the researcher's own criteria ("structural reality") is discussed in A. F. C. Wallace, "The Problems of the Psychological Validity of Componential Analysis," *American Anthropologist*, 67, Part 2, 1965.

[16] The studies in ethnoscience which have been concerned with classification systems, e.g., C. A. Frake, "The Diagnosis of Disease among the Subanun of Mindanao," *American Anthropologist*, 63, 1961, pp. 113–132; A. F. C. Wallace and J. Atkins, "The Meaning of Kinship Terms," *American Anthropologist*, 62, 1960, pp. 58–80, can be contrasted with Garfinkel's analysis of how jurors decide the correctness of a verdict or how suicides are classified. See H. Garfinkel, *Studies in Ethnomethodology*, Englewood Cliffs, N.J.: Prentice-Hall, 1967.

[17] R. G. D'Andrade, Introduction in *American Anthropologist*, Special Publication, 66, Part 2, 1964.

There is an assumption that communication and language form the basis for cultural life. The significant cognitive features of the shared symbolic system of the culture are presumed to be codifiable into language. Language can therefore be analyzed to determine the shared code or set of rules that members have and use in constructing and interpreting messages about their world. Their understanding of the code need not be explicit but the ethnoscientist assumes that there is such a code and that it can be discerned. Once it is discovered, he will have arrived at a description of the world as viewed by the native, i.e., an insight into his categories and conceptualizations. This reliance on an analysis of how members of the society talk *about* their world as a means of understanding it does not allow the ethnoscientist to examine non-verbal but nevertheless experienced aspects of the real world. Thus, he is not faithful to the phenomenological concern with *all* of man's experience and not solely his categorized, linguistically organized experience.

This is, therefore, a fundamental criticism of the ethnoscientist: he is not faithful to the phenomena of the social world which constitute themselves in a variety of ways.

Ethnomethodology

Ethnomethodology is the term coined by Garfinkel and his students[18] to refer to their work. Garfinkel has defined ethnomethodology as: "the investigation of the rational properties of indexical expressions and other practical actions as contingent ongoing accomplishments of organized artful practices of everyday life."[19] An elaboration of the particular meanings of these terms, as Garfinkel defines them, is beyond the scope of this paper. We shall only note that he is concerned with the practical, everyday activities of men in society as they make accountable, to themselves and others, their everyday affairs, and with the methods they use for producing and managing those same affairs. He sees similarity in the activities of producing and making accountable. His concern with the everyday, routine and commonplace activities as phenomena in their own right, deserving of

---

[18] For representative works see the following: H. Garfinkel, "Studies of the Routine Grounds of Everyday Activities," *Social Problems*, 11, 1964, pp. 225–250; Garfinkel, "Studies in Ethnomethodology," *op. cit.*; E. Bittner, "The Police on Skid-Row," *American Sociological Review*, 32, 1967, pp. 669–715; A. Cicourel, *Method and Measurement in Sociology*, New York: The Free Press, 1964; D. Sudnow, "Normal Crimes," *Social Problems*, 12, 1965, pp. 255–276; L. Churchill, "Everyday Quantitative Practices," paper presented to meetings of the American Sociological Association, August, 1966. For critical reviews of Garfinkel, see "The Review Symposium on *Studies in Ethnomethodology*," *American Sociological Review*, 33, 1968, pp. 122–130. It is not clear whether ethnomethodology is to be regarded as a special field within sociology, as a method for "doing" sociology or as a school or movement which may remake the field. There are elements of each of these, so far as I can determine.

[19] Garfinkel, *op. cit.*, p. 11.

detailed study, is certainly consistent with the views of phenomenology.[20]

The ethnomethodologist seeks to discover the "methods" that persons use in their everyday life in society in constructing social reality and also to discover the nature of the realities they have constructed. In studying, for example, the way that jurors recognize the "correctness" of a verdict, he would focus on how the jurors make their activities "normal," on how the moral order of their world is created. They are seen as creating, through their activities, familiar scenes and procedures which are recognizable to them as the world they know in common and take for granted, by which and within which "correctness" of a verdict is determined. Only by examining their procedures and discovering what they consist of, can one fully understand what they mean by correctness, as *correctness is decided by those who construct it.* Further, as Garfinkel shows, some understanding of decision-making in daily life, i.e., in situations other than the jury-room, is also achieved.

In common with ethnoscience is the ethnomethodologist's effort to understand the world as it is interpreted by men in daily life. For example, Natanson, in his introduction to Schutz's collected papers, states "the social scientist's task is the reconstruction of the way in which men in daily life interpret their own world."[21] This is a basic position in the work of ethnomethodologists and in Schutz's own work.

The distinction between natural science and social science, as Natanson, Schutz and others clearly point out, is based on the fact that men are not only objects existing in the natural world to be observed by the scientist, but they are creators of a world, a cultural world, of their own. In creating this world, they interpret their own activities. Their overt behavior is only a fragment of their total behavior. Any social scientist who insists that he can understand all of man's behavior by focusing only on that part which is overt and manifested in concrete, directly observable acts is naive, to say the least. The challenge to the social scientist who seeks to understand social reality, then, is to understand the meaning that the actor's act has for him. If the observer applies only his own categories or theories concerning the meanings of acts, he may never discover the meanings

---

[20] For an elaboration of the notion of accounts, see M. Scott and S. M. Lyman, "Accounts," *American Sociological Review*, 33, 1968, pp. 46–62.

[21] M. Natanson, in A. Schutz, *Collected Papers*, Vol. 1, The Hague: Martinus Nijhoff, 1962, Editor's Introduction, p. lxvi. Schutz is the phenomenologist most frequently cited by ethnomethodologists though Garfinkel is also familiar with the work of Husserl. There is no question that Schutz's work is most relevant for the student of social life. Much of his work has now been translated, the third volume of his collected papers having appeared in 1966; a translation of his *Der Sinnhafte Aufbau der Sozialen Welt* has now been published under the title *The Phenomenology of the Social World*, Northwestern University Press, Evanston, Illinois, 1967. P. L. Berger and T. Luckmann have drawn extensively from Schutz's and Luckmann's work, *Die Strukturen der Lebenswelt*, also being prepared for publication, in their recent book, *The Social Construction of Reality*, New York: Doubleday, 1966.

these same acts have for the actors themselves. Nor can he ever discover how social reality is "created" and how subsequent acts by human actors are performed in the context of *their* understandings.

This, it seems to me, is similar to the problem of bracketing in phenomenological analysis. The scientist must bracket his own pre-supposition concerning the phenomena and seek to discover the suppositions which human actors, *in situ*, adopt and use. Further, he must also bracket these suppositions in an effort to analyze the phenomena themselves.[22]

Both ethnoscience and ethnomethodology are involved in the problem of cultural relativism, but ethnomethodology, in my estimation, may come closer to escaping the bounds of the particular culture that is studied because of the phenomenological sophistication which aids it. For example, the ethnoscientist in studying one culture's classification system has no reason to expect that another culture's classification system will be the same. His emic analysis refers to one society's culture, i.e., he may discover how the Subanun classify disease but he does not claim that any other culture will have the same system of classification. Certainly he can do cross-cultural comparisons to see if emic systems of different cultures share common elements. But he does not take the position that an emic analysis will produce a system which is universally true or valid. Similarly, the ethnomethodologist studying particular actors in particular groupings in a particular society cannot claim that what he discovers will be true generally for all men. Some aspects of decision-making by jurors, for example, may change depending on changes in legal rules and procedures at a later historical point, may differ from one culture to another depending on how the legal system is structured, etc.

However, the grounding of ethnomethodology in phenomenology implies that research problems will be defined and approached in such a way as to result in the discovery of the essential features of the social phenomena being studied. This may appear to be a contradiction. In one sense it is, but at another level it may not be. For example, if one looks at the problem of jurors making decisions as a study of the general phenomenon of decision-making, an analysis of their procedures has implications for the understanding of the essence of the process of decision-making, of how groups, in contrast to individuals, make decisions, and of the rules of decision-making in everyday life. By taking a phenomenological position in which one tries to discover the basic essence of the process, it is possible for the ethnomethodologist to discover that which is more generally true and not be limited to culturally and temporally relative conclusions. As an example from what is more clearly a phenomenological analysis, the "natural attitude" and the "inter-subjective world of everyday life"[23] are presented

---

[22] Spiegelberg, *op. cit.*, p. 690.
[23] A. Schutz, *Collected Papers*, Vol. I, The Hague: Martinus Nijhoff, 1962.

as being characteristic not only of Western man, but probably of all men living in society. They are part of the basic human condition, so to speak. For example, that men assume, and assume that others assume, that if "I change places with the other, so that his 'here' becomes mine, I shall be at the same distance from things and see them with the same typicality that he does; moreover, the same things would be in my reach which are actually in his (and that the reverse is also true)" (*Ibid.* p. 12); that the world is taken for granted to be an inter-subjective world; that the world existed yesterday and will exist tomorrow; that my actions are based on my believing that others can interpret those actions as intelligible, given their understanding of what we know in our culture, etc. If we take the position that the basic features of the "natural attitude" and of the "inter-subjective world of everyday life" may represent essences of the human condition which are universally true—and there is certainly much to indicate in Schutz's analysis that the natural attitude is a taken-for-granted aspect of everyday life—then it is on this background or within this frame that men perform meaningful acts in their everyday activities. The meanings which are then added to behavior are based on the pre-suppositions of the natural attitude. If this is so, then it is possible to look for those common elements in a variety of cultures, based on the natural attitude and the inter-subjectivity of knowledge, that may affect the meanings assigned to activities. What I am saying here is that it is possible that, given this background, some restrictions are placed on how men can perceive and interact. The use of drugs to "escape" the taken-for-granted aspects of everyday life and throw these into sharp question is some indication that men are somehow tied down, bound by, the "facts" of human existence. It is only with some effort, such as the taking of drugs, that one can escape the bounds of the world of everyday life and enter other realities.

Given this grounding in phenomenology (of Schutz and others), the ethnomethodologist's approach to problems, it seems to me, is somewhat different from that of the ethnoscientist's. One contrast is that the former is directed more towards problems of *meaning* in everyday life situations. But even more basic is his concern with discovering those basic features (essences, perhaps) of everyday interaction so that the problem of how meanings are constructed and how social reality is created out of the interlocked activity of human actors becomes an important and critical topic for examination.[24]

Starting from the taken-for-granted, everyday world analyzed by the

---

[24] Another expression of this view in the sociological literature, again drawing heavily from Schutz, is that of P. L. Berger and T. Luckmann, *op. cit.* Although they subtitle their book a treatise on the sociology of knowledge, they are concerned with knowledge in the same sense that Garfinkel is, i.e., the everyday, ordinary knowledge that men have about themselves and their social world and with how the knowledge that men have comes to be established as reality for them.

phenomenologist, the ethnomethodologist takes the position that this is the basis for all other strata of man's reality. This is the ground on which all other realities are constructed. If so, it is important to know what it is that is basic, since one is concerned with the reality of everyday-life-as-seen-by-men-in-society, and one wants to learn how men perceive, experience, and construct the social reality in which they live.[25] This represents, in a real sense, I believe, a phenomenological position of "going to the things themselves," to the social phenomena rather than to previously developed theories to be tested by the formulation of deductive hypotheses.

Both approaches emphasize the importance of investigating the taken-for-granted aspects of man's existence in the world. The ethnoscientists investigate what they call components and the ethnomethodologists what they call background expectancies. Both are concerned with the "methods" which men use to make their world meaningful. The difference between the two approaches is that ethnoscience tends to emphasize the static thing-ness of the phenomena being studied, whereas ethnomethodology is concerned with the active processes whereby things (mainly activities) are constituted in the world of social action.[26]

It is important to note, in this connection, the effort by Garfinkel in his article "Studies in the Routine Grounds of Everyday Activities"[27] to demonstrate the existence of the natural attitude and the intersubjectivity of knowledge drawing from Schutz's analysis. In what Garfinkel calls "demonstration experiments," the technique used was that of disturbing or introducing a "nasty surprise" in interacting with others in order to demonstrate the presence of much that was taken for granted. The technique is simple though limited, and if imaginative variation were used,[28] would possibly not be necessary. Garfinkel disturbed others by simply not performing those acts which they expected—or by performing acts which others did not have any "reason" to expect. For example, his students were instructed to treat their parents at home as though they, the students, were guests in the home rather than the sons or daughters of the parents. The politeness and small acts of kindness they performed were then taken by their parents to be signs of hostility, antagonism or fatigue. For example, to ask one's parents if one may be allowed to look in the refrigerator or the pantry for something to eat—or to ask permission to eat in the first place —was greeted with perplexity, confusion and surprise.

Garfinkel reports going up to a customer standing in line in a restau-

---

25 It is possible to go into an analysis of the convergences between symbolic interaction theory, ethnomethodology and phenomenology, but this is beyond the scope of the present paper. There is without doubt much overlap in the work of W. I. Thomas, Cooley, Mead, William James, and more recent symbolic interactionist theorists such as Strauss, Shibutani, Goffman, Lindesmith, Becker and Garfinkel and his students.

26 I am grateful to Martin Kozloff for the recognition of this distinction.

27 Garfinkel, *op. cit.*

28 Spiegelberg, *op. cit.*, p. 680.

rant and treating him as though he were the waiter, or revealing to a friend during a conversation that he, Garfinkel, had a tape recorder and was recording the entire conversation. What can be learned from such demonstrations? A great deal, though I would not wish to recommend these procedures to others since I do not feel that these are necessarily the only, or even the best, ways of obtaining data concerning the taken-for-granted assumptions of the common sense world of everyday life. They may certainly reveal the variety and complexity of the pre-suppositions or taken-for-granteds that exist in everyday life. The grounds of man's social existence can be discovered. Such discovery can have tremendous possibilities not only for understanding particular social worlds but also for changing or even destroying them altogether.

From my own work,[29] I would like to refer to the study of how cab drivers locate addresses. In order to understand this activity, it is necessary to understand not only the cab driver and his world but also the phenomenon of an address or, even more basic, the phenomenon of a location in space. A phenomenological analysis would lead us to the essence of "location" on which are imposed, in layers of meaning, so to speak, the more unique and specific elements and relationships among elements that constitute locations for the cab driver in a particular kind of socio-cultural space, e.g., the urban environment.

In this research we have thus far studied the constitution of addresses in radio-dispatched orders transmitted to the driver. The order represents a constitution of a location made by the radio dispatcher and understood by the cab driver. There is thus a shared system of relevances. Following the model of componential analysis, we sought to discover the components underlying particular orders. For example, a place that is a frequent source of passengers, that can have more than one potential passenger waiting at the same time, which has more than one point within it at which a passenger may be waiting, and which can be identified by a proper name will be referred to by messages that contain the name of the place, possible information concerning the location of the passenger (to find him within the location) and, as a further possibility, the name of the passenger (to differentiate him from others). For example, "Hanley and Olive, The A&P, for Bush." In contrast, a complete order which consists of a street name and number (e.g., 6604 Pershing) can be used to indicate single or small multi-family residences, where no ambiguity concerning entrances and exits exists and where no more than one potential passenger is likely to be waiting.

We thus found, in examining a large number of radio-dispatched orders, that for places lacking the criteria mentioned but whose location is unambiguous and well-known, name of place alone is sufficient. If the place is distinguished by the regularity of the customer who uses it, the cus-

[29] Psathas and Henslin, *op. cit.*

tomer's name alone may be sufficient. If the place is a residence or otherwise poses no problems concerning the location of the passenger within it, then descriptions of the passenger or where to find him are not needed. We can then arrive at the meaning of "complexity" or "difficulty" in locating a place and passenger *as complexity is defined within the cab driver's world*. Further, a phenomenological analysis would reveal the essential relationships among the elements of the phenomenon, i.e., an address, and from this, what essential possibilities exist for referring to addresses. That is, by determining the essential properties of an address, we can then understand how these make possible particular ways of referring to it. For example, its location *on* one side of a street *between* other structures gives it a position with reference to other streets and with reference to other buildings that makes it locatable in terms of a number (if discrete numbers are assigned to buildings) and a street name (if names are assigned to streets). If such numbers and names are not assigned, it can still be located in terms of those features which distinguish it from other structures (size, color, shape, texture, etc.) and which distinguish its street from other streets (width, compass direction, right or left from some other street, etc.).

I do not claim to have completed the analysis, but this brief description may serve to illustrate what is possible.

The last point I want to make concerns the importance of understanding subjective reality. It is indeed significant that the problem of understanding the *manner* by which men understand other men's minds has not been solved in social science. It is a basic fact of everyday life, however, that men claim to and act as though they can and do understand others, i.e., that they can "know others' minds." They can, at least, know that which is relevant to be known, given the interaction in which they are engaged. Men in everyday society do not doubt that they can know others' minds. They further assume that other men can know their minds, as well.

For the social scientist, a major task in any study is to discover the understandings that the actor and the other have *of one another*.[30] His task is to explicate those understandings. It is not his concern to analyze, in all their detail, the subjective aspects of the actor's behavior, nor of his own (the scientist's) perceptions. His task is to form objective, ideal constructs relating to the understandings and the typifications that men have of one another. (Ethnomethodology, more than ethnoscience, is involved in this task.) In so doing he need not elaborate all of the variations that are involved in some of these typifications. Rather, it is his task to mke typifications of those typifications; to make abstractions, to make constructs, and to de-

---

[30] It is this meaning of *verstehen* which, as Wax argues, is the meaning which is of greatest relevance to the actual work of the sociologist. M. L. Wax, "On Misunderstanding *Verstehen*: A Reply to Abel," *Sociology and Social Research*, 51, 1967, pp. 323–333. Wax calls it "intra-cultural" *verstehen* involving "socialization into the meanings of the members of the culture."

termine the essences of the typifications which actors make. It is significant that phenomenologists are also undertaking the analysis of some of these problems and have discussed methods whereby men can determine how other men perceive. For example, Spiegelberg[31] shows that "imaginative self transposal" can occur, and sets out some of the elements of this process. One of these elements is what he calls "imaginative projection in thought"[32] in which one begins to "construct the other in his world on the basis of the clues which we find in the situation into which we have put ourselves imaginatively . . . and try to build, from these elements, his self and the world as he is likely to see it." The aim, as stated by Spiegelberg, is one which could not have been stated better by sociologists or anthropologists. It is to "see the world through another person's eyes" and consider the "whole 'frame' of existence which the other occupies."[33]

The other method, that of cooperative encounter or cooperative exploration, involves exploring the other's world with his helpful cooperation in a prolonged and extended dialogue involving the sympathetic probing, exploring and interrogation of the other. Anthropologists who have used native informants for long periods of time have experienced the phenomenon of coming to see the world through the other's eyes aided by the checks and qualifications introduced by the other in response to questions and comments. A better example, though it is a model which has not been extensively used for the development of scientific or phenomenological accounts of the other's world, is that of the patient-therapist relationship. Here the psychiatrist can achieve an encounter in which he comes to understand the other "in his entirety."

The method of participant observation in the social sciences has some of these possibilities also.[34] The extension of this method into *disguised* participant observation, in which the observer actually becomes a member of the group and performs a role within the group which others take to be his real identity rather than a role "put on" for the sake of collecting data, enables the observer-researcher to experience the role from within. That is, by having to perform *in that world,* he must develop and adopt the perspective that goes with that world. An example from my own experience is that of being a person who was asking others for directions in order to experience the receiving of directions; also vice versa—offering others di-

[31] H. Spiegelberg, "Phenomenology Through Vicarious Experience," in E. Strauss, *Phenomenology: Pure and Applied,* Pittsburgh: Duquesne University Press, 1964.
[32] This concept is drawn by Spiegelberg from Hans Kunz, who termed it *phantasierend-denkendes Entwerfen. Ibid.,* p. 122.
[33] H. Spiegelberg, "Toward a Phenomenology of Imaginative Understanding of Others," *Proceedings of XIIth International Congress of Philosophy,* Brussels, 1953, p. 237.
[34] For a recent analysis of the methodology of participant observation which makes explicit reference to its relation to phenomenology, see S. Bruyn, *The Human Perspective: The Methodology of Participant Observation,* Englewood Cliffs, N.J.: Prentice-Hall, 1966.

rections in order to experience the giving of directions. This could be extended to many roles which I as a sociologist could take, even to that of being a sociologist presenting a paper to a sociological convention. By then examining my own feelings, ideas, behavior, etc., I can construct possible typifications of the social role and the perspective which it provides for *me*. I can then use myself as a model of what others who perform this role are like, i.e., what the world is as seen by typical others from this perspective.

It is to be hoped that ethnomethodologists will turn their attention to methods whereby it is possible to "know other men's minds." It is often taken for granted in research done by those in the symbolic interactionist tradition in social psychology (influenced by G. H. Mead, C. H. Cooley, W. I. Thomas and others) and ethnomethodologists that it is possible for the researcher to "know the mind" of the subjects studied. A necessary extension is the determination of how members of society know other members' minds. What ethnoscientists are doing is calling our attention to the possibility of devising strict and rigorous procedures for the determination of the other's "mind" and furthermore making possible the replication of results. However, their methodology may have built-in limitations stemming from the assumption that linguistic categories and their underlying components can provide adequate understanding of men in society. It remains to be seen whether more "imaginative," "introspective" and "subjective" approaches to the understanding of others can produce *replicable* results in a manner similar to the methods used in linguistic and semantic analysis.[35]

There is much to be expected from these approaches. Phenomenology has a great deal to offer the social scientist. We may hope that attention now being directed to phenomenology by the ethnomethodologists will stimulate the selection of those aspects of phenomenological methods and insights which are most relevant and significant for the social scientist's endeavor.

Both approaches promise to affect the course of research by focusing attention on the world of everyday life. Since the world is so vast and complex, they virtually guarantee that scientific activity will never end. More important, however, than guaranteeing us jobs forever is that they guarantee a better understanding of human behavior-in-society, which I take to be the main aim of social science, that is, not an understanding of behavior-in-the-laboratory, or behavior-in-the-sociologists' society, but rather behavior where it occurs, in everyday life.

[35] In the study of cab drivers, Psathas and Henslin, *op. cit.*, I try to show how this might be possible.

Selected Bibliography I

Blumer, Herbert. *Symbolic Interactionism: Perspective and Method.* Englewood Cliffs, New Jersey: Prentice-Hall, Inc., 1969. A collection of writings by the chief progenitor of the Chicago School of symbolic interactionism.

Bolton, Charles D. "Behavior, Experience and Relationships." *American Journal of Sociology,* vol. 64 (July 1958), pp. 45–58. A criticism of symbolic interactionism, along with an attempt to indicate remedies for its deficiencies on the basis of concepts derived from George Herbert Mead, Emile Durkheim, and Kurt Riezler.

Bruyn, Severn. "The New Empiricists: The Participant Observer and Phenomenologist." *Sociology and Social Research,* vol. 51 (April 1967), pp. 317–322. Contrasts participant observation and phenomenology to traditional empiricism and to each other.

Cooley, Charles Horton. "The Roots of Social Knowledge." *The American Journal of Sociology,* vol. 32 (July 1926), pp. 59–79. A classic statement of the "sympathetic introspection" method in the study of human behavior.

Denzin, Norman K. *The Research Act.* Chicago: Aldine Publishing Company, 1970. The most comprehensive exposition available on methods appropriate to the perspective of symbolic interactionism. See also the set of readings edited by Denzin, *Sociological Methods: A Sourcebook.* Chicago: Aldine Publishing Company, 1970.

Garfinkel, Harold. *Studies in Ethnomethodology.* Englewood Cliffs, New Jersey: Prentice-Hall, Inc., 1969. By a major exponent of a variant form of symbolic interactionism, this is one of several recent books expounding ethnomethodology.

Hickman, C. Addison, and Manford H. Kuhn. *Individuals, Groups, and Economic Behavior.* New York: Dryden Press, 1956, pp. 21–45. A comprehensive statement of self-theory, the Iowa School of symbolic interaction. Contrasts this approach with Freudian, field, and learning theories.

Kuhn, Manford H. "Kinsey's View of Human Nature." *Social Problems,* vol. 1 (April 1954), pp. 119–125. A devastating critique of the neo-behavioristic, zoomorphic assumptions underlying Kinsey's approach to human sexual behavior.

Lindesmith, Alfred R., and Anselm L. Strauss. "A Critique of Culture–Personality Writings." *American Sociological Review,* vol. 15 (October 1950), pp. 587–600. By the authors of an outstanding symbolic interactionist textbook in social psychology. Indicates some significant deficiencies of an approach favored by many psychoanalytically oriented anthropologists.

McKinney, John C. "Methodological Convergence of Mead, Lundberg and Parsons." *American Journal of Sociology,* vol. 59 (May 1954), pp. 565–574. Indicates several points of both explicit and implicit convergence in the methodologies of three important sociologists who are rarely considered together.

Mead, George Herbert. *Mind, Self and Society.* Chicago: The University of Chicago Press, 1934. The single most influential book, to date, on symbolic interactionism.

Petras, John W. (ed.) *George Herbert Mead: Essays on His Social Philosophy.* New York: Teachers College Press, Columbia University, 1968. A group of articles related to Mead's theory of mind, self, and society, emphasizing his concern with applied pragmatism. Also see the articles by Petras in the *Journal of the History of the Behavioral Sciences* on John Dewey (vol. 4, January 1968, pp. 18–27), James Mark Baldwin and William James (vol. 4, April 1968, pp. 132–142), and W. I. Thomas (vol. 6, January 1970, pp. 70—79).

Rose, Arnold M. (ed.) *Human Behavior and Social Processes.* Boston: Houghton Mifflin Company, 1962. A collection of 34 articles in the symbolic interactionist tradition, most of which were prepared specifically for the book. The editor's introductory essay presents an overview of that tradition.

Schwartz, Morris S., and Charlotte G. Schwartz. "Problems in Participant Observation." *American Journal of Sociology*, vol. 60 (January 1955), pp. 343–353. An evaluation of one of the favorite research techniques of symbolic interactionists.

Strauss, Anselm (ed.) *George Herbert Mead: On Social Psychology.* Chicago: The University of Chicago Press, 1964. A collection of important selections from Mead's major writings.

Sullivan, Harry S. *Conceptions of Modern Psychiatry.* Washington, D.C.: The William Alanson White Psychiatric Foundation, 1940, 1945. The outstanding exponent of a theory of interpersonal relationships presents a theory of the formation of personality which closely parallels Mead's at several points.

Vaughan, Ted R., and Larry T. Reynolds. "The Sociology of Symbolic Interactionism." *The American Sociologist*, vol. 3 (August 1968), pp. 208–214. A sociometric study of the varieties of symbolic interaction theory.

part II

Society

Symbolic interactionists view society as a process of ongoing activity, of varied interactions, not as a relatively static system, structure, or organization. The symbolic interactionist conception of society tends to focus attention on interpersonal relationships rather than on whole societies or groups. As a consequence, some critics have questioned the applicability of the microsociological approach of symbolic interactionism to macrosociological phenomena.

In present American sociology, the developing emphases on structural-functional analysis and on historical and comparative studies have brought a focus on social systems and subsystems. Such analyses have stressed the role of larger social units in shaping component, smaller units. For many exponents of symbolic interactionism, this stress has been accompanied by an unacceptable collective determinism of human conduct. That is, the individual presented in such schemes is often merely a passive, pliant, taken-for-granted recipient of relatively inflexible societal influences.

On two counts, this presentation is held to be inadequate. In the first place, it overlooks the mutual, bilateral relationship between society and the individual. Most symbolic interactionists reject collective determinism almost as strongly as they reject biological determinism. Second, the assumption of a fixed or durable societal structure contradicts the symbolic interactionists' conception of a dynamic society ever in the process of "becoming."

In the essay, "Society as Symbolic Interaction," Herbert Blumer presents the basic premises and methodological implications of this position. He focuses on the distinctive character of human relationships—the learned ability of human beings to construct and share their social worlds. He links this focus with a microsociological approach to understanding human society.

The importance of communication in social life is stressed in the selection by John Dewey. Here Dewey suggests a conception of society as existing in the process of communication. Through communication, individuals are linked in a dynamic social process.

The excerpt from one of Charles Horton Cooley's books constitutes his classic statement of the centrality of the family and other intimate group relationships in forming what he calls "human nature." This selection, written in 1909, remains valuable despite his obsolete reference to race differences. A fairly good synopsis of Cooley's contribution to social psychology can be gained by reading this selection along with his article in Part III.

Reference group theory, first formulated by Herbert Hyman, has been congruent with the ideas of symbolic interactionism. Tamotsu Shibutani analyzes the ways the concept has been used and points out its specific relevance to communication and social relationships. Manford H. Kuhn's article reconsiders the reference group in light of recent theory and research. The distinction between "group" and "category" leads him to propose new ways of defining the idea of "others."

Norman K. Denzin's article, based on a distinction Kuhn makes, reports an attempt to identify both the role-specific "significant others" and the more broadly influential "orientational others" of a sample of college students.

The selection by Hans Gerth and C. Wright Mills concerns the ways institutions and roles are treated by symbolic interactionists, considered in the contexts of self-conceptions and interpersonal relations.

Ceremony and ritual are frequently considered in conjunction with status elevation—confirmation, graduation, marriage. The selection by Harold Garfinkel shows how moral indignation is used to reduce or degrade the position of individuals. In Clark McPhail's article, we find an empirical challenge to the customary separation of explanations of collective, "unstructured" behavior and routine social behavior. While these two concluding articles do not use large samples, highly standardized questionnaires, or sophisticated statistical techniques, their observations provide increased understanding of complex and relatively neglected aspects of social life.

While differing in focus and technique, the articles in Part II have a common perspective: They suggest that human relationships are neither static nor abstract, but reflect the constructed, emergent quality of individual behavior. This central feature helps to account for both the stability and the changeability of human society.

Society as Symbolic Interaction

A view of human society as symbolic interaction has been followed more than it has been formulated. Partial, usually fragmentary, statements of it are to be found in the writings of a number of eminent scholars, some inside the field of sociology and some outside. Among the former we may note such scholars as Charles Horton Cooley, W. I. Thomas, Robert E. Park, E. W. Burgess, Florian Znaniecki, Ellsworth Faris, and James Mickel Williams. Among those outside the discipline we may note William James, John Dewey, and George Herbert Mead. None of these scholars, in my judgment, has presented a systematic statement of the nature of human group life from the standpoint of symbolic interaction. Mead stands out among all of them in laying bare the fundamental premises of the approach, yet he did little to develop its methodological implications for sociological study. Students who seek to depict the position of symbolic interaction may easily give different pictures of it. What I have to present should be regarded as my personal version. My aim is to present the basic premises of the point of view and to develop their methodological consequences for the study of human group life.

The term "symbolic interaction" refers, of course, to the peculiar and distinctive character of interaction as it takes place between human beings. The peculiarity consists in the fact that human beings interpret or "define" each other's actions instead of merely reacting to each other's actions. Their "response" is not made directly to the actions of one another but instead is based on the meaning which they attach to such actions. Thus, human interaction is mediated by the use of symbols, by interpretation, or by ascertaining the meaning of one another's actions. This mediation is equivalent to inserting a process of interpretation between stimulus and response in the case of human behavior.

The simple recognition that human beings interpret each other's actions as the means of acting toward one another has permeated the thought and writings of many scholars of human conduct and of human group life. Yet few of them have endeavored to analyze what such interpretation implies about the nature of the human being or about the nature of human association. They are usually content with a mere recognition that "interpretation" should be caught by the student, or with a simple realization that symbols, such as cultural norms or values, must be introduced into their analyses. Only G. H. Mead, in my judgment, has sought to think through what the act of interpretation implies for an understanding of the human being, human action, and human association. The essentials of his analysis are so penetrating and profound and so important for an understanding of human group life that I wish to spell them out, even though briefly.

The key feature in Mead's analysis is that the human being has a self. This idea should not be cast aside as esoteric or glossed over as something that is obvious and hence not worthy of attention. In declaring that the human being has a self, Mead had in mind chiefly that the human being can be the object of his own actions. He can act toward himself as he might act toward others. Each of us is familiar with actions of this sort in which the human being gets angry with himself, rebuffs himself, takes pride in himself, argues with himself, tries to bolster his own courage, tells himself that he should "do this" or not "do that," sets goals for himself, makes compromises with himself, and plans what he is going to do. That the human being acts toward himself in these and countless other ways is a matter of easy empirical observation. To recognize that the human being can act toward himself is no mystical conjuration.

Mead regards this ability of the human being to act toward himself as the central mechanism with which the human being faces and deals with his world. This mechanism enables the human being to make indication to himself of things in his surroundings and thus to guide his actions by what he notes. Anything of which a human being is conscious is something which he is indicating to himself—the ticking of a clock, a knock at the door, the appearance of a friend, the remark made by a companion, a recognition that he has a task to perform, or the realization that he has a cold. Conversely, anything of which he is not conscious is, *ipso facto*, something which he is not indicating to himself. The conscious life of the human being, from the time that he awakens until he falls asleep, is a continual flow of self-indications—notations of the things with which he deals and takes into account. We are given, then, a picture of the human being as an organism which confronts its world with a mechanism for making indications to itself. This is the mechanism that is involved in interpreting the actions of others. To interpret the actions of another is to point out to oneself that the action has this or that meaning or character.

Now, according to Mead, the significance of making indications to oneself is of paramount importance. The importance lies along two lines. First, to indicate something is to extricate it from its setting, to hold it apart, to give it a meaning or, in Mead's language, to make it into an object. An object—that is to say, anything that an individual indicates to himself—is different from a stimulus; instead of having an intrinsic character which acts on the individual and which can be identified apart from the individual, its character or meaning is conferred on it by the individual. The object is a product of the individual's disposition to act instead of being an antecedent stimulus which evokes the act. Instead of the individual being surrounded by an environment of pre-existing objects which play upon him and call forth his behavior, the proper picture is that he constructs his objects on the basis of his on-going activity. In any of his countless acts—whether minor, like dressing himself, or major, like organizing himself for a professional career—the individual is designating different objects to himself, giving them meaning, judging their suitability to his action, and making decisions on the basis of the judgment. This is what is meant by interpretation or acting on the basis of symbols.

The second important implication of the fact that the human being makes indications to himself is that his action is constructed or built up instead of being a mere release. Whatever the action in which he is engaged, the human individual proceeds by pointing out to himself the divergent things which have to be taken into account in the course of his action. He has to note what he wants to do and how he is to do it; he has to point out to himself the various conditions which may be instrumental to his action and those which may obstruct his action; he has to take account of the demands, the expectations, the prohibitions, and the threats as they may arise in the situation in which he is acting. His action is built up step by step through a process of such self-indication. The human individual pieces together and guides his action by taking account of different things and interpreting their significance for his prospective action. There is no instance of conscious action of which this is not true.

The process of constructing action through making indications to oneself cannot be swallowed up in any of the conventional psychological categories. This process is distinct from and different from what is spoken of as the "ego"—just as it is different from any other conception which conceives of the self in terms of composition or organization. Self-indication is a moving communicative process in which the individual notes things, assesses them, gives them a meaning, and decides to act on the basis of the meaning. The human being stands over against the world, or against "alters," with such a process and not with a mere ego. Further, the process of self-indication cannot be subsumed under the forces, whether from the outside or inside, which are presumed to play upon the individual to produce his behavior. Environmental pressures, external stimuli, organic drives, wishes, attitudes, feelings, ideas, and their like do not cover or explain the process of self-indication. The process of self-indication stands over against them in that the individual points out to himself and interprets the appearance or expression of such things, noting a given social demand that is made on him, recognizing a command, observing that he is hungry, realizing that he wishes to buy something, aware that he has a given feeling, conscious that he dislikes eating with someone he despises, or aware that he is thinking of doing some given things. By virtue of indicating such things to himself, he places himself over against them and is able to act back against them, accepting them, rejecting them, or transforming them in accordance with how he defines or interprets them. His behavior, accordingly, is not a result of such things as environmental pressures, stimuli, motives, attitudes, and ideas but arises instead from how he interprets and handles these things in the action which he is constructing. The process of self-indication by means of which human action is formed cannot be accounted for by factors which precede the act. The process of self-indication exists in its own right and must be accepted and studied as such. It is through this process that the human being constructs his conscious action.

Now Mead recognizes that the formation of action by the individual through a process of self-indication always takes place in a social context. Since this matter is so vital to an understanding of symbolic interaction it needs to be explained carefully. Fundamentally, group action takes the form of a fitting together of individual lines of action. Each individual aligns his action to the action of others by ascertaining what they are doing or what they intend to do—that is, by getting the meaning of their acts. For Mead, this is done by the individual "taking the role" of others—either the role of a specific person or the role of a group (Mead's "generalized other"). In taking such roles the individual seeks to ascertain the intention or direction of the acts of others. He forms and aligns his own action on the basis of such interpretation of the acts of others. This is the fundamental way in which group action takes place in human society.

The foregoing are the essential features, as I see them, in Mead's analysis of the bases of symbolic interaction. They presuppose the following: that human society is made up of individuals who have selves (that is, make indications to themselves); that individual action is a construction and not a release, being built up by the individual through noting and interpreting features of the situations in which he acts; that group or collective action consists of the aligning of individual actions, brought about by the individuals' interpreting or taking into account each other's actions. Since my purpose is to present and not to defend the position of symbolic interaction I shall not endeavor in this essay to advance support for the three premises which I have just indicated. I wish merely to say that the three premises can be easily verified empirically. I know of no instance of human group action to which the three premises do not apply. The reader is challenged to find or think of a single instance which they do not fit.

I wish now to point out that sociological views of human society are, in general, markedly at variance with the premises which I have indicated as underlying symbolic interaction. Indeed, the predominant number of such views, especially those in vogue at the present time, do not see or treat human society as symbolic interaction. Wedded, as they tend to be, to some form of sociological determinism, they adopt images of human society, of individuals in it, and of group action which do not square with the premises of symbolic interaction. I wish to say a few words about the major lines of variance.

Sociological thought rarely recognizes or treats human societies as composed of individuals who have selves. Instead, they assume human beings to be merely organisms with some kind of organization, responding to forces which play upon them. Generally, although not exclusively, these forces are lodged in the make-up of the society, as in the case of "social system," "social structure," "culture," "status position," "social role," "custom," "institution," "collective representation," "social situation," "social norm," and "values." The assumption is that the behavior of people as members *of a society* is an expression of the play on them of these kinds of factors or forces. This, of course, is the logical position which is necessarily taken when the scholar explains their behavior or phases of their behavior in terms of one or other of such social factors. The individuals who compose a human society are treated as the media through which such factors operate, and the social action of such individuals is regarded as an expression of such factors. This approach or point of view denies, or at least ignores, that human beings have selves—that they act by making indications to themselves. Incidentally, the "self" is not brought into the picture by introducing such items as organic drives, motives, attitudes, feelings, internalized social factors, or psychological components. Such psychological factors have the same status as the social factors mentioned: they are regarded as factors which play on the individual to produce his action. They do not constitute the process of self-indication. The process of self-indication stands over against them, just as it stands over against the social factors which play on the human being. Practically all sociological conceptions of human society fail to recognize that the individuals who compose it have selves in the sense spoken of.

Correspondingly, such sociological conceptions do not regard the social actions of individuals in human society as being constructed by them through a process of interpretation. Instead, action is treated as a product of factors which play on and through individuals. The social behavior of people is not seen as built up by them through an interpretation of objects, situations, or the actions of others. If a place is given to "interpretation," the interpretation is regarded as merely an expression of other factors (such as motives) which precede the act, and accordingly disappears as a factor in its own right. Hence, the social action of people is treated as an outward flow or expression of forces playing on them rather than as acts which are built up by people through their interpretation of the situations in which they are placed.

These remarks suggest another significant line of difference between general sociological views and the position of symbolic interaction. These two sets of views differ in where they lodge social action. Under the perspective of symbolic interaction, social action is lodged in acting individuals who fit their respective lines of action to one another through a process of interpretation; group action is the collective action of such individuals. As opposed to this view, sociological conceptions generally lodge social action in the action of society or in some unit of society. Examples of this are legion. Let me cite a few. Some conceptions, in treating societies or human groups as "social systems," regard group action as an expression of a system, either in a state of balance or seeking to achieve balance. Or group action is conceived as an expression of the "functions" of a society or of a group. Or group action is regarded as the outward expression of elements lodged in society or the group such as cultural demands, societal purposes, social values, or institutional stresses. These typical conceptions ignore or blot out a view of group life or of group action as consisting of the collective or concerted actions of individuals seeking to meet their life situations. If recognized at all, the efforts of people to develop collective acts to meet their situations are subsumed under the play of underlying or transcending forces which are lodged in society or its parts. The individuals composing the society or the group become "carriers," or media for the expression of such forces; and the interpretative behavior by means of which people form their actions is merely a coerced link in the play of such forces.

The indication of the foregoing lines of variance should help to put the position of symbolic interaction in better perspective. In the remaining discussion I wish to sketch somewhat more fully how human society appears in terms of symbolic interaction and to point out some methodological implications.

Human society is to be seen as consisting of acting people, and the life of the society is to be seen as consisting of their actions. The acting units may be separate individuals, collectivities whose members are acting together on a common quest, or organizations acting on behalf of a constituency. Respective examples are individual purchasers in a market, a play group or missionary band, and a business corporation or a national professional association. There is no empirically observable activity in a human society that does not spring from some acting unit. This banal statement needs to be stressed in light of the common practice of sociologists of reducing human society to social units that do not act—for example, social classes in modern society. Obviously, there are ways of viewing human society other than in terms of the acting units that compose it. I merely wish to point out that in respect to concrete or empirical activity human society must necessarily be seen in terms of the acting units that form it. I would add that any scheme of human society claiming to be a realistic analysis has to respect and be congruent with the empirical recognition that a human society consists of acting units.

Corresponding respect must be shown to the conditions under which such units act. One primary condition is that action takes place in and with regard to a situation. Whatever be the acting unit—an individual, a family, a school, a church, a business firm, a labor union, a legislature, and so on—any particular action is formed in the light of the situation in which it takes place. This leads to the recognition of a second major condition, namely, that the action is formed or constructed by interpreting the situation. The acting unit necessarily has to identify the things which it has to take into account—tasks, opportunities, obstacles, means, demands, discomforts, dangers, and the like; it has to assess them in some fashion and it has to make decisions on the basis of the assessment. Such interpretative behavior may take place in the individual guiding his own action, in a collectivity of individuals acting in concert, or in "agents" acting on behalf of a group or organization. Group life consists of acting units developing acts to meet the situations in which they are placed.

Usually, most of the situations encountered by people in a given society are defined or "structured" by them in the same way. Through previous interaction they develop and acquire common understandings or definitions of how to act in this or that situation. These common definitions enable people to act alike. The common repetitive behavior of people in such situations should not mislead the student into believing that no process of interpretation is in play; on the contrary, even though fixed, the actions of the participating people are constructed by them through a process of interpretation. Since ready-made and commonly accepted definitions are at hand, little strain is placed on people in guiding and organizing their acts. However, many other situations may not be defined in a single way by the participating people. In this event, their lines of action do not fit together readily and collective action is blocked. Interpretations have to be developed and effective accommodation of the participants to one another has to be worked out. In the case of such "undefined" situations, it is necessary to trace and study the emerging process of definition which is brought into play.

Insofar as sociologists or students of human society are concerned with the behavior of acting units, the position of symbolic interaction requires the student to catch the process of interpretation through which they construct their actions. This process is not to be caught merely by turning to conditions which are antecedent to the process. Such antecedent conditions are helpful in understanding the process insofar as they enter into it, but as mentioned previously they do not constitute the process. Nor can one catch the process merely by inferring its nature from the overt action which is its product. To catch the process, the student must take the role of the acting unit whose behavior he is studying. Since the interpretation is being made by the acting unit in terms of objects designated and appraised, meanings acquired, and decisions made, the process has to be seen from the standpoint of the acting unit. It is the recognition of this fact that makes the research work of such scholars as R. E. Park and W. I. Thomas so notable.

To try to catch the interpretative process by remaining aloof as a so-called "objective" observer and refusing to take the role of the acting unit is to risk the worst kind of subjectivism—the objective observer is likely to fill in the process of interpretation with his own surmises in place of catching the process as it occurs in the experience of the acting unit which uses it.

By and large, of course, sociologists do not study human society in terms of its acting units. Instead, they are disposed to view human society in terms of structure or organization and to treat social action as an expression of such structure or organization. Thus, reliance is placed on such structural categories as social system, culture, norms, values, social stratification, status positions, social roles and institutional organization. These are used both to analyze human society and to account for social action within it. Other major interests of sociological scholars center around this focal theme of organization. One line of interest is to view organization in terms of the functions it is supposed to perform. Another line of interest is to study societal organization as a system seeking equilibrium; here the scholar endeavors to detect mechanisms which are indigenous to the system. Another line of interest is to identify forces which play upon organization to bring about changes in it; here the scholar endeavors, especially through comparative study, to isolate a relation between causative factors and structural results. These various lines of sociological perspective and interest, which are so strongly entrenched today, leap over the acting units of a society and bypass the interpretative process by which such acting units build up their actions.

These respective concerns with organization on one hand and with acting units on the other hand set the essential difference between conventional views of human society and the view of it implied in symbolic interaction. The latter view recognizes the presence of organization in human society and respects its importance. However, it sees and treats organization differently. The difference is along two major lines. First, from the standpoint of symbolic interaction the organization of a human society is the framework inside of which social action takes place and is not the determinant of that action. Second, such organization and changes in it are the product of the activity of acting units and not of "forces" which leave such acting units out of account. Each of these two major lines of difference should be explained briefly in order to obtain a better understanding of how human society appears in terms of symbolic interaction.

From the standpoint of symbolic interaction, social organization is a framework inside of which acting units develop their actions. Structural features, such as "culture," "social systems," "social stratification," or "social roles," set conditions for their action but do not determine their action. People—that is, acting units—do not act toward culture, social structure or the like; they act toward situations. Social organization enters into action only to the extent to which it shapes situations in which people act, and to the extent to which it supplies fixed sets of symbols which people use in interpreting their situations. These two forms of influence of social organization are important. In the case of settled and stabilized societies, such as isolated primitive tribes and peasant communities, the influence is certain to be profound. In the case of human societies, particularly modern societies, in which streams of new situations arise and old situations become unstable, the influence of organization decreases. One should bear in mind that the most important element confronting an acting unit in situations is the actions of other acting units. In modern society, with its increasing criss-crossing of lines of action, it is common for situations to arise in which the actions of participants are not previously regularized and standardized. To this extent, existing social organization does not shape the situations. Correspondingly, the symbols or tools of interpretation used by acting units in such situations may vary and shift considerably. For these reasons, social action may go beyond, or depart from, existing organization in any of its structural dimensions. The organization of a human society is not to be identified with the process of interpretation used by its acting units; even though it affects that process, it does not embrace or cover the process.

Perhaps the most outstanding consequence of viewing human society as organization is to overlook the part played by acting units in social change. The conventional procedure of sociologists is (*a*) to identify human society (or some part of it) in terms of an established or organized form, (*b*) to identify some factor or condition of change playing upon the human society or the given part of it, and (*c*) to identify the new form assumed by the society following upon the play of the factor of change. Such observations permit the student to couch propositions to the effect that a given factor of change playing upon a given organized form results in a given new organized form. Examples ranging from crude to refined statements are legion, such as that an economic depression increases solidarity in the families of workingmen or that industrialization replaces extended families by nuclear families. My concern here is not with the validity of such propositions but with the methodological position which they presuppose. Essentially, such propositions either ignore the role of the interpretative behavior of acting units in the given instance of change, or else regard the interpretative behavior as coerced by the factor of change. I wish to point out that any line of social change, since it involves change in human action, is necessarily mediated by interpretation on the part of the people caught up in the change —the change appears in the form of new situations in which people have to construct new forms of action. Also, in line with what has been said previously, interpretations of new situations are not predetermined by conditions antecedent to the situations but depend on what is taken into account and assessed in the actual situations in which behavior is formed. Variations in interpretation may readily occur as different acting units cut out different objects in the situation, or give different weight to the objects which they note, or piece objects together in different patterns. In formulating propositions of social change, it would be wise to recognize that any given line of such change is mediated by acting units interpreting the situations with which they are confronted.

Students of human society will have to face the question of whether their preoccupation with categories of structure and organization can be squared with the interpretative process by means of which human beings, individually and collectively, act in human society. It is the discrepancy between the two which plagues such students in their efforts to attain scientific propositions of the sort achieved in the physical and biological sciences. It is this discrepancy, further, which is chiefly responsible for their difficulty in fitting hypothetical propositions to new arrays of empirical data. Efforts are made, of course, to overcome these shortcomings by devising new structural categories, by formulating new structural hypotheses, by developing more refined techniques of research, and even by formulating new methodological schemes of a structural character. These efforts continue to ignore or to explain away the interpretative process by which people act, individually and collectively, in society. The question remains whether human society or social action can be successfully analyzed by schemes which refuse to recognize human beings as they are, namely, as persons constructing individual and collective action through an interpretation of the situations which confront them.

11   JOHN DEWEY

Communication, Individual and Society

We often fancy that institutions, social custom, collective habit, have been formed by the consolidation of individual habits. In the main this supposition is false to fact. To a considerable extent customs, or widespread uniformities of habit, exist because individuals face the same situation and react in like fashion. But to a larger extent customs persist because individuals form their personal habits under conditions set by prior customs. An individual usually acquires the morality as he inherits the speech of his social group. The activities of the group are already there, and some assimilation of his own acts to their pattern is a prerequisite of a share therein, and hence of having any part in what is going on. Each person is born an infant, and every infant is subject from the first breath he draws and the first cry he utters to the attentions and demands of others. These others are not just persons in general with minds in general. They are beings with habits, and beings who upon the whole esteem the habits they have, if for no other reason than that, having them, their imagination is thereby limited. The nature of habit is to be assertive, insistent, self-perpetuating. There is no miracle in the fact that if a child learns any language he learns the language that those about him speak and teach, especially since his ability to speak that language is a pre-condition of his entering into effective connection with them, making wants known and getting them satisfied. Fond parents and relatives frequently pick up a few of the child's spontaneous modes of speech and for a time at least they are portions of the speech of the group. But the ratio which such words bear to the total vocabulary in use gives a fair measure of the part played by purely individual habit in forming custom in comparison with the part played by custom in forming individual habits. Few persons have either the energy or the wealth to build private roads to travel upon. They find it convenient, "natural," to use the roads that are already there; while unless their private roads connect at some point with the highway they cannot build them even if they would.

These simple facts seem to me to give a simple explanation of matters that are often surrounded with mystery. To talk about the priority of "society" to *the* individual is to indulge in nonsensical metaphysics. But to say that some pre-existent association of human beings is prior to every particular human being who is born into the world is to mention a commonplace. These associations are definite modes of interaction of persons with one another; that is to say they form customs, institutions. There is no problem in all history so artificial as that of how "individuals" manage to form "society." The problem is due to the pleasure taken in manipulating concepts, and discussion goes on because concepts are kept from inconvenient contact with facts. The facts of infancy and sex have only to be called to mind to see how manufactured are the conceptions which enter into this particular problem.

The problem, however, of how those established and more or less deeply grooved systems of interaction which we call social groups, big and small, modify the activities of individuals who perforce are caught up within them, and how the activities of component individuals remake and redirect previously established customs is a deeply significant one. Viewed from the standpoint of custom and its priority to the formation of habits in human beings who are born babies and gradually grow to maturity, the facts which are now usually assembled under the conceptions of collective minds, group-minds, national-minds, crowd-minds, etc., etc., lose the mysterious air they exhale when mind is thought of (as orthodox psychology teaches us to think of it) as something which precedes action. It is difficult to see that collective mind means anything more than a custom brought at some point to explicit, emphatic consciousness, emotional or intellectual.[1]

The family into which one is born is a family in a village or city which interacts with other more or less integrated systems of activity, and which includes a diversity of groupings within itself, say, churches, political parties, clubs, cliques, partnerships, trade-unions, corporations, etc. If we start with the traditional notion of mind as something complete in itself, then we may well be perplexed by the problem of how a common mind, common ways of feeling and believing and purposing, comes into existence and then forms these groups. The case is quite otherwise if we recognize that in any case we must start with grouped action, that is, with some fairly settled system of interaction among individuals. The problem of origin and development of the various groupings, or definite customs, in existence at any particular time in any particular place is not solved by reference to psychic causes, elements, forces. It is to be solved by reference to facts of action, demand for food, for houses, for a mate, for someone to talk to and to listen to one talk, for control of others, demands which are all intensified by the fact already mentioned that each person begins a helpless, dependent creature. I do not mean of course that hunger, fear, sexual love, gregariousness, sympathy, parental love, love of bossing and of being ordered about, imitation, etc., play no part. But I do mean that these words do not express elements or forces which are psychic or mental in their first intention. They denote *ways of behavior*. These ways of behaving involve interaction, that is to say, and prior groupings. And to understand the existence

---

[1] Mob psychology comes under the same principles, but in a negative aspect. The crowd and mob express a disintegration of habits which releases impulse and renders persons susceptible to immediate stimuli, rather than such a functioning of habits as is found in the mind of a club or school of thought or a political party. Leaders of an organization, that is of an interaction having settled habits, may, however, in order to put over some schemes, deliberately resort to stimuli which will break through the crust of ordinary custom and release impulses on such a scale as to create a mob psychology. Since fear is a normal reaction to the unfamiliar, dread and suspicion are the forces most played upon to accomplish this result, together with vast vague contrary hopes. This is an ordinary technique in excited political campaigns, in starting war, etc. But an assimilation like that of Le Bon of the psychology of democracy to the psychology of a crowd in overriding individual judgment shows lack of psychological insight. A political democracy exhibits an overriding of thought like that seen in any convention or institution. That is, thought is submerged in habit. In the crowd and mob, it is submerged in undefined emotion. China and Japan exhibit crowd psychology more frequently than do western democratic countries. Not in my judgment because of any essentially Oriental psychology but because of a nearer background of rigid and solid customs conjoined with the phenomena of a period of transition. The introduction of many novel stimuli creates occasions where habits afford no ballast. Hence great waves of emotion easily sweep through masses. Sometimes they are waves of enthusiasm for the new; sometimes of violent reaction against it—both equally undiscriminating. The war has left behind it a somewhat similar situation in western countries.

of organized ways or habits we surely need to go to physics, chemistry and physiology rather than to psychology.

There is doubtless a great mystery as to why any such thing as being conscious should exist at all. But *if* consciousness exists at all, there is no mystery in its being connected with what it is connected with. That is to say, if an activity which is an interaction of various factors, or a grouped activity, comes to consciousness it seems natural that it should take the form of an emotion, belief or purpose that reflects the interaction, that it should be an "our" consciousness or a "my" consciousness. And by this is meant both that it will be shared by those who are implicated in the associative custom, or more or less alike in them all, and that it will be felt or thought to concern others as well as one's self. A family-custom or organized habit of action comes into contact and conflict for example with that of some other family. The emotions of ruffled pride, the belief about superiority or being "as good as other people," the intention to old one's own are naturally *our* feeling and idea of *our* treatment and position. Substitute the Republican party or the American nation for the family and the general situation remains the same. The conditions which determine the nature and extent of the particular grouping in question are matters of supreme import. But they are not, as such, subject-matter of psychology, but of the history of politics, law, religion, economics, invention, the technology of communication and intercourse. Psychology comes in as an indispensable tool. But it enters into the matter of understanding these various special topics, not into the question of what psychic forces form a collective mind and therefore a social group. That way of stating the case puts the cart a long way before the horse, and naturally gathers obscurities and mysteries to itself. In short, the primary facts of social psychology center about collective habit, custom. In addition to the general psychology of habit—which *is* general not individual in any intelligible sense of that word—we need to find out just how different customs shape the desires, beliefs, purposes of those who are affected by them. The problem of social psychology is not how either individual or collective mind forms social groups and customs, but how different customs, established interacting arrangements, form and nurture different minds.

12 CHARLES HORTON COOLEY

Primary Group and Human Nature

Primary groups are primary in the sense that they give the individual his earliest and completest experience of social unity, and also in the sense that they do not change in the same degree as more elaborate relations, but form a comparatively permanent source out of which the latter are ever springing. Of course they are not independent of the larger society, but to some extent reflect its spirit; as the German family and the German school bear somewhat distinctly the print of German militarism. But this, after all, is like the tide setting back into creeks, and does not commonly go very far. Among the German, and still more among the Russian, peasantry are found habits of free cooperation and discussion almost uninfluenced by the character of the state; and it is a familiar and well-supported view that the village commune, self-governing as regards local affairs and habituated to discussion, is a very widespread institution in settled communities, and the continuator of a similar autonomy previously existing in the clan. "It is man who makes monarchies and establishes republics, but the commune seems to come directly from the hand of God."[1]

In our own cities the crowded tenements and the general economic and social confusion have sorely wounded the family and the neighborhood, but it is remarkable, in view of these conditions, what vitality they show; and there is nothing upon which the conscience of the time is more determined than upon restoring them to health.

These groups, then, are springs of life, not only for the individual but for social institutions. They are only in part molded by special traditions, and, in larger degree, express a universal nature. The religion or government of other civilizations may seem alien to us, but the children or the family group wear the common life, and with them we can always make ourselves at home.

By human nature, I suppose, we may understand those sentiments and impulses that are human in being superior to those of lower animals, and also in the sense that they belong to mankind at large, and not to any particular race or time. It means, particularly, sympathy and the innumerable sentiments into which sympathy enters, such as love, resentment, ambition, vanity, hero-worship, and the feeling of social right and wrong.[2]

Reprinted by permission of Charles Scribner's Sons from *Social Organization*, pages 26–31, by Charles Horton Cooley. Copyright 1909 Charles Scribner's Sons; renewal copyright 1937 Elsie Jones Cooley.

[1] De Tocqueville, *Democracy in America*, vol. i, chap. 5.

[2] These matters are expounded at some length in the writer's *Human Nature and the Social Order*.

Human nature in this sense is justly regarded as a comparatively permanent element in society. Always and everywhere men seek honor and dread ridicule, defer to public opinion, cherish their goods and their children, and admire courage, generosity, and success. It is always safe to assume that people are and have been human.

It is true, no doubt, that there are differences of race capacity, so great that a large part of mankind are possibly incapable of any high kind of social organization. But these differences, like those among individuals of the same race, are subtle, depending upon some obscure intellectual deficiency, some want of vigor, or slackness of moral fibre, and do not involve unlikeness in the generic impulses of human nature. In these all races are very much alike. The more insight one gets into the life of savages, even those that are reckoned the lowest, the more human, the more like ourselves, they appear. Take for instance the natives of Central Australia, as described by Spencer and Gillen,[3] tribes having no definite government or worship and scarcely able to count to five. They are generous to one another, emulous of virtue as they understand it, kind to their children and to the aged, and by no means harsh to women. Their faces as shown in the photographs are wholly human and many of them attractive.

And when we come to a comparison between different stages in the development of the same race, between ourselves, for instance, and the Teutonic tribes of the time of Caesar, the difference is neither in human nature nor in capacity, but in organization, in the range and complexity of relations, in the diverse expression of powers and passions essentially much the same.

There is no better proof of this generic likeness of human nature than in the ease and joy with with which the modern man makes himself at home in literature depicting the most remote and varied phases of life—in Homer, in the Nibelung tales, in the Hebrew Scriptures, in the legends of the American Indians, in stories of frontier life, of soldiers and sailors, of criminals and tramps, and so on. The more penetratingly any phase of human life is studied the more an essential likeness to ourselves is revealed.

To return to primary groups: the view here maintained is that human nature is not something existing separately in the individual, but a *group-nature or primary phase of society,* a relatively simple and general condition of the social mind. It is something more, on the one hand, than the mere instinct that is born in us—though that enters into it—and something less, on the other, than the more elaborate development of ideas and sentiments that makes up institutions. It is the nature which is developed and expressed in those simple, face-to-face groups that are somewhat alike in all societies; groups of the family, the playground, and the neighborhood. In the essential similarity of these is to be found the basis, in experience, for

[3] *The Native Tribes of Central Australia.* Compare also Darwin's views and examples given in chap. 7 of his *Descent of Man.*

similar ideas and sentiments in the human mind. In these, everywhere, human nature comes into existence. Man does not have it at birth; he cannot acquire it except through fellowship, and it decays in isolation.

If this view does not recommend itself to common sense I do not know that elaboration will be of much avail. It simply means the application at this point of the idea that society and individuals are inseparable phases of a common whole, so that wherever we find an individual fact we may look for a social fact to go with it. If there is a universal nature in persons there must be something universal in association to correspond to it.

What else can human nature be than a trait of primary groups? Surely not an attribute of the separate individual—supposing there were any such thing—since its typical characteristics, such as affection, ambition, vanity, and resentment, are inconceivable apart from society. If it belongs, then, to man in association, what kind or degree of association is required to develop it? Evidently nothing elaborate, because elaborate phases of society are transient and diverse, while human nature is comparatively stable and universal. In short the family and neighborhood life is essential to its genesis and nothing more is.

Here as everywhere in the study of society we must learn to see mankind in psychical wholes, rather than in artificial separation. We must see and feel the communal life of family and local groups as immediate facts, not as combinations of something else. And perhaps we shall do this best by recalling our own experience and extending it through sympathetic observation. What, in our life, is the family and the fellowship; what do we know of the we-feeling? Thought of this kind may help us to get a concrete perception of that primary group-nature of which everything social is the outgrowth.

13   TAMOTSU SHIBUTANI

Reference Groups as Perspectives

Although Hyman coined the term scarcely more than a decade ago, the concept of reference group has become one of the central analytic tools in social psychology, being used in the construction of hypotheses concerning a variety of social phenomena. The inconsistency in behavior as a person

Tamotsu Shibutani, "Reference Groups as Perspectives," *American Journal of Sociology*, vol. 60 (May 1955), pp. 562–569, by permission of The University of Chicago Press. Copyright 1955 by the University of Chicago.

moves from one social context to another is accounted for in terms of a change in reference groups; the exploits of juvenile delinquents, especially in interstitial areas, are being explained by the expectations of peer-group gangs; modifications in social attitudes are found to be related to changes in associations. The concept has been particularly useful in accounting for the choices made among apparent alternatives, particularly where the selections seem to be contrary to the "best interests" of the actor. Status problems— aspirations of social climbers, conflicts in group loyalty, the dilemmas of marginal men—have also been analyzed in terms of reference groups, as have the differential sensitivity and reaction of various segments of an audience to mass communication. It is recognized that the same generic processes are involved in these phenomenally diverse events, and the increasing popularity of the concept attests to its utility in analysis.

As might be expected during the exploratory phases in any field of inquiry, however, there is some confusion involved in the use of this concept, arising largely from vagueness of signification. The available formal definitions are inconsistent, and sometimes formal definitions are contradicted in usage. The fact that social psychologists can understand one another in spite of these ambiguities, however, implies an intuitive recognition of some central meaning, and an explicit statement of this will enhance the utility of the concept as an analytic tool. The literature reveals that all discussions of reference groups involve some identifiable grouping to which an actor is related in some manner and the norms and values shared in that group. However, the relationship between these three terms is not always clear. Our initial task, then, is to examine the conceptions of reference group implicit in actual usage, irrespective of formal definitions.

One common usage of the concept is in the designation of that group which serves as the point of reference in making comparisons or contrasts, especially in forming judgments about one's self. In the original use of the concept Hyman spoke of reference groups as points of comparison in evaluating one's own status, and he found that the estimates varied according to the group with which the respondent compared himself. Merton and Kitt, in their reformulation of Stouffer's theory of relative deprivation, also use the concept in this manner; the judgments of rear-echelon soldiers overseas concerning their fate varied, depending upon whether they compared themselves to soldiers who were still at home or men in combat. They also propose concrete research operations in which respondents are to be asked to compare themselves with various groups. The study of aspiration levels by Chapman and Volkmann, frequently cited in discussions of reference-group theory, also involves variations in judgment arising from a comparison of one's own group with others.[1] In this mode of application,

[1] H. H. Hyman, "The Psychology of Status," *Archives of Psychology*, XXXVIII (1942), 15; R. K. Merton and A. Kitt, "Contributions to the Theory of Reference Group Behavior," in R. K. Merton and P. F. Lazarsfeld (eds.), *Studies in the Scope and Method of*

then, a reference group is a standard or check point which an actor uses in forming his estimate of the situation, particularly his own position within it. Logically, then, *any* group with which an actor is familiar may become a reference group.

A second referent of the concept is that group in which the actor aspires to gain or maintain acceptance: hence, a group whose claims are paramount in situations requiring choice. The reference group of the socially ambitious is said to consist of people of higher strata whose status symbols are imitated. Merton and Kitt interpret the expressions of willingness and felt readiness for combat on the part of inexperienced troops, as opposed to the humility of battle-hardened veterans, as the efforts of newcomers to identify themselves with veterans to whom they had mistakenly imputed certain values.[2] Thus, the concept is used to point to an association of human beings among whom one seeks to gain, maintain, or enhance his status; a reference group is that group in which one desires to participate.

In a third usage the concept signifies that group whose perspective constitutes the frame of reference of the actor. Thus, Sherif speaks of reference groups as groups whose norms are used as anchoring points in structuring the perceptual field,[3] and Merton and Kitt speak of a "social frame of reference" for interpretations.[4] Through direct or vicarious participation in a group one comes to perceive the world from its standpoint. Yet this group need not be one in which he aspires for acceptance; a member of some minority group may despise it but still see the world largely through its eyes. When used in this manner, the concept of reference group points more to a psychological phenomenon than to an objectively existing group of men; it refers to an organization of the actor's experience. That is to say, it is a structuring of his perceptual field. In this usage a reference group becomes any collectivity, real or imagined, envied or despised, whose perspective is assumed by the actor.

Thus, an examination of current usage discloses three distinct referents for a single concept: (1) groups which serve as comparison points; (2) groups to which men aspire; and (3) groups whose perspectives are assumed by the actor. Although these terms may be related, treating together what should be clearly delineated as generically different can lead only to further confusion. It is the contention of this paper that the restriction of the concept of reference group to the third alternative—that group whose

---

"The American Soldier" (Glencoe, Ill.: Free Press, 1950), pp. 42–53, 69; D. W. Chapman and J. Volkmann, "A Social Determinant of the Level of Aspiration," *Journal of Abnormal and Social Psychology*, XXXIV (1939), 225–38.

[2] *Op. cit.*, pp. 75–76.

[3] M. Sherif, "The Concept of Reference Groups in Human Relations," in M. Sherif and M. O. Wilson (eds.), *Group Relations at the Crossroads* (New York: Harper & Bros., 1953), pp. 203–31.

[4] *Op. cit.*, pp. 49–50.

perspective constitutes the frame of reference of the actor—will increase its usefulness in research. Any group or object may be used for comparisons, and one need not assume the role of those with whom he compares his fate; hence, the first usage serves a quite different purpose and may be eliminated from further consideration. Under some circumstances, however, group loyalties and aspirations are related to perspectives assumed, and the character of this relationship calls for further exploration. Such a discussion necessitates a restatement of the familiar, but, in view of the difficulties in some of the work on reference groups, repetition may not be entirely out of order. In spite of the enthusiasm of some proponents there is actually nothing new in reference-group theory.

Culture and Personal Controls

Thomas pointed out many years ago that what a man does depends largely upon his definition of the situation. One may add that the manner in which one consistently defines a succession of situations depends upon his organized perspective. A perspective is an ordered view of one's world—what is taken for granted about the attributes of various objects, events, and human nature. It is an order of things remembered and expected as well as things actually perceived, an organized conception of what is plausible and what is possible; it constitutes the matrix through which one perceives his environment. The fact that men have such ordered perspectives enables them to conceive of their ever changing world as relatively stable, orderly, and predictable. As Riezler puts it, one's perspective is an outline scheme which, running ahead of experience, defines and guides it.

There is abundant experimental evidence to show that perception is selective; that the organization of perceptual experience depends in part upon what is anticipated and what is taken for granted. Judgments rest upon perspectives, and people with different outlooks define identical situations differently, responding selectively to the environment. Thus, a prostitute and a social worker walking through a slum area notice different things; a sociologist should perceive relationships that others fail to observe. Any change of perspectives—becoming a parent for the first time, learning that one will die in a few months, or suffering the failure of well-laid plans—leads one to notice things previously overlooked and to see the familiar world in a different light. As Goethe contended, history is continually rewritten, not so much because of the discovery of new documentary evidence, but because the changing perspectives of historians lead to new selections from the data.

Culture, as the concept is used by Redfield, refers to a perspective that is shared by those in a particular group; it consists of those "conventional understandings, manifest in act and artifact, that characterize societies."[5] Since these conventional understandings are the premises of action, those who share a common culture engage in common modes of action. Culture is not a static entity but a continuing process; norms are creatively reaffirmed from day to day in social interaction. Those taking part in collective transactions approach one another with set expectations, and the realization of what is anticipated successively confirms and reinforces their perspectives. In this way, people in each cultural group are continuously supporting one another's perspectives, each by responding to the others in expected ways. In this sense culture is a product of communication.

In his discussion of endopsychic social control Mead spoke of men "taking the role of the generalized other," meaning by that that each person approaches his world from the standpoint of the culture of his group. Each perceives, thinks, forms judgments, and controls himself according to the frame of reference of the group in which he is participating. Since he defines objects, other people, the world, and himself from the perspective that he shares with others, he can visualize his proposed line of action from this generalized standpoint, anticipate the reactions of others, inhibit undesirable impulses, and thus guide his conduct. The socialized person is a society in miniature; he sets the same standards of conduct for himself as he sets for others, and he judges himself in the same terms. He can define situations properly and meet his obligations, even in the absence of other people, because, as already noted, his perspective always takes into account the expectations of others. Thus, it is the ability to define situations from the same standpoint as others that makes personal controls possible.[6] When Mead spoke of assuming the role of the generalized other, he was not referring to people but to perspectives shared with others in a transaction.

The consistency in the behavior of a man in a wide variety of social contexts is to be accounted for, then, in terms of his organized perspective. Once one has incorporated a particular outlook from his group, it becomes his orientation toward the world, and he brings this frame of reference to bear on all new situations. Thus, immigrants and tourists often misinterpret the strange things they see, and a disciplined Communist would define each situation differently from the non-Communist. Although reference-group behavior is generally studied in situations where choices seem possible, the actor himself is often unaware that there are alternatives.

The proposition that men think, feel, and see things from a standpoint

[5] R. Redfield, *The Folk Culture of Yucatan* (Chicago: University of Chicago Press, 1941), p. 132. For a more explicit presentation of a behavioristic theory of culture see *The Selected Writings of Edward Sapir in Language, Culture and Personality*, ed. D. G. Mandelbaum (Berkeley: University of California Press, 1949), pp. 104–9, 308–31, 544–59.

[6] G. H. Mead, "The Genesis of the Self and Social Control," *International Journal of Ethics*, XXXV (1925), 251–77, and *Mind, Self and Society* (Chicago: University of Chicago Press, 1934), pp. 152–64. Cf. T. Parsons, "The Superego and the Theory of Social Systems," *Psychiatry*, XV (1952), 15–25.

peculiar to the group in which they participate is an old one, repeatedly emphasized by students of anthropology and of the sociology of knowledge. Why, then, the sudden concern with reference-group theory during the past decade? The concept of reference group actually introduces a minor refinement in the long familiar theory, made necessary by the special characteristics of modern mass societies. First of all, in modern societies special problems arise from the fact that men sometimes use the standards of groups in which they are *not* recognized members, sometimes of groups in which they have never participated directly, and sometimes of groups that do not exist at all. Second, in our mass society, characterized as it is by cultural pluralism, each person internalizes several perspectives, and this occasionally gives rise to embarrassing dilemmas which call for systematic study. Finally, the development of reference-group theory has been facilitated by the increasing interest in social psychology and the subjective aspects of group life, a shift from a predominant concern with objective social structures to an interest in the experiences of the participants whose regularized activities make such structures discernible.

A reference group, then, is that group whose outlook is used by the actor as the frame of reference in the organization of his perceptual field. All kinds of groupings, with great variations in size, composition, and structure, may become reference groups. Of greatest importance for most people are those groups in which they participate directly—what have been called membership groups—especially those containing a number of persons with whom one stands in a primary relationship. But in some transactions one may assume the perspective attributed to some social category—a social class, an ethnic group, those in a given community, or those concerned with some special interest. On the other hand, reference groups may be imaginary, as in the case of artists who are "born ahead of their times," scientists who work for "humanity," or philanthropists who give for "posterity." Such persons estimate their endeavors from a postulated perspective imputed to people who have not yet been born. There are others who live for a distant past, idealizing some period in history and longing for "the good old days," criticizing current events from a standpoint imputed to people long since dead. Reference groups, then, arise through the internalization of norms; they constitute the structure of expectations imputed to some audience for whom one organizes his conduct.

The Construction of Social Worlds

As Dewey emphasized, society exists in and through communication; common perspectives—common cultures—emerge through participation in common communication channels. It is through social participation that perspectives shared in a group are internalized. Despite the frequent recitation of this proposition, its full implications, especially for the analysis of mass societies, are not often appreciated. Variations in outlook arise through differential contact and association; the maintenance of social distance—through segregation, conflict, or simply the reading of different literature—leads to the formation of distinct cultures. Thus, people in different social classes develop different modes of life and outlook, not because of anything inherent in economic position, but because similarity of occupation and limitations set by income level dispose them to certain restricted communication channels. Those in different ethnic groups form their own distinctive cultures because their identifications incline them to interact intimately with each other and to maintain reserve before outsiders. Different intellectual traditions within social psychology—psychoanalysis, scale analysis, *Gestalt*, pragmatism—will remain separated as long as those in each tradition restrict their sympathetic attention to works of their own school and view others with contempt or hostility. Some social scientists are out of touch with the masses of the American people because they eschew the mass media, especially television, or expose themselves only condescendingly. Even the outlook that the *avant-garde* regards as "cosmopolitan" is culture-bound, for it also is a product of participation in restricted communication channels—books, magazines, meetings, exhibits, and taverns which are out of bounds for most people in the middle classes. Social participation may even be vicarious, as it is in the case of a medievalist who acquires his perspective solely through books.

Even casual observation reveals the amazing variety of standards by which Americans live. The inconsistencies and contradictions which characterize modern mass societies are products of the multitude of communication channels and the ease of participation in them. Studying relatively isolated societies, anthropologists can speak meaningfully of "culture areas" in geographical terms; in such societies common cultures have a territorial base, for only those who live together can interact. In modern industrial societies, however, because of the development of rapid transportation and the media of mass communication, people who are geographically dispersed can communicate effectively. Culture areas are coterminous with communication channels; since communication networks are no longer coterminous with territorial boundaries, culture areas overlap and have lost their territorial bases. Thus, next-door neighbors may be complete strangers; even in common parlance there is an intuitive recognition of the diversity of perspectives, and we speak meaningfully of people living in different social worlds—the academic world, the world of children, the world of fashion.

Modern mass societies, indeed, are made up of a bewildering variety of social worlds. Each is an organized outlook, built up by people in their interaction with one another; hence, each communication channel gives rise to a separate world. Probably the greatest sense of identification and solidarity is to be found in the various communal structures—the underworld, ethnic minorities, the social elite. Such communities are frequently spatially segregated, which isolates them further from the outer world, while the "grapevine" and foreign-language presses provide internal contacts. Another common type of social world consists of the associational structures— the world of medicine, of organized labor, of the theater, of café society. These are held together not only by various voluntary associations within each locality but also by periodicals like *Variety*, specialized journals, and feature sections in newspapers. Finally, there are the loosely connected universes of special interest—the world of sports, of the stamp collector, of the daytime serial—serviced by mass media programs and magazines like *Field and Stream*. Each of these worlds is a unity of order, a universe of regularized mutual response. Each is an area in which there is some structure which permits reasonable anticipation of the behavior of others, hence, an area in which one may act with a sense of security and confidence.[7] Each social world, then, is a culture area, the boundaries of which are set neither by territory nor by formal group membership but by the limits of effective communication.

Since there is a variety of communication channels, differing in stability and extent, social worlds differ in composition, size, and the territorial distribution of the participants. Some, like local cults, are small and concentrated; others, like the intellectual world, are vast and the participants dispersed. Worlds differ in the extent and clarity of their boundaries; each is confined by some kind of horizon, but this may be wide or narrow, clear or vague. The fact that social worlds are not coterminous with the universe of men is recognized; those in the underworld are well aware of the fact that outsiders do not share their values. Worlds differ in exclusiveness and in the extent to which they demand the loyalty of their participants. Most important of all, social worlds are not static entities; shared perspectives are continually being reconstituted. Worlds come into existence with the establishment of communication channels; when life conditions change, social relationships may also change, and these worlds may disappear.

Every social world has some kind of communication system—often nothing more than differential association—in which there develops a special universe of discourse, sometimes an argot. Special meanings and symbols further accentuate differences and increase social distance from outsiders. In each world there are special norms of conduct, a set of values, a special prestige ladder, characteristic career lines, and a common outlook toward life—a *Weltanschauung*. In the case of elites there may even arise a code of honor which holds only for those who belong, while others are dismissed as beings somewhat less than human from whom bad manners

---

[7] Cf. Riezler, *Man: Mutable and Immutable* (Chicago: Henry Regnery Co., 1950), pp. 62–72; L. Landgrebe, "The World as a Phenomenological Problem," *Philosophy and Phenomenological Research*, I (1940), 38–58; and A. Schuetz, "The Stranger: An Essay in Social Psychology," *American Journal of Sociology*, XLIX (1944), 499–507.

may be expected. A social world, then, is an order conceived which serves as the stage on which each participant seeks to carve out his career and to maintain and enhance his status.

One of the characteristics of life in modern mass societies is simultaneous participation in a variety of social worlds. Because of the ease with which the individual may expose himself to a number of communication channels, he may lead a segmentalized life, participating successively in a number of unrelated activities. Furthermore, the particular combination of social worlds differs from person to person; this is what led Simmel to declare that each stands at the point at which a unique combination of social circles intersects. The geometric analogy is a happy one, for it enables us to conceive the numerous possibilities of combinations and the different degrees of participation in each circle. To understand what a man does, we must get at his unique perspective—what he takes for granted and how he defines the situation—but in mass societies we must learn in addition the social world in which he is participating in a given act.

Loyalty and Selective Responsiveness

In a mass society where each person internalizes numerous perspectives there are bound to be some incongruities and conflicts. The overlapping of group affiliation and participation, however, need not lead to difficulties and is usually unnoticed. The reference groups of most persons are mutually sustaining. Thus, the soldier who volunteers for hazardous duty on the battlefield may provoke anxiety in his family but is not acting contrary to their values; both his family and his comrades admire courage and disdain cowardice. Behavior may be inconsistent, as in the case of the proverbial office tyrant who is meek before his wife, but it is not noticed if the transactions occur in dissociated contexts. Most people live more or less compartmentalized lives, shifting from one social world to another as they participate in a succession of transactions. In each world their roles are different, their relations to other participants are different, and they reveal a different facet of their personalities. Men have become so accustomed to this mode of life that they manage to conceive of themselves as reasonably consistent human beings in spite of this segmentalization and are generally not aware of the fact that their acts do not fit into a coherent pattern.

People become acutely aware of the existence of different outlooks only when they are successively caught in situations in which conflicting demands are made upon them, all of which cannot possibly be satisfied. While men generally avoid making difficult decisions, these dilemmas and contradictions of status may force a choice between two social worlds. These conflicts are essentially alternative ways of defining the same situation, arising from several possible perspectives. In the words of William

James, "As a man I pity you, but as an official I must show you no mercy; as a politician I regard him as an ally, but as a moralist I loathe him." In playing roles in different social worlds, one imputes different expectations to others whose differences cannot always be compromised. The problem is that of selecting the perspective for defining the situation. In Mead's terminology, which generalized other's role is to be taken? It is only in situations where alternative definitions are possible that problems of loyalty arise.

Generally such conflicts are ephemeral; in critical situations contradictions otherwise unnoticed are brought into the open, and painful choices are forced. In poorly integrated societies, however, some people find themselves continually beset with such conflicts. The Negro intellectual, children of mixed marriages or of immigrants, the foreman in a factory, the professional woman, the military chaplain—all live in the interstices of well-organized structures and are marginal men.[8] In most instances they manage to make their way through their compartmentalized lives, although personal maladjustments are apparently frequent. In extreme cases amnesia and dissociation of personality can occur.

Much of the interest in reference groups arises out of concern with situations in which a person is confronted with the necessity of choosing between two or more organized perspectives. The hypothesis has been advanced that the choice of reference groups—conformity to the norms of the group whose perspective is assumed—is a function of one's interpersonal relations; to what extent the culture of a group serves as the matrix for the organization of perceptual experience depends upon one's relationship and personal loyalty to others who share that outlook. Thus, when personal relations to others in the group deteriorate, as sometimes happens in a military unit after continued defeat, the norms become less binding, and the unit may disintegrate in panic. Similarly, with the transformation of personal relationships between parent and child in late adolescence, the desires and standards of the parents often become less obligatory.

It has been suggested further that choice of reference groups rests upon personal loyalty to significant others of that social world. "Significant others," for Sullivan, are those persons directly responsible for the internalization of norms. Socialization is a product of a gradual accumulation of experiences with certain people, particularly those with whom we stand in primary relations, and significant others are those who are actually involved in the cultivation of abilities, values, and outlook.[9] Crucial, apparently, is the character of one's emotional ties with them. Those who think

---

[8] Cf. E. C. Hughes, "Dilemmas and Contradictions of Status," *American Journal of Sociology*, L (1945), 353–59, and E. V. Stonequist, *The Marginal Man* (New York: Charles Scribner's Sons, 1937).

[9] H. S. Sullivan, *Conceptions of Modern Psychiatry* (Washington, D.C.: W. H. White Psychiatric Foundation, 1947), pp. 18–22.

the significant others have treated them with affection and consideration have a sense of personal obligation that is binding under all circumstances, and they will be loyal even at great personal sacrifice. Since primary relations are not necessarily satisfactory, however, the reactions may be negative. A person who is well aware of the expectations of significant others may go out of his way to reject them. This may account for the bifurcation of orientation in minority groups, where some remain loyal to the parental culture while others seek desperately to become assimilated in the larger world. Some who withdraw from the uncertainties of real life may establish loyalties to perspectives acquired through vicarious relationships with characters encountered in books.[10]

Perspectives are continually subjected to the test of reality. All perception is hypothetical. Because of what is taken for granted from each standpoint, each situation is approched with a set of expectations; if transactions actually take place as anticipated, the perspective itself is reinforced. It is thus the confirming responses of other people that provide support for perspectives.[11] But in mass societies the responses of others vary, and in the study of reference groups the problem is that of ascertaining *whose* confirming responses will sustain a given point of view.

The Study of Mass Societies

Because of the differentiated character of modern mass societies, the concept of reference group, or some suitable substitute, will always have a central place in any realistic conceptual scheme for its analysis. As is pointed out above, it will be most useful if it is used to designate that group whose perspective is assumed by the actor as the frame of reference for the organization of his perceptual experience. Organized perspectives arise in and become shared through participation in common communication channels, and the diversity of mass societies arises from the multiplicity of channels and the ease with which one may participate in them.

Mass societies are not only diversified and pluralistic but also continually changing. The successive modification of life-conditions compels changes in social relationships, and any adequate analysis requires a study of these transformational processes themselves. Here the concept of reference group can be of crucial importance. For example, all forms of social mobility, from sudden conversions to gradual assimilation, may be regarded essentially as displacements of reference groups, for they involve a loss of

10 Cf. R. R. Grinker and J. P. Spiegel, *Men under Stress* (Philadelphia: Blakiston Co., 1945), pp. 122–26; and E. A. Shils and M. Janowitz, "Cohesion and Disintegration in the Wehrmacht in World War II," *Public Opinion Quarterly*, XII (1948), 280–315.

11 Cf. G. H. Mead, *The Philosophy of the Act* (Chicago: University of Chicago Press, 1938), pp. 107–73; and L. Postman, "Toward a General Theory of Cognition," in J. H. Rohrer and M. Sherif (eds.), *Social Psychology at the Crossroads* (New York: Harper & Bros. 1951), pp. 242–72.

responsiveness to the demands of one social world and the adoption of the perspective of another. It may be hypothesized that the disaffection occurs first on the level of personal relations, followed by a weakening sense of obligation, a rejection of old claims, and the establishment of new loyalties and incorporation of a new perspective. The conflicts that characterize all persons in marginal roles are of special interest in that they provide opportunities for cross-sectional analyses of the processes of social change.

In the analysis of the behavior of men in mass societies the crucial problem is that of ascertaining how a person defines the situation, which perspective he uses in arriving at such a definition, and who constitutes the audience whose responses provide the necessary confirmation and support for his position. This calls for focusing attention upon the expectations the actor imputes to others, the communication channels in which he participates, and his relations with those with whom he identifies himself. In the study of conflict, imagery provides a fertile source of data. At moments of indecision, when in doubt and confusion, who appears in imagery? In this manner the significant other can be identified.

An adequate analysis of modern mass societies requires the development of concepts and operations for the description of the manner in which each actor's orientation toward his world is successively reconstituted. Since perception is selective and perspectives differ, different items are noticed and a progressively diverse set of images arises, even among those exposed to the same media of mass communication. The concept of reference group summarizes differential associations and loyalties and thus facilitates the study of selective perception. It becomes, therefore, an indispensable tool for comprehending the diversity and dynamic character of the kind of society in which we live.

14   MANFORD H. KUHN

The Reference Group Reconsidered

The Other

What I really have in mind to do is to attempt an exploration of the whole *idea of the other* in the symbolic interaction orientation as a context for the consideration of the *idea of the reference group.*

I wish to observe at the outset that while *the other* plays an incontest-

Manford H. Kuhn, "The Reference Group Reconsidered," *The Sociological Quarterly,* vol. 5 (Winter 1964), pp. 6–21. Reprinted by permission.

ably crucial role in the conceptions of Cooley, Dewey, Mead, Faris, and the other writers who developed the symbolic interaction orientation, nevertheless *the other* is never attended to with the discerning and analytic interest which they give to the actor. Cooley, Dewey, and Mead all thought of the individual and society as inseparable aspects of the same reality, to use Cooley's phrase. They all shared the idea that meaning, thought, and the self arise alike in the relationships between the actor and his alters.

We are all familiar, I am sure, with Mead's conception that meaning grows out of the gesture of an actor to another, the responding gesture of the other, and the uncompleted phases of the act to which the gestures refer. Thus the omission of the other from these "relata," as Mead calls them, leaves the activity without meaning. Cooley, as we are abundantly aware, saw the self as drawn from the common life—that is, the life of the actor as immersed in a context of others. "The social self," he wrote, "is simply any idea, or system of ideas, drawn from the communicative life, that the mind cherishes as its own."[1] And his ubiquitously quoted looking-glass-self statement, "A self-idea of this sort seems to have three principal elements: the imagination of our appearance to the other person, the imagination of his judgment of that appearance, and some sort of self-feeling, such as pride or mortification," quite apparently makes the others the looking glass in which one is able to be an object to himself, and without which he would lack even self-feelings.[2] The self is indeed only an eddy of the general communicative current.

Thinking, for all the symbolic interactionists, is an internal conversation among the self and internalized others. And the meaning of internalization is simply the covert segment of the general communicative process. The figures of speech differ—an internal audience, an inner forum, a covert conversation of gestures—but the meanings coincide. They all make the other crucial to the self and to meaningful action.

Cooley insisted on the reality of the internalized other. Again universally quoted is his statement that "the imaginations which people have of one another are the solid facts of society," and he went on to say that "to observe and interpret these must be a chief aim of sociology."[3] He insisted on this idea, and extended it to say that the imaginative idea is logically prior—as far as the actor is concerned—in reality to the physical organism of the other. He wrote, for example, that "I do not see how any one can hold that we know persons directly except as imaginative ideas in the mind," and "a corporeally existent person is not socially real unless he is imagined."[4] In fact he says, after rhetorically raising the question about the

[1] Charles Horton Cooley, *Human Nature and the Social Order*, New York: Scribner's, 1902, p. 179.
[2] *Ibid.*, p. 184.
[3] *Ibid.*, p. 121.
[4] *Ibid.*, pp. 120, 123.

reality of the dead and of fictional characters: "I should say that in so far as we imagine them they are [real]."[5]

The well-known notions of Mead regarding the process by which the self arises in taking the role of the other similarly stress this internally imagined other of Cooley's. For both, "the social person is primarily *a fact of the mind*."[6]

The elder Faris, in his not-so-well-known critique of the concept of the primary group, expresses much the same set of ideas when he disparages the notion that the quality of face-to-face existence is a necessary attribute of the primary group relation. In fact he invokes Cooley's own ideas endemic to these several quotations I have given, in suggesting that Cooley himself must have had in mind the essential characteristic of identification with the others as the basic condition for the existence of the primary group. "If there is a group consciousness, esprit-de-corps—a feeling of 'we' —then we have a primary group that will manifest attitudes appropriate and recognizable."[7]

Subsequently, Harry Stack Sullivan made similarly crucial use of the other in his formulation. His "significant other" is not basically different in its reference from Mead's other. His self, resting on "reflected appraisals of others," is very much the same self as the self of Cooley or Dewey or Mead. His analysis of communications and interpersonal relations reflects his professional focus on misunderstandings, distortions and anxiety, but otherwise his notions are very similar to those of the earlier interactionists.[8]

We might go further to explore Mead's use of the other in the constituting of *social objects*—the "things" of experience—or in the formation of the generalized other, the abstract principles of conduct. But these really but extend his general notion that the other is crucial to the rise of all meaning, all reality.[9]

Kimball Young in one of several definitions of the *social act* defined it as any act which is qualified by the act of another.[10]

---

[5] *Ibid.*, p. 122. It should be noted that Cooley took pains to dissociate this stance from any overtones of naive solipsism, in the following disclaimer: "In saying this I hope I do not seem to question the independent reality of persons or to confuse it with personal ideas. The man is one thing and the various ideas entertained about him are another; but the latter, the personal idea, is the immediate social reality, the thing in which men exist for one another and work directly upon one another's lives." (*Ibid.*, pp. 123–124.)

[6] *Ibid.*, p. 124.

[7] Ellsworth Faris, "The Primary Group: Essence and Accident," Chapter 4 in Faris, *The Nature of Human Nature*, New York: McGraw-Hill, 1937. Quotation from p. 40.

[8] Harry Stack Sullivan, *Conceptions of Modern Psychiatry*, Washington, D. C.: W. A. White Psychiatric Foundation, 1940. See especially pp. 18–22.

[9] George Herbert Mead, *Mind, Self and Society*, Chicago: University of Chicago Press, 1934. See especially pp. 117–125, 152–164, and 375–377.

[10] Kimball Young, *Personality and Problems of Adjustment* (2nd edition), New York: Appleton-Century-Crofts, 1952, p. 154.

Such, in brief summary, is the role of the other in the symbolic interactionist orientation. The other turns out to be the other as the actor sees him. But the actor's own view of himself is gained only through the image he imagines the other to have of him. His objects, his reality in short, derive from the same source of shared perspectives with imagined others. Even his conscience and his purposes arise in the same process. But the imagination as a process has a solid basis in communication, being in effect the very process of communication by which meaning exists in his social group. "We are able to act together because we are able to take one another's point of view." There is a singularity, unity and consensus, in this point of view, because the symbols on which it rests are significant symbols: they call out in the actor the incipient anticipations of the responses they call out in the other. In short, they have common *universal referents,* with only moderate exception and qualification.

Now there is nothing much that is incorrect in this orientation as far as we know. But by very virtue of the fact that it is only an orientation, it suffers many shortcomings as a basis for a social psychology.

To be more specific: By what process do one's others get selected? Are any features of this process accessible to observation? Is this a process characterized by regularities, and if so of what kind? Or are we to take the mechanism of identification to be essentially whimsical and capricious?

Cooley wrote that we must imagine the imaginings of the members of the groups we wish to study. This is not a very complete recipe for research, nor does its flavor suggest much that is compatible with contemporary notions of social psychological investigation. Is all social investigation to be limited to the ambiguities and imprecisions of *Einfühlung* and *Verstehen?* To speak of the inseparability of self and other, as many of these early writers did, is not very helpful except in a broadly explanatory way. We would want to have some verifiable ways of discovering just who the others are from whom the self is inseparable.

Thus, while we are led through the cogent rhetoric of the early writers to accept the crucial importance of the subjective life and of the covert features of experience, we are given by them relatively few leads on how to make this subjective life accessible to observation or systematic inquiry. Mead rightly caricatured J. B. Watson for ordering "off with their heads" respecting all problems having to do with covert events such as thought, meaning, purpose, self and the like;[11] yet in retrospect one must credit Watson for insisting on the necessity for empirical demonstrability of generalizations, i.e., the "openness of evidence."

[11] Mead, *op. cit.,* pp. 2–3.

The Reference Group Concept

In 1942 Herbert Hyman proposed the reference group concept in his monograph "The Psychology of Status."[12] The concept is a simple one. It assumes
that people make fundamental judgments and self-assessments based on
psychological identifications rather than on formal memberships in groups.
So stated there is nothing about the idea that in any way differentiates it
from the general phenomenological position of symbolic interactionists. His
research use of the idea, however, was in terms of the self-assignments to
social categories of his subjects. There was thus in the operationalization
of the term a rotation of the sociological conception of the *group*. This
conception has it that a *group* involves reciprocal role-playing, a common
vocabulary, and a common body of values and norms. In fact, it is the
nearly ubiquitous assumption of sociologists in their use of the term *group*
that group membership is predicated upon some degree of group *identification.*

The reference group concept did not come immediately to the attention
of sociologists. It remined for Merton and Kitt, in their widely known
chapter published in 1950 on the utilization of the reference group idea by
Stouffer and associates in *The American Soldier*, to introduce sociologists
to the term.[13] They took the concept of "relative deprivation," used in *The
American Soldier*, as an example of a special and effective use of Hyman's
reference group concept. The "Continuities in Research" volume, *Studies
in the Scope and Method of "The American Soldier,"* was—and continues
to be—widely distributed and widely read. The Merton-Kitt chapter is one
of the most persuasive and influential chapters in the book. Since then the
chapter, together with another attempting to revise and to take into account
criticisms, has appeared in the revised and enlarged edition of *Social Theory
and Social Structure*, a collection of Robert Merton's papers, another influential, widely distributed book.[14]

In the meantime the idea had been having its impact on the psychological social psychologists, many of whom have a considerable audience among
sociologists—men such as Sherif, Newcomb and others.[15]

With such sponsors as Robert Merton, Theodore Newcomb, Muzafer

[12] In *Archives of Psychology*, vol. 269.
[13] Robert K. Merton and Alice S. Kitt, "Contributions to the Theory of Reference
Group Behavior," in Merton and Paul F. Lazarsfeld (eds.), *Continuities in Social Research: Studies in the Scope and Method of "The American Soldier,"* Glencoe, Ill.: Free
Press, 1950, pp. 40–105.
[14] Robert K. Merton, *Social Theory and Social Structure* (revised edition), Glencoe,
Ill.: Free Press, 1957, Chapters 8 and 9.
[15] Muzafer Sherif and Carolyn W. Sherif, *An Outline of Social Psychology* (revised
edition), New York: Harper and Brothers, 1956; Theodore M. Newcomb, *Social Psychology*, New York: Dryden Press, 1950.

Sherif, and, by implication, the late Sam Stouffer and his associates, it is little wonder the concept enjoyed—as one observer put it—a meteoric rise in popularity. This popularity has endured.

The persistence of the popularity of this concept does not owe entirely to the prestige of its initial users. First of all, it was proposed at the time when survey research was just coming into large-scale use by sociologists and social psychologists on the sociological side. The operationalizations by Hyman and by Stouffer and associates were peculiarly adapted to use in survey research. That is to say, the operationalizations were in the form of simple questions regarding self-assignment to social categories or regarding comparisons of self with members of such categories. They were questions that were neither particularly subtle nor likely to arouse sensitivities. The demonstrations of their validity could be made through the use of other, similar questions, obviating the need for indirect, open-ended, probing or depth forms of inquiry—kinds of inquiry not at all well adapted to large-scale survey research. And while the establishment of their validity by means of this tactic of "triangulation" left necessary a certain amount of inference, this inference could easily be of the open and direct form rather than the ambiguously varied and idiosyncratic or secretive or *ad hoc* Freudian form of logically unverifiable inference. But the very fact that the inference used in these operationalizations of the reference group concept was relatively open to verification has itself tended to obscure the correlative fact that it has not, to this day, yet been concretely verified.

A second reason for the persistence in popularity of the concept (as well as for its meteoric acceptance, for that matter) was the fact that the concept represents a vast simplification and fairly sharp specification of the idea of the other. When we canvass the notion of the other as we did earlier, we can appreciate how many directions one might go with the translation of the perspective into concrete inquiry. There is always some mental relief associated with the implication in any operation that a broad and elliptical idea is "nothing but" these marks on these pieces of paper. Such relief tends to suit the mind to further logical examination of the idea involved.

This is especially true when the operation in question has even one or a few strong logical connections with the logical or orientational idea, which in this case is undeniable. It is not only undeniable, but it is called forcefully to the attention of all readers of the Merton-Kitt commentary in a section which the reference group concept (and its use by Stouffer under the aegis of the notion of relative deprivation) is compared with the general *idea of the other* as formulated by Mead.[16] These authors suggest

---

[16] Merton, *op. cit.*, pp. 236–241. It is interesting to note that it is in this very passage that Merton and Kitt make a resounding pass at Mead and his followers by observing that Mead's theory "was not exposed to *systematic* empirical evidence" and that he, with

that the empirical use of the reference group concept and the auxiliary one of relative deprivation will enable conceptual clarification, reformulation, and useful elaboration of earlier ideas of the other. Their analysis, in their own view, yields several instances of such: e.g., (1) they find that under certain circumstances men "report . . . the objective situation rather than a socially reflected image";[17] (2) they find a sharp discrepancy between operations that inquire into "attitudes" and those which elicit "self-images";[18] and (3) they find that there are multiple reference groups which provide contexts for evaluation by individuals—some of which are conflicting and some of which are mutually sustaining.[19]

Now it may well be that sometimes a human being confronts reality directly while at other times he sees only a socially reflected image. But if this is so, there is no continuity here between the earlier formulations of Cooley, Dewey, Mead, Faris, Thomas, Blumer, *et al.*, for the whole epistemology of symbolic interaction, from Cooley to Cassirer, rests on the proposition that language is necessarily interposed between man and raw reality so that he can *never* confront it directly. If reference group theory rests on some new and different epistemology, that epistemology ought to be spelled out. It cannot rest purely on a pair of empirical findings without explanation.

But this gives one pause. The idea of the reference group is that it is a special kind of other, one with which a person feels psychologically identified as opposed to one with which he is merely socially associated. Yet this was the idea central to the concept of the other (or of the group, for that matter) all along. Are we now to think in terms of two kinds of others—those whose behavior qualifies ours, and those who are merely physically real? Where does this *new* distinction differ from that in Cooley's corridor illustration?

Then, too, what shall we make of the difference between an attitude and a self-image? What is meant by the self as being an object to oneself if it is not that the self *is attitudes*—symbolic proposals for action toward or with respect to the self? And of what use is the self in any theoretical formulation unless it is the anchoring object in one's system of objects? The crucial object with respect to which the other objects have meaning? The victorious manner in which Merton and Kitt "discover" this distinction between attitude and self-image seems to imply that they are happy to be able to *dismiss all consideration* of self-image as of no significance to

---

"those of his followers who also eschew empirical research, had little occasion to move ahead to the question of conditions under which non-membership-groups may also constitute a significant frame of reference." (*Ibid.*, p. 239).

[17] *Ibid.*, p. 257.

[18] *Ibid.*, p. 253.

[19] *Ibid.*, pp. 241–250.

their research interests. If the self has no relevance to their theory of action, again what continuity is there between the symbolic interaction orientation and reference group theory? For certainly the self is central to all social acts as Mead, Dewey and Cooley saw the matter. One behaves in terms of the kind of person he thinks he is, and for the ends such a person seeks. If "reference groups," operationalized as researcher-proposed, subject-accepted reference *categories*, do not yield meaningful results having to do with the self, is it perhaps that the operationalization has netted relatively insignificant or superficial others as opposed to the ones on which the self is based?

And is not this suspicion strengthened by their third conceptual reformulation—that of multiple reference groups, sometimes conflicting, sometimes mutually reinforcing? It is indeed very plausible that one finds his own categories of self-assignation sometimes conflicting. It is even probable that groups, with which he finds himself only moderately identified or only situationally committed, present such conflicting claims. Yet one supposes the others on which his self-conception crucially rests are only rarely or occasionally such as to put him under such cross-pressures.

However, it ought to be evident that this third proposal, unlike the other two, is not a theoretical or logical discontinuity with earlier symbolic interaction notions. There has always been uncertainty in the formulations about the consistency of the others (cf. Mead's problematic others as making development of the generalized other itself problematic)[20] and the stability of the self (cf. Anselm Strauss' notion that self shifts with each episode).[21] It is only possibly—in my view probably—a quantitative overstatement of the likelihood of inconsistency and conflict among others.

Group and Category in Symbolic Interactionism

Since so much is being made here of the prevalence of social categories in reference group operationalization, it is desirable to pause and examine the significance of social categories in symbolic interaction theory. In this theory they are not conceptualized as social categories but must be searched for in other guises.

The social group is paramount for the theory in that it provides both the language through which interaction takes place and the mutual others with whom interaction occurs. The group is antecedent to the individual and so is its language (from a basic standpoint this is redundant, since the group exists *in* its communication). As a new individual is inducted

---

[20] Mead, *op. cit.*, pp. 307–311.
[21] Anselm Strauss, *Mirrors and Masks*, Glencoe, Ill.: Free Press, 1959. See especially Chapters 3 and 4.

into the group, he takes on its objects, whose attributes derive from the group's communicative categories. That is to say, the qualities of objects which are meaningful to the group in its ongoing activity must be contained as distinctions in its vocabulary. Otherwise one could not perceive objects differentially in terms of these qualities. The most important objects to the ongoing, mutually reciprocal role activity of the group are human beings. The lexical categories that refer to them make possible differential discernment of the kinds of people there are and the differential activity that may be directed toward them or with respect to them. Universal categories, found in all groups, are age and sex. Thousands of other categories exist, many of them unique to particular groups. In fact, there is no logical limit to the number of categories that might exist. Cultural relativism as an idea may be fairly well summed up in terms of the culturally unique categories which exist in specific societies—particularly for human actors. The self of a given person is in part a set of assignments of the self to relevant categories. But these assignments reflect group assessments: in the *broad*, because there is but one vocabulary to use; in the *specific*, because one cannot behave conjointly with others without consensus on one's assignment to categories (or put another way, without consensus on one's possession of role-relevant attributes).

Thus *category membership* is in any social system a *derivative* matter. It is the *group* or groups with whom one feels identified which are the source of the very vocabulary creating the categories and their meanings. Therefore, the other with whom one has a we-feeling, that is, a self which includes him, is an altogether different kind of other than the one with whom one shares a similar age or sex or number of years of overseas service. The dynamics for the support or modification of the self and, therefore, the dynamics for the organization and redirection of action, *lie* in one's *group relationships*. They will only *refer* to his category assignments.

It is difficult to look into the vocabulary of one's own society with any likelihood of finding generic differentia among its categories which will be instructive in delineating the processes of which I have just been speaking. The vernacular yields a rich bag of terms by which we regularly differentiate among our others and with respect to the different ways we confront them. A small but completely unsystematically assembled sampling of them from my own smattering recollection gives the following: dutch uncle; wet hen; party pooper; blood brother; traitor; hypocrite; snob; underdog; lover; sissy; man; other members of the team; final oral committee; old maid (of either sex); someone in the same boat (used in *The American Soldier*); sucker; the Joneses; pig; hero; clown; cry-baby; lion; mouse; boon companion; financial angel; sidewalk superintendent; customer; having somebody as one's "property" (e.g. a movie star); operator; promoter. Words for *collectivities of others* include: audience; forum;

clique; the boys; guys like me; committee; cabinet; huddle; rescue team; them bums; the officials; passersby; mob; the crew; those cave-dwellers.

How can one distill from these any generic classes of others? I do not think one can. One *can*, however, make a beginning by starting with such elementary distinctions as those based on time, continuity, physical and social space, and the like: we can differentiate present others from absent others; proximal others from distal others; contemporary others from past others; continuous others from intermittent others; in-category from out-category others; immediate, impulsive, passing others from considered others. Behind these proffered distinctions lie testable hypotheses of considerable importance for the extension of symbolic interaction theory. It is simple to see what these might be, so I will not burden you with specific formulations of them. One cannot help acknowledging the debt symbolic interaction theory has to reference group theory, if only in the demonstration that the problem of the other may be approached systematically and empirically. But the examination of regularities with respect to the implicit hypotheses in the distinctions I suggested may not necessarily be best approached through survey research. It is especially important—given the assumptions of symbolic interactionism—to note what amounts to an aside made by Merton and Kitt to the effect that it is important to find out *what others the subject himself will give most saliently*—that is, presumably in answers to open-ended questions.[22] Although this kind of question may be used in survey research, it is the kind of question which evidently requires other forms of inquiry for the validation of its answers and to provide a broad base of understanding for their meaning.

It may be that some kind of orderliness lies in a possible hierarchy with which an actor holds—and invokes—his others. This kind of notion best fits the mechanistic models of Parsons and Homans and learning theory of several varieties. It tends to be incompatible with the all-or-none types of others envisaged in symbolic interactionism—others whose importance to one's self-conception rests on inclusion in groups with which one's self is coextensive and inclusive.

The dramatistic model of Burke, Goffman, Duncan and others suggests a process of casting acquaintances in various roles of others, depending on the kind of act to be presented and the circumstances and audience involved.[23] Such a casting process presents complexity which baffles imaginative attempts to categorize aspects and procedures for the purposes of finding regularities about which one might form useful generalizations.

---

[22] Merton, *op. cit.*, pp. 249–250.

[23] Kenneth Burke, *A Grammar of Motives*, New York: Prentice-Hall, 1945; Erving Goffman, *The Presentation of Self in Everyday Life*, Garden City, N.Y.: Doubleday, 1959; and Hugh Dalziel Duncan, *Communication and Social Order*, New York: Bedminister Press, 1962.

Much introspective experience supports the use of this model. We ought to be reminded that sociological inquiry must be directed toward events as they occur rather than toward fictions that please or seem to represent efficiencies or economies of investigation. It would be an error to create models of processes from a consideration of the tools we have readily available for research rather than from a consideration of the evidences of the processes we already have available for examination. If there is further evidence that we cast our others on the basis, not of conditioned or habitual experience, but at least partially on the basis of anticipated self-fulfillment by or in others of traits, qualities and potentialties for enactment, then the notions of hierarchy may not be at all relevant.

One of the claimed advantages of the reference group concept, as far as it was employed in such a study as *The American Soldier,* is that it enables us to examine the regularities with which social structure influences the creation and invocation of others, particularly in the process of self-evaluation and in the development of attitudes of relative deprivation. This is a cogent argument, deserving serious examination. It would seem, however, that if the major regularities of individual behavior hang on categorical memberships in social systems, there is little need for a social psychology in general or for the concept of the other in particular. The intervening factors between system regularity and individual regularity are in the nature of constants rather than of variables. One need not pry open the lid of the little black box or even worry about what's in it. It is when systems crosscut, or when personality processes and structures deriving from the diversity of past statuses and roles in other systems make difficult the discovery of regular relation between present social system and individual behavior, that we need to understand how the self and self-appraisal work and from whence they derive.

But in our kind of society, cross-cutting memberships are the rule rather than the exception—and so is diversity of past role-playing and past others. Furthermore, the situations in which most people find themselves are seldom so close to the nature of total institutions as those in which the subjects of *The American Soldier* found *themselves.* In such tight circumstances, others presumably are often nearly prefabricated, certainly predesignated, by the norms of the system itself. Independence of judgment and autonomy of conduct are rather uncommon in the services in wartime. It is not such regularized and routinized, subservient and ordered behavior which an understanding of self-conception assists us in understanding. Even the attitudinal reactions to these regularities and routines are to some large degree contained within the controlling framework of the total institution itself rather than being, as they normally are, inclusive of possible elections and choices that would get one to "leave the field," in Lewin's term.

Thus, if a study of the other is to assist us in the general study of social psychology, it has considerably larger tasks to perform in the area of the *lack* of regularity of relation between present social system and individual acts. In my view we have far more use for concepts of self and other, say, in studying the family than in the study of the prison. This is not to say that the concept of other has *no* utility in the study of behavior in the total institution, but that its use is more or less one which inverts that to which it is put by Merton and Kitt.

The Orientational Other

If what I have just suggested makes sense, I should like to advance the implicit idea in it by proposing a new concept—a new category of the other, which I shall call, for want of a better name, the *orientational other*. (It is singular by language convention only. It refers to a social object which may be a single other or a group). I should have preferred to call it by the name of *significant other*, but since that term has become so solidly entrenched in our usage as meaning something not basically different from simply "the other," in Mead's terms, I will suggest the rather less desirable name "orientational other." The orientational other has, in my proposal four defining attributes: (1) The term refers to the others to whom the individual is most fully, broadly and basically committed, emotionally and psychologically; (2) it refers to the others who have provided him with his general vocabulary, including his most basic and crucial concepts and categories; (3) it refers to the others who have provided and continue to provide him with his categories of self and other and with the meaningful roles to which such assignments refer; (4) it refers to the others in communication with whom his self-conception is basically sustained and/or changed.

This orientational other has some kinship with the concept of the primary self advanced some years ago by Bingham Dai, but Dai's notion begged the essential question of sequence and assumed that the primary self—and presumably the primary others—are necessarily primary in the life trajectory—that is, they are events and objects of infancy and childhood only.[24]

The study of the orientational other would be one which would lie quite at the opposite end of the scale of significance from the study of the reference group. It would attempt, that is, to study the processes by which the self is formed and sustained and to discover if there are regularities in the relation between orientational other and the self which can account *for the discrepancies* between regularities of social system and the phenomena

[24] Bingham Dai, "A Socio-Psychiatric Approach to Personality Organization," *American Sociological Review*, 1952, 17:44–49.

of individual behavior. It would afford the opportunity for inquiry regarding the possible relation between absence or diversity of orientational others and disoriented behavior.

It might be pointed out in conclusion that one has a *history* in his relations with his orientational others, but he has *only spent abstract time* in his social categories. When his reference categories have "come alive" for him, they have done so in terms of vivid role events vis-à-vis his orientational others, not in tilting windmills vis-à-vis all green recruits.

Summary

I know from several oblique comments that Professor Merton believes symbolic interactionists have an orientational aversion to empirical research—and from my own earlier-voiced doubts about Professor Blumer, you can guess that I at least have once *entertained thoughts* that *some* of them do. (Notice my perfidious shift from *us* to *them!*) But I want to remind myself and also Professor Merton that Professor Cooley's early study of the uses of personal pronouns by his children as a clue to the development of the self was one of the earliest empirical studies in social psychology.[25] And Professor Bain's replication of it was one of the earliest replication studies.[26] Now, in these days of survey research and of IBM 7070's, such studies of one's own children are to be looked upon, I suppose, as in the same genre as analysis by introspection! But I digress.

It had never occurred to me until the other day that one might study the other in much the same way that Cooley studied the self—through the use of pronouns by children. My ten-year-old daughter Abigail reported at dinner table the other day that "when she was *very* young and her older brother came home from school to report what 'they' did—she thought 'they' meant little people dressed in white clothes—people about six inches tall who lived under the furniture." Suddenly it occurred to me that questions like "Compared with the chances of promotion for *raw recruits*, what do you think of your chances?" might have something in common with the notion that "they" refers to people under the furniture who wear little white coats. I think perhaps we are in the infancy of our study of the other.

I hope that this—or for that matter, my previous remarks—will not be taken as an indication that I wish to scrap the reference group concept altogether. I do think it should be amended to be the "reference *category*" concept. But I have no intention of suggesting that those who are persuaded by the cogency of the arguments behind it cease their research efforts. My

[25] Charles Horton Cooley, "A Study of the Early Use of the Self-Words by a Child," *Psychological Review*, 1908, 15:339–357.

[26] Read Bain, "The Self-and-Other Words of a Child," *American Journal of Sociology*, 1936, 41:767–775.

proposal of the concept of *orientational other* was in no sense intended as a proposal of an *alternative* to the reference category concept.

The burden of what I have been attempting to say is that there are serious *discontinuities* between the symbolic interaction orientation and the reference-group concept of the other as it has generally been employed, and that whatever empirical successes have been achieved in its employment are not very large or persuasive when one considers the context of the research—a war, for example, is extraordinarily framed off from the rest of life, both in time and space. It is important to consider and to explore how far reference categories are coextensive with significant others. I have suggested that they may not even be of the same order. I am inclined to think that, if one is to demonstrate that they *are* of the same order, one must demonstrate that reference categories have major importance in the development and maintenance of the self as an object to the person. Ordinarily one keeps himself together and headed in the right direction by remembering who he is. If he remembers saliently that he is a second lieutenant, it is not, dynamically, because all second looies clutch him to their bosoms and think of him as one of them, but because the people with whom he is in a continual interchange of communicative symbols think of him saliently, and in respects significant to themselves and their mutual interaction, as a second lieutenant. If members of the faculty of the University of Wisconsin are asked, "Compared with those who got their B.A.'s at the University of Wisconsin, how good do you think your chances for promotion at the University of Wisconsin are?" regularities in their responses do not carry proof to me that faculty members there regularly and saliently divide in their self-conceptions between those who think of themselves as University of Wisconsin B.A.'s and "elsewhere B.A.'s."

Yet symbolic interactionism owes a considerable debt to this new development, for it has demonstrated that the other can probably be empirically researched and that it is very likely to be quite important to do so.

If these remarks have seemed excessively concerned with terminological distinctions, it might remind us of Stephen Leacock's wonderful characterization of our whole enterprise: "Ignorance, in its wooden shoes, shuffles around the portico of the temple of learning, stumbling among the litter of terminology. The broad field of human wisdom has been cut into a multitude of little professional rabbit warrens. In each of these a specialist burrows deep, scratching a shower of terminology, head down in an unlovely attitude which places an interlocutor at a grotesque conversational disadvantage."

15 NORMAN K. DENZIN

The Significant Others
of a College Population

Sociologists have long recognized that man learns his self-definitions and the definitions of his subsidiary social objects through interaction with various generic classes of social others.[1] In the theoretical works of Mead, Dewey, Faris, and Sullivan, the term "other" occupied a central role, Sullivan coined the term "significant other" to refer to those others whose evaluation of his behavior and attitudes the individual held in high esteem.[2] It was through interaction with such others that the self, meaning, and thought arose.

In a recent attempt to explore the role the concept of other had in the theories of Mead, Sullivan, and Faris, Manford Kuhn felt the need to make a distinction between the "social other" of Mead and the "significant other" of Sullivan and a class of social others which he felt oc-

Norman K. Denzin, "The Significant Others of a College Population," *The Sociological Quarterly*, vol. 7 (Summer 1966), pp. 298–310. Reprinted by permission.

The author would like to thank Evelyn K. Denzin, George J. McCall, and Harold Mulford for their comments and criticisms on earlier versions of this paper.

[1] Harold A. Mulford, "The Significant Others of a General Population," paper presented at the Midwest Sociological Meetings, 1964. Various classes of social others that have been identified include Goffman's informer, shill, imposter, go-between, nonperson and colleague. See his *Presentation of Self in Everyday Life* (New York: Doubleday, 1959), pp. 141–66, for an excellent discussion of these discrepant roles. Other classes of others include Newcomb's positive and negative reference group others; see his text *Social Psychology* (New York: 1950); those others contained in primary and secondary groups as discussed by Cooley in *Human Nature and the Social Order* (Glencoe, Ill.: 1956); those others contained in membership and reference groups as noted originally by Herbert Hyman, "The Psychology of Status," *Archives of Psychology*, vol. 38, no. 269 (1942), and later expanded by Merton and Kitt, in "Contributions to the Theory of Reference Group Behavior," in R. K. Merton and P. F. Lazarsfeld (eds.), *Continuities in Social Research: Studies in the Scope and Method of "The American Soldier"* (Glencoe, Ill.: Free Press, 1950); those others who contribute to the actor's "frame of reference" as discussed by Sherif and Sherif in *An Outline of Social Psychology*, rev. ed. (New York: Harper and Brothers, 1956). For an excellent recent discussion of the concept "other" see also Everett C. Hughes, "What Other?" in Arnold M. Rose (ed.), *Human Behavior and Social Processes* (Boston: Houghton Mifflin, 1962), pp. 119–27.

[2] Manford H. Kuhn, "The Reference Group Reconsidered," *Sociological Quarterly*, 5:5–24 (1964). There is some doubt as to whether Sullivan intended his term "significant other" to refer to those others responsible for socializing the actor or to all those persons the actor holds in high esteem. Recent usage has tended to employ the latter interpretation.

cupied a role of more central importance to the individual.[3] This new category of other was labeled "orientational other" and had four defining attributes: (1) the term refers to the others to whom the individual is most fully, broadly, and basically committed, emotionally and psychologically; (2) it refers to the others who have provided him with his general vocabulary, including his most basic and crucial concepts and categories; (3) it refers to the others who have provided and continue to provide him with his categories of self and other, and with the meaningful roles to which such assignments refer; (4) it refers to the others in communication with whom his self-conception is basically sustained or changed.[4]

The "orientational other," as Kuhn introduced the term, was distinguished from the significant other or other of Mead in that the individual tends to have a history of relationships with the orientational others, whereas the relationships with the significant other tend to be more situationally determined. Thus Kuhn was making a distinction between those others who are significant for individuals in a highly role-specific sense (Mead's social other) and those social others who are significant for the individual, regardless of the social role presently enacted or the social situation in which the behavior occurs.[5]

Kuhn's term appears to have a great deal of heuristic appeal, but if it is to be useful at all for future theory and research, investigations must be undertaken to demonstrate (1) that such a class of others can be identified; and (2) that they operate differently for the individual than do the social others of Mead and Sullivan.

This paper reports a purely exploratory attempt to locate the role-specific-significant others (Sullivan's significant others) and the orientational others of a small sample of college students enrolled in a large midwestern university.[6]

---

[3] Kuhn, *op. cit.*, p. 18.

[4] *Ibid.*

[5] A recent paper by Carl J. Couch and John S. Murray, "Significant Others and Evaluation," *Sociometry*, 27:502–9 (1964), did not make the distinction between role-specific and orientational others when asking their subjects for significant others. The authors note (p. 507) that "this variation in technique imposed limitations on comparisons between the two role groups studied." The paper lends support to the importance of Kuhn's distinction by noting that within complex organizations where roles are highly unspecific, actors will select significant others within the organization who facilitate the maintenance of social relationships, but where the role is highly specific the selection of significant others is not contingent upon maintenance of social relationships.

[6] The research design employed was cross-sectional, but because students in all phases of the college career were sampled, it was possible to treat the data as approximating the longitudinal or "simulated before-after" type. Such a decision is of course beset with limitations, not the least of which is the assumption that the groups under consideration are similar in all relevant background and social characteristics.

Methods

Data were gathered from 67 college students enrolled in an introductory sociology class at a large midwestern state university. Twenty-six of the subjects were males and 41 were females. Forty-three were between the ages of 18 and 20, and 27 were over 20. Three were enrolled in the school of business, 19 in nursing, 10 in education, 4 in music and 31 in the liberal arts and sciences. Forty were freshmen and sophomores, 18 were juniors and 9 were seniors.

Two open-end questions were asked in an attempt to locate empirically role-specific significant others and orientational others. The question designed to operationalize *role-specific significant others* was a version of Mulford's Significant Others Test (SOT) and read as follows:

> Would you please give me a list of those persons or groups of people whose evaluation of you as a *student* on the —— campus concern you the *most*. (You need only give the relationship of these persons to you and not their names.)[7]

The following was employed to operationalize orientational other:

> Would you please give me a list of those persons or groups of people whose evaluation of you as a *person* concern you the *most*.

The question designed to tap orientational other is a highly abstracted version of Kuhn's original definition of the concept. It was felt, however, that to ask a question consisting of the four attributes listed by Kuhn would be too cumbersome and difficult to communicate to the respondent. The question employed is, however, only one of many which could be used to operationalize the concept.[8]

[7] Mulford, *op. cit.*, p. 1; see also Mulford's original formulation of the instrument in "Toward an Instrument to Identify and Measure the Self, Significant Others and Alcohol in the Symbolic Environment: An Empirical Study," unpublished doctoral dissertation, University of Iowa, 1955.

[8] Two questions are in order at this point. The first deals with the role we placed our respondents in when they answered the role-specific question. The role of student is very encompassing and perhaps overlaps with the role of "person." Future investigations should test the hypothesis on roles that are more narrowly defined as Couch and Murray, *op. cit.*, did. Furthermore the fact that all respondents answered both questions may have led to contamination in the categories of others given (i.e., mention of one class of other in question one may have led the respondent's not mentioning that class of other on question two). Future studies should either divide the sample into two groups and administer one question to each or at least reverse the order of questioning if both questions are to be answered.

TABLE 1. Role-specific significant others reported by a sample of college students: frequency by sex and year in college

	Percentage Who Mention								
Role-specific significant others	Total		Male		Female		Fresh/Soph		Jun/Senior	
	67		26		41		40		27	
	%	N	%	N	%	N	%	N	%	N
Faculty	84	(56)	77	(20)	89	(36)	85	(34)	81	(22)
Friends	69	(46)	50	(13)	81	(33)	68	(27)	70	(19)
Family	43	(29)	38	(10)	46	(19)	33	(13)	59	(16)
Students	39	(26)	35	(9)	41	(17)	35	(14)	44	(12)
Soc. Organ.	21	(14)	27	(7)	17	(7)	25	(10)	15	(4)
Work	15	(10)	15	(4)	15	(6)	18	(7)	11	(3)
Univ. Admin.	13	(9)	19	(5)	10	(4)	15	(6)	11	(3)
Other	13	(9)	8	(2)	17	(7)	5	(2)	26	(7)
Religious	12	(8)	4	(1)	17	(7)	15	(6)	7	(2)

Findings

ROLE SPECIFIC SIGNIFICANT OTHERS

In answer to question one, our attempt at operationalizing role-specific significant other (RSO), we obtained 271 discrete responses from the 67 subjects with a mean of 4.04 responses from each person. A total of nine discrete categories of others were listed (see Table 1). The three most frequently appearing classified others were faculty, 84 percent mentioned, friends mentioned by 69 percent, and family members mentioned by 43 percent. Students were mentioned by barely a third of the subjects, only 39 percent. Thus, while there appeared to be consensus among the respondents on the importance of faculty, friends, and family, there is little agreement among the choices of the remaining five categories of others. We find that one-fifth mention members of social organizations (i.e., fraternities and sororities), 15 percent mention persons related to their work, or future employers, 12 percent mention persons related to religious organizations, and 13 percent mention university administration as well as a category of other coded simply as "other" (i.e., self, people of Iowa City, Doctor). There appears to be a large residual category of RSO which occupy differential roles of importance for only a small portion of the students. It remains for further analyses to identify which types of students pick others from this rather large residual category.

TABLE 2. Orientational others reported by a sample of college students: frequency of mention by sex and year in college

Percentage Who Mention

Orienta-tional other	Total		Male		Female		Fresh/Soph		Jun/Senior	
	67		26		41		40		27	
	%	N	%	N	%	N	%	N	%	N
Friends	79	(53)	69	(18)	56	(35)	83	(33)	74	(20)
Family	62	(41)	62	(16)	61	(25)	58	(23)	67	(18)
Faculty	48	(32)	50	(13)	46	(19)	50	(20)	44	(12)
Religious	21	(14)	19	(5)	22	(9)	28	(11)	11	(3)
Social Organ.	21	(14)	15	(4)	24	(10)	30	(12)	7	(2)
Other	16	(11)	35	(9)	5	(2)	10	(5)	22	(6)
Students	12	(8)	12	(3)	12	(5)	5	(2)	22	(6)
Univ. Admin.	9	(6)	4	(1)	12	(5)	5	(2)	15	(4)
Work	9	(6)	19	(5)	2	(1)	5	(2)	15	(4)
Campus Deviants	4	(3)	...	...	7	(3)	8	(3)	...	...

ORIENTATIONAL OTHERS

In answer to question two, 273 discrete responses were given, with a mean of 4.07 per subject. A total of 10 discrete categories of others were given with the only new category being a class of other coded as "campus deviant." Others coded under this category consisted of persons defined as "art crowd," "beatniks," and "long hairs."

A consideration of the most frequently appearing categories again reveals a skewed distribution, with three categories of others receiving the most choices and a large residual category remaining. The most popular orientational other was friend, mentioned by 79 percent; this was followed closely by family, 62 percent and then faculty, not quite 50 percent mentioned. As can be seen in Table 2 there is a definite shift in the choice pattern of orientational others. For example, 84 percent of the students mentioned faculty as RSO but only 48 mentioned them as orientational others (OO). Further, while less than half selected family as RSO, nearly two-thirds selected family as OO. It is also of interest to note that while only 12 percent selected religious persons as RSO, 21 percent selected such persons as OO. Another interesting switch in ratings is that given to students. On question two only 12 percent mentioned students as compared to 39 percent on question one. Statistical analysis conducted to assess the significance of the change in preference patterns for social others between questions one and two confirms the observation that significant switching did occur (P < .001, Wilcoxen test).

When we compare the responses from the two questions it becomes apparent that (1) approximately the same number and general categories of others are chosen for each question, but (2) the order of preference for the categories changes, depending on the situation in which the student finds himself. It appears that university students have a limited set of others which they regard as important when their behavior and attitudes as *students* and *persons* are under consideration. These others seem to occupy a hierarchical pattern for the student, with university-related persons occupying uppermost positions when the role of college student is salient. When their situation is changed, and the role now becomes nonspecific, the relative ordering of others shifts and friends and family members occupy primary positions with university-related persons given more secondary roles.[9]

We turn now to the effects of the respondent's sex and year in college on the choice patterns for the two types of significant others.

SEX AND CHOICE OF ROLE-SPECIFIC SIGNIFICANT OTHERS

Table 1 presents the choice patterns of males and females for RSO. It can be seen that males and females appear to be in agreement as to the importance of faculty, students, and university administration. They disagree, however, when choice of friends is under consideration; only one-half of the males select friends, whereas 81 percent of the females make this selection. Choice of family members also indicates a *slight* sex difference; 38 percent of the males select family related others, while 46 percent of the females makes this selection. Males appear to be more closely tied to social organizations than are girls, 27 percent selected social organizations, while only 17 percent of the girls mentioned them. We find another sex disagreement on choice of religion: 17 percent of females mention religious-related others, but only 4 percent of males.

Thus the analysis by sex discloses some interesting differences in choice patterns of the RSO. For example, females appear to be more prone to mention family-related others. It is now becoming clearer who is accounting for the mentions of the six residual categories of others. Females ac-

---

[9] This finding appears to be similar to Stouffer's finding in "An Analysis of Conflicting Social Norms," *American Sociological Review*, 14:707–17 (1949), that obligations to various classes of others are contingent upon the social situation. See also the paper by W. W. Charters, Jr., and Theodore M. Newcomb, "Some Attitudinal Effects of Experimentally Increased Salience of a Membership Group," in Eleanor E. Maccoby, Theodore M. Newcomb, and Eugene L. Hartley (eds.), *Readings in Social Psychology* (New York: Henry Holt, 1958), pp. 276–80; Newcomb found that the effect of religious member groups upon attitudes was "a function of the relative momentary potency of his relevant group memberships."

count for the most mentions of religion, students, and family. Males are more likely to mention social organizations.

YEAR IN COLLEGE AND CHOICE OF ROLE-SPECIFIC SIGNIFICANT OTHERS

The sample was divided into two groups: freshmen and sophomores as one group and juniors and seniors in the other group. Table 1 presents the results of this analysis. It can be seen that there is approximate agreement between these two groups on the choices of faculty, friends, and students. There is disagreement on choice of family members. Juniors and seniors are twice as likely to mention family related others as compared to freshmen and sophomores. Freshmen are more likely to mention religious others and others in social organizations than are juniors and seniors (25 percent to 15 percent, and 15 percent to 7 percent).

Analysis by year in college indicates that juniors and seniors appear to be more family oriented in their choices than are freshmen and sophomores; furthermore, upperclassmen are more likely to mention fellow students as RSO, whereas freshmen and sophomores will more likely mention members of social organizations, religious related others, faculty, and friends.

SEX AND MENTION OF ORIENTATIONAL OTHER

From Table 2 it can be seen that approximately the same number of males and females select family members and faculty but that two-thirds of the males select friends while scarcely one-half of the females make this selection. Males and females appear to agree on the choice of religious related others (19 percent as compared to 22 percent). Females account for all of the mentions of campus deviants and males account for the majority of the mentions of work-related others. From this analysis, it is apparent that males are more likely to select friends than are females (nearly 3 to 1), that girls will select campus deviants, and that both sexes agree on the importance of the roles of family members and faculty.

YEAR IN COLLEGE AND CHOICE OF ORIENTATIONAL OTHER

Freshmen and sophomores are more likely to mention friends, faculty members, religious-related persons, and persons from social organizations. On the other hand, juniors and seniors make more references to "others" (i.e., self, people of Iowa City, etc.), students, work-related, and family-related others. The mention of family-related others more frequently parallels the finding from question one, where it was determined that upperclassmen mentioned family-related persons as RSO more frequently than underclassmen.

TABLE 3. Role-specific significant others by year in college and sex

Percentage Who Mention

Role-specific Significant Others	Freshman/Sophomore (40)				Junior/Senior (27)				Total
	Male		Female		Male		Female		
	14		26		12		15		
	%	N	%	N	%	N	%	N	67
Faculty	93	(13)	81	(21)	67	(8)	93	(14)	(56)
Friends	57	(8)	73	(19)	42	(5)	93	(14)	(46)
Family	57	(8)	19	(5)	42	(5)	73	(11)	(29)
Social Organ.	29	(4)	27	(7)	25	(3)	...	...	(14)
Students	21	(3)	46	(12)	58	(7)	27	(4)	(26)
Univ. Admin.	21	(3)	12	(3)	17	(2)	7	(1)	(9)
Work	14	(2)	19	(5)	17	(2)	7	(1)	(10)
Religious	7	(1)	19	(5)	17	(2)	...	...	(8)
Other	...	...	12	(3)	17	(2)	27	(4)	(9)

While the investigation of the effects of sex and year in college upon the choice patterns of RSO and OO yield interesting results, the crucial test of the relationship between these variables comes only after we have simultaneously controlled the effects of both upon the choice patterns. We now turn to this analysis.

ROLE-SPECIFIC SIGNIFICANT OTHERS
BY YEAR IN COLLEGE AND SEX

Table 3 presents the results of this analysis. When we look at males only, by year in college, we note a very interesting *inverse* relationship between choice of faculty members, friends, and family. It will be noted that males in the freshman and sophomore years of college choose a very high number of faculty members as RSO (93 percent) but by the time they are juniors and seniors this identification with faculty has decreased substantially as evidenced by the fact that only 67 percent make that selection at this point in their college careers. A similar pattern holds for choices of friends and family. An interesting question arising at this point may be phrased, "Who do the males select as RSO when they are juniors and seniors?" Table 3 also presents evidence which bears on this question for it may be observed that males begin to identify with the following classes of others as they progress through their college careers: students, religious others, and "others." For example, while only 21 percent of the freshmen and sophomores mentioned students as RSO, nearly 60 percent of them made this mention when they were juniors and seniors. Similarly, while only 7 percent selected religious others as freshmen, 17 percent selected them as

TABLE 4. Orientational others by year in college and by sex

Percentage Who Mention

Orienta- tional others	Freshman/Sophomore (40)				Junior/Senior (27)				Total
	Male		Female		Male		Female		
	14		26		12		15		
	%	N	%	N	%	N	%	N	67
Faculty	50	(7)	50	(13)	50	(6)	40	(6)	(32)
Friends	86	(12)	81	(21)	67	(8)	80	(12)	(53)
Family	79	(11)	46	(12)	58	(7)	73	(11)	(41)
Univ. Admin.	...	...	12	(3)	8	(1)	13	(2)	(6)
Religious	7	(1)	38	(10)	25	(3)	...	...	(14)
Work	7	(1)	12	(3)	8	(1)	7	(1)	(6)
Social Organ.	7	(1)	35	(9)	17	(2)	12	(2)	(14)
Campus Deviants	...	...	12	(3)	...	...	...	...	(3)
Students	7	(1)	4	(1)	33	(4)	12	(2)	(8)
Other	29	(4)	8	(2)	25	(3)	12	(2)	(11)

juniors and seniors. Thus it seems that college males have a history of relationships with their RSO and that as they appear in different phases of their careers as students, different RSO become more salient and other RSO become less salient.

If we turn now to females by year in college, Table 3 presents the results of this analysis. Several points are at once noticeable: (1) the longer females are in college, the more likely it is they will mention family-related RSO (i.e., we note an increase from 19 percent mentioned as freshmen and sophomores to 73 percent mentioned as juniors and seniors); (2) we note also the increase in mention of friends by year in college, an increase of from 73 to 93 percent. Furthermore, it is clear that females display fewer choices of students, social organizations, religion-related and work-related others, the longer they are in college. Females, as do males, appear to have careers with their RSO, and as they move through college, different RSO appear and others drop out. A vivid example of this point is mention of religious others by year in college. Nineteen percent mention religious others as freshmen and sophomores but by the time they are seniors *not one* female mentions religious others.

ORIENTATIONAL OTHERS BY YEAR IN COLLEGE AND BY SEX

The results of this analysis are contained in Table 4. If we look at males first it can be seen that the same inverse relationship between choice of family and friends holds as we observed for choices of RSO in Table 1. It can be seen however, that choice of faculty member has changed. Now the same number of males select faculty members as OO when under-classmen, as they do when upperclassmen. The choice pattern of students is similar to that for RSO, only slightly lower, now the shift is from 7 percent as freshmen to 17 percent as juniors and seniors.

It is interesting to note that choice of religious others and others in social organizations increases as the male moves through college (i.e., religion goes from 7 percent to 25 percent and social organizations from 7 percent to 17 percent). Choice of work-related others is relatively low with only an increase of 1 percent from the first year to the last year (7 to 8 percent). The category of "other" is chosen by a relatively large percentage of males when they are underclassmen (29 percent) but when they are juniors and seniors this percentage decreases to 25 percent. Thus we note from this analysis that as males move through college, friends and family members are less frequently chosen as orientational others and fellow students, religious organizations and social organizations begin to account for more of their choices.

Turning to females we note from Table 4 that family others are chosen by nearly one-half of the freshmen and nearly three-fourths of the juniors and seniors. The friend choice pattern remains about the same throughout college for females (81 percent as freshmen and 80 percent as juniors and seniors). It can be seen that choice of faculty members declines as females move through college (50 to 40 percent). The choice of religious others also decreases with time in college. Whereas females account for nearly all mentions of religious others in the total analysis, it is disclosed by the partial analysis that this choice occurs only in the freshman years, for juniors and seniors make no mention of this category.

Interpretation and Discussion

While the predictive power of the significant other concept has only recently begun to be realized, it promises to occupy a central role in any social psychological formulations which attempt to link individual behavior and attitudes to social groupings.[10] The present investigation has attempted to conceptually distinguish two related dimensions of the familiar term significant other. Following Kuhn's formulation, we suggested that there exist for every individual two classes of significant others: those significant

[10] See Couch (*op. cit.*), Mulford (*op. cit.*), Kuhn (*op. cit.*), and Hughes (*op. cit.*), for recent uses of the concept. In addition to these recent formulations it is only sufficient to note the central role his concept has occupied in the self theory of Carl Rogers, the person perception studies of Bruner, the career studies of Hughes, Strauss, Becker, and Goffman, the reference group research of Merton and Kitt, Hyman, Erhlich, Newcomb, Sherif, Kelly, and Turner, the social exchange theories of Homans, Thibaut and Kelly and Blau, and also the more recent social structural formulations of the Parsonians.

for him when he enacts his many special roles and those significant for him in a transituational, trans-role sense (i.e., his orientational others). We suggested that individuals have longer histories of relationships with orientational others than they do with role-specific others, and hence it is to the orientational other that we must turn if we are to learn anything about the more basic, underlying dimensions of an individual's personality. It is these persons who provide the individual with his basic vocabularies and his conceptions of role and self.[11]

The data gathered in this exploratory study support the contention that these two classes of significant others exist for individuals. We noted for example, that for females the mention of family members as orientational others provided one of the more consistent patterns in all of the choice patterns observed. This is consistent with the observation that females are socialized into family roles early in childhood and that such roles provide the basis for their social identities throughout adult life.[12] The autonomy of the male in middle class American society is brought out in the data presented in Tables 2 and 4.[13] Here we noted that males are very unlikely to mention family members as sources of orientational others. Rather, they mention persons who appear in their life-cycle of interactive relationships at various crucial points. Thus we note the appearance of fellow students as orientational others, and we note that this choice increases as the male progresses through college. Furthermore, the male appears to add others from religious and social organizations as he moves through college, all the while he is breaking away from the influence of the family as well as the omnipresent faculty. Thus, very dramatically with the male, do we observe the disjuncture of interactive relationships with orientational others. He begins selecting a high percentage of friends, family, and faculty (up to 90 percent) and by the time he is a junior or senior, these choices have decreased drastically and he has now added others from the previously mentioned areas.

Thus, the data seem to support Kuhn's hypothesis that individuals do have histories of relationships with their orientational others.[14]

If we turn to the selection of role-specific significant others, we note that for females, family members, friends, and faculty occupy stable roles

---

[11] Kuhn, *op. cit.*, pp. 18–21.

[12] See Talcott Parsons, "Age and Sex in the Social Structure of the United States," *American Sociological Review*, 7:604–17 (1942).

[13] *Ibid.*

[14] We can only infer that actors have longer histories of relationships with their orientational others than they do with their role specific others. Because of limitations of sample size and phrasing of the questions, the analysis was not able to determine the exact point in time when all the various categories of others such as friends were added to the actor's previously existing set of "relevant others." We can say with some assurance, however, that mention of campus social organizations, fellow students, faculty members, and family members are categories of others added at specific points in time (i.e., either before or after coming to the college campus).

throughout the college career. Fellow students are not prominent and religious choices begin at a high point and decrease to zero. This is also the case with mention of social organizations, work-related others, and university administration.

In the case of males we note that faculty and friends do not occupy central roles at the end of the college career, although they do in the beginning. Students are acquired as RSO later in the college career, as are religious others.

Kuhn would hypothesize that as the student role moves through periods of transition (from freshman to senior year) he would be responding to new sets of RSO and consequently we would expect changes in choice patterns. The data from males and females seem to support this contention, and the females seem to be more stable than the males.

One possible reason why choice patterns of orientational others appear to vary to such a large extent may be due to the fact that college students are in fact going through a crucial period in their lives, in which they try out new social identities and social roles.[15] The variations in choices of orientational others may well reflect this fundamental change process which is occurring for the student. Further research would do well to focus on changes in orientational others in other age periods of the life cycle. Another avenue of future research suggested by the present investigation is the degree to which orientational others continue to serve as role-specific others for the actor as he proceeds through his career of interactive relationships. In the present study it can be noted that friends and parents appeared under both categories of others. This suggests that certain highly salient categories of others operate for individuals in dual roles. The isolation of *those* categories of others which serve this dual function for *which* types of actors would contribute to our knowledge of the vicissitudes of socialization and personality change in late adolescence and early adulthood. It does not seem unreasonable to assume that role-specific others may take over many of the socialization functions served by earlier orientational others for the actor. In fact it appears that certain of ego's orientational others may be such that no history of relationships is needed. One's role-

[15] See especially the following: Manford H. Kuhn, "The Relation of Critical Experiences and of Certain Characteristics of Self-Attitudes to Subsequent Changes in Self-Attitudes," paper read at the American Sociological Society Meetings, 1958; Walter L. Wallace, "Institutional and Life-Cycle Socialization of College Freshmen," *American Journal of Sociology*, 70:303–18 (1964).

Perhaps the classic study in the area of changes in self-other relationships during college is that of Newcomb, *Personality and Social Change* (New York: Holt, Rinehart and Winston, 1943), which examines in great detail changes in reference groups of college students throughout their entire college histories. For a briefer report of the Bennington study see also Newcomb's "Attitude Development as a Function of Reference Groups: The Bennington Study," in Maccoby, Newcomb, and Hartley *op. cit.*, pp. 265–75. An excellent review of studies explicitly examining the experiences of college students is *The American College: A Psychological and Social Interpretation of Higher Learning*, Nevitt Sanford (ed.) (New York: John Wiley, 1962). Particularly relevant sections in this context are Parts 4–6.

specific others may indeed *at times* become one's orientational others. Questions which arise on this point include the extent to which role-specific others provide the actor with new vocabularies, new role models, new self-attitudes and new frames of reference with which to judge his own and others' behavior.[16]

It seems reasonable to conclude that Kuhn's concept, the "orientational other" has more than heuristic use to the sociologist. The data support the contention that individuals have different types of interactive relationships with role-specific significant others and orientational others and that changes in these interactive relationships can be linked to specific points in the individual's college career. The present investigation was only exploratory in nature, but suggestions for future research would seem to involve a need for studies dealing with variations in choices of orientational others at various points in the age cycle, studies linking conceptions of orientational others with conceptions of self and further investigations highlighting more vividly than the present study was able to do, the difference between role-specific significant others and orientational others and the consequences of this difference for continuities and discontinuities in individual behavior.

[16] Recent studies which have dealt with the influence of immediate or role-specific others on changes in personality include Newcomb (*op. cit.*), Wallace (*op. cit.*), and the career studies of Becker. See his recent work in this area: "Personal Change in Adult Life," *Sociometry*, 27:40–53 (1964), which reviews the literature on studies dealing with changes in adult life. Also important is the recent work of Barney G. Glaser, "Variations in the Importance of Recognition in Scientist's Careers," *Social Problems*, 10:268–76 (1964); also Fred Reif and Anselm Strauss, "The Impact of Rapid Discovery upon the Scientist's Career," *ibid.*, 12:297–310 (1965). Goffman's discussion of the effects of mental hospital staff upon mental patients illustrates the influence role-specific others can have upon self-attitudes and even the basic vocabulary of patients. See his *Asylums* (Garden City, N. Y., Doubleday: 1961).

16 HANS GERTH & C. WRIGHT MILLS

Institutions and Persons

If we shift our view from the external behavior of individual organisms and from explanations of such behavior in terms of physiological elements and mechanisms, and view man as a person who acts with and against other persons, we may then (1) examine the patterns of conduct which men enact together, and (2) avail ourselves of the direct experiences which persons have of one another and of themselves. At its minimum, social conduct consists of the actions of one person oriented to another, and most of the actions of men are of this sort. Man's action is interpersonal. It is often informed by awareness of other actors and directly oriented to their expectations and to anticipations of their behavior.

Out of the metaphors of poets and philosophers, who have likened man's conduct to that of the stage actor, sociologists have fashioned analytical tools. Long-used phrases readily come to mind: "playing a role" in the "great theater of public life," to move "in the limelight," the "theater of War," the "stage is all set." More technically, the concept "role" refers to (1) units of conduct which by their recurrence stand out as regularities and (2) which are oriented to the conduct of other actors. These recurrent interactions form patterns of mutually oriented conduct.

By definition, roles are interpersonal, that is, oriented to the conduct and expectations of others. These others, who expect things of us, are also playing roles: we expect them to do things in certain ways and to refrain from doing and feeling things in other ways. Interpersonal situations are thus built up and sets of roles held in line by mutual expectation, approbation, and disfavor.

Much of our social conduct, as we know from direct experience, is enacted in order to meet the expectations of others. In this sense, our enemies often control us as much as our friends. The father of a patriarchal family is expected by his wife and children to act in certain ways when confronted with given situations, and he in turn expects them to act in certain regular ways. Being acquainted with these simple facts about patriarchal families we expect regularities of conduct from each of their members, and having experienced family situations, we expect, with some degree of probability, that each of these members will experience his place and his self in a certain way.

Man as a person is an historical creation, and can most readily be understood in terms of the roles which he enacts and incorporates. These roles are limited by the kind of social institutions in which he happens to be born and in which he matures into an adult. His memory, his sense of time and space, his perception, his motives, his conception of his self . . . his psychological functions are shaped and steered by the specific configuration of roles which he incorporates from his society.

Perhaps the most important of these features of man is his image of his self, his idea of what kind of person he is. This experience of self is a crucially interpersonal one. Its basic organization is reflected from surrounding persons to whose approbation and criticism one pays attention.

What we think of ourselves is decisively influenced by what others think of us. Their attitudes of approval and of disapproval guide us in learning to play the roles we are assigned or which we assume. By internalizing these attitudes of others toward us and our conduct we not only gain new roles, but in time an image of our selves. Of course, man's "looking-glass self" may be a true or a distorted reflection of his actual self. Yet those from whom a man continually seeks approval are important determinants of what kind of man he is becoming. If a young lawyer begins to feel satisfaction from the approval of the boss of the local political machine, if the labels which this boss uses to describe his behavior matter a lot to the lawyer, he is being steered into new roles and into a new image of his self by the party machine and its boss. Their values may in time become his own and he will apply them not only to other men but to his own actions as well.[1] The self, Harry Stack Sullivan once said, is made up of the reflected appraisals of others.[2]

The concept of role does not of course imply a one person–one role equation. One person may play many different roles, and each of these roles may be a segment of the different institutions and interpersonal situations in which the person moves. A corporation executive acts differently in his office than in his child's nursery. An adolescent girl enacts a different role when she is at a party composed of members of her own clique than when she is at her family's breakfast table. Moreover, the luxury of a certain image of self implied in the party role is not often possible in her family circle. In the family circle the party role might be amusing, as a charming attempt at sophistication "beyond her age and experience," but at the party it might bring prestige and even the adulation of young males. She cannot, usually, act out the self-conception of a long-suffering lover before her grandfather, but she can when she is alone with her young man.

The chance to display emotional gestures, and even to feel them, varies with one's status and class position. For emotional gestures, expected by others and by one's self, form important features of many social roles. The Victorian lady could dramatize certain emotions in a way that today would be considered silly, if not hysterical. Yet the working girl who was her contemporary was not as likely to faint as was the lady; there would probably not have been anyone to catch the working girl. During the nineties in America it was expected that women who were also ladies, that is, members

---

[1] The mechanism by which persons thus internalize roles and the attitudes of others is language. Language is composed of gestures, normally verbal, which call forth similar responses in two individuals. Without such gestures man could not incorporate the attitudes of others, and could not so easily make these attitudes a condition of his own learning and enactment of roles of his own image of self.

These conceptions will be discussed in greater detail in Chapters III: Organism and Psychic Structure and IV: The Person. Here we are only concerned with setting forth in the most general way the sociological model of explanation. [Ed. Note: reference is to chapters in *Character and Social Structure*.]

[2] "Conceptions of Modern Psychiatry," *Psychiatry*, Vol. III, No. 1 (February 1949), pp. 10–11. Compare also C. H. Cooley's *Human Nature and the Social Order* (rev. ed.; New York: Scribner's, 1922). The tradition is well documented by Fay B. Karpf, *American Social Psychology* (New York: McGraw-Hill, 1932).

of an upper status group, would faint upon very exciting occasions. The role of the delicate and fainting lady was involved in the very being of a lady.[3] But the "same" occasions would not elicit fainting on the part of the ladies' maid, who did not conceive of her "place," and of her self, as a fainting lady; fainting requires a certain amount of leisure and gentlemanly attention, and accordingly offers opportunities to the gentleman to demonstrate that chivalry is not dead.

The roles allowed and expected, the self-images which they entail, and the consequences of these roles and images on the persons we are with are firmly embedded in a social context. Inner psychological changes and the institutional controls of a society are thus interlinked.

An institution is an organization of roles, which means that the roles carry different degrees of authority, so that one of the roles—we may call it the "head" role—is understood and accepted by the members of the other roles as guaranteeing the relative permanence of the total conduct pattern. An *institution* is thus (1) an organization of roles, (2) one or more of which is understood to serve the maintenance of the total set of roles.

The "head role" of an institution is very important in the psychic life of the other members of the institution. What "the head" thinks of them in their respective roles, or what they conceive him to think, is internalized, that is, taken over, by them. In a strictly patriarchal family, the head, the father, is looked up to; his is the most important attitude toward the child that may determine the child's attitude toward his, the child's, own conduct and perhaps toward his self: in taking over this attitude the child builds up an "other" within his self, and the attitude he conceives this other to have toward him is a condition for his attitude toward his own self. Other persons in other roles also have attitudes toward him and each of these may be internalized, and eventually form segments of his self-conception. But the attitude of the head of the major institution in which we play a role is a decisive one in our own maturation. If "he says it is all right," we feel secure in what we are doing and how we are conceiving our self. When his attitudes are taken over into the self, this head constitutes in a concrete form, a "particular other." But he is not seen merely as a particular person; he is the symbol and the "mouth piece" of the entire institution. In him is focused the "final" attitudes toward our major roles and our self within this institution; he sums them up, and when we take over these attitudes and expectations we control our institutional conduct in terms of them. It is by means of such internalized others that our conduct, our playing of roles within institutions, is "self-controlled."

By choosing the social role as a major concept we are able to reconstruct the inner experience of the person as well as the institutions which make up an historical social structure. For man as a *person* (from the Latin *persona*, meaning "mask") is composed of the specific roles which he enacts

---

[3] Cf. Ralph Linton, *The Study of Man* (New York: Appleton-Century, 1936).

and of the effects of enacting these roles upon his self. And society as a *social structure* is composed of roles as segments variously combined in its total circle of institutions. The organization of roles is important in building up a particular social structure; it also has psychological implications for the persons who act out the social structure.

Most of the various interpersonal situations in which we are involved exist within institutions, which make up a social structure; and changes of social structure make up the main course of human history. In order to understand men's conduct and experience we must reconstruct the historical social structures in which they play roles and acquire selves. For such regularity of conduct, and of the motives for this conduct, as we may find will rest upon the historical regularities of these social structures, rather than upon any suprahistorical, biological elements assumed to be innate and constant within the organism. From the sociological point of view, man as a person is a social-historical creation. If his view of his self and of his motives is intimately connected with the roles which are available to him and which he incorporates, then we may not expect to learn much that is very concrete about individual men unless we investigate a number of his specific roles in a number of varied social-historical settings.

Rather than constant elements within a physiological organism, the sociologist rests his primary model of explanation upon the interpersonal situations, and in the last analysis, the social structures within which persons live out their lives.

17 HAROLD GARFINKEL

Conditions of Successful Degradation Ceremonies[1]

Any communicative work between persons, whereby the public identity of an actor is transformed into something looked on as lower in the local scheme of social types, will be called a "status degradation ceremony." Some restrictions on this definition may increase its usefulness. The identities

Harold Garfinkel, "Conditions of Successful Degradation Ceremonies." Reprinted from *The American Journal of Sociology*, vol. 61 (March 1956), pp. 420–424, by permission of The University of Chicago Press. Copyright 1956 by The University of Chicago.

[1] Acknowledgment is gratefully made to Erving Goffman, National Institute of Mental Health, Bethesda, Maryland, and to Sheldon Messinger, Social Science Research Council pre-doctoral fellow, University of California, Los Angeles, for criticisms and editorial suggestions.

referred to must be "total" identities. That is, these identities must refer to persons as "motivational" types rather than as "behavioral" types,[2] not to what a person may be expected to have done or to do (in Parsons' term,[3] to his "performances") but to what the group holds to be the ultimate "grounds" or "reasons" for his performance.[4]

The grounds on which a participant achieves what for him is adequate understanding of why he or another acted as he did are not treated by him in a utilitarian manner. Rather, the correctness of an imputation is decided by the participant in accordance with socially valid and institutionally recommended standards of "preference." With reference to these standards, he makes the crucial distinctions between appearances and reality, truth and falsity, triviality and importance, accident and essence, coincidence and cause. Taken together, the grounds, as well as the behavior that the grounds make explicable as the other person's conduct, constitute a person's identity. Together, they constitute the other as a social object. Persons identified by means of the ultimate "reasons" for their socially categorized and socially understood behavior will be said to be "totally" identified. The degradation ceremonies here discussed are those that are concerned with the alteration of total identities.

It is proposed that only in societies that are completely demoralized, will an observer be unable to find such ceremonies, since only in total anomie are the conditions of degradation ceremonies lacking. Max Scheler[5] argued that there is no society that does not provide in the very features of its organization the conditions sufficient for inducing shame. It will be treated here as axiomatic that there is no society whose social structure does not provide, in its routine features, the conditions of identity degradation. Just as the structural conditions of shame are universal to all societies by the very fact of their being organized, so the structural conditions of status degradation are universal to all societies. In this framework the critical question is not whether status degradation occurs or can occur within any given society. Instead, the question is: Starting from any state of a society's organization, what program of communicative tactics will get the work of status degradation done?

---

[2] These terms are borrowed from Alfred Schutz, "Common Sense and Scientific Interpretation of Human Action," *Philosophy and Phenomenological Research*, Vol. XIV, No. 1 (September, 1953).

[3] Talcott Parsons and Edward Shils, "Values, Motives, and Systems of Action," in Parsons and Shils (eds.), *Toward a General Theory of Action* (Cambridge: Harvard University Press, 1951).

[4] Cf. the writings of Kenneth Burke, particularly *Permanence and Change* (Los Altos, Calif.: Hermes Publication, 1954), and *A Grammar of Motives* (New York: Prentice-Hall, Inc., 1945).

[5] Richard Hays Williams, "Scheler's Contributions to the Sociology of Affective Action, with Special Attention to the Problem of Shame," *Philosophy and Phenomenological Research*, Vol. II, No. 3 (March, 1942).

First of all, two questions will have to be decided, at least tentatively: *What are we referring to behaviorally when we propose the product of successful degradation work to be a changed total identity?* And *what are we to conceive the work of status degradation to have itself accomplished or to have assumed as the conditions of its success?*

I

Degradation ceremonies fall within the scope of the sociology of moral indignation. Moral indignation is a social affect. Roughly speaking, it is an instance of a class of feelings particular to the more or less organized ways that human beings develop as they live out their lives in one another's company. Shame, guilt, and boredom are further important instances of such affects.

Any affect has its behavioral paradigm. That of shame is found in the withdrawal and covering of the portion of the body that socially defines one's public appearance—prominently, in our society, the eyes and face. The paradigm of shame is found in the phrases that denote removal of the self from public view, i.e., removal from the regard of the publicly identified others "I could have sunk through the floor; I wanted to run away and hide; I wanted the earth to open up and swallow me." The feeling of guilt finds its paradigm in the behavior of self-abnegation—disgust, the rejection of further contact with or withdrawal from, and the bodily and symbolic expulsion of the foreign body, as when we cough, blow, gag, vomit, spit, etc.

The paradigm of moral indignation is *public* denunciation. We publicly deliver the curse: "I call upon all men to bear witness that he is not as he appears but is otherwise and *in essence*[6] of a lower species."

The social affects serve various functions both for the person as well as for the collectivity. A prominent function of shame for the person is that of preserving the ego from further onslaughts by withdrawing entirely its contact with the outside. For the collectivity, shame is an "individuator." One experiences shame in his own time.

Moral indignation serves to effect the ritual destruction of the person denounced. Unlike shame, which does not bind persons together, moral indignation may reinforce group solidarity. In the market and in politics, a degradation ceremony must be counted as a secular form of communion. Structurally, a degradation ceremony bears close resemblance to ceremonies of investiture and elevation. How such a ceremony may bind persons to the

---

[6] The man at whose hands a neighbor suffered death becomes a "murderer." The person who passes on information to enemies is really, i.e., "in essence," in the first place," "all along," "in the final analysis," "originally," an informer.

collectivity we shall see when we take up the conditions of a successful denunciation. Our immediate question concerns the meaning of ritual destruction.

In the statement that moral indignation brings about the ritual destruction of the person being denounced, destruction is intended literally. The transformation of identities is the destruction of one social object and the constitution of another. The transformation does not involve the substitution of one identity for another, with the terms of the old one loitering about like the overlooked parts of a fresh assembly, any more than the woman we see in the department store window that turns out to be a dummy carries with it the possibilities of a woman. It is not that the old object has been overhauled; rather it is replaced by another. One declares, "*Now,* it was otherwise in the first place."

The work of the denunciation effects the recasting of the objective character of the perceived other: The other person becomes in the eyes of his condemners literally a different and *new* person. It is not that the new attributes are added to the old "nucleus." He is not changed, he is reconstituted. The former identity, at best, receives the accent of mere appearance. In the social calculus of reality representations and test, the former identity stands as accidental; the new identity is the "basic reality." What he is now is what, "after all," he was all along.[7]

The public denunciation effects such a transformation of essence by substituting another socially validated motivational scheme for that previously used to name and order the performances of the denounced. It is with reference to this substituted, socially validated motivational scheme as the essential grounds, i.e., *the first principles,* that his performances, past, present, and prospective, according to the witnesses, are to be properly and necessarily understood.[8] Through the interpretive work that respects this rule, the denounced person becomes in the eyes of the witnesses a different person.

---

[7] Two themes commonly stand out in the rhetoric of denunciation: (1) the irony between what the denounced appeared to be and what he is seen now really to be where the new motivational scheme is taken as the standard and (2) a re-examination and redefinition of origins of the denounced. For the sociological relevance of the relationship between concerns for essence and concerns for origins see particularly Kenneth Burke, *A Grammar of Motives.*

[8] While constructions like "Substantially a something" or "essentially a something" have been banished from the domain of scientific discourse, such constructions have prominent and honored places in the theories of motives, persons, and conduct that are employed in handling the affairs of daily life. Reasons can be given to justify the hypothesis that such constructions may be lost to a group's "terminology of motives" only if the relevance of socially sanctioned theories to practical problems is suspended. This can occur where interpersonal relations are trivial (such as during play) or, more interestingly, under severe demoralization of a system of activities. In such organizational states the frequency of status degradation is low.

II

How can one make a good denunciation?[9]

To be successful, the denunciation must redefine the situations of those that are witnesses to the denunciation work. The denouncer, the party to be denounced (let us call him the "perpetrator"), and the thing that is being blamed on the perpetrator (let us call it the "event") must be transformed as follows:[10]

1. Both event and perpetrator must be removed from the realm of their everyday character and be made to stand as "out of the ordinary."

2. Both event and perpetrator must be placed within a scheme of preferences that shows the following properties:

A. The preferences must not be for event A over event B, but for event of *type A* over event of *type B*. The same typing must be accomplished for the perpetrator. Event and perpetrator must be defined as instances of a uniformity and must be treated as a uniformity throughout the work of the denunciation. The unique, never recurring character of the event or perpetrator should be lost. Similarly, any sense of accident, coincidence, indeterminism, chance, or monetary occurrence must not merely be minimized. Ideally, such measures should be inconceivable; at least they should be made false.

B. The witnesses must appreciate the characteristics of the typed person and event by referring the type to a dialectical counterpart. Ideally, the witnesses should not be able to contemplate the features of the denounced person without reference to the counterconception, as the profanity of an occurrence or a desire or a character trait, for example, is clarified by the references it bears to its opposite, the sacred. The features of the mad-dog murderer reverse the features of the peaceful citizen. The confessions of

[9] Because the paper is short, the risk must be run that, as a result of excluding certain considerations, the treated topics may appear exaggerated. It would be desirable, for example, to take account of the multitude of hedges that will be found against false denunciations; of the rights to denounce; of the differential apportionment of these rights, as well as the ways in which a claim, once staked out, may become a vested interest and may tie into the contests for economic and political advantage. Further, there are questions centering around the appropriate areas of denunciation. For example, in our society the tribal council has fallen into secondary importance; among lay persons the denunciation has given way to the complaint to the authorities.

[10] These are the effects that the communicative tactics of the denouncer must be designed to accomplish. Put otherwise, in so far as he denouncer's tactics accomplish the reordering of the definitions of the situation of the witnesses to the denunciatory performances, the denouncer will have succeeded in effecting the transformation of the public identity of his victim. The list of conditions of this degrading effect are the determinants of the effect. Viewed in the scheme of a project to be rationally pursued, they are the adequate means. One would have to choose one's tactics for their efficiency in accomplishing these effects.

the Red can be read to teach the meanings of patriotism. There are many contrasts available, and any aggregate of witnesses this side of a complete war of each against all will have a plethora of such schemata for effecting a "familiar," "natural," "proper," ordering of motives, qualities, and other events.

From such contrasts, the following is to be learned. If the denunciation is to take effect, the scheme must not be one in which the witness is allowed to elect the preferred. Rather, the alternatives must be such that the preferred is morally required. Matters must be so arranged that the validity of his choice, its justification, is maintained by the fact that he makes it.[11] The scheme of alternatives must be such as to place constraints upon his making a selection "for a purpose." Nor will the denunciation succeed if the witness is free to look beyond the fact that he makes the selection for evidence that the correct alternative has been chosen, as, for example, by the test of empirical consequences of the choice. The alternatives must be such that, in "choosing," he takes it for granted and beyond any motive for doubt that not choosing can mean only preference for its opposite.

3. The denouncer must so identify himself to the witnesses that during the denunciation they regard him not as a private but as a publicly known person. He must not portray himself as acting according to his personal, unique experiences. He must rather be regarded as acting in his capicity as a public figure, drawing upon communally entertained and verified experience. He must act as a bona fide participant in the tribal relationships to which the witnesses subscribe. What he says must not be regarded as true for him alone, not even in the sense that it can be regarded by denouncer and witnesses as matters upon which they can become agreed. In no case, except in a most ironical sense, can the convention of true-for-reasonable-men be invoked. What the denouncer says must be regarded by the witnesses as true on the grounds of a socially employed metaphysics whereby witnesses assume that witnesses and denouncer are alike in essence.[12]

4. The denouncer must make the dignity of the supra-personal values of the tribe salient and accessible to view, and his denunciation must be delivered in their name.

5. The denouncer must arrange to be invested with the right to speak in the name of these ultimate values. The success of the denunciation will be undermined if, for his authority to denounce, the denouncer invokes the personal interests that he may have acquired by virtue of the wrong done to him or someone else. He must rather use the wrong he has suffered as a tribal member to invoke the authority to speak in the name of these ultimate values.

---

[11] Cf. Gregory Bateson and Jurgen Ruesch, *Communication: The Social Matrix of Psychiatry* (New York: W. W. Norton & Co., 1951), pp. 212–27.

[12] For bona fide members it is not that these are the grounds upon which we are agreed but upon which we are *alike*, consubstantial, in origin the same.

6. The denouncer must get himself so defined by the witnesses that they locate him as a supporter of these values.

7. Not only must the denouncer fix his distance from the person being denounced, but the witnesses must be made to experience their distance from him also.

8. Finally, the denounced person must be ritually separated from a place in the legitimate order, i.e., he must be defined as standing at a place opposed to it. He must be placed "outside," he must be made "strange."

These are the conditions that must be fulfilled for a successful denunciation. If they are absent, the denunciation will fail. Regardless of the situation when the denouncer enters, if he is to succeed in degrading the other man, it is necessary to introduce these features.[13]

Not all degradation ceremonies are carried on in accordance with publicly prescribed and publicly validated measures. Quarrels which seek the humiliation of the opponent through personal invective may achieve degrading on a limited scale. Comparatively few persons at a time enter into this form of communion, few benefit from it, and the fact of participation does not give the witness a definition of the other that is standardized beyond the particular group or scene of its occurrence.

The devices for effecting degradation vary in the feature and effectiveness according to the organization and operation of the system of action in which they occur. In our society the arena of degradation—whose product, the redefined person, enjoys the widest transferability between groups—has been rationalized, at least as to the institutional measures for carrying it out. The court and its officers have something like a fair monopoly over such ceremonies, and there they have become an occupational routine. This is to be contrasted with degradation undertaken as an immediate kinship and

---

[13] Neither of the problems of possible communicative or organizational conditions of their effectiveness have been treated here in systematic fashion. However, the problem of communicative tactics in degradation ceremonies is set in the light of systematically related conceptions. These conceptions may be listed in the following statements: (1) The definition of the situation of the witnesses (for ease of discourse we shall use the letter S) always bears a time qualification. (2) The S at t_2 is a function of the S at t_1. This function is described as an operator that transforms the S at t_1. (3) The operator is conceived as a communicative work. (4) For a successful denunciation, it is required that the S at t_2 show specific properties. These have been specified previously. (5) The task of the denouncer is to alter the S's of the witnesses so that these S's will show the specified properties. (6) The "rationality" of the denouncer's tactics, i.e., their adequacy as a means for effecting the set of transformations necessary for effecting the identity transformation, is decided by the rule that the organizational and operational properties of the communicative net (the social system) are determinative of the size of the discrepancy between an intended and an actual effect of the communicative work. Put otherwise, the question is not that of the temporal origin of the situation but always and only how it is altered over time. The view is recommended that the definition of the situation at time 2 is a function of the definition at time 1 where this function consists of the communicative work conceived as a set of operations whereby the altered situation at time 1 is the situation at time 2. In strategy terms the function consists of the program of procedures that a denouncer should follow to effect the change of state S_{t1} to S_{t2}. In this paper S_{t1} is treated as an unspecified state.

tribal obligation and carried out by those who, unlike our professional degraders in the law courts, acquire both right and obligation to engage in it through being themselves the injured parties or kin to the injured parties.

Factors conditioning the effectiveness of degradation tactics are provided in the organization and operation of the system of action within which the degradation occurs. For example, timing rules that provide for serial or reciprocal "conversations" would have much to do with the kinds of tactics that one might be best advised to use. The tactics advisable for an accused who can answer the charge as soon as it is made are in contrast with those recommended for one who had to wait out the denunciation before replying. Face-to-face contact is a different situation from that wherein the denunciation and reply are conducted by radio and newspaper. Whether the denunciation must be accomplished on a single occasion or is to be carried out over a sequence of "tries," factors like the territorial arrangements and movements of persons at the scene of the denunciation, the numbers of persons involved as accused, degraders, and witnesses, status claims of the contenders, prestige and power allocations among participants, all should influence the outcome.

In short, the factors that condition the success of the work of degradation are those that we point to when we conceive the actions of a number of persons as group-governed. Only some of the more obvious structural variables that may be expected to serve as predicters of the characteristics of denunciatory communicative tactics have been mentioned. They tell us not only how to construct an effective denunciation but also how to render denunciation useless.

18   CLARK McPHAIL

Student Walkout: A Fortuitous Examination of Elementary Collective Behavior

Sociologists have traditionally separated crowd behavior, if not all elementary collective behavior, from routine social behavior. The separation has involved more than the recognition that behavior patterns can differ substantively in the crowd vis-à-vis the routine social encounter. More frequently

Clark McPhail, "Student Walkout: A Fortuitous Examination of Elementary Collective Behavior, *Social Problems*, vol. 16, no. 4 (Spring 1969), pp. 441–455. Reprinted by permission of The Society for the Study of Social Problems and the author.

Revised version of a paper presented at the annual meetings of The Midwest Sociological Society, 1967. The critical reading and suggestions of Robert L. Stewart, Carl J.

than not, distinctively different explanatory principles have been employed to account for the behavior patterns in these substantively separated areas.[1]

One of the most influential interpretations of collective behavior for the past two decades has been that of Herbert Blumer. He clearly separates the principles by which he accounts for conventional social behavior from those which he introduces to account for collective behavior.

> From one point of view practically all group activity can be thought of as collective behavior. Group activity means that individuals are acting together in some fashion; that there is some fitting together of the different lines of individual conduct. In this sense, group activity is a collective matter. In the classroom, for example, there is a division of labor between the teacher and the students. The students act in expected ways and the teacher, likewise, has a different kind of activity which is expected of him. The activities of the different students and of the teacher fit together to form orderly and concerted group conduct.[2]
>
> . . . the great bulk of collective behavior among human beings occurs because people have common understandings and expectations.[3]

On the other hand:

> A highly excited mob, a business panic, a state of war hysteria, a condition of social unrest represent instances of collective behavior which are [not] of this character. In these instances, the collective behavior arises spontaneously and is not due to pre-established understandings or traditions.[4]

Blumer refers to these phenomena as elementary forms of collective behavior.

> Its elementary nature is suggested by its short life, its spontaneity, its simple forms of emotional interplay, its lack of the delicate and complicated alignment that occurs between self-conscious individuals, and its lack of any intricate organization.[5]

Couch, and Charles W. Tucker have been incorporated into the present version. The data were provided by students at a midwestern college in 1965. The participation and contribution of all the aforementioned persons is gratefully acknowledged.

[1] E. A. Ross, *Social Psychology*, New York: Macmillan, 1908; R. E. Park, "Collective Behavior," in E. R. A. Seligman, editor, *Encyclopedia of the Social Sciences*, New York: Macmillan, 1930, 31, p. 631; H. A. Blumer, "Collective Behavior," in A. M. Lee, editor, *Principles of Sociology*, New York: Barnes and Noble, 1946; R. H. Turner and L. M. Killian, *Collective Behavior*, Englewood Cliffs, N.J.: Prentice-Hall, 1957; K. Lang and G. L. Lang, *Collective Dynamics*, New York: Crowell, 1961; T. Shibutani, "Suggestibility and Behavioral Contagion," in his *Improvised News*, Indianapolis: Bobbs-Merrill, 1966, pp. 95–128. The influence of LeBon on this American tradition is quite clear. Each of those cited above makes extensions and refinements of LeBon's ideas but maintains his separation and separate explanations of collective behavior from conventional human behavior. G. LeBon, *La Psychologie des Foules*, Paris: Olean, 1895; *The Crowd*, New York: Viking, 1960.

[2] Blumer, *op. cit.*, p. 167.

[3] *Ibid.*, p. 168.

[4] *Ibid.*

[5] H. Blumer, "Collective Behavior," in J. B. Gittler, editor, *Review of Sociology*, New York: Wiley, 1957, p. 131.

Based on this characterization, Blumer developed a separate set of explanatory principles to account for this different behavior. These separate principles emphasize spontaneous and "circular reaction" among individual participants resulting in the development of homogenous patterns of behavior.[6] This emphasis has directed the attention of students of collective behavior away from the principles Blumer employs to account for routine social behavior, viz., the fitting together of individual lines of conduct in terms of the common expectations and understandings of the participants.

The present paper is addressed to two questions concerning the traditional treatment of elementary collective behavior by sociologists in general and by Blumer in particular. First, are different principles of explanation required for the substantively different patterns which may be observed in collective versus routine social behavioral settings? Second, are the principles Blumer employs to account for social behavior restricted to such routine settings as the classroom?

Recent theoretical treatments of collective behavior have emphasized convergence with interpretations of more routine social behavior. Smelser[7] and Turner[8] have developed or applied explanatory principles which they contend are applicable to both collective and routine social behavioral settings. Irrespective of the merits of their somewhat different sets of explanatory principles, credit is due their attempts to develop parsimonious approaches to human social behavior across substantively different areas. The present paper is an additional effort toward such parsimonious development.[9]

Descriptions of and reports by participants in panic crowds and disaster situations question the restriction of many of Blumer's explanatory principles to routine social behavioral settings.[10] Participants report attention to one another's behavior and the construction of coordinated, differential, and similar lines of behavior based upon those cues.[11] Such illustrative evidence

---

[6] Blumer, 1946, *op. cit.*, pp. 170–171.

[7] N. J. Smelser, *Theory of Collective Behavior*, New York: Free Press, 1963, p. 23.

[8] R. H. Turner, "Collective Behavior," in R. E. L. Faris, editor, *Handbook of Modern Sociology*, Chicago: Rand McNally, 1964, p. 384.

[9] Another recent effort to accomplish such a convergence is R. R. Dynes and E. L. Quarantelli, "Group Behavior Under Stress: A Required Convergence of Organizational and Collective Behavior Perspectives," *Sociology and Social Research*, 52 (1968), pp. 416–428.

[10] W. H. Form and C. P. Loomis, "The Persistence and Emergence of Social and Cultural Systems in Disaster," *American Sociological Review*, 21 (1956), pp. 180–185. E. L. Quarantelli, "The Behavior of Panic Participants," *Sociology and Social Research*, 41 (1957), pp. 187–194, and "Images of Withdrawal Behavior in Disasters: Some Basic Misconceptions," *Social Problems*, 8 (1960), pp. 68–79.

[11] Human beings fit together similar and different lines of behavior in routine and problematic situations. Attention must be given to one's behavior in relation to that of another when fitting together the similar behaviors involved in exciting a classroom, walking through shopping center malls, or turning over an automobile. The same is

questions the separation of routine from collective behavioral phenomena maintained by Blumer's position. The present paper presents data which further challenge such a separation.

The principles of social behavior suggested by Mead, Blumer, and others of their theoretical persuasion, require attention to what people do with and in relation to one another. In routine encounters, the regularities in participants' behavior toward one another are based upon shared identifications and expectations for regularities in the behavior of persons so identified.[12] As long as the behavior of each participant permits the other participants to maintain their identification of and claims upon one another, their respective performances will be coordinated in routine fashion. An ongoing course of coordinated behavior can be deflected by an act or acts of the participants or by some intruder. When the complementary activities of the participants are deflected, a problematic situation is said to exist. A fundamental sociological notion is that the responses of the participants to the deflecting act or acts will determine the resolution of the problematic course of action; it may continue, or it may be terminated, modified, or replaced with a different course of action.[13]

An empirical examination of these views requires observations of: 1) participants fitting together a routine sequence of behaviors; 2) the deflection of that sequence of behaviors;[14] and 3) participants' efforts at resolving the problematic sequence of behaviors. Most frequently, problematic lines of coordinated behavior resume their original form with only minor adjustments. Less frequently participants are unable to fit together either their previous routine or some alternate line of behaviors and must, consequently, go their separate ways. On other occasions, alternated lines of behavior are fitted together in the construction of a new course of collective behavior. Opportunities are rare to observe such sequences and to obtain detailed data about and/or from participants during and immediately after their routine behaviors are deflected. Such an opportunity was recently afforded the present writer.

---

true when fitting the different behaviors together necessary for a symphony orchestra performance, for purchasing cigarettes from a clerk, engaging in sexual intercourse, or engaging in a fistfight.

[12] N. Foote, "Identification as a Basis for a Theory of Motivation," *American Sociological Review*, 16 (1951), pp. 14–21.

[13] G. H. Mead, *The Philosophy of the Act*, Chicago: U. of Chicago, pp. 82–83. An extension of this line of reasoning to interpret the production and development of interest groups is found in N. Foote and C. W. Hart, "Public Opinion and Collective Behavior," in M. Sherif and M. O. Wilson, editors, *Group Relations at the Crossroads*, N.Y.: Harper, 1953, pp. 308–333.

[14] If the assumption is granted that human beings are continuously active, then only portions of activity are deflected and in turn modified, replaced, or terminated at any one time, i.e., total activity is terminated only in death.

Source and Analysis of Data

While lecturing to a class of 25 students, all but two members of the class walked out of the room ten minutes before the end of the writer's lecture. The lecturer recovered in a sufficiently brief period of time to contact the majority of the students on the same afternoon as the walkout. Detailed written reports were obtained from 21 of the students involved, including the two students who did not walk out. Verbatim statements were extracted from these reports to construct a description of the sequence of events.[15] These descriptive data, provided by the participants, are used to outline and illustrate some rudimentary principles of human social behavior in routine and non-routine situations. The theoretical framework within which these principles are developed is briefly outlined in the following section.

Theoretical Perspective

Students of social behavior frequently use such expressions as the aligning, coordinating, or fitting together of the respective lines of behavior of participants. How this fitting together is accomplished remains a central question. George H. Mead suggested that human beings accomplish this by calling out in themselves the response of the other to their own conduct.[16] Two classes of behaviors are viewed as central to this anticipatory process of "taking the attitude of the others:" designating behaviors and prescribing behaviors.[17] Designating behaviors locate and identify acting units.[18] Designating behaviors are the answers given to questions such as "Who am I?," "Who are we?," "Who is he?," "Who are they?," and "What is that?" To establish the identities of acting units is to construct a relationship between the namer and the named.[19] Thus, designating behaviors establish social relationships. Prescribing behaviors specify some course of action toward or

---

[15] All statements included in the descriptive sequence of events should be considered representative unless otherwise indicated. Where appropriate, the proportion of respondents citing a particular phenomenon is indicated. The names of persons mentioned by respondents have been replaced by pseudonyms. The numbers preceding the verbatim statements are respondent code numbers, e.g., R. *01–21*, and are not to be confused with frequencies.

[16] G. H. Mead, "The Genesis of the Self and Social Control," *International Journal of Ethics*, 35 (1924–1925), pp. 251–277.

[17] Robert L. Stewart first directed my attention to the importance of designating and prescribing behaviors and suggested many of the basic ideas stated in this paper concerning the consequence of those classes of behaviors in the organization of social behavior.

[18] I am using the term designating behavior as synonymous with but more generic than such prevalent terms as identification, naming, and labeling. For a similar usage see Charles W. Morris, *Signification and Significance*, Cambridge: M.I.T., 1964, pp. 1–15.

[19] A. Strauss, following K. Burke, discusses naming as an act of relational placement. See, respectively, *Mirrors and Masks*, Glencoe: Free Press, 1959, p. 19; and *A Grammar of Motives*, N.Y.: Prentice-Hall, 1945, p. 24.

from designated acting units and thus provide the substantive content of social relationships. Prescribing behaviors are answers given to the question: "What is expected from designated acting units and what may be done to them?"

Congruent designating and prescribing behaviors among acting units make possible the coordination of their respective individual lines of behavior.[20] Further, a coordinated line of behavior will be maintained or will recur until rendered problematic by some deflecting action.[21] Ordinarily, then, social relationships between students and teachers, husbands and wives, or majority and minority group members are performed in routine fashion. In the absence of deflecting actions, designating and prescribing behaviors continue and permit the ongoing coordination of individual lines of behavior.

It is clear that some departures from conventional performances are ignored or squelched and participants continue in their respective, complementary lines of behavior.[22] Nonetheless, the departure from routine performances gives evidence to all who observe that such action can be taken; the response of participants to that action determines whether it will be continued, modified, or terminated.[23] Garfinkel's research on the routine grounds of everyday activities clearly illustrates the deflecting consequences of violating common expectations for participants' behaviors in routine

[20] Blumer's formulation allows for congruent designating and prescribing behaviors and consequent coordinated behavior, but, only in routine settings. Blumer, *op. cit.* The writer's observations of the behaviors taken *among* demonstrators with regard to police (and presumably among police with regard to demonstrators) suggest that presence or absence of congruent designating and prescribing behaviors is consequential for coordination of behavior in these non-routine settings as well.

[21] W. Catton argues that an axiom of inertia is fundamental for a naturalistic sociology. Such an axiom holds that a pattern of social behavior will continue to manifest itself at unaltered rates unless some social force modifies the pattern or rate. *From Animistic to Naturalistic Sociology*, N.Y.: McGraw-Hill, 1966, p. 235. My preference is to explicitly attend to the behaviors of individual and collective acting units, vis-à-vis "social forces," which can deflect coordinated lines of behavior.

[22] T. Scheff suggests that much "residual deviance" is either transitory or denied. "The Role of the Mentally Ill and the Dynamics of Mental Disorder," *Sociometry*, 26 (1963), pp. 441–442. Some evidence bearing on this is M. Yarow *et al.*, "The Psychological Meaning of Mental Illness in the Family," *Journal of Social Issues*, 11 (1955), pp. 12–24. See Table 2: Wives' "Initial Interpretations of the Husband's Behavior."

[23] Labeling theory has emphasized the importance of other's designations for the stabilization of deviant behavior. See Scheff, *op. cit.*, p. 451. These designating or labeling behaviors are of consequence, however, in terms of the alteration in relationships between designators and designated and the alteration in coordinated performances permitted, required, or precluded by the relationship. New or alternate designations may permit or preclude the continued coordination of similar performances, may permit or require the coordination of alternate performances, or may preclude any coordination of similar or alternate performances in terms of the relationship established by the designations. From this perspective the reciprocity of participants' responses to a deviant performance must be examined rather than assigning singular responsibility for the outcome to the behavior of the designator or the designated.

social encounters.[24] The performance of a line of conduct which departs from what is expected of or prescribed for a designated acting unit can deflect the coordination of behaviors among participants. Gross and Stone's research suggests that such departures can require altered identifications of performers. As a consequence, "when inappropriate identities are established or appropriate identities are lost, role performance is impossible."[25] Thus, alternate designations can and do deflect the coordination of behaviors. Garfinkel's specification of the sequence of actions necessary to transform the "public identity" of a person illustrates the consequences of alternate designating behaviors for social relationships and contingent coordinated behavior.[26] The following reports of participants in a classroom walkout suggest that the interdependence of designations, prescriptions, and performances are of central importance for maintaining an old or developing a new line of coordinated behavior.

Routine and New Lines of Behavior

New lines of coordinated behavior are initiated in response to the deflection of previous lines of behavior. One type of deflection is a performance which departs from what is routinely prescribed.

> R.08 . . . the idea of staging a classroom walkout first came when the professor told the class about an experiment in which the lecturer nonchalantly left the room in the middle of the class and in the middle of a sentence.
> R.10 . . . the professor mentioned the fact that he had considered walking out of class during a lecture and not returning. He not only said he had considered doing it, he demonstrated by walking out the door how he would have done it.

It was noted earlier, however, that the response to the deflection is crucial in determining whether the problematic course of action will be continued, modified, terminated, or replaced. *The development of a new line of coordinated behavior requires the proposal and organization of those behaviors by at least some of the participant acting units.* Without that organization, a new line of coordinated behavior cannot develop.

> R.16 . . . several of us were walking to class and discussing the feasibility of 'out experimenting the experimenter' and walking out of class in the

[24] H. Garfinkel, "Studies in the Routine Grounds of Everyday Activities," *Social Problems*, 11 (1964), pp. 225–250.
[25] E. Gross and G. Stone, "Embarrassment and the Analysis of Role Requirements," *American Journal of Sociology*, 70 (1964), p. 3.
[26] H. Garfinkel, "Conditions of Successful Degradation Ceremonies," *American Journal of Sociology*, 61 (1956), pp. 420–424.

middle of a lecture. . . . On this day, however, our professor arrived just after we'd taken our seats and there was no time to discuss the idea with the rest of the class.

On a subsequent day, the proposal and organization of the new line of co-ordinated behavior did develop among some of the participant acting units.

> R.16 When we reached the class, our professor had not arrived, so we sat around talking about what a beautiful day it was, and how none of us felt like studying. At this time a girl suggested asking the professor if we could have class . . . in the union so we could all get a cup of coffee. Suddenly, I remembered our idea from the preceding class period. "Hey," I broke in, "He's not here yet; today would be a perfect day to stage the walkout."

Turner[27] and Couch[28] have recently discussed a rather prevalent mis-conception about the spontaneity of new patterns of coordinated behavior. They suggest a continuity between old and new lines of behavior. One aspect of that continuity, noted above, is that the latter emerges or develops in response to some deflection of the former. Another aspect is that *new lines of coordinated behavior always involved a new or different sequencing of old elements of behavior, skill, and/or knowledge.* Whether the new pattern of behavior involved preparing and hurling a molotov cocktail, taking an item from a store and walking out with it, or walking out of a class-room, the component activities do not spontaneously emerge; rather, there is a new and different sequencing of the component behaviors.

Establishing New Relationships

If routine patterns of coordinated behavior are the product of routine social relationships, then new patterns of coordinated behavior must be similarly produced. Routine social relationships can impede if not preclude participation in new lines of social behavior.[29] If the person is to participate in a new line of behavior with others, old relationships must be altered or replaced. *New relationships among participant acting units are required for the development and implementation of a new line of coordinated behavior.*[30]

In his discussion of the construction of a new line of conduct, Ralph Turner has mentioned, in order, the following three factors: a concern on

---

[27] Turner, *op. cit.*, p. 384.

[28] C. J. Couch, "Collective Behavior: An Examination of Some Stereotypes," *Social Problems*, 15 (Winter, 1968), pp. 310–322.

[29] G. Marx reports data showing an inverse relationship between implication in religious activities and support for militant civil rights activities. "Religion: Opiate or Inspiration," *American Sociological Review*, 32 (1967), pp. 64–72.

[30] Couch, *op. cit.*, p. 320.

the part of participants with rules; attempts to define the situation; and determination of leaders who will legitimate the rules and initiate action.[31] While each of these phenomena *may* occur, the order of their appearance and consequence must be somewhat different from that suggested by Turner. In line with my earlier comments, designating behaviors locate and differentiate "leaders" from "other participants" and thus make all designated acting units liable for corresponding prescriptions for behavior. These acts constitute a "definition of the situation." Thus, *new relationships are established by new or alternate designations of participant acting units.*[32]

The reports of the participants in the walkout included new or alternate designations of both professor and students. These designations established new relationships among the students as well as between the students and the professor. The following report illustrates some of the acts involved in establishing a new relationship among the students.

> R.11 When I walked into the classroom . . . I could tell something was going on. There were relatively few students in the room but most of them were whispering to each other. After a minute or so [Ann] turned to me and whispered: "The whole class is going to walk out at 1:40 to see what the professor will do." I thought that was a good idea so I said, "That's cool; do you think everybody will do it?" She said, "Yeah, [R.16] started it."

Nine of the 21 respondents designated R.16 as "the leader" and/or "a senior sociology major who had taken several courses with the professor and knew him quite well." While this was in fact erroneous, it served to designate R.16 as one who could propose such an alternate course of action. Similarly, designating acts were taken which constructed an alternate relationship between the students and the professor. The professor was designated as one who had suggested walking out of class earlier himself; as one supportive of students "experimenting" with ideas acquired in classes; and as one deserving of the walkout given his own past manipulations of students in similar situations.

> R.04 . . . the professor would realize that this was a sort of experiment, that we had only missed eight minutes of class, and would merely laugh the whole thing off as a combination student prank and experiment pertaining to the subject matter of the course.
> R.05 After all, a lot of other experiments were instigated by the professor around town and on campus. . . . It seemed only right and natural that we try an experiment on him especially one which he himself had suggested.
> R.16 There were a few people who worried about whether the professor would be angry, but we decided if we left at 1:45, only five minutes be-

---

[31] Turner, *op. cit.*, p. 395.
[32] This seems to be a fundamental principle in H. Garfinkel's discussion of successful degradation ceremonies, *op. cit.*

fore the class was supposed to end, he would not be too upset; besides, he himself had experimented on many classes.

The students clearly designated the professor as one toward whom a new line of behavior could be taken. At the same time, however, the students scheduled their performance of the new line of behavior sufficiently late in the lecture period so that it would preclude the professor's designation of them as totally disinterested or irresponsible.

> R.19 . . . a time for the walkout had to be decided upon and 1:15 was suggested as a possibility. But someone remarked that this was too early and the professor might be irritated if we left that early. Next the time of 1:45 was suggested and everyone seemed to agree that it was a good time because it was near the end of the period and we wouldn't miss too much of the lecture material.

Proposals for and Commitments to a New Line of Behavior

The suggestion was made earlier that at least some of the participant acting units must be involved in the proposal and organization of a new line of behavior to assure its development. The participants' reports indicate that all the students were not involved in the proposal and organization of the walkout.

> R.02 Although the girls asked everyone who was in the class *early* if they would walk out of the class at "a quarter to two" and most answered that they would, it appeared to me that many students did not know beforehand what was coming. (Respondent's emphasis.)
> R.20 I was asked, "Say, do you know about the walkout?" and then was asked, "Well, are you going to do it?" At this point I had still not heard any attempted formulation of the purpose of the walkout or any true confirmation that it was an . . . experiment. These thoughts had an influence on my reply, which amounted to a series of noncommittal mumblings, ending up with, "I don't see any purpose in it."

It should come as no surprise that R.20 did not participate in the walkout and that R.02 was the last student to leave the room at the time of the walkout.

R.20's report suggests another aspect of the organization of a new line of coordinated behavior, namely, the presence or absence of overt acts of commitment to participate in the new line of behavior. Public declarations of intention to commit some line of action involve a self-designation in the presence of others who can place appropriate claims on one who is so designated. Thus, *the successful implementation of a new line of coordinated conduct is directly related to the commitments which acting units make to one another to perform the new line of conduct.*[33]

> R.21 Many of us enthusiastically joked about . . . [the walkout] . . . but [R.16] asked seriously if we'd go along with it. Students looked around at each other first, then most affirmed the action either vocally or with some gesture. I myself said I'd go anytime but not first.

Sixteen of the 21 participants mentioned their intention, at this point, to take part in the walkout; less than half this number, however, reported a public statement of commitment to participate in the new line of behavior. An important consideration, then, is the proportion of participants who must make public commitments in order for the new line of behavior to be implemented, and the manner in which that proportion is secured.

> R.14 Then someone turned to me and said, "Will you go along with it?" Without much thought about purpose or consequence I said I would. My only thoughts were that if *everyone else was going to do it, it would be safe for me to do it also,* and I did not want to hold out and ruin it for the other people. (Emphasis supplied.)

The preceding participant's report of attention to an inferred majority in the formulation of his own decision to walk out, points to an important phenomenon in the development of a new line of collective behavior. Turner suggests that "if the ability to carry out a [new or unusual] course of action successfully is often a consideration in judging it legitimate, the apparent power of the crowd adds to its displacements of the usual behavioral anchorages."[34] The course of action at issue here is the student's public commitment to participate in the walkout. Following Turner's reasoning, as more students followed this course of action without deflection in the form of challenge or dissent, the course of action was increasingly viewed as legitimate. It may be the case that the proportion of students taking the action, i.e., the size of the majority, is not so important as the absence of challenge or dissent to the course of action. Asch's research, for example, showed that a majority of three produced as much compliance as a majority of 10–15. However, he also found that a majority of three without a dissenter produced more compliance than a majority of eight with one dis-

---

[33] H. S. Becker, "Notes on the Concept of Commitment," *American Journal of Sociology,* 62 (1960), pp. 32–40. Empirical evidence bearing on the consequence of commitments to others is found in R. R. Blake and J. S. Mouton, "Loyalty of Representatives to Ingroup Positions during Intergroup Competition," *Sociometry,* 24 (1961), p. 181.

[34] Turner, *op. cit.,* p. 386. This notion dates back as early as LeBon's statement that "An isolated individual knows well enough that alone he cannot set fire to a palace or loot a shop. [but making him a part of a crowd] . . . *he is conscious of the power given him by number . . ." op. cit.,* p. 38. (Emphasis supplied.) It is interesting to note that on this point, LeBon contradicts his contention that members of a crowd are not conscious of their actions.

senter.[35] A tentative principle summarizing the foregoing suggests that *when any proportion of acting units engage in a course of action which is not deflected, the likelihood of compliance on the part of the remaining acting units is increased.* This appears to provide behavioral referents for what Turner and other students have referred to as "the apparent power of the crowd."[36]

Synchronizing New Lines of Behavior

Even though the participants agreed that the new line of conduct should take place near the end of the forthcoming lecture period, there was no consensus as to the specific time at which the walkout would occur nor was there any specification of a keynoting activity or acting unit. Six of the 21 reports mentioned 1:40, 11 mentioned 1:45, and the rest made no mention or indicated confusion about the time of the walkout. Congruent designating and prescribing behaviors, establishing "who" will do "what," are necessary for the coordination of individual lines of conduct. In addition, the specification of "when" acting units will perform is necessary in order to synchronize their respective lines of behavior. For example, students are expected to be seated in the classroom, to direct their attention to the front of the room, take notes, refrain from talking, etc. However, these behaviors are prescribed for specified time frames designated by such activities as the ringing of a bell, a professor's actions, etc. Similarly, students are expected to leave the classroom at the end of a specified time frame which is designated by the ringing of a bell, a professor's action, etc. Without the timing of these prescribed performances, the routine coordination of behaviors would be impossible. The independent deviation of one or two students from this routine does not deflect the continued coordination of behaviors among others, e.g., some students may arrive late, look out the window, or leave early without disturbing the class routine. But, if the late arrival, looking out the window, or early departure is a joint enterprise involving the fitting together of two or more individual lines of conduct, some synchronizing of these lines of conduct must be consensually established. The participants in the walkout did not attend to this aspect of con-

---

[35] S. Asch, "Effects of Group Pressure Upon the Modification and Distortion of Judgments," in H. Proshansky and B. Seidenberg, editors, *Basic Studies in Social Psychology*, N.Y.: Holt, Rinehart and Winston, 1966, pp. 309 and 310.

[36] It remains an empirical question as to what proportion of participants in a crowd must follow a course of action *in the presence of deflection*, before compliance is forthcoming from the remaining participants. Casual observations suggest that although some participants may initially express reservations about pursuing a new course of action, these deflections are squelched or ignored as an increasing proportion of participants advocate or pursue the new course of action.

structing the new line of action and their failure to do so handicapped the smooth implementation of their plan.

Routine Relationships and Behaviors

The specification of a keynoting activity or acting unit might have been accomplished had the professor not arrived at this point. His arrival initiated the classroom routine which in turn interrupted the planning activities of the students.

> R.07 When the professor entered, students immediately prepared to take notes and because of the standard atmosphere that existed, (class behavior seemed to be like any other day), I completely forgot about the intended walkout.
> R.19 Since I was sitting in the front of the room, I became very engrossed with the lecture of the day and hardly noticed the time go by.
> R.18 I didn't think about the walkout very much (I was busy taking notes) until a few moments before we were supposed to leave.

So far as the professor observed, the students' behavior seemed to be like any other day. Correspondingly, 11 of the 21 participants, including the three quoted above, reported that they had given the majority of their attention to the lecture and had forgotten about what had been planned. On the other hand, eight of the participants reported difficulty in concentrating on the lecture or in forgetting about the pending walkout.

> R.12 The thought of the walkout ruined all lines of concentration for me and I continued to stare out the window. . . . It was such a beautiful day outside I just wanted to get out in it. I thought about how tired I was and lit a cigarette so that I wouldn't fall asleep.
> R.09 Once the plan had been formed, it was extremely difficult to sit through 45 minutes of class.

Even these participants, however, did not behave in a manner noticeably different from the rest. The result was to facilitate the continuation of routine classroom behaviors and to leave the tasks of establishing the time of departure and the keynoting activities incomplete.

The professor lectured during the first 30 minutes of the class period. This activity elicited attention to him and made it difficult for students to further organize their departure. After the first 30 minutes, at about 1:30, the professor shifted from lecturing to answering questions from and asking questions of students about the lecture. This not only permitted students to attend to each other but required that they do so. It also allowed students to look at a clock or at watches and thus to take up again the problem of synchronizing. Correspondingly, some of the participants reported giving attention to time at this point.

R.19 When I finally glanced at my watch, it was 1:30.

R.07 I suddenly remembered our intentions as I glanced down at my watch —it was 1:30.

After the question and answer session proceeded for approximately ten minutes, the professor shifted back to the final portion of his lecture. Again this shift in his activity deflected the students' activities. One student reports:

R.16 As the appointed time drew close, I grew more nervous and excited. At 1:40 [ten minutes prior to the end of the period] I glanced to my left and panicked as I saw one of the girls toward the back begin to fold up her notebook and get her books together. I tried to signal her that she was too early and that we weren't leaving until 1:45, but I only succeeded in confusing her. She began looking around for validation. Since no one else in the class appeared to be getting ready to depart, she merely sat with her hands folded and her books in a pile. At this point, I began to get very nervous wondering if others in the class were similarly confused, and if so, would they still have the courage to take part.

The approximate time for the walkout was approaching but the absence of a specified time or keynoting action to synchronize the participants' individual lines of action proved problematic. Prior to the lecture, 16 of the 21 students reported their intention to participate in the walkout near the end of the period. However, as that point approached, 13 of the 21 reported doubts: whether or not the walkout would now occur; who would have the courage to take the first step; whether others would participate; or whether they would themselves participate.

R.12 At 1:40 no one moved. I started to put my things away quietly so that the professor wouldn't notice anything. [Fran] did the same thing and so did some of the other kids around me. But still, no one moved. Well, I wasn't going to be the first to go because I thought maybe they had changed their minds and wouldn't follow.

R.11 One point is important, however. I didn't want to initiate action when the plan was endangered by some changes in the planned time for the walkout. I suppose now that I wanted to slip back into the established routine, instead of doing something drastic . . .

R.09 I wanted to do it, but I didn't want to be the leader. I wondered if everyone else would walk out or if they would just sit there. Part of me hoped we'd just forget the idea and yet I wanted to get up and leave.

Implementing a Proposed Line of Behavior

When acting units have committed themselves to a line of coordinated action but have not specified procedures by which their respective actions will be synchronized, the coordinated action cannot develop. In such situations the attention of the acting units will invariably be directed to one another rather than to the object of the proposed action. Participants may then claim prior commitments of one another in the form of reminders, challenges, or taunts.

> R.18 At 1:40, several people were still looking around, apparently waiting for someone to take a line of action. I was hesitant about initiating the walkout by myself, preferring to let someone else make the first move. At this point, [R.06], sitting next to me, and I asked each other something like, "Well, are we going to leave or not?" Then we both got up simultaneously and began walking toward the door . . . I'm not sure whether or not I would have initiated the walkout by myself. I know that I would have been hesitant.

The confederate keynoter reports:

> R.06 Before the walkout, I weighed the pro's and con's of getting out from my desk. I figured that if no one followed I'd go straight to the professor's office and wait for him. [R.18] and I looked at each other, said, "Shall we?" and left the room. My thoughts at the time were directed at the doorknob, turning it, and getting out. To my delightful surprise, once I did get out I noticed everyone was coming.

Altogether, 18 of the 21 participants report their attention to the actions of their fellows prior to their own departure from the classroom.

> R.14 A general restlessness began as people started closing their notebooks and the boy who had taken the leadership position on himself stood up. . . . I knew that he had to be followed or the whole plan would fall through. In a matter of seconds everyone was up and heading for the door, so my momentary hesitation was gone and I felt secure in the knowledge that I was not alone.
>
> R.19 I then waited for more students to leave before I made any preparation to leave. I guess I was waiting for my . . . activity to be confirmed by more students. As soon as I saw other students leaving I grabbed my books as fast as I could and headed for the door.
>
> R.11 Then several others, among them [Joyce] and her girlfriend stood up, too, and within seconds most of the class was nervously on its feet, . . . We exchanged grins to affirm each others' behavior. I stood up and put on my coat. Then I saw that [Ann] was still sitting down; so I said, "Come on, it's gonna work!" and she got up too and walked out.

"Human group life consists of the fitting together of the lines of action of the participants."[37] An examination of these data suggests that this fundamental principle holds for new as well as routine lines of social behavior. Contrary to Blumer's position that any new line of collective (i.e., social) behavior ". . . arises spontaneously and is not due to pre-established understanding or traditions,"[38] these data suggest that social behavior

---

[37] H. Blumer, "Reply to Woelfel, Stone and Farberman," *American Journal of Sociology*, 72 (1967), p. 411.
[38] Blumer, 1947, *op. cit.*, p. 167.

is not spontaneous; rather, acts are taken in relation to acts. Further, "shared understandings" are continually, although not continuously, constructed in the actions of participants with one another.[39] The preceding participants' reports have clearly demonstrated this to be the case for the lines of action taken by the students in relation to one another.

Unanticipated Consequences

An examination of the response of the professor to the students' new line of collective action suggests another fundamental principle. *The development of a new line of conduct toward an acting unit not implicated in its proposal and organization is facilitated by that acting unit's continued performance of old lines of conduct and/or disorganized response to the new line of conduct.*

> R.04 [The professor] was not upset when he saw the two boys stand up to leave, for there are many times when students will have to leave classes early for a number of common reasons. When the entire class followed, however, his sentences became disconnected until he finally stopped speaking with a bewildered expression on his face. He made no attempt to try to stop the class and seemed stunned, merely wanting an explanation of what was going on.
>
> R.18 At no time did the professor attempt to stop the walkout. If he had become upset and ordered the class to return, I'm sure we would have done so.
>
> R.07 The professor's reaction was unexpected—"Hey, did the bell ring already?"—and then as we were almost out [of the room] "Well, I'll finish the lecture for you two." These two comments, especially the first one, coupled with the look on his face, had a sort of sanctioning effect on me. I can remember thinking as I was walking, that if he had said or made some kind of dissenting word or objection that our action might have been different.

The behavior of the professor was deflected by the early departure of the two students who were seated near the back of the classroom. Such a departure, as noted above, is not unusual. Unfortunately, the professor made reference to the departure in the context of his comments. Alluding to some just-mentioned incidents of violent gang behavior, the professor wryly remarked: "I hope I didn't offend you two with the examples" and then glanced back at his lecture notes. When he looked up again, the entire class, save two, was either rising to its feet or on the way out the back door of the classroom. His next responses were: "What—what's going on, is class over already?" and "Hey, did the bell ring already?" "Did my watch stop?"

The professor's responses had two significant consequences for the devel-

---

[39] Strauss, *op. cit.*, p. 25.

opment of the new line of behavior. First, his comments to the two key-noting students clearly indicated to the remaining students that the time for the walkout had arrived. The comments had the unanticipated consequence of synchronizing the participants respective lines of behavior. Second, the sputtering and stammering of the professor, in his attempt to account for the behavior which had been deflected—his own—did nothing to render problematic the developing new line of behavior undertaken by the students. Quite the contrary, his actions facilitated the development of the new line of behavior.

The Deviant Cases

Two students did not join their fellows in the new line of behavior. An examination of the acts which they took at the time the walkout was proposed and organized, as well as their actions at the time of implementation, provides a partial explanation of their deviant performance. One of the two deviants had initially agreed to participate in the walkout. As the lecture period developed, however, he reports a reconsideration of that intention.

> R.21 When [R.16] suggested the walkout, I consented uncritically. However, after the class began, the situation became questionable to me. I first wondered what the purpose of the walkout was. If no one stayed, the professor would simply leave and nothing would be accomplished [i.e., we wanted to observe his reactions] . . . I began to wonder if [R.16] was trying some experiment on her own, or if she was a confederate of the professor in some type of study. . . . As the time grew near, I started feeling uncomfortable. My stomach grew tense.

When the keynoting action was taken and the majority of the students had followed course, the same student—sitting in the back row of the classroom—gave the following report.

> R.21 When the students filed out, I felt very conspicuous; nervous but defiant. I noticed [R.20] and wondered if he was going to leave. When he didn't I felt a little relieved. Still my face was stinging and I couldn't understand much of what the professor said.

The reader will recall that R.20 declined to commit himself to participate in the walkout when this line of action was proposed and organized prior to the lecture period. He had arrived late and had not ". . . heard any attempted formulation of the purpose of the walkout or any true confirmation that it was an . . . experiment." This student, sitting in the front row of the classroom, reported the following:

> R.20 Realization of the start of the walkout came when I heard a great rustling behind me and almost simultaneously I saw the professor look

at his watch [and] say, "What-what's going on, is class over already?" In about one to two minutes the room was empty with the exception of myself and another student. The professor was bewildered and I was uncontrollably blushing. I remember turning around to the other remaining student [R.21] and raising my hands in a bewildered expression. By this action I think I was looking for some sort of confirmation or support for my actions. I believe he replied with almost the same actions.

And what of the professor's subsequent actions? One of the departing students, quoted earlier, recalled the professor's comments to the remaining students: ". . . as we were almost out [of the room, he said], 'Well, I'll finish the lecture for you two.' " The professor did have five minutes of prepared comments remaining and there were two students left to listen to those comments. "In the classroom . . . there is a division of labor between the teacher and the students. The students act in expected ways and the teacher, likewise, has a different kind of activity which is expected of him."[40] Had all the students left, there would have been no one to teach; had the teacher left, the remaining students would have had no one to study. While this does not provide a conclusive interpretation, the interdependence of the respective behaviors of the professor and students cannot be ignored.

Summary

The reports of participants in a classroom walkout have been used to construct the sequence of events involved in deflecting routine and constructing new lines of social behavior. These data provide an empirical record of the initiation and development of an elementary form of collective behavior. Repeated examples are provided of some rudimentary principles of social behavior which have previously been restricted to the ongoing construction of routine lines of social behavior. The applicability of these principles to the production, maintenance, and alteration of social behavior in routine and collective behavioral settings follows Turner's suggestions. The examination of collective behavior events may possibly ". . . undermine all of the traditional dynamic distinctions between collective behavior and organizational behavior and suggest that no special set of principles is required to deal with this subject matter."[41]

[40] Blumer, *op. cit.*, p. 167.
[41] Turner, *op. cit.*, p. 384.

Selected Bibliography II

Couch, Carl J. "Dimensions of Association in Collective Behavior Episodes." *Sociometry*, vol. 33 (December 1970), pp. 457–471. Challenges the need for a special set of concepts in the examination of collective, as opposed to societal, behavior.

Coutu, Walter. "Role-Playing vs. Role-Taking: An Appeal for Clarification." *American Sociological Review*, vol. 16 (April 1951), pp. 180–187. Precursor of Turner's paper, below. Shows the need for a clearer distinction between two useful and closely related concepts.

Davis, Fred. "The Cab Driver and His Fare: Facets of a Fleeting Relationship." *American Journal of Sociology*, vol. 65 (September 1959), pp. 158–165. Participant-observation study of a special kind of human encounter.

———. "Deviance Disavowal: The Management of Strained Interaction by the Visibly Handicapped." *Social Problems*, vol. 9 (Fall 1961), pp. 120–132. Empirical study of the way in which individuals with visible physical handicaps seek to normalize interaction with others.

Duncan, Hugh Dalziel. *Symbols in Society*. New York: Oxford University Press, 1968. Focuses on the symbolic act as the unit of social performance, presenting over seventy semi-intuitive, axiomatic, theoretical, and methodological propositions.

Garfinkel, Harold. "Studies of the Routine Grounds of Everyday Activities." *Social Problems*, vol. 11 (Winter 1964), pp. 225–250. Inspired by Alfred Schuetz's phenomenology. An insightful delineation of taken-for-granted elements in everyday human relationships.

Goffman, Erving. *Asylums*. Garden City, New York: Doubleday & Company, Inc., 1961. Description of "total institutions" (prisons, mental hospitals, convents, orphanages, and other societies-in-miniature) and the kinds of interaction typifying them.

———. "On Face-Work: An Analysis of Ritual Elements in Social Interaction." *Psychiatry*, vol. 18 (August 1955), pp. 213–231. Discusses the elaborate social rituals that function primarily to reduce the likelihood of invalidation of self-image, particularly in casual contacts.

Gross, Edward, and Gregory P. Stone. "Embarrassment and the Analysis of Role Requirements." *American Journal of Sociology*, vol. 60 (July 1964), pp. 1–15. Study of 1,000 instances of recalled embarrassment, revealing some major sociological functions of deliberate embarrassment.

Mead, George Herbert. *Mind, Self and Society*. Chicago: The University of Chicago Press, 1934, pp. 260–328. Mead here explores the complex relationship between society and the individual.

Riezler, Kurt. "Comment on the Social Psychology of Shame." *American Journal of Sociology*, vol. 48 (January 1943), pp. 457–465. Insightful speculations about a common human sentiment. A precursor to articles by Goffman and by Gross and Stone on embarrassment.

Schatzman, Leonard, and Anselm Strauss. "Social Class and Modes of Communication." *American Journal of Sociology*, vol. 60 (January 1955), pp.

329–338. Observed differences in role-taking and standpoints revealed by interviews with lower-class and middle-class persons.

Stryker, Sheldon. "Relationships of Married Offspring and Parent: A Test of Mead's Theory." *American Journal of Sociology,* vol. 62 (November 1956), pp. 308–319. Empirical tests of hypotheses on role-taking drawn from propositions of Mead.

Swanson, Guy E. "On Explanations of Social Interaction." *Sociometry,* vol. 28 (June 1965), pp. 101–123. A lengthy and difficult but rewarding analysis of the assumptions underlying various conceptions of the nature of human interaction.

Turner, Ralph H. "Role-Taking: Process versus Conformity." In Arnold M. Rose (ed.) *Human Behavior and Social Processes.* Boston: Houghton Mifflin Company, 1962, pp. 20–40. Makes an important distinction between role-taking and role-making.

———. "Role-Taking, Role Standpoint, and Reference-Group Behavior." *American Journal of Sociology,* vol. 61 (January 1956), pp. 316–328. Clarification of certain important social-psychological concepts.

Vernon, Glenn M. *Human Interaction: An Introduction to Sociology.* New York: The Ronald Press Company, 1965. A thoroughgoing effort to present the concepts and principles of an introductory sociology course within the symbolic interactionist framework.

Warriner, Charles K. *The Emergence of Society.* Homewood, Illinois: Dorsey Press, 1970. Examines the social-psychological phenomena involved in the formation and persistence of social forms and processes.

part III

Self

During the late nineteenth century, the concept of the self received considerable attention by philosophers and psychologists. To William James, Josiah Royce, James Mark Baldwin, and others, the development and functioning of the self were central in the study of social life. With the rise of Watsonian behaviorism, however, the concept was rejected as subjective and unscientific. In turn, behaviorism has been criticized for neglecting important, though covert, aspects of human behavior.

Mead's social behaviorism stressed the processes by which the individual becomes aware of and learns to guide his own behavior. The article by Meltzer summarizing Mead's approach (in Part I) discussed the major contributions and problems of his concept of self. The ambiguity in Mead's work was paralleled by recent divergences in definitions and methods of empirical study of the concept.

Among current symbolic interactionists, those who see the self as a dynamic process—of viewing and responding to one's own behavior—emphasize participant-observation, interviews, and Cooley's "sympathetic introspection." Those who see the self as a structure of internalized roles stress such devices as the Who Am I Test. Finally, some investigators, conceiving the self as a set of attitudes or evaluations, use self-rating scales in their research.

The first two selections in Part III deal with two distinct facets of the self: object and actor. The selection from Cooley's work describes how the individual comes to experience himself as an object. Through the attitudes of others, each person learns to "see" and to evaluate his own appearance, attitudes, and behavior. It is in this sense that the self is sometimes defined as "the individual as known to the individual." Cooley's depiction of the "looking-glass self" is in close accord with his suggested method for the acquisition of social knowledge.

The Erving Goffman article concerns the individual as subject rather than object. Here the self is considered in its active aspect. The individual is capable not only of viewing his own behavior, but also of directing and guiding this behavior and of shaping the images of himself available to others. In explaining his view of the self, Goffman draws on drama, literature, and observation. His perspective is dramaturgical—interpreting the individual as an actor in a theatrical performance.

John W. Kinch seeks to clarify self theory by formal or axiomatic logic. He states the theory's basic postulates, then deduces their logical consequences. Because it is a recent formulation, its heuristic value cannot be certain at this time. However, some of its deductions correspond to findings of prior research.

The theoretical distinction between the "I" and the "Me" receives critical scrutiny by William L. Kolb. Although these concepts have been analytically useful, Kolb points out their lack of clarity. The absence of empirical research using these concepts may stem from their ambiguity.

A series of experiments by Kinch, summarized in his second article, were designed to test a proposition he derived from the Mead-Cooley theory of the self-conception. Four hypotheses test the basic proposition that the individual's self-conception is based on his conception of others' behavior toward him.

E. L. Quarantelli and Joseph Cooper describe a study of professional self-conception and its relation to the generalized other. Using a structured questionnaire, which is not often employed by symbolic interactionists, they apply a ten-point scale to measure development of the professional self-image.

Research findings based on the Twenty Statements Test are described in the next two articles. Carl J. Couch, a student of Kuhn, presents empirical confirmation of the influence of family relationships. He uses the Twenty Statements Test to explore the relationship between family roles and individual self-images. His study is an example of the kinds of research suggested by the first selection by Sheldon Stryker in Part V.

No theory of human behavior can be restricted to a single human grouping. Edwin D. Driver's comparison of self-conceptions in India and the United States, however, is among the few cross-cultural studies. His data are used to assess the validity of the Twenty Statements Test.

The concluding article, by Charles W. Tucker, raises crucial questions about Kuhn's self theory and its most common research techniques. His analysis makes a valuable contribution to what he has called the "age of inquiry" in symbolic interactionism.

While these articles represent substantial divergences in interpretation and research orientation, they agree in their central thesis that self-conceptions are largely derived from experiences with others and are crucial sources of individual and interpersonal behavior. No other aspect of symbolic interactionism has received more attention than the individual's sense of self. The articles in this part are only a small segment of the rapidly growing theoretical and empirical literature on what might be considered the core of the human personality.

19   CHARLES HORTON COOLEY

Looking-Glass Self

In a very large and interesting class of cases the social reference takes the form of a somewhat definite imagination of how one's self—that is any idea he appropriates—appears in a particular mind, and the kind of self-feeling one has is determined by the attitude toward this attributed to that other mind. A social self of this sort might be called the reflected or looking-glass self:

> "Each to each a looking-glass
> Reflects the other that doth pass."

As we see our face, figure, and dress in the glass, and are interested in them because they are ours, and pleased or otherwise with them according as they do or do not answer to what we should like them to be; so in imagination we perceive in another's mind some thought of our appearance, manners, aims, deeds, character, friends, and so on, and are variously affected by it.

A self-idea of this sort seems to have three principal elements: the imagination of our appearance to the other person; the imagination of his judgment of that appearance, and some sort of self-feeling, such as pride or mortification. The comparison with a looking-glass hardly suggests the second element, the imagined judgment, which is quite essential. The thing that moves us to pride or shame is not the mere mechanical reflection of ourselves, but an imputed sentiment, the imagined effect of this reflection upon another's mind. This is evident from the fact that the character and weight of that other, in whose mind we see ourselves, makes all the difference with our feeling. We are ashamed to seem evasive in the presence of a straightforward man, cowardly in the presence of a brave one, gross in the eyes of a refined one, and so on. We always imagine, and in imagining

Reprinted by permission of Charles Scribner's Sons from *Human Nature and the Social Order* by Charles Horton Cooley.

share, the judgments of the other mind. A man will boast to one person of an action—say some sharp transaction in trade—which he would be ashamed to own to another.

. . .

The process by which self-feeling of the looking-glass sort develops in children may be followed without much difficulty. Studying the movements of others as closely as they do they soon see a connection between their own acts and changes in those movements; that is, they perceive their own influence or power over persons. The child appropriates the visible actions of his parent or nurse, over which he finds he has some control, in quite the same way as he appropriates one of his own members or a plaything, and he will try to do things with this new possession, just as he will with his hand or his rattle. A girl six months old will attempt in the most evident and deliberate manner to attract attention to herself, to set going by her actions some of those movements of other persons that she has appropriated. She has tasted the joy of being a cause, of exerting social power, and wishes more of it. She will tug at her mother's skirts, wriggle, gurgle, stretch out her arms, etc., all the time watching for the hoped-for effect. These performances often give the child, even at this age, an appearance of what is called affectation, that is, she seems to be unduly preoccupied with what other people think of her. Affectation, at any age, exists when the passion to influence others seems to overbalance the established character and give it an obvious twist or pose. It is instructive to find that even Darwin was, in his childhood, capable of departing from truth for the sake of making an impression. "For instance," he says in his autobiography, "I once gathered much valuable fruit from my father's trees and hid it in the shrubbery, and then ran in breathless haste to spread the news that I had discovered a hoard of stolen fruit."[1]

The young performer soon learns to be different things to different people, showing that he begins to apprehend personality and to foresee its operation. If the mother or nurse is more tender than just, she will almost certainly be "worked" by systematic weeping. It is a matter of common observation that children often behave worse with their mother than with other and less sympathetic people. Of the new persons that a child sees, it is evident that some make a strong impression and awaken a desire to interest and please them, while others are indifferent or repugnant. Sometimes the reason can be perceived or guessed, sometimes not; but the fact of selective interest, admiration, prestige, is obvious before the end of the second year. By that time a child already cares much for the reflection of himself upon one personality and little for that upon another. Moreover, he soon claims intimate and tractable persons as *mine*, classes them among

[1] *Life and Letters of Charles Darwin*, by F. Darwin, p. 27.

his other possessions, and maintains his ownership against all comers. M., at three years of age, vigorously resented R.'s claim upon their mother. The latter was "*my* mamma," whenever the point was raised.

Strong joy and grief depend upon the treatment this rudimentary social self receives. In the case of M. I noticed as early as the fourth month a "hurt" way of crying which seemed to indicate a sense of personal slight. It was quite different from the cry of pain or that of anger, but seemed about the same as the cry of fright. The slightest tone of reproof would produce it. On the other hand, if people took notice and laughed and encouraged, she was hilarious. At about fifteen months old she had become "a perfect little actress," seeming to live largely in imaginations of her effect upon other people. She constantly and obviously laid traps for attention, and looked abashed or wept at any signs of disapproval or indifference. At times it would seem as if she could not get over these repulses, but would cry long in a grieved way, refusing to be comforted. If she hit upon any little trick that made people laugh she would be sure to repeat it, laughing loudly and affectedly in imitation. She had quite a repertory of these small performances, which she would display to a sympathetic audience, or even try upon strangers. I have seen her at sixteen months, when R. refused to give her the scissors, sit down and make-believe cry, putting up her under lip and snuffling, meanwhile looking up now and then to see what effect she was producing.[2]

In such phenomena we have plainly enough, it seems to me, the germ of personal ambition of every sort. Imagination co-operating with instinctive self-feeling has already created a social "I," and this has become a principal object of interest and endeavor.

Progress from this point is chiefly in the way of a greater definiteness, fulness, and inwardness in the imagination of the other's state of mind. A little child thinks of and tries to elicit certain visible or audible phenomena, and does not go back of them; but what a grown-up person desires to produce in others is an internal, invisible condition which his own richer experience enables him to imagine, and of which expression is only the sign. Even adults, however, make no separation between what other people think and the visible expression of that thought. They imagine the whole thing at once, and their idea differs from that of a child chiefly in the comparative richness and complexity of the elements that accompany and interpret the visible or audible sign. There is also a progress from the naive to the subtle in socially self-assertive action. A child obviously and simply, at first, does things for effect. Later there is an endeavor to suppress the appearance of doing so; affection, indifference, contempt, etc., are simulated to hide the real wish to affect the self-image. It is perceived that an obvious seeking after good opinion is weak and disagreeable.

[2] This sort of thing is very familiar to observers of children. See, for instance, Miss Shinn's Notes on the Development of a Child, p. 153.

The Presentation of Self to Others

When an individual enters the presence of others, they commonly seek to acquire information about him or to bring into play information about him already possessed. They will be interested in his general socio-economic status, his conception of self, his attitude toward them, his competence, his trustworthiness, etc. Although some of this information seems to be sought almost as an end in itself, there are usually quite practical reasons for acquiring it. Information about the individual helps to define the situation, enabling others to know in advance what he will expect of them and what they may expect of him. Informed in these ways, the others will know how best to act in order to call forth a desired response from him.

For those present, many sources of information become accessible and many carriers (or "sign-vehicles") become available for conveying this information. If unacquainted with the individual, observers can glean clues from his conduct and appearance which allow them to apply their previous experience with individuals roughly similar to the one before them or, more important, to apply untested stereotypes to him. They can also assume from past experience that only individuals of a particular kind are likely to be found in a given social setting. They can rely on what the individual says about himself or on documentary evidence he provides as to who and what he is. If they know, or know of, the individual by virtue of experience prior to the interaction, they can rely on assumptions as to the persistence and generality of psychological traits as a means of predicting his present and future behavior.

However, during the period in which the individual is in the immediate presence of the others, few events may occur which directly provide the others with the conclusive information they will need if they are to direct wisely their own activity. Many crucial facts lie beyond the time and place of interaction or lie concealed within it. For example, the "true" or "real" attitudes, beliefs, and emotions of the individual can be ascertained only indirectly, through his avowals or through what appears to be involuntary expressive behavior. Similarly, if the individual offers the others a product or service, they will often find that during the interaction there will be no time and place immediately available for eating the pudding that the proof can be found in. They will be forced to accept some events as conventional or natural signs of something not directly available to the senses. In Ichheiser's terms,[1] the individual will have to act so that he intentionally or unintentionally *expresses* himself, and the others will in turn have to be *impressed* in some way by him.

The expressiveness of the individual (and therefore his capacity to give impressions) appears to involve two radically different kinds of sign activity: the expression that he *gives,* and the expression that he *gives off.* The first involves verbal symbols or their substitutes which he uses admittedly and solely to convey the information that he and the others are known to attach to these symbols. This is communication in the traditional and narrow sense. The second involves a wide range of action that others can treat as symptomatic of the actor, the expectation being that the action was performed for reasons other than the information conveyed in this way. As we shall have to see, this distinction has an only initial validity. The individual does of course intentionally convey misinformation by means of both of these types of communication, the first involving deceit, the second feigning.

Taking communication in both its narrow and broad sense, one finds that when the individual is in the immediate presence of others, his activity will have a promissory character. The others are likely to find that they must accept the individual on faith, offering him a just return while he is present before them in exchange for something whose true value will not be established until after he has left their presence. (Of course, the others also live by inference in their dealings with the physical world, but it is only in the world of social interaction that the objects about which they make inferences will purposely facilitate and hinder this inferential process.) The security that they justifiably feel in making inferences about the individual will vary, of course, depending on such factors as the amount of information they already possess about him, but no amount of such past evidence can entirely obviate the necessity of acting on the basis of inferences. As William I. Thomas suggested:

> It is also highly important for us to realize that we do not as a matter of fact lead our lives, make our decisions, and reach our goals in everyday life either statistically or scientifically. We live by inference. I am, let us say, your guest. You do not know, you cannot determine scientifically, that I will not steal your money or your spoons. But inferentially I will not, and inferentially you have me as a guest.[2]

Let us now turn from the others to the point of view of the individual who presents himself before them. He may wish them to think highly of

[1] Gustav Ichheiser, "Misunderstandings in Human Relations," Supplement to *The American Journal of Sociology.* LV (September, 1949), pp. 6–7.

[2] Quoted in E. H. Volkart, editor, *Social Behavior and Personality.* Contributions of W. I. Thomas to Theory and Social Research (New York: Social Science Research Council, 1951), p. 5.

him, or to think that he thinks highly of them, or to perceive how in fact he feels toward them, or to obtain no clear-cut impression; he may wish to ensure sufficient harmony so that the interaction can be sustained, or to defraud, get rid of, confuse, mislead, antagonize, or insult them. Regardless of the particular objective which the individual has in mind and of his motive for having this objective, it will be in his interests to control the conduct of the others, especially their responsive treatment of him.[3] This control is achieved largely by influencing the definition of the situation which the others come to formulate, and he can influence this definition by expressing himself in such a way as to give them the kind of impression that will lead them to act voluntarily in accordance with his own plan. Thus, when an individual appears in the presence of others, there will usually be some reason for him to mobilize his activity so that it will convey an impression to others which it is in his interests to convey. Since a girl's dormitory mates will glean evidence of her popularity from the calls she receives on the phone, we can suspect that some girls will arrange for calls to be made, and Willard Waller's finding can be anticipated:

> It has been reported by many observers that a girl who is called to the telephone in the dormitories will often allow herself to be called several times, in order to give all the other girls ample opportunity to hear her paged.[4]

Of the two kinds of communication—expressions given and expressions given off—this report will be primarily concerned with the latter, with the more theatrical and contextual kind, the non-verbal, presumably unintentional kind, whether this communication be purposely engineered or not. As an example of what we must try to examine, I would like to cite at length a novelistic incident in which Preedy, a vacationing Englishman, makes his first appearance on the beach of his summer hotel in Spain:

> But in any case he took care to avoid catching anyone's eye. First of all, he had to make it clear to those potential companions of his holiday that they were of no concern to him whatsoever. He stared through them, round them, over them—eyes lost in space. The beach might have been empty. If by chance a ball was thrown his way, he looked surprised; then let a smile of amusement lighten his face (Kindly Preedy), looked round dazed to see that there *were* people on the beach, tossed it back with a smile to himself and not a smile *at* the people, and then resumed carelessly his nonchalant survey of space.

---

[3] Here I owe much to an unpublished paper by Tom Burns of the University of Edinburgh. He presents the argument that in all interaction a basic underlying theme is the desire of each participant to guide and control the responses made by the others present. A similar argument has been advanced by Jay Haley in a recent unpublished paper, but in regard to a special kind of control, that having to do with defining the nature of the relationship of those involved in the interaction.

[4] Willard Waller, "The Rating and Dating Complex," *American Sociological Review*, II, p. 730.

But it was time to institute a little parade, the parade of the Ideal Preedy. By devious handlings he gave any who wanted to look a chance to see the title of his book—a Spanish translation of Homer, classic thus, but not daring, cosmopolitan too—and then gathered together his beach-wrap and bag into a neat sand-resistant pile (Methodical and Sensible Preedy), rose slowly to stretch at ease his huge frame (Big-Cat Preedy), and tossed aside his sandals (Carefree Preedy, after all).

The marriage of Preedy and the sea! There were alternative rituals. The first involved the stroll that turns into a run and a dive straight into the water, thereafter smoothing into a strong splashless crawl towards the horizon. But of course not really to the horizon. Quite suddenly he would turn on to his back and thrash great white splashes with his legs, somehow thus showing that he could have swum further had he wanted to, and then would stand up a quarter out of water for all to see who it was.

The alternative course was simpler, it avoided the cold-water shock and it avoided the risk of appearing too high-spirited. The point was to appear to be so used to the sea, the Mediterranean, and this particular beach, that one might as well be in the sea as out of it. It involved a slow stroll down and into the edge of the water—not even noticing his toes were wet, land and water all the same to *him!*—with his eyes up at the sky gravely surveying portents, invisible to others, of the weather (Local Fisherman Preedy).[5]

The novelist means us to see that Preedy is improperly concerned with the extensive impressions he feels his sheer bodily action is giving off to those around him. We can malign Preedy further by assuming that he has acted merely in order to give a particular impression, that this is a false impression, and that the others present receive either no impression at all, or worse still, the impression that Preedy is affectedly trying to cause them to receive this particular impression. But the important point for us here is that the kind of impression Preedy thinks he is making is in fact the kind of impression that others correctly and incorrectly glean from someone in their midst.

I have said that when an individual appears before others his actions will influence the definition of the situation which they come to have. Sometimes the individual will act in a thoroughly calculating manner, expressing himself in a given way solely in order to give the kind of impression to others that is likely to evoke from them a specific response he is concerned to obtain. Sometimes the individual will be calculating in his activity but be relatively unaware that this is the case. Sometimes he will intentionally and consciously express himself in a particular way, but chiefly because the tradition of his group or social status require this kind of expression and not because of any particular response (other than vague acceptance or approval) that is likely to be evoked from those impressed by the expression. Sometimes the traditions of an individual's role will lead him to give a well-designed impression of a particular kind and yet he may be neither consciously nor unconsciously disposed to create such an impression. The

[5] William Sansom, *A Contest of Ladies* (London: Hogarth, 1956), pp. 230–32.

others, in their turn, may be suitably impressed by the individual's efforts to convey something, or may misunderstand the situation and come to conclusions that are warranted neither by the individual's intent nor by the facts. In any case, in so far as the others act *as if* the individual had conveyed a particular impression, we may take a functional or pragmatic view and say that the individual has "effectively" projected a given definition of the situation and "effectively" fostered the understanding that a given state of affairs obtains.

There is one aspect of the others' response that bears special comment here. Knowing that the individual is likely to present himself in a light that is favorable to him, the others may divide what they witness into two parts; a part that is relatively easy for the individual to manipulate at will, being chiefly his verbal assertions, and a part in regard to which he seems to have little concern or control, being chiefly derived from the expressions he gives off. The others may then use what are considered to be the ungovernable aspects of his expressive behavior as a check upon the validity of what is conveyed by the governable aspects. In this a fundamental asymmetry is demonstrated in the communication process, the individual presumably being aware of only one stream of his communication, the witnesses of this stream and one other. For example, in Shetland Isle one crofter's wife, in serving native dishes to a visitor from the mainland of Britain, would listen with a polite smile to his polite claims of liking what he was eating; at the same time she would take note of the rapidity with which the visitor lifted his fork or spoon to his mouth, the eagerness with which he passed food into his mouth, and the gusto expressed in chewing the food, using these signs as a check on the stated feelings of the eater. The same woman, in order to discover what one acquaintance (A) "actually" thought of another acquaintance (B), would wait until B was in the presence of A but engaged in conversation with still another person (C). She would then covertly examine the facial expressions of A as he regarded B in conversation with C. Not being in conversation with B, and not being directly observed by him, A would sometimes relax usual constraints and tactful deceptions, and freely express what he was "actually" feeling about B. This Shetlander, in short, would observe the unobserved observer.

Now given the fact that others are likely to check up on the more controllable aspects of behavior by means of the less controllable, one can expect that sometimes the individual will try to exploit this very possibility, guiding the impression he makes through behavior felt to be reliably informing.[6] For example, in gaining admission to a tight social circle, the participant observer may not only wear an accepting look while listening to

---

[6] The widely read and rather sound writings of Stephen Potter are concerned in part with signs that can be engineered to give a shrewd observer the apparently incidental cues he needs to discover concealed virtues the gamesman does not in fact possess.

an informant, but may also be careful to wear the same look when observing the informant talking to others, observers of the observer will then not as easily discover where he actually stands. A specific illustration may be cited from Shetland Isle. When a neighbor dropped in to have a cup of tea, he would ordinarily wear at least a hint of an expectant warm smile as he passed through the door into the cottage. Since lack of physical obstructions outside the cottage and lack of light within it usually made it possible to observe the visitor unobserved as he approached the house, islanders sometimes took pleasure in watching the visitor drop whatever expression he was manifesting and replace it with a sociable one just before reaching the door. However, some visitors, in appreciating that this examination was occurring, would blindly adopt a social face a long distance from the house, thus ensuring the projection of a constant image.

This kind of control upon the part of the individual reinstates the symmetry of the communication process, and sets the stage for a kind of information game—a potentially infinite cycle of concealment, discovery, false revelation, and rediscovery. It should be added that since the others are likely to be relatively unsuspicious of the presumably unguided aspect of the individual's conduct, he can gain much by controlling it. The others of course may sense that the individual is manipulating the presumably spontaneous aspects of his behavior, and seek in this very act of manipulation some shading of conduct that the individual has not managed to control. This again provides a check upon the individual's behavior, this time his presumably uncalculated behavior, thus re-establishing the asymmetry of the communication process. Here I would like only to add the suggestion that the arts of piercing an individual's effort at calculated unintentionality seem better developed than our capacity to manipulate our own behavior, so that regardless of how many steps have occurred in the information game, the witness is likely to have the advantage over the actor, and the initial asymmetry of the communication process is likely to be retained.

When we allow that the individual projects a definition of the situation when he appears before others, we must also see that the others, however passive their role may seem to be, will themselves effectively project a definition of the situation by virtue of their response to the individual and by virtue of any lines of action they initiate to him. Ordinarily the definitions of the situation projected by the several different participants are sufficiently attuned to one another so that open contradiction will not occur. I do not mean that there will be the kind of consensus that arises when each individual present candidly expresses what he really feels and honestly agrees with the expressed feelings of the others present. This kind of harmony is an optimistic ideal and in any case not necessary for the smooth working of society. Rather, each participant is expected to suppress his immediate heartfelt feelings, conveying a view of the situation which he feels the others will be able to find at least temporarily acceptable. The maintenance of this surface of agreement, this veneer of consensus, is facilitated by each participant concealing his own wants behind statements which assert values to which every- one present feels obliged to give lip service. Further, there is usually a kind of division of definitional labor. Each participant is allowed to estab- lish the tentative official ruling regarding matters which are vital to him but not immediately important to others, e.g., the rationalizations and justifica- tions by which he accounts for his past activity. In exchange for this courtesy he remains silent or non-committal on matters important to others but not immediately important to him. We have then a kind of interac- tional *modus vivendi.* Together the participants contribute to a single over- all definition of the situation which involves not so much a real agreement as to what exists but rather a real agreement as to whose claims concern- ing what issues will be temporarily honored. Real agreement will also exist concerning the desirability of avoiding an open conflict of definitions of the situation.[7] I will refer to this level of agreement as a "working con- sensus." It is to be understood that the working consensus established in one interaction setting will be quite different in content from the working consensus established in a different type of setting. Thus, between two friends at lunch, a reciprocal show of affection, respect, and concern for the other is maintained. In service occupations, on the other hand, the spe- cialist often maintains an image of disinterested involvement in the prob- lem of the client, while the client responds with a show of respect for the competence and integrity of the specialist. Regardless of such differences in content, however, the general form of these working arrangements is the same.

    In noting the tendency for a participant to accept the definitional claims made by the others present, we can appreciate the crucial importance of the information that the individual *initially* possesses or acquires concern- ing his fellow participants, for it is on the basis of this initial information that the individual starts to define the situation and starts to build up lines of responsive action. The individual's initial projection commits him to what he is proposing to be and requires him to drop all pretenses of being other things. As the interaction among the participants progresses, additions and modifications in this initial informational state will of course occur, but it is essential that these later developments be related without con- tradition to, and even built up from, the initial positions taken by the sev-

---

[7] An interaction can be purposely set up as a time and place for voicing differences in opinion, but in such cases participants must be careful to agree not to disagree on the proper tone of voice, vocabulary, and degree of seriousness in which all arguments are to be phrased, and upon the mutual respect which disagreeing participants must carefully continue to express toward one another. This debaters' or academic definition of the situation may also be invoked suddenly and judiciously as a way of translating a serious conflict of views into one that can be handled within a framework acceptable to all present.

eral participants. It would seem that an individual can more easily make a choice as to what line of treatment to demand from and extend to the others present at the beginning of an encounter than he can alter the line of treatment that is being pursued once the interaction is underway.

In everyday life, of course, there is a clear understanding that first impressions are important. Thus, the work adjustment of those in service occupations will often hinge upon a capacity to seize and hold the initiative in the service relation, a capacity that will require subtle aggressiveness on the part of the server when he is of lower socio-economic status than his client. W. F. Whyte suggests the waitress as an example:

> The first point that stands out is that the waitress who bears up under pressure does not simply respond to her customers. She acts with some skill to control their behavior. The first question to ask when we look at the customer relationship is, "Does the waitress get the jump on the customer, or does the customer get the jump on the waitress?" The skilled waitress realizes the crucial nature of this question . . .
> The skilled waitress tackles the customer with confidence and without hesitation. For example, she may find that a new customer has seated himself before she could clear off the dirty dishes and change the cloth. He is now leaning on the table studying the menu. She greets him, says, "May I change the cover, please?" and, without waiting for an answer, takes his menu away from him so that he moves back from the table, and she goes about her work. The relationship is handled politely but firmly, and there is never any question as to who is in charge.[8]

When the interaction that is initiated by "first impressions" is itself merely the initial interaction in an extended series of interactions involving the same participants, we speak of "getting off on the right foot" and feel that it is crucial that we do so. Thus, one learns that some teachers take the following view:

> You can't ever let them get the upper hand on you or you're through. So I start out tough. The first day I get a new class in, I let them know who's boss . . . You've got to start off tough, then you can ease up as you go along. If you start out easy-going, when you try to get tough, they'll just look at you and laugh.[9]

Similarly, attendants in mental institutions may feel that if the new patient is sharply put in his place the first day on the ward and made to see who is boss, much future difficulty will be prevented.[10]

Given the fact that the individual effectively projects a definition of the

---

[8] W. F. Whyte, "When Workers and Customers Meet," Chap. VII, *Industry and Society*, ed. W. F. Whyte (New York: McGraw-Hill, 1946), pp. 132–33.

[9] Teacher interview quoted by Howard S. Becker, "Social Class Variations in the Teacher-Pupil Relationship," *Journal of Educational Sociology*, XXV, p. 459.

[10] Harold Taxel, "Authority Structure in a Mental Hospital Ward" (unpublished Master's thesis, Department of Sociology, University of Chicago, 1953).

situation when he enters the presence of others, we can assume that events may occur within the interaction which contradict, discredit, or otherwise throw doubt upon this projection. When these disruptive events occur, the interaction itself may come to a confused and embarrassed halt. Some of the assumptions upon which the responses of the participants had been predicated become untenable, and the participants find themselves lodged in an interaction for which the situation has been wrongly defined and is now no longer defined. At such moments the individual whose presentation has been discredited may feel ashamed while the others present may feel hostile, and all the participants may come to feel ill at ease, nonplussed, out of countenance, embarrassed, experiencing the kind of anomy that is generated when the minute social system of face-to-face interaction breaks down.

In stressing the fact that the initial definition of the situation projected by an individual tends to provide a plan for the co-operative activity that follows—in stressing this action point of view—we must not overlook the crucial fact that any projected definition of the situation also has a distinctive moral character. It is this moral character of projections that will chiefly concern us in this report. Society is organized on the principle that any individual who possesses certain social characteristics has a moral right to expect that others will value and treat him in an appropriate way. Connected with this principle is a second, namely that an individual who implicitly or explicitly signifies that he has certain social characteristics ought in fact to be what he claims he is. In consequence, when an individual projects a definition of the situation and thereby makes an implicit or explicit claim to be a person of a particular kind, he automatically exerts a moral demand upon the others, obliging them to value and treat him in the manner that persons of his kind have a right to expect. He also implicitly forgoes all claims to be things he does not appear to be[11] and hence forgoes the treatment that would be appropriate for such individuals. The others find, then, that the individual has informed them as to what is and as to what they *ought* to see as the "is."

One cannot judge the importance of definitional disruptions by the frequency with which they occur, for apparently they would occur more frequently were not constant precautions taken. We find that preventive practices are constantly employed to avoid these embarrassments and that corrective practices are constantly employed to compensate for discrediting occurrences that have not been successfully avoided. When the individual employs these strategies and tactics to protect his own projections, we may refer to them as "defensive practices"; when a participant employs them to save the definition of the situation projected by another, we speak of "pro-

---

[11] This role of the witness in limiting what it is the individual can be has been stressed by Existentialists, who see it as a basic threat to individual freedom. See Jean-Paul Sartre, *Being and Nothingness*, trans. by Hazel E. Barnes (New York: Philosophical Library, 1956), p. 365 ff.

tective practices" or "tact." Together, defensive and protective practices comprise the techniques employed to safeguard the impression fostered by an individual during his presence before others. It should be added that while we may be ready to see that no fostered impression would survive if defensive practices were not employed, we are less ready perhaps to see that few impressions could survive if those who received the impression did not exert tact in their reception of it.

In addition to the fact that precautions are taken to prevent disruption of projected definitions, we may also note that an intense interest in these disruptions comes to play a significant role in the social life of the group. Practical jokes and social games are played in which embarrassments which are to be taken unseriously are purposely engineered.[12] Fantasies are created in which devastating exposures occur. Anecdotes from the past— real, embroidered, or fictitious—are told and retold, detailing disruptions which occurred, almost occurred, or occurred and were admirably resolved. There seems to be no grouping which does not have a ready supply of these games, reveries, and cautionary tales, to be used as a source of humor, a catharsis for anxieties, and a sanction for inducing individuals to be modest in their claims and reasonable in their projected expectations. The individual may tell himself through dreams of getting into impossible positions. Families tell of the time a guest got his dates mixed and arrived when neither the house nor anyone in it was ready for him. Journalists tell of times when an all-too-meaningful misprint occurred, and the paper's assumption of objectivity or decorum was humorously discredited. Public servants tell of times a client ridiculously misunderstood form instructions, giving answers which implied an unanticipated and bizarre definition of the situation.[13] Seamen, whose home away from home is rigorously he-man, tell stories of coming back home and inadvertently asking mother to "pass the fucking butter."[14] Diplomats tell of the time a near-sighted queen asked a republican ambassador about the health of his king.[15]

To summarize, then, I assume that when an individual appears before others he will have many motives for trying to control the impression they receive of the situation. This report is concerned with some of the common techniques that persons employ to sustain such impressions and with some of the common contingencies associated with the employment of these techniques. The specific content of any activity presented by the individual participant, or the role it plays in the interdependent activities of an ongoing social system, will not be at issue; I shall be concerned only with

---

[12] Goffman, *op. cit.*, pp. 319–27.

[13] Peter Blau, "Dynamics of Bureaucracy" (Ph.D. dissertation, Department of Sociology, Columbia University, forthcoming, University of Chicago Press), pp. 127–29.

[14] Walter M. Beattie, Jr., "The Merchant Seaman" (unpublished M. A. Report, Department of Sociology, University of Chicago, 1950), p. 35.

[15] Sir Frederick Ponsonby, *Recollections of Three Reigns* (New York: Dutton 1952), p. 46.

the participant's dramaturgical problems of presenting the activity before others. The issues dealt with by stagecraft and stage management are sometimes trivial but they are quite general; they seem to occur everywhere in social life, providing a clear-cut dimension for formal sociological analysis.

It will be convenient to end this introduction with some definitions that are implied in what has gone before and required for what is to follow. For the purpose of this report, interaction (that is, face-to-face interaction) may be roughly defined as the reciprocal influence of individuals upon one another's actions when in one another's immediate physical presence. An interaction may be defined as all the interaction which occurs throughout any one occasion when a given set of individuals are in one another's continuous presence; the term "an encounter" would do as well. A "performance" may be defined as all the activity of a given participant on a given occasion which serves to influence in any way any of the other participants. Taking a particular participant and his performance as a basic point of reference, we may refer to those who contribute the other performances as the audience, observers, or co-participants. The pre-established pattern of action which is unfolded during a performance and which may be presented or played through on other occasions may be called a "part" or "routine."[16] These situational terms can easily be related to conventional structural ones. When an individual or performer plays the same part to the same audience on different occasions, a social relationship is likely to arise. Defining social role as the enactment of rights and duties attached to a given status, we can say that a social role will involve one or more parts and that each of these different parts may be presented by the performer on a series of occasions to the same kinds of audience or to an audience of the same persons.

[16] For comments on the importance of distinguishing between a routine of interaction and any particular instance when this routine is played through, see John von Neumann and Oskar Morgenstern, *The Theory of Games and Economic Behavior* (2nd ed.; Princeton: Princeton University Press, 1947), p. 49.

A Formalized Theory of the Self-Concept

In recent years many sociologists have become concerned with the relation between the research process and existing theory. The use of formal mathematical models to enhance this relationship has not proved completely satisfactory. In this note we discuss the use of a type of formalization[1] which has many of the advantages of the mathematical model, yet at the same time maintains some of the values of the more subjective theoretical approach with which we are familiar in sociology. The interactionist notions about the self-concept will be used to exemplify what is involved in this type of formalization. The strategy is very simple: First, we scrutinize the theory to search out what seem to be its basic propositions and make these postulates explicit; second, the variables or concepts are identified and carefully defined; third, all interrelationships between the variables that can be derived from the basic postulates are considered. We will use those rules of logic which are part of ordinary language rather than the rules of mathematics. Finally, after the formalized theory has been explicated, we can consider the conditions under which each of the basic postulates will be expected to hold. Let us now proceed by stating the formalized theory of the self-concept, considering an example of its application, and finally evaluating this approach as a method of handling theory.

The Self-Concept

The interactionist notions about the self-concept, based on the writings of G. Mead, Cooley, and several others, are well known to social psychologists. The theory attempts to explain the conception that the individual has of himself in terms of his interaction with those about him.

John W. Kinch, "A Formalized Theory of the Self-Concept." Reprinted from *The American Journal of Sociology*, vol. 68 (January 1963), pp. 481–486, by permission of the University of Chicago Press. Copyright 1963 by the University of Chicago.

[1] Terminology is always a problem in this area. Some have talked about axiomatic theories, some about formal theories. We prefer the term "formalized theory" because it connotes a process of dealing with existing theory which is our concern. Also, one finds several words used in the literature to refer to the statements of a theory; words like postulates, propositions, axioms, theorems, and hypotheses. Here we will use the word "proposition" to refer to any statement which involves an empirical claim. Those propositions which the theory starts with we have called basic "postulates." Statements which are used to define a concept will be referred to simply as "definitions."

Although there have been a variety of words used in describing what is meant by an individual's conception of himself, it appears that general agreement could be reached on the following definition: *The self-concept is that organization of qualities that the individual attributes to himself.* It should be understood that the word "qualities" is used in a broad sense to include both *attributes* that the individual might express in terms of adjectives (ambitious, intelligent) and also the *roles* he sees himself in (father, doctor, etc.).[2]

The general theory.—In very general terms the basic notions of the theory can be stated in one sentence: *The individual's conception of himself emerges from social interaction and, in turn, guides or influences the behavior of that individual.*

Basic Propositions of Formalized Theory of Self-Concept

The following statements are at least implicit in most treatments of the self-concept using this tradition and will be used as the basic postulates of our formalized theory.

1. The individual's self-concept is based on his perception of the way others are responding to him.
2. The individual's self-concept functions to direct his behavior.
3. The individual's perception of the responses of others toward him reflects the actual responses of others toward him.

(These postulates are not expected to hold under all conditions: The formalization procedure described below allows us to consider under what conditions they will hold.)

These three statements make up the postulates of the theory. The reason for this selection will become apparent later. Within these propositions there are four basic concepts or variables:

1. The individual's self-concept (S). (Defined above.)
2. His perception of the responses of others toward him (P). (The response of the individual to those behaviors of others that he perceives as directed toward him.)
3. The actual responses of others toward him (A). (The actual behavior of the others, that is, in response to the individual.)

---

[2] The language used in this definition comes mainly from Theodore R. Sarbin, "Role Theory," in Gardner Lindzey (ed.), *Handbook of Social Psychology* (Cambridge, Mass.: Addison-Wesley Publishing Co., 1954), 223–58.

4. His behavior (B). (The activity of the individual relevant to the social situation.)

At this point it is possible to see the first advantage from our formalized theory. By the use of simple logic we may take the three basic propositions and deduce from them three more. For example, from postulates 1 and 2 we can conclude that the way an individual perceives the response of others toward him will influence his behavior, for if his perception determines his self-concept and his self-concept guides his behavior, then his perception will determine his behavior. In symbolic form,

$$\begin{aligned} \text{if } &P{\to}S \quad \text{postulate 1} \\ \text{and } &S{\to}B \quad \text{postulate 2} \\ \hline \text{then } &P{\to}B \quad \text{proposition 4} \end{aligned}$$

Therefore, the fourth proposition of the theory (call it a derived proposition) is:

4. The way the individual perceives the responses of others toward him will influence his behavior.

In like manner from postulates 1 and 3 we deduce a fifth proposition:

5. The actual responses of others to the individual will determine the way he sees himself (his self-concept).

And, finally, by combining either propositions 5 and 2, or 3 and 4 we get the sixth proposition:

6. The actual responses of others toward the individual will [a]ffect the behavior of the individual.

Our theory so far can be summarized in the following statement: The actual responses of others to the individual will be important in determining how the individual will perceive himself; this perception will influence his self-conception which, in turn, will guide his behavior. Symbolically,

$$A{\to}P{\to}S{\to}B \quad {\to} = \text{"leads to"}$$

Before proceeding further into the analysis of the theory let us consider a short anecdote to clarify what we have said so far. The following story is alleged by some to be true; however, the present author has no confirmation of this and the story is presented only as a helpful device to make a point.

A group of graduate students in a seminar in social psychology became interested in the notions implied in the interactionist approach. One evening after the seminar five of the male members of the group were discussing some of the implications of the theory and came to the realization that it might be possible to invent a situation where the "others" systematically manipulated their responses to another person, thereby changing that person's self-concept and in turn his behavior. They thought of an experiment to test the notions they were dealing with. They chose as their subject (victim) the one girl in the seminar. The subject can be described as, at best, a very plain girl who seemed to fit the stereotype (usually erroneous) that many have of graduate student females. The boys' plan was to begin in concert to respond to the girl as if she were the best-looking girl on campus. They agreed to work into it naturally so that she would not be aware of what they were up to. They drew lots to see who would be the first to date her. The loser, under the pressure of the others, asked her to go out. Although he found the situation quite unpleasant, he was a good actor and by continually saying to himself "she's beautiful, she's beautiful . . ." he got through the evening. According to the agreement it was now the second man's turn and so it went. The dates were reinforced by the similar responses in all contacts the men had with the girl. In a matter of a few short weeks the results began to show. At first it was simply a matter of more care in her appearance; her hair was combed more often and her dresses were more neatly pressed, but before long she had been to the beauty parlor to have her hair styled, and was spending her hard-earned money on the latest fashions in women's campus wear. By the time the fourth man was taking his turn dating the young lady, the job that had once been undesirable was now quite a pleasant task. And when the last man in the conspiracy asked her out, he was informed that she was pretty well booked up for some time in the future. It seems there were more desirable males around than those "plain" graduate students.

Our story suggests that the girl perceived the actual response of others (the men) in such a way as to require a change in her self-concept which in turn eventually changed her behavior. So their behavior influenced hers. However, the story brings to light another proposition that has so far been overlooked. At the end of the experiment we saw that the men's responses to the girl's behavior had changed, and they were now reacting to her as a desirable young lady. A new postulate then would be:

7. The behavior that the individual manifests influences the actual responses of others toward that individual.

We are not dealing with any new variables but rather with a new combination of the old ones. The theory at this point becomes circular:

$$
\begin{array}{ccc}
 & P & \\
\nearrow & & \searrow \\
A & & S \\
\nwarrow & & \swarrow \\
 & B &
\end{array}
$$

It will be noted that with the addition of this new postulate a whole new set of derived propositions emerge. There are now sixteen inter-related propositions in our simple theory which has only four variables. Rather than laboriously listing these propositions, let us now consider some of the factors which modify one of the propositions.

It is apparent that as the theory now stands it has not gone far enough in explaining the phenomena under consideration, and it might prove mis-leading if left as is. The major problem lies in the fact that the proposi-tions are presented as if there was a one-to-one relationship between the variables dealt with. It is obvious that in reality these propositions hold only in varying degrees under certain conditions. To illustrate the type of thing that might be done, we will briefly consider the conditions under which we would expect proposition 3 to hold.

This postulate states that the individual's perception of the responses of others toward him reflects the actual responses of others. We have a rather generous supply of evidence relating to the accuracy of this postu-late: Studies of role-taking ability have, almost without exception, oper-ationally defined role-taking ability in terms of the relationship between the individual's perception of the responses of others and the actual re-sponses. *The evidence seems to suggest that the accuracy of postulate 3 varies with (1) the individual's familiarity with the others, (2) his famili-arity with the situation, (3) the social visibility[3] of the situation, (4) the individual's past experience in interpersonal situations, and (5) other factors which relate to all types of perception (conditions of body, immediate past, etc.).* Briefly, what this proposition says is that the more familiar the indi-vidual is with the situation and the others in the situation, the more socially visible the situation is, the more experience the individual has had in inter-personal situations and the less interference there is from irrelevant condi-tions, the more likely it is that postulate 3 will hold.

Evaluation

With the formalized statement of the basic postulates and derived proposi-tions of the theory and an example of how the postulates must be condi-tioned, it is now possible to evaluate, at least to some extent, the usefulness of this method of dealing with theory in the social sciences. The following evaluation will be concerned primarily with the advantages and disadvan-tages of this approach over the informal, unsystematic approaches usually

---

[3] Here we are using Merton's definition of "visibility": "the extent to which the structure of a social organization provides occasion to those variously located in that structure to perceive the norms obtaining in the organization and the character of role-performance by those manning the organization. In reference to an attribute of social structure, not to the perceptions which individuals happen to have" see Robert K. Merton, *Social Theory and Social Structure* (rev. ed.; Glencoe, Ill.: Free Press, 1957), p. 350.

used in sociology. The advantages seen in this approach are listed below. No rank order is implied.

1. *The formalized theory offers the most parsimonious summary of antici-pated or actual research findings.*[4] By designing our research so that we test four postulates of our theory and by the use of logical deductions we obtain support for sixteen propositions by testing only the four. Al-though this is an obvious virtue of the formalized theory, our modifying propositions make it clear that it must be taken with a certain degree of caution. Hypothesis-testing in sociology is such that the confirmation of propositions 1 and 2 at a certain level will not necessarily mean that proposition 4 can be stated at the same level of significance. Zetterberg cautions, "it is at present desirable that we in sociological research do not claim too much from the transfer of probability since our deductions are not too precise so long as our concepts are defined in normal prose and the deduction rules of ordinary language are used."[5] Even with some awareness of the factors which modify the postulates, words like "guides," "directs," and "influences" cannot be translated into rigorous mathematical operations.

Zetterberg also points out another type of parsimony seen by com-paring the results of sixteen isolated hypotheses (say, sixteen different investigators testing each of our propositions) with sixteen interrelated hypotheses (say, the same investigator does all the research using our theory).[6] It is obvious that the same data will provide more confirmation with the systematic theory than with the isolated hypotheses.

2. *The formalized theory will make the present knowledge on the subject accumulative and point to gaps if they exist.* The theory provides a way of bringing together the evidence that has emerged on the subject of the self. For example, we find that there is a good bit of evidence accumulat-ing on the relationship between perception and the self-concept, and there is some evidence on the actual responses of others as these re-sponses relate to perception and self-concepts.[7] However, very little has been done in relating the self-concept of a person to his behavior.[8]

[4] Here we borrow extensively from Hans Zetterberg's discussions of axiomatic theory (*On Theory and Verification in Sociology* [New York: Tressler Press, 1954], pp. 16–28).

[5] *Ibid.*, p. 22.

[6] *Ibid.*, p. 21.

[7] There are a great number of articles on this topic. The following is only a sample: Leo G. Reeder, George Donohoe, and Arturo Biblarz, "Conception of Self and Others," *American Journal of Sociology*, LXVI, No. 2 (September, 1956), 153–59; S. Frank Miya-moto and Sanford Dornbusch, "A Test of the Symbolic Interactionist Hypothesis of Self-Conception," *American Journal of Sociology*, LXI, No. 5 (March, 1956), 339–403; William R. Rosengren, "The Self in the Emotionally Disturbed," *American Journal of Sociology*, LXVI, No. 5 (March, 1961), 454–62; Carl J. Couch, "Self-Attitudes and De-gree of Agreement with Immediate Others," *American Journal of Sociology*, LXIII (1958), 491–96.

[8] For an example of the type of thing that might be done see Thomas S. McPartland, John H. Cumming, and Wynona S. Garretson, "Self-Conception and Ward Behavior," *Sociometry*, XXIV, No. 2 (June, 1961), 111–24.

3. *The formalized theory requires a clear distinction between statements that define the concepts of the theory and statements that are empirical propositions.* Careless writers on the topic of the self have often used a definition such as: "The self is defined as that organization of qualities *originating in social interaction* . . ." Then the author goes on to attempt to convince his readers that that self is a social phenomena and not something innate or individualistic. Of course, he turns out to be right *by definition.* If he wishes to consider the social origin of the self as an empirical hypothesis (such as our postulate 1) then he is required to define his concept "self" independently of the concept of social interaction. The formalized theory should eliminate errors of this type by clearly differentiating those statements that are definitions and those statements that are empirical claims (postulates or propositions).[9]

4. *The formalized theory allows for careful consideration of the conditions under which the theory is expected to hold.* In our discussion of postulate 3 we attempted to show how a proposition could be scrutinized to find the conditions under which it would hold. This procedure requires empirical evidences outside the theory itself, since the limitations are in no way implicit in the propositions.

5. *The formalized theory provides a systematic procedure for scrutinizing the theory in terms of hidden implications and conceptual problems.* The requirement that all the propositions which are derived from the basic postulates be considered individually should reveal any hidden implications within the theory itself. The requirement for clear definitions of major concepts should go a long way in eliminating, or at least clarifying, conceptual problems.

6. *The formalized theory enables the investigator to bridge gaps in his data.* Often in empirical research there are situations in which it is impossible to gather data on one or more of the variables of the theory. In these situations a formalized theory may make it possible to bridge the gap between the data available by providing a conceptual link between these data. Suppose we have a situation where the only source of data is through direct observation (say participant-observation technique). If we wish to test our notions about the self, it is obvious that only two of our four variables can be measured. We can observe the variable we called "the actual responses of others," and we can observe the individual's behavior. However, we know of no way of directly observing the individual's perception or his self-concept. Our data then consist of observations of the actual responses of other persons toward the subject and the subject's actual behavior. Our theory allows us to "make sense" of these observations by suggesting that the relationship might be explained in terms of the two intervening variables of perception and self-

[9] For an excellent statement of this point see Clarence C. Schrag, review of Talcott Parsons and Edward Shils (eds.), *Toward a General Theory of Action* in *American Sociological Review*, XVII (1952), 247–49.

concept. This was the case in the anecdotal example we used earlier. The girl's perceptions and self-concept were never observed, but we inferred something about them by applying the theory to the observations that were available. The theory stated in a formalized manner enabled us to bridge the gap in our data.

7. *The formalized theory facilitates communication.* A major problem that the sociologist faces today is understanding what his colleagues are talking about. We read passage after passage only to wonder what in the world the author is trying to say. If the theorist was required to formalize his notions as we have suggested in this paper, many of the misunderstandings would disappear. Many of us would find ourselves exclaiming, "Was that what he was saying?" The author cannot help but feel that some theorists, if required to handle their theories in this manner, might themselves end up saying, "Was that what I've been saying?"

The one disadvantage to this approach is that the formalized theory must not be treated as a set of logically and conceptually tight statements complete within themselves. Throughout this paper we tried to make it clear that the formal statements of the theory must be limited by statements of conditions. Our present state of development in sociology requires that we temper our statements even more with some "common-sense" notions we have about the subject with which we are concerned. We are suggesting here that, since the formalized theory may look like a mathematical model, some may assume that the conclusions can be treated with the rigor of a mathematical derivation. This could prove disastrous. The careful investigator can reap the benefits of the advantages mentioned in this paper and avoid the disadvantages if he does not expect the theory to do more than it is capable of doing.

The purpose of this note has been to suggest the possibility of developing models that are not so restrictive as the conventional mathematical models, yet are formal and systematic enough to be a considerable improvement over the general run of theory in sociology. The hope is that this paper might stimulate other attempts at formalizing existing sociological and social psychological theories. The results of a trend in this direction may prove extremely valuable in unscrambling the present state of theory.

A Critical Evaluation of Mead's
"I" and "Me" Concepts

Social scientists have finally come to the realization that the task of a specific systematic science is not the exhasutive explanation of the empirical reality from which it draws its data, but rather the verifying of a series of abstract hypotheses which can then be used in conjunction with the concepts of other sciences to explain a specific situation in reality.[1] The infinite divisibility of reality makes any other approach impossible; any empirical situation is made up of a multiplicity of systems, physical, biological and social. These variables combine in determining the structure of the situation, and any attempt to explain this tangled web of phenomena within the frame of reference offered by any one science can only end in disaster. Conversely, any attempt to construct a systematic science on the basis of all these variables can only result in the crudest form of eclecticism and inconsistent systematization. The social psychologist has been one of the most persistent offenders of this unalterable canon of science. This inability or disinclination to deal only with that which falls properly within the sphere of social psychology is reflected in the unsystematic character of textbooks that are purported to be systematic analyses of personality or of other social psychological phenomena.[2]

Of all social psychologists the one that would seem least guilty of this desire to explain everything about personality is G. H. Mead.[3] Yet, even

William L. Kolb, "A Critical Evaluation of Mead's 'I' and 'Me' Concepts," *Social Forces*, vol. 22 (March 1944), pp. 291–296. Reprinted by permission of The University of North Carolina Press.

[1] Cf. Talcott Parsons, *The Structure of Social Action* (New York, 1937), pp. 3–42. Here the emphasis is on the relation between a given body of theory and empirical fact. See also Florian Znaniecki, *The Method of Sociology* (New York, 1934), *passim*. Both of these works are concerned with the necessity of abstraction in what might be called sociology proper, but their strictures are applicable to any systematic body of knowledge.

[2] Since the writer is unfamiliar with any social psychology text which has not been conceived in too grandiose a fashion, it is unfair to single out any particular offender, but for a somewhat similar criticism pointed at a specific text see H. H. Gerth's review of Steuart Henderson Britt, *Social Psychology of Modern Life* (New York, 1941), in *American Sociological Review*, 6 (December 1941), 915–916.

[3] G. H. Mead, *Mind, Self, and Society* (Chicago 1934). See also his "The Social Self," *Journal of Philosophy, Psychology and Scientific Method*, X (1913), 374–380; "The Mechanism of Social Consciousness," *Journal of Philosophy, Psychology and Scientific Method*, IX (1912), 401–406; "What Social Objects Must Psychology Presuppose," *Journal of Philosophy, Psychology and Scientific Method*, VII (1910), 174–180; "A Behavioristic Account of the Significant Symbol," *Journal of Philosophy*, XIX (1922), 157–163; and "Genesis of the Self and Social Control," *International Journal of Ethics*, XXXV (1924–1925), 251–277.

here, it is possible to discover the results of an attempt to explain aspects of personality and self that more properly belong to other sciences. In his logical development of a systematic theory of the social nature of the growth of the self and of the personality through social interaction and role-taking, Mead gives no explicit explanation of the facts of social change or of the fact that the actions of individuals never exactly correspond to the roles which they are expected to play, prior to the introduction of the "I" and "me" concepts. If he had closed his system without taking these phenomena into consideration, the personality and social structures formed by the processes delineated in his analysis would have been constant, i.e., personality would not vary from the various roles defined by the culture of the society. This is not an a priori impossibility, since as we have seen, a systematic science may not explain everything concerning a particular phenomenon, and thus all differences in personality not accounted for by differentiated roles might conceivably be due to differences generated by other than social factors. Nevertheless, Mead was perfectly justified in attempting to discover whether or not some of these differences could be explained within his frame of reference. In so doing, however, he erred in attempting to explain these residual phenomena under one concept, the "I," and in attempting to close his system by enclosing within it heterogeneous phenomena. The "I" becomes accountable for everything that cannot be explained by the organized set of roles which the individual takes over in the processes of social interaction.[4] This conceptualizing of a residual category of phenomena as being homogeneous has been a source of confusion for both Mead and his interpreters; the nature of this confusion can be demonstrated by an analysis of the characteristics which have been attributed to the "I" as opposed to the "me."

The first characteristic of the "I," that we do not experience it until it passes into memory, fails to distinguish it from the "me," if we define the latter behavioristically. Since this point of view involves defining attitude as an early stage of an act, the "me," which consists of organized internalized attitudes of others, can and must be regarded, unless one is willing to disregard the behavioristic aspects of Mead's work, as realizing itself only in responses. In other words, unless one regards the aspects of the active "me" as existing in various responses called out by various stim-

[4] For Mead's basic discussion of the "I" see *Mind, Self, and Society*, pp. 173–178 and 192–199. It should be noted that the chronological development of Mead's thinking is not involved here. It may well be that Mead first made the distinction between the "I" and "me" long before other elements of his system had been chronologically developed; but the fact remains, the reader of *Mind, Self, and Society* is more interested in the logic of Mead's discussion as it is developed in this book; and in the logical argument social change and personal uniquenesses are only accounted for after the "I" and "me" have been introduced on p. 173. After the "I" is introduced it is then used as an explanation of the emergence of the novel, pp. 196–200.

uli, including earlier actions of the individual, the "me" becomes merely a fictional concept, useful, perhaps, but unrelated to a behavioristic psychology.[5] If then we are unconscious of what we are doing until we respond to our doing it, as Mead assumed when he speaks of our consciousness of the "I," we are unconscious of any specific active aspect of the "me" until we have responded to it. This being true, the first criterion by means of which we can distinguish the "I" from the "me" becomes meaningless: the assumption that we become conscious of the "I" only when it has passed into experience and become part of the "me." If we use a behavioristic definition of the "me" as outlined above, the "me" and the "I" become hopelessly confused because we are conscious of neither of them until they have passed into experience, i.e., until we respond to them.

Another criterion used to identify the "I" can, if properly developed, be used to differentiate between sectors of the self, but can hardly be used to account for the uniqueness of response which it is supposed to explain. We are told that one of the distinguishing characteristics of the "I" is that around it persists ". . . the sense of individuality of our own movements in relation to outer objects or persons, and of our activity in regard to these internalized "me's.""[6] If we use this conception of the "I" it becomes differentiated from the "me" only in that it is that segment of attitudes which will issue in overt action unless modified by the responses of other segments of attitudes. What is one time the "I" may next time be the "me." If, for example, a man sees someone beating a woman, his definition of the situation may be of such a nature that his immediate impulse is to strike the woman-beater; but this impulse calls out in him an attitude of discretion,[7] which may lead to inaction. In that case the "I" would be the anti-woman beating attitude, and the "me" would be the attitude of caution which nullified the active impulse. If, however, his wife does something of which he disapproves there may be called out in him a wife-beating response, which in turn may call out an anti-woman beating response of the nature described above. In that event, the "I" would consist of the wife-beating impulse, and the "me" of the anti-woman beating response. Thus this differentiation is merely a convenient method of distinguishing the original impulse from the modifying attitudes which prevent its fruition in

[5] *Ibid.*, pp. 1–41. In a social psychology devoted purely to the content of personality structures, i.e., those devoted to such phenomena as value hierarchies and their effect on action, little attention need be paid to this technical psychological point, for this relation between psychology and social action can be assumed; but it forms the center of a systematic analysis which is directed toward an explanation of the dynamics of personality and self-development.

[6] Kimball Young, *Personality and Problems of Adjustment* (New York, 1940), p. 175. *Cf.* Mead, *op. cit.*, pp. 177–178.

[7] No social action is as simple as this example might lead one to believe, but there still remains a convenient distinction to be drawn between the initial impulse to act and the various "me's" which are drawn out by it; it is the function of this example to illustrate this distinction in its simplest form.

overt action. Both attitudes are part of the generalized pattern of attitudes or generalized other which make up the personality of the individual, and offer no explanation of uniqueness of overt action.[8]

The third distinguishing feature of the "I" is that it is unpredictable. Thus we are given the illustration of the baseball player whose "me" calls for a throw to first base when a ground ball is hit in his direction, but who actually may either succeed in throwing the ball directly to his man or ten feet over his head.[9] It is in this example that we must take care not to fall into an erroneous conception of the relations of the various segments of the action: it is not the action of throwing the ball and throwing it ten feet over the first baseman's head which are related socially, but rather the attitude of throwing the ball to first base and the actual throwing of the ball that are bound together. If the "I" concept is meaningful at all in this case it must consist of the attitude which is called forth by the internalized attitudes of others, and its relation to the subsequent action. If we accept this as sound, there may or may not be a relation between the attitudes involved and the fact that the ball was thrown wild. If there is such a relation it can be explained only in terms of the uniqueness of the organized set of attitudes in terms of which the player was acting.[10] Any other explanation involves the appeal to another system of causation. Thus if the player in throwing had slipped on a banana peel, there would have been no relationship between the wild throw and the attitude which we have designated as the "I." To force the banana peel or an organic rheumatic twinge in the thrower's arm into a social frame of reference would of course be sheer nonsense.[11] There is then no significance to the concept of the "I" as the unpredictable unless we regard the "I" as that attitude, located in the generalized system of attitudes, which was called out by the situation and by the attitudes of the other players internalized in the same system. If this is so, then the problem becomes one of the analysis of the determinants of the uniqueness of the attitude configuration or of a specific attitude which renders unnecessary any division of the self into the "I" and the "me" unless it is

[8] In this analysis the sense of individuality would grow out of the set of attitudes which one took toward one's self as distinct from other objects in the environment, and not out of some mystical concept of "being." Thus this approach is in line with Mead's analysis of how the individual becomes self-conscious, but refutes any attempt to account for later self-consciousness in terms of the "I." Another somewhat related, although not identical, conception of the "I" is that it is that attitude which is issuing into response at any instant of time. In this case the conception of the "I" would be compatible with the "I" as not directly experienced, but would be undistinguishable from the "me" except as the latter concept is used to refer to attitudes in their *latent* state. This conception may be useful for some purposes, but cannot be used to explain the residual category of phenomena which it is intended to explain.

[9] Mead, *op. cit.*, pp. 175–76.

[10] Again we see that the concept of the "I" becomes functionally useless, since it is either part of the generalized other, or is part of another system of relations that has no place within a social frame of reference.

[11] If the banana peel and the rheumatic twinge become defined within the system of attitudes which constitutes the generalized other of the player, then they may be interpreted within sociological theory of personality, but not until that time.

used in the manner exemplified above, i.e., as a means of distinguishing between that attitude which is called out in any specific situation and all those others which respond to it and perhaps modify it.

This still leaves us, however, with the problem of the definite residual category that Mead introduced when he had practically finished his analysis. It is necessary to carve out of that category those sectors which contain factors related to the unpredictability of human behavior which can be analyzed within Mead's scheme and to separate them from those sectors which can only be handled within a different frame of reference. This is not an easy task to perform and the following schematization must be regarded as preliminary and provisional in nature.

Physical factors, of course, can be most easily eliminated, since the social psychologist has never insisted on including phenomena in his research that can only be explained on the basis of physical laws. Thus human behavior which is rendered deviant from expectations by changes in the physical environment must merely be regarded as something that complicates the task of prediction within the empirical sphere and about which nothing can be done within the framework of a systematic social psychology. Our ball player who slipped on a banana peel must be regarded as a phenomenon unexplainable in terms of our frame of reference, and we must recognize that the "I" has nothing to do with the outcome of a situation in which a man is kept from reaching his goal by reason of the fact that he is bound by iron chains.

When we come to the realm of biological phenomena, however, the problem becomes somewhat more complicated, since the relationship prevailing between biological and social phenomena is much more complex and subtle, and the effect of the biological is discernible even on that fundamentally social phenomenon, the pattern of integrated attitudes which Mead calls the "generalized other." While Mead himself attached no explicit biological significance to the "I," others have attempted to explain the "I" as being composed of basically biological elements. Young, for example, finds the roots of the "I" partly located in the biological or constitutional foundations of action.[12] While there is some validity in this conception of the "I," the issue is still basically confused. We cannot think of the "I" as being a biological response to the "generalized other" which is social in nature, since we know that the actual response is made up of an attitude called out from this generalized system of attitudes, and hence if they are social it too must be regarded as social. The solution to this dilemma is to be found in analyzing the "generalized other" as the product of social interaction in which an individual with certain biological characteristics has engaged. Thus the "me" or the "generalized other" of a given individual is unique in that as a biological specimen he is unique.

The question then arises as to the possibility of explaining this unique-

---

12 Young, *op. cit.*, p. 178.

ness within a social frame of reference. It is the writer's position that this is an impossibility if we intend to develop a systematic social psychology of personality. Since the set of attitudes is the product of both biological and social factors which present almost infinite possibilities of combining with one another, attempts to explain the importance of shifting biological conditions while at the same time analyzing the effect of socialization can only result in the conclusion that each personality is incapable of being compared with any other. This does not mean, however, that we should ignore the biological, but rather that we should assess it as a constant.[13] We must take the typical biological characteristics of man as man and consider them as dynamic factors in the development of personality, not merely as the preconditions of social development. In doing this we forego the urge to explain differences of behavior arising within the same social group as a product of biological differences between the members, but we are enabled to open up a new realm of research to Mead's frame of reference: the phenomenon which Kardiner calls basic personality structure.[14]

Thus we find a connective link between the work of a cultural psychoanalyst and Mead, which will make Mead's work more dynamic and the research of Kardiner more relevant for the sociologist and the social psychologist. If Mead's theory is used as an explanation of the process of socialization and Kardiner's work used as a means of delineating the dynamic relationship between the socially incorporated attitudes and the constant biological drives of men, there is some possibility of the two theories merging into one.[15] Even if this is not accomplished, there is still some benefit to be derived from the addition of a dynamic biologic element to Mead's theory; and the work of tracing the relation between socially de-

---

[13] Mead treats the biologic individual as a constant, but tends to emphasize the non-dynamic aspects of the constant. See *Mind, Self, and Society*, p. 139, 347–353, and *passim.*

[14] Abram Kardiner, *The Individual and His Society* (New York, 1939). Basic personality structure is defined by Linton in the foreword of Kardiner's study as "the constellation of personality characteristics which would appear to be congenial with the total range of institutions comprised within a given culture." p. vi. The importance of this concept is that with it Kardiner emphasizes the dynamic relationships existing between the demands of the society and the basic biological characteristics of man. This is not a reversion to instinct theory, since it is recognized that the drives are generalized and that all that is necessary is that they be satisfied some way, not in any specific. Thus: "If, in a particular culture, the biological need for sexual gratification is systematically interfered with, from infancy on, from our knowledge of human nature we can expect that this will give rise to a series of reactions, and that these reactions may eventually become petrified in institutions which offer some expression for the effects created by the frustrations concerned." p. 11. Since any institution is the result of human action we have here a situation in which the internalization of attitudes interfering with a basic drive result in something new: a culture complex which was not present before, and which is due to just this dynamic interaction between internalized attitude and biological drives.

[15] It must be remembered that this convergence becomes possible only after we have reopened Mead's system by throwing out the concept of the "I" and re-examining the residual category of phenomena which Mead cloaked with this concept.

rived attitudes, the basic personality structure, and the secondary institutions, which are the product of the dynamic interaction of basic drives and social attitudes, will not suffer because of an increased knowledge of how the incorporation of social attitudes into the personality actually takes place. Attempts to reconcile different bodies of theory that stem from such divergent origins as do these two is obviously dangerous, but since the psychoanalysts are gradually approaching a social point of view the gap between the two bodies of theory is much more apparent than real.[16]

The application of this point of view which considers biological factors as dynamic elements in the formation of the personality also makes it possible to explain widely divergent overt behavior where the difference between the social attitudes involved seems very slight. If one family adds just a slightly higher degree of emphasis on anti-masturbation attitudes than does another, with the result that the sexual behavior of the offspring of the two families varies widely, it might be possible to explain this difference on the basis of the relation between the sex drive and the two sets of attitudes.

In all the above analysis of the relation of biological factors to social factors in the formation of unique attitudes and behavior, we have approached the central problem which faces us, but have not quite come to grips with it. That problem is, of course, whether there is any source of uniqueness of attitudes and behavior that is definitively social in nature, and that does not involve extra-social considerations. The generic answer to this question is probably in the negative. Given absolutely the same biological makeup, the identical geographic environment, a constancy in the time element, and identical physical conditions, there seems no reason to believe that there is anything in the process of socialization that would lead to divergent attitudes and hence to divergent behavior. This, however, is scarcely a relevant answer. Once a process of attitude differentiation sets in, for whatever reason, it should be obvious that the operation of purely social factors will increase that differentiation. This is most apparent in the social interaction that takes place between people who have divergent backgrounds. The personality structures of both are modified, usually in an unpredictable direction, and in a direction which perhaps has never been manifested before in either of the social groups from which the individuals originated. If either of these individuals returns to his group the result is the differentiation of attitudes within the group, provided the individual is not removed

---

[16] The dangers inherent in the reconciling of divergent bodies of theory grow primarily from two sources: premature reconciliation and crude eclecticism. This attempt to bring together the work of Kardiner and Mead may be somewhat premature since the cultural psychoanalysts are still hazy in their ideas concerning the influence and nature of social factors, and since such convergence also depends on the validity of the writer's arguments concerning the "I"; but it certainly does not suffer from eclecticism since there is no picking and choosing involved, but rather a conjunction of the theories in their totality has been suggested.

in order to remove the danger of change. The literature which we have accumulated concerning culture contact, acculturation, and social change within a society bears witness to this analysis. Thus a unique set of attitudes is the produce of the social interaction in which one engages with an individual who has a different set of attitudes, and at least part of this change can be viewed as brought about by purely social factors.

The result of continued differentiation of this sort is a growing discrepancy between the various basic attitudes which are the common property of the group, and a child born into this type of society is likely to inherit a set of attitudes which are not consistently related to one another. The analysis of this situation is best carried out in terms of Mead's theory of internal conversation.[17] When a situation arises which is governed by conflicting attitudes, unless the self of the individual is compartmentalized, a conversation between various aspects of the self ensues and the resultant attitude is likely to diverge significantly from both of the previously existing ones, so that the overt action may be greatly different from what anyone expected.

Finally, there are shifts in attitudes which occur as a result of success or failure in reaching the goals or values defined by the attitudes so that the behavior becomes unpredictable. Success is almost certain to result in the reinforcement of the attitude, but prolonged and persistent failure may result in shifts in attitudes in at least two basic fashions. The first is simply that if the defined value is important enough, the ethically enjoined attitudes toward the means will gradually lose their strength so that the goal may be sought by a new pattern of activity.[18] The second involves an evaluation of failure. If, for example, the culture places a high premium on success, prolonged failure is likely to result in self-condemnation which in turn violates basic security attitudes. In turn the interaction of these attitudes may result in what Horney has called neurotic trends, set up to protect the individual.[19] The nature of this trend is likely to depend on other techniques for gaining security which are approved by the society.

---

[17] Mead, *op cit.*, pp. 61–75.

[18] An analysis of this type of attitude shift is to be found in Robert K. Merton's article, "Social Structure and Anomie," *American Sociological Review*, III (1938), 672–682.

[19] While the cultural psychoanalysis of Kardiner is oriented about the interplay of biological and social factors, Karen Horney's studies are concerned with the nature of conflict between social attitudes within the individual. If we disregard her undue emphasis on security, her research delineates quite clearly certain types of personality conflict based on the presence of conflicting attitudes, or of attitudes conflicting with actual performance, and traces the conflicts back to their origin in the culture pattern of our society. The same things may be said of the possible convergence of Horney's theory with that of Mead as were said in the case of Kardiner and Mead, except that in this case Horney offers a technique for unraveling the relations existing between conflicting attitudes within Mead's frame of reference. See Karen Horney, *New Ways in Psychoanalysis* (New York, 1939); *The Neurotic Personality of Our Time* (New York, 1937); and "Culture and Neurosis, "*American Sociological Review*, I (1936), pp. 221–230.

It is manifestly impossible to present all the various forms of attitude differentiation which arise out of the dynamic interplay between differing social attitudes and the situation in which they are expressed, but we have succeeded, perhaps, in pointing out the scientific benefits to be derived from the breaking down of the residual category which Mead called the "I" into some of its various components. We have discovered that some uniquenesses in behavior are unexplainable in terms of a social frame of reference; that others can be explained only in terms of the dynamic interaction of a constant biological factor and various social factors; and finally, that there does exist a realm of attitude differentiation which analytically belongs wholly within the field of social interaction. We must remember that these various forms are intermixed in the real world, but nevertheless, they are analytically separable.

One more result of this breakdown of the residual category should now be apparent: Within the framework of Mead's theory certain aspects of behavior which were unexplainable except by the use of the ambiguous concepts of the "I" and the "me" are now not only explainable but have been processed so that they may to some extent even become predictable. If we recognize the basic social factors at work in attitude differentiation, it should be possible to discover predictable features in their recurrence. The way has already been opened by the cultural psychoanalysts, and with the reopening of Mead's system to include the basic findings of these researchers, it seems plausible to expect that future research will discover that variation from the dominant sets of attitudes of any society are not random but follow a pattern that can be discovered, provided one stays within the limits of the social frame of reference. That there always will be unexplainable differences in attitude and action is obvious, but that the area not only of theoretical unpredictability but of empirical unpredictability will be cut down can certainly be anticipated. In that case the extremely high probabilities that of necessity accompany all theoretical prediction will be of more significance, in that they will serve to increase the somewhat low probabilities which attend our present efforts at empirical prediction. We shall never know all about reality, but if we recognize the nature of systematic science and its limitations, we can approach closer and closer to the goal.

Experiments on Factors
Related to Self-Concept Change

A. Theoretical Framework

The Cooley-Mead formulations concerning the self-concept are primarily focused on the relationships between other persons' responses to an individual and his conception of himself. More specifically, they argue that a person's conception of himself comes about as a result of the way he perceives the responses of others toward him [Cooley's "looking-glass self" (5) and Mead's "taking-the-role-of-the-other" (14)]. This, they aver, is particularly important, since the way the individual sees himself (his self-concept) has the function of directing, or influencing, the way he will behave.

This approach has had wide acceptance among social psychologists, but not without some reservations. The vague concepts and general propositions make its application very difficult. However, when the basic ideas are used as a general framework from which more specific statements are developed, the theory is most fruitful. These extensions or elaborations are not necessarily derived from the theory in a logical sense, but are intervening claims that reduce the generality or abstractness of the framework and bring it conceptually closer to the specific phenomena it purports to explain.

In the study reported here, previous work on one of the propositions is used as a framework from which specific hypotheses are developed to be tested. The proposition may be stated as follows: *The individual's conception of himself is based on his perception of the way others are responding to him.* There is ample research evidence supporting this general relationship between individuals' perceptions of others and their self-concepts. However, few writers in this tradition have paid specific attention to how this process works. It is obvious that the theorists are not arguing that every time a new response is directed toward an individual there will be a corresponding change in his self-concept. What is needed is an expansion of this general proposition so that the relationships are made explicit. The basic question seems to be: *Under what conditions do the perceptions of the others' responses have an effect on the individual's self-conception?*

The theoretical framework and what evidence there is available in the

John W. Kinch, "Experiments on Factors Related to Self-Concept Change," *Journal of Social Psychology*, vol. 74 (1968), pp. 251–258. Reprinted by permission.

literature suggest that the effect of perceived responses on the self-concept is a function of a series of factors involved in interpersonal contacts. They are (*a*) the *frequency* of responses in the course of these interpersonal contacts, (*b*) the perceived *importance* of the contacts, (*c*) the *temporal proximity* of the contacts, and (*d*) the *consistency* of the responses resulting from the contacts. It should be understood that each of the hypotheses that follows is preceded by an implied "other-factors-being-equal."

1. HYPOTHESIS 1 (FREQUENCY)

The more frequently the individual perceives others as responding toward him in a particular way, the more likely he is to align his self-concept with the perceived responses.

Although very little attention is given to the direct test of this notion, there are many studies that implicitly do so. For example, experimental studies have for the most part given the subjects specific ratings or evaluations which, in effect, increase the frequency of these responses, thus indirectly testing this hypothesis (4, 9, 13, 17).

2. HYPOTHESIS 2 (IMPORTANCE)

The more important the individual perceives the contact between himself and the others to be, the more likely it is that the individual's perceptions of the responses of the others will be used in defining his self-image. It is widely accepted that contacts with "significant others" are required before the individual's self-concept will be affected. These "significant others" may take the form of prestigeful persons (experts) or of personal acquaintances (friends). However, the research evidence available is not completely consistent on this subject (4, 10, 11).

3. HYPOTHESIS 3 (TEMPORAL PROXIMITY)

The individual's concept of himself is a function of (a) the earliest evaluations he receives on a particular attribute and (b) the most immediate evaluations. This hypothesis has two parts. First, it is contended that the *first contacts* which the individual perceives as favoring a particular self-concept are of extreme importance. Self-conceptions that develop in early childhood are likely to persist throughout life. No direct evidence is available on this hypothesis, but there is considerable indirect evidence when one considers the *selective* aspect of early evaluations. If the author's basic contention is true that the responses of others are used in the original formation of the self-concept, there is ample evidence in the literature to suggest that persons choose friends and join groups which they perceive as evaluating them congruently with their perception of themselves (2, 3, 8, 15). Therefore, once an individual develops a conception of himself, he will interact as much as possible with others who will reinforce this conception for him. The second part of Hypothesis 3 suggests that those *most immediate contacts* are important in understanding the individual's self-concept at any given time. Almost without exception those studies which have compared perceived responses of others to self-concepts have dealt with responses of others in the immediate situation (7, 16). In one study that directly confronted this issue, it was found that the most exaggerated changes were observed immediately following the experiment. However, some significant change still remained six weeks following the experiment, which suggests some lasting effects (9).

4. HYPOTHESIS 4 (CONSISTENCY)

The more the individual perceives a consistent pattern in the responses of others, the more likely he is to let this affect his self-concept.

B. Research Design

The research presented here empirically evaluates certain aspects of the hypotheses suggested above. It employs a series of experiments—each following the classical design with before and after tests on both experimental and control groups. The dependent variable concerns changes in one aspect of an individual's self-concept and the independent, or experimental, variables consist of the "factors" (frequency, importance, temporal proximity, and consistency) which are varied, one at time, in the experimental situations.

In the present study the notion of the self-concept is defined as the *organization of qualities which the individual attributes to himself.* Although this self-concept is "organized," it cannot be measured on a single continuum of self-regard (as many social psychologists have used the concept), but must be analyzed in terms of individual attributes or clusters of attributes. There seems to be substantial evidence for this contention (1, 6, 13, 17). In the present study, subjects were required to evaluate themselves on several descriptive objectives by use of a seven-point scale. Rather than attempt to accumulate these self-evaluations, the investigation concentrated on one adjective, "leadership."

As in other experimental studies of the self, the subjects were asked to evaluate themselves before and after they were involved in an experimental situation. In the set of experiments, conditions were varied in order to demonstrate the effect of those factors which the hypotheses suggest should influence self-concept change. In order to specify the procedure more clearly, a detailed description follows: Each experiment followed a design whereby all participants, with one exception, were confederates of the investigator. During the activity in the experimental setting, the one naive student was assigned a position of leadership and was required to direct the others. On completion of this activity the confederates were presented to the naive subject as students who were experts in organizational dynamics, all having taken advanced courses on the subject. They were then asked by the investigator to rate the naive subject's performance as a leader. This was done according to a prearranged system, *independent of the subject's actual performance*. The ratings were communicated by the verbal response of each confederate and were marked on a scale on the blackboard in front of all the participants. The confederates were pre-instructed to perform the task reasonably well regardless of the naive subject's orders, so that the prearranged ratings did not appear out of line.

Four variations in the confederates' ratings made up what were called "experimental conditions" and were designed to test several of the hypotheses. In Experimental Condition 1, each subject was rated favorably by all experts with very little variation in ratings. In the second condition (E.C. 2) each subject was involved in two sessions, thus doubling the number of evaluations which they received. Experimental Conditions 3 and 4 followed the same pattern as E.C. 1, except that in E.C. 3 only five confederates were used and a sixth rating was given by the investigator conducting the experiment, and in E.C. 4 the six ratings were more dispersed and less consistent than in E.C. 1, although the average ratings were the same for both. These categories were compared with a control group: a matched category of students who did not participate in the experiment.

All the prearranged ratings were *higher* than the individual had rated himself before the experiment. The question of the consequence of lower ratings was not examined. In a limited experiment in which negative ratings were given a number of subjects, the results seemed to suggest that these ratings were even more influential in changing self-concepts than were the positive ratings. However, for ethical reasons this study was limited to only a few students and was not continued after the first responses were considered (12). About half of the naive students were interviewed and questioned about their impressions of the experiment. Although there were several reasons for these interviews, one major concern was with establishing some idea of the subjects' perception of the ratings they were given. Since the theory suggests that it is the way the individual *perceives* the responses of others that changes his self-concept, it was felt that the investigators must make certain that the favorable ratings which were given the subjects were perceived as such.

The difficulty of setting up an experiment that would test the hypotheses of this theory is apparent. The experimental situation had to be somewhat artificial. The ratings were rather formal compared with the ratings that one gets in everyday life. The student participation in the experiment took a relatively short time (10 minutes). Four to five weeks elapsed between the before and after tests. During that time these freshmen in college were experiencing many other situations relevant to their self-concept. For these reasons the sensitivity of the experiment and its significance for the respondents was seen as one of the major problems to be dealt with in the research presented here. Several devices were employed to increase the significance of the situation for the subjects. The subjects were required to work with the other members of the experiment "as a team," and it was this "team" that rated them. In other experiments of this type, the subjects were rated by some*one* (expert, stranger, or friend) who was not engaged with them in the experiment. In the interviews, the subjects indicated considerable concern over what ratings they received and considered the ratings as favorable. This suggests that the others in the experiment were significant to them.

The problem of sample size is particularly difficult in this type of design, since, for each subject, there must be a separate experiment, plus complete before and after test information. When the total number of cases is divided into four experimental conditions and a control group, the number of cases in any one condition is likely to be cut seriously low. This was the case in the present study, which started with 105 subjects, 21 assigned to each of the four experimental conditions and 21 to the control group. Some of the disadvantages of the small numbers were reduced by precision matching and randomization of assignments.

C. Results

By comparing before-after changes in self-concept ratings on leadership for the subjects in each of the conditions, evidence is brought to bear on at least part of three of the four hypotheses mentioned above. The complete results are reported in Table 1.

There are several ways in which these data may be applied to Hypothesis 1. In this hypothesis it is suggested that the more frequently a person perceives a particular type of response directed toward him, the more likely he is to use that response in changing his self-concept. Since all those taking part in the experiments had a particular type of response (favorable ratings on leadership) directed toward them, we can assume that "on the average" this group has had more of this type of response than the control group. Therefore, one test of the hypothesis is a simple comparison of those in the experimental groups with those in the control group. The results are in the expected direction with mean changes of +.65 of a unit on the rating scale for those in the experimental groups ($N = 71$) and only +.23 of a unit for the control group ($N = 21$). The differences between the two changes are statistically significant at the .05 level of significance ($t = 1.76$, difference between independent mean test).

TABLE 1. Mean self-ratings on leadership before and after experimental evaluations by experimental conditions

Experimental condition	N	Before		After		Before-after differences		
		M	SD	M	SD	M	SD	t
E.C. 1 (Standard)	19	4.26	1.02	4.63	.93	.37	.98	1.59
E.C. 2 (Repeat)	18	4.28	1.04	5.28	.73	1.00	1.15	3.57**
E.C. 3 (Importance)	19	4.26	1.12	4.89	.73	.63	.74	3.62**
E.C. 4 (Dispersed)	15	4.20	1.11	4.80	.83	.60	.92	2.36*
All experimental conditions	71	4.25	1.07	4.90	.83	.65	.99	5.45**
Control group	21	4.29	1.16	4.52	.96	.23	.75	1.42

Note: All tests are one-tailed. The *t*'s above refer to the difference between the before and after means of dependent samples.
* $p < .05$.
** $p < .01$.

A more refined test on this hypothesis involves comparing those in E.C. 2 with those in E.C. 1 and the control group, since the subjects in E.C. 2 had more of a particular type of response directed toward them than did the subjects in E.C. 1. The results support the hypothesis. Those who performed under E.C. 2 showed a mean change in their self-conceptions of one complete unit on the rating scale, while those in E.C. 1 changed only .37 of a unit. This difference is statistically significant ($t = 2.29$, difference between independent mean test).

From Hypothesis 2 (Importance) it was felt that the added prestige of the investigator's rating in E.C. 3 would lead to greater changes than in the comparable E.C. 1. Here the results are in the expected direction; however, the difference between the two experimental groups was small and not statistically significant (means of .37 and .63 for E.C. 1 and 3, respectively— $t = .93$).

Hypothesis 4 suggests that the consistency of responses is important and would lead to the expectation of a greater before-after difference in E.C. 1 than in E.C. 4. Here the results show just the opposite. Those students who were given about the same ratings by all the raters changed less than those subjects who were given more dispersed ratings (mean changes of .37 in E.C. 1 as compared with a change of .60 in E.C. 4).

D. Summary

The study described here is one in a series of studies proposed by the author designed to vary systematically factors relevant to changes in self-conceptions. Although experimental studies of this type are hampered by the several difficulties apparent in this report, the valuable manipulative power that the investigator has over his variables allows crucial tests which could not be accomplished by other methods. The need for systematic empirical support or investigation of social psychological theory is recognized by all. This study has attempted to provide that type of support for the Mead-Cooley notions about the self-concept.

References

1. Akeret, R. U. Interrelationships among various dimensions of the self concept. *J. Counsel. Psychol.*, 1959, 6, 199–201.
2. Backman, C. W., & Secord, P. F. The effect of perceived liking on interpersonal attraction. *Hum. Relat.*, 1959, 12, 379–384.
3. ————. Liking, selective interaction, and misperception in congruent interpersonal relations. *Sociometry*, 1962, 25, 321–335.
4. Bergin, A. The effect of dissonant persuasive communications upon changes in a self-referring attitude. *J. Personal.*, 1962, 30, 423–438.
5. Cooley, C. H. Human Nature and the Social Order. New York: Scribner, 1902.
6. Couch, C. Family role specialization and self-attitudes in children. *Sociolog. Quart.*, 1962, 3, 115–122.
7. Davidson, H. H., & Lang, G. Children's perceptions of their teachers' feelings toward them related to self-perception, school achievement and behavior. *J. Exper. Educ.*, 1960, 29, 107–118.
8. Dittes, J. E. Attractiveness of group as a function of self-esteem and acceptance by group. *J. Abn. & Soc. Psychol.*, 1959, 59, 77–82.
9. Haas, H. L., & Moehr, M. L. Two experiments on the concept of self and the reactions of others. *J. Personal. & Soc. Psychol.*, 1965, 1, 100–105.
10. Harvey, O. J., Kelley, H. H., & Shapiro, M. M. Reactions to unfavorable evaluations of the self made by other persons. *J. Personal.*, 1957, 25, 393–411.
11. Kennedy, J. L., & Lasswell, H. D. A cross-cultural test of self-image. *Hum. Organization*, 1958, 17, 41–43.
12. Kinch, J. W. The manipulation of subjects in experiments. Unpublished paper presented at the Pacific Sociological Association Meetings, Vancouver, British Columbia, Canada, 1966.
13. Maehr, M., Mensing, J., & Nafager, S. Concept of self and the reaction of others. *Sociometry*, 1962, 25, 353–357.
14. Mead, G. H. *Mind, Self, and Society.* Chicago, Ill.: Univ. Chicago Press, 1934.
15. Reese, H. W. Relationships between self-acceptance and sociometric choices. *J. Abn. & Soc. Psychol.*, 1961, 62, 472–474.
16. Rosengren, W. R. The self in the emotionally disturbed. *Amer. J. Sociol.*, 1961, 66, 454–462.
17. Videbeck, R. Self-conception and the reaction of others. *Sociometry*, 1960, 23, 351–359.

Self-Conceptions and Others:
A Further Test of Meadian Hypotheses

In this paper we attempt to do the following with respect to the symbolic interactionist approach to social psychological phenomena: (1) to add to its relatively meager empirical base; (2) to develop a neglected aspect of the position, namely, the time dimension; and (3) to contribute to both the replication and the extension of the limited systematic research which has used this particular framework to focus on the key concept of self.

That the symbolic interactionist approach does not rest on a substantial body of empirical research has been noted by even such a sympathetic critic as Merton.[1] Proponents of the approach have tended to substitute discursive illustrations for hypothesis testing especially when setting forth the ideas of George H. Mead, the major progenitor of the scheme. In fact, some of the major commentators on Mead have àt times suggested that his prime contribution is an abstract frame of reference with which an observer can look at behavior rather than a set of specific hypotheses to be tested.[2] We try to show it is possible to test a key Meadian notion on the relationship between self-conception and social others, through an examination of concrete data.

E. L. Quarantelli and Joseph Cooper, "Self-Conceptions and Others: A Further Test of Meadian Hypotheses," The Sociological Quarterly, vol. 7, no. 3 (Summer 1966), pp. 281–297. Reprinted by permission.

This investigation was supported in part by Public Health Service Research Grant DH–00014–04, The Division of Dental Public Health and Resources. Margaret Helfrich played an important role in gathering a major part of the data used in the analysis. The authors are also indebted to Albert Schwartz for his suggestions and advice on earlier drafts. James Ross helped with some of the data processing.

[1] Robert K. Merton, Social Theory and Social Structure, rev. and enlarged (Glencoe, Ill.: Free Press, 1957), p. 239. See also Manford Kuhn, "Major Trends in Symbolic Interaction Theory in the Past Twenty-Five Years," Sociological Quarterly, 5:61–84 (Winter, 1964).

[2] For example, Strauss once wrote in a preface to a compilation of Mead's work: "The truth of the matter seems to be that Mead offers us not so much specific hypotheses, or even a theory, as a rather abstract frame of reference." See Anselm Strauss (ed.), The Social Psychology of George Herbert Mead (Chicago: Univ. of Chicago Press, 1956), p. xvi. These remarks are not in the preface to the 1964 second edition of the same book entitled George Herbert Mead on Social Psychology. See also, Guy E. Swanson, "Mead and Freud: Their Relevance for Social Psychology," Sociometry, 24: 319–39 (Dec., 1961). A somewhat contrasting viewpoint is presented by John Kinch, "A Formalized Theory of the Self Concept," American Journal of Sociology, 68:481–86 (Jan., 1963).

Stryker has noted the general paucity of symbolic interactionist studies which systematically deal with the time dimension in the stream of human conducts.[3] This is a telling criticism, since the processual aspects of behavior are central to the interactionist frame of reference. Recent efforts to formulate and test hypotheses based on Mead's view of the self as product of social interaction are cases in point.[4] Although these studies unambiguously view self-conceptions as dynamic consequences of interaction, self-attitudes are typically analyzed either with reference to some static instant or against a time period of short duration.[5] In contrast, our study utilizes data covering time periods of up to two years.

Finally, the symbolic interactionist approach suffers, as does most sociology, from a lack of replication and cumulation. To be sure, findings from innumerable studies can be interpreted in Meadian terms. However, such analyses do not represent any kind of systematic testing of the framework. Even a number of the studies recently brought together by Rose, as being within the symbolic interactionist framework, are neither clearly drawn from the basic propositions in the formulation nor built upon earlier research.[6] This paper instead reports a partial replication of two prior studies specifically testing hypotheses based on Mead's notion of the social origins of the self. It also extends the range of these earlier studies by offering data in support of derived hypotheses which focus on future oriented self-conceptions.

Theoretical Background

As many observers have noted, the dynamic nature of the symbolic interactionist framework has made its empirical test exceedingly difficult. This has been particularly true with respect to a central thesis of the scheme,

[3] Sheldon Stryker, "The Interactional and Situational Approaches" in Harold Christensen (ed.), *Handbook of Marriage and the Family* (Chicago: Rand McNally, 1964), p. 162. Neglect of the time dimension in sociological studies has been stressed by Wilbert Moore in his *Man, Time and Society* (New York: Wiley, 1963).

[4] For example, S. Frank Miyamoto and Sanford Dornbusch, "A Test of the Symbolic Interactionist Hypothesis of Self-Conception," *American Journal of Sociology*, 617:399–403 (Mar., 1956); Lee Reeder, George Donohue, and Arturo Biblarz, "Conceptions of Self and Others," *American Journal of Sociology*, 66:153–59 (Sept., 1960); Carl Couch, "Self-Attitude and Degree of Agreement with Immediate Others," *American Journal of Sociology*, 63:491–96 (Mar., 1958); Martin Maehn, Josef Mensing and Samuel Nafager, "Concept of Self and the Reactions of Others," *Sociometry*, 25:353–57 (Dec., 1962); and John J. Sherwood, "Self Identity and Referent Others," *Sociometry*, 28:66–81 (Mar., 1965).

[5] At most the time period is a matter of weeks. For example, a six week period was used by Melvin Manis in "Social Interaction and the Self Concept," *Journal of Abnormal and Social Psychology*, 51:362–70 (Nov., 1955).

[6] Arnold Rose (ed.), *Human Behavior and Social Processes* (Boston: Houghton Mifflin, 1962).

the view that the self is social in that it is derived from responses of other persons. Nevertheless, some aspects of this particular idea have been investigated, first by Miyamoto and Dornbusch and later by Reeder, Donohue, and Biblarz.[7]

Miyamoto and Dornbusch, using ten somewhat miscellaneous semi-groupings from fraternities, sororities, and college sociology classes, ask their respondents to give self-ratings and also to rate every other group member on four specified personal characteristics. They conclude that their findings from 195 individuals not only show the possibility of empirically studying self-conception within the symbolic interactionist framework, but also support three general propositions. First, the response of others is related to self-conceptions; second, the subject's perception of that response is more closely related to self-conceptions than the actual response of others; and third, an individual's self-conception is more closely related to his estimate of the generalized attitude toward him than to the perceived responses of members of a particular group.

Reeder, Donohue, and Biblarz are particularly interested in the relation between self-conception and both the actual and the perceived ratings by members of given groups. They report on nine work crews (totaling 54 enlisted men), at a small military base. Each respondent was asked to rank every member of his crew (including himself) in terms of two criteria: best worker and best leader. Further, each respondent was asked to indicate how he thought most of the men in his group would rank him on these dimensions. Reeder and his co-workers find, in general, that the responses of others have "an influence in shaping one's self-definition" and that his self-definition is "derived chiefly from the perception of the generalized other."[8] In essence, the findings parallel those reported by Miyamoto and Dornbusch.

Both sets of authors judge their research as supporting key notions implicit in the Meadian conception of the social nature of the self. Yet both acknowledge the limited conclusions of their studies, while also indicating that future research should go beyond duplicating their own work. Hence our work is not merely a replication of their research on a different and much larger population. More important, we try to develop three lines of new research suggested to us by these previous studies.

First, a better indicator of self-conception is desirable. Miyamoto and Dornbusch use self-ratings of intelligence, self-confidence, physical attractiveness and likableness as an index of self-conception. But no evidence is presented that any or all of these features were salient in the self-conception of their respondents. While there is no reason to question that some of these characteristics were central to parts of the self-definition of some of their

---

[7] Miyamoto and Dornbusch, *op. cit.*; Reeder, Donohue, and Biblarz, *op. cit.*
[8] *Ibid.*, p. 158.

subjects,[9] their centrality to the selves of all of the participants in the study is neither subjectively nor objectively argued or documented. Similarly, Reeder and his co-workers do not particularly justify their use of ranking along the dimensions of best leader and best worker as a valid measure of the individual's self-conception. They simply say that "it is assumed that the self-rank is an expression of the individual's self-conception."[10] An index of self-conception for which a case for saliency in the life of the individual can be made would be more in keeping with Mead's view.

Second, neither of the previous studies takes into account the time dimension in the emergence and maintenance of the self. The questions put to respondents are confined to the instant of questioning. If the Meadian formulation—that the individual learns to define and to identify himself as he begins to perceive (and later to share) the responses of others toward him—is correct, this neglect of time is a serious omission in the research design. There are two ways to remedy this oversight. One way is through a longitudinal study which catches the individual's self-conceptions at two or more points in time. Another way is by having the respondent project his self-conceptions at future times. The latter procedure has the advantage of being less likely to be confused by the attempts of individuals to reconcile what they wish they were with what they perceive themselves to be.

Third, both previous studies struggle to operationalize the somewhat abstract concept of the "generalized other" and seem, in part, to deviate from what its originator had in mind. Miyamoto and Dornbusch take the position that Mead treats the "generalized other" as the individual's conception of the organized social process of which he is a part, and that he sees it "composed of numerous specialized roles."[11] They note, however, that persons often enter into social relationships wherein there is a response to a "generalized other," but where the organization of roles is obscure or minimal. In fact, the Miyamoto and Dornbusch study relies upon social groupings "whose members were, at best, loosely joined by friendships and had no definite organized group activity within which to identify their respective roles."[12] Accordingly, their index of the generalized other is based on the respondent's perception of the *typical* attitudes of others toward him. Operationally, they ask: "How intelligent . . . do most people think you are?"[13]

[9] Studies that have used the "Who Am I?" instrument would cast some doubt about the saliency of all four characteristics in the self-conceptions of many persons. See Manford Kuhn, "Self-Attitudes by Age, Sex, and Professional Training," *Sociological Quarterly*, 1:40–55 (Jan., 1960).

[10] Reeder, Donohue, and Biblarz, *op. cit.*, p. 154.

[11] Miyamoto and Dornbusch, *op. cit.*, p. 400.

[12] *Ibid.*

[13] *Ibid.*, p. 410. There is an interesting assumption here that the "typical" is equivalent to the "most."

In other words, Miyamoto and Dornbusch use the term "generalized other" to refer to the nonparticular other taken into account by the individual in situations which are lacking organization for him.[14] This seems a partial, albeit conscious, departure from the Meadian formulation. Mead, in a frequently cited passage, speaks of the generalized other as the process whereby the person "takes the attitudes of the organized social group to which he belongs."[15] As suggested in his account on the game stage in the development of the self, the internalization of the generalized other requires the individual to define and regulate his conduct with regard for the expectations of a complexly organized multiplicity of other actors.

Reeder and his co-workers capture part of this formulation. As an index of the generalized other, they use the participant's "estimated objective group rating." In turn, this rating is based on the respondent's indication of the rank which he thinks most of his work group assign him with respect to two criteria—leadership and workmanship. Unlike the procedure used by Miyamoto and Dornbusch, this technique has the merit of conceiving the generalized other in terms of the attitudes of an organized and on-going group.

Reeder and his co-authors, however, assume "that the individual, in making an estimate of how the group ranks him, is taking the role of the generalized other."[16] In this research the group is treated as the equivalent of the small number of immediately present individuals in any given work crew. This is not inconsistent with one of Mead's two somewhat different uses of the term "organization." In the research of Reeder and his colleagues, the work crews seem analogous to Mead's famous example of the ball team, where the team is seen as the generalized other "insofar as it enters —as an organized process or social activity—into the experience of any one of the individual members."[17] Mead's other use of the term "organization," however, appears to place greater stress on the actor's organizing of attitudes towards himself than on the possibility that these attitudes may be derived from an organized activity. Even while discussing games, it is noted: "We get then an organization of attitudes of those involved in the same process."[18] Clearly the process can extend beyond any group. In fact, most of Mead's discussion of the generalized other is in terms of the socialization of the child. In this context, the child's organization of the attitudes of others is of greater importance than the organized nature of the activity wherein he draws his self-conception.

At still another point, Mead observes that the individual enters into

[14] *Ibid.*, p. 400.
[15] Charles W. Morris (ed.), *Mind, Self and Society* (Chicago: University of Chicago Press, 1934), p. 155.
[16] Reeder, Donohue, and Biblarz, *op. cit.*, p. 154.
[17] Morris, *op. cit.*, p. 154.
[18] *Ibid.*, p. 154.

two kinds of social relations: "Some of them are concrete social classes or subgroups. . . . The others are abstract social classes or subgroups . . . in terms of which their individual members are related to one another only more or less indirectly and which only more or less indirectly function as social units. . . ."[19] A research effort centered on the latter formulation seems called for. The generalized other would be viewed as the individual's perception of the responses of others as he sees them with regard to some salient aspect of himself. The perceiving individual and the others whose responses he organizes need not be members of any particular group. They do, however, stand in some role relationship to him (e.g., as friend or teacher). Analysis along these lines emphasizes process rather than structure. Such an analysis proceeds from the actor's point of view and not from the standpoint of an outside observer.

Given these considerations, this study seeks to develop a more salient index of self-conception, to incorporate the temporal aspect of the process of self-identification and to operationalize the generalized other so as to reflect Mead's concern with the self-as-process.

Methods and Techniques

We draw data for this study from a much broader investigation of factors influencing the professionalization of dental students. In the larger effort on career lines, we are following two successive waves of students panel-like from the time of entrance into dental school until graduation. (Two other waves are under study for shorter periods.) This report is based on a small segment of the extensive questionnaire data obtained from all students at the very beginning of each academic year. The larger study is still in progress; but data are available from 600 freshmen (waves 1, 2, 3, 4) and from 450 sophomores (waves 1, 2, 3).[20] No doubt our findings would be strengthened if all the longitudinal data (ultimately to cover the entire four years' experience of 300 dental students) were available. However, the particular hypotheses to be examined are testable just as readily with the information already in hand; that is, with data covering one year's actual experience, as well as a two-year projection of self-ratings.

Among many other questions, we asked each student at the start of every academic year to complete the following professional labeling scale. The line in the diagram represents an arbitrary distance between a dental student and a dentist.

---

[19] *Ibid.*, p. 157.
[20] Because of dropouts and failures to answer relevant questions we have data for only 594 freshmen and 432 sophomores.

Using *ONE* of the *WHOLE* numbers on this line write in *below:*

A. Where would you place yourself at this time?———

B. Which point on the line is closest to where you think you will be one year from now?———

C. In general, where do you think you will be about two years from now, i.e., when you start to work in the clinic?———

D. Where do you think that the dental faculty now sees you?———

E. Where do you think that the faculty will expect you to be one year from now?———

F. Where do you think your parents now see you?———

G. (IF MARRIED) Where do you think your wife now sees you?———

H. Where do you think that your non-dental school friends and acquaintances now see you?———

I. Where do you think that your classmates now see you?———

J. Where do you think that the advanced dental students now see you?———

We use the respondent's self-placement on the scale (Item A) as a salient index of self-conception. The student's very presence in a professional school is taken as a firm indication that a dental career is of considerable importance to him. Entering dental school is not only a voluntary act on the part of the student but it also follows upon a series of necessarily rather self-conscious decisions. Even without assuming total or identical commitment to the profession, the embarkation upon a long and expensive educational career argues for the importance of the undertaking to the participant. In this respect the dental student differs from the typical social club member, the student in a sociology class, or the worker on a military crew.

In addition to recording his current location (or actual self-conception) on the professional labeling scale, each respondent projected the locations he expected to occupy in one or two years' time (Items B–C). We discuss these as projected self-ratings or self-conceptions. Further, each respondent noted his perception of current and projected placements by a variety of others: (Items D–J) these we treat as *perceived*—actual or projected—ratings by others. A parallel questionnaire completed by 86 percent of the dental school's faculty (N–93), provides data on the actual faculty ratings of the students at three points in their academic careers: these data we refer to as the *actual* ratings—current or projected—by others. Table 1 summarizes the data considered in this study. The means of both

TABLE 1. Means of actual and projected ratings by self and others

			Freshmen			
	High		Low		Total	
	x̄	N	x̄	N	x̄	N
		Self-ratings				
Current	3.18	91	1.00	503	1.33	594
Projection						
One-Year	4.90	91	2.87	502	3.18	593
Two-Year	6.86	91	5.46	499	5.67	590
		Perceived Ratings by Others				
Current						
Faculty	2.12	89	1.04	494	1.21	583
Upperclassmen	2.07	91	1.05	501	1.20	592
Classmates	2.80	91	1.12	492	1.39	583
Nondental Friends	3.95	91	2.46	501	2.69	592
Parents	4.15	88	2.31	495	2.58	583
Wives	4.60	20	1.88	130	2.25	150
Aggregate 1*	3.08	—	1.61	—	1.84	—
Aggregate 2†	3.15	—	1.73	—	1.94	—
Projection						
One-Year Faculty	4.36	91	2.91	502	3.13	593
		Actual Ratings by Faculty				
Current	1.71	80	1.71	80	1.71	80
Projection						
One-Year	2.94	80	2.94	80	2.94	80
Two-Year	4.96	80	4.96	80	4.96	80

* Includes classmates.
† Excludes classmates.

current and projected ratings at the onset of two academic years are recorded for three analytical categories: self-ratings, perceived ratings by others, and actual ratings by faculty.[21]

We distinguish between particular others and the generalized other. Particular others are specific social alters we assume to be saliently related to our respondents in their role as dental students. Six categories of particular others are used: faculty, classmates, upperclassmen, nondental school friends, parents, and in appropriate cases, wives. Potentially at least, these categories appear to exhaust the likely sources of major interaction within which the process of self-identification could be developed. Furthermore, and important to our case, we take the perceived responses of these others toward a salient aspect of the student self-conception—his position on the professional labeling scale.

[21] We do not have comparable faculty ratings of sophomores.

TABLE 1 (cont.)

	High		Low		Total	
	x̄	N	x̄	N	x̄	N
Self-ratings						
Current	3.56	214	1.84	218	2.69	432
Projection						
One-Year	6.14	214	4.26	218	5.19	432
Two-Year	—	—	—	—	—	—
Perceived Ratings by Others						
Current						
Faculty	2.94	213	1.78	216	2.36	431
Upperclassmen	3.22	212	1.85	216	2.54	428
Classmates	3.62	2.0	2.14	2.4	2.89	424
Nondental Friends	5.07	208	4.27	217	4.66	425
Parents	5.03	203	4.02	214	4.51	417
Wives	4.73	73	3.00	80	3.81	153
Aggregate 1*	4.01	—	2.83	—	3.41	—
Aggregate 2†	4.10	—	2.98	—	3.53	—
Projection						
One-Year Faculty	5.80	213	4.47	216	5.13	429
Actual Ratings by Faculty						
Current	—	—	—	—	—	—
Projection						
One-Year	—	—	—	—	—	—
Two-Year	—	—	—	—	—	—

The columns High, Low, Total are under the heading *Sophomores*.

* Includes classmates.
† Excludes classmates.

We operationally define the generalized other as the aggregate of the student's perceptions of the ratings awarded to him by particular others. This definition of the generalized other differs from the concept as it appears in the work of Miyamoto and Dornbusch and in the paper by Reeder, Donohue, and Biblarz. As noted above, the earlier studies exhibit a partial adherence to the Meadian formulation. The present operationalization, however, has a somewhat different focus. We assume the aggregated data to relate to the respondent's organization of ratings by others of a salient part of himself. We think this is consistent with one reading of the Meadian formulation, and in combination with the time element discussed before, may better capture the processual aspect supposedly involved in the emergence of salient self-conceptions. We claim no more.

Following the analytical lead provided in the two previous studies, we classify (where appropriate) the average ratings of our respondents into "high" and "low." In the case of the freshmen we treat statistical means of one as "low," all others as "high." For sophomores, we classify means of three and over as "high," all below that figure as "low."[22]

Hypotheses and Findings

Hypothesis 1. Self-conception is closer to the mean perceived response of others to the actor than to the mean actual response of others. Drawn directly from Miyamoto and Dornbusch, this hypothesis rests on the assumption that the perceived behavior of others towards the actor has a more direct influence than their actual behavior. For purposes of testing this notion, we match the mean self-rating of freshmen against their perception of faculty rankings, as well as against actual faculty rating of students.

Our data fully support the hypothesis. Freshmen perceive themselves at a mean of 1.33 on the scale; they think the faculty sees them at 1.21; the faculty actually ranks them at 1.71. Thus, there is only a mean difference of .12 (in the direction of a lower estimate) between perceived rating by faculty and self-rating in contrast to a mean difference of .38 between self-rating and actual rating by faculty members.

Although partly dictated by its easier accessibility, the choice of data from faculty members to test this hypothesis is also guided by a substantive consideration. In one respect, it seems reasonable to expect that freshmen might be more sensitive to faculty judgments of their relative position on the path to becoming a dentist, than they are to the judgment of most others. The institutional structure is such that, by virtue of the assignment of grades, only faculty members decide whether a freshman can move through the professional school. This is a point sometimes explicitly made by students in personal interviews. Other persons may influence what a student thinks of himself, but only faculty members, particularly in the crucial first year, decide if a freshman can even remain on the path to becoming a dentist. (The poor underestimation by freshmen of how far along faculty members actually see them is of course the kind of finding that would be anticipated by this kind of reasoning.)

Hypothesis 2. The mean of the perceived responses by others is higher for those persons with high self-rating than for those with low self-rating. This hypothesis is also directly drawn from Miyamoto and Dornbusch.[23]

---

[22] The rationale for treating sophomores in this fashion is that it gives us an approximate median distribution of the respondents. Unfortunately our data, as was also true in the case of the data obtained by Miyamoto and Dornbusch, and by Reeder and his co-workers, preclude the application of tests of significance. Consequently, as they did, we primarily search for gross differences in examining the validity of the hypotheses.

[23] Most of the hypotheses said to be set forth by Miyamoto and Dornbusch are more indirectly stated also by Reeder and his co-workers.

The reasoning here is that if self-conceptions are primarily determined by the perceived responses of others toward the person, those seeing themselves accorded higher ranking should reflect a higher self-evaluation than those visualizing themselves as less highly regarded.

In our examination of this hypothesis, we not only choose to focus on the perceived rather than the actual responses of others, but attempt to strengthen the testing of the hypothesis by taking into account the range of others that could likely be salient to our students. Thus, we examine how both freshmen and sophomores perceive the rating accorded them by faculty members, upperclassmen, classmates, nondental-school friends, parents, wives. Without pretending that all possible others who might be important for every single respondent is included, it seems reasonable to argue that we encompass in our categories most all who would be salient —in the sense of being an "other"—to the mass of our students.

As indicated in Table 1 this hypothesis is supported for each category of others (i.e., faculty, etc.). High self-raters perceive all others as according them a higher rank than do low self-raters. This is equally true for freshmen and sophomores with no mean difference in the twelve comparisons made lower than .80. It is of interest that low self-raters as sophomores perceive themselves ranked higher by only one other category (nondental-school friends), than do high self-raters see others ranking them as freshmen.

Whereas the previous hypotheses were confined to a particular point in time, the following set of hypotheses deals with projections through time.

Hypothesis 3. Anticipated self-rating is closer to the mean perceived future response of others to the actor than to the mean actual future response of others. Of course this is an extension of Hypothesis 1 through time. It assumes that even in future projections, the perceived rather than the actual behavior of others is the more important influence as far as self-conception is concerned.

We again use faculty members as the example of the other in the test of the hypothesis. We contrast the self-ratings which the freshmen project into their sophomore year, first, with their perceptions of the faculty's projected ratings, and second, with the faculty's actual anticipation.

The mean anticipated self-rating is 3.18. The perception of the projected rating by the faculty is 3.13; the actual projected rating is 2.94. Thus, the mean differences between self and perceived projected faculty rating is .05, but it is .24 between self and actual projected faculty rating. Thus, Hypothesis 3 is supported, though perhaps not as strongly as Hypothesis 1.

Hypothesis 4. The mean of the perceived future responses by others is higher for those persons with high present self-rating than for those with present low self-rating. This hypothesis makes the same basic assumption as is made in Hypothesis 2. It differs only in that it involves a projection into the future. The hypothesis assumes that those presently according themselves a high self-rating compared with those who visualize themselves as lower on the scale, will project a higher future self-ranking by others.

We test this hypothesis for both freshmen and sophomores. That is, we examine the freshmen's perceptions of the faculty's projected placement of them as sophomores and the sophomore's perceptions of the faculty's expectations of them as juniors. For this hypothesis, unfortunately, we do not have perceived projections by the students of all possible salient others as we do have for Hypothesis 2.

We find that the high self-raters project a sophomore mean score by others of 4.36 whereas the low self-raters see others as only rating them 2.91. This is a mean difference of 1.45 in the direction of supporting the hypothesis. The same relationship holds for sophomore perceived projections by the faculty into the junior year. The high self-raters project a junior mean score by the faculty of 5.80; the low self-raters see the professional staff as rating them but 4.47. The mean difference here is 1.33. Thus, both sets of data support Hypothesis 4.

Hypothesis 5. The mean anticipated self-rating is higher for those whose present self-rating is high than for those whose present self-rating is low. This hypothesis derives from some of our previous findings. We observe that the anticipated self-conception of our respondents appears to be related to their perception of the future response of others towards them. Likewise, we note that the perceived future responses of others seems to be linked to whether or not the respondent presently rates himself high or low. It follows then that there ought to be some relationship between anticipated self-rating and present high or low self-rating. In the light of Hypothesis 4, the proposition is stated as above.

In testing this hypothesis, we examine the freshman respondents' projected self-ratings as sophomores and as juniors. Present high self-raters project a mean rank of 4.90 as sophomores, whereas low self-raters foresee a mean rank of 2.87: the mean difference of 2.03 is substantial. The mean difference for projected junior ranking is also high, being 1.40. The present high self-raters give themselves an anticipated mean rank of 6.86, but the low self-raters only 5.46. The general hypothesis is thus supported. Similarly, the sophomores who are low self-raters project a self-rating of 4.26 as juniors, while their high self-rating peers anticipate a rating of 6.14. Thus, all comparisons allowed by our data point to a relationship between present self-conception and future oriented self-expectations.

Hypothesis 6. Those persons who have high self-rating have a higher mean perception of the generalized other than those with low self-rating. Although our formulation of the generalized other is somewhat different from theirs, this hypothesis is also directly drawn from Miyamoto and Dornbusch. Basically, however, the hypothesis tests the notion that self-conception is derived from multiple perspectives, and that persons seeing themselves accorded generally higher ranking should reflect a higher self-evaluation than those visualizing themselves as in general less highly regarded.

We test this hypothesis by comparing summations of the respondents' perceptions of ratings assigned to them by others. In this instance, all other categories are utilized in the analysis of the effects of the generalized other. Both freshman and sophomore data are examined.

The results are clear-cut. The high freshman self-raters have an aggregate mean score of 3.08 while the low self-raters have a score of 1.61. This mean difference of 1.47 compares with a mean difference of 1.18 among the sophomores. In that group, the high self-raters have an aggregate mean score of 4.01 whereas the low self-raters have a mean score of 2.83. Thus both freshman and sophomore high self-raters perceive themselves as being ranked higher from multiple perspectives than do low self-raters. We thus find support for Hypothesis 6.

Hypothesis 7. Self-conception corresponds more closely to the mean perception of the generalized other than to the mean of the perceived response of particular others. Again this is a hypothesis derived from Miyamoto and Dornbusch. Its rests on the assumption that self-conception as a whole emerges from interaction in divergent relationships. Thus, self-conception should more closely reflect the way most potentially meaningful others are perceived as viewing the subject than the perception of the responses of any particular collection of individuals to the actor.

In testing this hypothesis, we treat the student's classmates as particular others. The rationale for this is that classmates represent those persons with whom the freshman in the dental school has the most social contact, at least in the quantitative sense. (Also, in using this group we have the nearest equivalent in our study to the fraternity, sorority, and school class groupings Miyamoto and Dornbusch used, and the work teams Reeder and his co-workers employed in their study.) For purposes of this analysis, the category of classmates is left out of the aggregated data for the generalized other.

The data do *not* support the hypothesis. Both for freshmen and sophomores the mean perceived response of particular others (i.e., classmates) are closer to the actual self-conception of students than the mean perception of the generalized other. Among freshmen the mean difference between self and particular others is only .06, but it is .61 between self and generalized other. Among sophomores the mean difference between the self and generalized other is .84, whereas it is only .20 between self and particular other. Thus, Hypothesis 7 is not supported.

It is significant that both prior studies of which ours is a partial replication also encountered some unexpected findings in testing variants of this hypothesis. Miyamoto and Dornbusch find that only for the characteristic of self-confidence was there "marked deviations from the expected direction."[24] That is, the findings were not much better than chance when ratings on self-confidence were used to test the hypothesis that self-conceptions should correspond more closely with the generalized other than with the mean of the perceived response of others (i.e., how each individual predicted every other member of his grouping ranked him as to self-confidence). As distinguished from intelligence, physical attractiveness, and likeableness, self-confidence is the one characteristic which most closely approximates the index of self we use in our study—where our subjects rank themselves on a dental student to dentist scale. Hence, the absence of a positive finding along these lines in both studies may be more than a coincidence.

As part of their demonstration of the weight to be given to the perceived response of the generalized other in accounting for self-conception, Reeder and his co-researchers compare subject self-rating with the rankings actually awarded them by work-related others. They find a difference between high and low self-raters. They attribute this difference to the possibility that high self-raters have more reference groups than low self-raters, and thus are less responsive to the actual attitudes of particular others towards the self. (In their study this would be the actual attitudes of the other members of the work crews.)

Following the lead of Reeder and his co-workers, we also examine our data to see if there is a similar high-low self-rating difference. We proceed as in testing Hypothesis 7, except that we divide our subjects into high and low self-raters.

The results are not consistent. For the freshmen we find the same difference found by Reeder and co-workers. That is, the mean self-conception of the low self-raters corresponds more closely to the perceived mean attributed to particular others than to the generalized other. The high self-raters show a reverse pattern. However, the pattern does not hold for the sophomores, where the mean self-conception of the high self-raters corresponds more closely to the perceived mean attributed to particular others than to their perceptions of ratings by the generalized other. The low self-raters among the sophomore students exhibit the same pattern. These findings are not a direct test of the observation by Reeder and his co-workers (i.e., that there is considerable correspondence between self-conception and the actual response of others only for persons who rate themselves low

---

24 Miyamoto and Dornbusch, *op. cit.*, p. 403.

and not for those whose self-rating is high). They, however, do raise questions about its generality.

It is of interest that both prior studies and ours have encountered unhypothesized results when examining roughly the same general proposition.[25] At least it is suggestive of the possibility that the findings are not idiosyncratic to particular pieces of research or specific analytical procedures. It could indicate that something more fundamental may be involved. However, it would probably be most fruitful in future research to attempt to get at the relationship between the generalized other and particular others in still some different way. For instance, it may be that the findings in all three studies are confounded by a research failure to separate the category of significant other from particular others. If this is what accounts for the findings, the basic hypothesis may only require modification and may not need a major alteration.

Conclusion

The results of our study reinforce the suggestion of the earlier researchers that it is possible to test and also to find some empirical support for those aspects of the symbolic interactionist framework examined. The posited relationships are clearly supported for six of the seven major hypotheses, even when in our opinion a more rigorous index of self-conception is introduced, when the neglected time dimension is incorporated into some of the data, and when a somewhat different operational measure of the generalized other is utilized.

As did Miyamoto and Dornbusch, we find that it is the perceived rather than the actual response of others that is the more important in the formation of self-conception. Furthermore, this holds true not only for self-conception at a given point in time, but also for anticipated self-rating. It is the same whether a general comparison is made or whether subjects are divided into high and low self-raters. Furthermore, the data indicate that not only is self-definition chiefly derived from the perceived rather than the actual response of others, but that it is also a reflection of the perceived response of the generalized other. The latter statement, however, has to be qualified insofar as the key hypothesis concerning it is not fully supported. Since there have been difficulties with variants of this hypothesis in prior studies, the need for future research to take this as a prime point of attack is obvious.

[25] Vaughan, in a test of three hypotheses which are similar in some respects to the hypothesis in question above, also failed to find anticipated results. See Ted R. Vaughan, "Group Determinants of Self-Conception: An Empirical Assessment of Symbolic Interaction Theory," (Unpublished Ph. D. dissertation, University of Texas, 1964), pp. 102–6.

The possibility of attaining empirical results should be of some comfort to many who, while advocating the symbolic interactionist position, have been bothered with the suspicion that there was no way of either confirming or disproving the basic notions involved. We hope our research, crude and gross as it is, will encourage others towards far more systematic and more rigorous empirical testing not only of the ideas of Mead examined in this paper, but of many others. After all, whether in the course of the development of sociology, Mead is to be eventually ranked with the alchemists or as a Lavoisier is yet to be decided.

25   CARL J. COUCH

Family Role Specialization and Self-Attitudes in Children

For those social psychologists subscribing to self-role theory, the proposition that the self arises through interaction is a crucial one. In the past few years there have been several procedures developed to put into operational form the concepts "self" and "role," thereby rendering them useful in the formulation of empirical propositions. One of these, the Twenty Statements Test (TST),[1] has been validated by the demonstration that dimensions of the self, abstracted from responses to the TST, are related to other aspects of behavior.[2] In addition, Kuhn has found professional training, age, and sex to be related to the nature of the self as measured by the TST,[3] while

Carl J. Couch, "Family Role Specialization and Self-Attitudes in Children," *The Sociological Quarterly*, vol. 3 (April 1962), pp. 115–121. Reprinted by permission.

The author wishes to thank Bernard Meltzer for his critical reading of the manuscript.

[1] The TST consists of a single sheet of paper with the following instructions: "In the twenty blank spaces provided below please make 20 different statements in response to the question, "Who am I?" Give these answers as if you were giving them to yourself, not to somebody else. Write fairly rapidly, for the time is limited."

The TST was originally discussed in Manford H. Kuhn and Thomas S. McPartland, "An Empirical Investigation of Self-Attitudes," *American Sociological Review*, 19:68–78 (1954).

[2] Carl J. Couch, "Self-Attitudes and Degree of Agreement with Immediate Others," *The American Journal of Sociology*, 63:491–96 (1958). Thomas S. McPartland, John H. Cumming, and Wynona S. Garretson. "Self-Conception and Ward Behavior in Two Psychiatric Hospitals," *Sociometry*, 24:111–24 (1961).

[3] Manford H. Kuhn, "Self Attitudes by Age, Sex, and Professional Training," *The Sociological Quarterly*, 1:39–55 (1960).

McPartland and Cumming report a relationship between social class and self-conception.[4]

The research reported here is a limited attempt to investigate a relationship between the role structure of a group and the way members of the group define themselves. Specifically, this research attempts to discern relationships between the role structure within families and the self-identifications of children of the families. That such relationships should prevail derives from our awareness that the family is a pervasive group in our society, and that the development and maintenance of the self for most individuals depends in large part upon the interaction that occurs within the family group. As families differ in structure this difference should be reflected in the ways children define themselves.

The subjects for the research were college students, the majority of them freshmen, enrolled in introductory sociology classes. In an ideal research design, the structure of the families would be delineated by a direct study of the families of the subjects. The practical difficulties of this procedure forced an indirect approach. The students were asked to complete a questionnaire which was designed to measure the degree of role specialization within their families. The instructions took the following form:

> This questionnaire is to determine what tasks various members of your family perform. There are no right or wrong answers. In order for this research to be successful it is necessary that you attempt to be as accurate as possible in describing your family. In the spaces provided below write in one of the following words: "Usually," "sometimes," "seldom," or "never."

Below these instructions, on the left-hand side of the questionnaire, were seventeen items. Sample items are: "Shops for groceries," "Earns money for family," "Helps children with school work," "Shows affection for children in presence of others," etc. To the right of these items were four columns with the headings: mother, father, female teenager, and male teenager.

On the basis of the responses, role-specialization scores for "father-mother" and for "male-female teenagers" were computed. "Usually" was scored as four, "sometimes" as three, "seldom" as two, and "never" as one. On the item "Drives family car," for example, if the respondent indicated "usually" for the father and "never" for the mother, the difference would be three points. As there were seventeen items on the questionnaire, a score of 51 was possible for each measure. The highest observed role-specialization score for the parents was 30, and the lowest was four. For the teenagers the highest role-specialization score observed was 24 and the lowest 2.

---

[4] Thomas S. McPartland and John H. Cumming, "Self-conception, Social Class, and Mental Health," *Human Organization*, 17:24–29.

To standardize family background in some respects other than degree of role specialization, all respondents with any of the following characteristics were discarded: (1) those who were married, (2) those who reported step-children in the family, (3) those who reported they were living with only one parent or with neither parent, and (4) those who did not have a sibling of the opposite sex within five years of their age. Of approximately 200 who completed the questionnaire, only 64 met all qualifications, leaving a rather small sample. Moreover, of these 64, only 60 had completed the TST, so that the total sample of this study was 60, composed of 22 males and 38 females. The average age of the males was 19.3, ranging from 17 to 23 with only two over 21 years old. For the females the average age was 18.3, ranging from 17 to 21 years of age. With the above controls and with all subjects being students at a specific college, the sample is quite homogeneous.

Fundamental to George Herbert Mead's orientation is the proposition that humans perceive and define themselves as they believe others perceive and define them.[5] It appears logical to assume that families with a high degree of role specialization would be more likely to define their members in terms of sex statuses than would families marked by a low degree of role specialization. Therefore, the empirical hypothesis tested is: The greater the reported role specialization is between sexes within a family, the more frequently will the children use their sex status as a means of self-identification in responding to the TST.

As a test of the hypothesis, it was noted whether or not respondents had identified themselves on the TST as male or female, boy or girl, or man or woman. Self-identifications as son or daughter or reference to interest in activities that are traditionally male or female, were not considered in this test. [R]eported role specialization of [neither] parent nor . . . teenagers appeared to be associated with identification or nonidentification of self on the TST by sex. A parallel analysis was performed for association between self-identification as son or daughter and role-specialization scores. No associations were noted. In short, the data completely failed to support the hypothesis.

The data were then reanalyzed for each sex separately, and an interesting pattern emerged. As Table 1 indicates, while an *inverse* association obtains between degree of reported role specialization and identification of self by sex for female respondents, a *positive* association is present for male respondents.

The TST protocols were also examined for mentioning or failing to mention son or daughter status. The mean parental role-specialization scores of those girls who identified themselves as daughters was slightly higher than was the mean of those who did not, a direct association (see Table 2). This difference, while slight, is in the opposite direction from

[5] G. H. Mead, *Mind, Self, and Society* (Chicago: Univ. of Chicago Press, 1934).

TABLE 1. Mean role-specialization scores of males and females by identification or non-identification of self by sex

	Females			Males		
	Mean Score of Parental Role-Specialization	N	Mean Score of Teenager Role-Specialization	Mean Score of Parental Role-Specialization	N	Mean Score of Teenager Role-Specialization
Self-identification by sex	13.83*	30	11.97	18.14	14	11.00
No self-identification by sex	17.88*	8	13.25	14.37	8	10.13

* Difference significant at the .06 level.

TABLE 2. Mean role-specialization scores of males and females by identification or non-identification of self as son or daughter

	Females			Males		
	Mean Score of Parental Role-Specialization	N	Mean Score of Teenager Role-Specialization	Mean Score of Parental Role-Specialization	N	Mean Score of Teenager Role-Specialization
Self-identification as son or daughter	15.08	24	10.92†	19.17*	12	11.25
No self-identification as son or daughter	14.00	14	14.50†	13.90*	10	10.00

* Difference significant at the .05 level.
† Difference significant at the .02 level.

the general pattern observed. For males, the mean parental role-specialization score of those who identified themselves as sons was significantly higher than the mean for those who did not.

A consideration of the relationship between children's role specialization and self-identification as son or daughter indicates that role specialization is inversely associated with self-identification as daughter, while there is a slight positive association of role specialization with self-identification as son (see Table 2).

Table 3 presents the results when it is noted whether the respondent identifies himself by both sex and son or daughter statuses, by one or the other, or fails to make either type of self-identification. The number who failed to make either type of self-identification is small, but there is consistency in the results obtained. Females with neither form of self-identi-

TABLE 3. Mean role-specialization scores of males and females by self-identification by sex and son or daughter, by sex or son or daughter, and neither

	Females			Males		
	Mean Score of Parental Role-Specialization	*N*	*Mean Score of Teenager Role-Specialization*	*Mean Score of Parental Role-Specialization*	*N*	*Mean Score of Teenager Role-Specialization*
Identified self by sex and as son or daughter	14.42	19	10.89	19.75	8	10.37
Identified self by sex or as son or daughter	14.31	16	12.94	16.80	10	12.30
Failed to identify self by sex or as son or daughter	18.33	3	17.00	10.75	4	7.25

fication tend to have high scores on both measures of role specialization. In contrast, males with neither form of self-identification tend to have low role-specialization scores on both measures.

In summary, despite some minor exceptions, the data rather consistently display (1) a direct association between degree of role specialization within the family and self-identification as son or by sex status for male respondents and (2) an inverse association between degree of role specialization within the family and self-identification as daughter or by sex status for female respondents.

Any interpretation of the findings of this research must take into account other common findings relevant to self-identification by sex and family statuses. It has been rather consistently observed that females of college age use their sex status and family status as means for self-identification more frequently than do males in responding to the TST.[6] In this sample 30 of 38 females (79 percent) made a sex reference, compared to 14 of 22 males (64 percent). Also 24 of 38 females (63 percent) indentified themselves as daughters compared to 12 of 22 males (56 percent) identifying themselves as sons. Kuhn has reported that members of minority groups commonly identify themselves by reference to their ethnic background. In conjunction with the use by females of their sex and family statuses more frequently than by males, he offers: "One . . . hypothesis is that the salience of defining oneself as a woman is related to the status of women as a minority group (sociologically speaking) in our society."[7] Members of a minority group are rather continually made aware of their status by restric-

[6] Kuhn, *op. cit.*, pp. 46–49; Couch, *op. cit.*, p. 496.
[7] Kuhn, *op. cit.*, p. 48.

tions placed upon their behavior and, therefore, tend to utilize this status as a means of self-identification.

While this could account for the difference in frequency between the sexes in defining themselves by sex, this interpretation makes it difficult to understand the finding that females from families with the highest degree of role specialization are the very ones who fail to identify themselves by reference to sex. It would seem that these persons would be most saliently aware of their "minority" status and, therefore, if awareness is the crucial variable, would identify themselves by sex.

It has been frequently observed that people do not always think of themselves as they are consensually defined by others. Self-conceptions are not a mere replication of the definitions applied to the person by others. Perhaps the findings of this study and the observation that self-conceptions are not a direct reflection of definitions furnished by others can be interpreted as follows. The acquisition of a self involves, in nearly all cases, learning to place positive value upon the self as a general object.[8] Humans also learn techniques or means for the maintenance of positive self-conceptions. One way humans learn to acquire and maintain a positive self-conception is to acquire those statuses that are positively valued within their groups and to avoid acquiring those statuses that are negatively valued.

It seems highly probable that those families with a high degree of role specializations are patriarchal families, in which high role specialization is associated with high evaluation of male and son statuses. This leads to self-identification as male or son by the males, for the value assigned to both statuses is consistent with the value placed upon the self as a general object. In contrast, females with a family background of high role specialization learn that the statuses of female and daughter are somewhat negatively evaluated. This is in conflict with the positive value placed upon the self as a general object. As a consequence, they think of themselves less frequently as daughters and as females than do females from families with low role specialization.

The above interpretation assumes a level of awareness by females of their sex and daughter statuses that is of sufficient intensity that variation in role specialization within the family has no appreciable effect upon it. An alternative interpretation may be that in the case of those females with a family background of high role specialization the negative evaluation of these statuses is of such intensity as to override the effect of greater awareness.

---

[8] Although this proposition needs intensive investigation, it is tentatively accepted.

Self-Conceptions in India and the United States: A Cross-Cultural Validation of the Twenty Statement Test

The Twenty Statement Test (TST) was first reported by Kuhn and Mc-Partland (1954) as a valid instrument for identifying and measuring self-attitudes as they are defined in the self theory of C. H. Cooley, G. H. Mead, H. S. Sullivan, T. Newcomb, and others. Since 1954 the TST has been used in studies of the general adult population, businessmen, students, the professions, and other populations in order to learn how self-conceptions vary and how they are related to changes in age, the reference set, and other social variables. Although this instrument and its associated theory have been assessed in several ways (see Wylie, 1961; Kuhn, 1964; Kemper, 1966), it has not been assessed in terms of its cross-cultural adequacy in eliciting self-conceptions. Yet, this evaluation is quite important both because self theory is not viewed as having subcultural or cultural boundaries and because the users of the TST implicitly suggest its rather general applicability.

Purpose and Method

We are therefore interested in determining the validity of the TST when used in India, a society whose cultural system differs appreciably from that of the United States. The data for this study were collected in 1966 as a part of a larger project, involving interviews with a stratified sample of 440 adults residing in a large city, small town, and three small and contiguous villages in South India. Except for the use of interviews rather than questionnaires, we have replicated as closely as possible the procedures of Kuhn and McPartland. In order to prevent the influence of answers to direct questions in the interview on TST responses, the TST material was sought at the beginning of the interview. The TST responses were "content analyzed" by the Beta system devised by Kuhn (n.d.), which requires

Edwin D. Driver, "Self-Conceptions in India and the United States: A Cross-Cultural Validation of the Twenty Statement Test," *The Sociological Quarterly*, vol. 10, no. 3 (Summer 1969), pp. 341–354. Reprinted by permission.

placement of each statement of a respondent in one of the five categories: "(1) social groups and classifications (the statuses and roles of the subject); (2) ideological beliefs (his explanation of the cosmos, life, society— and his part in them); (3) interests (approach and avoidance with respect to social objects—the familiar adience-abience of the psychologist); (4) ambitions (status and role intentions; anticipations and expectations respecting positions in the social system); (5) self-evaluations ('a kind of pride or mortification over the way the subject imagines he appears to others who matter to him')." The second part of the "content analysis" involved assigning the statements to either the consensual group or the sub-consensual group. The difference between them is that the former type is a reference which unquestionably and pointedly places the individual in a social system, whereas, the latter type requires interpretation by the speaker before its relevance to a social system, if any, can be ascertained. In establishing the two groups, we have simply merged together statements of self-evaluation, ideological beliefs, ambitions, and interests to form the subconsensual reference. Both the five-fold and the two-fold systems of classifying the responses were necessary in order to show the unique features of the India protocols and to examine the cross-cultural validity of the claims made for the TST.

What then are the claims made for the TST and how do they relate to the theoretical position of the symbolic-interactionist school, as represented primarily by Kuhn and McPartland? The claims (propositions) for the TST, or what it in effect elicits, are explicitly stated in the conclusions drawn by Kuhn and McPartland (1954:75–76) from their study of university students:

1) The consensual (more directly socially anchored) component of the self-conception is the more salient component. Stated differently, consensually supported self-attitudes are at the top of the hierarchy of self-attitudes.

2) Persons vary over a rather wide range in the relative volume of consensual and subconsensual components in their self-conceptions . . .

3) The variation indicated in 1) and 2) can be established and measured by the empirical techniques of attitude research—specifically, the Guttman scaling technique. This . . . furthers the presumption that the locus variable is a unitary one . . .[1]

4) Locus scores vary with differential social anchorage in (a) large, con-

---

[1] Kuhn and McPartland point out that a respondent tends to exhaust his consensual references before giving any subconsensual ones and it is therefore possible to assign a score (the locus variable) which indicates both the number of consensual references made by the respondent and their positions among the twenty statements. If, for example, the last consensual statement is his seventh statement, then it is very probable (9/10 cases) that the preceding six statements are also consensual ones (Kuhn and McPartland, 1954:70–71).

ventional . . . and influential groups; (b) small, weak, or . . . ambivalently viewed . . . groups; or (c) no groups at all . . .[2]

5) Religious affiliation references are significantly more salient among the
self-attitudes of members of "differentistic" religious groups than among
members of "majority" or conventional religious groups.

6) Corroboratively, the religious group as a reference group appears far
more frequently . . . among members of "differentistic" religious groups.

These conclusions seem then to correspond with some key ideas of
self theory: "man is an object to himself—an object whose meaning to
himself and others can only be derived from the system of social objects
in which he is enmeshed" (Kuhn, 1960:53), the most important objects being his roles and statuses in the social system (Conclusions 1, 2, and 3);
individuals in a society vary in the ways in which "they have cast their
lot within the range of possible reference groups" (Kuhn and McPartland,
1954:72), and in what they interiorize from them (Conclusions 2, 4, 5, and
6); and the "self," defined as a set of attitudes (plans for action)[3] which the
individual holds toward himself, is organized (Conclusions 1 and 3) (Kuhn
and McPartland, 1954:69).

Findings

In order to confirm the cross-cultural validity of the TST our India data
must, then, support the above mentioned propositions.

General Pattern of Responses. The total responses per respondent range
from one for two persons to twenty—the maximum—for 121 persons, with
the median number being 12.3. (The median is 17.0 in the Kuhn-McPartland study.) Responses are mainly subconsensual ones, especially of the

[2] This is the one conclusion which we have drastically reconstructed. It originally
read: "Locus scores vary with religious affiliation, as our initial validation test shows,
members of the 'differentistic' religious groups having significantly higher locus scores
than do members of the 'conventional' religious groups" (Kuhn and McPartland,
1954:75). What we have given as the fourth conclusion is the merging of parts of
two quotes from Kuhn and McPartland (1954:73, 75) which we feel communicate the
larger propositions which the writers seemingly viewed as central to the validation
of the TST, namely: the type of religious affiliation may be regarded as an index of
majority group affiliation; persons having majority group affiliation are believed to
have greater social anchorage in general than persons having minority group affiliation;
and it follows, therefore, that persons who are known to have majority religious affiliation will have high locus scores if the TST is a valid measure of social anchorage.

[3] Kuhn and McPartland (1954:68) note that the 'self' has been called an image, a
conception, a concept, a feeling, a self looking at oneself, and so on. They believe that
their conceptualization of the 'self' as a set of attitudes is most consistent with Mead's
view and further that it has certain theoretical advantages. For other conceptualizations
of the self, see Lowe (1961).

TABLE 1. Percentage distribution of 440 respondents in India to the Twenty Statement Test, according to number of responses and Kuhn's five inclusive categories

Number of Responses	Consensual Statements — Social Groups and Categories	Subconsensual Statements — Self-Evaluative Statements	Ideological Beliefs	Ambitions	Interests	Total
0	25.23	1.59	56.36	83.86	39.55	...
1	25.23	2.50	33.64	12.50	18.41	0.45
2	14.55	5.91	8.18	2.73	10.91	0.91
3	12.05	6.36	1.36	0.45	7.95	1.14
4	8.18	12.27	0.23	...	4.55	5.23
5	6.14	9.77	...	...	5.68	6.36
6	2.95	10.23	...	...	4.55	5.91
7	2.50	8.41	...	0.23	2.95	7.73
8	1.14	6.36	0.23	...	2.05	5.91
9	1.14	6.14	...	0.23	1.82	4.55
10	0.45	5.00	...	...	1.14	7.05
11	...	4.32	...	...	0.23	3.64
12	0.23	4.09	...	...	0.23	3.64
13	0.23	3.64	...	...	...	1.59
14	...	3.41	...	...	...	3.18
15	...	2.95	...	...	...	2.50
16	...	1.82	...	...	...	2.95
17	...	1.82	...	...	...	4.55
18	...	2.05	...	...	...	2.73
19	...	0.45	...	...	...	2.50
20	...	0.91	...	...	...	27.50
Total	100.0	100.0	100.0	100.0	100.0	100.0
Mean	2.19	7.65	0.57	0.23	2.08	12.72
S.D.	2.26	4.53	0.81	0.72	2.61	5.60
S.E.	0.11	0.22	0.04	0.03	0.12	0.29

self-evaluative kind (see Table 1), and these patterns are vivid contrasts to those observed for United States respondents. Among the Indian respondents, there are, however, wide variations in the ratios of consensual to subconsensual responses, and this finding confirms proposition two.

Detailed analysis of the consensual responses suggests that the TST has successfully elicited information on each of the five general kinds of statuses which, according to Ralph Linton (1954), are found in every society. The percentage of respondents mentioning each of these statuses is as follows: 1) 18.7 and 12.5 for age and sex categories, respectively; 2) 54.7 for family groups (kinship); 3) 12.5 and 8.4 for primary group and secondary group identities, respectively (voluntary association); 4) 27.9 for specialized occupational groups; 5) 27.8 and 7.5 for social class and caste identities, respectively (the ordering of individuals or prestige systems).

TABLE 2. The scale of locus, showing scale-types, frequency, total responses* in each scale type and the coefficient of reproducibility for each scale type, United States and India

		United States**		
Scale Type	Frequency	Total Responses	Errors	C. R.
20	19	380	41	.892
19	5	100	13	.870
18	1	20	1	.950
17	4	80	7	.913
16	1	20	3	.850
15	6	120	24	.800
14	8	160	9	.937
13	8	160	19	.875
12	4	80	10	.875
11	13	260	21	.915
10	7	140	15	.893
9	9	180	19	.895
8	9	180	15	.912
7	7	140	9	.936
6	10	200	15	.925
5	11	220	24	.891
4	8	160	11	.932
3	12	240	24	.900
2	2	40	5	.875
1	4	80	8	.900
0	3	60	0	1.000
	151	3020	293	.903

The Pattern of Consensual Responses. Consensual statements constitute 16.9 percent of the total responses but 29.9 percent of the first responses, 22.3 percent of the second responses, and 20.9 percent of the third responses. Consensual references are, then, more salient than are the subconsensual ones. But, the strength of this pattern for our India respondents is much less than it is for Kuhn and McPartland's respondents and as a result the India data do not show the same scalability (see Table 2). These findings confirm the first proposition (the salience of consensual references), but are too weak statistically to support the third proposition (the scalability of consensual-subconsensual statements).

The data also confirm the fourth proposition: persons having majority, i.e., dominant, group affiliation have relatively high locus scores. Using education as an index to majority group affiliation,[4] we find that the highly educated—the dominant group—have appreciably higher scores than those having less education and those without any education (see Table 3). *Religious Affiliation and Identification.* "Other Religions"—Christians (85.0 percent of total), Muslims, Sikhs, Jains, and Parsis—are viewed by us as

[4] There are high intercorrelations among education, occupation, and caste in India (See Driver, 1962; Gist, 1954).

TABLE 2 (cont.)

| | | India | | |
Scale Type	Frequency	Total Responses	Errors	C. R.
20	16	320	246	.23
19	16	320	217	.48
18	10	200	129	.36
17	14	280	184	.34
16	14	280	167	.40
15	8	160	80	.50
14	14	280	130	.54
13	11	220	103	.53
12	14	280	112	.60
11	10	200	77	.62
10	18	360	118	.68
9	20	400	129	.68
8	16	320	81	.75
7	17	340	73	.79
6	14	280	61	.79
5	15	300	44	.85
4	21	420	42	.90
3	21	420	25	.94
2	27	540	17	.97
1	30	600	0	1.00
0	114	2280	0	1.00
	440	8800	2035	.77

* We followed the procedure of Kuhn and McPartland in counting the failure to respond to a blank as a response to the subconsensual type.
** From Table 1 of Kuhn and McPartland (1954: 71).

TABLE 3. Mean scores on "locus variable" by educational groups*

	No.**	Mean Score on 'Locus Variable'***	Significance of Difference in Means, Computed from	
			Matriculation or Above	Uneducated
Matriculation or Above	192	2.7	. . .	P < .0001
Below Matriculation	166	2.0	P < .0046	P < .05
Uneducated	81	1.5	P < .0001	. . .

* The level of education is viewed by us as an index of one's affiliation with the majority, i.e. dominant, group in India.
** Excludes one person whose education is unknown.
*** Our procedure for establishing these mean scores is identical with that used by Kuhn and McPartland. The score is "simply the mean number of consensual reference statements made by respondents."

the minority or "differentistic" religious groups in India. Compared with Hinduism, they stress congregate worship and other forms of grouping and they do not provide comprehensive philosophies and codes of living.[5] As might be expected, and in support of propositions five and six, members of the "Other Religions" make many more references to their religion (see Table 4) and these references are more salient[6]—the difference between their mean score of 1.500 and that of Hindus, 0.618, having a probability of less than .01.

TABLE 4. Religious affiliation and identification with religious groups

	Identification		
	Yes	No	Total
Hinduism	14 (20.1)*	326 (319.9)	340
Other Religions	12 (5.9)	88 (94.1)	100
Total	26	414	440

Chi Square: 8.69. $.01 > p > .001$; $Q = .523$.
* Figures in parentheses are expected frequencies.

Discussion and Interpretation

The India data, then, confirm all the propositions stated by Kuhn and McPartland in validating the TST except the one relating to the scalability of responses. One way of explaining the non-scalability of the India responses is to point to the small number of consensual references (an average of 2.2 in contrast to the average of 10.0 in Kuhn and McPartland's study) and to argue that scalability is, to a degree, a function of the number of consensual references. We will not go into the merits of this argument because the non-scalability of the India responses seems more strongly to suggest reformulation of one part of Kuhn and McPartland's statement of self theory than an adequate reason for rejecting the cross-cultural applicability of the TST. What we do wish to consider is whether the small num-

---

[5] Hinduism does not provide the individual with a standard form of worship or what to worship. One has a choice among 1) the Absolute (which is the highest form), 2) a personal god, 3) incarnations like Rama, Krsna, Buddha, 4) deities and sages, 5) petty forces and spirits. Futher, "while fixed intellectual beliefs mark off one religion from another, Hinduism sets itself no such limits. Intellect is subordinated to intuition, dogma to experience, outer expression to inner realization. . . . Religion is a specific attitude of the self, itself, and no other, though it is mixed up generally with intellectual views, aesthetic forms, and moral valuations" (Radhakrishnan, 1927:15, 32). (See also Wach, 1944.)

[6] Following Kuhn and McPartland (1954:74), the score on the 'salience of religious reference' is simply the mean of the *ranks* of "religious reference (if any was made) on the page of twenty statements, mention of religious affiliation in first place being scored 20, mention in last place scoring 1, and omission of reference to religious affiliation arbitrarily scored zero."

ber and lesser salience of consensual statements in the India data can be explained either by 1) our difference with Kuhn and McPartland in methodology; or 2) the fact that consensual references are not, really, primary aspects of self-conceptions in India to the same degree that they are in the United States.

Methodological Issues. In the area of methodology we differ from Kuhn and McPartland in using interviews rather than questionnaires and in having to "content analyze" materials obtained in a bilingual context. If our findings are associated with simply the interviewing process, then this would mean that the TST merely elicits the attitudes which the person holds toward himself in relation to the test administrator. We are inclined to reject this kind of "situationality" as an explanation of TST findings on the following grounds: the self-conceptions of persons in the United States are quite similar when presented in autobiographical material and in interview or questionnaire responses to the TST; and the oral and written responses of persons in India to the TST are quite similar.

The second methodological issue, bilingualism, is a very complex matter and its possible impact on the TST content can be considered here in only the most general manner. As we mentioned earlier, our interviews were recorded in English but the interviewer employed English, Tamil, Telegu, or another language common to him and the interviewee in giving the TST instruction and clarifying statements. Thus, the oral communications might be in the *mother-tongue* of both the interviewer and the interviewee, or neither, or of one but not the other. Bias, which in this instance means the use of terms which unintentionally connote other than the desired meaning may, therefore, arise with the interviewee or interviewer: the former as he translates instructions or self-conceptions from the common language into his mother-tongue, and vice versa; and the latter as he translates the interviewee's statements into his own mother-tongue and then into English. Bias would most often arise where there is not equivalence between English and the other language(s) in vocabulary, idiom, or grammar.[7] This could give rise to two kinds of distortion in meaning. On the one hand, conceptions of a consensual kind may appear as subconsensual statements, or vice versa;[8] on the other hand, a given type of con-

---

[7] Examples of the lack of equivalence between the English language and the languages of India are the English words: uncle, aunt, and cousin. As one writer puts it, they "are the most confusing to a Hindu. One can never know what relation is meant" (Karve, 1965:114).

[8] Kuhn certainly gave attention to the Sapir-Whorf-Cassirer 'language and culture orientation' but, in our opinion, did not stress strongly the subtleties of language within a culture and across cultures.

In analyzing our data we have become acutely aware that many terms connote a mixture of sentiment, and obligation or expectation. It is our belief that this is one of the more fruitful areas for investigation by persons involved in recording and analyzing TST material. It may very well be that terms which are now classified as consensual are really intended by the speaker to convey primarily his sentiment rather than obliga-

sensual or subconsensual conceptualization may appear as a different type when stated verbally or in writing. The manner in which the latter problem could arise may be seen by reference to the terms in Tamil for father. The sets of terms include: 1) *tantai, tantay, entai, muntai*; 2) *ai, aiyan*; 3) *appā, appaṉ, appu, takappan*; 4) *annan, annā*; 5) *attaṉ, accan*; 6) *ammān*. "Except *tantai* all the words . . . seem to be used for any elderly or powerful or respected person and only gradually seem to have acquired their fairly [clear] definition. Even now the connotation is not as definite as, e.g., the word *pitā* in Sanskrit" (Karve, 1965:228, 230). Further, the term *annā* is also used to denote elder brother (Karve, 1965:245). Confronted with the complex meaning of *annā*, for example, and the lack of an equivalent term in the other languages of India, including English, the translator must decide what aspect of its meaning he wishes to convey. A correct decision in South India seems to depend, as it does in North India, on knowledge of usage by localities and social strata (Gumperz, 1958).

The extent to which our findings are biased because of bilingualism cannot be precisely measured. But, two procedures convince us that the bias does not nearly approach the high level which is possible in such material. First, we sometimes had a second interviewer, who differed in mother-tongue from the first one, re-interview various persons; and secondly, we have compared the TST content with some "known characteristics" (such as caste and membership in voluntary associations) of the interviewee. Neither procedure, and we do not contend that they alone are adequate for the purpose at hand, yielded any great discrepancy between the two measurements being compared.

Substantive Issues. We may now turn to the second question which we asked at the beginning of this section: is the low frequency and salience of consensual statements in our data related to the fact that groups are not, really, primary aspects of self-conceptions in India to the same degree that they are in the United States? The writings of Morris, Hsu, McClelland, and Coehlo suggest an affirmative answer to this question.

There are sharp differences among students in the United States, China, and India in their responses to the "Ways of Living" document devised by Charles Morris. Factor analysis of the thirteen "ways" yields the same five factors for all three societies, and this suggests that there may

---

tion toward another person. The manner in which the sentiment component is expressed in choosing a term of reference from a group of terms which are usually considered to be synonymous is well-documented by Schneider and Homans (1955). Another writer (Ghurye, 1955:93) observes that the sentiments-system is closely integrated with even affinal relatives in some kinship terminologies. But, Karve (1965:242) states that the dichotomy of status and sentiments found in certain North India terms is absent in the South. Lastly, Kuhn (1960:55), after noting that fifteen to thirty percent of the responses of his groups were explicitly of a self-evaluation nature, states that "many of the other responses explicitly referring to status have an implicit self-evaluation dimension."

be a common "value space" for them. But, the societies differ in their rankings on the factors, with the United States having first place on factor e, self-indulgence, and with India having first place on factor a, social restraint and self-control. When asked to give their comments on the adequacy of the document, the few United States students who complied showed a dissatisfaction with all the "ways," a rejection of all definite codes for living, and said that the "ways" needed to stress more "orientation to self" and personal possessions. The most general criticism of the document was that it did not stress *social co-operation* enough. The comments of the India students were twice as numerous, did not reject any of the "ways" and formulated some new "ways." They, in particular, emphasized "service to one's fellow men" and the need of combining the "cultivation of the inner life with outward and socially responsible action" (Morris, 1956:36, 44, 46, 47, 53–54).

Somewhat similar contrasts between persons in the two countries are provided by Hsu (1963) and McClelland (1967). Hsu compares them in terms of responses to Cards 1 and 12 BG of the Thematic Apperception Test and finds that the images of United States students more often show *involvement with other persons (especially peers)*, insensitivity to the physical environment, and an absence of mutability. The India students more often pictured themselves as *being alone* in general and even when the specific response (to Card 12BG) is Enjoyment. "In addition . . . there is a kind of Enjoyment response which is highly impersonal that the Indians give but the Chinese and Americans do not give" (Hsu, 1963:263–311, especially (Tables A-2, A-3, A-6).

Using different measuring procedures, McClelland (1967:198) likewise finds more United States boys than India boys emphasizing group activity and egocentric virtue—Morris' self-indulgence factor. It is important to note, finally, that the intercultural differences found by Morris, Hsu, and McClelland are based on their studies of populations which are very similar in age, sex, education, and social class.

Possible reasons for the consensual-subconsensual variation between the United States and India may be adduced from the writings of Hsu and McClelland. Hsu provides evidence of the universality of sociability, security, and status as primary social needs and says that the type of cultural system affects the degree to which the family (the basic organization everywhere) or other organizations fulfill these needs. Further, cultural systems may be differentiated by the degree to which they stress one of the social needs over the others. An unusual emphasis on sociability and its corollary, membership in many voluntary associations, or "clubs," exists in the United States. In India and China, the respective combinations are caste and status, and kinship and security.[9]

[9] See Hsu (1963), especially Chapter 10, "Culture pattern and human grouping." The contrasts have led Hsu to characterize the societies in Durkheim's terms of 'kinship

McClelland attributes the tendency of persons to affiliate themselves with many organizations, and quite often with each one on a short-term basis, with the strong other-directed orientation which is now present in the United States. Voluntary associations, "particularly those in school, may serve the important social function of training people to pay attention to the wishes and opinions of others." In turn, the development of other-directedness, or the tendency of ego to be motivated to interact on the basis of pressures primarily from peers, probably heightens the need for sociability and the stress on self-development values (McClelland, 1967:201). In traditional, or less other-directed, societies such as India, there is "less dependence on the opinion of others, therefore less need for group activities to make people sensitive to such opinions, and correspondingly greater stress on such sociocentric virtues as kindness, loyalty, and obligations to others as defined and prescribed in traditional social institutions" (McClelland, 1967:201). The strength of tradition in India is evident from the way in which many people even today turn to the *Ramayana, Mahabharata,* and other classics for cultural models, norms, and values.[10]

The preceding evidence lends considerable support to our belief that the low frequency and salience of consensual references in the TST protocols of respondents in India may actually reflect a cultural system which does not stress sociability as strongly as the United States system. If culture is such a key variable, then one might reasonably expect that long exposure of a person to a new cultural system would modify his self-conceptions.

The studies of the Useems (1955: esp. Chapter 2, "Change in the character and outlook of the individual"), Hsu, and Coehlo (see also Lambert and Bressler, 1956:80–89) suggest that such changes, or acculturation, do, in fact, occur after long and intensive exposure to a different culture. Hsu observes how the TST responses of persons in India who have experienced United States culture through the educational system or the Indo-American Society resemble those of persons in the United States. The study by Coehlo (1958) of students from India presents some dramatic shifts in the dominance of certain themes and reference groups as the exposure to United States culture increases. From initial contact—one week or less— with the host culture to last contact—four years or more—there is a decline in themes which are diplomatic-political, educational-cultural, and eco-

---

solidarity' (premodern China), 'hierarchic solidarity' (India), and 'contractual solidarity' (United States).

Other researchers confirm the U.S. emphasis on peer group, or nonhierarchical, relations (See, Dahlberg and Stone, 1966:589–602; Kluckhohn and Strodtbeck, *et al.,* 1961:144, 147).

[10] Sanskritization, or the process whereby groups low in status or groups just being assimilated into Hinduism from a tribal background adopt the ideology, rituals and customs of high castes, strengthens the traditional orientation. Sanskritization is strong today and raises questions about the actual impact of Westernization (see Srinivas, 1966).

nomic-industrial, and an increase in the themes which are social-personal and religious-philosophical-theoretical. Persons who mentioned reference groups in the United States initially spoke of either the "average middle-class American" (67 percent) or the University Group (27 percent), but at the end of their stay they spoke of friends (13 percent), localized groups (27 percent), and the international group (27 percent). At the end, the University Group is as strong a reference as it was in the beginning but the undifferentiated "middle-class American" disappears altogether (Coehlo, 1958:8, 21, 31, 35, 68–70). The shifts in the organization of content do not occur smoothly and the student customarily experiences what Erik Erikson calls an "identity crisis" toward the end of phase two, i.e., from three to nine months in the United States. For the Indian students who continue their sojourn here the crisis is resolved through a greater assimilation of United States culture, with the result that in phase four they show the same "privatistic outlook" (Coehlo, 1958:103) as do other United States students (Dahlberg and Stone, 1966:601). As Coehlo (1958:88) remarks, "the major characteristic of Phase 4 is that the Indian student devotes an intense, if not exclusive, attention to his social and personal relations with those around him."

Conclusions

Our data for respondents in India indicate, therefore, that the TST is a valid instrument for eliciting self-conceptions in different cultural settings. We were able to confirm five of the six propositions which Kuhn and McPartland offered as evidence of the validity of the test for United States respondents. The one proposition which is not supported is not a crucial one insofar as validation is concerned, but its non-verification suggests that self theory, as presented by Kuhn, needs to be modified so as to view consensual (social system) references as central in only some cultural systems rather than universally. This modification in theory formulation is suggested not only by our data but also by an early study of Kuhn's in which an unexpected and glaringly high percentage of Amish, in contrast to Mennonites and "Gentiles," mentioned abstract moral and religious attributes rather than primary group or secondary group models when asked to define ideal persons as well as persons whom they would least like to be (Kuhn, 1954:57–59, 63).

In addition to assessing the cross-cultural validity of the TST, our data have also permitted us to make comparisons of self-conceptions in India and the United States. These comparisons bring out many similarities with respect to anchorage in both consensual and subconsensual types of objects and also the vivid contrast between the two societies with respect to emphasis on self-evaluation and involvement with groups.

References

Coehlo, George V. 1958. Changing Images of America. Glencoe: The Free Press.

Dahlberg, Francis M. and Philip J. Stone. 1966. "Cross-cultural contrasts in interpersonal structure." Pp. 589–602 in Philip J. Stone et al., The General Inquirer: A Computer Approach to Content Analysis. Cambridge: Massachusetts Institute of Technology Press.

Driver, E. D. 1962. "Caste and occupational structure in central India." Social Forces 41:26–31.

Ghurye, Govind S. 1955. Family and Kin in Indo-Aryan Culture. University of Bombay Publications in Sociology Series No. 4. Bombay: Oxford University Press.

Gist, N. P. 1954. "Caste differentials in south India." American Sociological Review 19: 126–137.

Gumperz, J. J. 1958. "Dialect differences and social stratification in a north Indian village." American Anthropologist 60:668–682.

Hsu, Francis L. K. 1963. Clan, Caste and Club. Princeton: D. Van Nostrand Company.

Karve, Irawate. 1965. Kinship Organization in India. Second Revised Edition. Bombay: Asia Publishing House.

Kemper, T. D. 1966. "Self-conceptions and the expectation of significant others." The Sociological Quarterly 7:323–343.

Kluckhohn, Florence Rockwood; Fred L. Strodtbeck, et al. 1961. Variations in Value Orientations. Evanston: Row, Peterson and Company.

Kuhn, Manford H. 1964. "Major trends in symbolic interaction theory in the past twenty-five years." The Sociological Quarterly 5:61–84.

———. 1960. "Self attitudes by age, sex, and professional training." The Sociological Quarterly 1:53.

———. 1954. "Factors in personality: socio-cultural determinants as seen through the Amish." Pp. 43–65 in Francis L. K. Hsu (ed.), Aspects of Culture and Personality. New York: Abelard-Schuman.

———. (n.d.) Procedure for Content Analysis of the TST in Five Inclusive Categories. Mimeographed paper. Ames: Iowa State University.

Kuhn, M. H. and T. S. McPartland. 1954. "An empirical investigation on self-attitudes." American Sociological Review 19:68–77.

Lambert, Richard D. and Marvin Bressler. 1956. Indian Students on an American Campus. Minneapolis: University of Minnesota Press.

Linton, Ralph. 1954. "What we know and what we don't know about society, culture and the individual." Pp. 187–210 in Francis L. K. Hsu (ed.), Aspects of Culture and Personality. New York: Abelard-Schuman.

Lowe, C. M. 1961. "The self-concept: fact or artifact?" Psychological Bulletin 58:325–336.

McClelland, David C. 1967. The Achieving Society. New York: The Free Press.

Morris, Charles W. 1956. Varieties of Human Value. Chicago: University of Chicago Press.

Radhakrishnan, Sarvepalli. 1927. The Hindu View of Life. London: George Allen and Unwin.

Schneider, D. M. and G. C. Homans. 1955. "Kinship terminology and the American kinship system." American Anthropologist 57:1194–1208.

Srinivas, Mysore N. 1966. Social Change in Modern India. Berkeley and Los Angeles: University of California Press.

Useem, John and Ruth Hill Useem. 1955. The Western-Educated Man in India. New York: Dryden Press.

Wach, Joachim. 1944. The Sociology of Religion. Chicago: University of Chicago Press.

Wylie, Ruth C. 1961. The Self Concept: A Critical Survey of Pertinent Research Literature. Lincoln: University of Nebraska Press.

Some Methodological Problems
of Kuhn's Self Theory

Manford Kuhn in his review of twenty-five years of symbolic interaction theory noted that the "oral tradition" had sustained the theory during the years preceding the "age of inquiry."[1] And, as Kuhn has accurately noted, this "age of inquiry" has utilized different subtheories and there was little consensus or "formalization" which preceded the empirical studies.[2] This is true for Kuhn's own theory as well as for the other subtheories of the orientation.

It is the purpose of this paper to correct this condition for Kuhn's theory. In doing this I have brought together, in a systematic manner, the ideas, definitions, assumptions, and propositions of the work of Kuhn and his students.[3] With this foundation, I discuss several methodological problems of the theory which have not been previously investigated. It is hoped that this effort will contribute to the "age of inquiry" in Symbolic Interaction Theory.

I

This part includes the assumptions, propositions and terms of the theory.[4] Initially, it is important to recognize that Kuhn distinguished between the cultural-institutional view and the social-psychological view of human activity. He considered the latter view, which he held, to be a complement to the former, rather than a substitute for it. The social-psychological view

Charles W. Tucker, Some Methodological Problems of Kuhn's Self Theory," *The Sociological Quarterly*, vol. 7, no. 3 (Summer 1966), pp. 345–358. Reprinted by permission.

[1] Manford H. Kuhn, "Major Trends in Symbolic Interaction Theory in the Past Twenty-five Years," *Sociological Quarterly*, 5:61–84 (Winter, 1964).

[2] *Ibid.*, p. 63.

[3] For a list of studies by Kuhn's students see Harold A. Mulford and Winfield W. Salisbury II, "Self-Conceptions in a General Population," *Sociological Quarterly*, 5:35–46 (Winter, 1964). In addition, for titles of dissertations by Kuhn's students see footnotes 20–25, and 33–36 in Kuhn *op. cit., ibid.*

[4] As the reader will notice, I am using C. A. Hickman and M. H. Kuhn, *Individuals, Groups, and Economic Behavior* (New York: Holt, Rinehart and Winston, 1956) extensively in the formulation of this theory. Although this book is seldom mentioned in the discussions of self theory, it seems to be the most complete treatment of this theory yet published.

attempts to account for human behavior in situations not completely structured, while the other view assumes structured or rigidly normative situations. In order to predict a person's behavior in a variety of situations it is necessary, according to Kuhn, that we measure "an individual's own hierarchy of identities at a time of rapid social change."[5] So, assuming this distinction regarding views of human behavior and the purpose of the social-psychological view, Kuhn set out his theoretical formulation.

According to this theory, society as ongoing human behavior, precedes any individual. The child is born into some specific family "context" where the procedures of living are being established. Then by means of simple act symbols the child learns the appropriate behaviors from others. As part of this process, a child is shown what to do with the objects in his environment. In fact, it is assumed that any introduction to an object is by use of the appropriate behaviors for employing that object. Hence, all objects are social *before* they are physical.

From these basic notions, the self theorist makes the following assumptions regarding human behavior:[6]

> Man lives in a universe of events and objects which do not have intrinsic meaning for human experience and behavior. Rather, the universe is endowed with meaning, by man himself, through social definitions in language.
> The meaning of any object is in terms of the behavior that is taken with regard to that object. "Those concatenations of events which we think of as objects have become objects as a result of structuring by language." So, the name for an object is simply a way of collapsing the meaning for the object.
> "The individual is not a passive agent who *automatically* responds to the group-assigned meaning of objects. Rather, he is constantly engaged in telling himself what he must pay attention to, what he must look for, what the significance of some object is, and how he must act on the basis of the objects about him."
> The process indicated above is commonly called "thinking." Thinking, it is assumed, is made possible through man's ability to internally manipulate language symbols. These language symbols are acquired by the person through his interaction with others. Therefore, his thinking is limited by his language and further, by the "others" who have interacted with him.

From these assumptions we go to the basic concepts and propositions of this theory.

First, the definition of "self" or "self-conception" as used in the theory is "the individual's attitudes (plans of action) toward his own mind and body, viewed as an object";[7] or similarly, "the individual as viewed

[5] Hickman and Kuhn, *op. cit.*, p. 46.
[6] *Ibid.*, pp. 25f, 43.
[7] *Ibid.*, p. 43.

(defined) by the individual, a social object among social objects."[8] The classes of "attitudes" may include identities, in terms of roles and statuses, interests and aversions, conceptions of goals, an ideological view, and evaluative statements.[9] The phrase "among social objects" implies a "context of behavior" or "situation" in which the self-attitudes are observed. Hence, unless the "situation" is specified the self-attitudes given by a person are meaningless.

With this definition of self we turn to a general statement of the theory:

> A person obtains attitudes toward himself from his "orientational others." These attitudes are similar to those he has obtained regarding other social objects. But, the self as a social object, unlike other objects, is present in all situations. This being the case, self-attitudes are anchoring attitudes or the "common frame of reference" upon which other attitudes are founded. Therefore, the self serves as the basis from which a person makes judgements and subsequent "plans of action" toward the many other objects that appear in each specific situation.[10]

Two propositions can be derived from this general statement. They are (1) a person's self is based on the behaviors that his "orientational others" direct toward him; (2) the self serves as the basis from which a person's behaviors are directed toward other objects. From these propositions, we derive a third proposition: The behavior of "orientational others" that are directed toward a person determines his behavior regarding all objects, including himself.[11] Now, the terms which seem to need defining in this theory are object, attitudes, and "orientational others." I will begin with the most important of these:

Object. As stated earlier, self theory asserts that man's experience in the world is in terms of objects. And, according to the theory, an object

---

[8] Manford H. Kuhn, "Self," in *A Dictionary of the Social Sciences*, ed. by J. Gould and W. L. Kolb (New York: The Free Press, 1964), p. 629. Most of the definitions by Kuhn in this volume had previously appeared in his "Definitions in Symbolic Interaction Theory," Department of Sociology, State University of Iowa, 1955 (mimeograph), which he utilized in his teaching.

[9] Manford H. Kuhn, "Self-Conception," *op. cit.*, p. 631.

[10] Hickman and Kuhn, *op. cit.*, pp. 21–45 *passim.*

[11] The difference between the above "formalization" and that of John Kinch in "A Formalized Theory of the Self-Concept," *American Journal of Sociology*, 68:481–86 (Jan., 1963), is seen clearly in his third proposition, which states: "The individual's perception of the responses of others toward him reflects the actual responses of others toward him" (p. 482). This proposition would, it seems to me, be questionable in Kuhn's theory, for he contends that "*perception* is *inextricably* bound up with *conception*, the conceptions have been learned with the language," therefore, "the individual acts not in terms of an intrinsically coercive and resistent outer reality, but in terms of the meanings he ascribes to units of that reality, as they are selected and defined for him by the symbols which constitute his language" (Hickman and Kuhn, *op. cit.*, p. 23). So, with this assertion there is no separation between "perceived" and "actual" which implies a dualistic notion of reality, but rather, what man *conceives* is reality.

which is experienced must have been socially defined, and hence is called a "social object." It refers to

> any distinguishable aspect of social reality. It may be a thing, a quality, an event, or a state of affairs. All that is necessary is that it have been given unity and disjunctiveness from other matters by having been given a name which distinguishes it and assigns it a meaning. The sum total of one's social objects constitute his social reality.[12]

Hence, it is asserted that the world man experiences is the world he symbolically or linguistically designates; there is no other world. And accordingly, the world varies according to the symbolic systems of designation which are utilized by men.

Related to the conception of social objects is the notion of "meaning" in self theory. The meaning of an object is "primarily a property of behavior and only secondarily a property of objects."[13] More specifically:

> The meaning of any object is only in part a set of assumptions or ascriptions regarding its nature—how it works, what it is made of, etc. It is also in part a prescription for behavior toward that object—how much it is valued, for what kinds of activity it has meaning, what one is supposed to do with it, etc. The language which we use to define an object or an event, regardless of how abstract, general, formal or objective it is, always indicates something about the object or event.[14]

Meaning is always relative to the "norms" of the group in which the activities are taking place. "The norms of the group constitute the relational 'plans of action' which gives meaning to (or creates) the object."[15] So, the meaning of any object is dependent upon the behavioral relationships and they are the limiting "factors" of meaning.

Attitudes. The behaviors which are observed as directed toward objects are called "plans of action." As Kuhn states:

> By "plan of action" we mean considerably more than seeking out or avoiding of an object. We mean also the ways in which the object is thought to behave, for these naturally have a bearing on the individual's own behavior toward or away from the object or state of affairs in question. And, too, we mean the affects (feelings and emotions) which the individual manifests in relation to others.[16]

All behaviors that are taken with regard to objects are considered as "plans of action." But not all "plans of action" are attitudes. Attitudes are

---

[12] Manford H. Kuhn, "Social Object," in Gould and Kolb, *op. cit.*, p. 659.

[13] See T. Shibutani, *Society and Personality* (Englewood Cliffs, N.J.: Prentice-Hall, 1961), pp. 98f. for a discussion of these ideas.

[14] Hickman and Kuhn, *op. cit.*, p. 24.

[15] Kuhn, "Social Object," *loc. cit.*

[16] Hickman and Kuhn, *op. cit.*, p. 223.

verbal statements that constitute blueprints for behavior in that they indicate the ends toward which action is directed, the justification for holding
these ends, the proper feelings and evaluations regarding the degree of
success and failure in achieving them.[17]

The main point is that attitudes, as used in this theory, are overt, observable
behavior which are directly amenable to scientific investigation. They are
considered to be verbal statements which can organize and direct other
behavior.[18]

Orientational others. In a recent article, Kuhn "reconsidered" the
concept of "reference group."[19] He indicated that Merton, Hyman, and
others have used this concept to refer to *categories* of others rather than
groups of others. To make a clear distinction between groups and categories,
he proposed a "new" concept which takes into account the ideas of those
who originally put forth the notion of "others" (e.g., Cooley, Dewey, and
Mead.) These "others" he called "orientational others," which is defined by
the following attributes:[20] (1) The term refers to the others to whom the
individual is most fully, broadly and basically committed, emotionally and
psychologically. (2) It refers to the others who have provided him with his
general vocabulary, including his most basic and crucial concepts and categories. (3) It refers to the others who have provided and continue to provide him with his categories of self and other, and with meaningful roles
to which such assignment refer. (4) It refers to the others in communication
with whom his self-conception is basically sustained and/or changes.
From this class of others, Kuhn specified several types or subclasses of
others which could be employed in research. For example there are "contemporary others" and "past others;" "proximal others" and "distal
others;" and "present others" and "absent others," and the like. Kuhn
believed that if we approach the investigation of "others" with this notion
of orientational others the empirical findings will be much more relevant to
ongoing human behavior than the approach which is now being used in
social psychology. Only empirical study can assess the correctness of this
"belief."

In the above I have attempted to summarize Kuhn's self theory by

---

[17] *Ibid.*, p. 87.

[18] Hickman and Kuhn expand on this notion in the following: "Such distinctions (between opinion and attitude) seem not only useless but misleading, first, because words
constitute a great deal—probably most—of man's activity, and hence, cannot be distinguished from deeds; and secondly, because we believe, like Merton, that nonverbal
overt acts can be and frequently are deceptive, as in the sense of 'posturing' or 'keeping
up a front.' Finally, if men's verbally communicated plans of action were not in fact
fairly accurate blueprints of their action, human societies could not exist. Societies rest
on reciprocal role-playing and consensual definitions of each situation" (p. 224).

[19] Manford H. Kuhn, "The Reference Group Reconsidered," *Sociological Quarterly*,
5:5–21 (Winter, 1964).

[20] *Ibid.*, p. 18.

using the Hickman and Kuhn book and incorporating some of Kuhn's last notions regarding the theory. In order to discuss the methodological problems of the theory it is necessary to look at some of the studies that have employed the Twenty Statements Test as an operational specification for the conception of self.[21] I will not consider each study separately, but I consider the problems mentioned as common to all the studies which employed this theory and technique. Therefore, the many "technical" problems which have plagued the self theorist will not be considered, but only those problems which clearly relate to the connection between the operational specifications and the theoretical framework. These connections will be specified in the section following the discussion of the Twenty Statements Test.

II

First, the question and the administration procedures of the Twenty Statements Test. Each prospective respondent is given a sheet of paper with twenty blank lines on it and a single question at the top of the page. The question usually reads as follows:

> In the spaces below, please give twenty different answers to the question, "Who Am I?" Give these as if you were giving them to yourself, not to somebody else. Write fairly rapidly, for the time is limited.

The respondents usually have a limited amount of time to answer the question. After the time limit has elapsed, the respondents are asked to complete other questions (e.g., face-data type questions), but told not to return to the self question. The instruments are collected after their completion.

By inspecting the question carefully we can note several assumptions which are implied by it. Then we can note whether these assumptions are consistent with the theoretical formulation. First, the respondent is asked to answer the question "Who Am I?" but he is to answer this question under a special circumstance. He is asked to answer the question "as if you were giving them (the answers) to yourself, *not to anyone else.*" If the directions are followed the person should refer to himself as an object. This specification seems to be consistent with the conception of self in this theory.

With further consideration, there is an assumption that the self theorist makes which is not always clearly stated. This assumption is stated by McPartland in a manual designed for using the Twenty Statements Test.[22]

[21] See note 3, above.

[22] T. S. McPartland, "Manual for the Twenty-Statements Problem" (Department of Research: The Greater Kansas City Mental Health Foundation, Jan. 3, 1959, mimeograph).

In order to answer the question it must be assumed that the person "knows" who he is and puts this "knowledge" into words. As McPartland states: ". . . respondents are confronted with the problem of identifying themselves and left to decide for themselves how this identification will be made."[23] This assumption is necessary for the self theorist and is not essentially inconsistent with the theory.

In addition to having a rather epistemological "tone" to it, the above assumption is related to several others which seem to be theoretically necessary. It is assumed that the person's "knowledge" of himself will be dependent upon the situation in which he finds himself. As stated, this "knowledge" comes from the behavior of the "orientational others" in various situations. Therefore, it is necessary to discard the notions of many personality theorists and "self-concept" theorists who employ "trait" notions with regard to their concepts. The self theorist finds this notion contrary to his assumptions.[24]

Secondly, the assumption that a person "knows" who he is precludes the use of a set of fixed responses to obtain theoretically meaningful information regarding the self. Giving the person a set of responses regarding himself assumes either (1) that the person does not "know" who he is or (2) that the researcher has the "knowledge" regarding the respondent's self-attitudes in this situation. The first alternative clearly contradicts the assumption of the self theorist, and the second alternative would question the necessity of any research on the problem. As Kuhn states, "responses resulting from suggestion have no predictive utility (regarding the self as defined in this theoretical framework) for they do not indicate the plans by which the individual organizes and directs his behavior."[25] So it is assumed that the "Who Am I?" question does not suggest specific answers to the respondent. Therefore, all the answers that are given are the respondent's own "plans of action" which can direct his subsequent behavior.

Finally, another assumption, related to the above is made by the self theorist. It is assumed that the question "Who Am I?" is general enough as not to elicit responses which are unique or particular to a limited situation, especially the testing situation. If this assumption was not made the responses to the question would have limited "predictive utility." That is, one could say very little about the person's behavior in a variety of circumstances with the information gathered from this question. This would, of course, make the theory so specific as to cast doubts on its scientific utility (i.e., the ability to make general statements regarding human behavior). So, as in the instance mentioned above, this final assumption seems to be required within the framework of self theory.

---

[23] *Ibid.*, p. 2.
[24] Hickman and Kuhn, *op. cit.*, p. 243.
[25] *Ibid.*

In summary, the following assumptions and assertions are made by the self theorist when he uses the Twenty Statements Test to operationalize the concept of self:

1. The person will refer the question "Who Am I?" to himself and not to anyone else.
2. The person is aware ("knows") of himself and he puts this "knowledge" into words.
3. The person's awareness of himself is dependent upon the behaviors of others in a situation and not a matter of "traits" or "instincts."
4. The person's awareness of himself precludes the use of any fixed responses; the responses must be the person's own plans of action.
5. The responses to the question are not limited to the testing situation, but have applicability in a variety of situations.

It seems that each of these assumptions or assertions, taken separately, is necessary within the theoretical framework and not essentially inconsistent with it.

The other area of importance regarding the Twenty Statements Test is the procedures that have been used for analyzing the data. I will discuss the procedures which have provided a *foundation* for the variety of analysis systems that have been employed. In this discussion, I will point out several assumptions which have not been mentioned previously. As before, I will assess the adequacy of these assumptions in terms of the theory.

Each answer of the respondent is content analyzed. Every statement is assigned to one of two categories: consensual or subconsensual (this latter category is sometimes called "nonconsensual"). Consensual statements are those which "require no further explanation in order to be understood by the analyst, or, for that matter, by anyone."[26] Examples are: "I am a man," "I am a student," or "I am a teacher." It is assumed that there is consensus by everyone regarding an object which is identified by this type of statement. The consensus is in terms of the behavior that one would take with regard to the object so identified. Another way of saying this is that the object, so identified, would have a common meaning for all concerned.

All statements which are not identified by the analyst as consensual are considered to be subconsensual. These statements refer to "groups, classes, attributes, traits, or any other matters which require interpretation by the respondent to be precise or to place him relative to other people."[27] They refer to "norms which may vary and into which the analyst must inquire if

---

[26] *Ibid.*, p. 244.
[27] Manford H. Kuhn and Thomas S. McPartland, "An Empirical Investigation of Self-Attitudes," *American Sociological Review*, 19:64 (Feb., 1954).

he is to grasp the denotation of the statements."[28] Examples of this type of statement are: "I am a good student," "I am an angry person," and so on. It is asserted, in these instances, that there is little consensus of meaning with regard to objects identified in a subconsensual manner. That is, others will not know how to behave consistently toward objects which are identified in these terms. This, of course, is the direct opposite of the interpretation for consensual statements.

One can see, I think, how the above analysis procedures relate to self theory. The main focus in these procedures is on the meaning of social objects. As mentioned earlier, meaning is defined in terms of behavior taken with regard to objects. Those objects which are identified in a consensual fashion will elicit the same responses from all who come in contact with them. So the person who has identified himself consensually can expect all others to behave toward him in a similar manner in a variety of situations. If that is so, it is further reasoned that those with the largest number of consensual statements have behaved in a greater number of different situations. They are, in other words, "socially anchored" in a variety of situations. And, the number of consensual statements "is a reflection of the degree to which a person is effectively anchored in the main (consensually agreed to) culture" and has "achieved a stable identification by, and in terms of, the larger culture."[29] All of these assumptions and assertions seem to be in accord with the theory and particularly the concepts of "social object" and "meaning." Now, with this discussion in mind, the next section will point out some methodological problems that appear between the theory and the procedures employed to investigate its notions.

III

The first problem to be discussed is what can be called "situationality." This problem is not only evident in self theory but it has plagued many a social scientist, especially social psychologist, for years. Essentially, the problem of "situationality" is concerned with the question: How do the social factors (i.e., behavior of others), *within the testing situation*, affect the observable behaviors one obtains from the respondent(s)?[30] I think the investigation of this question can be shown to be crucial to the development of social self theory.

---

[28] Hickman and Kuhn, *op. cit.*, p. 244.

[29] Robert L. Stewart and Glenn M. Vernon, "Four Correlates of Empathy in the Dating Situation," *Sociology and Social Research*, 43:284 (Mar., 1959).

[30] For an extended discussion of the issues involved in this question see Aaron V. Cicourel, *Method and Measurement in Sociology* (New York: The Free Press, 1964), pp. 157–171. This discussion should be useful to anyone concerned with the problems of social research, especially the type of research that obtains observations by asking people questions.

From the statements of the self theorists it can be seen that this problem is clearly relevant to their theory. Kuhn criticizes those who assume that the testing situation is "neutral," especially in an experimental study. He states that the researcher "must determine the subject's attitudes toward objects to be manipulated in the experiment . . . in order to have full knowledge of the variables."[31] Further, in the definitions of self and orientational others it is noted that these concepts are relative to the "definition of the situation." Finally, in one of Kuhn's latest articles, he points to this problem as one which has been "neglected" in symbolic interaction theory.[32] Yet, even with this recognition, the problem seems to have been ignored in most of the research. The question comes to mind: How could this "state of affairs" possibly have developed?

I think the problem developed from the "style" in which the theory was originally presented. The self theorist seldom attempted to order his theory as it has been done above. When he took each assumption and assertion *separately*, he could not discover the contrary assumptions which appear in the theory and research relationship. But when they are considered together the contradictions are quite noticeable.

To cite a case, one can see a direct contradiction between several ideas in self theory. First, is the idea that knowledge of the person's self-attitudes will enable an observer to predict that person's behavior in a variety of situations. This notion implies that there is a "core" self or a particular set of "basic self-attitudes" that a person utilizes in all, or at least a variety of, situations. This same notion is held by some "self-concept" theorists and is consistent *within their framework*.[33] But, *within this theoretical framework*, it is contradictory to the explicit and firm rejection of the "trait" notions of personality

In fact, it was one of Kuhn's expressed purposes to devise a theory which would show that the ideas of "traits" or "instincts" in human behavior are clearly metaphysical and beyond scientific investigation. But, it seems that the very ideas which he intended to challenge are to be found in his theory, particularly in the notion of "social anchoring" self-attitudes.

This same contradiction can be noted in the research operations. This appears when two ideas are contrasted. First is the idea that self-attitudes are derived within a particular "context of behavior" and are "meaningless" without the explication of that "context." But, in a contrary manner, it is assumed that the responses from the question "Who Am I?" are applicable to a *variety of situations*. This assumes that the others who are "present" and "contemporary" are irrelevant to the person's behavior. Now, it may be

31 Hickman and Kuhn, *op. cit.*, p. 26.

32 Manford H. Kuhn, "Major Trends in Symbolic Interaction Theory," p. 78.

33 The theorists who use this type of framework are reviewed in Ruth Wylie, *The Self-Concept* (Lincoln: The University of Nebraska Press, 1961), and in C. Marshall Lowe, "The Self-Concept: Fact or Artifact?" *Psychological Bulletin*, 58:325–336 (1961).

the case that *some* of the responses are applicable to the testing situation, while other responses are relevant to a variety of situations beyond the testing situation. But, it seems to me, before we can establish this assertion, an empirical investigation of the testing situation must be conducted.[34]

The second problem concerns the content analysis procedures that have been consistently used in the studies. Although this may appear to be a mere "technical" problem, I think that it can be demonstrated that these procedures are derived from the theory. This being the case, whatever problems that appear with these procedures have definite consequences for the development and utility of the theory.[35]

The content analysis categories and their assumptions were described briefly in the preceding part of this paper. As stated there, the ideas for these procedures were derived from the concepts of "meaning" and "social object." The statements obtained on the Twenty Statements Test are expected to refer to the respondent as an object. If the "meaning" of the statement has a high degree of agreement it is consensual; if not, then it is subconsensual. Now, because these procedures are related to several important ideas of the theory, we should take a closer look at them.

We noted that the self theorist assumes or asserts the following: (1) that fixed responses have little predictive utility; (2) that the person's "knowledge" of himself is contained in the responses on the Twenty Statement Test; (3) that the person's own perspective and "plans of action" is the focus of study. It was mentioned that the Twenty Statements Test does not violate any of these assumptions or assertions. But when it comes to the analysis of these statements from the Twenty Statements Test, the analyst *imposes the meaning on each of them from his own perspective.* In many theories this procedure would be appropriate. That is, they do not assume that the perspective or viewpoint of the respondent (actor) is the focus of study. In these theories the experience of the analyst is the focus of study. But, as the statements above point out, in self theory the experiences of the respondents are the focus of study. Therefore, the procedures employed in content analysis seem to contradict the assumptions and assertions of the theory.

Let us take a closer look at this contradiction. It seems that the self-theorist–researcher is using his notions of meaning on two different levels.

---

[34] At the present time, procedures are being devised to obtain observations which will be relevant to this problem. The main deviation from the previous operations include the use of post-test interview with respondents who have answered the "Who Am I?" question.

[35] The more "technical" problems which will not be discussed in the text of the paper include (1) the lack of any consistent set of coding instructions across all of the studies using the Twenty Statements Test, and (2) the lack of inter-coder reliability procedures which are clearly specified and reported in the studies under consideration here. Regarding this last issue, some studies have reported figures for inter-coder reliability, but the procedures used to obtain these figures were never clearly reported.

On one level, the researcher assumes that the person knows the meaning of himself and obtains that information on the Twenty Statements Test. But, at another point, the researcher determines the meaning for each of these responses without taking the person's perspective into account. He decides which responses have consensus in terms of another context (e.g., his own, the "culture," the "society," etc.) which *may* be irrelevant for the person who made the responses. The analyst's standard for consensus seems to be "common-sense," but as Cicourel points out,

> The social scientist cannot afford to rely upon his own common-sense understanding for his content analysis of communications. To do so would make it impossible for him to differentiate between what he can understand because of his theoretical framework and what he can understand as a member of the same society (or even the same audience) in which the communication was presented.[36]

Again, I think this problem stems from a lack of "systematic" formulation in the theory. In order to employ a content analysis type of procedure the theory should be precise. I agree with Cicourel when he states:

> The problem for the content analyst is to employ a theory which is sufficiently precise to enable the researcher to specify in advance what he should look for in some set of materials, how he is to identify and extract the material, how he must code it, and, finally, how its significance is to be decided.[37]

Even though the theory, as presented here, seems to be more "systematic" than others, in its original form it was not. If it had been, the self theorist might have noticed these problems. So, if these criticisms are valid, it seems that the self theorist should either investigate the notion of consensus or completely discard it.[38]

IV

Undoubtedly, those who have worked with this theory have thought of these and many other problems. Some other problems that could be explored are implied in the following questions:

[36] Cicourel, *op. cit.*, p. 155.

[37] *Ibid.*, p. 144.

[38] Several unpublished exploratory studies have been done regarding this problem. They include S. Clark McPhail, "Perceived Consensus Regarding Statements about the Self in Response to the Question, 'Who Am I?'" read at the Ohio Valley Sociological Society Meetings, Columbus, Ohio, 1964; and Charles W. Tucker, "The Dimensions of Self-Attitudes: A Working Paper" (mimeograph, 1965, Department of Sociology, Michigan State University).

1. Is there systematic empirical support for the assumptions and assertions that the self theorist states regarding the "self indication process"?
2. Is there systematic empirical support for the "interpretative process" that the self theorist and others posit as the basic process of social action?
3. What are the consequences for the theory of employing different types of questions, under a variety of conditions, which ask the respondent to refer to himself as an object?

These questions are rather "obvious" for those who have employed this theory in their research. But, as far as I know, the rationale for these questions, and the other problems mentioned in this paper, have not been specified by them. I think it is time for the self theorist to become openly "self-conscious" about his own work and limit the amount of effort expended on criticizing the other theories of social behavior. It is hoped that this paper is one minor step in that direction.

In summary, this paper has attempted to accomplish several tasks. First, it organizes the various ideas, assumptions, definitions, and propositions of Kuhn's self theory. Then, using this as a base, it points out two major methodological problems which have not been previously mentioned or investigated by the self theorists. These problems deal with the effects of the testing situation on the responses to the self question and the content analysis procedures which have been employed by the self-theorist–researchers. By indicating these problems in this way it is expected that further empirical work can be done with this theory on a more sturdy foundation than was heretofore available.

Selected Bibliography III

Bain, Read. "The Self-and-Other Words of a Child." *American Journal of Sociology*, vol. 41 (May 1936), pp. 767–775. Explores the relationship of society and self through the medium of language.

Baumann, Bedrich. "George H. Mead and Luigi Pirandello, Some Parallels Between the Theoretical and Artistic Presentation of the Social Role Concept." *Social Research*, vol. 34 (Autumn 1967), pp. 563–607. A lengthy and, at times, difficult illustration of the convergence between artistic and scientific expositions of human concept.

Cooley, Charles Horton. "A Study of the Early Use of Self-Words by a Child." *Psychological Review*, vol. 15 (November 1908), pp. 339–357. Forerunner of the study described by Bain, above.

Couch, Carl. "Self-Attitudes and Degree of Agreement with Immediate Others." *American Journal of Sociology*, vol. 63 (March 1958), pp. 491–496. Reveals the extent to which identification of oneself in terms of group membership affects agreement with estimated evaluations of others in a small-group situation.

Kuhn, Manford H. "Self-Attitudes by Age, Sex, and Professional Training." *Sociological Quarterly*, vol. 1 (January 1960), pp. 39–55. Research comparing self-identifications of individuals in different social roles.

Mead, George Herbert. *Mind, Self and Society*. Chicago: The University of Chicago Press, 1934, pp. 144–178. Mead's exposition of the genesis of the self.

Merrill, Francis E. "Stendhal and the Self: A Study in the Sociology of Literature." *American Journal of Sociology*, vol. 66 (March 1961), pp. 446–453. Presents an interpretative humanistic inquiry into the interactionist conception of the self in Stendhal's novel, *The Red and the Black*.

Miyamoto, S. Frank, and Sanford M. Dornbusch. "A Test of Interactionist Hypotheses of Self-Conception." *American Journal of Sociology*, vol. 61 (March 1956), pp. 399–403. Study of the relation of self-conceptions to the behavior of others, perception of others, and perception of the generalized other.

Natanson, Maurice. *The Journeying Self: A Study in Philosophy and Social Role.* Reading, Massachusetts: Addison-Wesley Publishing Company, 1970. Traces the genesis of self from a phenomenological and existential standpoint that is consistent with symbolic interactionism.

Pfuetze, Paul E. *The Social Self*. New York: Bookman Associates, 1954. A comparison and synthesis of Mead's ideas on the self with those of the eminent theologian Martin Buber.

Reckless, Walter C., Simon Dinitz, and Ellen Murray. "Self-Concept as an Insulator Against Delinquency." *American Sociological Review*, vol. 21 (December 1958), pp. 744–748. Research study of nondelinquents living in a high delinquency area.

Reeder, Leo G., George A. Donohue, and Arturo Biblarz. "Conceptions of Self and Others." *American Journal of Sociology*, vol. 66 (September 1960), pp.

153–159. Research among military personnel, comparing self-concepts with ratings by others in the group.

Schmitt, Raymond L. "Major Role Change and Self Change." *Sociological Quarterly*, vol. 7 (Summer 1966), pp. 311–322. Study of 48 girls in the process of becoming Catholic nuns.

Sherwood, J. J. "Self-Identity and Referent Others." *Sociometry*, vol. 28 (March 1965), pp. 66–81. Tests the proposition that "the individual's self-identity (and his self-evaluation) is dependent upon his subjectively held version of the peer group's actual ratings of him."

Spitzer, Stephan P. "Test Equivalence of Unstructured Self-Evaluation Instruments." *Sociological Quarterly*, vol. 10 (Spring 1969), pp. 204–215. Compares findings for six open-ended self-conception measures.

Wylie, Ruth C. *The Self Concept: A Critical Survey of Pertinent Research Literature.* Lincoln: University of Nebraska Press, 1961. A fairly comprehensive summary of research on the self, including studies based on symbolic interactionism.

part IV

Mind

For symbolic interactionists, "mind" refers to the processes of behavior through which a person carries on "transactions" with his environment. The processes, consisting of designations to oneself by means of symbols, enable the individual to construct his acts as he executes them and to "carve out" the objects constituting his environment.

The concept of mind refers to a mental process or activity, not a physical entity such as the brain. Although the activity is covert, it is behavior which closely resembles the overt communication between individuals. The inner processes of thought rely on the same symbols used in observable behavior. Thinking can be viewed as a process of internal conversation—of symbolic interaction between the individual and himself.

William Lewis Troyer's brief article presents Mead's major ideas on mind, stressing its social genesis and its adaptive, processual character. The crucial role of significant symbols in "minded behavior" emerges clearly in this summary.

The selection by John Dewey further underscores the functional view of mind. This pragmatic, instrumental conception stands in sharp contrast to the conception of mind in substantive terms. While this article focuses on the relation of mind to behavior, Dewey also stressed the importance of society and communication (see his article in Part II).

The excerpt from William I. Thomas's book discusses the indications to oneself entailed in thought-processes. That human beings act on the basis of their "definitions of the situation" is, of course, axiomatic for the symbolic-interactionist perspective.

Both Robert A. Stebbins and Harold Garfinkel present empirical studies of Thomas's concept. The selection by Stebbins shows how useful the concept can be in the explanation of motivated behavior, while Garfinkel's ethnomethodological experiment furnishes intensive illustration of the operation of situational definitions in human living.

Anselm L. Strauss carries the analysis further by showing some of the relationships between the symbols, labels, or definitions we apply to persons or other objects and our "plans of action" toward the objects. It is in the light of all the foregoing ideas that we can best understand the excerpt from Kurt Goldstein's book on aphasia. Here is empirical information demonstrating the importance of language (symbols) in cognition and action.

The selections by C. Wright Mills and by Marvin B. Scott and Stanford M. Lyman grapple with "motive," a concept that has proved troublesome to students of human behavior. It should be recalled, incidentally, that Stebbins's article addresses this concept. Mills and Scott and Lyman indicate the usefulness of treating motives as labels, or definitions, that humans apply to their own conduct and to the conduct of others. Scott and Lyman concern themselves especially with the "acceptable utterances" people make in accounting for untoward action. It is important to contrast the view presented in these articles with the more prevalent view of motives as internal stimuli which move the individual to behave in given ways.

These articles in Part IV should dispel the notion that "mind" is inevitably a mystical, unanalyzable phenomenon. To the symbolic interactionist, the term refers to an important process without which human behavior and society cannot be adequately understood. Indeed, "understanding" by the social psychologist involves the same process as "understanding" by his subjects.

The process of mind refers to the capacity of each socialized individual to communicate with himself just as he is able to communicate with others. While inner communication is not readily observable, the following articles reveal its importance and suggest techniques for its observation and analysis.

Mead's Social and Functional Theory of Mind

The development of an adequate theory of mind in relation to nature was a central interest of the late George Herbert Mead's philosophical career. His general position is best designated with the term "social behaviorism." The basic datum from this point of view is the social act. But this datum is by no means an obvious and simple element for observation. Before it can be used to explore and understand the nature and function of mind, supporting theories of society and of self require elaboration. Hence, the natural order of Mead's own thinking seems to have been that of society-self-mind, instead of the reverse as suggested by the title of the edited volume of his famous lectures in social psychology.[1] A well-proportioned and discerning outline of Mead's position should culminate rather than begin with his understanding of mind.

The Internal Organization of the Act

Mead, like John Dewey, was very critical of that form of behaviorism set forth by John Watson and his followers. These latter, he believed, had played a positive role in the development of a science of psychology but had, nevertheless, greatly oversimplified the concept and, consequently, the analysis of the act. They failed to take full account of the social character of the act, and what was worse yet, they limited analysis to fragmentary portions of the act. A thoroughgoing behaviorism would include within its purview the *complete* act, and particularly that portion of it which goes on "in the central nervous system as the beginning of the individual's act and as the organization of the act."[2] This larger inclusiveness would necessarily take the investigator beyond the field of direct observation, Watson's stopping point. An earlier retort that such procedure goes beyond science loses force in the light of a modern subatomic physics and a biochemistry of colloids and viruses.

Mead's criticism and his constructive development both begin with the

William Lewis Troyer, "Mead's Social and Functional Theory of Mind," *American Sociological Review*, vol. 11 (April 1946), pp. 198–202. Reprinted by permission.

[1] G. H. Mead, *Mind, Self, and Society* (Chicago: University of Chicago Press, 1934).
[2] *Ibid.*, p. 11.

concept of the reflex, or so-called stimulus-response arc. His position is essentially the same as that advanced by Dewey in his well-known article of 1896.[3] Both Mead and Dewey insisted that action is present in the living organism from the very outset. What has to be accounted for is not action but the direction which action takes. The process of responding is present in the entire act determining the very entertainment of stimuli. The living organism, in other words,

> . . . is not a sensitive protoplasm that is simply receiving these stimuli from without and then responding to them. It is primarily *seeking* for certain stimuli. . . . Whatever we are doing determines the sort of a stimulus which will set free certain responses which are merely ready for expression, and it is the *attitude* of action which determines for us what the stimulus will be.[4]

The use of the term "attitude" in this connection is highly important. Mead recognized that the functioning of the nervous system is as yet only partially explored, but he regarded the results already obtained as substantial enough to indicate an organization of the act in terms of social attitudes. Thus, he declared:

> There is an organization of the various parts of the nervous system that are going to be responsible for acts, an organization which represents not only that which is immediately taking place, but also the later stages that are to take place. If one approaches a distant object, he approaches it with reference to what he is going to do when he arrives there. If one is approaching a hammer, he is muscularly all ready to seize the handle of the hammer. *The later stages of the act are present in the early stages*—not simply in the sense that they are ready to go off, but in the sense that *they serve to control the process itself*. They determine how we are going to approach the object, and the steps in our early manipulation of it.[5]

Whatever may be found by biological research to be the actual physiological pattern of functioning in the nervous system, the important point emphasized by Mead probably will not be gainsaid; that is, that the complete act is present as a determining factor in the beginning of the overt phase of the act. The attitude, as Mead uses the term, stands simply for this internal organization of the act.

A closely associated fact, brought to emphasis in Mead's outlook, is that the central nervous system, among human beings at least, provides a mechanism of *implicit* response. Not only does the human organism select its stimuli on the basis of attitudes, but it may also test out implicitly the

---

[3] John Dewey, "The Reflex Arc Concept in Psychology," *Psychological Review*, III (July, 1896), 357–370.

[4] G. H. Mead, *Movements of Thought in the Nineteenth Century* (Chicago: University of Chicago Press, 1936), pp. 389–390 (italics not in the original).

[5] Mead, *Mind, Self, and Society*, p. 11 (italics not in the original).

various possible completions of an already initiated act in advance of the actual completion of that act. This it does through the employment of significant symbols. There is thus interposed between stimulus and response a process of selection. Mead referred to this phenomenon as "delayed reaction." To him this seemed to be the basis upon which it is legitimate to speak of choice and conscious control of behavior. It is this process, when considered in conjunction with the development of social attitudes, which constitutes intelligence or mind.[6] Obviously, this is far removed from the behaviorism of Watson; yet it is thoroughly behavioristic. It imports nothing from outside the act itself. It simply refuses to conceive the act narrowly as a mechanistic and individualistic reaction to external pressures.

Biological and Social Bases of Mind

Now, it should be clear from the foregoing that Mead emphasized the indispensability of the physiological organism in his account of mind. Individual experience and behavior was, in his thought, "physiologically basic" to social experience and behavior, and the processes and mechanisms essential to the origin and continued existence of society, self, and mind were dependent upon the social functioning of that which is physiologically individual.[7]

> The individual members of even the most advanced invertebrate societies do not possess sufficient physiological capacities for developing minds or selves, consciousness or intelligence, out of their social relations and interactions with one another; and hence these societies cannot attain either the degree of complexity which would be presupposed by the emergence of minds and selves within them, or the further degree of complexity which would be possible only if minds and selves had emerged or arisen within them. Only the individual members of human societies possess the required physiological capacities for such development of minds and selves, and hence only human societies are able to reach the level of complexity, in their structure and organization, which becomes possible as the result of the emergence of minds and selves in their individual members.[8]

For Mead the central nervous system, and particularly the cortex, furnished the physiological mechanism by means of which the "genesis of minds and selves out of the human social processes of experience and behavior—out of the human matrix of social relations and interactions—is made biologically possible in human individuals." Minds do not occur without brains. Looked at from the physiological angle, therefore, mind is an

---

[6] *Ibid.*, pp. 99–100; 117–118.
[7] *Ibid.*, pp. 1–2.
[8] *Ibid.*, p. 236 (footnote).

extraordinarily complex adjustment mechanism; an extension of distance receptors and motor effectors, a refined type of antennae, so to speak, by which more efficient adaptation of organism and environment as achieved.

Important as this grounding of mind and self-hood in physiology is, however, the repeated reference in the above quotations to *social relations and interactions* must be fully appreciated if Mead's notion of mind is not to be gravely misunderstood. Brains are necessary to the emergence of mind, but brains, *per se*, do not make mind. It is society—social interaction—using brains, which makes mind. Intelligent human behavior is "essentially and fundamentally social";

> . . . it involves and presupposes an ever on-going social life-process; and . . . the unity of that on-going social process—or any one of its component acts—is irreducible, and in particular cannot be adequately analyzed simply into a number of discrete nerve elements.[9]

If this be true, it follows that the psychologist should study social relations and social behavior primarily, rather than physiology, if he would know what mind is and how it functions.

In pursuing this line of approach, Mead took his students over ground dealing with the emergence of human society and the self. He focused attention on the gesture, particularly the *vocal gesture*, and especially upon the vocal gesture at the point where it becomes a *significant symbol*. He declared that mentality "resides in the ability of the organism to indicate that in the environment which answers to his responses, so that he can control these responses in various ways."[10]

In his discussion of society and the self this indicating process is designated as "taking the role of the other" or participation in the "conversation of attitudes." As a self can arise only in a society where there is communication, so mind can arise only in a self or personality within which this conversation of attitudes or social participation is taking place. It is this conversation, this symbolic interaction, interposed as an integral part of the act, which constitutes mind.[11] Looked at from one standpoint, it is mind; from another, it is communication. Functioning within the organismic processes and social activities of the specific individual, communication is mind. It is symbolic social interaction, the process which makes human life distinctive.

The concrete import of such a theory of mind cannot be better summarized than in Mead's own words.

> In defending a social theory of mind we are defending a functional, as opposed to any form of substantive or entitative, view as to its nature. And

[9] *Ibid.*, p. 118 (footnote).
[10] *Ibid.*, p. 132.
[11] Mead, *Movements of Thought*, pp. 384–385.

in particular, we are opposing all intracranial or intra-epidermal views as to its character and locus. For it follows from our social theory of mind that the field of mind must be co-extensive with, and include all the components of, the field of the social process or experience and behavior: i.e., the matrix of social relations and interactions among individuals, which is presupposed by it, and out of which it arises or comes into being. If mind is socially constituted, then the field or locus of any given individual mind must extend as far as the social activity or apparatus of social relations which constitutes it extends; and hence that field cannot be bounded by the skin of the individual organism to which it belongs.[12]

The advantage of this view of mind resides in its plausibility as an account and explanation of the genesis and development of mind without postulation of supernatural endowment or special Being.[13] It thoroughly naturalizes mind in such a way as to give the concept of mind heuristic value in any full-fledged science of human nature. In so far as originality can be assigned to Mead, this achievement in understanding, if sustained by later criticism, may well rank with those of Newton and Darwin in its importance to mankind.

The Object as a Collapsed Act

Mead's discussion of the self as an object to itself and also of the possibility of social responses toward inanimate objects raises a question as to the nature of objects and how they are known. While the ramifications of this phase of his thought are too varied for appropriate summary here, the matter does involve the concept of meaning and, therefore, warrants some consideration in the presentation of any rounded understanding of Mead's theory of mind.

In Mead's way of thinking, meaning arises only through communication. The significance of a gesture (symbol), for instance, is found in the response of others to it as a part of a social act. The various acts of individuals presuppose the social process, and

> . . . the gesture arises as a separable element in the social act, by virtue of the fact that it is selected out by the sensitivities of other organisms to it; it does not exist as a gesture merely in the experience of the single individual. The meaning of a gesture by one organism . . . is found in the response of another organism to what would be the completion of the act of the first organism which that gesture initiates and indicates.[14]

The relationship, in other words, between a stimulus as a gesture and the later phases of the social act constitutes the field within which meaning originates and exists.

[12] Mead, *Mind, Self, and Society*, p. 223 (footnote).
[13] *Ibid.*, pp. 223–225.
[14] *Ibid.*, pp. 145–146.

What is particularly of significance in such a statement is that meaning, as thus considered, is a development *objectively there* as a relation between certain phases of the social act. It is not to be thought of as a psychical addition" to the act. It is no mere "idea" in the traditional sense.[15] Meaning is implicit wherever there is present a certain "triadic relation of a gesture of one individual, a response to that gesture by a second individual, and completion of the given social act initiated by the gesture of the first individual."[16] Meaning is, therefore, thoroughly social in origin and nature.

According to Mead gestures may be either significant or non-significant. Below the human level of life the conversation of gestures is largely, if not completely, non-significant, non-meaningful, because it is not *self-conscious*. A lower organism acts, but its activity, from its own standpoint, or from that of any other non-human organism, is meaningless. There is gesture and response, as in the dog-fight, and things happen, but there is no self and no other; that is, no designation of objects. Any such designation would imply symbolic interaction. Meaning, as the object-matter of such symbolic interaction, or thought,

> . . . arises in experience through the individual stimulating himself to take the attitude of the other in his reaction toward the object. *Meaning is that which can be indicated to others while it is by the same process indicated to the indicating individual.*[17]

This point of view may be put in other terms. Mead laid emphasis, for example, upon the selective quality of organic activity. The living organism, within limits, but nevertheless definitely, selects or carves out its own environment. Among human beings this environment is distinctive in that it is composed of objects. At first the environment, or the world, is one of social objects, but as self and social other are acquired, physical objects and relationships may also be constructed by a process of abstraction. In this latter process the human hand, in conjunction with the eye, plays a major role.

Mead did not question that nature—or the extra-human world—is objectively there regardless of our experience of it. He was a pragmatist, not an idealist, in philosophy. He consequently held, however, that all objects are defined as such in and through human experience. Objective nature thereby comes to possess certain characteristics by virtue of its relationship to human experiencing or mind which it would not possess otherwise, or apart from this relationship. These characteristics, Mead held, constitute the meanings of objects to us, and to all intents and purposes, give definition and functional reality to the objects themselves.[18] An object is always in

---

[15] *Ibid.*, pp. 75–76.
[16] *Ibid.*, p. 81.
[17] *Ibid.*, p. 89 (italics not in the original).
[18] *Ibid.*, p. 131.

this sense a "construct," a resultant, the kind of response which will ensue after a certain type of activity. A blackboard, for example, is what it is for us, has certain properties associated with writing in black and white, because that is the way it responds to our activity. As a symbol, an object, it stands for certain consequences in activity. Certain qualities are there, but as parts of an act, and not of some independently existing "essence" or "extension." From this standpoint, an object may be defined as a "collapsed act"; the sign of what would happen if the act were carried to completion.[19]

Following this point to its conclusion, Mead declared:

> . . . The earliest objects are social objects, and all objects are social objects. Later experience differentiates the social from the physical objects, but the mechanism of the experience of things over against self as an object is the social mechanism. The identification of the individual with physical objects which appear in the effective occupation of space is a derivative of this.[20]

An object, thus, becomes a meaningful reality to a human being because of his ability to make indications, either imaginatively to himself, or directly to others. All objects, all symbols with semantic reference, represent telescoped acts. By means of the conversation of attitudes and the use of significant symbols—essentially a social process—the world (both social and physical) of each individual comes into being. Viewed, indeed, as consisting of objects and their relationships, the world is an out-and-out social world, as self and mind are also social, that is emergent within the human social process of activity itself. As Charles W. Morris, to whose labors we owe much for the possession of Mead's thought in print, declares in the introduction to the latest of the posthumous volumes,

> . . . Mind, as involving the symbolic internalization of the complete or social act, and the self, as an object that has itself for an object, are on this view seen as social emergents made possible through the process of linguistic communication within the social act. . . . In man, animal impulse becomes enormously elaborated and intelligently guided, sensitivity to stimuli becomes the perception of enduring objects, manipulation is elaborated into the physical world of science, and communication shares in the elaboration of impulse and its illumination through reason. Animals live in a world of events; man lives in a world of common meanings—and meaning for Mead is socially generated and sustained.[21]

[19] G. H. Mead, *The Philosophy of the Act* (Chicago: University of Chicago Press, 1938), pp. 368–370.
[20] *Ibid.*, pp. 428–430.
[21] *Ibid.*, pp. ix–x.

Mind, Experience, and Behavior

Let us begin with the technical side—the change in psychology. We are only just now commencing to appreciate how completely exploded is the psychology that dominated philosophy throughout the eighteenth and nineteenth centuries. According to this theory, mental life originated in sensations which are separately and passively received, and which are formed, through laws of retention and association, into a mosaic of images, perceptions and conceptions. The senses were regarded as gateways or avenues of knowledge. Except in combining atomic sensations, the mind was wholly passive and acquiescent in knowing. Volition, action, emotion, and desire follow in the wake of sensations and images. The intellectual or cognitive factor comes first and emotional and volitional life is only a consequent conjunction of ideas with sensations of pleasure and pain.

The effect of the development of biology has been to reverse the picture. Wherever there is life, there is behavior, activity. In order that life may persist, this activity has to be both continuous and adapted to the environment. This adaptive adjustment, moreover, is not wholly passive; is not a mere matter of the moulding of the organism by the environment. Even a clam acts upon the environment and modifies it to some extent. It selects materials for food and for the shell that protects it. It does something to the environment as well as has something done to itself. There is no such thing in a living creature as mere conformity to conditions, though parasitic forms may approach this limit. In the interests of the maintenance of life there is transformation of some elements in the surrounding medium. The higher the form of life, the more important is the active reconstruction of the medium. This increased control may be illustrated by the contrast of savage with civilized man. Suppose the two are living in a wilderness. With the savage there is the maximum of accommodation to given conditions; the minimum of what we may call hitting back. The savage takes things "as they are," and by using caves and roots and occasional pools leads a meagre and precarious existence. The civilized man goes to distant mountains and dams streams. He builds reservoirs, digs channels, and conducts the water to what had been a desert. He searches the world to find plants and animals that will thrive. He takes native plants and by selection and cross-fertilization improves them. He introduces machinery to till the soil and care for the harvest. By such means he may succeed in making the wilderness blossom like the rose.

John Dewey, "Mind, Experience, and Behavior." From *Reconstruction in Philosophy*, pp. 84–87, 90–92, by John Dewey, copyright 1920 by Henry Holt and Company, 1942 by John Dewey.

Such transformation scenes are so familiar that we overlook their meaning. We forget that the inherent power of life is illustrated in them. Note what a change this point of view entails in the traditional notions of experience. Experience becomes an affair primarily of doing. The organism does not stand about, Micawberlike, waiting for something to turn up. It does not wait passive and inert for something to impress itself upon it from without. The organism acts in accordance with its own structure, simple or complex, upon its surroundings. As a consequence the changes produced in the environment react upon the organism and its activities. The living creature undergoes, suffers, the consequences of its own behavior. This close connection between doing and suffering or undergoing forms what we call experience. Disconnected doing and disconnected suffering are neither of them experiences. Suppose fire encroaches upon a man when he is asleep. Part of his body is burned away. The burn does not perceptibly result from what he has done. There is nothing which in any instructive way can be named experience. Or again there is a series of mere activities, like twitchings of muscles in a spasm. The movements amount to nothing; they have no consequences for life. Or, if they have, these consequences are not connected with prior doing. There is no experience, no learning, no cumulative process. But suppose a busy infant puts his finger in the fire; the doing is random, aimless, without intention or reflection. But something happens in consequence. The child undergoes heat, he suffers pain. The doing and undergoing, the reaching and the burn, are connected. One comes to suggest and mean the other. Then there is experience in a vital and significant sense.

Certain important implications for philosophy follow. In the first place, the interaction of organism and environment, resulting in some adaptation which secures utilization of the latter, is the primary fact, the basic category. Knowledge is relegated to a derived position, secondary in origin, even if its importance, when once it is established, is overshadowing. Knowledge is not something separate and self-sufficing, but is involved in the process by which life is sustained and evolved. The senses lose their place as gateways of knowing to take their rightful place as stimuli to action. To an animal an affection of the eye or ear is not an idle piece of information about something indifferently going on in the world. It is an invitation and inducement to act in a needed way. It is a clue in behavior, a directive factor in adaptation of life in its surroundings. It is urgent not cognitive in quality. The whole controversy between empiricism and rationalism as to the intellectual worth of sensations is rendered strangely obsolete. The discussion of sensations belongs under the head of immediate stimulus and response, not under the head of knowledge.

* * *

When experience is aligned with the life-process and sensations are seen to be points of readjustment, the alleged atomism of sensations totally disappears. With this disappearance is abolished the need for a synthetic faculty of super-empirical reason to connect them. Philosophy is not any longer confronted with the hopeless problem of finding a way in which separate grains of sand may be woven into a strong and coherent rope—or into the illusion and pretence of one. When the isolated and simple existences of Locke and Hume are seen not to be truly empirical at all but to answer to certain demands of their theory of mind, the necessity ceases for the elaborate Kantian and post-Kantian machinery of *a priori* concepts and categories to synthesize the alleged stuff of experience. The true "stuff" of experience is recognized to be adaptive courses of action, habits, active functions, connections of doing and undergoing; sensori-motor co-ordinations. Experience carries principles of connection and organization within itself. These principles are none the worse because they are vital and practical rather than epistemological. Some degree of organization is indispensable to even the lowest grade of life. Even an amoeba must have some continuity in time in its activity and some adaptation to its environment in space. Its life and experience cannot possibly consist in momentary, atomic, and self-enclosed sensations. Its activity has reference to its surroundings and to what goes before and what comes after. This organization intrinsic to life renders unnecessary a super-natural and super-empirical synthesis. It affords the basis and material for a positive evolution of intelligence as an organizing factor within experience.

Nor is it entirely aside from the subject to point out the extent in which social as well as biological organization enters into the formation of human experience. Probably one thing that strengthened the idea that the mind is passive and receptive in knowing was the observation of the helplessness of the human infant. But the observation points in quite another direction. Because of his physical dependence and impotency, the contacts of the little child with nature are mediated by other persons. Mother and nurse, father and older children, determine what experiences the child shall have; they constantly instruct him as to the meaning of what he does and undergoes. The conceptions that are socially current and important become the child's principles of interpretation and estimation long before he attains to personal and deliberate control of conduct. Things come to him clothed in language, not in physical nakedness, and this garb of communication makes him a sharer in the beliefs of those about him. These beliefs coming to him as so many facts form his mind; they furnish the centres about which his own personal expeditions and perceptions are ordered. Here we have "categories" of connection and unification as important as those of Kant, but empirical not mythological.

The Definition of the Situation

One of the most important powers gained during the evolution of animal life is the ability to make decisions from within instead of having them imposed from without. Very low forms of life do not make decisions, as we understand this term, but are pushed and pulled by chemical substances, heat, light, etc., much as iron filings are attracted or repelled by a magnet. They do tend to behave properly in given conditions—a group of small crustaceans will flee as in a panic if a bit of strychnia is placed in the basin containing them and will rush toward a drop of beef juice like hogs crowding around swill—but they do this as an expression of organic affinity for the one substance and repugnance for the other, and not as an expression of choice or "free will." There are, so to speak, rules of behavior but these represent a sort of fortunate mechanistic adjustment of the organism to typically recurring situations, and the organism cannot change the rule.

On the other hand, the higher animals, and above all man, have the power of refusing to obey a stimulation which they followed at an earlier time. Response to the earlier stimulation may have had painful consequences and so the rule or habit in this situation is changed. We call this ability the power of inhibition, and it is dependent on the fact that the nervous system carries memories or records of past experiences. At this point the determination of action no longer comes exclusively from outside sources but is located within the organism itself.

Preliminary to any self-determined act of behavior there is always a stage of examination and deliberation which we may call *the definition of the situation*. And actually not only concrete acts are dependent on the definition of the situation, but gradually a whole life-policy and the personality of the individual himself follow from a series of such definitions.

But the child is always born into a group of people among whom all the general types of situation which may arise have already been defined and corresponding rules of conduct developed, and where he has not the slightest chance of making his definitions and following his wishes without interference. Men have always lived together in groups. Whether mankind has a true herd instinct or whether groups are held together because this has worked out to advantage is of no importance. Certainly the wishes in general are such that they can be satisfied only in a society. But we have only

From *The Unadjusted Girl*, pp. 41–50, by William I. Thomas (Boston: Little, Brown and Company, 1931), reprinted by permission of Social Science Research Council.

to refer to the criminal code to appreciate the variety of ways in which the wishes of the individual may conflict with the wishes of society. And the criminal code takes no account of the many unsanctioned expressions of the wishes which society attempts to regulate by persuasion and gossip.

There is therefore always a rivalry between the spontaneous definitions of the situation made by the member of an organized society and the definitions which his society has provided for him. The individual tends to a hedonistic selection of activity, pleasure first; and society to a utilitarian selection, safety first. Society wishes its member to be laborious, dependable, regular, sober, orderly, self-sacrificing; while the individual wishes less of this and more of new experience. And organized society seeks also to regulate the conflict and competition inevitable between its members in the pursuit of their wishes. The desire to have wealth, for example, or any other socially sanctioned wish, may not be accomplished at the expense of another member of the society—by murder, theft, lying, swindling, blackmail, etc.

It is in this connection that a moral code arises, which is a set of rules or behavior norms, regulating the expression of the wishes, and which is built up by successive definitions of the situation. In practice the abuse arises first and the rule is made to prevent its recurrence. Morality is thus the generally accepted definition of the situation, whether expressed in public opinion and the unwritten law, in a formal legal code, or in religious commandments and prohibitions.

The family is the smallest social unit and the primary defining agency. As soon as the child has free motion and begins to pull, tear, pry, meddle, and prowl, the parents begin to define the situation through speech and other signs and pressures: "Be quiet," "Sit up straight," "Blow your nose," "Wash your face," "Mind your mother," "Be kind to sister," etc. This is the real significance of Wordsworth's phrase, "Shades of the prison house begin to close upon the growing child." His wishes and activities begin to be inhibited, and gradually, by definitions within the family, by playmates, in the school, in the Sunday school, in the community, through reading, by formal instruction, by informal signs of approval and disapproval, the growing member learns the code of his society.

In addition to the family we have the community as a defining agency. At present the community is so weak and vague that it gives us no idea of the former power of the local group in regulating behavior. Originally the community was practically the whole world of its members. It was composed of families related by blood and marriage and was not so large that all the members could not come together; it was a face-to-face group. I asked a Polish peasant what was the extent of an "okolica" or neighborhood—how far it reached. "It reaches," he said, "as far as the report of a man reaches—as far as a man is talked about." And it was in communities of this kind that the moral code which we now recognize as valid originated. The customs of the community are "folkways," and both state and church have in their more formal codes mainly recognized and incorporated these folkways.

The typical community is vanishing and it would be neither possible nor desirable to restore it in its old form. It does not correspond with the present direction of social evolution and it would now be a distressing condition in which to live. But in the immediacy of relationships and the participation of everybody in everything, it represents an element which we have lost and which we shall probably have to restore in some form of cooperation in order to secure a balanced and normal society—some arrangement corresponding with human nature.

Very elemental examples of the definition of the situation by the community as a whole, corresponding to mob action as we know it and to our trial by jury, are found among European peasants. The three documents following, all relating to the Russian community or *mir*, give some idea of the conditions under which a whole community, a public, formerly defined a situation.

25. We who are unacquainted with peasant speech, manners and method of expressing thought—mimicry—if we should be present at a division of land or some settlement among the peasants, would never understand anything. Hearing fragmentary, disconnected exclamations, endless quarreling, with repetition of some single word; hearing this racket of a seemingly senseless, noisy crowd that counts up or measures off something, we should conclude that they would not get together, or arrive at any result in an age. . . . Yet wait until the end and you will see that the division has been made with mathematical accuracy—that the measure, the quality of the soil, the slope of the field, the distance from the village—everything in short has been taken into account, that the reckoning has been correctly done and, what is most important, that every one of those present who were interested in the division is certain of the correctness of the division or settlement. The cry, the noise, the racket do not subside until every one is satisfied and no doubter is left.

The same thing is true concerning the discussion of some question by the *mir*. There are no speeches, no debates, no votes. They shout, they abuse each other, they seem on the point of coming to blows. Apparently they riot in the most senseless manner. Some one preserves silence, silence, and then suddenly puts in a word, one word, or an ejaculation, and by this word, this ejaculation, he turns the whole thing upside down. In the end, you look into it and find that an admirable decision has been formed and, what is most important, a unanimous decision.[1]

26. As I approached the village, there hung over it such a mixed, varied violent shouting, that no well brought-up parliament would agree to recognize itself, even in the abstract, as analogous to this gathering of peasant deputies. It was clearly a full meeting today. . . . At other more quiet village meetings I had been able to make out very little, but this was a real lesson to me. I felt only a continuous, indistinguishable roaring in my ears,

[1] A. N. Engelgardt: "Iz Derevni: 12 Pisem" ("From the Country; 12 Letters"), p. 315.

sometimes pierced by a particularly violent phrase that broke out from the general roar. I saw in front of me the "immediate" man, in all his beauty. What struck me first of all was his remarkable frankness; the more "immediate" he is, the less able is he to mask his thoughts and feelings; once he is stirred up the emotion seizes him quickly and he flares up then and there, and does not quiet down till he has poured out before you all the substance of his soul. He does not feel embarrassment before anybody; there are no indications here of diplomacy. Further, he opens up his whole soul, and he will tell everything that he may ever have known about you, and not only about you, but about your father, grandfather, and great-grandfather. Here everything is clear water, as the peasants say, and everything stands out plainly. If any one, out of smallness of soul, or for some ulterior motive, thinks to get out of something by keeping silent, they force him out into clear water without pity. And there are very few such small-souled persons at important village meetings. I have seen the most peaceable, irresponsible peasants, who at other times would not have thought of saying a word against any one, absolutely changed at these meetings, at these moments of general excitement. They believed in the saying, "On people even death is beautiful," and they got up so much courage that they were able to answer back the peasants commonly recognized as audacious. At the moment of its height the meeting becomes simply an open mutual confessional and mutual disclosure, the display of the widest publicity. At these moments when, it would seem, the private interests of each reach the highest tension, public interests and justice in turn reach the highest degree of control.[2]

27. In front of the volost administration building there stands a crowd of some one hundred and fifty men. This means that a volost meeting has been called to consider the verdict of the Kusmin rural commune "regarding the handing over to the [state] authorities of the peasant Gregori Siedov, caught red-handed and convicted of horse-stealing." Siedov had already been held for judical inquiry; the evidence against him was irrefutable and he would undoubtedly be sentenced to the penitentiary. In view of this I endeavor to explain that the verdict in regard to his exile is wholly super-fluous and will only cause a deal of trouble; and that at the termination of the sentence of imprisonment of Siedov the commune will unfailingly be asked whether it wants him back or prefers that he be exiled. Then, I said, in any event it would be necessary to formulate a verdict in regard to the "non-reception" of Siedov, while at this stage all the trouble was premature and could lead to nothing. But the meeting did not believe my words, did not trust the court and wanted to settle the matter right then and there; the general hatred of horse-thieves was too keen. . . .

The decisive moment has arrived; the head-man "drives" all the judges-elect to one side; the crowd stands with a gloomy air, trying not to look at Siedov and his wife, who are crawling before the *mir* on their knees. "Old men, whoever pities Gregori, will remain in his place, and whoever does not forgive him will step to the right," cries the head man. The crowd wavered and rocked, but remained dead still on the spot; no one dared to be first to take the fatal step. Gregori feverishly ran over the faces of his

[2] N. N. Zlatovratsky: "Ocherki Krestyanskoy Obshchiny" ("Sketches of the Peasant Commune"), p. 127.

judges with his eyes, trying to read in these faces pity for him. His wife wept bitterly, her face close to the ground; beside her, finger in mouth and on the point of screaming, stood a three-year-old youngster (at home Gregori had four more children). . . . But straightway one peasant steps out of the crowd; two years before some one had stolen a horse from him. "Why should we pity him? Did he pity us?" says the old man, and stooping goes over to the right side. "That is true; bad grass must be torn from the field," says another one from the crowd, and follows the old man. The beginning had been made; at first individually and then in whole groups the judges-elect proceeded to go over to the right. The man condemned by public opinion ran his head into the ground, beat his breast with his fists, seized those who passed him by their coat-tails, crying: "Ivan Timofeich! Uncle Leksander! Vasinka, dear kinsman! Wait, kinsmen, let me say a word. . . . Petrushenka." But, without stopping and with stern faces, the members of the *mir* dodged the unfortunates, who were crawling at their feet. . . . At last the wailing of Gregori stopped; around him for the space of three *sazen* the place was empty; there was no one to implore. All the judges-elect, with the exception of one, an uncle of the man to be exiled, had gone over to the right. The woman cried sorrowfully, while Gregori stood motionless on his knees, his head lowered, stupidly looking at the ground.[3]

The essential point in reaching a communal decision, just as in the case of our jury system, is unanimity. In some cases the whole community mobilizes around a stubborn individual to conform him to the general wish.

28. It sometimes happens that all except one may agree but the motion is never carried if that one refuses to agree to it. In such cases all endeavor to talk over and persuade the stiff-necked one. Often they even call to their aid his wife, his children, his relatives, his father-in-law, and his mother, that they may prevail upon him to say yes. Then all assail him, and say to him from time to time: "Come now, God help you, agree with us too, that this may take place as we wish it, that the house may not be cast into disorder, that we may not be talked about by the people, that the neighbors may not hear of it, that the world may not make sport of us!" It seldom occurs in such cases that unanimity is not attained.[4]

A less formal but not less powerful means of defining the situation employed by the community is gossip. The Polish peasant's statement that a community reaches as far as a man is talked about was significant, for the community regulates the behavior of its members largely by talking about them. Gossip has a bad name because it is sometimes malicious and false and designed to improve the status of the gossiper and degrade its object, but gossip is in the main true and is an organizing force. It is a mode of defining the situation in a given case and of attaching praise or blame. It is one of the means by which the status of the individual and of his family is fixed.

[3] "V. Volostnikh Pisaryakh" ("A Village Secretary"), p. 283.
[4] F. S. Krauss: "Sitte und Brauch der Südslaven", p. 103.

The community also, particularly in connection with gossip, knows how to attach opprobrium to persons and actions by using epithets which are at the same time brief and emotional definitions of the situation. "Bastard," "whore," "traitor," "coward," "skunk," "scab," "snob," "kike," etc., are such epithets. In "Faust" the community said of Margaret, "She stinks." The people are here employing a device known in psychology as the "conditioned reflex." If, for example, you place before a child (say six months old) an agreeable object, a kitten, and at the same time pinch the child, and if this is repeated several times, the child will immediately cry at the sight of the kitten without being pinched; or if a dead rat were always served beside a man's plate of soup he would eventually have a disgust for soup when served separately. If the word "stinks" is associated on people's tongues with Margaret, Margaret will never again smell sweet. Many evil consequences, as the psychoanalysts claim, have resulted from making the whole of sex life a "dirty" subject, but the device has worked in a powerful, sometimes a paralyzing way on the sexual behavior of women.

Winks, shrugs, nudges, laughter, sneers, haughtiness, coldness, "giving the once over" are also language defining the situation and painfully felt as unfavorable recognition. The sneer, for example, is incipient vomiting, meaning, "you make me sick."

And eventually the violation of the code even in an act of no intrinsic importance, as in carrying food to the mouth with the knife, provokes condemnation and disgust. The fork is not a better instrument for conveying food than the knife, at least it has no moral superiority, but the situation has been defined in favor of the fork. To smack with the lips in eating is bad manners with us, but the Indian has more logically defined the situation in the opposite way; with him smacking is a compliment to the host.

In this whole connection fear is used by the group to produce the desired attitudes in its member. Praise is used also but more sparingly. And the whole body of habits and emotions is so much a community and family product that disapproval or separation is almost unbearable.

Studying the Definition of the Situation: Theory and Field Research Strategies

For over forty years, since Thomas and Znaniecki published *The Polish Peasant*, the phrase "the definition of the situation" has been in the American sociologist's lexicon. What is remarkable, given this longevity, is the paucity of research that focuses on the definitions of specific situations by groups of actors as explanations for the behaviour of these actors in the immediate environment. Those few studies that have been carried out under the name of definition of the situation (for example, Gorden, 1952; Lerner and Becker, 1962; Deutscher, 1964) have either inadequately operationalized this notion or have considered as the situation to be defined something far larger and less specific than a typical instance of ongoing social interaction.[1] However, it should be noted that there is one very recent exception to this indictment, and we shall consider it briefly later on. It is Peter McHugh's ingenious laboratory study of the definition of the situation (1968).

It seems that tradition as well as genuine conceptual and measurement difficulties have combined to produce a reluctance to investigate, in a systematic fashion, people's definitions of situations. The myth, outside and to some extent within the field of symbolic interactionism, that the ideas of George Herbert Mead (and therefore those of his followers) cannot be empirically examined still lingers. There is the very real problem of concretizing or establishing working definitions for a concept so subjective and abstract as the definition of the situation. Finally, there has been the tendency to consider the definition of the situation in terms of the single individual who holds it, a practice not conducive to the development of nomothetic science. With respect to this last point, we must strive instead to make general statements about *classes* of definitions used by identifiable *groups* of men in particular but recurrent situations.

Robert A. Stebbins, "Studying the Definition of the Situation: Theory and Field Research Strategies." Reprinted from *The Canadian Review of Sociology and Anthropology*, 6:4 (1969), by permission of the author and the publisher.

The author wishes to express his gratitude to Professors Jean L. Briggs, Frank E. Jones, and Robert W. Habenstein for their helpful comments on various drafts of the manuscript.

[1] It is this latter kind of situation in which we are interested. It has been defined more formally by Stebbins (1967:150) as the "subjective situation" or "the immediate social and physical surroundings and the current physiological and psychological state of the actor . . . *as seen by him*."

Although it will be a long time before anything like "grounded" theories of the definitions of specific kinds of situations by specific categories of actors appear, it is evident that a set of research strategies must be devised to assist us in our efforts to reach this goal. The aim of this paper is to offer, along with certain strategies for research, some refinements in the theory of the definition of the situation that was presented in an earlier essay by the author (Stebbins, 1967). An exploratory type of field experimental demonstration follows this discussion, and we conclude with a review of the implications of the refined theory for sociological motivation.

Theory and Research Strategies

The goal of making general statements about classes of definitions used by identifiable groups of men in particular but recurrent situations, is best attained by employing the following concepts. The groups of men to be studied are those in different *social identities*, the conventionally recognized categories in community life into which human actors place themselves and others.[2] Most of our definitions of the countless situations that we enter, whatever identity we are in, may be classified as belonging to one of the following modes: *cultural definitions* (Wolff, 1965:182), *habitual personal definitions*, or *unique personal definitions*.[3] The chief difference between the first two lies in the distinction between consensual and non-consensual sharing of meanings. Cultural definitions are collective representations; the standard meanings of events embedded in the community culture as a whole or some sub-part of it (sub-culture) that we learn either through primary socialization or secondary socialization or both. A given cultural definition is consensually shared to the extent that those who are members of a particular group are aware that others in it recognize and utilize that definition in the same way that they do. Thus, in North America bar rooms are generally defined as places where people drink alcoholic beverages and talk sociably with others, and offices at places of work are typically conceived as locations for occupationally related activity—two widely held cultural definitions.

But sharing of the definition need not be consensual. The non-consensual sharing characteristic of the habitual personal definition refers to the circumstances in which the same category of situation holds roughly the same meaning for a particular class of actor participating in it, but in which

[2] "Identity" is preferred over closely related ideas such as "status," "position," and "rank" because of its apparently broader scope. For example, one can have the identity of neighbour, but we would not ordinarily call this a position or a status.

[3] These three modes of the definition of the situation represent an expansion of the "cultural" and "personal definitions" discussed by the author in his earlier paper (Stebbins, 1967:158).

each individual participant is more or less *unaware* that people like him who are having the same kind of experiences elsewhere define them in the same way. Present research by the author into the ways teachers define certain classroom situations has disclosed that they are largely unaware of how their colleagues deal with routine instances of disorderly behaviour. That Johnny was discovered whispering the other day or that Susan was daydreaming this morning are apparently not of sufficient importance to the teachers investigated so far in the project to warrant comment to other teachers in the same kind of setting. Still, each teacher defined situations such as these, usually as calling for a specific action designed to curb the undesirable behaviour of the student or students involved.

Habitual definitions are the regular meanings employed by categories of actors in specific kinds of periodic situations that for one reason or another (such as, the insignificance of the event or the unavailability of like actors to each other while behaving in the situation) are not communicated. These meanings can be distinguished from unique personal definitions, which refer to the person's interpretation of events rarely or never encountered in the community. To wit, events that occur for which, so far as he is concerned, no cultural or habitual meaning exists. Thus, he must improvise his own interpretation, usually basing his synthesis on the nearest personal or collective equivalent. Presumably, the recent earth tremors in the midwestern portion of North America led to many unique definitions of that situation.

Although they are infrequent, unique personal definitions are apparently shared on a non-consensual basis under some circumstances. Hill and Hansen (1962:186), after examining several studies concerning the family in disasters, concluded that there is a general tendency for family members to seek each other under these circumstances, if geographical location does not prevent this. It seems that people's definitions of disaster situations regularly include family considerations, if their families are believed to be in any danger.

The relationship between these three modes of definitions of the situation is complicated and must await empirical specification. Because they are multidimensional they cannot be placed on a single continuum. At this stage of the development of the theory, they are best viewed as ideal types, functioning heuristically to inform us how closely a given empirical case approximates the pure conceptualization of the phenomenon.

The aim of research in this field should be the development of "grounded theories" of definitions of recurrent situations encountered by the incumbents of a particular identity.[4] Since cultural and habitual definitions are seen as forming the foundation on which actors build unique defi-

---

[4] Grounded theory is theory discovered "from data systematically obtained from social research" (Glaser and Strauss, 1967:2).

nitions, and since they refer to recurrent settings, it should be clear that we must begin any research program with the aim just suggested by concentrating initially on the first two modes of definitions. And by studying the definitions of situations of those in a given identity, a theoretical link to the social structure of the community is also gained, thereby permitting us as well to view our findings in terms of their relevance at the macrosociological level of analysis.

A cultural definition, since it is categorical and impersonal, must be given additional specification by the actor using it with reference to any particular setting. Once a cultural definition is determined to be relevant for the events at hand, it is idiosyncratically tailored so as to better serve the user. As we shall indicate shortly, this is done, in part, through activated predispositions. The usage of the term "predisposition" in this paper is similar to the modern conceptualization of Newcomb, Turner, and Converse (1965:40–46, 67–73) and Campbell (1963:97–112). Campbell, who limits his statement strictly to acquired states, stresses the importance of the fact that predispositions (he calls them "acquired behavioural dispositions") are enduring and that they remain dormant until activated by situational stimuli. When activated, these products of past experience impinge upon our awareness, equip us with a specific view of the world, and guide behaviour in the immediate present.

The following sequential model indicates the location of the definition of the situation in relation to the initial reaction of the individual to the setting.[5] 1. Typical actors in a given identity enter a typical setting with a specific intention or action orientation in mind. 2. Certain aspects of these surroundings, some of which are related to the intention, activate or awaken some of the predispositions the actors characteristically carry with them. 3. The aspects of the surroundings, the intention, and the activated predispositions, when considered together, lead to the selection of a cultural or habitual definition. 4. This definition directs subsequent action in the situation, at least until a reinterpretation occurs.

From what has been said so far, it is possible to formulate two research problems to guide actual study. 1. What cultural or habitual definitions are available to those in a given social identity for use in one or more specified kinds of recurring situations? 2. For classes of actors within an identity, what common predispositions are activated by elements in the ongoing setting that influence the selection of one of these definitions instead of another?[6]

---

[5] This is, of course, a highly simplified version of a more complicated process. For a more detailed discussion of this model, see Stebbins (1967).

[6] McHugh's treatment of the process of "emergence" seems to come closest in meaning to the cultural and habitual definitions, when compared with the rest of the concepts in our framework. Following Mead, emergence refers to the past and future in-

OPERATIONALIZATION

Once one discovers some of the more important recurring situations for the actors in an identity (by means of some form of observation), one can, if not already aware of them, begin to search for the cultural or habitual definitions available for each setting. This can be done most efficaciously by a combination of further direct observation and questionnaire interviewing. Here observation performs a single important function: it gives the investigator a crude idea of the definition that the subject has chosen in response to the situation at hand. Having acquired this knowledge it is possible for the former to question the latter about that event, the intention being to establish a more detailed and consequently more valid picture of the meaning that the incident held for the respondent. In order to avert problems of recall, interviewing should take place as soon as possible after the situation under observation has ended.

The interviewing, if it is to fulfil its function, must be conducted along the lines of programmatically developed statements operationalizing the concept of the definition of the situation, thirteen of which are listed below. Each of these has been theorized and often empirically demonstrated by social psychologists to play an important role in situationally based and situationally focused explanations of behaviour.[7] The merit of the theory of the definition of the situation is that it pulls together these theoretical strands, which are in themselves incomplete as explanations, within a more coherent and comprehensive framework (some of which we have yet to discuss). There is a degree of overlap between some of the statements, but for our purposes this may be advantageous. 1. Identification by the identity incumbents of the relevant others present (Ball, forthcoming; Foote, 1951: 17–21; McHugh, 1968:43; Stone, 1962:89–90; Strauss, 1959:47; Turner,

---

fluence on contemporary behaviour (McHugh, 1968:24–25). The process of emergence partly manifests itself in everyday life by leading the actor to expect a familiar "theme" in all or most of his dealings with others (McHugh, 1968:37). The other major parameter of the definition of the situation found in McHugh's study is that of the "relativity" of standpoints from which we judge the setting (1968:28, 42–45). However, his evidence suggests that relativity, as he uses this term, operates mostly where the assumption of a theme breaks down. This approaches our notion of unique personal definition, which is peripheral to our interests here. While there are several places where aspects of the process of emergence and those of the cultural or habitual definition seem to correspond, we shall retain the operational terminology developed earlier. It better relates to the previously developed theory and, because of its greater comprehensiveness, better serves field research.

7 The phrase "situationally based and situationally focused explanations" refers to those propositions in social psychology that fix on behaviour in the immediate setting and that are consistent with the assumption that human action is, at least in part, a product of what is happening there. They are clearly of a different genre than constitutionally based or social structurally based explanations.

1956; Weinstein and Deutschberger, 1963; 1964).[8] 2. The incumbents' perception of the evaluation that those others have made of the situation, including the moral and emotional or sentimental connotations of the immediate setting as they are established with reference to the others' identification of themselves (Ball, forthcoming; Jones and Davis, 1965:226–227; McHugh, 1968:44; Newcomb, 1958:180; Shand, 1920; Shibutani, 1961: 332–334; Stone, 1962:97–101; Strauss, 1959:59; Thomas, 1951:69; Turner, 1956:321; Weber, 1947:90–95). 3. The incumbents' perception of the goals or intentions of the others while in the setting (Ball, forthcoming; Jones and Davis, 1965:222–223; Schutz, 1964:32; Strauss, 1959:59; Turner, 1956; Weber, 1947:90–95). 4. The incumbents' perception of the plans of action (strategies for reaching the goals) of the relevant others (Turner, 1956:321). 5. The incumbents' perception of the justifications or vocabularies of motives associated with the others' plans of action (Mills, 1940; Schutz, 1964:32). 6. The incumbents' evaluation of the situation (Ball, forthcoming; Cooley, 1922:183–184; Foote, 1951:20–21; McCall and Simmons, 1966:136; Shand, 1920; Shibutani, 1961:332–334; Stone, 1962:93, 97–101; Strauss, 1959:59; Turner, 1956:322). 7. The incumbents' plans of action (Jones and Thibaut, 1958:158–174). 8. The incumbents' justifications of the plans (Burke, 1945; 1950; MacIver, 1964:293; Mills, 1940; Schutz, 1964:11).

And as through the looking glass: 9. The identity incumbents' perception of the identification of them by the relevant others (McCall and Simmons, 1966:140–142; Stone, 1962:93; Turner, 1956:321–323; 1962:34). 10. The incumbents' perception of the evaluation of the situation imputed to them by the others (Cooley, 1922:183–184; Jones, 1964; Stone, 1962:97–101; Turner, 1956:321–323; 1962:34). 11. The incumbents' perception of the intentions imputed to them while in the situation (Jones, 1964; Turner, 1956:321–323; 1962:34). 12. The incumbents' perception of the plans of action imputed to them (Foote, 1951; Strauss, 1959:51; Turner, 1956: 321–323). 13. The incumbents' perception of the justifications of the plans imputed to them (Mills, 1940; Schutz, 1964:32–33; Strauss, 1959:52).

All of these perceptions by a given set of identity holders can, theoretically, be said to be part of their definitions of a particular kind of situation. However, not all of them will necessarily be obtained in any given investigation, for the actors may not be able to get such information for their own use in the interaction. They might, for example, be able to identify the relevant others, their meanings, and their intentions, but they might not have time to reflect about their plans of action or their justifications for them.

---

[8] The citations at the end of each of these statements refer to some of the relevant theoretical and empirical literature. They do not, in any way, represent an exhaustive inventory of pertinent entries. Also the operational statements presented in this paper are occasionally couched in language rather different from that found in the works cited.

Moreover, we may not need or desire the type of knowledge contained in each of these perceptions. We, as social persons, require only *adequate* knowledge about the others present and their perceptions of us so that we can act; additional information, while perhaps desirable, is less essential.[9] Jones and Thibaut (1958:151–152) cite research demonstrating that not all information is equally useful in assessing other actors in the environment. They believe that much of the perceiver's energy will be directed toward his own future response (his plan of action) and not toward the stable characteristics of the others present (Jones and Thibaut, 1958:74). Ichheiser (1949:46–48) points out that there is a tendency to overestimate the role of personal factors in the environment, while underestimating the role of situational factors. We are often blind to situational factors as others see them. Finally, it has been suggested by Gerth and Mills (1954:115) that unless one's anticipated behaviour is contrary to the expectations of those present, there is no felt need to justify it.

The investigator can isolate the cultural or habitual definitions used by those in an identity in certain circumstances by combining their responses to the operational statements as they appear in the questionnaire. This is exemplified in the field experiment reported later. Such a procedure permits one to obtain something of the actors' organic views of the immediate circumstances, which is in keeping with the belief that a definition or meaning of the situation is a synthesis, interpretation, and interrelation of predispositions, intentions, and elements of the setting (Stebbins, 1967:158).

PHASES OF THE DEFINITION OF THE SITUATION

In our sequential model presented earlier we stated that on the basis of the situational factors, the actors' predispositions, and their goals, a cultural or habitual personal mode of definition was selected. Although generally correct this statement is oversimplified. In actuality, the choice of standard definitions seems to take place in two phases occurring in rapid succession. Phase I is that of identifying the ongoing events as an instance of some category of situation. Here the incumbents have a choice: (i) a set of events is for them an instance of "X" category of situation, or (ii) a set is not such an instance and therefore is an instance of another category of situation (say, situation "A," "B," or "C"). However, recurrent situations are not free from associated meanings in the individual mind; they do not occur as neutral, uninterpreted happenings. In the very process of identifying the category of setting we are in, we have also selected a portion of our cultural or habitual definition because it is associated by means of socializa-

---

[9] Or, lacking direct information one may assume a certain amount about the others, relying on what Simmel (1950:318) called "confidence" in their meanings, intentions, etc. These assumptions are still part of the definition of the situation.

tion with the events at hand. More specifically, some or all of operational statements 1 through 5 and 9 through 13 appear simultaneously merely from identifying a set of events as "X" or "B" or whatever.

Phase II of the selection of a cultural or habitual definition amounts to choosing a standard personal evaluation, plan of action, and justification (operational statements 6 through 8). This can only be done after some answers, no matter how tentative, have been provided to the questions posed by the operational statements that comprise Phase I. There must be a modicum of information about the situation to evaluate, and to respond to with a plan of action. In Phase II, choice is guided by the immediate intentions of the actors, the actors' identification of the setting in Phase I, and the activated predispositions resulting from this identification.[10] When the intentions and activated predispositions play a role in the selection of a certain cultural definition (as compared with a habitual definition), they also direct the tailoring of that definition to the individual user. In this subjective sense the intentions and the predispositions are very much a part of the definition of the situation (both as a process and a product).

There are a couple of formulations in the literature that speak for the tenability of conceptualizing the defining of a situation in terms of two rapidly occurring successive phases. For instance, Fritz Heider (1958:76) has enunciated the general principle that perception influences action by arousing motivational states in the actor. Shand's theory of emotional expression (1920) also fits our model: as manifestations of underlying sentiments, behaviour-directing emotions are responses to certain kinds of settings. If I hate the man next door, I will be revolted when I see him in his garden and pleased when I notice that he has a flat tire.

Once we have identified one or more common purposes for a set of identity incumbents in any typical situation, then, having observed the events there, our problem is just as we stated earlier: to isolate the activated predispositions for classes of actors. These predispositions, which are many and varied (e.g., attitudes, values, general life goals, ideal self-conceptions, internalized role expectations, interests, and so forth),[11] can be measured in almost as many diverse ways. The most critical procedural

---

[10] In the interest of clarity it should be pointed out that the immediate intentions with which an actor enters the setting and his general life goals or long-range goals are two distinct, albeit, related ideas. A general life goal is a predisposition that is too complex and abstract from the individual's point of view to be realized in one or a few situations. The immediate intention, on the other hand, although it may be in service of a long-range goal is envisaged by the actor as being realized in the ongoing setting or in a short sequence of such settings. This latter type of goal is not a predisposition because it is not an enduring state that may be activated from time to time or that equips us with a special view of the world.

[11] A longer though still incomplete list is available in Campbell (1963:100–101). In fact, some phenomena that traditionally have been considered in objective terms, can also be treated as predispositions. See, for example, the author's papers on interpersonal relationships and social networks and subjective career (Stebbins, 1969; 1970).

problem facing the researcher in this area is how to record this activation of predispositions. Its solution demands much more than simply finding out which people hold a particular attitude or self-conception. Rather it involves determining if that disposition has played a role in the selection of a particular cultural or habitual definition. Fortunately, we are aided by common sense here, since it will be obvious to the long-time occupants of an identity (and to the observer who taps their knowledge) that some predispositions are not usually associated with certain social situations, while others are. Thus, teacher attitudes toward other races are not likely to be activated in an all-white classroom situation where mathematics is being taught.

Appropriate knowledge about an identity, then, enables us to be reasonably confident that a relevant predisposition has been activated and has been a factor in the selection of a particular definition when those who have chosen it are found to hold both the disposition and the definition in a significantly greater proportion than we would expect from their observed frequency in the study sample.

Parenthetically, it should be noted that any cultural or habitual definition may be replaced by another if, for some reason, the events in the setting change in some significant way. If this happens, then the same processes of selection recur (also see Ball's discussion of this point, forthcoming). Major changes in the affairs of the moment have been said, in fact, to signal the emergence of a new situation. The problems of establishing temporal, social, and physical boundaries of situations, both old and new, are considered by Stebbins (1967:151–154).

A Field Experiment

The experiment was conducted during a series of controversial lectures on the theory of evolution in an introductory sociology and anthropology course in a community where religious matters are taken seriously. Although there were no outright contests between instructor and students, it was clear that the latter were taking an unusual interest in the lecture material of the former, thereby indicating its concern (both positive and negative) to them.

With the co-operation of the instructor, two well-dressed male sociology students, ages 22 and 38, entered the lecture hall just before class was to begin and sat in the front row. After the instructor had begun summarizing some of his previous lectures on evolution, one of the men abruptly interrupted him with a contentious question about the validity of his information. For approximately five minutes a heated debate raged between instructor and the experimenter's confederates over the merits of the biblical versus the scientific versions of creation and the development of man. The instructor, not from the community in which the university is located, was branded, among other things, an outsider, an atheist, and a Communist. He was accused of defiling the minds of students and inciting pernicious social change. In the end the interlopers were expelled without ceremony.

The experimenter (who was listening outside the door) appeared immediately, and disclosed the true nature of the preceding events. Thereupon each student was asked to fill in a questionnaire containing a small number of open-ended items which were constructed along the lines of some of the thirteen operational statements of the definition of the situation.[12] Although individual interviewing would have been preferable, this procedure was successful enough to provide some definitive information about their interpretation of the experimental situation. Most students were able to complete the form in approximately twenty minutes.

An hour later (at the second meeting of that class) each student was requested to take, in the order of their appearance here, the Kuhn-McPartland Twenty-Statements Test, an interest ranking test, and a goal ranking test.[13] These measures provided the experimenter with a modicum of data about the predispositions of the students. The Twenty-Statements Test, though successfully administered, was unusable because the numbers of respondents, even in the largest cells, were not sufficient for meaningful cross tabulation. With respect to the other tests the students were asked to rank order six major interests: theoretical, economic, aesthetic, social, political, and religious. There were also ten general life goals to be ranked (see Newcomb, 1961:39–40).

RESULTS

The following six operational statements were used: (i) identification of the two men; (ii) their perceived evaluation of the class and its activities; (iii) their perceived intentions; (iv) the students' evaluation of the behaviour of the men; (v) the students' plans of action; and (vi) their justifications for them. Tables I through IV summarize the distribution of responses to the questionnaire items constructed with reference to the first four of these. There were not enough responses to the items on plans of action and their justifications to be useful for our purposes.

By cross tabulating the data in Table I with those in Tables II through IV, two cultural definitions were isolated.

---

[12] The instructions that appeared at the top of the first page, which were also read aloud to the students, requested that they record only those reactions to the two men that they had *up to the time the experimenter entered the room*. By means of this procedure it was hoped that retrospective definitions would be minimized.

[13] Both the interest ranking and goal ranking tests were taken from Newcomb (1961:39–40).

TABLE I. Student identifications of the two men

Identifications	Number	Percent
Religious figures (clergymen, zealous laymen, theology students, etc.)	25	20.8
Non-student intruders or outsiders	16	13.3
Troublemakers, fanatics, cranks, etc.	10	8.3
Narrow-minded, conservative men	7	5.8
Know them by name	3	2.5
Suspect or know they are students	8	6.7
Newcomers to the course	6	5.0
Have been invited by the instructor (teaching assistants, graduate students, professors, etc.)	7	5.8
More than one identification	2	1.7
Other	2	1.7
Unable to make any identification	34	28.4
Totals	120	100.0

Definition I. These two men are religious figures of some sort. Their beliefs are being seriously threatened by the lectures, and as a result they want them either corrected or stopped. Their activities are outrageous and highly resented.

Definition II. These two men are only non-student intruders. They somehow feel that the lectures are having a bad influence upon us students, and as a result want them either corrected or stopped. Their activities are mildly disgusting.

For Definition I, 44.2 percent of those who identified the two men as religious figures also felt that the lectures posed a threat to their beliefs, whereas the expected proportion was only 29.2 percent as based on the marginal totals of the over-all cross tabulation between Tables I and II. Using the chi-square one-sample test, this association can be expected by chance in less than 3 percent of the cases ($\chi^2 = 4.60$; $0.025 > p > 0.01$).[14] Similarly, 52.7 percent of those who identified the men as religious figures also identified them as wanting to correct the instructor's views, while the expected proportion was only 30.5 percent ($\chi^2 = 4.36$; $0.025 > p > 0.01$). Finally, 50.0 percent of those identifying the men as religious figures felt that their activities and intentions were highly outra-

[14] All of the chi-squares reported here are one-tailed. This practice is justified by the observation that, for a cross tabulation to yield a meaningful association, it has to be of a *higher* frequency than expected from the margin totals. Also, in three of the chi-square tests presented in this paper, one of the expected frequencies was slightly below 5, the minimum allowed for their optimal application. The decision was made to use them in spite of this weakness since the research is only demonstrative, and the only alternative appeared to be the binomial test, which with our data is prohibitively laborious. See Siegel (1956:36–47).

TABLE II. Student perceptions of the evaluation of the class by the men

Perceived evaluations	Number	Percent
The lectures threaten their beliefs	63	52.5
The lectures have a bad influence on the students	14	11.7
The lectures will promote social and cultural change in the community	13	10.8
The lectures have made them curious about the class	5	4.2
An opportunity to make a disturbance or to show off	3	2.5
Other	3	2.5
Unable to establish any meaning	19	15.8
Totals	120	100.0

TABLE III. Student perceptions of the men's intentions

Perceived intentions	Number	Percent
They have come to correct the instructor's views	21	17.5
They have come to encourage the students to reject the lectures	5	4.2
They have come to test the student's reaction to the lectures	7	5.8
They have come to make a disturbance, harass, or to show off	25	20.8
They have come at the instructor's invitation to stimulate discussion	5	4.2
Other	3	2.5
Unable to establish any intentions	54	45.0
Totals	120	100.0

TABLE IV. Student feelings about the activities of the two men

Feelings	Number	Percent
Ambivalence, confusion	4	3.3
Disgust, dislike	56	46.7
Disappointment, shame, embarrassment that this happens in our community	6	5.0
Outrage, anger, resentment	17	14.2
Surprise, shock	3	2.5
Amusement	5	4.2
More than one sentiment (sequentially)	7	5.8
Other	4	3.3
No answer	18	15.0
Totals	120	100.0

geous, although this was expected in only 29.1 percent of those cases (χ^2 = 2.53; $0.10 > p > 0.05$). If these proportions seem low, it must be remembered that sizeable percentages of respondents were either unable to establish meaning or intention or else did not answer the questions. Hence, the proportions presented above would have been considerably higher if we had chosen to state them in relation to the total number of respondents who answered each item.

The association between the operational statements in Definition II is weaker because there were smaller numbers of respondents to work with and the ratios between observed and expected proportions were low in two of the three instances. Thirty-three percent of those who identified the two men as non-student intruders also saw them as holding the view that the lectures were a bad influence on the students. This was expected in only 19.1 percent of the cases ($\chi^2 = 1.22$; $0.15 > p > 0.10$). Those making this same identification of the men perceived them as intending to correct the instructor's ideas in 21.1 percent of the cases, whereas this was expected in only 15.3 percent of them ($\chi^2 = 0.39$; $0.35 > p > 0.25$). Thirty-one percent of those who looked on the men as intruders harboured feelings of mild disgust toward their activities, though this was expected in only 20.3 percent of their responses ($\chi^2 = 3.87$; $0.025 > p > 0.01$).

Only in the case of Definition I were we able to link it with a generally held predisposition, and this was only partially successful. By cross-tabulating the responses of those who placed religious interests either first, second, or third (out of six possible ranks) with the data presented in Tables I through IV, we were able to discover two associations. Thus, those who ranked religious interests in one of these positions were found to identify the two men as religious figures more often than expected; 64.0 percent were observed in contrast to the 55.0 percent expected ($\chi^2 = 0.78$; $0.25 > p > 0.15$). They also imputed the intention of wanting to correct the instructor's views beyond the frequency expected; 89.9 percent were observed as compared with an expected 55.0 percent ($\chi^2 = 5.63$; $0.01 > p > 0.005$). A similar response pattern was found in the ordering of the general life goal "living in accordance with religious principles." For the ranking of both goals and interests, no association was discernible with the perceived evaluation of the class by the two men or with the feelings that the students had toward their activities. In conclusion, common sense leads us to anticipate that religious predispositions will be found to be linked to our four operational statements, but the data only partly bear this out. Hopefully, the use of more precise data gathering techniques would eradicate this discrepancy in the findings in favour of our expectations.

DISCUSSION

The field experiment presented in this section was expressly designed to demonstrate some of the research strategies discussed in the preceding pages. However, as usually happens in exploratory undertakings such as this, one learns a great deal in the process of carrying them out, the significance of which sometimes embarrasses his earlier ideas. This has happened here. The research strategies presented earlier are, in part, remodelled products of hindsight made possible by the experiment.

For example, the demonstration was planned with the notion in mind that it should be a startlingly different experience so that one could observe the creative defining of a situation. This strategy was adopted when the author was still labouring under the belief that study of the innovative and therefore relatively idiosyncratic aspects of interpreting events, that is, the study of unique personal definitions, was the best way to make an initial thrust into the complexities of this area. In spite of these intentions a good case can be made for cultural definitions of situations such as the one contrived here for experimental purposes, since outbursts by the religiously conservative are not uncommon in this community. However, there was no program of observation over time that could help us determine if such cultural definitions do exist among students. For the sake of demonstration we have referred to the standard definitions of the situation that appeared in the experiment as cultural definitions, despite this shortcoming. Also, only six of the thirteen operational statements were employed because the remaining ones were conceived too late to incorporate them into the questionnaire.

Our demonstration of the research strategies has probably raised many more questions than it has solved. Space limitations allow us to deal with only two of these.

First of all, those engaged in studying definitions of situations empirically will find themselves in something of a dilemma with respect to the form of interviewing they choose to do. If the investigator has observed a large number of people define a situation, he is committed to using some type of self-administered questionnaire in order to obviate problems of recall, since it would be impossible to interrogate each person individually. This form of data collection enables one to survey all who are willing to participate in the project in a short period of time, perhaps much closer to the actual occurrence of the event under consideration, than if a special appointment had to be made for a face-to-face interview. However, it does restrict one to certain operational statements. Statements 9 through 13 are more subtle than the rest, and require additional explanation for most subjects; they would only spawn confusion in a self-administered form of questionnaire. Moreover, since the investigator depends entirely upon the benevolence of his respondents for co-operation and accurate reporting of their views, he must take care not to antagonize them. This means that he must eliminate not only subtle (and hence confusing) items from his instrument, but also ones that appear to be repetitious because the differences are not large enough for laymen to discriminate. Several of the operational statements, when transformed into questionnaire items, could easily seem repetitious to the average respondent.

When only one or a few persons are observed as they define situations, the author's more recent experiences in this field indicate that the personal interview is the more desirable method of gathering information relating to the operational statements. However, this approach is more time consuming, although it is also more thorough since the ambiguities and ambivalences typical of human definitions of situations can be examined by careful probing.

This dilemma concerning the more appropriate kind of data collection can only be solved through extensive research, where we have the advantage of viewing the strengths and weaknesses of both techniques. It is true, no doubt, that the relative novelty of our experimental situation contributed to the presence of a large variety of answers to the questions. More familiar events probably would not invite such a range of responses.

The second question also pertains to the amount of novelty in our experiment. Presumably it was this feature of it that led to the large number of "no answer" and "don't know" responses. Some of the students simply needed more time to reflect on the events that had just unfolded before their eyes. Had they been given this time they would have, by answering our questions, expanded the size of some of the substantive categories, while the size of the "no answer" and "don't know" cells would have shrunk.

Actually, we can expect a certain proportion of these responses in research involving definitions of the situation, even when we are dealing with recurrent settings. For not all of the recurring situations encountered by those in an identity will be equally familiar. Some reflection will be needed to sort out and interpret the novel elements present (which occur in every situation in some degree), and the more that is required the greater the number of incomplete questionnaires that will be turned in. Waiting for this reflection to take place before beginning the interviewing or distributing the questionnaire forms is not a solution either, since there will be the tendency for those who have already selected a definition to think further about the event, thereby changing its initial meaning through retrospective interpretation. This in itself is an interesting aspect of human behaviour which is worthy of study. But it is the ongoing definition of the situation that interests us and that guides behaviour in the immediate setting. In investigating it, it is wise to keep it as separate as possible from subsequent redefinitions beyond that setting.

When we speak of definition of the situation, we speak of motivation according to Nelson Foote (1951:15):

> In a sentence, we take motivation to refer to the degree to which a human being, as a participant in the ongoing social process in which he necessarily finds himself, defines a problematic situation as calling for performance of a particular act, with more or less anticipated consummations and consequences, and *thereby* his organism releases the energy appropriate to performing it.

Foote's paper and an earlier one by C. Wright Mills (1940) have been the two most significant advances in sociology's attempt to develop a situational theory of motivation. Yet, two curious facts exist: the last major theoretical progress was nearly twenty years ago, and there has been very little, if any, empirical work on this approach to motivation either before or since.[15] There are, no doubt many reasons for this situation including, perhaps, the vicissitudes of the fads of social science. The explanations given at the beginning of this paper for the lack of research on the definition of the situation could also be cited. Finally, there is still another reason, and it is this one that we shall consider now.

It seems that, in their haste to denounce the place of predispositions in a sociological theory of motivation, Mills and Foote worked themselves, and consequently the possibilities for further development of such a theory, into a logical *cul-de-sac*. Foote launched the strongest attack. As we have just seen he looked on motivation as a definition of a situation, though it should be added that he placed special emphasis on the process of identification of self and others within that setting. Predispositions were allowed into this scheme only as "memory . . . by virtue of which we call up in the present images of past consummations of acts" (1951:20). Memory plus organic mobilization (after the definition of the situation) were said to equal motivation.

This reaction against the inclusion of predispositions was reasonable fifteen years ago, but recent thought on their nature and on their location in a theory of the definition of the situation makes such a position untenable today. Foote (and Mills) appeared to be reacting to the organismically based, situation-free models of predispositions and motivation. But in this paper, following Campbell (1963), their prior activation by stimuli within the situation is taken as essential for their influence on behaviour. Here predispositions are viewed as developing from past experience, and once activated they are seen to impinge upon our awareness as specialized views of the world. There is little in this conceptualization with which a sociologist can disagree.

Nevertheless, the sociologist might assert that there is still no place in the theory of the definition of the situation for predispositions. Foote, for example, believed that "definitions of the situation account for attitudes, not the reverse" (1951:15). Our earlier discussion, however, indicates that defining a situation is a complicated process that takes place in two phases; and that predispositions do enter into the second phase, both in directing the selection of the cultural definition and in tailoring that definition to the peculiar requirements of the individual.

---

[15] This statement refers only to progress toward a theory of motivation in the name of such a theory. There have been many advances in closely related areas such as identification, situational studies, and, as I intend to show here, the social psychology of predispositions.

Predispositions as they have been incorporated into the model used in this paper are considerably more than just general "memory" of past acts. They are those peculiar (activated) perspectives in any immediate present so characteristic of the interchanges among men, although, of course, memory serves to make them available to us in the ongoing setting. Because they are enduring states, their recurrent activation also helps explain why human beings are motivated in the same way in the same class of situation at various points in time. Predisposing orientations such as attitudes of racial prejudice or ideals such as fair play or self-conceptions such as "I am a competent golfer," are impossible to ignore in any theory of motivation.[16] It is doubtful that Mills or Foote intended to do this either, but the state of knowledge about predispositions at that time led them toward a blind alley.

The problem of motivation is "to account for the *patterning, timing, and direction of behavior,* especially for persistent movement toward a goal" (Shibutani, 1961:181). There is good reason to believe that the theory of the definition of the situation is the best solution available; that is, as long as we include an adequate up-to-date statement about the nature and location of predispositions within it.

Summary and Conclusions

Contrary to some long-established beliefs, the definition of the situation can be studied empirically. That is, it can be studied with the aid of a certain number of research strategies, which it has been the objective of this paper to provide. Two problems should guide the investigator in this field. 1. What cultural or habitual personal definitions are available to those in a given social identity for use in one or more specified kinds of recurring situations? 2. For classes of actors within an identity, what predispositions are activated by elements in the ongoing setting that lead to the selection of one of these definitions instead of another? Observation is an indispensable part of any research program focusing on definitions of situations. When carried out over time it gives the social scientist a rough idea of the standard definitions identity incumbents have to choose from in typical situations. Later it facilitates precision in the interviewing when one begins to sharpen his picture of these definitions by questioning the actors along the lines of the various operationalizations with respect to specific ongoing settings. Cultural and habitual definitions are constructed by combining the responses to these questions. Theoretically, it is believed that selecting such definitions occurs in two relatively distinct temporal phases occurring in rapid succession.

[16] The use of "predisposition" here is compatible with the general scheme presented by Shibutani. He includes under the section heading of "motivation" discussion of self-concept, reference groups as perspectives, and the internalization of social control (1961:179–319). All of these have predispositional qualities about them.

At its present stage of technical development and theoretical accumulation, research on the definition of the situation can amount to little more than a program of description. Without knowledge of the cultural and habitual definitions available to sets of actors within an identity and without knowledge of their patterns of choice of these definitions in given kinds of situations, we have little on which to base prediction or higher-order explanation. Until such substantive propositions are established, we can only provide descriptive data. Through time and in conjunction with the general theory of the definition of the situation, bodies of descriptive data will form the bases for grounded theories of definitions of situations for particular identities.

Description of standard definitions and recurrent situations is probably best carried out by means of some type of field research. However, once a substantive theory begins to take shape, experimentation as a mode of testing hypotheses becomes a feasible alternative. But until we know a particular kind of situation in sufficient detail, it will be impossible to simulate it adequately in the laboratory. We also need an elementary knowledge of the possible cultural and habitual definitions available to the incumbents in such a situation so that we know which variables we wish to control.

This discussion of the definition of the situation has certain implications for a sociological theory of motivation. There is good reason to believe that the theory of the definition of the situation is the best explanation for motivated behaviour that is available; that is, as long as we include an adequate and contemporary statement about the nature and location of predispositions within it.

References

Ball, D. W. Forthcoming. "The definition of the situation: some theoretical and methodological consequences of taking W. I. Thomas seriously," in J. D. Douglas (ed.), Existential Sociology. New York: Appleton-Century-Crofts.

Burke, K. 1945. A Grammar of Motives. New York: Prentice-Hall.

———. 1950. A Rhetoric of Motives. New York: Prentice-Hall.

Campbell, D. T. 1963. "Social attitudes and other acquired behavioral dispositions." Pp. 94–172 in S. Koch (ed.), Psychology: A Study of a Science, vol. 6. New York: McGraw-Hill.

Cooley, C. H. 1922. Human Nature and the Social Order. New York: Charles Scribner's Sons.

Deutscher, I. 1964. "The quality of postparental life: definitions of the situation." Journal of Marriage and the Family 26:52–59.

Foote, N. N. 1951. "Identification as the basis for a theory of motivation." American Sociological Review 16:14–21.

Gerth, H. and C. W. Mills. 1954. Character and Social Structure. London: Routledge & Kegan Paul.

Glaser, B. G. and A. L. Strauss. 1967. The Discovery of Grounded Theory. Chicago: Aldine.

Gorden, R. L. 1952. "Interaction between attitude and the definition of the situation in the expression of opinion." American Sociological Review 17:50–58.

Heider, F. 1958. The Psychology of Interpersonal Relations. New York: John Wiley.

Hill, R. and D. A. Hansen. 1962. "Families in Disaster," pp. 185–221 in G. W. Baker and D. W. Chapman (eds.), Man and Society in Disaster. New York: Basic Books.

Ichheiser, G. 1949. "Misunderstandings in human relations." American Journal of Sociology 55 (September, Part II): 1–70.

Jones, E. E. 1964. Ingratiation. New York: Appleton-Century-Crofts.

Jones, E. E. and K. E. Davis. 1965. "From acts to dispositions." Pp. 220–266 in L. Berkowitz (ed.), Advances in Experimental Social Psychology, Vol. 2. New York: Academic Press.

Jones, E. E. and J. W. Thibaut. 1958. "Interaction goals as bases of inference in interpersonal perception." Pp. 151–178 in R. Tagiuri and L. Petrullo (eds.), Person Perception and Interpersonal Behavior. Stanford, Calif.: Stanford University Press.

Lerner, M. J. and S. Becker. 1962. "Interpersonal choice as a function of ascribed similarity and definition of the situation." Human Relations 15:27–34.

McCall, G. J. and J. L. Simmons. 1966. Identities and Interactions. New York: The Free Press.

McHugh, P. 1968. Defining the Situation. Indianapolis: Bobbs-Merrill.

MacIver, R. M. 1964. Social Causation (rev. ed.). New York: Harper & Row.

Mills, C. W. 1940. "Situated actions and vocabularies of motives." American Sociological Review 5:904–913.

Newcomb, T. M. 1958. "The cognition of persons as cognizers." Pp. 179–190 in R. Tagiuri and L. Petrullo (eds.), Person Perception and Interpersonal Behavior. Stanford, Calif.: Stanford University Press.

———. 1961. The Acquaintance Process. New York: Holt, Rinehart & Winston, Inc.

Newcomb, T. M., R. H. Turner, and P. E. Converse. 1965. Social Psychology: The Study of Human Relations. New York: Holt, Rinehart & Winston.

Schutz, A. 1964. Collected Papers II: Studies in Social Theory. The Hague: Martinus Nijhoff.

Shand, A. F. 1920. The Foundations of Character. London: MacMillan, Ltd.

Shibutani, T. 1961. Society and Personality. Englewood Cliffs, NJ: Prentice-Hall.

Siegel, S. 1956. Nonparametric Statistics for the Behavioral Sciences. New York: McGraw-Hill.

Simmel, G. 1950. The Sociology of Georg Simmel. New York: The Free Press.

Stebbins, R. A. 1967. "A theory of the definition of the situation." The Canadian Review of Sociology and Anthropology 4:148–164.

———. 1969. "Social network as a subjective construct: a new application for an old idea." The Canadian Review of Sociology and Anthropology 6:1–14.

———. 1970. "Career: the subjective approach." The Sociological Quarterly, forthcoming.

Stone, G. P. 1962. "Appearance and the self." Pp. 86–118 in A. M. Rose (ed.), Human Behavior and Social Processes. Boston: Houghton Mifflin.

Strauss, A. L. 1959. Mirrors and Masks. New York: The Free Press.

Thomas, W. I. 1951. Social Behavior and Personality, ed., E. H. Volkart. New York: Social Science Research Council.

Turner, R. H. 1956. "Role-taking, role standpoint, and reference-group behavior." American Journal of Sociology 61:316–328.

———. 1962. "Role-taking: process versus conformity." Pp. 20–40 in A. M. Rose (ed.), Human Behavior and Social Processes. Boston: Houghton Mifflin.

Weber, M. 1947. The Theory of Social and Economic Organization. New York: Oxford University Press.

Weinstein, E. A. and P. Deutschberger. 1963. "Some dimensions of altercasting." Sociometry 26:454–466.

———. 1964. "Tasks, bargains, and identities in social interaction." Social Forces 42:451–456.

Wolff, K. H. 1964. "Definition of the situation." P. 182 in J. Gould and W. L. Kolb (eds.), A Dictionary of the Social Sciences. New York: The Free Press.

Common Sense Knowledge
of Social Structures: The Documentary
Method of Interpretation

Sociologically speaking, "common culture" refers to the socially sanctioned grounds of inference and action that people use in their everyday affairs[1] and which they assume that other members of the group use in the same way.   Socially-sanctioned-facts-of-life-in-society-that-any-bona-fide-member-of-the-society-knows depict such matters as conduct of family life; market organization; distributions of honor, competence, responsibility goodwill, income, motives among members; frequency, causes of, and remedies for trouble; and the presence of good and evil purposes behind the apparent workings of things. Such socially sanctioned facts of social life consist of descriptions from the point of view of the collectivity member's[2] interests in the management of his practical affairs. Basing our usage upon the work of Alfred Schutz,[3] we shall call such knowledge of socially organ-

Reprinted with permission of The Macmillan Company from *Theories of the Mind* by Jordan Scher. © by The Free Press of Glencoe, a Division of The Macmillan Company, 1962.

This investigation was supported by a Senior Research Fellowship SF-81 from the U.S. Public Health Service. The materials for this paper are taken from a book in preparation by the author, *Common-Sense Actions as Topic and Features of Sociological Inquiry*. I wish to thank my colleagues Egon Bittner, Aaron V. Cicourel, and Eleanor Bernert Sheldon for many conversations about these materials. Thanks are due to Peter McHugh for his help with the experiment and for many useful ideas in his report.

[1] The concept "everyday affairs" is intended in strict accord with Alfred Schutz' usage in his articles, "On multiple realities," *Philosophy and Phenomenological Research*, 1945, 4:533–575; "Common sense and scientific interpretation of human action," *Philosophy and Phenomenological Research*, 1953, 14:1–37.

[2] The concept of "collectivity membership" is intended in strict accord with Talcott Parsons' usage in *The Social System*, The Free Press of Glencoe, New York, 1951, and in *Theories of Society*, Vol. I, Part Two, The Free Press of Glencoe, New York, 1961, pp. 239–240.

[3] Alfred Schutz, *Der sinnhafte Aufbau der sozialen Welt*, Verlag von Julius Springer, Wien, 1932; "The problem of rationality in the social world," *Economica*, 1943, 10:130–149; "Some leading concepts in phenomenology," *Social Research*, 1945, 12:77–97; "On multiple realities," *Philosophy and Phenomenological Research*, 1945, 4:533–575; "Choosing among projects of action," *Philosophy and Phenomenological Research*, 1951, 12:161–184; "Common sense and scientific interpretation of human action," *Philosophy and Phenomenological Research*, 1953, 14:1–37; "Concept and theory formation in the social sciences," *American Journal of Philosophy*, 1954, 51: 257–274; "Symbol, reality,

ized environments of concerted actions "common sense knowledge of social structures."

The discovery of common culture consists of the discovery *from within* the society by social scientists of the existence of common-sense knowledge of social structures, and the treatment by social scientists of knowledge, and of the procedures that societal members use for its assembly, test, management, and transmission as objects of mere theoretical sociological interest.

This paper is concerned with common-sense knowledge of social structures as an object of theoretical sociological interest. It is concerned with descriptions of a society that its members, *sociologists included,* as a condition of their enforceable rights to manage and communicate decisions of meaning, fact, method, and causal texture without interference, use and treat as known in common with other members, and with other members take for granted.

As an obect of theoretical sociological interest, such knowledge is both a topic as well as a feature of sociological inquiry. One facet of this assertion will be treated in this paper. Its interests are directed to a description of the work whereby decisions of meaning and fact are managed, and a body of factual knowledge of social structures is assembled in common-sense situations of choice.

The Documentary Method of Interpretation

There are innumerable situations of sociological inquiry in which the investigator—whether he be a professional sociologist or a person undertaking an inquiry about social structures in the interests of managing his practical everyday affairs—can assign witnessed actual appearances to the status of an event of conduct only by imputing biography and prospects to the appearances, which he does by embedding the appearances in presupposed knowledge of social structures. Thus it frequently happens that in order for the investigator to decide what he is now looking at he must wait for future developments, only to find that these futures in turn are informed by *their* history and future. By waiting to see what will have happened he learns what it was that he previously saw. Either that, or he takes imputed history and prospects for granted. Motivated actions, for example, have exactly these troublesome properties.

It, therefore, occurs that the investigator frequently must elect among alternative courses of interpretation and inquiry to the end of deciding matters of fact, hypothesis, conjecture, fancy, and the rest despite the fact

---

and society," *Symbols and Society,* Fourteenth Symposium of the Conference of Science, Philosophy, and Religion, edited by Lyman Bryson and others, Harper and Brothers, New York, 1955, pp. 135–202.

that in the calculable sense of the term "know," he does not and even cannot "know" what he is doing *prior to or while he is doing it*. Field workers, most particularly those doing ethnographic and linguistic studies in settings where they cannot presuppose a knowledge of social structures, are perhaps best acquainted with such situations, but other types of professional sociological inquiry are not exempt.

Nevertheless, a body of knowledge of social structures is somehow assembled. Somehow decisions of meaning, facts, method, and causal texture are made. How, in the course of the inquiry during which such decisions must be made, does this occur?

In his concern for the sociologist's problem of achieving an adequate description of cultural events, an important case of which would be Weber's familiar "behaviors with a subjective meaning attached and governed thereby in their course," Karl Mannheim[4] furnished an approximate description of one process. Mannheim called it "the documentary method of interpretation." It contracts with the methods of literal observation, yet it has a recognizable fit with what many sociological researchers, lay and professional, actually do.

According to Mannheim, the documentary method involves the search for ". . . an identical, homologous pattern underlying a vast variety of totally different realizations of meaning."[5]

The method consists of treating an actual appearance as "the document of," as "pointing to," as "standing on behalf of" a presupposed underlying pattern. Not only is the underlying pattern derived from its individual documentary evidences, but the individual documentary evidences, in their turn, are interpreted on the basis of "what is known" about the underlying pattern. Each is used to elaborate the other.

The method is recognizable for the everyday necessities of recognizing what a person is "talking about" given that he doesn't say exactly what he means, or in recognizing such common occurrences as mailmen, friendly gestures, and promises. It is recognizable as well in deciding the sociologically analyzed occurrence of events like Goffman's strategies for the management of impressions, Erickson's identity crises, Riesman's types of conformity, Florence Kluckhohn's value premises, Malinowski's magical practices, Bales' interaction counts, Merton's type of deviance, Lazarsfeld's latent structure of attitudes, and the U.S. Census' occupational categories.

How is it done by the investigator that from replies to a questionnaire he finds the respondent's "attitude"; that via interviews with office person-

[4] Karl Mannheim, "On the interpretation of weltanschauung," *Essays on the Sociology of Knowledge*, translated and edited by Paul Kecskemeti, Oxford University Press, New York, 1952, pp. 53–63.
[5] *Ibid.*, p. 57.

nel he reports their "bureaucratically organized activities"; that by consulting crimes known to the police, estimates are made of the parameters of "real crime"? More literally, what is the work whereby the investigator sets the observed occurrence and the intended occurrence into a correspondence of meaning such that the investigator finds it reasonable to treat witnessed actual appearances as evidences of the event he means to be studying?

To answer these questions it is necessary to detail the work of the documentary method. To this end a demonstration of the documentary method was designed to exaggerate the features of this method in use and to catch the work of "fact production" in flight.

An Experiment

Ten undergraduates were solicited by telling them that research was being done in the Department of Psychiatry to explore alternative means to psychotherapy "as a way of giving persons advice about their personal problems" [sic]. Each subject was seen individually by an experimenter who was falsely represented as a student counselor in training. The subject was asked to first discuss the background to some serious problem on which he would like advice, and then to address to the "counselor" a series of questions each of which would permit a "yes" or "no" answer. The subject was promised that the "counselor" would attempt to answer to the best of his ability. The experimenter-counselor heard the questions and gave his answers from an adjoining room, via an intercommunication system. After describing his problem and furnishing some background to it, the subject asked his first question. After a standard pause, the experimenter announced his answer, "yes" or "no." According to instructions, the subject then removed a wall plug connecting him with the counselor so that the "counselor will not hear your remarks" and tape-recorded his comments on the exchange. After these were completed, the subject plugged the microphone in and asked his next question. After he received the answer, he again recorded his comments, and thus proceeded through at least ten questions and answers. The subject had been told, "Most people want to ask at least ten questions."

The sequence of answers, evenly divided between yes's and no's, was predecided with a table of random numbers. All subjects asking the same number of questions were administered the same series of yes and no answers. Following the exchange of questions and answers the subject was asked to summarize his impressions of the entire exchange. An interview followed.

The following are illustrative unedited protocols.

CASE 1

Subject: Ok, this is the situation that I am presented with. I happen to be of the Jewish faith and I have been dating a Gentile girl now for about two months. My dad is not directly opposed to this situation, but I feel at the same time that he is not exactly pleased with it. Mother feels that as long as dad is not directly opposed to this situation that I should go ahead and continue dating until he makes some direct statement to the contrary. My reason for feeling why he is not too pleased with this is that he has never said don't date her, but at the same time he will come up with digs and sayings that make me feel very ill at ease about dating the girl. My question is, do you feel under the present circumstances that I should continue or stop dating this girl? Let me put that in a positive way. Do you feel that I should continue dating this girl?

Experimenter: My answer is no.

Subject: No. Well, that is kind of interesting. I kinda feel that there is really no great animosity between Dad and I but well perhaps he feels that greater dislike will grow out of this. I suppose or may be it is easier for an outsider to see certain things that I am blind to at this moment.

I would like to ask my second question now.

Experimenter: Okay.

Subject: Do you feel that I should have a further discussion with Dad about this situation or not? Should I have further discussion with Dad over this subect about dating the Gentile girl?

Experimenter: My answer is yes.

Subject: Well I feel that it is reasonable but I really don't know what to say to him. I mean he seems to be not really too understanding. In other words he seems to be afraid really to discuss the situation. I mean at least it appears that way to me so far. But I guess if it is worthwhile to me, if I really want to continue to date her that I will go on and have this discussion with Dad. I really don't know what to say because I mean I am dating her. I am not in love with her or anything but I really never know what is going to come out. I guess we should have a discussion based on what the future possibilities might be and how he would feel about that. He may not be too strongly opposed now because we are only dating but perhaps he sees future complications that he would really like to get off his chest at the moment. I am ready for my third question now.

If after having my conversation with Dad and he says to continue dating her but at the same time he gives me an impression that he is really not, he really does not want me to date her, but he is only doing it because he wants to be a good dad, should under these conditions, should I still date the girl?

Experimenter: My answer is yes.

Subject: Well I am actually surprised at the answer. I expected a no answer on that. Perhaps this is because you are not quite aware of my dad and his reactions and he seems to be the type of person that is sensitive and therefore he is very careful in the way that he will handle things. Even though he might have said go ahead and date her I perhaps would feel guilty in knowing that he really did not want me to continue to date her. Though I don't know that it would actually help the situation any. So, well, perhaps we will look into this further and that is another question. I am ready for the fourth question now.

If after having this discussion with Dad and getting a positive answer from him but at the same time felt that this was not his honest opinion do you think that it would be proper for me to have my mother have a serious talk with him and therefore try and get a truer reaction to Dad's opinion on the situation?

Experimenter: My answer is yes.

Subject: Well this seems fair to me. I feel perhaps that he would be honester with Mother about the situation. Of course that might present a problem. Would Mother come back and be completely honest with me? She seems to be more liberal than Dad, not to say that Mother would lie about it, but she would be a little more liberal about things like this and perhaps in her course of conversation with Dad she would try and present my side to him and therefore once again I get two answers. If I look at it that way I don't think that I am going to get to first base anyway, but at least I feel that we are moving along some way. I am ready for my fifth question now.

Do you think I should tell this Gentile girl who I am dating the problem that I am having with my folks at home or should I wait until, well that is another question. Do you feel that I should tell the girl that I am dating the problems that I am having at home over her religion?

Experimenter: My answer is no.

Subject: Well once again I am surprised. Of course, that might depend on how much you care for the girl and how much longer I feel that I am going to be dating her. But I personally feel that it is only right to tell her for if she is perhaps thinking more serious than I am, she might, it might be best for us to understand the full situation and if she feels that this will be a block then I feel perhaps that would end the situation right there without telling her. I feel that perhaps I am going to show this in different ways and she will be unaware of what the real situation is and perhaps react back to me in a certain way spoiling our dating and everything else like that. I am ready for my sixth question.

If I was to fall in love with this girl and want to make plans for marriage do you feel that it is fair that I should ask her to change her religion over to my belief?

Experimenter: My answer is no.

Subject: Well, no. Well, this has me stymied. No. Well, I honestly feel that I have been brought up in a certain way and I believe that she has too, and I feel pretty strong about the way that I believe. Not that I am completely orthodox or anything, but of course there is always family pressure and things like that. And I am quite sure that she feels, unfortunately I have never seen a family with a split in religion that really has been able to make a success out of it. So I don't know. I think that perhaps I would be tempted to ask her to change. I don't think that I would be able to really. I am ready for number seven.

Do you feel that it would be a better situation if we were to get married and neither one of us were willing to talk about the religious difference or to give in on either one side, that we bring our children up in a neutral religion other than the two that we believe in?

Experimenter: My answer is yes.

Subject: Well perhaps this would be a solution. If we could find a religion that would incorporate our two beliefs to a certain extent. I realize that perhaps this might be literally impossible to do. Perhaps in a sense this neutral religion might be something almost made up by ourselves because I honestly feel that religious training no matter which belief it is if not carried to extremes is good, for everyone should have a certain amount of religious training along these lines. Perhaps this might be a solution to the problem. I guess I should follow this along a little bit further and see exactly what happens. I am ready for number eight.

If we were to get married would it be best for us to live in a new community where we will not be in contact with our parents if we were getting a lot of family pressure over religious differences?

Experimenter: My answer is no.

Subject: Well, I kinda tend to agree with this answer. I feel that you wouldn't be accomplishing too much by running away from the issue and that perhaps it would be one of those things in life that eventually you would just be willing to accept it and that the families and we would get along harmoniously together. At least I hope it would work out if that situation comes about. I think it would be best for both families together that we are not going to work it out if we run away from our problem. So we best remain there and try and work it out. I am ready for number nine.

If we did get married and were to raise our children do you think that we should explain and tell our children that we once had this religious difference or would we just bring them up in this new religion, that is their religion, that we talked about, and let them believe that that is what we originally believed in?

Experimenter: My answer is no.

Subject: Once again I kinda agree with this. I think they should be told because undoubtedly they will find out. And if they did find out that there was this difference that we once had they would feel that we were sneaking or trying to hide something from them and this would not be the best situation either. So I believe this would be the best situation. I am ready for number ten.

Do you feel that our children, if there were any, would have any religious problems themselves because of us the parents and our difficulties?

Experimenter: My answer is no.

Subject: Well I really don't know if I agree with that or not. Perhaps they would have trouble if confusion set in and they were to feel that they did not know which is right and which is wrong or what side to pick if they did not want to stick with their religion. But I kinda feel that if their religion was a wholesome one which supplied the needs of a religion and that which a religion does supply that there would not be any problems with them. But I suppose that only time will tell if such problems would come about. I am finished with my comments now.

Experimenter: Okay, I will be right in.

The experimenter appeared in the room with the subject, handed him a list of points that he might comment on, and left the room. The subject commented as follows.

Subject: Well the conversation seemed to be one-sided because I was doing it all. But, I feel that it was extremely difficult for Mr. McHugh to answer these questions fully without having a complete understanding of the personalities of the different people involved and exactly how involved the situation was itself. The answers I received I must say that the majority of them were answered perhaps in the same way that I would answer them to myself knowing the differences in types of people. One or two of them did come as a surprise to me and I felt that the reason perhaps he answered these questions the way he did is for the reason that he is not aware of the personalities involved and how they are reacting or would react to a certain situation. The answers that I received were most of them I felt that he was for the most part aware of the situation as we moved along in that I was interpreting his answers even though they were yes or no answers as fully meditating over these situations that I presented to him and they had a lot of meaning to me. I felt that his answers as a whole were helpful and that he was looking out for the benefit to the situation for the most part and not to curtail it or cut it short in any means. I heard what I wanted to hear in most of the situations presented at time. Perhaps I did not hear what I really wanted to hear but perhaps from an objective standpoint they were the best answers because someone involved in a situation is blinded to a certain degree and cannot take this objective viewpoint. And therefore these answers may differ from the person who is involved in the situation and the person who is outside and can take an objective viewpoint. I honestly believe that the answer that he gave me, that he was completely aware of the situation at hand. Perhaps I guess that should be qualified. Perhaps when I said should I talk to Dad for instance he was not positive. When I said should I talk to Dad for instance he was not positive what I was going to talk to Dad about. In a full capacity. He knew the general topic but he is not aware how close I am to Dad or how involved the conversation might get. And if his saying "do talk" in knowing that Dad will not listen, well this perhaps isn't best, or if Dad is very willing to listen he says it may not help. Or don't talk. Well this once again is bringing in personalities which he is not aware of. The conversation and the answers given I believe had a lot of meaning to me. I mean it was perhaps what I would have expected for someone who fully understood the situation. And I feel that it had a lot of sense to me and made a lot of sense. Well I felt that the questions that I asked were very pertinent and did help in understanding the situation on both sides, that is myself and the answerer and my reaction to the answers like I have stated before were mostly in agreement. At times I was surprised but understood that because he is not fully aware of the situation and the personalities involved.

Here is another protocol.

CASE 2

Subject: I would like to know whether or not I should change my major at the present time. I have a physics major with quite a deficit in grade points to bring up to get my C average in physics. I would like to switch over to mathematics. I have a litle difficulty in it but I think maybe I could handle it. I have failed several math courses here at U.C.L.A. but I have always repeated them and had C's. I have come close to getting a B in math in one specific course because I studied a little more than in others but my question is still should I change my major?
Experimenter: My answer is no.
Subject: Well he says no. And if I don't then I will have to make up my deficit in grade points which will be awfully difficult because I am not doing too well this semester. If I pull through this semester with seven units of A then I can count on possibly going on to get my degree in physics in February but then I have this stigma of nuclear physics facing me. I thoroughly dislike the study of nuclear physics. Nuclear Physics 124 will be one of my required courses to get a degree in physics.

Do you think I could get a degree in physics on the basis of this knowledge that I must take Physics 124?
Experimenter: My answer is yes.
Subject: He says yes. I don't see how I can. I am not that good of a

theorist. My study habits are horrible. My reading speed is bad, and I don't spend enough time studying.

Do you think that I could successfully improve my study habits?

Experimenter: My answer is yes.

Subject: He says that I can successfully improve my study habits. I have been preached to all along on how to study properly but I don't study properly. I don't have sufficient incentive to go through physics or do I?

Do you think I have sufficient incentive to get a degree in physics?

Experimenter: My answer is yes.

Subject: He says my answer is yes. I think possibly so if I didn't have a bad scholastic record behind me to follow me up. It would be awfully difficult to get that degree.

Do you think I could successfully do my studying while trying to keep happy relations at home with my wife and still get my work done? I don't do my studying well at school and I don't have much incentive to study when I am at home. But when my wife comes home, I like to study. Yet this keeps us from doing things, and whenever she doesn't do things, it gets on my nerves because there is all this work piling up. Do you think I could successfully do my studying at home?

Experimenter: My answer is no.

Subject: He says no. I don't think so either.

Should I come to school every night after supper and do my studying?

Experimenter: My answer is no.

Subject: He says I shouldn't come to school and study. Where should I go? Should I go to the library on campus to do my studying?

Experimenter: My answer is yes.

Subject: He says I should go to the library to do my studying. Which library? They may not have all the references there that I may need but that is not always necessary. I need at least three more questions. Do you think I can develop sufficiently good study habits and incentive to actually achieve developing those habits such that I wouldn't have to stay up late at night and not get the work done in the first place?

Experimenter: My answer is no.

Subject: He says no. I can't develop the study habits properly to be able to pull myself through. If you don't think that I can develop the proper study habits and carry them through to reach my goal do you on the basis of this still believe that I can get a degree in physics?

Experimenter: My answer is no.

Subject: According to that I won't get a degree. What should I do? Are you still there?

Experimenter: Yes, I am.

Subject: If you don't think I will make the–achieve the necessary goal of improving my study habits and getting a degree in physics do you recommend that I quit school?

Experimenter: My answer is yes.

Subject: He says I should quit school. Are you still there?

Experimenter: Yes.

Subject: I have one more question. I would like to get a commission in the Air Force. I have completed the Air Force R.O.T.C. training program but to get a commission I need a degree. If I don't get the degree the chances are very strong that I may not get the commission although there are in's and out's that there is still some possibility that I may still get a commission without a degree, although this is not desirable. The question is, will I get a commission in the Air Force?

Experimenter: My answer is yes.

Subject: He says I will get a commission in the Air Force and that is what I am looking forward to, but will I ever get a degree? If I get a commission without a degree will I ever get a degree in anything?

Experimenter: My answer is no.

Subject: This leaves me somewhat unhappy although I don't really need a degree in the type of work that I desire to do. Are you there? Come back in.

The subject commented as follows. Well, as far as what I got from the conversation, it is rather foolish for me to pursue my work any further as far as getting a degree in anything. Actually I have felt all along that the type of work I am interested in which is inventing is not something that requires a degree necessarily. It requires a certain knowledge of math and physics but it doesn't require a degree to do inventing. From the conversation I gather that I should just quit school and go ahead and get my commission but how I don't know. But it would be awfully nice to have a degree. That degree would be able to get me into other schools. Otherwise I will have the statement that I went through college but I never got out. I also get the impression that my study habits will never improve as much as I would like them to anyway. I will not get a degree. I will get a commission and it is fruitless for me to study either at home or at school. Especially in the evening. I wonder if I should do any studying at all, or if I should learn to do all my studying at school. What to do? I have the feeling that my parents would be very unhappy and also my wife's parents would be very unhappy if I never did get a degree or at least especially right now. I have the feeling that this past conversation is based on what one should have learned to do years ago, that is, as a growing child. To ask themselves questions and give himself an answer of some type, yes or no, and to think out reason why either yes or no holds or might hold and upon the validity or the anticipation of the validity of that answer what one should do accomplish his goal or just exist. I personally think I can do better in math than I can in physics. But I won't know until the end of the summer.

FINDINGS

An examination of the protocols revealed the following:

A. *Getting through the exchange.*
None of the subjects had difficulty in accomplishing the series of ten questions, and in summarizing and evaluating the advice.

B. *Answers were perceived as "answers-to-questions."*
1. Typically the subjects heard the experimenter's answers as answers-to-the-question. Perceptually, the experimenter's answers were motivated by the question.
2. Subjects saw directly "what the adviser had in mind." They heard "in a glance" what he was talking about, i.e., what he meant, and not what he had uttered.
3. The typical subject assumed over the course of the exchange, and during the post-experimental interview, that the answers were advice to the problem, and that this advice as a solution to the problem was to be found via the answers.
4. All reported the "advice that they had been given" and addressed their appreciation and criticism to that "advice."

C. *There were no pre-programed questions; the next question was motivated by the retrospective-prospective possibilities of the present situation that were altered by each actual exchange.*
1. No subject administered a pre-programed set of questions.
2. Present answers altered the sense of previous exchanges.
3. Over the course of the exchange the assumption seemed to operate that there was an answer to be obtained, and that if the answer was not obvious, that its meaning could be determined by active search, one part of which involved asking another question so as to find out what the adviser "had in mind."
4. Much effort was devoted to looking for meanings that were intended but were not evident from the immediate answer to the question.
5. The present answer-to-the-questions motivated the succeeding set of possibilities from among which the next question was selected. The next question emerged as a product of reflections upon the previous course of the conversation and the presupposed underlying problem as the topic whose features each actual exchange documented and extended. The underlying "problem" was elaborated in its features as a function of the exchange. The sense of the problem was progressively accommodated to each present answer, while the answer motivated fresh aspects of the underlying problem.

6. The underlying pattern was elaborated and compounded over the series of exchanges and was accommodated to each present "answer" so as to maintain the "course of advice," to elaborate what had "really been advised" previously, and to motivate the new possibilities as emerging features of the problem.

D. *Answers in search of questions.*

1. Over the course of the exchange, subjects sometimes started with the reply as an answer and altered the previous sense of their question to accommodate this to the reply as the answer to the retrospectively revised question.

2. The identical utterance was capable of answering several different questions simultaneously, and of constituting an answer to a compound question that in terms of the strict logic of propositions did not permit either a yes or no or a single yes or no.

3. The same utterance was used to answer several different questions separated in time. Subjects referred to this as "shedding new light" on the past.

4. Present answers provided answers to further questions that were never asked.

E. *Handling incomplete, inappropriate, and contradictory answers.*

1. Where answers were unsatisfying or incomplete, the questioners were willing to wait for later answers in order to decide the sense of the previous ones.

2. Incomplete answers were treated by subjects as incomplete because of the "deficiencies" of this method of giving advice.

3. Answers that were inappropriate were inappropriate for "a reason." If the reason was found, the sense of the answer was thereupon decided. If an answer made "good sense" this was likely to be what the answerer had "advised."

4. When answers were incongruous or contradictory, subjects were able to continue by finding that the "adviser" had learned more in the meantime, or that he had decided to change his mind, or that perhaps he was not sufficiently acquainted with the intricacies of the problem, or the fault was in the question so that another phrasing was required.

5. Incongruous answers were resolved by imputing knowledge and intent to the adviser.

6. Contradictories faced the subject with electing the real question that the answer answered which they did by furnishing the question with additional meanings that fit with the meanings "behind" what the adviser was advising.

7. In the case of contradictory answers much effort was devoted to reviewing the possible intent of the answer so as to rid the answer of contradiction or meaninglessness, and to rid the answerer of untrustworthiness.

8. More subjects entertained the possibility of a trick than tested this possibility. All suspicious subjects were reluctant to act under the belief that there was a trick involved. Suspicions were quieted if the adviser's answers made "good sense." Suspicions were most unlikely to continue if the answers accorded with the subject's previous thought about the matter and with his preferred decisions.

9. Suspicions transformed the answer into an event of "mere speech" having the appearance of coincidental occurrence with the occasion of the questioner's question. Subjects found this structure difficult to maintain and manage. Many subjects saw the sense of the answer "anyway."

10. Those who became suspicious simultaneously, though temporarily, withdrew their willingness to continue.

F. *"Search" for and perception of pattern.*

1. Throughout, there was a concern and search for pattern. Pattern, however, was perceived from the very beginning. Pattern was likely to be seen in the first evidence of the "advice."

2. Subjects found it very difficult to grasp the implications of randomness in the utterances. A predetermined utterance was treated as deceit in the answers instead of as an utterance that was decided beforehand and that occurred independently of the subject's questions and interests.

3. When the possibility of deception occurred to the subjects, the adviser's utterance documented the pattern of the deceit instead of the pattern of advice. Thus the relationship of the utterance to the underlying pattern as its document remained unchanged.

G. *Answers were assigned a scenic source.*

1. Subjects assigned to the adviser as his advice the thought formulated in the subject's questions. For example, when a subject asked, "Should I come to school every night after supper to do my studying," and the experimenter said, "My answer is no," the subject in his comments said, "He said I shouldn't come to school and study." This was very common.

2. All subjects were surprised to find that they contributed so actively and so heavily to the "advice that they had received from the adviser."

3. Upon being told about the deception the subjects were intensely chagrined. In most cases they revised their opinions about the pro-

cedure to emphasize its inadequacies for the experimenter's purposes (which they understood still to be an exploration of means of giving advice).

H. *The vagueness of every present situation of further possibilities remained invariant to the clarification furnished by the exchanges of questions and answers.*

    1. There was vagueness (a) in the status of the utterance as an answer, (b) in its status as an answer-to-the-question, (c) in its status as a document of advice with respect to the underlying pattern, and (d) in the underlying problem. While, after the course of an exchange, the utterances furnished "advice about the problem," their function of advice also elaborated the entire scheme of problematic possibilities so that the over-all effect was that of a transformation of the subject's situation in which the vagueness of its horizons remained unchanged and "problems still remained unanswered."

I. *In their capacity as members, subjects consulted institutionalized features of the collectivity as a scheme of interpretation.*

    1. Subjects made specific reference to the social structures in deciding the sensible and warranted character of the adviser's advice. Such references, however, were not made to any social structures whatever. In the eyes of the subject, if the adviser was to know and demonstrate to the subject that he knew what he was talking about, and if the subject was to consider seriously the adviser's descriptions of his circumstances as grounds of the subject's further thoughts and management of these circumstances, the subject did not permit the adviser, nor was the subject willing to entertain, *any* model of the social structures. References that the subject supplied were to social structures which he treated as actually or potentially known in common with the adviser. And then, not to *any* social structures known in common, but to normatively valued social structures which the subject as a collectivity member accepted as *conditions* that his decisions, with respect to his own sensible and realistic grasp of his circumstances and the "good" character of the adviser's advice, had to satisfy. These social structures consisted of normative features of the social system *seen from within* which, for the subject, were definitive of his memberships in the various collectivities that were referred to.

    2. Subjects gave little indication, prior to the occasions of use of the rules for deciding fact and nonfact, what the definitive normative structures were to which their interpretations would make reference. The rules for documenting these definitive normative orders seemed to come into play only after a set of normative features had been

motivated in their relevance to his interpretive tasks, and then as a function of the fact that the activities of interpretation were underway.

3. Subjects presupposed known-in-common features of the collectivity as a body of common-sense knowledge subscribed to by both. They drew upon these presupposed patterns in assigning to what they heard the adviser talking about, its status of documentary evidence of the definitive normative features of the collectivity settings of the experiment, family, school, home, occupation, to which the subject's interests were directed. These evidences and the collectivity features were referred back and and forth to each other, with each elaborating and being thereby elaborated in its possibilities.

J. *Deciding warrant was identical with assigning the advice its perceivedly normal sense.*

Through a retrospective-prospective review, subjects justified the "reasonable" sense and sanctionable status of the advice as grounds for managing their affairs. Its "reasonable" character consisted of its compatability with normative orders of social structures presumed to be subscribed to and known between subject and adviser. The subject's task of deciding the warranted character of what was being advised was identical with the task of assigning to what the adviser proposed (1) its status as an instance of a class of events; (2) its likelihood of occurrence; (3) its comparability with past and future events; (4) the conditions of its occurrence; (5) its place in a set of means-ends relationships; and (6) its necessity according to a natural (i.e., moral) order. The subjects assigned these values of typicality, likelihood, comparability, causal texture, technical efficacy, and moral requiredness while using the institutionalized features of the collectivity as a scheme of interpretation. Thus, the subject's task of deciding whether or not what the adviser advised was "true" was identical with the task of assigning to what the adviser proposed its perceivedly normal values.

K. *Perceivedly normal values were not so much "assigned" as managed.*

Through the work of documenting—i.e., by searching for and determining pattern, by treating the adviser's answers as motivated by the intended sense of the question, by waiting for later answers to clarify the sense of previous ones, by finding answers to unasked questions—the perceivedly normal values of what was being advised were established, tested, reviewed, retained, restored; in a word, managed. It is misleading, therefore, to think of the documentary method as a procedure whereby the advice was admitted to membership in a common-sense corpus in the same way that the rule of observation is a procedure whereby propositions are accorded membership in an ideal scientific corpus. Rather the documentary method developed the advice so as to be continually "membershipping" it.

Examples in Sociological Inquiry

Examples of the use of the documentary method can be cited from every area of sociological investigation.[6] Its obvious application occurs in community studies where warrant is assigned to statements by the criteria of "comprehensive description" and "ring of truth." Its use is found also on the many occasions of survey research when the researcher, in reviewing his interview notes or in editing the answers to a questionnaire, has to decide "what the respondent had in mind." When a researcher is addressed to the "motivated character" of an action, or a theory, or a person's compliance to a legitimate order and the like, he will use what he has actually observed to "document" an "underlying pattern." The documentary method is used whenever selected features of an object are used to epitomize the object. For example, just as the lay person may say of something that "Harry" says, "Isn't that just like Harry?" the investigator may use some observed feature of the thing he is referring to as a characterizing indicator of the intended matter. Complex scenes like industrial establishments, communities, or social movements are frequently described with the aid of "excerpts" from protocols and numerical tables which are used to epitomize the intended events. The documentary method is used whenever the investigator constructs a life history or a "natural history." The task of historicizing the person's biography consists of using the documentary method to select and order past occurrences so as to furnish the present state of affairs its relevant past and prospects.

The use of the documentary method is not confined to cases of "soft" procedures and "partial descriptions." It occurs as well in cases of rigorous procedures where descriptions are intended to exhaust a definite field of possible observables. In reading a journal account for the purpose of literal replication, researchers who attempt to reconstruct the relationship between the reported procedures and the results frequently encounter a gap of insufficient information. The gap occurs when the reader asks how the investigator decided the correspondence between what was actually observed and the intended event for which the actual observation is treated as its evidence. The reader's problem consists of having to decide that the reported observation is a literal instance of the intended occurrence, i.e.,

---

[6] In his article, "On the interpretation of weltanschauung," Mannheim argued that the documentary method is peculiar to the social sciences. There exist in the social sciences many terminological ways of referring to it, viz., "the method of understanding," "sympathetic introspection," "method of insight," "method of intuition," "interpretive method," "clinical method," "emphatic understanding," and so on. Attempts by sociologists to identify something called "interpretive sociology" involve the reference to the documentary method as the basis for encountering and warranting its findings.

that the actual observation and the intended occurrence are identical *in sense*. Since the relationship between the two is a sign relationship, the reader must consult some set of grammatical rules to decide this correspondence. This grammar consists of some theory of the intended events on the basis of which the decisions to code the actual observations as findings are recommended. It is at this point that the reader must furnish the account an investment of interpretive work and an assumption of "underlying" matters "just known in common" about the society in terms of which, what the respondent said, is treated as synonymous with what the observer meant. Correct correspondence is apt to be meant and read on reasonable grounds. Correct correspondence is the product of the work of investigator and reader as members of a community of cobelievers. Thus, even in the case of rigorous methods, if a researcher is to recommend, and the reader is to appreciate, published findings as members of the corpus of sociological fact, the work of the documentary method is employed.

Sociological Situations of Inquiry as Common-Sense Situations of Choice

It is not unusual for professional sociologists to speak of their "fact production" procedures as processes of "seeing through" appearances to an underlying reality; of brushing past actual appearances to "grasp the invariant." Where our subjects are concerned, their processes are not appropriately imagined as "seeing through," but consist instead of coming to terms with a situation in which factual knowledge of social structures—factual in the sense of warranted grounds of further inferences and actions —must be assembled and made available for potential use despite the fact that the situations it purports to describe are, in any calculable sense, unknown; in their actual and intended logical structures are essentially vague; and are modified, elaborated, extended, if not indeed created, by the fact and manner of being addressed.

If many of the features of our subject's documentary work are recognizable in the work of professional sociological fact production, similarly many situations of professional sociological inquiry have precisely the features that our subjects' situations had. Such features of situations of professional sociological inquiry may be more exactly specified as follows.

1. In the course of an interview an investigator is likely to find himself addressing a series of present situations whose *future states that a contemplated course of treatment will produce* are characteristically vague or even unknown. With overwhelming frequency these as of here-and-now possible future states are only sketchily specifiable prior to undertaking the action that is intended to realize them. There is a necessary distinction be-

tween a "possible future state of affairs" and a "how-to-bring-it-about-fu-ture-from-a-present-state-of-affairs-as-an-actual-point-of-departure." The "possible future state of affairs" may be very clear indeed. But such a future is not the matter of interest. Instead we are concerned with the "how to bring it about from a here-and-now future." It is this state—for convenience, call it an "operational future"—that is characteristically vague or unknown.

An illustration. A trained survey researcher can describe with re-markably clarity and definiteness what questions he wishes answers to in a questionnaire. How actual replies of actual subjects are to be evaluated as "replies to the questions" are incorporated in a set of procedural deci-sions known as "coding rules." Any distribution of replies to the questions that is possible under the coding rules is a "possible future state of affairs." After suitable exploratory work such distributions are clearly and definitely imaginable to trained field workers. But with overwhelming frequency it occurs that even late in the *actual* course of the inquiry the questions and answers that will *in effect* have been asked and answered under the various ways of evaluating actual subjects' responses as "replies to the question," given the practical exigencies that must be accommodated in accomplish-ing the actual work of the inquiry, remain sketchy and open to "reasonable decision" even up to the point of composing the results of the inquiry for publication.

2. Given *a* future, any future, that is known in a definite way, the alternative paths to actualize the future state as a set of stepwise operations upon some beginning present state are characteristically sketchy, incoher-ent, and unelaborated. Again it is necessary to stress the difference between an inventory of available procedures—investigators can talk about these quite definitely and clearly—and the deliberately pre-programmed stepwise procedures, a set of predecided "what-to-do-in-case-of" strategies for the manipulation of a succession of actual present states of affairs *in their course.* In actual practices such a program is characteristically an unelabo-rated one.

For example, one of the tasks involved in "managing rapport" consists of managing the stepwise course of the conversation in such a way as to permit the investigator to commit his questions in profitable sequence while retaining some control over the unknown and undesirable directions in which affairs, as a function of the course of the actual exchange, may actu-ally move.[7] Characteristically the researcher substitutes for a pre-programed stepwise solution, a set of *ad hoc* tactics for adjusting to present oppor-tunity, with these tactics only generally governed by what the investigator would hope to have finally found out by the end of the conversation. Under

---

[7] Cf. Robert K. Merton and Patricia L. Kendall, "The focused interview," *American Journal of Sociology*, 1946, 51:541–557.

these circumstances, it is more accurate to talk of investigators acting in fulfillment of their hopes, or in avoidance of their fears, than of acting in the deliberate and calculated realization of a plan.

3. It frequently occurs that the investigator takes an action, and only upon the actual occurrence of some product of that action do we find him reviewing the accomplished sequences in a retrospective search therein for their decided character. Insofar as the *decision that was taken* is assigned by the work of the retrospective search, the outcome of such situations can be said to occur *before* the decision. Such situations occur with dramatic frequency at the time the journal article is being written.

4. Prior to his actually having to choose among alternative courses of action on the basis of anticipated consequences, the investigator, for various reasons, is frequently unable to anticipate the consequences of his alternative courses of action and may have to rely upon his actual involvement in order to learn what they might be.

5. Frequently, after encountering some actual state of affairs, the investigator may count it as desirable, and thereupon treat it as the goal toward which his previously taken actions, as he reads them retrospectively, were directed "all along" or "after all."

6. It frequently occurs that only in the course of actually manipulating a present situation, and as a function of his actual manipulation, does the nature of an investigator's future state of affairs become clarified. Thus, the goal of the investigation may be progressively defined as the consequence of the investigator's actually taking action toward a goal whose features as of any present state of his investigative action he does not see clearly.

7. Characteristically such situations are ones of imperfect information. The result is that the investigator is unable to assess, let alone calculate, the difference that his ignorance in the situation makes upon the accomplishment of his activities. Nor, prior to having to take action, is he able either to evaluate their consequences or to assess the value of alternative courses of action.

8. The information that he possesses, that serves him as the basis for the election of strategies, is rarely codified. Hence, his estimates of the likelihood of success or failure characteristically have little in common with the rational mathematical concept of probability.

In their investigative activities, investigators characteristically must manage situations with the above features, given the following additional conditions: that some action must be taken; that the action must be taken by a time and in pace, duration, and phasing that is coordinate with the actions of others; that the risks of unfavorable outcomes must somehow be managed; that the actions taken and their products will be subject to review by others and must be justified to them; that the elections of courses of action and the resultant outcome must be justified within the procedures of "reasonable" review; and that the entire process must occur within the conditions of, and with his motivated compliance to, corporately organized social activity. In their "shop talk" investigators refer to these features of their actual situations of inquiry and to the necessity for managing them as their "practical circumstances."

Because their features are so easily recognized in the activities of daily life, situations with such features may appropriately be called "common-sense situations of choice." The suggestion is recommended that when researchers call upon "reasonableness" in assigning the status of "findings" to their research results, they are inviting the use of such features as these as a context of interpretation for deciding sensibility and warrant. Findings as outcomes of documentary work, decided under circumstances of common-sense situations of choice, define the term "reasonable findings."

The Problem

Much of "core sociology" consists of "reasonable findings." Many, if not most, situations of sociological inquiry are common-sense situations of choice. Nevertheless, textbook and journal discussions of sociological methods rarely give recognition to the fact that sociological inquiries are carried out under common-sense auspices *at the points where decisions about the correspondence between observed appearances and intended events are being made.* Instead, available descriptions and conceptions of investigative decision-making and problem-solving assign to the decision-maker's situation contrasting features[8] as follows.

1. From the decision-maker's point of view there exists as a feature of each of his here-and-now states of affairs a recognizable goal with specifiable features. Where sociological inquiry is concerned, this goal consists of the investigator's present problem for the solution to which the investigation will have been undertaken. The goal's specifiable features consist of the criteria whereby, as of any present state of affairs, he decides the adequacy with which his problem has been formulated. In their terms, too, the event, "adequate solution," is defined as one of a set of possible occurrences.

2. The decision-maker is conceived to have set for himself the task of devising a program of manipulations upon each successive present state of affairs that will alter each present state so that over their succession they

[8] I wish to thank Drs. Robert Boguslaw and Myron A. Robinson of the System Development Corporation, Santa Monica, California, for the many hours of discussion that we had about calculable and noncalculable situations of choice when we were trying together to work through the problem of how consistently successful play in chess is possible.

are brought into conformity with an anticipated state, i.e., the goal, the solved problem.[9]

These features may be restated in terms of the rules of evidence. As a calculable state of affairs, an investigator's problem may be regarded as a proposition whose "application" for membership, i.e., whose warranted status, is under review. The rules of procedure whereby its warranted status is decided thereby operationally define what is meant by "adequate solution." In ideal scientific activities an investigator is required to decide the steps that define an adequate solution prior to his taking the decided steps. He is required to make this decision before he carries out the operations whereby the possibilities that the proposition proposes will be decided as to their having actually occurred or not. The task of deciding an adequate solution thereby has logical precedence over the actual observation. The observation is said thereby to be "programed," or, alternatively, the intended event is given an "operational definition," or, alternatively, the conditions for the occurrence of an intended event are furnished, or, alternatively, a "prediction" is made.

A prominent argument on behalf of this emphasis is that the documentary method is a scientifically erroneous procedure; that its use distorts the objective world in a mirror of subjective prejudice; and that where common-sense situations of choice exist they do so as historical nuisances. Protagonists for methods such as those used in survey research and laboratory experimentation, for example, assert their increasing exemption from situations with common-sense characteristics and documentary dealings with them. After World War II a flood of textbooks on methods was written to provide remedies for such situations. These methods are intended to depict the ways of transforming common-sense situations into calculable ones. Most particularly, the use of mathematical models and statistical schemes of inference are invoked as calculable solutions to the problems of deciding sensibility, objectivity, and warrant in a rigorous way. Immense sums of foundation money, criteria defining adequate research designs, and many careers rest on the conviction that this is so.

Yet it is common knowledge that in the overwhelming number of researches that are methodologically acceptable, and, paradoxically, precisely to the extent that rigorous methods are used, dramatic discrepancies are visible between the theoretical properties of the intended *sociological* findings of inquirers and the mathematical assumptions that must be satisfied if the statistical measures are to be used for the literal description of the in-

---

[9] In some cases, students of decision-making have been interested in those programs that represent fully calculated solutions to the decision-maker's problems. In other cases studies have addressed the fact that the decision-maker may invoke probabilistic rules to decide the differential likelihood that alternative courses of action would alter a present state of affairs in the desired direction.

tended events. The result is that statistical measurements are most frequently used as indicators, as signs of, as representing or standing on behalf of the intended findings rather than as literal descriptions of them. Thus, at the point where sociological findings must be decided from statistical results,[10] rigorous methods are being asserted as solutions to the tasks of literal description on the grounds of "reasonable" considerations.

Even if it is demonstrable that these features are present, let alone prominent, in sociological inquiries, is it not nevertheless true that a situation of inquiry might receive documentary treatment and still the factual status of its products would be decided differently? For example, is it not the case that there are strictures against ex post facto analysis? And is it not so that a field worker who learned after he consulted his notes what problems he had "in the final analysis" obtained answers to, might reapply for a grant to perform a "confirmatory study" of the "hypotheses" that his reflections had yielded? Is there, therefore, any *necessary* connection between the features of common-sense situations of choice, the use of documentary method, and the *corpus of sociological fact*? Must the documentary method necessarily be used by the professional sociologist to decide sensibility, objectivity, and warrant? Is there a necessary connection between the theoretical subject matter of sociology, as this is constituted by the attitude and procedures for "seeing sociologically" on the one hand, and the canons of adequate description, i.e., evidence, on the other?

Between the methods of literal observation and the work of documentary interpretation the investigator can choose the former and achieve rigorous literal description of physical and biological properties of sociological events. This has been demonstrated on many occasions. Thus far the choice has been made at the cost of either neglecting the properties that make events sociological ones, or by using documentary work to deal with the "soft" parts.

The choice has to do with the question of the conditions under which literal observation and documentary work necessarily occur. This involves the formulation of, and solution to, the problem of sociological evidence in terms that permit a descriptive solution. Undoubtedly, scientific sociology is a "fact," but in Felix Kaufmann's sense of fact, i.e., in terms of a set of procedural rules that *actually* govern the use of sociologists' recommended methods and asserted findings as grounds of further inference and inquiries. The problem of evidence consists of the tasks of making this fact intelligible.

[10] The term "results" is used to refer to the set of *mathematical* events that are possible when the procedures of a statistical test, like chi square, for example, are treated as grammatical rules for conceiving, comparing, producing, etc., events in the mathematical domain. The term "findings" is used to refer to the set of *sociological* events that are possible when, under the assumption that the sociological and mathematical domains correspond in their logical structures, sociological events are interpreted in terms of the rules of statistical inference.

33 ANSELM L. STRAUSS

Language and Identity

Central to any discussion of identity is language. The word "central" is used advisedly. Language is ofttimes construed as just one more kind of behavior—encompassing speaking, reading, writing, and hearing—within a long listing of other kinds of behavior. An important and recurring theme of this essay is that a proper theoretical account of men's identities and action must put men's linguistics into the heart of the discussion.

Names

Consider, as a beginning, that *distinctive appelation by which a person is known:* his name. A name can be very revealing, both of its donor and its owner; if we are observant we shall find it speaks volumes. First generation Jewish immigrants to this country were called by old-fashioned names resounding with rich historical overtones, names like Isaac, Benjamin, Abraham, Hannah, and Ruth; but the children of their children are hardly ever named after such Biblical models, since as their styles of life change, so have their ideals and aspirations. The children's names represent this change if not as precisely, at least as surely, as pink litmus signifies acid. Any name is a container; poured into it are the conscious or unwitting evaluations of the namer. Sometimes this is obvious, as when post-civil war Negroes named their children after the Great Emancipator; sometimes the position of the namer has to be sought and one's inference buttressed by other evidence.

If the name reveals the judgments of the namer, what of the person who receives it? How does he react to this attempt to fix his identity in some way, beforehand? There is a range here running from relative indifference to violent rejection or prideful acceptance. There is the name that announces its bearer to be the third of a line of famous personages, destined not to be the last to do it honor. Probably more common in this country are those names over which children have blushed and been ashamed as their teachers stuttered over pronunciation, these names often later to be shortened, discarded, or relegated to alphabetized shorthand. The point is not whether or not a man can be wholly indifferent to his name but that an extensive range of reaction can be evoked by his imaginings of what he must look like to certain audiences if he bears the name that he does.

The names that are adopted voluntarily reveal even more tellingly the indissoluble tie between name and self-image. The changing of names marks a rite of passage. It means such things as that the person wants to have the kind of name he thinks represents him as a person, does not want any longer to be the kind of person that his previous name signified. The commonest and perhaps least emotionally charged instance of name-changing occurs when a bride takes over her husband's last name and so signifies her changed status. Suppose the wife of an American male were to insist that he change his last name to hers! The phenomenon of "passing" is often marked by name-changing: you disguise who you were or are in order to appear what you wish to be. Benny Ginsburgh may become Basil Gainsborough to express—not necessarily passing and secrecy—but only mobility aspirations. Secrecy sometimes gets mingled with personality transition, as when revolutionists adopt new names and thus seek to bury publicly their pasts; but the new names also mark passage to new self-images. Conversion, religious or otherwise, is often marked by a complete change of name, that act signifying the person's new status in the eyes of God, the world, and himself—marking status and setting a seal upon it.

Less complete changes of status are commonly marked by the partial qualifications of name through the addition of a title, as if to say "this man is now a member of the Senate, so let us accord him his due and address him as Senator." There are some names, like titles, that have to be earned; having earned them, one tells himself that this is what he is and that other people think so too or they would not so address him. Some Indian tribes, for instance, recognized a warrior's major achievement in battle by sanctioning an entire change of name. Americans use a similar device in applying nicknames to express earned status, and by them, can denote a change in status. . . .

Naming as an Act of Placement

The philosophers, John Dewey and Arthur Bentley, in *Knowing and the Known*, have argued that to name is to know, and that the extent of knowing is dependent upon the extent of the naming. By this they do not mean to suggest anything magical about the act of naming, but to make that act central to any human's cognition of his world. This view informs much of the discussion that will follow.

Suppose a mother wishes her very young child to pay attention to an object. She moves his body so that his eyes focus somewhere near the object and then she points toward it. But when he is at an age when he can respond to a word, she will hope to attract his attention more efficiently to some thing by naming it. This is what is called "ostensive definition," meaning an indication of an object without any description whatever; it is the simplest kind of identification. The first identifications are singular; they indicate particular objects. But the child soon learns that certain objects can be called by the same word, albeit his groupings are frequently amusing and seem incorrect to his elders. At first parents often bow to the child's peculiar classification of objects, in order to keep peace in the family, but in the end they win the game, for the youngster must eventually conform to more conventional, if less colorful, lexicology.

To name, then, is not only to indicate; it is to identify an object as some kind of object. An act of identification requires that the thing referred to be placed within a category. Borrowing from the language of logic, we may say that any particular object that is referred to is a member of a general class, a representative of that class. An orange is a member of a class called oranges; but note that this class itself receives its placement, or definition, only by virtue of its relationships with other classes. These relationships are of quite a systematic sort. Thus oranges may be defined in relation to such classes as fruits, foods, tropical growths, tree products, and moderately priced objects. Defining any class, then, means relating it to systematically associated classes. "To tell what a thing is, you place it in terms of something else. This idea of locating, or placing, is implicit in our very word for definition itself: to *define*, or *determine* a thing, is to mark its boundaries.[1]

It should be noted, however, that any particular object can be named, and thus located, in countless ways. The naming sets it within a context of quite differently related classes. The nature or essence of an object does not reside mysteriously within an object itself but is dependent upon how it is defined by the namer. An object which looks so much like an orange—in fact which really is an orange—can also be a member of an infinite number of other classes. If it is in its nature to be an orange, it is also in its nature to be other things. In the case of an orange, we may choose to view it within different contexts for other equally legitimate purposes. It may thus be viewed as a spherical object, with rough, warm-colored skin, suitable for catching and casting lights, hence eminently definable as a model for a beginning art student. Essentially it is just that. This is only to repeat a point made earlier that to name or designate is always to do this from some point of view. From a single identical perspective, otherwise seemingly different things can be classed together. Justification lies in the perspective, not in the things. If you do not agree with your neighbor's classification, this may only signify that you have a somewhat or wholly different basis for drawing symbolic circles around things.

The way in which things are classed together reveals, graphically as

---

[1] Kenneth Burke, *A Grammar of Motives* (New York: Prentice-Hall, 1945), p. 24.

well as symbolically, the perspectives of the classifier. For instance, an anthropologist (Robert Pehrson) studying the Laplanders recently discovered that a single word is used to encompass both "people" and "reindeer." The life of the Laplander revolves around activities having to do with reindeer. Is a reindeer a human or is a human a reindeer? The question is senseless; the people and reindeer are identified, they go together, and the very fact of their identification in terminology gives the anthropologist one of his best clues to the Laplander's ordering of the world and its objects.

Any group of people that has any permanence develops a "special language," a lingo or jargon, which represents its way of identifying those objects important for group action. Waitresses classify types of customers and other workers in the restaurant, give shorthand names to foods, and have special signs and gestures standing for important activities. So do criminals; and even ministers are not immune from the necessity of classifying their clientele and colleagues, otherwise how could they organize activity in an orderly and sensible manner?

The propensity for certain categories invented by any group to be slanderous, to partake of epithet, derogation and innuendo, has been bemoaned by liberals, debunkers, teachers, and all others who have wished to set other's classifications straight. Since groups inevitably are in conflict over issues—otherwise they would not be different groups—and since events inevitably come to be viewed differently by those who are looking up or down opposite ends of the gun, it is useless to talk of trying to eradicate from the human mind the tendency to stereotype, to designate nastily, and to oversimplify. This is not to say that humans are brutish, but that they are thoroughly human. Animals do not name-call, neither do they possess or assign identities in the elaborate sense in which we are discussing identity.

Classification and the Direction of Action

This necessity for any group to develop a common or shared terminology leads to an important consideration: the direction of activity depends upon the particular ways that objects are classified. This can be simply illustrated. Not so long ago, children used to be fed large quantities of spinach according to the syllogism that spinach contained iron and that iron was needed for building bones. Now it appears that excessive consumption of spinach reduces body calcium and therefore is bad for the bones. Spinach is thus reclassified and only if you wish to reduce calcium content should you overindulge. The renaming of any object, then, amounts to a reassessment of your relation to it, and *ipso facto* your behavior becomes changed along the line of your reassessment. In any event it is the definition of what the object "is" that allows action to occur with reference to what it is taken to be. Mark Twain tells how as an apprentice pilot he mistook a wind reef (not dangerous) for a bluff reef (deadly dangerous) and, to the hilarity of his boss who "properly" read the signs, performed miraculous feats of foolishness to avoid the murderous pseudo-bluff.

The naming of an object provides a directive for action, as if the object were forthrightly to announce, "You say I am this, then act in the appropriate way toward me." Conversely, if the actor feels he does not know what the object is, then with regard to it his action is blocked. Suppose that in the dark one reached for a glass of milk, raised it to his lips, recoiled at the strange taste, and stood immobilized until he was able to label the taste as tomato juice. Energy for action was there, but was temporarily unharnessed, immobilized, until naming occurred. Of course, in this example the moment of immobilization would be fleeting, since as soon as one set about to discover what the taste was he would be acting toward something belonging to the category of "unidentified liquid, whose nature is to be discovered." A person need not be certain that he knows what an object is in order to organize a line of action toward it—he merely has to be willing to take a chance on his judgment.

Classification and Evaluation

An act of classification not only directs overt action, but arouses a set of expectations toward the object thus classified. A chair ought to hold anyone who sits on it, not turn into a piano or a cat, and a buzzing housefly should not piteously ask us not to swat her, saying she is a fairy in disguise. We are surprised only if our expectations are unfulfilled, as when a presumed salesman in a department store assures us that he is just an ordinary shopper like ourselves, or when milk turns out to be strongly spiked with rum. When we classify, our expectations necessarily face both past and future. Expectations have to do with consequential relations between ourselves and the object. However expectations rest also upon remembrances of past experiences with objects resembling—we believe— the one currently before us.

Since this is so, classifications not only carry our anticipations but also those values that were experienced when we encountered the things, persons, or events now classified. For example, the Japanese have a food called "tofu" which is a soy-bean product. Let us imagine that the first time we meet tofu it is served cold with soy sauce over it and that it strikes us as unpalatable. Tofu is for us an indifferent food, and if at some future time we should see tofu or hear the word our images would likely be of the indifferent experience we had with a whitish jellied object covered with brown sauce. But suppose that some time later we are treated to a delicious soup in which there are pieces of a mushy substance. "What is that good stuff in the soup?" we ask, and are surprised to find it is cooked tofu. Now we revise our evaluation: tofu in soup, good; tofu uncooked, not so good. This substance, as used by the Japanese, appears in several guises, so yet more surprises may be in store for us. The range of our experience with tofu is both what we know of it and how we value it. The wider grows this range, the better we know the object—what it can do and what can be done with it—and likewise the more extensive become our judgments of its capacities and qualities. It would appear that classification, knowledge and value are inseparable.

There are several more lessons suggested by the illustration. One is that values attributed to any object—like "good" or "hateful"—really are not "in" the object. In having an experience one does not put value into it like water into a kettle. Value is not an element; it has to do with a relation between the object and the person who has experiences with the object. This is just another way of stating that the "essence" or "nature" of the object resides not in the object but in the relation between it and the namer. Value as a relation is easily seen in conjunction with such an adjective as "useful"—useful for whom, under what conditions, for which of his purposes? Precisely the same is true whether the object is a thing or an event, and whether the value is "useful" or, say, "sinful." Sinfulness is not fixed in the event, a quality of it within the eye of God. An act is sinful to particular definers when perceived as committed under certain circumstances by persons of specified identities.

Since values are not in objects but are evaluations of objects, it follows that persons must do their own experiencing in order to do their own evaluating. This does not mean that I cannot teach you the meaning of something prior to your direct experience of it. I can say that the dust rises off the city streets in a certain country and constantly hangs so heavy in the air that it is hard to breathe. You have experienced similar conditions, so readily understand. But when you are introduced to a new terminology, the best you can do is draw upon possibly analogous experiences, and these may or may not lead to accurate conceptions. To experience, hence to evaluate, a Balinese trance as do the Balinese probably cannot even be approximated by an American. Everyone has at some time been introduced to new terms representing new ways of looking at objects, as when entering upon a new job. Such occupational terms cannot be fully grasped, the objects and events be perceived as others perceive them, until we have undergone similar experiences ourselves. Of course an articulate informant drawing colorfully and accurately upon whatever is similar in his and your experiences can bring you to closer comprehension and appreciation; hence the great usefulness of some novels and biographies. But no amount of description in advance, if the shift in perspective called for is radical, will teach you how you yourself will finally evaluate. You yourself must do, suffer, and undergo—to use John Dewey's terms.[2]

[2] John Dewey, *Reconstruction in Philosophy* (New York: Henry Holt, 1920), p. 86.

As people "undergo," their evaluations change. Values are not eternal. Expectations cannot always be fulfilled. Things change; so do we. "Good things change and vanish not only with changes in the environing medium but with changes in ourselves."[3] Even without direct new experience something novel may be learned about an object—such as one might learn something new about life in prison, or as when a college student studies about geological strata and rainfall and so comes into somewhat different relationships with rocks, rain, and water. As long as learning ccntinues, revision of concepts continues; and as long as revision takes place, reorganization of behavior takes place.

The naming or identifying of things is, then, a continual problem, never really over and done with. By "continual" I do not mean "continuous"—one can lie in a hammock contentedly watching the moon rise and raising no questions about it, the world, or oneself. Nevertheless, some portion of one's classificatory terminology, the symbolic screen through which the world is ordered and organized, is constantly under strain—or just has been—or will be. George H. Mead (who asserted that classifications are really hypotheses) would say it necessarily must be, from the very nature of action which brings in its train the reconstruction of past experience and the arising of new objects.[4]

[3] John Dewey, *Experience and Nature* (Chicago: Open Court, 1925), p. 399.
[4] George H. Mead, *Mind, Self and Society* (Chicago: University of Chicago Press, 1934).

34   KURT GOLDSTEIN

Speech and Thinking

The impairment of the abstract attitude is clearly revealed in characteristic changes in the speech of patients with brain lesions. We know various forms of speech defects in such patients and usually class them together as aphasia.[1] No other pathological material can teach us so much about the organization of the human being. Since we cannot deal with all the various types of aphasia, I shall confine the discussion to a special form, known as

Reprinted by permission of the publishers from Kurt Goldstein, *Human Nature in the Light of Psychopathology*. Cambridge, Mass: Harvard University Press, Copyright, 1940, by the President and Fellows of Harvard College.
[1] See Henry Head, *Aphasia and Kindred Disorders of Speech* (New York, 1926); Theodore Weisenburg and Katherine McBride, *Aphasia* (New York, 1935); Kurt Goldstein, *Uber Aphasie* (Zurich, 1927).

amnesic aphasia,[2] which in my opinion is particularly well suited to give us an insight into the nature of man.

If one examines a patient with this type of aphasia one observes as a striking symptom that he is totally or partially unable to find names for concrete things. This is especially noticeable in cases where he has the task of naming presented objects, but it is also apparent in his spontaneous language, which is conspicuously lacking in nouns and verbs. Usually this symptom is considered as the characteristic change, but closer examination shows that other changes also occur. Many circumlocutions are used where we would use single words. A patient shown a cup, for example, may respond with, "This is for drinking," or say, on seeing a penholder, "That is for writing," etc. In another case, a patient of mine said, "That is something for the rain," in a situation in which we should merely say, "That is an umbrella." Or she said: "I must have it for the rain," or, "I have three umbrellas at home." In the last sentence she used the right word in her periphrasis, yet she was unable to repeat it in reply to a repeated question, "What is that?" soon afterward. Evidently such a patient has not lost the word itself but for some reason is unable to use it in naming an object. Further, his entire behavior shows peculiarities. All his acting and thinking seems to center, to an unusual degree, around his own personality and its relation to the world. He is acting in the world rather than thinking or speaking about it. His speech is accompanied to a marked degree by expressive movements. Very often we observe that he seems unable to express his meaning by words but can do so quite well by movements.

The change involving the whole behavior appears still more strikingly in special examinations. I shall begin by presenting the results of one examination with a sorting test because the results seem particularly well suited to carry us into the core of our problem, namely, the basic change in patients with amnesic aphasia.

We place before the patient a heap of colored woolen skeins— Holmgren's well-known samples used for testing color efficiency. We ask him to pick out all the red skeins and put them together. (There are, of course, many different shades of red.) Or we pick out one particular skein —for example, a dark red one—and ask him to choose strands of the same and similar colors.

In the first task a normal person with good color efficiency usually selects a great number of different shades of the same ground color—that is, for example, different reds, without regard to intensity, purity, lightness, etc. In the same task patients with amnesic aphasia behave quite differently,

---

[2] See Kurt Goldstein and Adhemar Gelb, *Psychologische Analysen hirnpathologischer Falle* (Leipsig, 1920); Kurt Goldstein, "The Problem of the Meaning of Words Based upon Observation of Aphasic Patients," *Journal of Psychology*, vol. II, 1936; Ernst Cassirer, *Philosophie der symbolischen Formen*, vol. II (Berlin, 1928).

and exhibit varying types of behavior. For example, when he is told to choose all the skeins that are similar to a given skein, one patient chooses only skeins of the very same or of a closely similar shade. Though urged to go on he chooses a small number because there are only a few very similar ones in the heap. Another patient matches a given bright shade of red with a blue skein of similar brightness. At first such a patient may seem to be color-blind, but it can be demonstrated beyond doubt that his color efficiency is normal and that he is able to differentiate very distinctly between colors that are much alike. More precise observations disclose that in this case the choice is determined by a particular color attribute of the given skein, its brightness. We observe, further, that the choice may be decided by a number of different attributes—at one time by brightness, at another by softness, or coldness, warmth, etc. However—and this is a very amazing thing—a patient who seems to be choosing according to a certain attribute is not able to follow this procedure voluntarily if it is demanded of him—that is, if he is asked to choose only bright skeins, etc. Further, we observe that he does not seem to be able to hold to a certain procedure. He has chosen, for instance, some bright skeins. Suddenly he begins selecting on the basis of another attribute—the coldness of the color or some other factor. In another case, the patient arranges the skeins as if guided by a scale of brightness. He begins with a very bright red, then adds one less bright, and so on to a dull one. But if we ask him to place the skeins in a succession according to their brightness he shows himself incapable of the performance, even if it is demonstrated to him.

To understand the behavior of our patients, it is necessary to examine the procedure of normal persons in such tasks. If we normal persons want to choose a color, we select various nuances, even though we see that they have various attributes not equal to one another, because we recognize that they belong together in respect to their *basic* quality. The several shades are merely examples of this quality, and we treat the skeins not as different individual things but as representatives of that one basic color. For the moment we ignore all differences in shade and disregard all singular attributes. We are able to do this because we can abstract and because we can hold fast to a procedure once initiated.

There is another approach, however, which is open to the normal person. We can start with one particular skein and move it about over the heap, *passively* surrendering ourselves to the impressions that emerge. Then either of two things will take place. If we find skeins resembling our sample in *all* attributes, all these immediately cohere in a unitary sensory experience with the sample. If we find skeins which match our sample in some respects, we experience a characteristic unrest concerning the heap, and an alternating sense of relationship between skeins in the heap and the sample, according to different attributes. No matter whether we experience rivalry or matching, the coherence we feel results directly from sense data and takes place passively; we do not experience a definite attitude toward any attribute.

There is an essential difference between the more passive kind of approach and the former, in which we definitely choose a particular color. In the one, a definite ordering principle determines our actions; in the other, there is no such principle, and our actions are passively determined by outer impressions. These two kinds of behavior correspond to what we have called abstract and concrete behavior and what we may now call categorical and concrete behavior.

A particular kind of language belongs to each of these types of behavior. Our behavior is abstract when we give a name to an object. When we speak of "table" we do not mean a special given table with all its accidental properties; we mean table in general. The word is used as a representative of the category "table" even when naming a particular table. Thus, if we are asked to group together all reds, upon hearing the word "red" we are immediately prepared to select colors in a categorical fashion. In this approach language plays a great role, and the particular form it takes here may be designated by Karl Buehler's term, *darstellende Sprache,* which may be translated as "representative speech."

In the second form of behavior language does not play much of a role at all. Our words merely accompany our acts and express a property of the object itself, like other properties, such as color, size, etc. This fact is shown in the particular kind of words we use in such situations. The words are especially adapted to the individuality of the given object. We use words like "rose-red," "violet"; we do not say "red," but "pink," "dark red," "strawberry-red," "sky-blue"; not green but "grass-green," etc. Often we have no word for naming a given object, and then we do it in a roundabout way. Words are used here less as representative of categories than as individual properties which, like other properties, belong to the object in question. We call such words "individual" words.

Now when we consider the behavior of the patient in the light of these elucidations we may say that it is similar to the second approach of normal persons. He is able to assume only the more concrete, the more realistic, attitude. Therefore he chooses identical skeins or skeins which are similar in an outstanding property, such as brightness. This interpretation finds confirmation in the greater concreteness of the patient's general behavior, in the predominance of acting over thinking, in the accompaniment of speech by expressive movements.

Our assumption is finally substantiated by the results of another type of sorting test. If a normal person tries to arrange a number of objects lying before him—say, on the writing table of a very busy man—he may do it in various ways, according to various attitudes. He may arrange them by size, by color, by function, by the importance of their situation, in terms of activity, of thought, etc. Further, he is able both to shift from one attitude and one kind of order to another as the situation demands it, and to effect a particular arrangement on demand. A patient with amnesic aphasia, confronted with miscellaneous objects with the instruction to group them, will exhibit the same behavior as in the color test. He is capable of proceeding only in a manner that indicates that he is guided by *concrete* promptings.

A particularly instructive example is the following. Among a number of different objects there were placed on a table before a patient a cork-screw and a bottle with a cork loosely set in its neck. The patient, asked to arrange these, did not put the bottle and the corkscrew together. Asked if these two objects did not belong together, he said, "No," very positively, backing his answer up with the explanation, "The bottle is already opened." Under these circumstances most normal people would pay no attention to the fact that the cork was not fast. For the immediate task —the grouping together of objects that belong together—it is quite incidental and unimportant whether the cork is loose or fast. With the abstract attitude, in a form of sorting which involves grouping objects according to categories, we assume that bottle and corkscrew belong together, independently of their occurrence in any particular situation. But for the patient who is able to take the objects only as they are given in sense experience, the corkscrew does not belong to the bottle and the cork if the cork is already loose. From this and similar cases it is plain that he takes the concrete attitude toward objects as well—we may say toward all objects, toward the world in its entirety.

Our conclusion is that the patient's inability to name objects is a consequence of his inability to assume the abstract attitude, for this is a prerequisite for the naming of objects. As we have shown in the example of the umbrella, he has not lost the words themselves, but he is unable to use them in situations which demand their use as categories. Often a patient, asked to name a color presented to him, calls out over and over various color names: red, blue, yellow, etc. He may even utter the appropriate name, but in spite of this he is still unable to connect it with the color itself. Furthermore, it does not help him when we say the different color names for him to repeat after us.

But what makes these words unsuitable for use in connection with objects in the normal way—that is, as names? Why can they not be used as symbols for objects? This may be disclosed in observations of patients who utter appropriate words in connection with some objects but, as closer analysis shows, do not use them in a normal categorical fashion. Here we learn that the patients have the same *concrete* attitude toward the words that they have toward objects they are asked to sort.

Asked to mention the names of several different kinds of animals, the patient may be at first unable to do so. In one case it was not until we had given a patient such examples as dog, cat, mouse, that she replied to the question at all. Then suddenly she said: "A polar bear; a brown bear; a lion; a tiger." Asked why she named these particular animals, she said, "If we enter the zoological gardens, we come at first to the polar bear and then to the other animals."[3] Obviously she had recalled the animals as they were situated in the zoological gardens, and had used the words only as belonging to the concrete situation, not as names for objects. It was very characteristic that she did not simply say "bear," a word which represents the category of all bears, and which we would use when asked to name animals, but that instead she selected the words "polar bear," "brown bear." The same fact appeared when the patient was asked to recite different female first names. She said: "Grete, Paula, Clara, Martha," and, asked why she had mentioned these particular names, answered, "These are all G——s" (G—— was her family name), and went on, "one sister died of a heart neurosis." The last sentence demonstrates very clearly that the patient did not recite names but only uttered words which belonged to a particular concrete situation, namely, to her family situation.

How very concretely such words are apprehended may be demonstrated by the following example. When, to such a patient of ours, a knife was offered with a pencil, she called the knife a "pencil sharpener"; when the knife was offered with an apple, it was to her an "apple parer"; when offered with a potato, it was a "potato peeler"; in company with a piece of bread, it became a "bread knife"; and with a fork it was "knife and fork." The word "knife" alone she never uttered spontaneously, and when she was asked, "Could we not always call it simply 'knife?'" she replied promptly, "No."

With different mental sets the same word may mean for the normal person different things. For example, in German the word *Anhänger* is used for a lavalier which hangs on a chain around a girl's neck, or for a follower of a personage, or for the second car which is customarily attached to a street-car in Germany. Our patient was unable to use the word in more than one sense or in connection with more than one object. If she understood the word in a particular sense she could not understand that it could be used in another sense. This observation shows clearly that the words themselves are qualitatively different for such patients as compared with normal people, by whom the same word can be used for various totally different objects. By patients with amnesic aphasia they can be used only in a concrete way, for they seem to have lost the characteristic that is necessary if they are to be used in a categorical sense—that is, as symbols. They may be useful as properties belonging

[3] Eva Rothmann, "Untersuchung eines Falles von umschriebener Hirnschadigung mit Storungen auf verschiedenen Leistungsgebieten," *Schweizer Archiv fur Neurologie und Psychiatrie*, vol. XXXIII, 1933.

to a definite object, but they have become unfit to serve as symbols for ideas. *They have lost their meaning.*

It has usually been assumed, even by those authors who recognize that these patients have lost the categorical attitude toward objects, that the cause of this lack is the loss of words, or a difficulty in evoking words. This cannot be the case. There is no doubt that words provide a very important means of helping us to assume the categorical attitude and of stabilizing concepts, but, as we have explained, our patients have not really lost the words. Instead, the words have lost their character of being usable in the abstract, and this change in language is only one expression of the basic change in our patients, *the lack of the capacity to create any sort of abstraction.*

These observations are important for understanding the character of the capacity for naming objects. This apparently simple performance does not represent a superficial connection between a thing and a word; naming objects presupposes the abstract attitude and is an expression of a very high mental function. But these observations reveal another point still more important for our discussion. They show that speech is one of the essential characteristics of human nature, inasmuch as it is tied to man's highest capacity, the capacity for abstract behavior.

Another significant point appears. The patients we have been discussing have not lost the capacity to use words in a concrete way, and from the advantage this type of speech gives them we can infer what role it may play in normal life.

A patient of mine could name pure colors with their respective color names—red, blue, and so on—but she declined to extend the same word to the several shades of a given color. The words were at her disposal only as individual, concrete things belonging to definite objects. In the course of time, after repeated examinations, she came to call various shades by the same name; for instance, she would use the word "red" for all shades of red. Superficially she seemed to behave like a normal person. One might have thought that she had improved, that she had regained the *meaning* of the words. But it was not so. Asked why she now called all these different shades by the same word, she answered, "The doctors have told me that all these colors are named red. Therefore I called them all red." Asked if this was not correct, she laughed and said, "Not one of these colors is red, but I am told to call them by this word." It is clear that she had not used the words as symbols but had learned to build a quite external connection between one word and a diversity of things, a quite meaningless connection, which, however, because she had a good memory, helped her to carry out a task, if only in a very external way.

Thus we must distinguish very definitely between two ways of using words in connection with objects: real naming, which is an expression of the categorical attitude toward the world in general, and pseudo-naming of objects, which is simply a use of words held in memory. The incidence of this pseudo-naming depends on the extent of the individual's verbal possessions. In it words are used as properties of objects just as other properties—color, size, hue—are used; they belong to concrete behavior. To this type of words belong the speech automatisms of ordinary people —the alphabet, numbers in series, the days of the week, and many other longer or shorter speech expressions of everyday life. This use of words plays a great role in ordinary speech. In learning a foreign language, for example, as long as we have no real conception of it as a language, we possess its words only by such superficial connections with the words of our own language. If we understand their meaning within the realm of the foreign language itself, then the words achieve an absolutely different character; then they become representative of a category.

Important as these speech possessions are for our everyday language, they obtain their significance only from their position against a background of representational, meaningful speech. This may be gathered from the fact that to a certain extent speech automatisms are developed only if a human being possesses the function of meaning. Certainly a child acquires many automatisms by repeated imitation of his own speech and that of others. If he is not able to use them later in connection with meaningful speech, however, his learning of these words is limited, and he forgets many that he has learned. We know that children with an inborn deficiency in the attitude toward the abstract are not able to develop speech automatisms to any extent, and that they forget them, in spite of a good memory, if the words are not practiced constantly. In the same way, patients with a loss of categorical behavior may lose their speech automatisms if they are not continuously kept in use by the demands of concrete situations. Thus, for example, if the meaning of numbers is lost, these patients lose the ability to count and the knowledge of the simple multiplication table, which are usually regarded as well-established possessions of memory.

Speech automatisms may be designated as "tools," but it is false to consider language in general as a mere tool. Even speech automatisms are dependent upon the categorical attitude both in their building and in their use. This point is most important. The use of speech automatisms alone is not real language. Our patients, despite their lack of the categorical attitude, may be able to use speech automatisms which they acquired at a time when they were capable of the categorical attitude, but the fact that their speech lacks the spontaneity and fluidity which characterizes normal language, and that they are not able to use the words as symbols, demonstrates very clearly that language without a categorical background is not real language. Whenever human beings use language to establish natural connections between themselves and the world, particularly with their fellow men, language is not merely a tool. It is not merely a superficial means of communication, not a simple naming of objects through words; it represents a particular way of building up the world—namely, by means of abstractions. "Language," said Wilhelm von Humboldt, "never represents objects themselves but the concepts which the mind has formed of them in the autonomous activity by which it creates language." It is this that makes language so important, so essential to the development of a culture. It becomes a manifestation both of all that is human, the human being at his deepest, and of man's psychic bond with his fellows; in none of his cultural creations does man reveal himself so fully as in the creation of language itself. It would be impossible for animals to create a language, because they do not have this conceptual approach toward the world. If they had, they would be not animals but human beings. Nothing brings this home to us more strikingly than observing in patients with amnesic aphasia the parallelism between the changes which occur in personality and the loss of the meaning of words.

35   C. WRIGHT MILLS

Situated Actions and Vocabularies of Motive

The major reorientation of recent theory and observation in sociology of language emerged with the overthrow of the Wundtian notion that language has as its function the "expression" of prior elements within the individual. The postulate underlying modern study of language is the simple one that we must approach linguistic behavior, not by referring it to private states in individuals, but by observing its social function of coordinating diverse actions. Rather than expressing something which is prior and in the person, language is taken by other persons as an indicator of future actions.[1]

Within this perspective there are suggestions concerning problems of motivation. It is the purpose of this paper to outline an analytic model

C. Wright Mills, "Situated Actions and Vocabularies of Motive," *American Sociological Review*, vol. 5 (December 1940), pp. 904–913. Reprinted by permission.
Revision of a paper read to The Society for Social Research, University of Chicago, August 16–17, 1940.
[1] See C. Wright Mills, "Bibliographical Appendices," Section I, 4: "Sociology of Language" in *Contemporary Social Theory*, Ed. by Barnes, Becker & Becker, New York, 1940.

for the explanation of motives which is based on a sociological theory of language and a sociological psychology.[2]

As over against the inferential conception of motives as subjective "springs" of action, motives may be considered as typical vocabularies having ascertainable functions in delimited societal situations. Human actors do vocalize and impute motives to themselves and to others. To explain behavior by referring it to an inferred and abstract "motive" is one thing. To analyze the observable lingual mechanisms of motive imputation and avowal as they function in conduct is quite another. Rather than fixed elements "in" an individual, motives are the terms with which interpretation of conduct *by social actors* proceeds. This imputation and avowal of motives by actors are social phenomena to be explained. The differing reasons men give for their actions are not themselves without reasons.

First, we must demarcate the general conditions under which such motive imputation and avowal seem to occur.[3] Next, we must give a characterization of motive in denotable terms and an explanatory paradigm of why certain motives are verbalized rather than others. Then, we must indicate mechanisms of the linkage of vocabularies of motive to systems of action. What we want is an analysis of the integrating, controlling, and specifying function a certain type of speech fulfils in socially situated actions.

The generic situation in which imputation and avowal of motives arise, involves, first, the *social* conduct or the (stated) programs of languaged creatures, i.e., programs and actions oriented with reference to the actions and talk of others; second, the avowal and imputation of motives is concomitant with the speech form known as the "question." Situations back of questions typically involve *alternative* or *unexpected* programs or actions which phases analytically denote "crises."[4] The question is distinguished in that it usually elicits another *verbal* action, not a motor response. The question is an element in *conversation.* Conversation may be concerned with the factual features of a situation as they are seen or believed to be or it may seek to integrate and promote a set of diverse

---

[2] See G. H. Mead, "Social Psychology as Counterpart of Physiological Psychology," *Psychol. Bul.,* VI: 401–408, 1909; Karl Mannheim, *Man and Society in an Age of Reconstruction,* New York, 1940; L. V. Wiese-Howard Becker, *Systematic Sociology,* part I, New York, 1932; J. Dewey, "All psychology is either biological or social psychology," *Psychol. Rev.,* vol. 24: 276.

[3] The importance of this initial task for research is clear. Most researches on the verbal level merely ask abstract questions of individuals, but if we can tentatively delimit the situations in which certain motives *may* be verbalized, we can use that delimitation in the construction of *situational* questions, and we shall be *testing* deductions from our theory.

[4] On the "question" and "conversation," see G. A. DeLaguna, *Speech: Its function and Development,* 37 (and index), New Haven, 1927. For motives in crises, see J. M. Williams, *The Foundations of Social Science,* 435 ff, New York, 1920.

social actions with reference to the situation and its normative pattern of expectations. It is in this latter assent and dissent phase of conversation that persuasive and dissuasive speech and vocabulary arise. For men live in immediate acts of experience and their attentions are directed outside themselves until acts are in some way frustrated. It is then that awareness of self and of motive occur. The "question" is a lingual index of such conditions. The avowal and imputation of motives are features of such conversations as arise in "question" situations.

Motives are imputed or avowed as answers to questions interrupting acts or programs. Motives are words. Generically, to what do they refer? They do not denote any elements "in" individuals. They stand for anticipated situational consequences of questioned conduct. Intention or purpose (stated as a "program") *is* awareness of anticipated consequence; motives are names for consequential situations, and surrogates for actions leading to them. Behind questions are possible alternative actions with their terminal consequences. "Our introspective words for motives are rough, shorthand descriptions for certain typical patterns of discrepant and conflicting stimuli."[5]

The model of purposive conduct associated with Dewey's name may briefly be stated. Individuals confronted with "alternative acts" perform one or the other of them on the basis of the differential consequences which they anticipate. This nakedly utilitarian schema is inadequate because: (a) the "alternative acts" of *social* conduct "appear" most often in lingual form, as a question, stated by one's self or by another; (b) it is more adequate to say that individuals act in terms of anticipation of named consequences.

Among such names and in some technologically oriented lines of action there may appear such terms as "useful," "practical," "serviceable," etc., terms so "ultimate" to the pragmatists, and also to certain sectors of the American population in these delimited situations. However, there are other areas of population with different vocabularies of motives. The choice of lines of action is accompanied by representations, and selection among them, of their situational termini. Men discern situations with particular vocabularies, and it is in terms of some delimited vocabulary that they anticipate consequences of conduct.[6] Stable vocabularies of motives link anticipated consequences and specific actions. There is no need to invoke "psychological" terms like "desire" or "wish" as explanatory, since they themselves must be explained socially.[7] Anticipation is a subvocal or overt naming of terminal phases and/or social consequences

[5] K. Burke, *Permanence and Change*, 45, New York, 1936. I am indebted to this book for several leads which are systematized into the present statement.

[6] See such experiments as C. N. Rexroad's "Verbalization in Multiple Choice Reactions," *Psychol. Rev.*, Vol. 33: 458, 1926.

[7] Cf. J. Dewey, "Theory of Valuation," *Int. Ency. of Unified Science*, New York, 1939.

of conduct. When an individual names consequences, he elicits the behaviors for which the name is a redintegrative cue. In a *societal* situation,
implicit in the names for consequences is the social dimension of motives.
Through such vocabularies, types of societal controls operate. Also, the
terms in which the question is asked often will contain both alternatives:
"Love or Duty?" "Business or Pleasure?" Institutionally different situations have different *vocabularies of motive* appropriate to their respective
behaviors.

This sociological conception of motives as relatively stable lingual
phases of delimited situations is quite consistent with Mead's program
to approach conduct socially and from the outside. It keeps clearly in
mind that "both motives and actions very often originate not from within
but from the situation in which individuals find themselves. . . ."[8] It
translates the question of "why"[9] into a "how" that is answerable in terms
of a situation and its typical vocabulary of motives, i.e., those which
conventionally accompany that type situation and function as cues and
justifications for normative actions in it.

It has been indicated that the question is usually an index to the
avowal and imputation of motives. Max Weber defines motive as a complex of meaning, which appears to the actor himself or to the observer
to be an adequate ground for his conduct.[10] The aspect of motive which
this conception grasps is its intrinsically social character. A satisfactory
or adequate motive is one that satisfies the questioners of an act or program, whether it be the other's or the actor's. As a word, *a motive tends to
be one which is to the actor and to the other members of a situation an
unquestioned answer to questions concerning social and lingual conduct.*
A stable motive is an ultimate in justificatory conversation. The words
which in a type situation will fulfil this function are circumscribed by the
vocabulary of motives acceptable for such situations. Motives are accepted justifications for present, future, or past programs or acts.

To term them justification is *not* to deny their efficacy. Often anticipations of acceptable justification will control conduct. ("If I did this, what
could I say? What would they say?") Decisions may be, wholly or in part,
delimited by answers to such queries.

A man may begin an act for one motive. In the course of it, he may
adopt an ancillary motive. This does not mean that the second apologetic

---

[8] K. Mannheim, *Man and Society*, 249, London, 1940.

[9] Conventionally answerable by reference to "subjective factors" within individuals.
R. M. MacIver, "The Modes of the Question Why," *J. of Soc. Phil.*, April, 1940. Cf. also
his "The Imputation of Motives," *Amer. J. Sociol.*, July, 1940.

[10] *Wirtschaft und Gesellschaft*, 5, Tubingen, 1922, " 'Motiv' heisst ein Sinnzusammen-
hang, Welcher dem Handelnden selbst oder dem Beobachtenden als sinnhafter 'Grund'
eines Verhaltens in dem Grade heissen, als die Beziehung seiner Bestandteile von uns
nach den durchschnittlichen Denk-und Gefühlsgewohnheiten als typischer (wir pflegen
in sagen: 'richtiger') Sinzusammenhang bejaht Wird."

motive is inefficacious. The vocalized expectation of an act, its "reason," is not only a mediating condition of the act but it is a proximate and controlling condition for which the term "cause" is not inappropriate. It may strengthen the act of the actor. It may win new allies for his act.

When they appeal to others involved in one's act, motives are strategies of action. In many social actions, others must agree, tacitly or explicitly. Thus, acts often will be abandoned if no reason can be found that others will accept. Diplomacy in choice of motive often controls the diplomat. Diplomatic choice of motive is part of the attempt to motivate acts for other members in a situation. Such pronounced motives undo snarls and integrate social actions. Such diplomacy does not necessarily imply intentional lies. It merely indicates that an appropriate vocabulary of motives will be utilized—that they are conditions for certain lines of conduct.[11]

When an agent vocalizes or imputes motives, he is not trying to *de-* *scribe* his experienced social action. He is not merely stating "reasons." He is influencing others—and himself. Often he is finding new "reasons" which will mediate action. Thus, we need not treat an action as discrepant from "its" verbalization, for in many cases, the verbalization is a new act. In such cases, there is not a discrepancy between an act and "its" verbalization, but a difference between two disparate actions, motor-social and verbal.[12] This additional (or *"ex post facto"*) lingualization may involve appeal to a vocabulary of motives associated with a norm with which both members of the situation are in agreement. As such, it is an integrative factor in *future* phases of the original social action or in other acts. By resolving conflicts, motives are efficacious. Often, if "reasons" were not given, an act would not occur, nor would diverse actions be integrated. Motives are common grounds for mediated behaviors.

Perry summarily states the Freudian view of motives "as the view that the real motives of conduct are those which we are ashamed to admit either to ourselves or to others."[13] One can cover the facts by merely saying that scruples (i.e., *moral* vocabularies of motive) are often efficacious and that men will alter and deter their acts in terms of such motives. One of the components of a "generalized other," as a mechanism of societal control, is vocabularies of acceptable motives. For example, a business man joins the Rotary Club and proclaims its public-spirited vocabulary.[14] If this man cannot act out business conduct without so do-

[11] Of course, since motives are communicated, they may be lies; but this must be proved. Verbalizations are not lies merely because they are socially efficacious. I am here concerned more with the social function of pronounced motives, than with the sincerity of those pronouncing them.

[12] See F. Znaniecki, *Social Actions*, 30, New York, 1936.

[13] *General Theory of Value*, 292–293, New York, 1936.

[14] *Ibid.*, 392.

ing, it follows that this vocabulary of motives is an important factor in his behavior.[15] The long acting out of a role, with its appropriate motives, will often induce a man to become what at first he merely sought to appear. Shifts in the vocabularies of motive that are utilized later by an individual disclose an important aspect of various integrations of his actions with concomitantly various groups.

The motives actually used in justifying or criticizing an act definitely link it to situations, integrate one man's action with another's, and line up conduct with norms. The societally sustained motive-surrogates of situations are both constraints and inducements. It is a hypothesis worthy and capable of test that typical vocabularies of motives for different situations are significant determinants of conduct. As lingual segments of social action, motives orient actions by enabling discrimination between their objects. Adjectives such as "good," "pleasant," and "bad" promote action or deter it. When they constitute components of a vocabulary of motives, i.e., are typical and relatively unquestioned accompaniments of typal situations, such words often function as directives and incentives by virtue of their being the judgments of others as anticipated by the actor. In this sense motives are "social instruments, i.e., data by modifying which the agent will be able to influence [himself or others]."[16] The "control" of others is not usually direct but rather through manipulation of a field of objects. We influence a man by naming his acts or imputing motives to them—or to "him." The motives accompanying institutions of war, e.g., are not "the causes" of war, but they do promote continued integrated participation, and they vary from one war to the next. Working vocabularies of motive have careers that are woven through changing institutional fabrics.

Genetically, motives are imputed by others before they are avowed by self. The mother controls the child: "Do not do that, it is greedy." Not only does the child learn what to do, what not to do, but he is given standardized motives which promote prescribed actions and dissuade those proscribed. Along with rules and norms of action for various situations, we learn vocabularies of motives appropriate to them. These are the motives we shall use, since they are a part of our language and components of our behavior.

The quest for "real motives" supposititiously set over against "mere rationalization" is often informed by a metaphysical view that the "real"

---

[15] The "profits motive" of classical economics may be treated as an ideal-typical vocabulary of motives for delimited economic situations and behaviors. For late phases of monopolistic and regulated capitalism, this type requires modification; the profit and commercial vocabularies have acquired other ingredients. See N. R. Danielian's *AT&T*, New York, 1940, for a suggestive account of the *noneconomic* behavior and motives of business bureaucrats.

[16] *Social Actions*, 73.

motives are in some way biological. Accompanying such quests for something more real and back of rationalization is the view held by many sociologists that language is an external manifestation or concomitant of something prior, more genuine, and "deep" in the individual. "Real attitudes" versus "mere verbalization" or "opinion" implies that at best we only infer from his language what "really" is the individual's attitude or motive.

Now what *could we possibly* so infer? Of precisely *what* is verbalization symptomatic? We cannot *infer* physiological processes from lingual phenomena. All we can infer and empirically check[17] is another verbalization of the agent's which we believe was orienting and controlling behavior at the time the act was performed. The only social items that can "lie deeper" are other lingual forms.[18] The "Real Attitude or Motive" is not something different in kind from the verbalization or the "opinion." They turn out to be only relatively and temporally different.

The phrase "unconscious motive" is also unfortunate. All it can mean is that a motive is not explicitly vocalized, but there is no need to infer unconscious motives from such situations and then posit them in individuals as elements. The phrase is informed by persistence of the unnecessary and unsubstantiated notion that "all action has a motive," and it is promoted by the observation of gaps in the relatively frequent verbalization in everyday situations. The facts to which this phrase is supposedly addressed are covered by the statements that men do not always explicitly articulate motives, and that *all* actions do not pivot around language. I have already indicated the conditions under which motives are typically avowed and imputed.

Within the perspective under consideration, the verbalized motive is not used as an index of something in the individual but *as a basis of inference for a typal vocabulary of motives of a situated action.* When we ask for the "real attitude" rather than the "opinion," for the "real motive" rather than the "rationalization," all we can meaningfully be asking for is the controlling speech form which was incipiently or overtly presented in the performed act or series of acts. There is no way to plumb behind verbalization into an individual and directly check our motive-mongering, but there is an empirical way in which we can guide and limit, in given historical situations, investigations of motives. That is by the construction of typal vocabularies of motives that are extant in types of situations and actions. Imputation of motives may be controlled by reference to the typical constellation of motives which are

[17] Of course, we could infer or interpret constructs posited in the individual, but these are not easily checked and they are not explanatory.

[18] Which is not to say that, physiologically, there may not be cramps in the stomach wall or adrenalin in the blood, etc., but the character of the "relation" of such items to social action is quite moot.

observed to be societally linked with classes of situated actions. Some of the "real" motives that have been imputed to actors were not even known to them. As I see it, motives are circumscribed by the vocabulary of the actor. The only source for a terminology of motives is the vocabularies of motives actually and usually verbalized by actors in specific situations.

Individualistic, sexual, hedonistic, and pecuniary vocabularies of motives are apparently now dominant in many sectors of twentieth-century urban America. Under such an ethos, verbalization of alternative conduct in these terms is least likely to be challenged among dominant groups. In this milieu, individuals are skeptical of Rockefeller's avowed religious motives for his business conduct because such motives are not *now* terms of the vocabulary conventionally and prominently accompanying situations of business enterprise. A medieval monk writes that he gave food to a poor but pretty woman because it was "for the glory of God and the eternal salvation of his soul." Why do we tend to question him and impute sexual motives? Because sex is an influential and widespread motive in our society and time. Religious vocabularies of explanation and of motives are now on the wane. In a society in which religious motives have been debunked on rather wide scale, certain thinkers are skeptical of those who ubiquitously proclaim them. Religious motives have lapsed from selected portions of modern populations and other motives have become "ultimate" and operative. But from the monasteries of medieval Europe we have no evidence that religious vocabularies were not operative in many situations.

A labor leader says he performs a certain act because he wants to get higher standards of living for the workers. A business man says that this is rationalization, or a lie; that it is really because he wants more money for himself from the workers. A radical says a college professor will not engage in radical movements because he is afraid for his job, and besides, is a "reactionary." The college professor says it is because he just likes to find out how things work. What is reason for one man is rationalization for another. The variable is the accepted vocabulary of motives, the ultimates of discourse, of each man's dominant group about whose opinion he cares. *Determination of such groups, their location and character, would enable delimitation and methodological control of assignment of motives for specific acts.*

Stress on this idea will lead us to investigations of the compartmentalization of operative motives in personalities according to situation and the general types and conditions of vocabularies of motives in various types of societies. The motivational structures of individuals and the patterns of their purposes are relative to societal frames. We might, e.g., study motives along stratified or occupational lines. Max Weber has observed:

> . . . that in a free society the motives which induce people to work vary with . . . different social classes. . . . There is normally a graduated scale of motives by which men from different social classes are driven to work. When a man changes ranks, he switches from one set of motives to another.[19]

The lingual ties which hold them together react on persons to constitute frameworks of disposition and motive. Recently, Talcott Parsons has indicated, by reference to differences in actions in the professions and in business, that one cannot leap from "economic analysis to ultimate motivations; the institutional patterns *always* consitute one crucial element of the problem."[20] It is my suggestion that we may analyze, index, and gauge this element by focusing upon those specific verbal appendages of variant institutionalized actions which have been referred to as vocabularies of motive.

In folk societies, the constellations of motives connected with various sectors of behavior would tend to be typically stable and remain associated only with their sector. In typically primary, sacred, and rural societies, the motives of persons would be regularly compartmentalized. Vocabularies of motives ordered to different situations stabilize and guide behavior and expectation of the reactions of others. In their appropriate situations, verbalized motives are not typically questioned.[21] In secondary, secular, and urban structures, varying and competing vocabularies of motives operate coterminously and the situations to which they are appropriate are not clearly demarcated. Motives once unquestioned for defined situations are now questioned. Various motives can release similar acts in a given situation. Hence, variously situated persons are confused and guess which motive "activated" the person. Such questioning has resulted intellectually in such movements as psychoanalysis with its dogma of rationalization and its systematic motive-mongering. Such intellectual phenomena are underlaid by split and conflicting sec-

---

[19] Paraphrased by K. Mannheim, *op. cit.*, 316–317.

[20] "The Motivation of Economic Activities," 67, in C. W. M. Hart, *Essays in Sociology*, Toronto, 1940.

[21] Among the ethnologists, Ruth Benedict has come up to the edge of a genuinely sociological view of motivation. Her view remains vague because she has not seen clearly the identity of differing "motivations" in differing cultures with the varied extant and approved vocabularies of motive. "The intelligent understanding of the relation of the individual to his society . . . involves always the understanding of the types of human motivations and capacities capitalized in his society . . ." "Configurations of Culture in North America," *Amer. Anthrop.*, 25, Jan.–Mar. 1932; see also: *Patterns of Culture*, 242–243, Boston, 1935. She turns this observation into a quest for the unique "genius" of each culture and stops her research by words like "Apollonian." If she would attempt constructively to observe the vocabularies of motives which precipitate acts to perform, implement programs, and furnish approved motives for them in circumscribed situations, she would be better able to state precise problems and to answer them by further observation.

tions of an individuated society which is characterized by the existence of competing vocabularies of motive. Intricate constellations of motives, for example, are components of business enterprise in America. Such patterns have encroached on the old style vocabulary of the virtuous relation of men and women: duty, love, kindness. Among certain classes, the romantic, virtuous, and pecuniary motives are confused. The asking of the question: "Marriage for love or money?" is significant, for the pecuniary is now a constant and almost ubiquitous motive, a common denominator of many others.[22]

Back of "mixed motives" and "motivational conflicts" are competing or discrepant situational patterns and their respective vocabularies of motive. With shifting and interstitial situations, each of several alternatives may belong to disparate systems of action which have differing vocabularies of motives appropriate to them. Such conflicts manifest vocabulary patterns that have overlapped in a marginal individual and are not easily compartmentalized in clear-cut situations.

Besides giving promise of explaining an area of lingual and societal fact, a further advantage of this view of motives is that with it we should be able to give sociological accounts of other theories (terminologies) of motivation. This is a task for sociology of knowledge. Here I can refer only to a few theories. I have already referred to the Freudian terminology of motives. It is apparent that these motives are those of an upper bourgeois patriarchal group with strong sexual and individualistic orientation. When introspecting on the couches of Freud, patients used the only vocabulary of motives they knew; Freud got his hunch and guided further talk. Mittenzwey has dealt with similar points at length.[23] Widely diffused in a postwar epoch, psychoanalysis was never popular in France where control of sexual behavior is not puritanical.[24] To converted individuals who have become accustomed to the psychoanalytic terminology of motives, all others seem self-deceptive.[25]

In like manner, to many believers in Marxism's terminology of power, struggle, and economic motives, all others, including Freud's, are due to hypocrisy or ignorance. An individual who has assimilated thoroughly only business congeries of motives will attempt to apply these motives to all situations, home and wife included. It should be

---

[22] Also motives acceptably imputed and avowed for one system of action may be diffused into other domains and gradually come to be accepted by some as a comprehensive portrait of *the* motive of men. This happened in the case of the economic man and his motives.

[23] Kuno Mittenzwey, "Zur Sociologie der psychoanalystischer Erkenntnis," in Max Scheler, ed., *Versuche zu einer Sociologie des Wissens*, 365–375, Munich, 1924.

[24] This fact is interpreted by some as supporting Freudian theories. Nevertheless, it can be just as adequately grasped in the scheme here outlined.

[25] See K. Burke's acute discussion of Freud, *op. cit.*, Part I.

noted that the business terminology of motives has its intellectual articulation, even as psychoanalysis and Marxism have.

It is significant that since the Socratic period many "theories of motivation" have been linked with ethical and religious terminologies. Motive is that in man which leads him to do good or evil. Under the aegis of religious institutions, men use vocabularies of moral motives: they call acts and programs "good" and "bad," and impute these qualities to the soul. Such lingual behavior is part of the process of social control. Institutional practices and their vocabularies of motives exercise control over delimited ranges of possible situations. One could make a typal catalog of religious motives from widely read religious texts, and test its explanatory power in various denominations and sects.[26]

In many situations of contemporary America, conduct is controlled and integrated by *hedonistic* language. For large population sectors in certain situations, pleasure and pain are now unquestioned motives. For given periods and societies, the situations should be empirically determined. Pleasures and pain should not be reified and imputed to human nature as underlying principles of all action. Note that hedonism as a psychological and an ethical doctrine gained impetus in the modern world at about the time when older moral-religious motives were being debunked and simply discarded by "middle class" thinkers. Back of the hedonistic terminology lay an emergent social pattern and a new vocabulary of motives. The shift of unchallenged motives which gripped the communities of Europe was climaxed when, in reconciliation, the older religious and the hedonistic terminologies were identified: the "good" is the "pleasant." The conditioning situation was similar in the Hellenistic world with the hedonism of the Cyrenaics and Epicureans.

What is needed is to take all these *terminologies* of motive and locate them as *vocabularies* of motive in historic epochs and specified situations. Motives are of no value apart from the delimited societal situations for which they are the appropriate vocabularies. They must be situated. At best, socially unlocated *terminologies* of motives represent unfinished attempts to block out social areas of motive imputation and avowal. Motives vary in content and character with historical epochs and societal structures.

Rather than interpreting actions and languages as external manifestations of subjective and deeper lying elements in individuals, the research task is the locating of particular types of action within typal frames of normative actions and socially situated clusters of motive. There is no explanatory value in subsuming various vocabularies of motives under some terminology or list. Such procedure merely confuses the task of ex-

---

[26] Moral vocabularies deserve a special statement. Within the viewpoint herein outlined many snarls concerning "value-judgments," etc., can be cleared up.

plaining specific cases. The languages of situations as given must be considered a valuable portion of the data to be interpreted and related to their conditions. To simplify these vocabularies of motive into a socially abstracted terminology is to destroy the legitimate use of motive in the explanation of social actions.

36   MARVIN B. SCOTT & STANFORD M. LYMAN

Accounts

From time to time sociologists might well pause from their ongoing pursuits to inquire whether their research interests contribute in any way to the fundamental question of sociology, namely, the Hobbesian question: How is society possible? Attempts to answer this question could serve to unite a discipline that may not yet have forgotten its founders, but may still have forgotten why it was founded.

Our purpose here is not to review the various answers to the Hobbesian question,[1] but rather to suggest that an answer to this macro-sociological problem might be fruitfully explored in the analysis of the slightest of interpersonal rituals and the very stuff of which most of those rituals are composed—talk.

Talk, we hold, is the fundamental material of human relations. And though sociologists have not entirely neglected the subject,[2] the sociology of talk has scarcely been developed. Our concern here is with one feature of talk: Its ability to shore up the timbers of fractured sociation, its ability to throw bridges between the promised and the performed, its ability to repair the broken and restore the estranged. This feature of talk involves the giving and receiving of what we shall call *accounts*.

Marvin B. Scott and Stanford M. Lyman, "Accounts," *American Sociological Review*, vol. 33 (December 1968), pp. 46–62. Reprinted by permission.
    [1] For a now classic statement and analysis of the Hobbesian question, see the discussion by Talcott Parsons, *The Structure of Social Action*, Glencoe, Ill.: The Free Press, 1949, pp. 89–94.
    [2] See, for instance, William Soskin and Vera John, "The Study of Spontaneous Talk," in *The Stream of Behavior*, edited by Roger Barker, N.Y.: Appleton-Century-Crofts, 1963, pp. 228–282. Much suggestive material and a complete bibliography can be found in Joyce O. Hertzler, *A Sociology of Language*, N.Y.: Random House, 1965.

An account is a linguistic device employed whenever an action is subjected to valuative inquiry.[3] Such devices are a crucial element in the social order since they prevent conflicts from arising by verbally bridging the gap between action and expectation.[4] Moreover, accounts are "situated" according to the statuses of the interactants, and are standardized within cultures so that certain accounts are terminologically stabilized and routinely expected when activity falls outside the domain of expectations.

By an account, then, we mean a statement made by a social actor to explain unanticipated or untoward behavior—whether that behavior is his own or that of others, and whether the proximate cause for the statement arises from the actor himself or from someone else.[5] An account is not called for when people engage in routine, common-sense behavior in a cultural environment that recognizes that behavior as such. Thus in American society we do not ordinarily ask why married people engage in sexual intercourse, or why they maintain a home with their children, although the latter question might well be asked if such behavior occurred among the Nayars of Malabar.[6] These questions are not asked because they have been settled in advance in our culture and are indicated by the language itself. We learn the meaning of a "married couple" by indicating that they are two people of opposite sex who have a legitimate right to engage in sexual intercourse and maintain their own children in their own household. When such taken-for-granted phenomena are called into question, the inquirer (if a member of the same culture group) is regarded as "just fooling around," or perhaps as being sick.[7]

---

[3] An account has a family resemblance to the verbal component of a "motive" in Weber's sense of the term. Weber defined a motive as "a complex of subjective meaning which seems to the actor himself or to the observer as an adequate ground for the conduct in question." Max Weber, *Theory of Social and Economic Organization*, translated by Talcott Parsons and A. M. Henderson, Glencoe: The Free Press, 1947, pp. 98–99. Following Weber's definition and building on G. H. Mead's social psychology and the work of Kenneth Burke, C. Wright Mills was among the first to employ the notion of accounts in his much neglected essay, "Situated Action and the Vocabulary of Motives," *American Sociological Review*, 6 (December, 1940), pp. 904–913. Contemporary British philosophy, following the leads of Ludwig Wittgenstein, has (apparently) independently advanced the idea of a "vocabulary of motives." An exemplary case is R. S. Peters' *The Concept of Motivation*, London: Routledge and Kegan Paul, 1958.

[4] The point is nicely illustrated by Jackson Toby in "Some Variables in Role Conflict Analysis," *Social Forces*, 30 (March, 1952), pp. 323–327.

[5] Thus by an account we include also those non-vocalized but linguistic explanations that arise in an actor's "mind" when he questions his own behavior. However, our concern is with vocalized accounts and especially those that are given in face-to-face relations.

[6] William J. Goode, *World Revolution and Family Patterns*, New York: The Free Press of Glencoe, 1963, pp. 254–256.

[7] Moreover, common-sense understandings that violate widespread cognitive knowledge, such as are asserted in statements like "The sun rises every morning and sets every night," or avowed in perceptions that a straight stick immersed in water appears

To specify our concerns more sharply we should at his point distinguish accounts from the related phenomenon of "explanations." The latter refers to statements about events where untoward action is not an issue and does not have critical implications for a relationship. Much of what is true about accounts will also hold for explanations, but our concern is primarily with linguistic forms that are offered for untoward action. With this qualification to our concern, we may now specify further the nature and types of accounts.

Types of Accounts

There are in general two types of accounts: *excuses* and *justifications*.[8] Either or both are likely to be invoked when a person is accused of having done something that is "bad, wrong, inept, unwelcome, or in some other of the numerous possible ways, untoward."[9] Justifications are accounts in which one accepts responsibility for the act in question, but denies the pejorative quality associated with it. Thus a soldier in combat may admit that he has killed other men, but deny that he did an immoral act since those he killed were members of an enemy group and hence "deserved" their fate. Excuses are accounts in which one admits that the act in question is bad, wrong, or inappropriate but denies full responsibility. Thus our combat soldier could admit the wrongfulness of killing but claim that his acts are not entirely undertaken by volition: he is "under orders" and must obey. With these introductory remarks, we now turn our focus to a more detailed examination of types of justifications and excuses.

Excuses are socially approved vocabularies for mitigating or relieving responsibility when conduct is questioned. We may distinguish initially four modal forms by which excuses are typically formulated:[10] *appeal to accidents, appeal to defeasibility, appeal to biological drives,* and *scapegoating*.

Excuses claiming *accident* as the source of conduct or its consequences

---

bent, are expected to be maintained. Persons who always insist on the astronomically exact statement about the earth's relation to the sun might be considered officious or didactic, while those who "see" a straight stick in a pool might be credited with faulty eyesight. For a relevant discussion of social reactions to inquiries about taken-for-granted phenomena, see Harold Garfinkel, "Studies of the Routine Grounds of Everyday Activities," *Social Problems*, 11 (Winter, 1964), pp. 225–250, and "A Conception of and Experiments with 'Trust' as a Condition of Concerted Action," in *Motivation and Social Interaction*, edited by O. J. Harvey, N.Y.: Ronald Press, 1963, pp. 187–238.

8 We have taken this formulation from J. L. Austin. See his *Philosophical Papers*, London: Oxford University Press, 1961, pp. 123–152.

9 *Ibid.*, p. 124.

10 These types of excuses are to be taken as illustrative rather than as an exhaustive listing.

mitigate (if not relieve) responsibility by pointing to the generally recognized hazards in the environment, the understandable inefficiency of the body, and the human incapacity to control all motor responses. The excuse of accident is acceptable precisely because of the irregularity and infrequency of accidents occurring to any single actor. Thus while hazards are numerous and ubiquitous, a particular person is not expected ordinarily to experience the same accident often. In other words, social actors employ a lay version of statistical curves whereby they interpret certain acts as occurring or not occurring by chance alone. When a person conducts himself so that the same type of accident befalls him frequently, he is apt to earn a label—such as "clumsy"—which will operate to stigmatize him and to warn others not to put him and themselves or their property in jeopardy by creating the environment in which he regularly has accidents. When the excuse is rooted in an accident that is unobservable or unable to be investigated—such as blaming one's lateness to work on the heaviness of traffic—frequent pleas of it are likely to be discredited. Excuses based on accidents are thus most likely to be honored precisely because they do not occur all the time or for the most part to the actor in question.[11]

Appeals to *defeasibility*[12] are available as a form of excuse because of the widespread agreement that all actions contain some "mental element." The components of the mental element are "knowledge" and "will." One defense against an accusation is that a person was not fully informed or that his "will" was not completely "free." Thus an individual might excuse himself from responsibility by claiming that certain information was not available to him, which, if it had been, would have altered his behavior. Further, an individual might claim to have acted in a certain way because of misinformation arising from intentional or innocent misrepresentation of the facts by others. An excuse based on interference with the "free will" of an individual might invoke duress or undue influence. Finally both will and knowledge can be impaired under certain conditions, the invocation of which ordinarily constitutes an adequate mitigation of

---

[11] Only where nothing is left to chance—as among the Azande, where particular misfortunes are accounted for by a ubiquitous witchcraft—is the excuse by accident not likely to occur. Azande do not assert witchcraft to be the sole cause of phenomena; they have a "practical" and "realistic" approach to events which would enjoy consensual support from Occidental observers. However, Azande account for what Occidentals would call "chance" or "coincidence" by reference to witchcraft. E. E. Evans-Pritchard writes: "We have no explanation of why the two chains of causation [resulting in a catastrophe] intersected at a certain time and in a certain place, for there is no interdependence between them. Azande philosophy can supply the missing link. . . . It is due to witchcraft. . . . Witchcraft explains the coincidence of these two happenings." *Witchcraft, Oracles and Magic Among the Azande*, London: Oxford University Press, 1937, p. 70.

[12] Defeasibility, or the capacity of being voided, is a concept developed by H. L. A. Hart. This section leans heavily on Hart's essay, "The Ascription of Responsibility and Rights," in *Logic and Language, First Series*, edited by Anthony Flew, Oxford: Basil Blackwell, 1960, pp. 145–166.

responsibility—intoxication (whether from alcohol or drugs) and lunacy (whether temporary or permanent) being examples.

In ordinary affairs and in law a person's actions are usually distinguished according to their intent. Further, a person's intentions are distinguished from the consequences of his actions. Under a situation where an action is questioned an actor may claim a lack of intent or a failure to foresee the consequences of his act, or both. If the action in question involves a motor response—such as knocking over a vase—the situation is not very different from that subsumed under the term accident. When actions going beyond motor responses are at issue, the actor's intentions and foresight can be questioned. "Why did you make her cry?" asks the accuser. The presentational strategies in reply to this question allow several modes of defeating the central claim implied in the question, namely, that the actor intended with full knowledge to make the lady weep. The accused may simply deny any intention on his part to have caused the admittedly unfortunate consequence. However, men ordinarily impute to one another some measure of foresight for their actions so that a simple denial of intent may not be believed if it appears that the consequence of the action in question was indeed what another person might expect and therefore what the actor intended.

In addition to his denial of intent an actor may also deny his knowledge of the consequence. The simplest denial is the cognitive disclaimer: "I did not *know* that I would make her cry by what I did." But this complete denial of cognition is often not honored, especially when the interactants know one another well and are expected to have a more complete imagery of the consequences of their acts to guide them. A more complex denial—the gravity disclaimer—includes admitting to the possibility of the outcome in question but suggesting that its probability was incalculable: "I knew matters were serious, but I did not know that telling her would make her weep."

Still another type of excuse invokes biological drives. This invocation is part of a larger category of "fatalistic" forces which in various cultures are deemed in greater or lesser degree to be controlling of some or all events. Cultures dominated by universalist-achievement orientations[13] tend to give scant and ambiguous support to fatalistic interpretations of events, but rarely disavow them entirely. To account for the whole of one's life in such terms, or to account for events which are conceived by others to be controlled by the actor's conscience, will, and abilities is to lay oneself open to

[13] For a general discussion of cultures in terms of their "fatalistic" orientations or universalist-achievement orientations, see Talcott Parsons, "A Revised Analytical Approach to the Theory of Social Stratification," in *Essays in Sociological Theory*, The Free Press of Glencoe, 1954, pp. 386–439. See also Parsons, *The Social System*, Glencoe: The Free Press, 1951.

the charge of mental illness or personality disorganization.[14] On the other hand, recent studies have emphasized the situational element in predisposing certain persons and groups in American society to what might be regarded as a "normalized" fatalistic view of their condition. Thus, for example, Negroes[15] and adolescent delinquents[16] are regarded and tend to regard themselves as less in control of the forces that shape their lives than Whites or middle-class adults.

Among the fatalistic items most likely to be invoked as an excuse are the biological drives. Despite the emphasis in Occidental culture since the late nineteenth century on personality and social environment as causal elements in human action, there is still a popular belief in and varied commitment to the efficacy of the body and biological factors in determining human behavior. Such commonplaces as "men are like that" are shorthand phrases invoking belief in sex-linked traits that allegedly govern behavior beyond the will of the actor. Precisely because the body and its biological behavior are always present but not always accounted for in science or society, invocation of the body and its processes is available as an excuse. The body and its inner workings enjoy something of the status of the sociological stranger as conceived by Simmel, namely, they are ever with us but mysterious. Hence, biological drives may be credited with influencing or causing at least some of the behavior for which actors wish to relieve themselves of full responsibility.

The invocation of biological drives is most commonly an appeal to natural but uncontrollable sexual appetite. Among first and second generation Italians in America the recognition and fear of biologically induced sexual intercourse serves men as both an excuse for pre- and extra-marital sexual relations and a justification for not being alone with women ineligible for coitus. Thus one student of Italian-American culture observes:

> What the men fear is their own ability at self-control. This attitude, strongest among young unmarried people, often carries over into adulthood.

[14] Thus, in the most famous study of the psychodynamics of prejudice, one of the characteristics of the intolerant or "authoritarian" personality is "externalization," i.e., the attribution of causality of events believed to be within the actor's power or rational comprehension to uncontrollable forces beyond his influence or understanding. See T. W. Adorno, *et al.*, *The Authoritarian Personality*, N.Y.: Harper and Row, 1950, pp. 474–475. See also Gordon W. Allport, *The Nature of Prejudice*, Garden City: Doubleday Anchor, 1958, p. 379. In a recent study an intermittently employed cab driver's insistence that there would inevitably be a revolution after which the world would be taken over by Negroes and Jews is recalled as one of several early warning cues that he is mentally ill. Marion Radke Yarrow, *et al.*, "The Psychological Meaning of Mental Illness in the Family," in Thomas J. Scheff, *Mental Illness and Social Process*, N.Y.: Harper and Row, 1967, p. 35.

[15] See Horace R. Cayton, "The Psychology of the Negro Under Discrimination," in Arnold Rose, editor, *Race Prejudice and Discrimination*, N.Y.: Alfred Knopf, 1953, pp. 276–290; and Bertram P. Karon, *The Negro Personality*, N.Y.: Springer, 1958, pp. 8–53, 140–160.

[16] David Matza, *Delinquency and Drift*, N.Y.: Wiley, 1964, pp. 88–90, 188–191.

The traditional Italian belief—that sexual intercourse is unavoidable when a man and a woman are by themselves—is maintained intact among second-generation Italians, and continues even when sexual interest itself is on the wane. For example, I was told of an older woman whose apartment was adjacent to that of an unmarried male relative. Although they had lived in the same building for almost twenty years and saw each other every day, she had never once been in his apartment because of this belief.[17]

Biological drive may be an expected excuse in some cultures, so that the failure to invoke it, and the use of some other excuse, constitutes an improper account when the appropriate one is available. Oscar Lewis provides such an example in his ethnography of a Mexican family. A cuckolded wife angrily rejects her wayward husband's explanation that the red stains on his shirt are due to paint rubbed off during the course of his work. She strongly suggests, in her retelling of the incident, that she would have accepted an excuse appealing to her husband's basic sex drives:

And he had me almost believing it was red paint! It was not that I am jealous. I realize a man can never be satisfied with just one woman, but I cannot stand being made a fool of.[18]

Homosexuals frequently account for their deviant sexual desires by invoking the principle of basic biological nature. As one homosexual put it:

It's part of nature. You can't alter it, no matter how many injections and pills they give you.[19]

Another of the biological elements that can be utilized as an excuse is the shape of the body itself. Body types are not only defined in purely anatomical terms, but also, and perhaps more importantly, in terms of their shared social meanings. Hence fat people can excuse their excessive laughter by appealing to the widely accepted proverb that fat men are jolly. Similarly persons bearing features considered to be stereotypically "criminal"[20] may be exonerated for their impoliteness or small larcenies on the grounds that their looks proved their intentions and thus their victims ought to have been on guard. The phrase, "he looks crooked to me," serves as a

[17] Herbert J. Gans, *The Urban Villagers*, N.Y.: The Free Press, 1962, p. 49. According to another student of Italian-American life, slum-dwelling members of this subculture believe that "a man's health requires sexual intercourse at certain intervals." William F. Whyte, "A Slum Sex Code," *American Journal of Sociology*, 49 (July, 1943), p. 26.

[18] Oscar Lewis, *The Children of Sanchez*, N.Y.: Random House, 1961, p. 475.

[19] Gordon Westwood, *A Minority*, London: Longmans, Green and Co., 1960, p. 46.

[20] For an interesting study showing that criminals believe that a fellow criminal's physical attractiveness will vary with type of crime—robbers are the most attractive, murderers the least; rapists are more attractive than pedophiles, etc.—see Raymond J. Corsini, "Appearance and Criminality," *American Journal of Sociology*, 65 (July, 1959), pp. 49–51.

warning to others to carefully appraise the character and intentions of the person so designated, since his features bespeak an illegal intent.

The final type of excuse we shall mention is *scapegoating*. Scapegoating is derived from another form of fatalistic reasoning. Using this form a person will allege that his questioned behavior is a response to the behavior or attitudes of another. Certain psychological theory treats this phenomenon as indicative of personality disorder, and, if found in conjunction with certain other characteristic traits, a signal of authoritarian personality.[21] Our treatment bypasses such clinical and pathological concerns in order to deal with the "normal" situation in which individuals slough off the burden of responsibility for their actions and shift it on to another. In Mexican working-class society, for example, women hold a distinctly secondary position relative to men, marriage causes a loss of status to the latter, and sexual intercourse is regarded ambivalently as healthy and natural, but also as a necessary evil.[22] Such a set of orientations predisposes both men and women to attribute many of their shortcomings to women. An example is found in the autobiography of a Mexican girl:

> I was always getting into fights because some girls are vipers; they get jealous, tell lies about each other, and start trouble.[23]

Similarly, a Mexican youth who tried unsuccessfully to meet a girl by showing off on a bicycle explains:

> She got me into trouble with my father by lying about me. She said I tried to run her down with my bike and that all I did was hang around spying on her.[24]

In another instance the same youth attributes his waywardness to the fact that the girl truly loved was his half-sister and thus unavailable to him for coitus or marriage:

> So, because of Antonia, I began to stay away from home. It was one of the main reasons I started to go on the bum, looking for trouble.[25]

Like excuses, *justifications* are socially approved vocabularies that neutralize an act or its consequences when one or both are called into question. But here is the crucial difference: to *justify* an act is to assert its positive value in the face of a claim to the contrary. Justifications recog-

---

[21] Adorno, *op. cit.*, pp. 233, 485; Allport, *op. cit.*, pp. 235–249, suggests the historicity and uniqueness of each instance of scapegoating.

[22] Arturo de Hoyos and Genevieve de Hoyos, "The Amigo System and Alienation of the Wife in the Conjugal Mexican Family," in Bernard Farber, editor, *Kinship and Family Organization*, N.Y.: Wiley, 1966, pp. 102–115, esp., pp. 103–107.

[23] Lewis, *op. cit.*, p. 143.

[24] *Ibid.*, p. 202.

[25] *Ibid.*, p. 86.

nize a general sense in which the act in question is impermissible, but claim that the particular occasion permits or requires the very act. The laws governing the taking of life are a case in point. American and English jurisprudence are by no means united on definitions or even on the nature of the acts in question, but in general a man may justify taking the life of another by claiming that he acted in self-defense, in defense of others' lives or property, or in action against a declared enemy of the state.

For a tentative list of types of justifications we may turn to what has been called "techniques of neutralization."[26] Although these techniques have been discussed with respect to accounts offered by juvenile delinquents for untoward action, their wider use has yet to be explored. Relevant to our discussion of justification are the techniques of "denial of injury," "denial of victim," "condemnation of condemners," and "appeal to loyalties."[27]

In *denial of injury* the actor acknowledges that he did a particular act but asserts that it was permissible to do that act since no one was injured by it, or since no one about whom the community need be concerned with was involved, or finally since the act resulted in consequences that were trifling. Note that this justification device can be invoked with respect to both persons and objects. The denial of injury to *persons* suggests that they be viewed as "deserving" in a special sense: that they are oversupplied with the valued things of the world, or that they are "private" persons ("my friends," "my enemies") who have no standing to claim injury in the public, or to be noticed as injured. Denial of injury to *objects* involves redefining the act as not injurious to it but only using it, e.g., car "borrowing" is not theft.

In *denial of the victim* the actor expresses the position that the action was permissible since the victim deserved the injury. Four categories of persons are frequently perceived as deserving injury. First, there are proximate foes, i.e., those who have directly injured the actor; second, incumbents of normatively discrepant roles, e.g., homosexuals, whores, pimps; third, groups with tribal stigmas, e.g., racial and ethnic minorities; and finally, distant foes, that is, incumbents of roles held to be dubious or hurtful, e.g., "Whitey" the "Reds," "politicians." Besides categories of persons, there are categories of objects perceived as deserving of injury. To begin with, the property of any of the above mentioned categories of persons may become a focus of attack, especially if that property is symbolic of the attacked person's status. Thus the clothing of the whore is torn, the gavel of the politician is smashed, and so on. Secondly, there are objects that have a neutral or ambiguous identity with respect to ownership, e.g., a

---

26 Gresham M. Sykes and David Matza, "Techniques of Neutralization," *American Sociological Review*, 22 (December, 1957), pp. 667–669.

27 One other neutralization technique mentioned by Sykes and Matza, "denial of responsibility," is subsumed in our schema under "appeal to defeasibility."

park bench. A final focus of attacked objects are those having a low or polluted value, e.g., junk, or kitsch.

Using the device of *condemnation of the condemners,* the actor admits performing an untoward act but asserts its irrelevancy because others commit these and worse acts, and these others are either not caught, not punished, not condemned, unnoticed, or even praised.

Still another neutralization technique is *appeal to loyalties.* Here the actor asserts that his action was permissible or even right since it served the interests of another to whom he owes an unbreakable allegiance or affection.[28]

Besides these "techniques of neutralization," two other sorts of justification may be mentioned: "sad tales," and "self-fulfillment." The *sad tale* is a selected (often distorted) arrangement of facts that highlight an extremely dismal past, and thus "explain" the individual's present state.[29] For example, a mental patient relates:

> I was going to night school to get an M.A. degree, and holding down a job in addition, and the load got too much for me.[30]

And a homosexual accounts for his present deviance with this sad tale:

> I was in a very sophisticated queer circle at the university. It was queer in a sense that we all camped like mad with "my dear" at the beginning of every sentence, but there was practically no sex, and in my case there was none at all. The break came when I went to a party and flirted with a merchant seaman who took me seriously and cornered me in a bedroom. There was I, the great sophisticate, who, when it came to the point, was quite raw, completely inexperienced; and I might tell you that seaman gave

[28] Note that appeal to loyalties could be an *excuse* if the argument runs that X did do A under the influence of Y's domination or love, or under the coercive influence of Y's injury to him were he not to act, e.g., loss of love, blackmail, etc. In other words, appeal to loyalties is an excuse if X admits it was bad to do A, but refuses to monopolize responsibility for A in himself.

[29] Erving Goffman, *Asylums,* Garden City: Doubleday Anchor, 1961, pp. 150–151. The sad tale involves the most dramatic instance of the general process of reconstructing personal biography whereby—for example—a husband may account for his present divorce by reconstructing the history of earlier events in an ascending scale leading up to the final dissolution. The idea of a reconstruction of biography is a continual theme in the writings of Alfred Schutz. See his *Collected Papers,* Vol. I, edited by Maurice Natanson, The Hague: Martinus Nijhoff, 1962. A short clear summary of Schutz's contribution on the reconstruction of biography is found in Peter L. Berger, *Invitation to Sociology,* Garden City: Doubleday Anchor, 1963, pp. 54–65. Drawing on Schutz, Garfinkel details the concept of reconstruction of biography in a series of experiments on the "retrospective reading" of social action. See his "Common Sense Knowledge of Social Structures," in *Theories of the Mind,* edited by Jordon M. Scher, Glencoe: The Free Press, 1962, pp. 689–712. The empirical use of the concept of retrospective reading of action is nicely illustrated by John I. Kitsuse, "Societal Reaction to Deviant Behavior," in *The Other Side,* edited by Howard S. Becker, N.Y.: The Free Press of Glencoe, 1964, pp. 87–102.

[30] Goffman, *op. cit.,* p. 152.

me quite a shock. I can't say I enjoyed it very much but it wasn't long after before I started to dive into bed with anyone.[31]

Finally we may mention a peculiarly modern type of justification, namely, *self-fulfillment*. Interviewing LSD users and homosexuals in the Haight-Asbury district of San Francisco, we are struck by the prominence of self-fulfillment as the grounds for these activities. Thus, an "acid head" relates:

> The whole purpose in taking the stuff is self-development. Acid expands consciousness. Mine eyes have seen the glory—can you say that? I never knew what capacities I had until I went on acid.[32]

And a Lesbian:

> Everyone has the right to happiness and love. I was married once. It was hell. But now I feel I have fulfilled myself as a person and as a woman.[33]

We might also note that the drug users and homosexuals interviewed (in San Francisco) who invoked the justification of self-fulfillment did not appear to find anything "wrong" with their behavior. They indicated either a desire to be left alone or to enlighten what they considered to be the unenlightened establishment.

Honoring Accounts, and Background Expectations

Accounts may be honored or not honored. If an account is honored, we may say that it was efficacious and equilibrium is thereby restored in a relationship. The most common situation in which accounts are routinely honored is encounters interrupted by "incidents"—slips, boners, or gaffes which introduce information deleterious to the otherwise smooth conduct of the interactants.[34] Often a simple excuse will suffice, or the other interactants will employ covering devices to restore the *status quo ante*. A related situation is that in which an individual senses that some incident or event has cast doubt on that image of himself which he seeks to present. "At such times," the authority on impression management writes, "the individual is likely to try to integrate the incongruous events by means of apologies, little excuses for self, and disclaimers; through the same acts, incidentally, he also tries to save his face."[35]

---

31 Westwood, *op. cit.*, p. 32.
32 Tape-recorded interview, May 1967.
33 Tape-recorded interview, June 1967.
34 Erving Goffman, *Encounters*, Indianapolis: Bobbs-Merrill, 1961, pp. 45–48.
35 *Ibid.*, p. 51.

One variable governing the honoring of an account is the character of the social circle in which it is introduced. As we pointed out earlier, vocabularies of accounts are likely to be routinized within cultures, sub-cultures and groups, and some are likely to be exclusive to the circle in which they are employed. A drug addict may be able to justify his conduct to a bohemian world, but not to the courts. Similarly kin and friends may accept excuses in situations in which strangers would refuse to do so. Finally, while ignorance of the consequences of an act or of its prohibition may exculpate an individual in many different circles, the law explicitly rejects this notion: "Ignorance of the law excuses no man; not that all men know the law but because 'tis an excuse every man will plead, and no man can tell how to confute him."[36]

Both the account offered by *ego* and the honoring or non-honoring of the account on the part of *alter* will ultimately depend on the *background expectancies* of the interactants. By background expectancies we refer to those sets of taken-for-granted ideas that permit the interactants to interpret remarks as accounts in the first place.[37] Asked why he is listless and de-pressed, a person may reply, "I have family troubles." The remark will be taken as an account, and indeed an account that will probably be honored, because "everyone knows" that "family problems" are a cause of depression.

This last illustration suggests that certain accounts can fit a variety of situations. Thus in response to a wide range of questions—Why don't you get married? Why are you in a fit of depression? Why are you drinking so heavily?—the individual can respond with "I'm having family problems." The person offering such an account may not himself regard it as a true one, but invoking it has certain interactional payoffs: since people cannot say they don't understand it—they are accounts that are part of our socially distributed knowledge of what "everyone knows"—the inquiry can be cut short.

Clearly, then, a single account will stand for a wide collection of events, and the efficacy of such accounts depends upon a set of shared back-ground expectations.

In interacting with others, the socialized person learns a repertoire of background expectations that are appropriate for a variety of others. Hence the "normal" individual will change his account for different role others. A wife may respond sympathetically to her depressed husband because his favorite football team lost a championship game, but such an account for

---

[36] John Selden, *Table Talk*, 1696, quoted in Harry Johnson, *Sociology*, New York: Harcourt, Brace and Co., 1960, p. 552n.

[37] The term is borrowed from Harold Garfinkel. Besides the footnote references to Garfinkel already cited, see his *Studies in Ethnomethodology*, Englewood Cliffs, N.J.: Prentice-Hall, 1968. For an original discussion on how the meaning of an account de-pends upon background expectancies and a methodology for its study, see Harvey Sacks, *The Search for Help*, unpublished doctoral dissertation, University of California, Berkeley, 1966.

depression will appear bizarre when offered to one's inquiring boss. Thus background expectancies are the means not only for the honoring, but also for the non-honoring of accounts. When the millionaire accounts for his depression by saying he is a failure, others will be puzzled since "everyone knows" that millionaires are not failures. The incapacity to invoke situationally appropriate accounts, i.e., accounts that are anchored to the background expectations of the situation, will often be taken as a sign of mental illness.[38] There are grounds then for conceptualizing normal individuals as "not stupid" rather than "not ill."[39] The person who is labeled ill has been behaving "stupidly" in terms of his culture and society: he offers accounts not situationally appropriate according to culturally defined background expectations.[40]

Often an account can be discredited by the appearance of the person offering an account. When a girl accounts for her late return from a date by saying the movie was overlong—that no untoward event occurred and that she still retains virgin status—her mother may discredit the account by noting the daughter's flushed appearance. Since individuals are aware that appearances may serve to credit or discredit accounts, efforts are understandably made to control these appearances through a vast repertoire of "impression management" activities.[41]

When an account is not honored it will be regarded as either *illegitimate* or *unreasonable*. An account is treated as *illegitimate* when the gravity of the event exceeds that of the account or when it is offered in a circle where its vocabulary of motives is unacceptable. As illustration of the former we may note that accidentally allowing a pet turtle to drown may be forgiven, but accidentally allowing the baby to drown with the same degree of oversight may not so easily be excused. As illustration of the latter, male prostitutes may successfully demonstrate their masculinity within the sub-

[38] On how background expectations are used to determine whether a person is judged criminal or sick see the neglected essay by Vilhelm Aubert and Sheldon L. Messinger, "The Criminal and the Sick," *Inquiry*, 1 (Autumn, 1958), pp. 137–160.

[39] This formulation is persistently (and we believe rightly) argued in the various writings of Ernest Becker. See especially *The Revolution in Psychiatry*, N.Y.: The Free Press of Glencoe, 1964; and his essay "Mills' Social Psychology and the Great Historical Convergence on the Problem of Alienation," in *The New Sociology*, edited by Irving L. Horowitz, N.Y.: Oxford University Press, 1964, pp. 108–133.

[40] In the case of schizophrenics, it has been noted that they are individuals who construct overly elaborate accounts, i.e., accounts that are perceived as being elaborately constructed. These accounts, it appears, take the form of "building up" the possibilities of a situation that others find improbable. Thus the paranoid husband accounts for his frenzied state by relating that his wife went shopping—and, to him, going shopping constitutes the most opportune occasion to rendezvous secretly with a lover. In response to the inquirer, the paranoid asks: "If you wanted to meet a lover, wouldn't you tell your spouse you're going shopping?" For a general discussion, see Becker, *The Revolution in Psychiatry, op. cit.*

[41] Erving Goffman, *Presentation of Self in Everyday Life*, University of Edinburgh, 1956.

culture of persons who regularly resort to homosexual acts by insisting that they are never fellators, but such a defense is not likely in heterosexual circles to lift from them the label of "queer."[42]

An account is deemed *unreasonable* when the stated grounds for action cannot be "normalized" in terms of the background expectancies of what "everybody knows." Hence when a secretary explained that she placed her arm in a lighted oven because voices had commanded her to do so in punishment for her evil nature, the account was held to be grounds for commitment to an asylum.[43] In general those who persist in giving unreasonable accounts for questioned actions are likely to be labeled as mentally ill. Or, to put this point another way, unreasonable accounts are one of the sure indices by which the mentally ill are apprehended. Conversely, those persons labeled as mentally ill may relieve themselves of the worst consequence of that label by recognizing before their psychiatrists the truth value of the label, by reconstructing their past to explain how they came to deviate from normal patterns, and by gradually coming to give acceptable accounts for their behavior.[44]

Beyond illegitimacy and unreasonableness are special types of situations in which accounts may not be acceptable. One such type involves the incorrect invocation of "commitment" or "attachment"[45] in account situations where one or the other, but only the correct one, is permitted. By commitment we refer to that role orientation in which one has through investiture become liable and responsible for certain actions. By attachment we refer to the sense of vesting one's feelings and identity in a role. Certain statuses, especially those dealing with distasteful activities or acts that are condemned except when performed by licensed practitioners, are typically expected to invest their incumbents with only commitment and not with attachment. Hangmen who, when questioned about their occupation, profess to be emotionally attracted to killing, are not likely to have their account honored. Indeed, distasteful tasks are often imputed to have a clandestine but impermissible allure, and so those who regularly perform them are often on their guard to assert their commitment, but not their attachment to the task.

Organizations systematically provide accounts for their members in a variety of situations. The rules of bureaucracy, for instance, make available accounts for actions taken toward clients—actions which, from the

[42] Albert J. Reiss, Jr., "The Social Integration of Queers and Peers," in *The Other Side, op. cit.*, pp. 181–210.

[43] Marguerite Sechehaye, *Autobiography of a Schizophrenic Girl*, New York: Grune and Stratton, 1951.

[44] See Thomas Scheff, *Being Mentally Ill*, Chicago: Aldine Press, 1966. See also Erving Goffman, *Asylums, op. cit.*

[45] These terms are adapted from Erving Goffman, *Behavior in Public Places*, N.Y.: The Free Press of Glencoe, 1963, p. 36n, and *Encounters, op. cit.*, pp. 105 ff.

viewpoint of the client, are untoward.[46] Again, these accounts "work" because of a set of background expectations. Thus when people say they must perform a particular action because it is a rule of the organization, the account is regarded as at least reasonable, since "everyone knows" that people follow rules. Of course, the gravity of the event may discredit such accounts, as the trials of Nazi war criminals dramatically illustrate.[47]

Under certain situations behavior that would ordinarily require an account is normalized without interruption or any call for an account. Typically such situations are social conversations in which the values to be obtained by the total encounter supersede those which would otherwise require excuses or justifications. Two values that may override the requirement of accounts are *sociability* and *information*.

In the case of *sociability* the desire that the interactional circle be uninterrupted by any event that might break it calls for each interactant to weigh carefully whether or not the calling for an account might disrupt the entire engagement. When the gathering is a convivial one not dedicated to significant matters—that is, matters that have a proactive life beyond the engagement itself—the participants may overlook errors, inept statements, lies, or discrepancies in the statements of others. Parties often call for such behavior but are vulnerable to disruption by one who violates the unwritten rule of not questioning another too closely. In unserious situations in which strangers are privileged to interact as a primary group without future rights of similar interaction—such as in bars—the interactants may construct elaborate and self-contradictory biographies without fear of being called to account.[48]

In some engagements the interactants seek to obtain *information* from the speaker which is incidental to his main point but which might be withheld if any of the speaker's statements were called into account. Among the Japanese, for example, the significant item in a conversation may be circumscribed by a verbal wall of trivia and superfluous speech. To interrupt a speaker by calling for an account might halt the conversation altogether or detour the speaker away from disclosing the particularly valued pieces of information.[49] Among adolescent boys in American society engaged in a "bull session" it is usually inappropriate to challenge a speaker describing his sexual exploits since, no matter how embellished and exaggerated the account might be, it permits the hearers to glean knowledge

---

[46] The theme is widely explored in the literature on formal organizations. For an early and perhaps still the clearest statement of the theme, see Robert K. Merton's widely reprinted "Bureaucratic Structure and Personality," available in *Complex Organizations*, edited by Amitai Etzioni, New York: Holt, Rinehart and Winston, 1962, pp. 48–60.

[47] For a literary illustration, see the play by Peter Weiss, *The Investigation*, N.Y.: Atheneum Books, 1967.

[48] See Sherri Cavan, *Liquor Licences*, Chicago: Aldine Press, 1966, pp. 79–87.

[49] Edward T. Hall, *The Hidden Dimension*, Garden City: Doubleday, 1966, pp. 139–144.

about sex—ordinarily withheld from them in the regular channels of education—with impunity. Calling for an account in the midst of such disclosures, especially when the account would require a discussion of the speaker's morality, might cut off the hearers from obtaining precisely that kind of information which is in no other way available to them.[50]

So far we have discussed accounts in terms of their content, but it should be pointed out that accounts also differ in form or style. Indeed, as we will now suggest, the style of an account will have bearing on its honoring or dishonoring.

Linguistic Styles and Accounts

We may distinguish five linguistic styles that frame the manner in which an account will be given and often indicate the social circle in which it will be most appropriately employed. These five styles, which in practice often shade into one another and are not unambiguously separated in ordinary life, are the *intimate, casual, consultative, formal,* and *frozen* styles.[51] These styles, as we shall see, are ordered on a scale of decreasing social intimacy.[52]

The *intimate* style is the socially sanctioned linguistic form employed among persons who share a deep, intense and personal relationship. The group within which it is employed is usually a dyad—lovers, a married pair, or very close friends. The group can be larger but not much larger, and when it reaches four or five it is strained to its limits. The verbal style employs single sounds or words, and jargon, to communicate whole ideas. An account given in this form may be illustrated by the situation in which a husband, lying beside his wife in bed, caresses her but receives no endearing response. His wife utters the single word, "pooped." By this term the husband understands that the account given in response to his unverbalized question, "Why don't you make love to me? After all I am your husband. You have wifely duties!" is "I realize that under ordinary circumstances I should and indeed would respond to your love making, but tonight I am too exhausted for that kind of activity. Do not take it to mean that I have lost affection for you, or that I take my wifely duties lightly."

[50] When a boy is interrupted by a call for an account in the midst of his own recounting of sexual exploits he may simply relapse into uncommunicative silence, change the subject, or withdraw from the group. To prevent any of these, and to aid in the continuity of the original story, the other members of the audience may urge the speaker to continue as before, assure him of their interest and support, and sharply reprove or perhaps ostracize from the group the person who called for the account.

[51] We have adapted these styles from Martin Joos, *The Five Clocks*, N.Y.: Harbinger Books, 1961.

[52] Each of these linguistic styles is associated with distinctive physical distances between the interactants. For a discussion of this point see Hall, *op. cit.*, pp. 116–122.

The *casual* style is used among peers, ingroup members and insiders. It is a style employed by those for whom the social distance is greater than that among intimates but is still within the boundaries of a primary relationship. Typically it employs ellipses, i.e., omissions, and slang. In casual style certain background information is taken for granted among the interactants and may be merely alluded to in order to give an account. Thus among those who are regular users of hallucinogenic drugs, the question "Why were you running about naked in the park?" might be answered, "I was 'on.'" The hearer will then know that the speaker was under the influence of a familiar drug and was engaged in an activity that is common in response to taking that drug.

While each style differs from that to which it is juxtaposed by degree, the difference between any two styles—skipping an interval on the aforementioned social intimacy scale—is one of kind. Thus intimate and casual styles differ only in degree from one another and suggest a slight but significant difference in social distance among the interactants, but the *consultative* style differs in kind from the intimate. Consultative style is that verbal form ordinarily employed when the amount of knowledge available to one of the interactants is unknown or problematic to the others. Typically in such an interaction the speaker supplies background information which he is unsure the hearer possesses, and the hearer continuously participates by means of linguistic signs and gestures which indicate that he understands what is said or that he requires more background information. In offering accounts in this form there is a definite element of "objectivity," i.e., of non-subjective and technical terms. The individual giving an account relies on reference to things and ideas outside the intimate and personal realm. In response to the question, "Why are you smoking marijuana? Don't you know that it's dangerous?", the individual might reply, "I smoke marijuana because everybody who's read the LaGuardia Report knows that it's not habit forming." But a casual response might be simply, "Don't be square."

Formal style is employed when the group is too large for informal co-participation to be a continuous part of the interaction. Typically it is suited to occasions when an actor addresses an audience greater than six. Listeners must then wait their turn to respond, or, if they interject comments, know that this will be an untoward event, requiring some kind of re-structuring of the situation. Speaker and audience are in an active and a passive role, respectively, and, if the group is large enough, may be obligated to speak or remain silent according to pre-established codes of procedure. Formal style may also be employed when speaker and auditor are in rigidly defined statuses. Such situations occur in bureaucratic organizations between persons in hierarchically differentiated statuses, or in the courtroom, in the interaction between judge and defendant.

Frozen style is an extreme form of formal style employed among those who are simultaneously required to interact and yet remain social strangers. Typically interaction in the frozen style occurs among those between whom an irremovable barrier exists. The barrier may be of a material or a social nature, or both. Thus pilots communicate to air scanners in a control tower in the same lingual style as prisoners of war to their captors or telephone operators to angered clients. Often the frozen accounts offered are tutored, memorized or written down in advance, and they may be applicable to a variety of situations. Thus the prisoner of war reiterates his name, rank and serial number to all questions and refers his interrogators to the Geneva Convention. The pilot replies to questions about his aberrant flight pattern, coming from the anonymous control tower, with a smooth flow of technical jargon quoted from his handbook on flying. The telephone operator refuses to become flustered or angered by the outraged demands and accusations of the caller unable to reach his party, and quotes from memory the rules of telephone conduct required of the situation.

In summary, then, accounts are presented in a variety of idioms. The idiomatic form of an account is expected to be socially suited to the circle into which it is introduced, according to norms of culture, subculture, and situation. The acceptance or refusal of an offered account in part depends on the appropriateness of the idiom employed. Failure to employ the proper linguistic style often results in a dishonoring of the account or calls for further accounts. Sometimes the situation results in requirements of compound accounting wherein an individual, having failed to employ idiomatic propriety in his first account, is required not only to reaccount for his original untoward act but also to present an account for the unacceptable language of his first account. Note that idiomatic errors on the part of a person giving an account provide an unusual opportunity for the hearer to dishonor or punish the speaker if he so wishes. Thus even if the content of the tendered account is such as to excuse or justify the act, a hearer who wishes to discredit the speaker may "trip him up" by shifting the subject away from the matter originally at hand and onto the form of the account given. Typical situations of this kind arise when persons of inferior status provide substantially acceptable accounts for their allegedly untoward behavior to their inquiring superiors but employ idiomatically unacceptable or condemnable form. Thus school children who excuse their fighting with others by not only reporting that they were acting in self-defense but also, and in the process, by using profanity may still be punished for linguistic impropriety, even if they are let off for their original defalcation.[53]

---

[53] Besides the five linguistic styles discussed, we may note that accounts may be usefully distinguished in the manner of their *delivery*. For a cogent typology see Robert E. Pittenger, *et al.*, *The First Five Minutes*, Ithaca, N.Y.: Paul Martineau, 1960, p. 255.

Strategies for Avoiding Accounts

The vulnerability of actors to questions concerning their conduct varies with the situation and the status of the actors. Where hierarchies of authority govern the social situation, the institutionalized office may eliminate the necessity of an account, or even prevent the question from arising. Military officers are thus shielded from accountability to their subordinates. Where culture distance and hierarchy are combined—as in the case of slaveholders vis-à-vis their new imported slaves—those enjoying the superior status are privileged to leave their subordinates in a perplexed and frightened state.[54]

Besides the invulnerability to giving accounts arising from the status and position of the actors are the strategies that can prevent their announcement. We may refer to these strategies as meta-accounts. Three such strategies are prominent: *mystification, referral,* and *identity switching.*[55]

When the strategy of *mystification* is employed an actor admits that he is not meeting the expectations of another, but follows this by pointing out that, although there are reasons for his unexpected actions, he cannot tell the inquirer what they are. In its simplest sense the actor says "It's a long story," and leaves it at that. Such accounts are most likely to be honored under circumstances which would normally hinder an elaborate account, as when students have a chance meeting while rushing off to scheduled classes.

More complicated versions of mystification are those that suggest that *alter* is not aware of certain facts—facts that are secret—which, if known, would explain the untoward action. Typically this is the response of the charismatic leader to his followers or the expert to his naive assistant. Thus does Jesus sometimes mystify his disciples and Sherlock Holmes his Dr. Watson. Finally, as already mentioned, certain statuses suggest mystification: in addition to charismatic leaders and experts at occult or little-understood arts are all those statuses characterized by specialized information including (but not limited to) doctors, lawyers, and spies.

Using the strategy of *referral,* the individual says, "I know I'm not meeting your expectations but if you wish to know why, please see. . . ." Typically referral is a strategy available to the sick and the subordinate. Illness, especially mental illness, allows the sick person to refer inquiries

[54] Another kind of invulnerability arises in those situations in which physical presence is tantamount to task performance. Students in a classroom, parishioners in a church, and soldiers at a drill may be counted as "present"–their very visibility being all that is required for routine performance–although they might be "away" in the vicarious sense of day-dreaming, musing on other matters, or relaxing into a reverie.

[55] For these terms, in the context of strategies for avoiding accounts, we are indebted to Gregory Stone.

about his behavior to his doctor or psychiatrist. Subordinates may avoid giving accounts by designating superiors as the appropriate persons to be questioned. A special example of group referral is that which arises when accounts for the behavior of a whole people are avoided by sending the interrogator to the experts. Thus juvenile delinquents can refer inquiries to social workers, Hopi Indians to anthropologists, and unwed Negro mothers to the Moynihan Report.

In *identity switching, ego* indicates to *alter* that he is not playing the role that *alter* believes he is playing. This is a way of saying to *alter*, "You do not know who I am." This technique is readily available since all individuals possess a multiplicity of identities. Consider the following example.[56] A working-class Mexican husband comes home from an evening of philandering. His wife suspects this and says, "Where were you?" He responds with: "None of your business, you're a wife." Here the husband is assuming that it is not the wife's job to pry into the affairs of her husband. She replies, "What kind of a father are you?" What the woman does here is to suggest that she is not a wife, but a mother—who is looking out for the welfare of the children. To this the husband replies: "I'm a man—and you're a woman." In other words, he is suggesting that, in this status of man, there are things that a woman just doesn't understand. We note in this example that the status of persons not only affects the honoring and non-honoring of accounts, but also determines who can call for an account and who can avoid it. Again it should be pointed out that the normal features of such interaction depend upon the actors sharing a common set of background expectancies.

Negotiating Identities, and Accounts

As our discussion of identity-switching emphasizes, accounts always occur between persons in roles—between husband and wife, doctor and patient, teacher and student, and so on. A normative structure governs the nature and types of communication between the interactants, including whether and in what manner accounts may be required and given, honored or discredited.

Accounts, as suggested, presuppose an identifiable speaker and audience. The particular identities of the interactants must often be established as part of the encounter in which the account is presented.[57] In other words,

---

[56] For this illustration we are again indebted to Gregory Stone. The illustration itself is derived from Oscar Lewis' *The Children of Sanchez, op. cit.*

[57] For an excellent discussion of this point as well as an insightful analysis of the concept of identity, see Anselm L. Strauss, *Mirrors and Masks*, The Free Press of Glencoe, 1959.

people generate role identities for one another in social situations. In an account-giving situation, to cast *alter* in a particular role is to confer upon him the privilege of honoring a particular kind of account, the kind suitable to the role identity conferred and assumed for at least the period of the account. To assume an identity is to don the mantle appropriate to the account to be offered. Identity assumption and "alter-casting"[58] are prerequisites to the presentation of accounts, since the identities thus established interactionally "set" the social stage on which the drama of the account is to be played out.

The identities of speaker and audience will be negotiated as part of the encounter. Each of the interactants has a stake in the negotiations since the outcomes of the engagement will often depend on these pre-established identities. In competitive or bargaining situations[59] the interactants will each seek to maximize gains or minimize losses, and part of the strategy involved will be to assume and accept advantageous identities, refusing those roles that are disadvantageous to the situation. *Every account is a manifestation of the underlying negotiation of identities.*[60]

The most elementary form of identification is that of human and fellow human negotiated by the immediate perceptions of strangers who engage in abrupt and involuntary engagements. Thus once two objects on a street collide with one another and mutually perceive one another to be humans, an apology in the form of an excuse, or mutually paired excuses, will suffice. Those persons not privileged with full or accurate perception—the blind, myopic, or blindfolded—are not in a position to ascertain immediately whether the object with which they have collided is eligible to call for an account and to deserve an apology. In overcompensating for their inability to negotiate immediately such elementary identities, the persons so handicapped may indiscriminately offer apologies to everyone and everything with which they collide—doormen and doors, street-walkers and street signs. On the other hand, their identification errors are forgiven as soon as their handicap is recognized.

Some objects are ambiguously defined with respect to their deserving of accounts. Animals are an example. House pets, especially dogs and cats are sometimes imputed to possess human attributes and are thus eligible for apologies and excuses when they are trodden upon by their masters. But insects and large beasts—ants and elephants, for example—do not appear

---

[58] The concept of "alter-casting" is developed by Eugene A. Weinstein and Paul Deutschberger, "Tasks, Bargains, and Identities in Social Interaction," *Social Forces*, V. 42 (May, 1964), pp. 451–456.

[59] See the brilliant discussion by Thomas C. Schelling, *The Strategy of Conflict*, N.Y.: Galaxy Books, 1963, pp. 21–52.

[60] The terms "identities" and "roles" may be used as synonymous in that roles are identities mobilized in a specific situation; whereas role is always situationally specific, identities are trans-situational.

to be normally eligible for accounts even when they are trodden upon by unwary (Occidental) humans.

However, there are instances wherein the anthropomorphosis of the human self is more difficult to negotiate than that of a dog. Racial minorities in caste societies often insist to no avail on the priority of their identity as "human beings" over their identification as members of a racial group.[61] Indeed the "Negro human-being" role choice dilemma is but one instance of a particular form of strategy in the negotiation of identities. The strategy involves the competition between ego and alter over particularistic versus universalistic role identities. In any encounter in which a disagreement is potential or has already occurred, or in any situation in which an account is to be offered, the particularistic or universalistic identity of the interactants might dictate the manner and outcome of the account situation. Each participant will strive for the advantageous identity. A Negro psychoanalyst with considerable experience in Europe and North Africa has shown how the form of address—either consultative or deprecatingly casual—and in the tone used, are opening moves in the doctor's designation of his patient as European or Negro:

> Twenty European patients, one after another, came in: "Please sit down . . . Why do you wish to consult me?" Then comes a Negro or an Arab: "Sit there, boy. . . ."[62]

And, as the psychoanalyst points out, the identity imputed to the patient might be accepted or rejected. To reject the particularistic identity in favor of a universalistic one, the Negro patient might reply, "I am in no sense your boy, Monsieur"[63] and the negotiations for identities begin again or get detoured in an argument.

In an account situation there is a further complication. Once identities have been established and an account offered, the individual has committed himself to an identity and thus seemingly assumed the assets and liabilities of that role for the duration of the encounter. If he accepts the identity as permanent and unchangeable, however, he may have limited his range of subsequent accounts. And if he wishes to shift accounts to one appropriate to another identity he may also need to account for the switch

---

[61] "An unconscious desire to be white, coupled with feelings of revulsion toward the Negro masses, may produce an assimilationist pattern of behavior at the purely personal level. Assimilation is in this sense a means of escape, a form of flight from 'the problem.' It involves a denial of one's racial identity which may be disguised by such sentiments as 'I'm not a negro but a human being'—as if the two were mutually exclusive. This denial is accompanied by a contrived absence of race consciousness and a belittling of caste barriers. By minimizing the color line, the assimilationist loses touch with the realities of Negro life." Robert A. Bone, *The Negro Novel in America*, New Haven: Yale University Press, 1965, p. 4.

[62] Frantz Fanon, *Black Skin, White Masks*, N.Y.: Grove Press, 1967, p. 32.

[63] *Ibid.*, p. 33.

in identities. Thus, in the face of a pejorative particularistic identity, a Negro might wish to establish his claim to a positive universalistic one devoid of the pejorative contents of the imputed one. However, once this new universalistic identity has been established, the Negro might wish to shift back to the particularistic one, if there are positive qualities to be gained thereby, qualities utterly lost by an unqualified acceptance of the universalistic identity.[64] But the switch might require an account itself.

Identity switching has retroactive dangers, since it casts doubt on the attachment the claimant had to his prior identity, and his attachment may have been a crucial element in the acceptability of his first account. On the other hand, the hearer of an account may have a vested interest in accepting the entire range of accounts and may thus accommodate or even facilitate the switch in identities. Thus the hearer may "rationalize" the prior commitment, or reinterpret its meaning so that the speaker may carry off subsequent accounts.[65] Another strategy available to a hearer is to engage in alter-casting for purposes of facilitating or frustrating an account. The fact that individuals have multiple identities makes them both capable of strategic identity change and vulnerable to involuntary identity imputations.

In ordinary life, accounts are usually "phased."[66] One account generates the question which gives rise to another; the new account requires re-negotiation of identities; the identities necessitate excuses or justifications, improvisation and alter-casting; another account is given; another question arises, and so on. The following interview between a Soviet social worker and his client, a young woman, nicely illustrates this phenomenon.[67]

A girl of about nineteen years of age enters the social worker's office and sits down sighing audibly. The interview begins on a note of *mystification* which ends abruptly when the girl establishes her identity—abandoned wife.

> "What are you sighing so sadly for?" I asked. "Are you in trouble?"
> Lyuba raised her prim little head with a jerk, sighed pianissimo and smiled piteously.
> "No . . . it's nothing much. I *was* in trouble, but it's all over now. . . ."
> "All over, and you are still sighing about it?" I questioned further. Lyuba gave a little shiver and looked at me. A flame of interest had leaped into her earnest brown eyes.
> "Would you like me to tell you all about it?"
> "Yes, do."

[64] Fanon, *ibid.*, provides one of the most graphic examples of this phenomenon. For a socio-literary treatment, see St. Clair Drake, "Hide My Face?–On Pan-Africanisms and Negritude," in Herbert Hill, editor, *Soon One Morning*, N.Y.: Alfred Knopf, 1963, pp. 77–105.

[65] Schelling, *op. cit.*, p. 34.

[66] For a discussion on the "phasing" of encounters, see Strauss, *op. cit.*, p. 44 ff.

[67] The following is from A. S. Mackarenko, *The Collective Family*, Garden City: Doubleday Anchor, 1967, pp. 230–232.

"It's a long story."
"Never mind. . . ."
"My husband has left me."

The interview carries on in what must be regarded as an unsuccessful approach by the social worker. He establishes that Lyuba still loves her wayward husband, has lost faith in men, and is unwilling to take his advice to forget her first husband and remarry. The abandoned wife turns out to be an identity with which the worker has difficulty coping. He, therefore, altercasts with telling effect in the following manner.

"Tell me, Lyuba, are your parents alive?"
"Yes, they are. Daddy and Mummy! They keep on telling me off for having got married."
"Quite right too."
"No, it's not. What's right about it?"
"Of course, they're right. You're still a child and already married and divorced."
"Well . . . what about it! What's that got to do with them?"
"Aren't you living with them?"
"I have a room of my own. My husband left me and went to live with his . . . and the room is mine now. And I earn two hundred rubles. And I'm not a child! How can you call me a child?"

Note that little bits of information provide the cues for alter-casting, so that Lyuba's volunteering the fact of her parents' disapproval of her first marriage, provides the grounds for the social worker's recasting her in the child role. However, this new identity is rejected by Lyuba by further evidentiary assertions: she supports herself and maintains her own residence. The child role has been miscast. Even the social worker gives up his attempt at switching Lyuba out from her role as abandoned wife. He writes: "Lyuba looked at me in angry surprise and I saw that she was quite serious about this game she played in life." Thus negotiations for identities—as in financial transactions—usually end with both parties coming to an agreeable settlement.

Conclusion

The sociologist has been slow to take as a serious subject of investigation what is perhaps the most distinctive feature of humans—talk. Here we are suggesting a concern with one type of talk: the study of what constitutes "acceptable utterances"[68] for untoward action. The sociological study of

---

[68] The term is borrowed from Noam Chomsky, *Aspects of a Theory of Syntax,* Cambridge, Mass.: MIT Press, 1965, p. 10.

communications has relegated linguistic utterances largely to linguists and has generally mapped out non-verbal behavior as its distinctive domain. We are suggesting that a greater effort is needed to formulate theory that will integrate both verbal and non-verbal behavior.[69]

Perhaps the most immediate task for research in this area is to specify the background expectations that determine the range of alternative accounts deemed culturally appropriate to a variety of recurrent situations. We want to know how the actors take bits and pieces of words and appearances and put them together to produce a perceivedly normal (or abnormal) state of affairs. This kind of inquiry crucially involves a study of background expectations.[70] On the basis of such investigations, the analyst should be able to provide a set of instructions on "how to give an account" that would be taken by other actors as "normal."[71] These instructions would specify how different categories of statuses affect the honoring of an account, and what categories of statuses can use what kinds of accounts.

Future research on accounts may fruitfully take as a unit of analysis the *speech community*.[72] This unit is composed of human aggregates in frequent and regular interaction. By dint of their association sharers of a distinct body of verbal signs are set off from other speech communities. By speech community we do not refer to language communities, distinguished by being composed of users of formally different languages. Nor do we refer simply to dialect communities, composed of persons who employ a common spoken language which is a verbal variant of a more widely used written language.

Speech communities define for their members the appropriate lingual forms to be used amongst themselves. Such communities are located in the

69 To our knowledge the most persuasive argument for this need is made by Kenneth L. Pike, *Language in Relation to a Unified Theory of the Structure of Human Behavior*, Glendale: Summer Institute of Linguistics, 1954. A short, clear programmatic statement is found in Dell Hymes' "The Ethnography of Speaking," in Thomas Gladwin and William C. Sturtevant, editors, *Anthropology and Human Behavior*, Washington, D.C.: Anthropological Society of Washington, 1962, pp. 72–85. For an argument that stresses the analytic separation of the content of talk from the forms of talk, see the brief but lucid statement by Erving Goffman, "The Neglected Situation," in The Ethnography of Communications, edited by John Gumperz and Dell Hymes, *American Anthropologist*, 66 (December, 1964), Part 2, pp. 133–136.

70 For the methodology of such studies sociologists may well investigate the anthropological technique of componential analysis, i.e., the study of contrast sets. The clearest statement of the method of componential analysis is that of Charles O. Frake, "The Ethnographic Study of Cognitive Systems," in *Anthropology and Human Behavior*, op. cit., pp. 72–85. A related methodology is developed by Sacks in *The Search for Help*, op. cit.

71 See Charles O. Frake, "How to Ask for a Drink in Subanun," in *The Ethnography of Communications*, op. cit., pp. 127–132.

72 The idea of a "speech community" is usefully developed by John J. Gumperz in "Speech Variation and the Study of Indian Civilization," in *Language in Culture and Society*, edited by Dell Hymes, N.Y.: Harper and Row, 1964, pp. 416–423; and "Linguistic and Social Interaction in Two Communities," in *Ethnography of Communications*, op. cit., pp. 137–153.

social structure of any society. They mark off segments of society from one another, and also distinguish different kinds of activities. Thus, the everyday language of lower-class teenage gangs differs sharply from that of the social workers who interview them, and the language by which a science teacher demonstrates to his students how to combine hydrogen and oxygen in order to produce water differs from the language employed by the same teacher to tell his inquisitive six-year-old son how babies are created. The types of accounts appropriate to each speech community differ in form and in content. The usage of particular speech norms in giving an account has consequences for the speaker depending upon the relationship between the form used and the speech community into which it is introduced.

A single individual may belong to several speech communities at the same time, or in the course of a lifetime. Some linguistic devices (such as teenage argot) are appropriate only to certain age groups and are discarded as one passes into another age grouping; others, such as the linguistic forms used by lawyers in the presence of judges, are appropriate to certain status sets and are consecutively employed and discarded as the individual moves into and out of interactions with his various status partners. Some individuals are dwellers in but a single speech community; they move in circles in which all employ the same verbal forms. The aged and enfeebled members of class or ethnic ghettoes are an obvious example. Others are constant movers through differing speech communities, adeptly employing language forms suitable to the time and place they occupy. Social workers who face teenage delinquents, fellow workers, lawyers, judges, their own wives, and children, all in one day, are an example.

In concluding we may note that since it is with respect to deviant behavior that we call for accounts, the study of deviance and the study of accounts are intrinsically related, and a clarification of accounts will constitute a clarification of deviant phenomena—to the extent that deviance is considered in an interactional framework.[73]

---

[73] We refer to the approach to deviance clearly summarized by Howard S. Becker, *The Outsiders*, N.Y.: The Free Press of Glencoe, 1963, esp. pp. 1–18.

Selected Bibliography IV

Berger, Peter L., and Thomas Luckman. *The Social Construction of Reality*. New York: Doubleday & Company, Inc., 1966. A valuable theoretical bridge between the sociology of knowledge and social psychology.

Blumer, Herbert. "Attitudes and the Social Act." *Social Problems*, vol. 3 (October 1955), pp. 59–65. A critique of "attitude," one of the most widely used concepts in social psychology.

Burke, Kenneth. *Permanence and Change*. New York: New Republic, 1936, pp. 30–53. An early statement on the relation between language and motives. Burke is also the author of the more recent *The Grammar of Motives* (New York: Prentice-Hall, Inc., 1945) and *The Rhetoric of Motives* (New York: Prentice-Hall, Inc., 1950), which present this relationship in much greater detail.

Carroll, John B. (ed.) *Language, Thought, and Reality: Selected Writings of Benjamin Lee Whorf*. New York: John Wiley & Sons, Inc., and the Technology Press of Massachusetts Institute of Technology, 1956. Includes articles on the role of language in shaping perception and thought.

Cassirer, Ernst. *An Essay on Man*. New Haven: Yale University Press, 1944, pp. 27–56. Expounds the nature and function of symbols, which account for the evolution "from animal responses to human responses."

Foote, Nelson N. "Identification as the Basis for a Theory of Motivation." *American Sociological Review*, vol. 16 (February 1951), pp. 14–21. A useful companion-piece to the selection in this part by Mills.

Langer, Suzanne. *Philosophy in a New Key*. New York: Penguin Books, Inc., 1942, pp. 42–63. On the logic of signs and symbols.

Levy, David M. "The Act as a Unit." *Psychiatry*, vol. 25 (November 1962), pp. 295–309. A psychiatrist adapts Mead's concept of "the act" to the analysis of mental disorder.

McCall, George J., and J. L. Simmons. *Identities and Interactions: An Examination of Associations in Everyday Life*. New York: The Free Press, 1966. A "refined version of symbolic interaction theory and the exchange theory of interaction."

Mead, George Herbert. *Mind, Self and Society*. Chicago: The University of Chicago Press, 1934, pp. 67–74 and 94–125. Descriptions of the development of significant symbols and the process of minded behavior.

Miyamoto, S. Frank. "The Social Act: Re-examination of a Concept." *Pacific Sociological Review*, vol. 2 (Fall 1959), pp. 51–55. Emphasizes the need for research on "the organized character of the interactional process."

Stevens, Edward. "Sociality and Act in George Herbert Mead." *Social Research*, vol. 34 (Winter 1967), pp. 613–631. A critical philosophical analysis of some of Mead's ideas.

Strong, Samuel W. "A Note on George H. Mead's 'The Philosophy of the Act.'" *American Journal of Sociology*, vol. 45 (July 1939), pp. 71–76. A good but difficult summary of the concept "the act."

Vigotsky, L. S. "Thought and Speech." *Psychiatry*, vol. 2 (February 1939), pp. 29–52. Argues for the identity of thought and speech, as opposed to the conception of speech as merely the means for expressing thought.

White, Leslie T. "Mind Is Minding." *Scientific Monthly*, vol. 48 (1939), pp. 169–171. An eminent anthropologist views mind as behavior, paralleling the functionalist views of Dewey and Mead.

part V

Research
implications & applications

The preceding parts of this book analyzed the concepts and propositions of symbolic interactionism. In this concluding section, the readings present heuristic implications and illustrative researches documenting the broad use this perspective has in research.

The first four articles deal with research in a variety of different settings: the family, awareness contexts, political role, and role-taking. Sheldon Stryker does much to refute the widely held view that symbolic interactionism does not generate researchable hypotheses. In the first of three articles, he indicates the kinds of answers such research can give to certain persistent questions on the family. Further, he describes some research questions that emerge from the theory.

Barney G. Glaser and Anselm L. Strauss direct attention to an important aspect of all human interaction—the identities actors assign themselves and their co-actors. The complexities of this topic are explored in the authors' impressionistic accounts of terminally ill patients in hospitals. Such cases illustrate how interaction is shaped by the identity each actor assigns himself, the identities he assigns others, the identity he believes others assign him, and the identity others actually assign him.

Self-conception, political ideology, and identification with major social institutions are examined in the article by Richard S. Brooks. His concern with left-wing and right-wing political roles offers a distinctive usage of the Twenty Statements Test.

The second selection by Stryker centers on the hypothesis that "the adjustment of the individual is a function of the accuracy with which he can take the role of the other(s) implicated with him in some social situation." The fact that this hypothesis is not fully supported by Stryker's data argues against a sectarian total commitment to symbolic interactionism and urges upon us, rather, a critical but open-minded orientation.

Although some critics of this orientation have argued it is relevant only to understanding "normal" behavior, a growing research literature is dispelling that notion. Symbolic interactionist perspectives have contributed greatly to understanding the sociology and social psychology of deviance. The selections on criminality and marihuana use are cases in point.

In an influential article, Daniel Glaser shows the images of human behavior underlying various theories of criminality. His "differential identification" theory, entirely consistent with symbolic interactionism, stresses the role of reference groups in criminal behavior. The theory is a modification of Edwin H. Sutherland's clearly social-psychological "differential association" explanation of crime.

Howard S. Becker's widely cited article describes how individuals learn to define the use of marihuana in terms favoring the continuation of such use. The compatibility of these findings with differential identification theory should be noted.

The four concluding articles also deal with deviant behavior—specifically, with mental disorder. The symbolic interactionist perspective is clearly supported in William R. Rosengren's study. His research reveals that changes in self-conception tend to be associated with changes in the overt behavior of a small sample of emotionally disturbed boys.

The article by Michael Schwartz, Gordon Fearn, and Sheldon Stryker considers the deviant as role-maker. On this premise, they hypothesize that commitment to the deviant role of "emotionally disturbed" results in better and more stable self-meanings.

Erving Goffman's earlier article (in Part III) is a useful preface to his study of the moral career of the mental patient. Although the concept of career is usually restricted to the professions, Goffman demonstrates its utility for explaining the changes in the self-conception of the patient in a mental institution.

The author, Arlene K. Daniels, describes the concluding article as "radical symbolic interactionism." Seemingly influenced by the phenomenologists and ethnomethodologists, this paper examines the way in which the label "mental illness" is assigned by military psychiatrists. The method and perspective of this paper attest to the viability and modifiability of symbolic interactionism.

A recurring criticism of symbolic interactionism has been its putative nonempirical character. Along with the selections in the preceding parts of this book, the articles in Part V may partially offset such criticism, although they represent only a small portion of the expanding body of symbolic-interactionist research.

Symbolic Interaction
as an Approach to Family Research

Various commentators have stated that the ideas covered by the label symbolic interaction are part of the intellectual baggage of almost all who concern themselves with human behavior. On the other hand, persons identifying themselves as symbolic interactionists commonly hold that this theory suffers from general, albeit certainly undeserved, neglect. There is a good deal of validity in both views. Many social psychologists have made at least some of the ideas of symbolic interaction part of their theoretical equipment, whether or not they are aware of their debt. Yet the implications of this theoretical scheme are not always perceived and appreciated even by men calling themselves symbolic interactionists. The problem seems to be that at least some of the once-novel ideas of the theory have become, for many, simple commonplaces or platitudes, and like most platitudes, more likely to defeat thought than to stimulate it.

This paper is above all an attempt at a straightforward review of symbolic interaction theory. Its aim is to stimulate renewed interest in a simple, but relatively powerful, set of ideas which remain largely unexploited. It is perhaps particularly in the family field that these are open to exploitation.

The theory being dealt with has a venerable tradition, beginning at least as far back as Hegel. Modern formulations have their roots in American pragmatism, in the writings of Peirce and James. Suggestions contained here were elaborated and systematized by James Mark Baldwin, John Dewey, Charles Horton Cooley and, most important of all, George Herbert Mead. Specifically in the family field, Waller, Burgess, Hill, and Foote represent persons whose work, to important degree, stems from this framework.

There is no single orthodoxy which is symbolic interaction theory. There is certainly a hard core of agreement, and there are certainly important differences, among representatives of the position. Some see it as no more than a set of concepts serving to sensitize one to aspects of social

Sheldon Stryker, "Symbolic Interaction as an Approach to Family Research," *Marriage and Family Living*, vol. 21 (May 1959), pp. 111–119. Reprinted by permission.
A slightly amended version of a paper presented to the 21st Groves Conference on Marriage and the Family, Washington, D.C., April 15, 1958.

life, some as a general theory of human behavior. The present discussion proceeds on another view, which sees the theory as addressing itself to a relatively modest series of questions.

Theory can be taken to mean a set of assumptions or postulates with which one approaches some part of the empirical world, a set of concepts in terms of which this part of the world is described, and a set of propositions, emerging from the assumptions and relating the concepts, about the way this part of the world "works" which are checked against observations of that world. This presentation begins by noting briefly the general questions to which symbolic interaction theory is addressed, and turns successively to the assumptions underlying the theory, the concepts provided by the theory, and illustrative instances of the propositions which are the answers to its questions. It concludes by considering some of the implications of the theory for family research.

The Problems to Which the Theory Is Addressed

As a social psychological theory, symbolic interaction addresses a set of interrelated questions, most of which take their place in the context of two major problems. The first is that of socialization: how the human organism acquires the ways of behaving, the values, norms and attitudes of the social units of which he is a part. The focus here is on development—that which happens over time to the human neophyte: the infant, the recruit entering the army, the student entering the university, the bride entering a new set of family relationships.

The twin of the problem of socialization is that of personality: the organization of persistent behavior patterns. Such organization cannot be assumed but must be demonstrated and accounted for. The task of a social psychology is to account for such organization insofar as it depends upon social relationships. It should be added that symbolic interaction addresses itself largely to the normal person—in the sense of the person without gross physical, physiological, or psychological defect.

To say that this position is oriented to the normal person is not to say that it is concerned only with personal organization, for the theory seeks to explore personal disorganization as well. As a matter of fact, one of the strengths of this position is that it treats personal organization and personal disorganization as facets of the same problem, rather than different problems, and that it can provide answers to both without invoking principles lying outside its theoretical scheme.

These are the major problems which symbolic interaction theory seeks to resolve. They have been stated in general form, for more specific formulation depends on the assumptions and concepts with which the theory approaches the parts of the world in which it has interest.

Assumptions

The initial assumption is that, insofar as interests are social psychological, man must be studied on his own level. The position of symbolic interactionism is anti-reductionist; it argues that valid principles of human social psychological behavior cannot be derived from, or inferred from, the study of non-human forms. This assertion rests on the principle of emergence. Emergence suggests the existence of qualitative differences as well as quantitative continuities among the precipitates of the evolutionary process. If man is qualitatively different in some respects from other animal forms, it follows that principles derived from other forms cannot completely account for his behavior. The task of at least some social psychologists is to focus on that which is different in man.

A second assumption is that the most fruitful approach to man's social behavior is through an analysis of society. This assumption involves no assertion of some metaphysical priority of society over the individual. Social psychologists of one stripe have argued that society is *the* ultimate reality; social psychologists of another variety give ontological precedence to the individual, denying the reality of society. Either position leads to confusion and contradiction. Symbolic interaction has not resolved the argument; but it has bypassed it. It has done so by beginning its analyses with the social act. Its basic unit of observation is interaction, and from interaction both society and individual derive. It is worth noting that this formulation permits an articulation between sociology and social psychology which alternative frameworks can forge, if at all, only with great difficulty. Both begin with the same "building bricks:" social actions. Sociology builds in one direction to the behavior of collectivities. Social psychology builds in another direction to the behavior of individuals. Those whose problems bridge the two fields, as is true of many students of the family, are provided with a framework facilitating movement from one level to the other, allowing systematic transactions between the two levels.

A third assumption concerns the equipment with which the newborn enters life. The human infant is, from this point of view, neither social nor antisocial, but rather asocial. It has the potentialities for social development. It is an active organism, it has "impulses," but these impulses are not channelized or directed toward any specific ends. Original nature is amorphous and plastic; it lacks organization.

A last assumption is that the human being is actor as well as reactor. The human being does not simply respond to stimuli occurring outside himself. In fact, what is a stimulus depends on the activity in which the organism is engaged: objects become stimuli when they serve to link impulses with satisfactions. The environment of the organism is a selected segment of the "real" world, the selection occurring in the interests of behavior which the human being himself has initiated. It is the assumption which leads to the fundamental methodological principle of symbolic interactions the demand that the investigator see the world from the point of view of the subject of his investigation.

These seem to be the assumptions underlying symbolic interaction theory. Not an assumption, but closely related to those discussed, is a predilection on the part of adherents of this theory to stay close to the world of everyday experience. The viewpoint develops out of such experience, and it is with such experience that it seeks to deal.

Major Concepts

An assumption of this theory, again, is emergence. The principle emergent on the human level is language behavior. The initial concern in this review of concepts thus must be with language and its correlatives.

The starting point is with the *act:* behavior by an organism stemming from an impulse requiring some adjustment to appropriate objects in the external world. A *social act* is one in which the appropriate object is another individual. But another individual does not "stand still"; he, too, acts with reference to the first actor. Thus every social act implicates at least two individuals, each of whom takes the other into account in the processes of satisfying impulses. Since such acts occur over time, they have a history. This makes possible the appearance of *gestures,* defined as any part of the act which stands for, or comes to be a sign of, those parts of the act yet to occur. Thus, in responding to one another, individuals may be involved in what Mead called a "conversation of gestures:" they may come to use early stages of one anothers' acts as indicators of later stages. Such gestures have meaning. Vocal sounds can serve as gestures, and they too may have meaning. The meaning of a gesture (an early stage of an act) is the behavior which follows it (the later stages of the act): meaning is, by definition, behavior. Some gestures have an additional property. They may mean the same thing, imply the same set of subsequent behaviors, to the organism which produces the gesture and that which perceives it. When this occurs, the gesture becomes a *significant symbol.* To illustrate: the cry of the infant may serve as a sign of hunger to the mother, and she responds by feeding the infant. The cry is a gesture whose meaning lies in the parental response. At a later stage, the child may call out "milk!" and, unless the appropriate parental response is made, protest vigorously. The word "milk" is here a significant symbol. Language, basically, is a system of significant symbols. This is equivalent to asserting that language is a system of shared meanings, and this in turn implies that language is a system of shared behavior. Communication between human beings presupposes these characteristics of language symbols.

Retreat is necessary before going forward. Symbols arise in the context of social acts, and they function in completing acts: they reflect the interests from which the acts stem. We respond to symbols as predicters of further behavior, our own as well as that of others. Since these symbols predict later behavior, they provide a basis for adjusting our activity before that later behavior has occurred. Thus symbols may be said to function in the context of the act in place of that which they symbolize, and may further be said to organize behavior with reference to that which is symbolized. Symbols entail a plan of action. To illustrate and summarize:

> Thus if one hunter shouts to another, "A duck!" the second hunter immediately looks into the air and makes appropriate preparations for shooting at a bird on the wing. If the first hunter shouts, "Rabbit!" his partner responds in a different manner. Language symbols do not merely stand for something else. They also indicate the significance of things for human behavior, and they organize behavior toward the thing symbolized.[1]

Some symbols represent generalizations of behavior toward objects; these are *categories*. To categorize is to apply a class term to a number of objects, to signify that a number of different things are, for certain purposes, to be treated as the same kind of thing. Classification or categorization is essential to activity, for life would be impossible if one were forced to respond to every object in the world as unique. Class terms, or categories, are of course symbols, and as such they share the characteristics of symbols. They have meaning, they are cues to behavior, and they organize behavior.

Humans respond to a classified world, one whose salient features are named and placed into categories indicating their significance for behavior. In short, humans do not respond to the environment as physically given, but to an environment as it is mediated through symbols—to a *symbolic environment*. Persons frequently enter situations in which their behavior is problematic. Before they can act, they must define the situation, that is, represent it to themselves in symbolic terms. The products of this defining behavior are termed "definitions of the situations."

A particularly important kind of category is that called "position."[2] Positions are socially recognized categories of actors, any general category serving to classify persons: father, sergeant, teacher are positions by this usage, as are playboy, intellectual, blacksheep.

---

[1] Alfred R. Lindesmith and Anselm L. Strauss, *Social Psychology*, New York: Dryden Press, 1956, p. 63.

[2] Others have used the term "status" here. I prefer "position" in order to avoid the hierarchical implications of status. Positions may certainly be hierarchized, but hierarchy and position are conceptually distinct and it is important to distinguish between them.

The significance of such categories is that they serve to organize behavior toward persons so categorized. An equivalent assertion is that in attaching one of these position designations to a person we are led to expect certain behaviors from him and we behave toward him on the basis of these expectancies. To the expectations with regard to behavior attached to a position the term "role" is given. These expectations are social in the same sense symbolic behavior is always social: the ultimate meaning of the positions to which these expectations apply is shared behavior. They are social in another and most important sense, namely, that it is impossible to talk about *a* position without reference to some context of *other* positions: one cannot talk about the behavior of father except with reference to the positions of mother, child, and so on. Thus every position assumes some counter-position, and every role presumes some counter-role. To use the term "role" is necessarily to refer to an interpersonal relation.

The discussion of categories has been couched in terms of an actor responding to objects in the external world, including people, by classifying them in functionally relevant ways. Under certain circumstances, an actor may apply such categories to himself: he may respond to himself as he responds to other people, by naming, defining, classifying himself. To engage in this kind of behavior is to have a *self*. Self can be defined in various ways, each calling attention to slightly different aspects of the same activity. Mead defined the self as that which is an object to itself. Others have discussed the self as a set of responses of an organism serving to organize other responses of the same organism. It is useful in the present context to define the self in terms of categories one applies to himself, as a set of self-identifications.

However defined, self refers to activity, to reflexive activity, and not to an object, thing, or essence. It is a necessary concept, from the standpoint of the symbolic interactionist, but it is one fraught with the dangers of reification. As Robert W. White notes:[3]

> The necessity of using the concept of self does not confer the privilege of misusing it. As we use concepts in our thinking, they tend to get firmer and harder. Thought about fluid events tends to curdle and form solid clots. Before long we begin to think of the self as if it were a lump in the personality. It becomes a region, an institution, an entity. . . . In the end the self is standing like a solid boulder of granite in the midst of personality, and one's thinking about it is as flexible as granite.

The self is defined in terms of socially recognized categories and their corresponding roles. Since these roles necessarily imply relationships to others, the self necessarily implies such relations. One's self is the way one describes to himself his relationships to others in a social process.

---

[3] Robert W. White, *The Abnormal Personality*, New York: Ronald Press, 1948, p. 140.

The discussion thus far has presumed but not made explicit the concept of "role-taking," or alternatively, "taking the role of the other." Role-taking refers to anticipating the responses of others implicated with one in some social act. The meaning of the concept can best be elucidated through illustration. Consider the classroom instructor who presents to his students an especially difficult conception. He perhaps finds that the words ordinarily used to cover the topic do not allow the discussion to proceed beyond the immediate issue. He then casts about for words which will allow him to clarify the conception, and so allow him to move beyond it to further materials. How shall he select such words? Presumably he will do so in terms of what he knows or guesses about the backgrounds or experiences of the students before him. He will, in other words, attempt to put himself in the place of the students; he will attempt to anticipate their responses to the words he will use. He takes the role of the other.

Role-taking may involve the anticipation of responses of some particular other. More frequently, it involves the anticipation of responses of what Mead called the "generalized other." To revert to the classroom illustration, the instructor must deal with the class not as discrete individuals but as an organized unit, the members of which can be expected to behave in differentiated yet related ways. To take the role of the generalized other is to see one's behavior as taking place in the context of a defined system of related roles. The concept of reference group, as it is currently used, represents partially a restatement and partially an extension of the generalized other concept.

In comparatively recent work, the concept of "significant other" has come into use. This concept represents the recognition that, in a fragmented and differentiated world, not all the persons with whom one interacts have identical or even compatible perspectives; and that, therefore, in order for action to proceed, the individual must give greater weight or priority to the perspectives of certain others. To speak, then, of significant others is to say that given others occupy high rank on an "importance" continuum for a given individual.

One last set of concepts must be mentioned. Symbolic interaction makes unashamed use of "mental" concepts such as thinking, volition, and self-consciousness. The case can be put in stronger fashion; its judgment is that any scheme which rules out such concepts distorts the facts of human experience. However, its usage of these terms is not traditional. Where frequently these concepts are defined in such way as to place them outside the bounds of scientific discourse, symbolic interaction defines these terms behavioristically and, in so doing, permits their treatment within the conventions of scientific procedure. Thus, thinking is defined as the internalized manipulation of language symbols. Volition becomes the process of selecting among alternatives symbolically present in the experience of the individual. And self-consciousness is the activity of viewing oneself from the standpoint of others.

The Answers Provided by the Theory: Illustrative Cases

It will be impossible, given limitations of space, to do full justice to the complexities of the problems raised or the explanations provided by symbolic interaction theory; all that can be done is to review these in barest outline.

The problem of socialization has a number of interrelated facets, among them questions of how meanings are obtained by the human infant, how the self develops and is structured, and how thinking and objectivity arises in the course of experience.

The human infant, active but unorganized, is born into an ongoing set of social relationships. Such relationships are premised upon a set of shared meanings. The infant acts, but randomly: he thrashes his arms, he exercises his vocal cords. The adult responds to these actions, say the crying of the infant, by doing something to the infant—he feeds it, or changes it, or turns it over on its stomach. He will eventually find that response which will complete the act in a desired way, that is, stop the crying. There is in this situation an "impulsive" act which is, incipiently, a gesture, and there is incipient meaning as well. The incipient meaning is that part of the act supplied by the adult. In time, both the cry of the infant and the response of the adult become specialized; when this occurs, the cry is a gesture in the previously-defined sense. The significant point is that, since it is the adult who completes the act, it is he who supplies the meaning of the gesture. What kinds of completions will he supply? He is, of course, limited by the repertory of meanings available in the social unit of which he is a part. Further, the adult will have defined the situation, including his positional relationship to the infant, for example, that of father to son, and this definition will invoke the set of expected behaviors we call the role of the father. If the father is a middle class American, and if he takes the cry of the infant to mean that the infant is thirsty, his response will be to supply milk or water—but not wine or whiskey. The meanings attached to the gestures of the infant are social meanings, and they are supplied through his relationships with already socialized participants in an ongoing society.

The early activity of the child will include random vocalization. Eventually, too, he will imitate sounds others make. Others respond to the initially random vocalization by selecting out particular sounds and responding to these. They respond to the imitated sounds as well by acts which contain the adult meanings of these sounds. For the child, the correspondence between sound and meaning will be initially vague, but in the process of interaction over time the correspondence will become more pronounced. So, for example, the child may use the sound "ba" to refer to any approximately round object and, having played this game with daddy, may be led to roll any such object—ball, orange, egg—around the floor. The response of parent to the rolling of an egg—especially an uncooked one—will soon make clear that an egg is not a "ba" and thus is not to be rolled on the floor. In the course of time, child and parent will come to agree on what is and is not a ball, and thus a significant symbol will have come into existence. A sound, initially meaningless to the child, comes to mean for the child what it already means for the adult.

The "self" comes into existence in the same way. Just as the sound "ba" took on meaning through the responses of others, so too the human organism as an object takes on meaning through the behavior of those who respond to that organism. We come to know what we are through others' responses to us. Others supply us with a name, and they provide the meaning attached to that symbol. They categorize us in particular ways—as an infant, as a boy, et cetera. On the basis of such categorization, they expect particular behaviors from us; on the basis of these expectations, they act toward us. The manner in which they act towards us defines our "self," we come to categorize ourselves as they categorize us, and we act in ways appropriate to their expectations.

The evolution of the self is, of course, gradual; moreover, it is continual. This development is one of increasing complexity, in a sense, for as the child moves into the social world he comes into contact with a variety of persons in a variety of self-relevant situations. He comes, or may come, into contact with differing expectations concerning his behavior, and differing identities on which these expectations are based. Thus he has, through the role-taking process, a variety of perspectives from which to view and evaluate his own behavior, and he can act with reference to self as well as with reference to others. In short, the socialization process as described makes possible the appearance of objectivity. Furthermore, since these processes may be internalized through the use of language symbols, it also makes possible the appearance of self-control.

The individual, at the same time and through time as well, occupies a variety of positions in sets of social relationships. If he responded in each of these in terms of unique sets of role-expectations and self-definitions, his behavior would be discontinuous. Usually, however, there is a continuity and organization among the behaviors of a given individual. The question is how such personal organization can be accounted for. The basic answer provided by symbolic interaction theory uses the concepts of self, role, and definition of the situation. On entering an ongoing social situation, one responds to that situation by defining it. This definition includes the assignment of positions to others, and thus the setting up of expectations concerning their behavior. It, further, includes an assessment of self, that is, the assignment of positional identities to oneself. Others in the situation are, of course, engaged in the same kind of activity. The behavior that ensues is a function of such definitions. A crucial question thus becomes one of the congruence of definitions, situation, role and self, of the interacting persons. Congruence permits efficient, organized behavior. Expanding this, again noting that the individual moves through a variety of interpersonal situations, the congruence of definitions, and so the behavioral expectations these imply, is fundamental to continuity of behavior. Personal organization is thus seen as a function, not simply of that which the individual carries around with him, but of the relationship between that which he carries with him—in the form of self-concepts—and the situations in which he interacts with others as these are mediated symbolically.

When one asks what kinds of social conditions foster or permit such congruence, the generalized answer is that when meanings are widely shared in a society, or among those persons within a society with whom one actually interacts, congruence is likely.

What happens when meanings are diverse among the others with whom one interacts? Reversing the above process, but maintaining the same explanatory principle, it may be said that incongruities in definition and so incongruities in expectations will result, and that personal disorganization is the outcome. A number of possible types of incongruity may be suggested: conflicts or lack of coordination between self concepts and the expectations of others; conflicts among aspects of self called into play in the same situation; the temporal succession of expectations which do not articulate, and so on.

It may be worthwhile to take one type of incongruity, say lack of coordination between self concepts and expectations of others, and note more closely its relevance to personal disorganization. At the same time, the question can be raised: under what circumstances do identities change? Suppose one enters a situation with a set of self identifications which include the name "professor," and suppose he defines the situation—for example, as a classroom—in such a way that this identity is appropriate. He will then presumably conduct himself in ways indicated by that identity. He speaks in judicious, measured tones, he adopts a knowledgeable air, and so on. He can behave this way only so long as his audience accepts this definition of himself and so responds in such ways as validate his behavior, by taking notes, by concentrating attention upon him, by directing questions at him. Suppose, however, the audience fails to accept this definition; they think him a fool rather than a professor (although perhaps the two are not completely incompatible). They disregard what he is saying, they challenge his competency, they pay more attention to friends in class than they do to him. In short, they fail to validate his self identification. How will he behave? It is highly probable that behaviors ordinarily inappropriate to the classroom will ensue. He will likely lose his judicious tones and become emotional. He is likely to act confused, uncertain, embarrassed, ambivalent. At the same time, since persons typically have considerable investment in identities, he very probably will attempt to defend himself. He may do so by redoubling his efforts to act the complete professor, by dismissing the incident as a joke, by regarding the audience as consisting of morons. But if, persistently, his identity as professor fails to be validated by others, he cannot retain that identity. Others validate identities by behaving in appropriate ways, ways which provide cues on the basis of which further performance in terms of the identity is possible. If these cues are not provided, then such performance is no longer possible, and the identity will fade.

Implications for Family Research

Rather than attempt to detail implications of symbolic interaction for family research, a few brief indications of researchable questions stimulated by this theory will be presented.

One question, or set of questions, has to do with differential commitment to family identities. It is obvious, for example, that not all persons who are objectively fathers are equally committed to such an identity. What accounts for such differentials, for the fact that for one man identity as father supersedes all other ways in which he sees himself, while for another the father identity is relatively low on the self totem pole? The theory suggests that this will be a function of the extent to which one is defined by significant others as a father. It also suggests that the degree of congruence of definitions by significant others will be of import. Borrowing a phrase from studies of political behavior, could the presence or absence of "cross-pressures" deriving from others with whom one interacts account for this differential commitment, at least in some degree?

Perhaps of greater significance to students of the family is the question of the consequences of differential commitment to familial identities. Foote[4] has contended that differences in motivation of role performances may fruitfully be seen in these terms. Political apathy seems to be in good part a consequence of lack of commitment to a clear-cut political identity; it seems reasonable to suspect that apathetic familial behavior has a similar source. It is also quite possible that, for example, the prediction of divorce would be on sounder ground when questions dealing with commitment to family identities are included in batteries of predictive items.

[4] Nelson N. Foote, "Identification as the Basis for a Theory of Motivation," *American Sociological Review*, 16 (February, 1951), pp. 14–21.

Closely related to these questions is another set. Are there extra-familial identities which are in varying degree compatible with familial identities? What are the effects of identities deriving from diverse spheres of activity on one another, and on behavior in these diverse spheres? Someone has suggested that the deviant behavior of a man in a work situation which appears to be idiosyncratic when viewed in this limited context, may rather be a consequence of his position and role within his family. That is, for example, the rate-buster on the job may not be acting "selfishly," but may simply be acting in accord with his conception of self as family breadwinner. It is certain that one's extra-familial identities operate within the family situation. Which identities so operate, their specific mode of articulation with family identities, and their consequences for family relationships are questions of obvious importance.

Another set of questions can be phrased around the relationship of crises to identity. Crises will always threaten identifications, for the latter depend on stable activities of others with reference to oneself; and crises are likely to be important in the process by which identities change. It may be that adaptation in crisis situations is a function of the ease with which identities alter; adaptation to the death of a spouse, for example, might profitably be approached in these terms. Yet that ease with which identities are altered is not always functional is suggested by Hill's[5] research on war separation and return; in such multi-phased crises it may be that, at least for some, easy alteration of identity at one point creates problems at still another point. Such questions, too, are worth the research energies of students of the family.

A different kind of question suggested by the theory may be prefaced by relating an overheard conversation. A young lady was speaking of her relationships with her boy friend. The two were, apparently, sufficiently involved to talk about marriage and their future. But, it seems, they argued when they engaged in such talk. The basis for the argument was this: she labelled such talks "plans," he called them "dreams," and each bridled at the other's conception of their conversations. Nonsense? Arguing over mere words? Not when one has in mind the significance of defining behavior and the consequences of classification. Plan implies a greater stake in a projected course of action than does dream. Dreams suggest freedom of action, plans a commitment. Suggested here is the potential fertility of studying the courtship process, marital role relationships, parent-child relationships, and so on, in terms of role-linked symbolic behavior: for example, the investigation of possible sex-linked differences in defining family situations, and the consequences of such differential definitions as may exist.

Finally, the theory suggests that studies focusing on the role-taking process may be rewarding. Role-taking is a variable; anticipation of the

[5] Reuben Hill, *Families Under Stress*, New York: Harpers, 1949.

responses of others is not always correct. Foote[6] and his associates have conducted an impressive series of studies designed to uncover means by which role-taking ability can be improved, on the assumption that role-taking ability, or empathy in their language, is one aspect of interpersonal competence. While this may well be justified, some research[7] indicates that if one expects that interpersonal adjustment will always result from accurate role-taking, he is likely to be disappointed. But this still leaves open questions of the specific consequences, under varying conditions, of role-taking accuracy. Are the consequences the same, for example, when husband and wife share the same value framework and when they do not? Might it not be that accurate role-taking differs in its consequences as role relationships change, when a couple moves through the sequential stages of courtship, early marital experience, and later family experience? These, too, are questions worth raising and answering.

One final remark: symbolic interaction is not a general theory of human behavior. That is, it does not incorporate all the variables presumably important in accounting for human behavior, but rather selects from these a few for concentrated attention. Thus it would not do to deny the contributions of alternative theoretical views from which human behavior can be approached. It is contended, however, that alternative views can be enriched by taking into account the set of ideas which have been developed.

[6] Nelson N. Foote, Editor, *Developing Interpersonal Competence: A Manual of Procedures for Family Life Educators*, unpublished manuscript.

[7] See for example, Sheldon Stryker, "Role-Taking Accuracy and Adjustment," *Sociometry*, 20 (December, 1957), pp. 286–296.

38 BARNEY G. GLASER & ANSELM L. STRAUSS

Awareness Contexts and Social Interaction

When men confront each other, each cannot always be certain—even when given seemingly trustworthy guarantees—that he knows either the other's identity or his own identity in the eyes of the other. An honest citizen may be taken in by a confidence man, a government official by

Barney G. Glaser and Anselm L. Strauss, "Awareness Contexts and Social Interaction," *American Sociological Review*, vol. 29 (October, 1964), pp. 669–679. Reprinted by permission.

Many of the examples used in this paper are taken from the author's study of Hospital Personnel, Nursing Care and Dying Patients, supported by National In-a foreign spy passing as his secretary, or a dying patient by his doctor. But the confidence man's mark may actually be from the local detective squad; the official, suspecting undercover play, may be pretending innocence while slipping the secretary false documents; and the dying patient may suspect his true condition but not reveal his suspicion to the physician. Thus, who is really being "taken in" is a matter of the awareness of both parties to the situation.

The phenomenon of awareness—which is central to the study of interaction—can be quite complex for at least two reasons. First, interaction may involve not merely two persons, but a third or quite a few more. For instance, when a homosexual flashes cues to another homosexual in the presence of many straight people, some may not notice and others may misread the cues, while others might be aware of their intended meaning. The identity of the homosexual is, therefore, unknown or suspect to some straights and known to still others. Conversely, a homosexual cannot always be certain who suspects or who is or is not aware of his true identity. Second, each person involved may be the representative of a system with specific requirements for, and perhaps a high stake in, how the person manages his own and the other's identity. Spies and counterspies are linked to such systems as often as are doctors and nurses.

These considerations highlight important features of the relation between interaction and awareness. To establish our basic notion, however, we shall content ourselves in this paper with the least complex situation: two interactants (whether persons or groups) who face the dual problem of being certain about both their identity in the other's eyes and the other's identity.

Contexts of Awareness

By the term *awareness context* we mean the total combination of what each interactant in a situation knows about the identity of the other and his own identity in the eyes of the other.[1] This total awareness is the

---

stitutes of Health, Grant GN9077. For a full discussion of awareness contexts related to social interaction in the hospital dying situation, see our . . . book, *Awareness of Dying: A Study of Social Interaction.* Jeanne Quint, a member of our project team, has worked closely with us on these data. We are indebted to Howard S. Becker, Fred Davis, Erving Goffman, Sheldon Messinger, and Melvin Sabshin for their helpful comments on this paper.

[1] The concept of awareness context is a structural unit, not a property of one of the standard structural units such as group, organization, community, role, position, etc. By "context" we mean it is a structural unit of an encompassing order larger than the other unit under focus: interaction. Thus, an awareness context surrounds and affects the interaction. Much as one might say that the interaction of staff with dying patients occurs within the context of a cancer ward or a veteran's hospital, one can also say that this interaction occurs within a type of awareness context. Note that ward or hospital are concrete, conventional social units, while awareness context is an analytic

context within which are guided successive interactions between the two persons over periods of time—long or short. Empirically the question of true identity may focus only on that of one of the two persons (the dying patient) or on that of both persons (spy and counterspy).

We have singled out four types of awareness context for special consideration since they have proved useful in accounting for different types of interaction. An *open* awareness context obtains when each interactant is aware of the other's true identity and his own identity in the eyes of the other. A *closed* awareness context obtains when one interactant does not know either the other's identity or the other's view of his identity. A *suspicion* awareness context is a modification of the closed one: one interactant suspects the true identity of the other or the other's view of his own identity, or both. A *pretense* awareness context is a modification of the open one: both interactants are fully aware but pretend not to be.

These types illustrate how the sociologist's total picture may differ from that held by each interactant, no matter how well informed or expert. For example, a doctor may state that a patient does not yet know that he is dying (his identity in the eyes of the doctor) while the patient may very well suspect the physician's definition. Thus, the doctor believes that closed awareness obtains when actually there is a suspicion context within which the patient is testing his suspicions. If the doctor recognizes those suspicions he may attempt to parry them. If the doctor believes himself successful, he may only report to the sociologist that as yet the patient is unaware, neglecting to mention the patient's suspicions. Therefore, delimiting an awareness context requires always that the sociologist ascertain independently the awareness of each interactant. The safest method is to obtain data, through observation or interview, from each interactant on his own state of awareness. To accept the word of only one informant is risky, even perhaps for the open awareness context.

The successive interactions occurring within each type of context tend to transform the context. As yet it is an empirical question as to the direction in which a change in one context will lead, or what are some patterns of successive transformations. Thus, a closed context can be shattered by arousing suspicions; but if suspicions are quelled, the closed context is reinstituted. If suspicions are validated, the context may change to either pretense or open awareness. With a change in identity of one interactant in the eyes of the other, an open context can easily become either closed or pretense. For instance, the government official who suspects that his secre-

---

social unit, constructed to account for similarities in interaction in many diverse conventional units.

A more general definition of awareness context is the total combination of what specific people, groups, organizations, communities or nations know what about a specific issue. Thus, this structural concept can be used for the study of virtually any problem entailing awareness at any structural level of analysis.

tary is a spy must now check his suspicions. If he discovers that she is a spy but does not reveal his knowledge, then she in turn misreads his view of her identity. Thus, a closed context now obtains! If she in turn surreptitiously learns of his new view of her but says nothing, the context is again closed. But if he unmasks her spying, then the context now becomes open, since each now fully acknowledges the other's true identity.

How long each context will last before it is transformed is also an empirical question. In the abstract none is inherently less stable than another; although within a given substantive area, differential degrees of stability may become apparent. For dying patients, a suspicion context is probably the least stable, becoming resolved by successive interactions with staff which confirm the patient's suspicions.

A Paradigm for the Study of Awareness Contexts

To organize a study of interaction within different awareness contexts, we have developed a paradigm or set of directives. These directives focus on the study of developmental interaction process—interaction that changes as it continues—as distinct from the relatively static study of the rules that govern interaction.[2]

The component parts of the paradigm are as follows: (1) a description of the given type of awareness context; (2) the structural conditions under which the awareness context exists;[3] (3) the consequent interaction; (4) changes of interaction that occasion transformations of context, along with the structural conditions for the transformations; (5) the tactics of various interactants as they attempt to manage changes of awareness context; and (6) some consequences of the initial awareness context, its transformation and associated interactions—for interactants and for the organizations or institutions notably affected.

To illustrate the use of this paradigm, we briefly sketch the closed awareness context surrounding dying patients.

[2] Cf. Erving Goffman, *Behavior in Public Places*, New York: Free Press of Glencoe, 1963.
[3] We use the phrase "structural conditions" to emphasize that the conditions are conceived of as properties of social structural units. These units may vary from the smallest (such as role, status, or relationship) to the largest (such as organization, community, nation or society) and may be either larger or smaller than the unit of discussion. Usually they are larger contextual units. Structural conditions tend to have a determining or guiding effect on the unit of discussion. Since structural conditions are the tools-in-trade of most sociologists, this footnote is not meant for them. The structural conditions under which interaction takes place, however, are not typically included in the work of social psychologists, especially those trained in departments of psychology.

(1) Hospitalized patients frequently do not recognize their impending death while staff does.[4] Thus interaction between staff and patient occurs within a closed awareness context about the patient's true identity.

(2) At least four major structural conditions determine this closed awareness context. First, most patients are not especially experienced at recognizing the signs of impending death. Second, the hospital is magnificently organized, both by accident and design, for hiding the medical truth from the patient. Records are kept out of reach. Staff is skilled at withholding information from him. Medical talk about him occurs generally in far-removed places. Also, the staff is trained or accustomed to act collusively around patients so as not to disclose medical secrets. Third, physicians are supported in their withholding of information by professional rationales: "Why deny them all hope by telling them they are dying?" Fourth, ordinarily the patient has no allies who can help him discover the staff's secret: even his family or other patients will withhold such information if privy to it.

(3) To prevent the patient's comprehension of the truth, the personnel utilize a number of "situation as normal" interaction tactics. They seek to act in his presence as if he were not dying but only ill. They talk to him as if he were going to live. They converse about his future, thus enhancing his belief that he will regain his health. They tell him stories about others (including themselves) who have recovered from similar or worse illnesses. By such indirect signaling they offer him a false biography. Of course, they may directly assure him that he will live, lying with a clear purpose.

To supplement these tactics the staff members use additional ones to guard against disclosure. They carefully guard against the patient's overhearing any conversation about his real condition. They engage also in careful management of expressions, controlling their facial and other gestures so as not to give the show away:[5] they must control the expression of any sadness they experience over the patient's approaching death. Almost inevitably they attempt, not always consciously, to reduce the number of potentially disclosing cues by reducing time spent with the patient or by restricting their conversations with him.

(4) In such collusive games, the teamwork can be phenomenal but the dangers of disclosure to the patient are very great. Unless the patient dies quickly or becomes permanently comatose, the patient tends to suspect or even clearly understand how others identify him. Patients do overhear occasional conversations about themselves. Personnel unwittingly may

---

[4] We shall assume that the staff members all share the same awareness and the staff's definition of a patient's identity (dying) is correct.

[5] Erving Goffman, *The Presentation of Self in Everyday Life*, Edinburgh, Scotland: University of Edinburgh, 1956; see also the Anchor edition.

flash cues or make conversational errors, which arouse the patient's suspicions. Day and night staff may give him contradictory information or divergent clues. The frequent practice of rotating personnel through the hospital services, or adding new personnel, may add to the danger of disclosure. The patient himself may become more knowledgeable about what is going on around him after some days in the hospital, or after repeated hospitalizations. Eventually he may also understand that the hospital is organized not to give him all the information about his condition but rather to withhold most information. He therefore takes what is told him with a grain of salt and some distrust of its accuracy. In short, the original structural conditions that sustain closed awareness begin to disappear, or are counteracted by new structural conditions that make for suspicion or open awareness. This is true even when the patient's symptoms do not badly worsen, but when he does turn worse this may cause him to ask new questions about his illness, which staff members need to handle cannily to keep from him their knowledge that he is dying.

(5) Some interactants may wish to move him along into other types of awareness context. If so, they can employ certain interactional tactics which are, for the most part, merely the opposites of the non-disclosure tactics. Intentionally, a staff member may give the show away wholly or partly, by improper management of face, by carefully oblique phrasing of words, by merely failing to reassure the patient sufficiently about a hopeful prognosis, by changing all talk about the future into concentration upon the present, or by increasing avoidance both of conversation and the patient himself. Of course, personnel occasionally may just plain tell him that he is dying.

(6) The closed awareness that "surrounds" the dying patient has many significant consequences for patient and staff. The patient, unaware of the other's view of his identity, cannot act as if he were aware of dying. Thus, he cannot talk to close kin about his fate. He cannot assuage their grief. Nor can he act toward himself as if he were dying, by facing his expected death gracefully—or with panic and hysteria.

The kinsmen and hospital personnel are saved from certain stressful scenes that accompany open awareness about death, but they are also blocked from participating in various satisfying rituals of passage to death. Wives cannot openly take farewells of husbands; personnel cannot share the patient's sometimes ennobling acceptance of death. A profound consequence for the hospital itself, as well as for staff, of the closed awareness context is an interesting division of labor wherein nurses carry the brunt of stressful verbal interaction during which dying and death talk must be avoided. The physicians escape much of this stress since only brief visits are required for patients seemingly on the mend, hence talk is held to a minimum. Moreover, the climate of certain hospital services would be quite different (usually less oppressive) if closed awareness contexts were completely absent—as they are on certain special types of hospital wards.[6]

Previous Analyses of Interaction

The notion of awareness context is useful for understanding other theoretical approaches to awareness as it relates to social interaction. Our paradigm for the study of interaction within awareness contexts may be used to locate, in a single scheme, the diverse aspects of awareness and social interaction attended to in sociological writings. To illustrate this application of both concept and paradigm, we shall discuss the theoretical work of George H. Mead and Erving Goffman as well as the researches of Donald Roy and Fred Davis. Rather than assess their work *per se,* we shall discuss the writings of these men as good examples of the current state of theory and research about social interaction.

GEORGE H. MEAD:

Mead's concern with social interaction was secondary to a lifetime preoccupation with the problems of social order and its orderly change. We interpret his analysis of interaction—also his writing about communication and thought—as bearing principally on an open awareness context. In a well known passage he wrote that: "In short, the conscious or significant conversation of gestures is a much more adequate and effective mechanism of mutual adjustment within the social act—involving, as it does, the taking, by each of the individuals carrying it on, the attitudes of the others toward himself—than is the unconscious or non-significant conversation of gestures."[7] For Mead, "awareness" was essentially an *accurate* awareness of how one's own gesture (vocal or otherwise) was being defined by others, followed by further action based on that awareness. Thus: "That process . . . of responding to one's self as another responds to it, taking part in one's own conversations with others, being aware of what one is saying and using that awareness of what one is saying to determine what one is going to say thereafter—that is a process with which we are all familiar" (p. 217). This perceptive social philosopher gave his readers a rich but highly generalized analysis of that universal situation in which men genuinely and openly communicate.

Mead was not always consistently concerned with shared communica-

---

[6] Cf. Renée Fox, *Experiment Perilous,* Glencoe, Ill.: The Free Press, 1959.

[7] Anselm Strauss (ed.), *The Social Psychology of George Herbert Mead,* Chicago: University of Chicago Press, 1956, p. 173. All references are to this volume.

tion but—as the preceding quotations suggest—also with how one guesses the other's perception of his behavior so as further to direct that behavior oneself. Whether on the basis of these guesses one then misleads the other or plays the game honestly is left ambiguous. Presumably Mead meant the ensuing interaction to be genuinely open and cooperative.[8] The full force of our commentary on this aspect of his work is best demonstrated by an unusual passage wherein Mead raises and dismisses those aspects of interaction that do not involve shared symbolization. He remarks:

> There is, of course, a great deal in one's conversation with others that does not arouse in one's self the same response it arouses in others. That is particularly true in the case of emotional attitudes. One tries to bully somebody else; he is not trying to bully himself. . . . We do at times act and consider just what the effect of our attitude is going to be, and we may deliberately use a certain tone of voice to bring about a certain result. Such a tone arouses the same response in ourselves that we want to arouse in somebody else. But a very large part of what goes on in speech has not this . . . status.
>
> It is the task not only of the actor but of the artist as well to find the sort of expression that will arouse in others what is going on in himself . . . the stimulus calls out in the artist that which it calls out on the other, but this is not the natural function of language . . . (pp. 224–226).

And what is the natural function of language? "What is essential to communication is that the symbol should arouse in one's self what it arouses in the other individual." Mead seems here to touch on interaction based on something different from open awareness and genuine communication. In deliberate bullying, for example, one's activity may frighten the other but does not frighten oneself. In writing poetry, one finds the means to arouse responses in others [to] what one finds in himself (and Mead remarks that Wordsworth took some years to turn those immediate responses into poetry). And in this same passage, Mead notes that "we do not assume that the person who is angry is calling out the fear in himself that he is calling out in someone else"; that is, in this spontaneous expression of feeling, actor and audience do not respond identically. We should not be surprised to find, sandwiched within this passage, Mead's laconic comment that though we can act—quite like the actor does—"It is not a natural situation; one is not an actor all of the time." Of course no one is! But what about the times when we do act?

Mead's analysis is especially pertinent to this paper because it emphasizes a property of interaction so often absent in other men's work: the

[8] Herbert Blumer, in pointing to the great value of Mead's approach, has also emphasized concerted action, whether accomplished or developed. See Blumer's "Society as Symbolic Interaction" in Arnold Rose (ed.), *Human Behavior and Social Processes,* Boston: Houghton Mifflin, 1962, esp. pp. 187–188.

developmental properties of interaction. In Mead's writing the concept of significant symbol not only underscores the consensual character of social order but also shows how social order is changed—how social objects are formed and transformed during the course of constructed acts. In current reading of Mead, this developmental aspect tends to be overlooked; so does his processual, rather than substantial, treatment of the self. The self as process insures that interaction is usually not static or merely repetitive. In Mead's world, acts are open-ended, frequently surprising to the actors themselves. And in some of his finest writings Mead emphasizes how even past events are reconstructed, powerfully influencing the directions taken by present events. In short, interaction always tends to go somewhere, but exactly where is not always known for certain by the interactants.

ERVING GOFFMAN:

Erving Goffman's work is probably the most influential among current theoretical analyses of interaction. If he does not stand at an opposite pole from Mead, he surely stands far removed—in style, temperament, theoretical perspective, and above all in his focus on the interplay of people. In his first book, *The Presentation of Self in Everyday Life*,[9] one can easily follow his detailed central analysis of interaction.

From the beginning, Goffman emphasizes an audience's need to define an individual's identity. "When an individual enters the presence of others, they commonly seek to acquire information about him or to bring into play information about him already possessed" (p. 2). Whether or not an actor wishes, his actions yield impressions of him to his audiences. Therefore, people most frequently "devote their efforts to the creation of desired impressions" rather than act completely without guile or contrivance. "Engineering a convincing impression" is an inescapable fact (p. 162). It is a way for each interactant "to control the conduct of others" (p. 2).

Because of such impression management, "events may occur within the interaction which contradict, discredit, or otherwise throw doubt upon the actor's projection of himself." Much of Goffman's book turns around the confusion or embarrassment that occurs when interaction is thus disrupted. He analyzes extensively the "preventive practices" consequent upon disruptions: "defensively by the actor himself, and protectively when the audience strives to save the definition of the situation projected by another" (p. 7).

In all of this, Goffman focuses on closed awareness. He has a section on "team collusion" (pp. 112–120), and another on the "maint[en]ance of expressive control" (pp. 33–37). Second, he explicitly treats pretense

[9] All references are to the original Edinburgh edition.

awareness contexts. For instance, "each team tends to suppress its candid view of itself and of the other team, projecting a conception of self and a conception of other that is relatively acceptable to the other. And to insure that communication will follow established, narrow channels, each team is prepared to assist the other team, tacitly and tactfully, in maintaining the impression it is attempting to foster" (page 107).[10] In general, Goffman, at least in this volume, is uninterested in open awareness contexts; and though he touches on contexts where audiences are suspicious of the actor's projected definition, he does not go into the ways in which the suspicion gradually grows and then is validated.

But whether pretense or closed awareness is at issue, Goffman's principal focus is on how the interaction is kept going, or if disrupted, how interactants manage to get it going again. He has little interest in awareness contexts that are transformed through the deliberate operations of the interactants or through the continued course of the interaction itself. Indeed, his analysis is geared to episodic or repeated interactions rather than to sustained interplay. Consistently with this non-developmental focus, his dramaturgical model refers to the *team* of stage actors who night after night seek to create an acceptable illusion, rather than to the *drama* itself, with its plot line and evolving, relatively unpredictable, sequence of transactions.[11] Particularly it is worth underscoring that the identity of Goffman's actor is rarely problematical to himself, but only and always to his audience.[12]

In this book Goffman tends to leave implicit the structural conditions imposed by the larger social unit. Rather, he focuses mainly on situational conditions such as setting and front and back regions. Of course, most interaction in *The Presentation of Self* occurs in establishments containing service personnel and clients, insiders and outsiders; that is, persons who are either relatively unknown to each other or respectively withhold significant aspects of their private lives from each other. Goffman leaves to his readers the task of considering what kinds of structural conditions might lead to interactions quite different from those described. For example, his discussions of impression management might have been very different had he studied neighborhood blocks, small towns, or families, where participants are relatively well known to each other. Similarly, he is not much concerned with systematically tracing various consequences of the interaction (especially for larger social units); although for interactants,

---

[10] This passage is a pretty fair description of the situation in which a dying patient and his nurses both engage in pretense by delicately avoiding talk about the patient's impending death.

[11] Many readers seemed to have missed this point. Cf. a similar comment in Sheldon Messinger, Harold Sampson and Robert Towne, "Life as Theater: Some Notes on the Dramaturgic Approach to Social Reality," *Sociometry*, 25 (March, 1962), p. 108.

[12] To Goffman, surprise means potential disruption of interaction—as compared with Mead's notion of the creative and surprising impulsivity of the "I."

of course, consequences are noted in terms of specific linkages with the disruption or smooth continuance of encounters.

Aside from its restricted range of awareness contexts, Goffman's world of interaction is non-developmental and rather static. In other writings, he is concerned with interaction of considerable duration, but characteristically his interest is in the rules that govern that interaction. Often interaction proceeds to its termination almost as inexorably as a Greek tragedy.[13] For these aspects, however, his analysis is a considerable advance beyond those of his predecessors.

Next we re-examine two useful papers, our aim being first, to locate the reported research within our awareness paradigm; second, to assess its contribution to interactional analysis; and third, to suggest what might be added to that analysis if one were now to undertake such research.

DONALD ROY:

In his "Efficiency and 'The Fix': Informal Intergroup Relations in a Piecework Machine Shop,"[14] Roy is interested in demonstrating "that the interaction of two groups in an industrial organization takes place within and is conditioned by a larger intergroup network of reciprocal influences." The interaction is a contest between management and the workers. The latter adroitly scheme, connive and invent methods for attaining quotas set by management; while management attempts to minimize the success of these "black arts of 'making out.'" These arts "were not only responses to challenge from management but also stimulations, in circular interaction, to the development of more effective countermagic in the timing process" established by management's timecheckers. An important segment of Roy's discussion deals with "intergroup collusion" among workers from other departments, who become allies in this unending contest with management.

Where shall we locate Roy's research in our awareness context paradigm? From Roy's description, the awareness contexts are not entirely clear since we do not always know the extent to which management was aware of what was going on among the workers. But in general, workers' attempts to keep closed awareness about their specific collusive games seem to have alternated with management's periodic awareness of such games. Whether this periodic awareness of management transformed the closed context temporarily into pretense or open awareness is difficult to determine. Roy does, however, clearly give the structural conditions that permit both the closed awareness context and its periodic, temporary transformation to pretense or open before the workers reinstitute the closed context with a new collusive game.

13 Cf. Messinger, *et al., op. cit.*
14 *American Journal of Sociology,* 60 (November, 1954), pp. 255–266.

Roy describes in great detail the interactional tactics of both sets of players which maintain, transform and reinstitute closed awareness. Teamwork on the worker's side is exceptionally well sketched. Managerial tactics, however, are described principally from "below," for two reasons. First, Roy was doing field work as an industrial worker, and could scarcely be privy to management's specific perspectives and decisions. Second, he did not need to scrutinize management's views because his research was designed to explore how workers organized their work.

In spite of the fact that Roy describes the phases through which the contest, and hence the awareness context, oscillates, true temporal development is lacking. This is because he conceives of the interaction as unendingly the same. Apparently the limits of the interaction were set by the time period devoted to the research itself. As Roy himself notes in passing: "How far the beginning of the series [of new rules] antedated the writer's arrival is not known. Oldtimers spoke of a 'Golden Age' enjoyed before the installation of the 'Booth System' of production control." An interest in interaction process must raise these questions: from what situation did the interaction phases develop, where did they end, and what happened if someone attempted to bring the collusive interaction out into the open?

The consequences of the interaction are noted sporadically—mainly in terms of work blockages and cumulative inefficiency—but again we might wish to know much more, especially about diverse consequences for the functioning of the organization at large.

FRED DAVIS:

A very different presentation of interaction is Fred Davis' "Deviance Disavowal: The Management of Strained Interaction by the Visibly Handicapped."[15] The sub-title accurately describes what this paper is all about. The visible stigma of the handicapped person presents a threat to sociability which "is, at minimum, fourfold: its tendency to become an exclusive focal point of the interaction, its potential for inundating expressive boundaries, its discordance with other attributes of the person and, finally, its ambiguity as a predicator of joint activity." These are "contextual emergents which, depending on the particular situation, serve singly or in combination to strain the framework of normative rules and assumptions in which sociability develops."

After a discussion of these various emergents, which constitute a grave threat to interaction, we are shown "how socially adept handicapped persons cope with it so as to either keep it at bay, dissipate it or lessen its impact upon the interaction." The analysis is aimed at delineating "in

[15] *Social Problems*, 9 (Winter, 1961), pp. 120–132.

transactional terms the stages through which a social relationship with a normal typically passes." The stages are: (1) fictional acceptance, (2) "breaking through" or facilitating normalized role-taking, and (3) institutionalization of the normalized relationship. From the viewpoint of the handicapped person, the "unfolding" of the stages represents deviance disavowal; from that of the normal person it is normalization. For each stage in the process, a certain number of interactional tactics are noted, though Davis is more interested in interactional stages than in the "tremendous variety of specific approaches, ploys and stratagems that the visibly handicapped employ in social situations."

This research deals with the transformation of pretense awareness ("fictional acceptance") to open awareness ("institutionalization of the normalized relationship"), chiefly but not solely under the control of transforming operations by the handicapped. As Davis describes it, the handicapped person attempts first to keep interaction in the fictional mode (both interactants mutually aware of his stigma but neither acting as though it existed); then, gradually, the handicapped person engineers matters to a final phase where it is openly "fitting and safe to admit to certain incidental capacities, limits, and needs"—that is, where both parties may openly refer to the stigma of the handicapped person.

Davis' discussion is additionally rich because he makes some very explicit remarks about how difficult the open awareness (normalization) phase is for either party to maintain. For instance: "to integrate effectively a major claim to 'normalcy' with numerous minor waivers of the same claim is a tricky feat and one which exposes the relationship to the many situational and psychic hazards of apparent duplicity. . . ." By implication, this relationship between the two parties has a future: because it is difficult to maintain, it cannot remain at a standstill. We say "by implication" because Davis is content to carry the story only to where something like normal sociability can take place. Said another way, Davis actually is analyzing a developmental—not merely an engineered—interaction situation. "As against the simplistic model of a compulsive deviant and a futile normalizer we would propose one in which it is postulated that both are likely to become engaged in making corrective interactional efforts toward healing the breach." Precisely because *both* are likely to make those correctional efforts, this is a developmental relationship. Our paradigm helps raise the question of where the relationship is going and what further transformations, under what conditions, may occur.

Our paradigm also suggests focusing on both parties to the interplay even when it is relatively adeptly controlled by one, since our understanding of the relationship's developmental aspects necessarily requires knowledge of the actions and awareness of both parties. Thus, how does the normal interactant see the handicapped, and the interaction, at various phases of the interaction—and what is he doing, or deciding to do, about it?

What will his tactics be, whether occasional or continual? Davis also assumes that the handicapped person has often been through this type of interaction—hence has evolved tactics for handling it—while the normal person is a novice. This may be so, but in actual life both players may have had similar experiences.

Lastly, Davis attempts to specify one class of structural conditions that permit the handicapped person to manage strained interaction. He begins his paper by referring to "that genre of everyday intercourse" which is characteristically face-to-face, not too prolonged but not too fleeting either, with a certain degree of intimacy, and "ritualized to the extent that all know in general what to expect but not so ritualized as to preclude spontaneity and the slightly novel turn of events." This explicit detailing is not a mere backdrop but an intrinsic part of the analysis of interaction in the presence of physical stigma. The consequences of interaction (e.g., the satisfaction of both parties and the possibility of a continuing relationship) are left mainly implicit.

General Implications of Paradigm

Our examination of these four writers indicates that future research and theory on interactional problems should encompass a far broader range of phenomena than heretofore. Of course, one need not do everything demanded by the paradigm. But it guides the researcher in exploring and perhaps extending the limits of his data, and in stating clearly what was done and left undone, perhaps adding why and why not. The paradigm helps the theorist achieve greater clarity, integration, and depth of analysis by encouraging reflection upon what he has chosen *not* to make explicit. It also raises questions about development and structure that a straight factor approach to the study of interaction typically does not:[16] How does one type of context lead to another; what are the structural conditions—including rules—in the relevant institutions that facilitate or impede existence of a context, and changes in it; what are the effects of a changing awareness context on the identity of a participant; why does one party wish to change a context while another wishes to maintain it or reinstate it; what are the various interactional tactics used to maintain or reinstate change; and what are the consequences for each party, as well as for sustaining institutional conditions?

---

[16] The factor approach is a standard one in sociology: it is legitimated by the notion that one can only consider so much at one time with precision and clarity, and therefore boundaries must be chosen, usually according to one's interests, provided they are theoretically relevant. For a discussion of "simultaneous *versus* sequential" factor models, see Howard S. Becker, *Outsiders*, New York: The Free Press, 1963, pp. 22–25.

This developmental focus helps to eliminate the static quality and restricted boundaries for analysis that are characteristic of the factor approach. The factor approach is useful only when the analyst is conscious of the location of his conceptual boundaries within a larger developmental, substantive scheme, and can thereby explain their relevance to his readers, rather than implicitly declaring all other substantive factors out of bounds. Only then is it sensible to leave out so much that other sociologists, in the light of present theory and knowledge, recognize as relevant to the area under consideration.

The focus on structural conditions increases the likelihood that the microscopic analysis of interaction will take into account the nature of the larger social structure within which it occurs. The usual structural approach in sociology tends to neglect microscopic analysis of interaction and also inhibits attention to its developmental character. Our paradigm encompasses in one developmental scheme the twin, but often divorced, sociological concerns with social structure and social interaction. Neither need be slighted, or forgotten, for a focus on the other.

Our discussion has touched on only four possible types of awareness contexts: open, closed, pretense and suspicion. These four types are generated by the substantively relevant combinations of four variables found in our study of the literature and in our data on awareness of identity and interaction. We have considered two variables as dichotomous—*two interactants; acknowledgment of awareness* (pretense or no pretense)—and two as trichotomous—*degree of awareness* (aware, suspicious, and unaware); and *identity* (other's identity, own identity, and own identity in the eyes of the other). Logical combination of these variables would yield 36 possible types, but to start research with all the logical combinations of these variables would be an unnecessarily complex task, considering that many or most types are empirically nonexistent. Therefore, the procedure used to develop awareness context types related to interaction was first, to search data for relevant types; second, to logically substruct the variables involved; and third, on the basis of these variables to judge whether other possible types would be useful or necessary for handling the data.

Presumably, more empirically relevant types can be found by scrutinizing the sociological literature, one's own data, and one's own life.[17] Another implication of the present analysis is that increasingly complex types of awareness contexts and their distinctive consequences should be systematically sought. We recommend our procedure for evolving types,

[17] We are working with the "unawareness" context, in which neither party knows the identity of the other or his identity in the other's eyes. This is illustrated by strangers meeting or passing each other on a dark street. If they stop to talk, the first task they are likely to engage in is to transform the "unawareness" context to facilitate interaction.

as opposed to starting out with the full set of logical combinations, each of which must then be screened for empirical relevance.

We suggested, at the beginning of the paper, two factors that further complicate awareness contexts: additional people, and people representing organized systems with a stake in certain types of awareness context. Certain types of social phenomena are probably strategic for extending our knowledge of awareness contexts: for example, research discoveries in science and in industry, spy systems, deviant communities whose actions may be visible to "square," types of bargaining before audiences, such as occurs in diplomatic negotiations, and unofficial reward systems like those depicted by Melville Dalton and Alvin Gouldner.[18]

[18] *Men Who Manage*, New York: Wiley, 1959; and *Patterns of Industrial Bureaucracy*, Glencoe, Ill.: The Free Press, 1954, respectively.

39   RICHARD S. BROOKS

The Self and Political Role: A Symbolic Interactionist Approach to Political Ideology

Symbolic interaction theory, though widely applied in the analysis of other areas of human behavior, has been used infrequently in the study of politics and almost never in the study of political ideology.[1] This paper illustrates the applicability of the theory as an approach to the latter. More specifically, it attempts to find a relation between differential self conceptions and the types of political roles individuals play. It attempts to provide a tentative answer to the following question: What kinds of self-views are associated with a left-wing or moderate or right-wing or some other political role?

Traditionally, an individual's social beliefs or ideology has been viewed as a product of economic class or social conditions. More recently,

Richard S. Brooks, "The Self and Political Role: A Symbolic Interactionist Approach to Political Ideology," *The Sociological Quarterly*, vol. 10 (Winter 1969), pp. 22–31. Reprinted by permission.

[1] Two exceptions are: Carl J. Couch, "Self-Identification and Alienation," *The Sociological Quarterly*, 7:255–64 (Summer, 1966); and William Kornhauser, "Social Bases of Political Commitment: A Study of Liberals and Radicals," in Arnold M. Rose (ed.), *Human Behavior and Social Processes* (Boston: Houghton-Mifflin, 1962), pp. 321–39.

a number of sociologists and political scientists have approached it as a correlate of status crystallization.[2] But most of the empirical research on political ideology has considered it to be a manifestation of personality.[3] In the personality studies it is assumed that ideological beliefs spring from an underlying personality structure or predisposing factors within the individual. In the research presented in the present article, political ideology is treated as role perception. It is viewed as a set of norms or a role incorporated into the individual's view of himself and the world he lives in. It develops out of symbolic interaction with significant others. Political role, as well as mind and self, is "the individual importation of the social process."[4]

Preliminary Definitions

Political acts are social acts, and all social acts are directed toward objects.[5] Therefore, "political behavior" may be defined as that part of human activity directed toward the social object government. Much political behavior is institutional behavior, that is to say, it is role performance within a well-defined interactional network or social system. But political behavior sometimes takes the form of activity directed toward changing or preventing change in the social system. In this case it lies wtihin the field of what is called collective behavior.[6]

The self refers to the individual's view of himself in all of the statuses and roles which organize and direct his behavior toward all of the objects of his experience; "political self identification" refers to the individual's view of himself in the single status-role of political participant or actor. An individual's perception of his political role consists of all the norms attached to his view of himself in the status of political actor. It is his beliefs concerning the appropriate ways of acting toward the social object government.

---

[2] The status crystallization research on political behavior will be discussed in a later section of this paper.

[3] Two critiques of the personality approach to politics are: M. Brewster Smith, Jerome S. Bruner, and Robert W. White, *Opinions and Personality* (New York: John Wiley and Sons, 1956), pp. 7–23; and Richard Christie and Marie Jahoda (eds.), *Studies in the Scope and Method of the Authoritarian Personality* (Glencoe, Illinois: The Free Press, 1954).

[4] George Herbert Mead, "Mind as the Individual Importation of the Social Process," in Alfred M. Lee (ed.), *Readings in Sociology* (New York: Barnes and Noble, 1951), pp. 84–90.

[5] For discussions of "the act" as the unit of analysis in symbolic interaction theory, see Bernard N. Meltzer, *The Social Psychology of George Herbert Mead* (Kalamazoo, Michigan: Western Michigan University, 1959), pp. 23–25; and Elsworth Faris, "The Retrospective Act and Education," *Journal of Educational Sociology*, 14:79–91 (October, 1940).

[6] Ralph H. Turner and Lewis M. Killian, *Collective Behavior* (Englewood Cliffs, New Jersey: Prentice-Hall, 1957), p. 308.

As used in this paper, the term "ideology" is linked with the individual's perception of his political role. It is a set of political norms incorporated into the individual's view of himself. However, it should be noted that many political roles are non-ideological. In ordinary usage, a political role is not considered ideological unless the individual assigns importance to it relative to other roles. All members of a nation-state do not interact with respect to political objects and, consequently, do not incorporate the status of political participant into their views of themselves. In the United States, for example, a large segment of the population is politically apathetic.[7] For many persons, politics is a minor part of their lives; they define the political role as subordinate or peripheral to other roles. For some, politics is a central life role.[8] Hence, political ideology, from the standpoint of the individual, may be defined as any set of beliefs about appropriate ways of acting toward the political institution which have been saliently incorporated into the individual's view of himself. While this definition excludes those who are politically apathetic, it is broad enough to include "moderates" and "middle-of-the-roaders" as well as extremists of the left and the right.

Hypothesis

The hypothesis tested in this research is that the differences in left-wing and right-wing political role perceptions are related to the manner in which individuals identify themselves with respect to the major institutions of society. Specifically, it is hypothesized that right-wingers primarily view themselves as acting *within* these institutions. They tend to anchor themselves and center their lives within societal and communal institutions such as the family, occupation, church, and state. They of course interact and identify themselves within other groups and play other roles, but these latter tend to be peripheral. Reciprocally, it is expected that political left-wingers will identify themselves as acting within these same institutions, to be sure, but they more often view themselves as acting *against* or *toward* them as well as within them. They may also tend to identify themselves more and organize a larger part of their activity within other groups. They identify themselves in a wider variety of statuses and roles.[9]

---

[7] Lester W. Milbrath, *Political Participation* (Chicago: Rand McNally, 1965).

[8] Kornhauser, *op. cit.*

[9] *Ibid.*, found that radicals had less commitment to family and occupational roles than liberals. It is also interesting to note a similarity between the hypothesis tested in this paper and a point in Marxism. According to Marx, the "forces of production" are dynamic while the "relations of production" tend to be static. The latter tends to be static because the dominant class resists the changes required by the "forces of production." That is, individuals who are anchored in the social system support the status quo.

Differences in behavior stemming from differential interaction and identification are probably in the direction of acceptance of the prevailing norms of the groups or systems within which the interaction occurs. And the prevailing norms in any group may include those that are relevant to supporting or maintaining the group. Individuals who interact primarily within the family, occupational group, church, and state acquire norms directed toward supporting these institutions. Individuals who interact within many groups in addition to the major institutions are more likely to acquire norms in conflict with the status quo.

Method

The data for this research were gathered over a period of three years (1964 through 1966), and the 254 respondents in the "sample" were selected because they were assumed to be ideologues (individuals who have internalized ideological political roles). The interviewing was conducted by persons trained for this specific project, and the respondents were selected by the interviewers on the basis of preset criteria.[10] Briefly, these criteria included such things as reputation as left- or right-winger, level of political activity, and demographic and status criteria. The 254 respondents are not representative of any larger population, and no attempt will be made to generalize beyond them. However, the distribution of the sample according to age, sex, occupation, religion, education, geography, and political party preference creates the possibility though not the probability, that they are somewhat representative of ideologues.

With only five or six exceptions, all of the respondents come from the 10 percent of the population who are most active politically.[11] They vote regularly, contribute money, attend political meetings, read the news, talk politics, and define themselves as having a strong interest in politics. The sample includes individuals who identify themselves as Marxists, Black Nationalists, Professional Revolutionists, Socialists, Liberals, Moderates, Moderate Republicans, Conservatives, Goldwater Republicans, proponents of Moral Rearmament, and John Birchers.

A ten-item Guttman Scale was used to observe and measure the re-

[10] In this study, "reputation" is from the standpoint of individuals in the respondents' home communities. The respondents were located by graduate students and undergraduate majors in sociology and political science, and the latter came from a wide variety of communities. The sample includes not only those reputed to be liberals, conservatives, Black Nationalists, etc., but those reputed to be political activists such as elective office holders, candidates for elective office, and party leaders and workers. In order to obtain a broader distribution of the sample, the interviewers were assigned quotas based on age, sex, occupation, religion, education, and geography.

[11] For a brief discussion of the extent of political participation in the United States see Fred I. Greenstein, *The American Party System and the American People* (Englewood Cliffs, New Jersey: Prentice-Hall, 1963), pp. 9–11.

spondent's political role perceptions. Forty-three items, selected from almost one hundred in a pretest schedule, were included in the interview schedule. It was possible to construct two or three scales with more than ten items, but many of the items in these scales were quite similar to each other and did not present as wide a variety of political topics as the ten-item scale. Conspicuously absent from the latter are items relating to foreign policy, labor relations, and Communism. These would not scale with the items used in the present scale.

Each item in the scale can be treated as a norm, because it expresses approval or disapproval of a plan of action toward the social object government. The items are statements relating to current, controversial political topics, and the respondents were asked to agree or disagree. The scale as a whole, however, does not present a complete picture of the political role, but only a role segment; for all of the 254 political activists in the sample obviously have internalized more political norms than the ten included in the scale.

The ten items are listed below with either "agree" or "disagree" in parentheses to indicate the direction of a left-wing response. The items are listed in the order into which they fall in the scale. That is, the first item received the smallest number of left-wing responses, and the last item received the largest number of left-wing responses.

1. It is too bad that some people consider patriotism old-fashioned. (Disagree)
2. A program of socialized medicine for the entire population would be better than the more limited program of compulsory health insurance for old people. (Agree)
3. The federal government should use its power to put an end to economic and social inequality. (Agree)
4. Negroes are moving too fast and pushing too hard in the Civil Rights movement. (Disagree)
5. The state and local governments should be left free to work out their social and economic problems without interference from the federal government. (Disagree)
6. The United States is leaning too much toward socialism. (Disagree)
7. There is too much government control of the economy. (Disagree)
8. Governmental expenditures for welfare, education, and social security should be greatly increased. (Agree)
9. Federal government aid for education should be increased. (Agree)
10. Barry Goldwater would make a great President. (Disagree)

Table 1 gives the number of respondents in each of the eleven scale types, the number of errors, and the pattern of response for each scale type. The eighteen individuals in Scale Type 1 are the farthest left, both polit-

TABLE 1. Left wing–right wing Guttman scale

Scale Type	No. in Scale Type	No. of Errors	Left-Wing Response on Items
(Left)			
1	18	12	All ten items
2	22	22	2 through 10
3	22	11	3 through 10
4	20	16	4 through 10
5	27	25	5 through 10
6	38	47	6 through 10
7	13	8	7 through 10
8	15	12	8 through 10
9	33	44	9 through 10
10	31	31	10
11	15	4	None of the items
(Right)			
Total	254	232	

C. R. = .91.

ically and in terms of scale order. The fifteen individuals in Scale Type 11 are the farthest right.

A second instrument employed in the study was the Twenty Statements Test, also known as the TST or the "Who am I?" This test was developed at the State University of Iowa by Manford H. Kuhn.[12] It is used in the present research to measure the individuals' identifications of themselves with respect to the major social institutions. The TST is a simple, open-ended, relatively unstructured test and is administered by giving the respondent a sheet of paper with twenty numbered blank spaces on it and asking him to make twenty different statements about himself in answer to the question, "Who am I?"

There are several methods for the analysis of the TST responses, and some of these are based on form and structure and ignore the content of the statements.[13] But the method used in the present paper was developed for this specific research and is based on the literal content of the statements.

The basic rule in the present method of scoring the TST was to count the number of mentions of the major social institutions: the family, the occupational or economic institution, the church or religious institution, the state or governmental or political institution, and civic and service or-

[12] Manford H. Kuhn and Thomas S. McPartland, "An Empirical Investigation of Self-Attitudes," *American Sociological Review,* 19:68–76 (February, 1954). For a criticism of the TST see Charles W. Tucker, "Some Methodological Problems of Kuhn's Self Theory," *The Sociological Quarterly,* 7:345–58 (Summer, 1966).

[13] "Manual for the Twenty-Statements Problem," Department of Research, The Greater Kansas City Mental Health Foundation, Rev. mimeograph (January, 1959).

ganizations.[14] However, two important exceptions to this rule should be noted. In the first place, a distinction was made between acting within an institution and acting against or toward it. For example, "I am a liberal," "I am a Democrat," and "I am nonpartisan" were counted as political mentions, for they seem to identify the individual as acting or playing a role in the political system. "I dislike politics" and "I am a radical" were not counted as major institutional mentions because they seem to identify the individual as playing a role toward or against the state rather than within it. The second exception to the rule was the counting of physical self-identification statements as implied references to major institutions. This included statements such as the following: "I am a blond," "I am overweight," "I own an automobile," and "I live on College Street." While these statements do not mention major social institutions, they are examples of what Kuhn and McPartland call "locus" or "consensual" references and indicate "anchorage or self-identification in a social system."[15]

The 254 respondents gave a total of 4083 statements on the TST. Of these, 2376 (58 percent) were references to major institutions. The average

TABLE 2. Distribution of total number of statements and of number of major institutional statements on the Twenty Statements Test, by political category

		Statements on the Twenty Statements Test			
*Political Category**		*TST Statements*		*Major Institutional Statements*	
	N	No.	$\overline{X}$	No.	$\overline{X}$
Left	40	609	15.2	296	7.4
Left of Center	42	670	16.0	356	8.5
Center	78	1274	16.3	747	9.6
Right of Center	48	775	16.1	485	10.1
Right	46	755	16.4	492	10.7
Total	254	4083	16.1	2376	9.4

* The "Left" consists of scale types 1 and 2; the "Left of Center," scale types 3 and 4; the "Center," scale types 5, 6, and 7; the "Right of Center," scale types 8 and 9; and the "Right," scale types 10 and 11.

[14] In addition to mentions of the family, occupation, church, and state, references to local community groups, service organizations, and "civic duties and responsibilities" are counted as major institutional mentions.

[15] Kuhn and McPartland, *op. cit.*, p. 70. The "physical self-identification" statements of this research are quite similar to the category "A" statements in Thomas S. McPartland, John H. Cumming, Wynona S. Garretson, "Self-Conception and Ward Behavior in Two Psychiatric Hospitals," *Sociometry*, 24:111–24 (June, 1961); and the "possession or location" statements in Couch, *op. cit.* Self-identification statements of this kind are quite clear and unambiguous, and others know how to behave consistently toward persons who identify themselves in this manner. According to McPartland, statements of this kind "refer to a more concrete level than that on which social interaction ordinarily is based. They contain information about the self which can be validated with a mirror, a yardstick, or a scale; . . ." "Manual for the Twenty Statements Problem," p. 6.

number of all statements was 16.1, while the average number of major institutional statements was 9.4 (Table 2).

Findings

The findings, presented in Tables 2, 3, and 4, support the hypothesis.[16] Table 2 shows an increase in the average number of mentions of major institutions, moving from the political left to the political right. The 40 leftists averaged 7.4 such mentions, while the 46 rightists averaged 10.7 such mentions. Only 49 percent of the statements made by the former refer to the major institutions, while 65 percent of the statements made by the latter are of this kind.

Tables 3 and 4 show an association in the direction of left-wingers not mentioning major institutions on the TST and right-wingers making such mentions. In Table 3 it can be seen that 16 of the 18 individuals in Scale Type 1 made fewer than the median number of 9 institutional mentions, while 10 out of 15 in Scale Type 11 mentioned the major institutions more than 9 times. In Table 4, 75 percent of the 40 individuals in the Left

TABLE 3. Distribution of mentions of major institutions on the Twenty Statements Test, by political scale type

Political Scale Type	*Mentions of Major Institutions*		Total
	*Median or Below**	*Above Median**	
	Percentage	Percentage	No.
(Left)			
1	89	11	18
2	64	36	22
3	73	27	22
4	55	45	20
5	56	44	27
6	47	53	38
7	38	62	13
8	13	87	15
9	48	52	31
10	35	65	31
11	33	67	15
(Right)			
Total	51	49	254

Gamma = .36; x^2 = 30.64; p < .001.
* The median number of mentions of major institutions is 9.

[16] Tables 1 and 3 present the data by political scale type; but in Tables 2 and 4, scale types 1 and 2 have been collapsed into the category "Left," 3 and 4 into "Left of Center," 5, 6, and 7 into "Center," 8 and 9 into "Right of Center," and 10 and 11 into "Right."

TABLE 4. Distribution of mentions of major institutions on the Twenty Statements Test, by political category

| Political Category* | Mentions of Major Institutions | | |
	Median or Below†	Above Median†	Total
	Percentage	*Percentage*	*No.*
Left	75	25	40
Left of Center	64	36	42
Center	49	51	78
Right of Center	38	62	48
Right	35	65	46
Total	51	49	254

Gamma $= .39$; $x^2 = 20.80$; $p < .001$.
* The "Left" consists of scale types 1 and 2; the "Left of Center," scale types 3 and 4; the "Center," scale types 5, 6, and 7; the "Right of Center," scale types 8 and 9; and the "Right," scale types 10 and 11.
† The median number of mentions of major institutions is 9.

made fewer than the median number of institutional mentions; and the percentage decreases through each political category, with only 35 percent of the 46 individuals in the Right making less than 9 mentions.[17]

Discussion

The most important contribution of the present research is its illustration of the utility of symbolic interaction theory as an approach to political ideology. It demonstrates an association of self identification with left-wing and right-wing political role perception. The limitations of the data do not permit a claim to superiority over other theoretical orientations, but this research does demonstrate that political ideology can be approached empirically within the framework of that theory. According to a recent statement, two of the major adverse criticisms of symbolic interaction theory are (1) "the limited researchability of some of its concepts" and (2) "its presumed inapplicability to broad, societal phenomena."[18] To some

[17] The Gamma (Goodman and Kruskal's coefficient of ordinal association) of .39 can be interpreted to mean that for every pair of individuals drawn at random from the 254 in the sample, the probability is 39 percent greater that the pair will confirm the hypothesis rather than contradict it. It should also be noted that the findings support the hypothesis when political mentions and physical self-identifications are not counted in the scoring of the TST. For example, when these statements are not counted, 29 percent of the statements of the 40 leftists are institutional mentions, while 39 percent of the statements of the 46 rightists refer to major institutions.
[18] Jerome G. Manis and Bernard N. Meltzer (eds.), *Symbolic Interaction, A Reader in Social Psychology* (Boston: Allyn and Bacon, 1967), p. 495.

extent, the present research surmounts these difficulties. It provides an empirical test for a hypothesis, derived from the theory, which relates the individual's self conception to his perception of the political role. It demonstrates an association between left-wing or right-wing political role perception and the way an individual views himself with respect to the major societal institutions. In answer to the second criticism, it should be noted that political ideology falls within the scope of the phrase "broad, societal phenomena"; and although this research is basically microsociological, it deals with intra- and interpersonal relations within the context of institutions and social systems. For the independent variable in this study is the way the individual views himself as an actor within the larger social system.

A number of recent studies have approached political ideology as a product of inconsistent or poorly crystallized status.[19] Because of the difference in orientation, it is interesting to contrast these studies to the symbolic interaction approach. This contrast is most apparent in the approach to status. In the status crystallization studies, status is assigned objectively by the observer on the basis of the subject's rank or membership in income, occupation, education, or ethnic categories. In symbolic interaction theory, an individual's statuses are his own view of his locations in various social systems, and the assignment is made by the individual himself in the process of interacting with others. That is, a person's status is not determined by the position he "really" occupies in a social category, it results from the way others behave toward him and the way he interprets that behavior. Status, in this view, reflects identification with significant others or reference groups, not mere membership in a group or collectivity. Income, occupation, education, and ethnic group are relevant to his behavior in a given status if, and only if, the individual incorporates them into his view of himself. The Twenty Statements Test is a projective instrument which permits the investigator to make an assessment of the subject's own interpretation of his statuses.

From the point of view of symbolic interaction, the status crystallization research seems to either omit "definitions of the situation" or assume a correspondence between "objective" status and perceived status. In the words of Herbert Blumer, "Human beings interpret or 'define' each other's

---

[19] Gary B. Rush, "Status Consistency and Right-Wing Extremism," *American Sociological Review*, 32:86–92 (February, 1967); Irwin W. Goffman, "Status Consistency and Preference for Change in Power Distribution," *American Sociological Review*, 22:275–81 (June, 1957); Emile Benoit-Smullyan, "Status, Status Types, and Status Interrelation," *American Sociological Review*, 9:289–94 (April, 1944); Gerhard E. Lenski, "Status Inconsistency and the Vote: A Four Nation Test," *American Sociological Review*, 32:296–301 (April, 1967). Gerhard E. Lenski, "Social Participation and Status Crystallization," *American Sociological Review*, 21:458 (August, 1956). Gerhard E. Lenski, "Status Crystallization: A Non-Vertical Dimension of Social Status," *American Sociological Review*, 19:412 (August, 1954).

actions instead of merely reacting to each other's actions."[20] They do not respond to or organize their activities in terms of what the situation or world "really" is, but to what they interpret it to be or believe it is. To see a pin and pick it up is to engage in activity. If the pin turns out to be an optical illusion, one gets the exercise nevertheless.

[20] Herbert Blumer, "Society as Symbolic Interaction," in Rose (ed.), *Human Behavior and Social Process, op. cit.*, p. 180.

40   SHELDON STRYKER

Role-Taking Accuracy and Adjustment[1]

The assumption that knowledge is necessarily adjustive and ignorance or lack of knowledge necessarily maladjustive may fairly be said to suffuse the thinking of current social science whether in its "pure" or "applied" forms (8, 19). This assumption is clearly, and perhaps especially, embedded in various therapeutic uses of role-playing techniques (2, 7, 20, 21, 27). It is present as well in the use of role-playing as a teaching aid (4, 15) and in the increased use of this technique in diverse business settings (3, 11, 17). In all these instances, it is assumed that role-playing will improve role-taking skills and that the increases in knowledge of others consequent to improved role-taking will mean more adjusted social relationships.

This line of thinking takes on wider interest with the observation that many who write in the tradition of George Herbert Mead argue the adjustment functions of accurate role-taking (5, 16, 22).[2] Here, it must be stressed that Mead's usage of the adjustment concept differs significantly from contemporary usage. For Mead, adjustment is synonymous with

Sheldon Stryker, "Role-Taking Accuracy and Adjustment," *Sociometry*, vol. 20 (December 1957), pp. 286–296. Reprinted by permission.
[1] This research was partially supported by a grant from the Graduate School, Indiana University.
[2] While our interest in the question being raised stems from Mead, and thus the paper is oriented to his work and interpretations of it, the fact that persons of somewhat different theoretical leanings present analogous arguments should not be overlooked. So, for example, Sullivan (26) discusses "selective inattention," describing this process as a "security operation" by which "we fail to recognize the actual import of a good many things we see, hear, think, do and say, not because there is anything the matter with our zones of interaction with others but because the process of inferential analysis is opposed by the self system." Sullivan clearly regards selective inattention in negative terms, a "powerful brake on personal and on human progress" and "more than any other of the inappropriate and inadequate performances of life, the classic means by which we do not profit from experience . . ." (26, pp. 374, 346).

adaptation, both terms referring to a *process* whereby one alters the course of his behavior in terms of the demands of the social situation (18, pp. 155–159). Adjustment, as it is currently used, is a static concept, typically referring to an *end-state* of happiness, satisfaction, and the like (10, pp. 48–49). Again, however, the implication of adjustment in the sense of happiness and satisfaction as an end-product of accuracy in the role-taking process had been drawn by many.

Thus, on both practical and theoretical grounds, the answer to the question of the relationship between role-taking and adjustment (as end-state) becomes important. This question may be formulated as an hypothesis: the adjustment of the individual is a function of the accuracy with which he can take the role of the other(s) implicated with him in some social situation.

This hypothesis and the design of the study stem from an interest in testing implications drawn from Mead's theory. Given this interest, we have utilized a conception of role-taking as anticipation of the responses of others implicated with one in an ongoing social situation (18, pp. 151, 242–243, 253–254). Accurate role-taking has been operationally defined as the correct prediction of the responses of others. Role-taking, so conceived, is obviously related to such concepts as empathy, insight, social sensitivity, and so on, studies of which have used similar measurement procedures. These concepts are not, however, synonyms; and the similarity of measurement procedures should not be taken to imply identical conceptualization or theoretical concern.[3]

[3] There is considerable confusion in the literature with regard to the concepts role-taking, empathy, sympathy, identification, insight, social sensitivity, etc. These are sometimes seen as independent, sometimes as overlapping and sometimes as essentially identical. We cannot attempt, here, to distinguish systematically among these concepts: Dymond (9) provides an extensive review of this literature, offering necessary distinctions. Suffice it to say that, for us, role-taking is anticipatory behavior; and that the emotional unity, participation in emotional life of others, "feeling-with" quality, and fellow-feeling that sometimes (although not always) are incorporated into these other concepts are not seen as part of the role-taking concept.

It is true that there may be diverse sources of accuracy when role-taking scores are based on correctness in prediction. From the standpoint of Mead's theory, which postulates that one's behavior is predicated on the symbolic anticipation of responses of others, the "impurity" of our role-taking index is of little consequence. This theory, as it has thus far been developed, does not require distinguishing the various possible bases of accuracy. The problem of "impurities" in studies of empathy, insight, etc., has been attacked by Hastorf and Bender (13), Cronbach (6), and Gage and Cronbach (12). Hastorf and Bender suggest that "projection" can be screened out by subtracting from an accuracy score a second score based on the coincidence of ascriber's own responses and his predictions for another. This technique is unable, however, to distinguish between correct ascriptions based on knowledge and correct ascriptions based on projection when, in fact, ascriber and other respond identically to an item. The technique has the same difficulty with correct predictions when ascriber and other disagree with respect to an item (12). Cronbach (6) develops a model which distinguishes four components of accuracy scores. The model is, however, premised on a research design which requires judges to predict responses of (the same) multiple others, rather than on a design strictly analogous to ours.

The role-taking conception requires that predictor and other be mutually implicated in an ongoing social situation, and that predictions be made with reference to responses meaningfully related to that social situation. These, and consideration of desirable controls, led to the selection of the family as the most appropriate setting for the study. Data pertinent to the hypothesis were gathered in the summer of 1954 from 46 family units, residents of Bloomington, Indiana. Each family unit consisted of a married pair and the parents of one, but not both, of this pair.[4] Each subject responded to a 20-item Likert-type attitude scale dealing with traditionalism in family-related matters.[5] He was asked for his own attitudes, and to predict or ascribe the responses the two other-generation members of his family would make to the items of this scale. An index of role-taking accuracy, consisting of the number of correct predictions person A makes of person B's responses, expressed as a percentage of total predictions of B's responses, was computed for each subject.[6]

From the same set of responses, an index of agreement between parent and offspring was devised, consisting of the percentage of items on which a given parent's own responses to the items of the scale corresponded with his offspring's responses.

Subjects also responded to a 40-item instrument indexing their adjustment to each of the persons for whom they ascribed attitudinal responses, and to a 10-item instrument indexing their dependence upon these persons. Odd-even correlations of from .88 to .92, and a test-retest correlation of .87, deriving from various pretests of the adjustment index provide evidence that this index meets minimal reliability requirements. That the index is, to a degree, a valid instrument is indicated by its ability to distinguish between groups, whose adjustment scores may be expected to differ: e.g., the scores of females with reference to their own relatives are higher than are those of males; scores with reference to own relatives are higher than those with reference to in-laws. We have no reliability data for the dependence index. Validity evidence includes the facts that, in accord with ex-

---

[4] In most instances, only the parents of one of the offspring pair resided in the community. When both sets of parents were available, the choice of one was determined by the desire to maintain a balance in the numbers within relationship categories. It should be stressed that "sampling" was not random. We have used statistical techniques based on random sampling, nonetheless, on the grounds that formal (objective) assessment of our data was preferable to nonformal (subjective).

[5] This instrument was adapted from a scale devised by P. E. Huffman (14) and entitled "Traditional Family Ideology Scale." There is evidence from this source that the instrument is reasonably reliable and valid.

[6] Subjects responded to the attitude items via a four-point continuum: Strongly Agree, Agree, Disagree, Strongly Disagree. The decision to use this set of response categories was reached after extensive pretesting designed to provide items which were relatively stable both when a subject responded for himself and when he predicted how another would respond. The requirement of item stability also dictated that the two agree, and the two disagree, responses be scored as identical for purposes of the role-taking index.

pectations, females indicate a greater degree of dependence upon their relatives than do males, and that there is greater "neutrality" on this index in relation to in-laws than in relation to own relatives. Further, unpublished data show that offspring scores indicating dependence on parent are associated with parent scores indicating dominance over offspring, and that offspring scores indicating dominance over parent are associated with parent scores indicating dependence on offspring.[7]

The study has available, then, indices of role-taking accuracy, agreement, adjustment, dependence, and subjects' own attitudes on family traditionalism.

Each subject ascribed the attitudes of two others. There are, consequently, 16 categories of subjects—8 parent and 8 offspring—each containing the responses of 23 persons. The notations in subsequent tables follow the convention of placing the role-taker first, the person whose role is taken second, and use the following abbreviations: son—S; son-in-law—IS; daughter—D; daughter-in-law—ID; father—F; father-in-law—IF; mother—M; mother-in-law—IM. Thus, for example, the notation S-IF refers to the category comprised of male offspring who ascribed the attitudes of their fathers-in-law.

The expectation from the initial hypothesis is that high role-taking accuracy will be associated with high adjustment. To test this expectation, subjects in the various relationship categories were dichotomized, using median role-taking or ascription accuracy scores as the breaking point. The eight parent and eight offspring categories were grouped and analyzed separately, using analysis of variance.

Table 1 presents the test of the hypothesis for the parent categories. The cell entries are mean adjustment scores, with higher scores indicating better adjustment. There is, it will be noted, a statistically significant difference between the weighted row means. However, the direction of the difference is not in accord with that hypothesized. That is, parents who are comparatively *poor* role-takers are significantly *better* adjusted with reference to their offspring than are parents who are comparatively accurate role-takers. The row mean difference in Table 2, for the offspring categories, is in the expected direction. However, this difference is not statistically significant.

What might explain the inverse, statistically significant relationship between role-taking accuracy and adjustment for the parent category?[8] Clues are provided through speculation concerning the parent-adult off-

---

[7] For more complete accounts of these indices, and the data on the basis of which many of these remarks are made, see (24). The unpublished data will be made available to anyone interested in them.

[8] It has been pointed out to me by Dr. Nathan L. Gage that the inverse relationship between role-taking accuracy and adjustment appearing in Table 1 could occur if there is also an inverse relationship between parent adjustment to offspring and off-

TABLE 1. Parent adjustment by high or low role-taking accuracy

	F–S	F–D	F–IS	F–ID	M–S	M–D	M–IS	M–ID	Row
High									
M	56.70	60.10	54.23	48.67	59.58	58.42	50.58	58.64	55.71
N	10	10	13	12	12	12	12	11	92
Low									
M	59.15	64.15	53.70	58.45	61.55	66.72	55.45	57.08	59.66
N	13	13	10	11	11	11	11	12	92

Completed Analysis of Variance

	Sums of Squares	d.f.	Mean Square	F
Columns	2372.58	7	338.94	2.24
Rows	616.95	1	616.95	4.07
Interaction	627.82	7	89.69	
Within groups	25470.82	168	151.61	

Weighted mean difference, rows: 3.68. F_{95} (1,168) = 3.90.

TABLE 2. Offspring adjustment by high or low role-taking accuracy

	S–F	S–M	S–IF	S–IM	D–F	D–M	D–IF	D–IM	Row*
High									
M	42.90	57.50	51.89	47.00	58.67	63.46	47.09	52.18	52.91
N	10	10	9	12	12	13	11	11	88
Low									
M	55.62	48.08	48.79	49.73	61.18	60.10	37.75	42.25	50.13
N	13	13	14	11	11	10	12	12	96

* Preliminary analysis of variance indicated no statistically significant difference between row means appears in this table.

spring relationship and the cited findings, and through a consideration of thinking and research already in the literature.

Theorizing about the parent-adult offspring relationship, the following assertions seem justified: (a) the self-identifications and respect of parents are bound up with the lives of their *adult* offspring to a greater degree

spring scores on the family traditionalism scale; and that, under these circumstances, the inferences drawn from the table are not warranted. Similarly, the implications drawn from subsequent Tables 3–8 would not be warranted if a negative relationship between parent adjustment and offspring traditionalism existed for the subjects represented in Tables 3, 5, and 7, and if a positive relationship between parent adjustment and offspring traditionalism obtained for the subjects represented in Tables 4, 6, and 8. These possibilities have been checked, using Pearsonian correlations and also using analysis of variance. The results of these analyses were negative; i.e., relationships between parent adjustment and offspring traditionalism which would call for an alternative interpretation of the findings did not occur.

than are those of such offspring with the lives of their parents. That is, (b) parents are psychologically more involved with their offspring than are offspring with their parents. Thus, (c) evidence of gaps between the attitudes and behaviors of parents and offspring are more likely to be resisted and distorted by parents; and (d) when such evidence becomes open and recognized by parents, its consequences for their adjustment to their offspring are likely to be accentuated.

More generally, Moore and Tumin argue that ". . . ignorance must be viewed not simply as a passive or dysfunctional condition, but as an active and often positive element in operating structures and relations" (19, p. 787). Robin Williams writes: "It is extremely important also that many of the implicit understandings that make society possible are not just *implicit* but are also resistant to statement: it is as if there is a tacit agreement not to express or become aware of what would be dysfunctional. . . . We suspect that a study of areas of blocked communication would often reveal conflicts that remain non-disabling only so long as they are kept from overt crystallization" (29, pp. 528–529). Pertinent are the researches of William F. Whyte (28) and Howard S. Becker (1). Whyte, describing the social structure of the restaurant, points out that, in a society in which males are expected to originate action for females, interposing a high counter as a physical barrier to free communication between waitresses and countermen filling their orders serves to protect the countermen. Becker suggests that platforms, pianos, chairs, and so on, perform the same function for the dance musician in relation to his audience.

The foregoing suggests an hypothesis which would serve to explain the finding that parents who are accurate in their role-taking are significantly less well adjusted to their offspring than are parents who are inaccurate role-takers, while the same finding does not hold for offspring role-takers. The hypothesis asserts that the greater one's vulnerability in a relationship, the greater the tendency to erect blocks to full knowledge of the other in that relationship.

Data are available to test this explanatory hypothesis. Earlier it was noted that the study provides scores on scales measuring traditional family attitudes, dependence, and agreement of parent and offspring with respect to familial attitudes. It may be expected that highly traditional parents will be more vulnerable in their relations to offspring than nontraditional parents; that parents who are dependent upon their children will be more vulnerable than independent parents; and that parents whose views do not agree with their offspring's will be more vulnerable than will parents whose views coincide with those of their offspring. Treating vulnerability as an intervening variable, from the hypothesis, then, it follows that the inverse relationship between role-taking and adjustment should be more marked for highly traditional parents than nontraditional, for dependent parents than independent, for low-agreement parents than high-agreement.

These expectations are examined in Tables 3–8. In each instance, analysis proceeded as follows: the parent sample was dichotomized, using median scores (on tradition, dependence, agreement). Then, each subsample was further broken down into two categories, accurate and inaccurate role-takers, on the basis of median scores within these subsamples. The cell entries in the tables are, as earlier, mean adjustment scores.

As the analyses of variance indicate, the expectations deriving from the vulnerability hypothesis are borne out. For highly traditional parents (Table 3), dependent parents (Table 5), and low-agreement parents (Table

TABLE 3. Parent adjustment, high-tradition parents only, by high or low role-taking accuracy

	F–S	F–D	F–IS	F–ID	M–S	M–D	M–IS	M–ID	Row
High									
M	53.50	57.20	51.00	42.50	57.80	61.57	48.86	60.20	53.80
N	4	5	7	6	5	7	7	5	46
Low									
M	67.83	62.50	59.83	60.25	65.00	65.40	60.60	60.83	62.87
N	6	8	6	4	6	5	5	6	46

Completed Analysis of Variance

	Sums of Squares	d.f.	Mean Square	F
Columns	1622.09	7	231.73	2.13
Rows	1588.41	1	1588.41	14.60
Interaction	586.78	7	83.83	
Within groups	8270.83	76	108.83	

Weighted mean difference, rows: 8.42. F_{99} (1, 76) = 6.99.

TABLE 4. Parent adjustment, low-tradition parents only, by high or low role-taking accuracy

	F–S	F–D	F–IS	F–ID	M–S	M–D	M–IS	M–ID	Row
High									
M	58.00	66.60	60.50	54.83	63.50	64.60	61.50	61.20	60.98
N	7	5	4	6	4	5	4	5	40
Low									
M	51.50	63.20	48.33	57.43	57.13	59.00	46.57	51.14	54.12
N	6	5	6	7	8	6	7	7	52

Completed Analysis of Variance

	Sums of Squares	d.f.	Mean Square	F
Columns	1356.93	7	193.85	1.37
Rows	1012.96	1	1012.96	7.17
Interaction	587.69	7	83.96	
Within groups	10735.66	76	141.26	

Weighted mean difference, rows: 6.75. F_{99} (1, 76) = 6.99.

TABLE 5. Parent adjustment, dependent parents only, by high or low role-taking accuracy

	F–S	F–D	F–IS	F–ID	M–S	M–D	M–IS	M–ID	Row
High									
M	52.75	57.00	58.00	48.33	57.57	64.43	59.86	60.57	57.65
N	8	4	6	6	6	7	7	7	51
Low									
M	64.80	66.29	57.17	64.17	67.40	67.83	63.00	62.33	64.00
N	5	7	6	6	5	6	7	6	48

Completed Analysis of Variance

	Sums of Squares	d.f.	Mean Square	F
Columns	1099.01	7	157.00	1.12
Rows	1119.86	1	1119.86	8.01
Interaction	642.53	7	91.79	
Within groups	11603.41	83	139.80	

Weighted mean difference, rows: 6.58. F_{99} (1, 83) = 6.95.

TABLE 6. Parent adjustment, independent parents only, by high or low role-taking accuracy

	F–S	F–D	F–IS	F–ID	M–S	M–D	M–IS	M–ID	Row*
High									
M	54.00	62.17	51.83	52.40	59.75	58.14	40.67	55.25	55.13
N	5	6	6	5	4	7	3	4	40
Low									
M	64.00	61.67	49.20	48.33	57.25	55.33	39.17	51.83	53.24
N	5	6	5	6	8	3	6	6	45

* Preliminary analysis of variance indicated no statistically significant difference between row means appears in this table.

7), accurate role-taking is accompanied by comparatively poor adjustment. In each of these cases, row differences are statistically significant. For nontraditional parents (Table 4), independent parents (Table 6), and high-agreement parents (Table 8) row differences are *reversed*—i.e., the mean adjustment scores for accurate role-takers are higher than they are for inaccurate role-takers, although only in the case of the nontraditional parents is the difference significant, and in one case (Table 8) the row difference is extremely slight. It should be noted, however, that in the independent parent table (Table 6), in seven of the eight relationship categories there are higher mean adjustment scores in the accurate role-taker cells; one large "reversal" in the F-S category probably accounts for the absence of statistically significant results. There is, it may also be noted, no particular consistency in the direction of the row differences in the high-agreement parents table (Table 8).

TABLE 7. Parent adjustment, low-agreement parents only, by high or low role-taking accuracy

	F–S	F–D	F–IS	F–ID	M–S	M–D	M–IS	M–ID	Row
High									
M	56.40	53.60	52.33	41.50	60.80	61.43	49.00	51.86	53.37
N	5	5	6	6	5	7	5	7	46
Low									
M	60.00	63.33	49.87	57.40	64.00	65.40	51.80	63.60	59.32
N	7	6	7	5	7	5	5	5	47

Completed Analysis of Variance

	Sums of Squares	d.f	Mean Square	F
Columns	2484.87	7	354.98	2.52
Rows	793.71	1	793.71	5.63
Interaction	710.24	7	101.46	
Within groups	10848.37	77	140.89	

Weighted mean difference, rows: 5.89. F_{95} (1, 77) = 3.97.

TABLE 8. Parent adjustment, high-agreement parents only, by high or low role-taking accuracy

	F–S	F–D	F–IS	F–ID	M–S	M–D	M–IS	M–ID	Row*
High									
M	56.00	66.60	56.17	55.83	60.20	66.33	53.00	64.50	59.40
N	6	5	6	6	5	6	7	6	47
Low									
M	59.60	64.86	62.00	60.83	56.50	57.20	57.00	52.40	58.95
N	5	7	4	6	6	5	6	5	44

* Preliminary analysis of variance indicated no statistically significant differences between row means appears in this table.

In over-all terms, the evidence clearly supports the hypothesis that vulnerability increases the likelihood of blocks to communication.

To return to our point of departure, the presumed adjustive consequences of knowledge of others: our findings clearly call into question any easy assumption on this score. Rather, they point to the conclusion that, at least under certain circumstances, such knowledge is maladjustive. Further, these findings serve to emphasize the lack of clarity in interpretations of Mead's social psychological theory. It may still be true, as Mead held, that the process of adapting one's behavior to others with whom one is socially implicated is dependent on role-taking.[9] That one will always

9 Recently, Steiner (23) has questioned the generality of this assertion, noting that empirical evidence with regard to the propositions that accurate social perceptions are responsible for interpersonal competence and for group efficiency is contradictory. His

become better adjusted, in the sense of happier or more satisfied, through role-taking must, on the basis of these findings, be doubted.

The reverse side of this coin should be noted. The assertion that knowledge is necessarily adjustive cannot be defended; it is highly probable that the unqualified assertion that ignorance is adjustive is equally invalid. The problem, now, is to specify further the conditions under which knowledge or ignorance is adjustive or maladjustive.[10]

References

1. Becker, H. S., "The Professional Dance Musician and His Audience," *American Journal of Sociology*, 1951, 57, 136–144.
2. Borden, R., "The Use of Psychodrama in an Institution for Delinquent Girls," *Sociometry*, 1940, 3, 81–90.
3. Chapman, E. A., "Role-Playing in a Cooperative Retail Training Class," *Occupations*, 1951, 29, 358–359.
4. Coleman, W., "Role-Playing as an Instructional Aid," *Journal of Educational Psychology*, 1938, 39, 427–435.
5. Coutu, W., *Emergent Human Behavior: A Symbolic Field Interpretation*, New York: Knopf, 1949.
6. Cronbach, L. J., "Processes Affecting Scores on 'Understanding of Others' and 'Assumed Similarity,' " *Psychological Bulletin*, 1955, 52, 177–193.
7. Curran, F. J., "The Drama as a Therapeutic Measure in Adolescents," *American Journal of Orthopsychiatry*, 1939, 9, 215–232.
8. Davis, K., "The Application of Social Science to Personal Relations," *American Sociological Review*, 1936, 1, 236–247.
9. Dymond, R. F., *Empathic Ability: An Exploratory Study*, Ph.D. dissertation, Cornell University, 1949.
10. Foote, N. N., and L. S. Cottrell, Jr., *Identity and Interpersonal Competence*, Chicago: University of Chicago Press, 1955.
11. French, J. R. P., "Role-Playing as a Method of Training Foremen," *Group Psychotherapy*, New York: Beacon House, 1945.
12. Gage, N. L. and L. J. Cronbach, "Conceptual and Methodological Problems in Interpersonal Perception," *Psychological Review*, 1955, 62, 411–422.
13. Hastorf, A. H., and I. E. Bender, "A Caution Respecting Measurement of Empathic Ability," *Journal of Abnormal and Social Psychology*, 1952, 47, 574–576.
14. Huffman, P. E., "Authoritarian Personality and Family Ideology," M.A. thesis, Western Reserve University, 1950.
15. Kay, L. W. "Role-Playing as a Teaching Aid," *Sociometry*, 1946, 9, 263–274.
16. Lindesmith, A. R., and A. L. Strauss, *Social Psychology*, New York: Dryden, 1949.
17. Liveright, A. A., "Role-Playing in Leadership Training," *Personnel Journal*, 1951, 29, 412–416.
18. Mead, G. H., *Mind, Self, and Society*, Chicago: University of Chicago Press, 1934.
19. Moore, W. E., and M. M. Tumin, "Some Social Functions of Ignorance," *American Sociological Review*, 1949, 14, 787–795.

---

analysis of assumptions concerning collective activity leads him to conclude that these propositions will hold when "(a) group members are motivated to cooperate; (b) the accurately perceived qualities are relevant to the activities of the group; (c) members are free to alter their own behaviors in response to their perceptions of other members; and (d) the behavioral changes which are a consequence of accurate social perceptions are the kinds which produce a more thoroughly integrated dyadic system" (23, p. 273).

[10] For materials suggestive of further conditions, see (25).

20. Moreno, J. L., "Psychodramatic Treatment of Marriage Problems," *Sociometry*, 1940, 3, 1–23.
21. Moreno, J. L., "Psychodramatic Treatment of Psychoses," *Sociometry*, 1940, 3, 115–132.
22. Newcomb, T. M., "Autistic Hostility and Social Reality," *Human Relations*, 1947, 1, 69–86.
23. Steiner, I. D., "Interpersonal Behavior as Influenced by Accuracy of Social Perception," *Psychological Review*, 1955, 62, 268–274.
24. Stryker, S., "The Adjustment of Married Offspring to Their Parents," *American Sociological Review*, 1955, 20, 149–154.
25. Stryker, S., "Relationships of Married Offspring and Parent: A Test of Mead's Theory," *American Journal of Sociology*, 1956, 62, 308–319.
26. Sullivan, H. S., *The Interpersonal Theory of Psychiatry*, New York: Norton, 1953.
27. Trendley, M. B., "Psychodrama and Social Case Work" *Sociometry*, 1944, 7, 169–177.
28. Whyte, W. F., "The Social Structure of a Restaurant," *American Journal of Sociology*, 1949, 54, 302–310.
29. Williams, R., *American Society: A Sociological Interpretation*, New York: Knopf, 1951.

41   DANIEL GLASER

Criminality Theories and Behavioral Images[1]

This article attempts to appraise the scientific utility of alternative theories proposed for the explanation of that individual behavior which is most uniformly designated "crime" in our society. All such theories are derived, explicitly or implicitly, from more general psychological or social-psychological theories applicable to the larger class of behavior of which crime is considered an instance.

Theories and Imagery

The language which explains a human act evokes imagery by which certain aspects of the act are abstractly conceived and are related to other phenomena. For example, an act may be explained as the rational pursuit of a purpose, as the expression of inner drives, as a conditioned neural re-

Daniel Glaser, "Criminality Theories and Behavioral Images." Reprinted from *The American Journal of Sociology*, vol. 61 (March 1956), pp. 433–444, by permission of The University of Chicago Press. Copyright 1956 by The University of Chicago.

[1] Acknowledgment is made of useful comments, leading to revisions of this article, which were received from Drs. J. E. Hulett, Jr., Alvin W. Gouldner, Bernard Farber, and others, all of the University of Illinois, and from Martin U. Martel, now of the University of Washington.

sponse, or as a mechanical resultant of external pressures. Each type of explanatory language evokes a somewhat different image of how human beings behave—as rational, as driven from within, as internally mechanical, or as atoms in fields of external forces. Each set of terms for explaining behavior and the associated imagery constitutes a psychological frame of reference. When made explicit, they are called "models" or "paradigms."

"Language is by its very nature and essence, metaphorical," Cassirer observed.[2] For example, such psychological concepts as "force," "stimulus," and "response" were imported from physics and physiology, where they were first developed to deal with phenomena other than those to which they are applied by psychologists. These concepts evoke images which give meaning to our observations by interrelating them. But since considerable compression, deletion, or extension of available observations of behavior are usually necessary to fit our observations into our frame of reference, these conceptual frameworks determine both what we look for and what we overlook.[3]

As a theory is more rigorously tested, it becomes increasingly formalized. Ultimately, it may be expressed as mathematical relations between quantitative variables which are operationally defined by objectively specified rules of observational procedure. It then evokes little in the way of concrete images. While any theory may be formalized, more or less adequately, the imagery evoked when the theory is first formulated limits what later testing seeks. As testing proceeds, the theory may be delimited on the basis of negative findings. But additions to scientific theory have always depended upon the introduction of new imagery, from the theory of evolution to time-space relativity to any hypothesis which is clearly new to a particular research situation (though probably metaphorically drawn from another situation). If we focus on explaining an empirical phenomenon, a theory may be sufficiently tested to provoke extensive revision before it is highly formalized. That is a justification for this article. If we focus on developing and applying techniques for formalizing theory, we are likely to select theories on the basis of their amenability to the techniques of formalization rather than by their relevance to the phenomenon which we initially sought to explain.[4]

Crime, like most topics in social psychology, refers to a class of be-

[2] Ernst Cassirer, *An Essay on Man* (Garden City, N.Y.: Doubleday, 1953), p. 142.

[3] Cf. Herbert Blumer, "Science without Concepts," *American Journal of Sociology*, XXXVI (January, 1931), 515–33; Kenneth Burke, *Permanence and Change* (New York: New Republic, 1936); Susanne K. Langer, *Philosophy in a New Key* (Cambridge: Harvard University Press, 1942), esp. chap. iv.

[4] Cf. A. H. Maslow, "Problem Centering versus Means Centering in Science," *Philosophy of Science*, XIII (October, 1946), 326–31; Gordon W. Allport, "The Psychologist's Frame of Reference," *Psychological Bulletin*, XXXVII (January, 1940), 1–28; Paul H. Furfey, "The Formalization of Sociology," *American Sociological Review*, XIX (October, 1954), 525–28.

havior the separate instances of which have many and diverse subjective and objective aspects.[5] Our theoretical conceptions of criminal or other behavior necessarily simplify this complexity, and in our effort to comprehend such behavior we may distort it. Nevertheless, we strive for the most valid theoretical image of actual behavior, assuming thereby that this effort will ultimately produce the most fruitful basis for prediction or control of behavior.

In distinguishing the images which various criminality theories evoke, a somewhat imperfect distinction will be made between (1) "monistic" theories, which are based upon a single type of simple behavioral image; (2) "pluralistic" theories, which involve two or more distinct behavioral images; and (3) "integrative" theories, which attempt to subsume the aspects of behavior dealt with in pluralistic theories under a single relatively complex behavioral image. These theories will be appraised with respect to the interconnectedness of their explanatory imagery,[6] their comprehensiveness (the types or aspects of crime to which they apply), and their implications for the continuity and validity of empirical research.

Monistic Theories

Underlying prevailing monistic criminality theories, the following types of imagery may be distinguished: spontaneity, possession, rationality, external forces, internal mechanism, and role.

[5] The term "crime" is here confined primarily to felonies, as felonies are defined by criminal courts in their prosecution and adjudication of cases, to which we add misdemeanors, such as petty larceny and assault, which are identified by lesser forms of the same attributes which identify felonies. This usage, which we believe corresponds to the usual connotation of "crime," excludes those misdemeanors which do not become felonies when "exaggerated," such as most disorderly conduct, vagrancy, and indecent exposure. It also excludes those "white-collar crimes" not commonly prosecuted as felonies. We also include as crime any act legally called "delinquency" if the only attribute which is the basis for its being considered delinquency rather than crime is the fact that the doer is below a particular age.

We believe that there is a predominantly stable and uniform content to this reference of "crime" in Western society, despite some variation in its limits under different legal jurisdictions. Indicative of the complexity of crime as a topic for social-psychological study are the facts that crimes (a) occur in diverse situations; (b) must be identified by the symbolic interpretation given the behavior by the actors in the situation (e.g., identifying the victim's property as "owned" or his compliance as "involuntary"); (c) can be experienced or imputed subjectively as symbolic processes (ideation) and feelings (reflected in such legal language as "willfully," "maliciously," etc.)

[6] The significance of interconnectedness in theory was indicated when, in a lecture at the University of Chicago in 1939, Bertrand Russell distinguished mysticism from science by saying that mysticism accepts the possibility of distance between cause and effect, while "science cannot accept action at a distance." As Hume suggested, this distinction is relative rather than absolute, since the connection is conceived rather than directly observed. In terms of that philosophy of science which eschews the language of "causality," disconnectedness refers to the failure to specify intervening variables between a dependent and an independent variable.

An image of behavior as spontaneous underlies that "pure" free-will criminality theory which is still voiced in lay discussions of crimes and is implicit in the judicial notion of "choosing" between right and wrong. Such an explanation is the epitome of disconnectedness, since it indicates inability or unwillingness to relate the behavior to anything else. Actually, "pure" free-will theory is seldom maintained continuously, for, when practical problems are considered, it must be modified to reflect other types of imagery.[7]

Possession imagery, which involves an image of a prepotent force resident in the person and determining his behavior, has been evoked by biological determinism theories of criminality, from Lombroso to Sheldon. While criminal behavior is asserted to be caused by malformed biological structures, no direct connection between the specific actions involved in crime and the defective structure is indicated, at least not in terms of specific known functions of organic structures. Much use of the term "psychopath," especially when explicitly or implicitly modified by the adjective "constitutional," still conveys this image of determination by an ill-defined condition. Another such disconnected explanation is that implied in the assertions that criminality is correlated with hypoglycemia or with organic brain damage. These hypotheses have never been tested on representative samples of persons with these ailments. However, if such correlation were established, there would be pressure to focus theory and research on establishing a conceptual connection between the correlated data. As an explanation for crime, it would still be "disconnected," as we use this adjective, because of the large conceptual gaps between organic phenomena and complex behavior.[8]

---

[7] We are implying that the free-will position in most debate on free-will versus determinism in criminology involves simultaneous employment of several definitions of "free will." No one endeavors to educate or to persuade without assuming that an individual's behavior is influenced by the experience to which he is exposed and that when this experience brings alternative choices to an individual's attention, he has the experience of choosing between alternative courses of action. Neither of these assumptions contradicts the notion of universal determinism in nature on which all science rests, nor has either the remotest relationship to the question of the [indeterminacy] of quantum particles, to which the free-will issue is often referred (cf. C. H. Cooley, *Social Organization* [New York: Charles Scribner's Sons, 1929], pp. 20–21; and *Human Nature and the Social Order* [rev. ed.; New York: Charles Scribner's Sons, 1922], pp. 38–43 and 55, n.).

[8] When comparing delinquents and non-delinquents from high-delinquency areas, the Gluecks found the delinquents to be stronger and more athletic (mesomorphic) anatomically than the non-delinquents, as well as more aggressive and extroverted in what they call "temperament." An example of conceptual connection between such "biological" data and criminality is the following earlier statement by Sutherland (which is amenable to empirical validation): "In an area where the delinquency rate is high a boy who is sociable, gregarious, active and athletic is very likely to come in contact with the other boys in the neighborhood, learn delinquent behavior from them, and become a gangster. . . . In another situation the sociable, athletic, aggressive boy may become a member of a scout troop and not become involved in

Freudian criminologists have ascribed criminality to instinct.[9] This conception also involves possession imagery. However, in psychoanalysis, controls by the rational mind (ego) and society (superego) are seen as repressing or redirecting the instinctive criminal force (id), latent and manifest criminality being ascribed to the failure of the controls. Like other possession images, this conception fails to explain any aspect of criminality in which learning can be observed (such as complex criminal techniques, pride in conception of self as criminal, and pious loyalty to a criminal group). In the purely Freudian conception, we are possessed of criminal impulses, and we learn or fail to learn to control them; there is no learning of distinctively new criminality.

The frustration-equals-aggression formula, an amalgamation of behavioristic and psychoanalytic theory, provides another variation of possession imagery. A sum of vaguely defined emotional energy is seen as fixed in an individual. If the steady and relatively moderate expression of this energy is blocked, one of two alternative results is predicted: either there is an immediate outburst of unusually violent and reckless behavior, or there is a slow accumulation of "blocked energy" which must ultimately be expressed. The immediate outburst may explain some "crimes of passion" which seem unplanned, but it is inapplicable where blockage does not lead to immediate aggression. The "blockage-leads-to-ultimate-expression-in-some-other-manner" formulation provides a disconnected explanation for any emotional behavior; early frustration, perhaps in infancy or even prenatal, can always be demonstrated or assumed and can then be cited as the cause of later behavior without a clearly connecting causal mechanism.

Observations of aggression following frustration are explained in less disconnected imagery by certain older theories of emotional behavior which also account more adequately for observations contradicting the frustration-equals-aggression formula. We may develop the habit of reacting to frustration by violence, growing more set in the habit with each occasion of it. The current reaction against extreme permissiveness in child-rearing, which had been advocated as preventing children from accumulating aggression, is based on the newer tenet that tolerance of their aggression develops aggressive children. The James-Lange theory of emotions, that "we are afraid because we run," can be restated as: When habitual be-

---

delinquent behavior" (E. H. Sutherland, *Principles of Criminology* [4th ed.; Chicago: J. B. Lippincott Co., 1947], p. 8; cf. also S. and E. Glueck, *Unravelling Juvenile Delinquency* [New York: Commonwealth Fund, 1950]).

[9] E. g., "The ideal criminal has not structured his personality in accordance with any value system. . . . Instinctual forces drive him on without any opposition from a restraining conscience" (K. R. Eissler, "General Problems of Delinquency," in K. R. Eissler, [ed.], *Searchlights on Delinquency* [New York: International Universities Press, 1949], p. 7). Similar quotations from several other psychoanalytic writers are presented in Albert K. Cohen, *Delinquent Boys* (Glencoe, Ill.: Free Press, 1955), pp. 181–82.

havior is frustrated, we mobilize attention and energy for initiating a new course of behavior. Emotions are sense-experiences of bodily changes concomitant with such mobilization. We experience anger when we react by mobilizing to strike, and fear when we mobilize to flee. Mobilization may be inhibited before completion; we may only raise our voice rather than strike. Different experience leads to different habits of mobilization for given types of frustrating situation: one person mobilizes to fight, another flees, another deliberates. Different emotional experience accompanies each of these behavioral patterns.

The "classical" theory of criminality, identified with utilitarian philosophy and expressed in most criminal law, implies free will but immediately modifies it with the notion that man's behavior is determined by the nearness and efficacy of the choosable means for obtaining happiness. (Crime is to be prevented by making it produce unhappiness.) This is really a pluralistic theory, since the image of man shifts from a purely spontaneous actor to a rational calculator and, finally, to an atom moved by its external field of pleasant and painful forces.

Economic determinism in criminology is simply classical theory which assumes that economic ends are the primary means to the ultimate end of happiness. Crime is viewed as an alternative means to such ends when other means fail. The behavioral image of rational man in classical theory provides an insufficiently comprehensive explanation of irrational habits, predilections, and prejudices in specific cases of criminality; it also does not explain the absence of criminality in people whose economic need is equal to, or greater than, that of criminals. The imagery of external forces does not connect economic, geographic, and other abstract forces to specific criminal techniques and loyalties. Extreme cultural determinism theories may also arouse an imagery of external forces. They have been criticized for implying greater homogeneity of criminal subcultures than can be established empirically.

An image of internal mechanism (personality) developing through conditioning underlies many psychological explanations of crime which dispense with the concept of instinct. Its adequacy depends in part on the answer to the question of whether conditioning explains the acquisition of new responses rather than the association of new stimuli with old responses. Indicative of the issue of disconnectedness is the current debate on reductionism in the behavioral sciences: whether "voluntary" human behavior, in which images and symbolic evaluations of completed acts continuously enter into the initiation of new acts, can usefully be reduced to the conditioned-reflex model which physiologists verify from the study of isolated muscles or glands.[10] The discovery of the extreme diversity of per-

---

[10] Still highly relevant are the questions raised in John Dewey, "The Reflex-Arc Concept in Psychology," *Psychological Review*, III (July, 1896), 357–70. New response

sonality in criminals and of the frequency of allegedly criminal categories of personality among non-criminals supports the view that ascribing criminality to the habitual modes of behavior which psychologists usually connote by the term "personality" is based on an invalid image of criminal behavior.[11]

The image of behavior as role-playing, borrowed from the theater, presents people as directing their actions on the basis of their conceptions of how others see them. The choice of another, from whose perspective we view our own behavior, is the process of identification. It may be with the immediate others or with distant and perhaps abstractly generalized others of our reference groups. (The "amateur" criminal may identify himself with the highly professional "master"-criminal whom he has never met.) Rationalization is seen as a necessary concomitant of voluntary behavior, particularly when role conflicts exist. Acceptance by the group with which one identifies one's self and conceptions of persecution by other groups are among the most common and least intellectual bases for rationalization by criminals. Role imagery provides the most comprehensive and interconnected theoretical framework for explaining the phenomena of criminality.[12] We shall take up the problem of articulating the specific relationship of role theory with criminality in discussing "integrative" criminality theories.

---

learning seems accounted for by the concept of operants as response components which are "emitted rather than elicited" and which are continuously shaped into even the most complex behavior through reinforcement of those components yielding favorable consequences and extinction of the remainder (cf. B. F. Skinner, *Science and Human Behavior* [New York: Macmillan Co., 1953]). While mechanistic data on animal learning may support this theory, such data are related only by gross analogy to human learning of complex "voluntary" behavior like crime, since we have negligible evidence of animal ability to learn complex behavior through symbolic communication (hence accumulation of learning from one generation to the next) or of animals reinforcing their acts by verbal rationalization. Apart from the need to learn those gross principles applicable to both human and animal learning, further "control" of such human learning as that involved in crime requires more discriminating analysis and more reliable data on human verbal processes, feelings, and relationships.

[11] Where the measure of personality is a measure of the extent of criminal behavior (psychopathy scales), the empirical correlation discovered is that between criminality and itself. This has no explanatory value and does not compare with the fruitful logical reduction of complex theories to quasi-tautological relations between distinct conceptual frameworks (cf. Karl F. Schuessler, review of Hathaway and Monachesi, "Analyzing and Predicting Juvenile Delinquency with the MMPI," *American Journal of Sociology*, LX [November, 1954], 321–22; Donald R. Cressey and Karl F. Schuessler, "Personality Characteristics of Criminals," *American Journal of Sociology*, LV [March, 1950], 476–84).

[12] Cf. Nelson N. Foote, "Identification as the Basis for a Theory of Motivation," *American Sociological Review*, XVI (February, 1951), 14–22; C. Wright Mills, "Situated Actions and Vocabularies of Motive," *American Sociological Review*, V (December, 1940), 904–13; Tamotsu Shibutani, "Reference Groups as Perspectives," *American Journal of Sociology*, LX (May, 1955), 562–69.

Pluralistic and Integrative Theories

Serendipity—the influence of "unanticipated, anomalous and strategic"[13] observations—in causing us to revise theory, has usually resulted in patchwork electicism rather than the systematic revision of criminality theory. Where one behavioral image does not fit, we skip to another. Most textbooks in criminology present a cluster of disparate monistic theories as "the theory of multiple causation." These should be regarded as temporary expedients in the course of revising theory. Instead, since the nineteenth-century writings of Enrico Ferri, they have been repeatedly extolled as the ultimate most satisfactory formulations.

Pluralistic theories evoke a mixed metaphorical image—the criminal is possessed, pushed, rationally chooses, or interpretively interacts. The major practical objection is that no rules are provided for interrelating component theories and for shifting from one to another. Starting an analysis from the standpoint of one theory, one is likely to persevere in that theory in analyzing behavior and thus may be blinded to observations which might be revealed, were one to start with another theory. For example, even sociologists repeatedly find themselves neglecting social relationships through the natural tendency to look only at individual traits when trying to explain an individual's criminality. Both the defects and the merits of the component theories thereby remain in the multiple-causation mixtures.

There are precedents in the physical sciences for the simultaneous acceptance of alternative theoretical images of phenomena, such as the wave and the corpuscular conceptions of light, each being employed to explain different types of observation. This is considered a temporary and unsatisfactory state of affairs pending the appearance of a more general integrative theory which will account for all the observations. The old theories often become special cases of the more general theory (e.g., as Newtonian physics is a special case of Einsteinian physics).

The outstanding attempt to formulate an integrative theory of criminality is the "differential association" theory, proposed by the late Edwin H. Sutherland, who summarized his theory in the statement: "A person becomes delinquent because of an excess of definitions favorable to violation of law."[14] Personality, economic conditions, and other elements of monistic criminality theories are related to crime by this theory only to the extent that they lead to the procurement of an excess of definitions favorable to

---

[13] Robert K. Merton, *Social Theory and Social Structure* (Glencoe, Ill.: Free Press, 1949), p. 98.
[14] E. H. Sutherland, *Principles of Criminology*, prepared by Donald R. Cressey (5th ed.; Chicago: J. B. Lippincott Co., 1955), p. 78 (p. 6 in 4th ed.).

violation of law. Unlike the pluralistic approaches, such theory interrelates the separate monistic factors in each case. Differential association theory channels research by knitting diverse data together, whereas multiple-factor conceptions lead to the collection of disparate observations.

Sutherland's formal statement of this theory actually conveys a rather mechanistic image of criminality, which differs from the multiple-factor conception in one major respect. While the multiple-factor imagery presents the criminal as an atom in a multidimensional field, the differential association conception involves imagery of the criminal on a unidimensional continuum. Criminality is at one extreme of this continuum and non-criminality at the other, with the individual's associations pushing him toward one extreme or the other. This imagery is not altered essentially when Sutherland observes that criminal and non-criminal associations may vary in "frequency, duration, priority and intensity." The phrase "excess of definitions" itself lacks clear denotation in human experience.

Probably, the failure of Sutherland's language to evoke a clearly recognizable behavioral image is responsible for the limited acceptance of his theory. The criticisms have been of two principal types. First, there have been assertions that the differential learning of crime is more complex than the critics assume Sutherland's conception of differential association to be. Some critics have interpreted "association" in Sutherland's writings as synonymous with "contact."[15] Sutherland seems to have been dismayed by an assumption that "association" is distinct from "identification."[16] Donald R. Cressey has suggested modification of differential association theory by:

> the substitution of a different conception of the process by which criminality is learned for the conception of a differential in the quantity and

[15] E.g.: "While this theory of crime explains the delinquent behavior of many juveniles, it does not adequately explain why some individuals who have extensive contacts with criminal norms and with persons who engage in criminal behavior do not themselves commit delinquencies" (Martin H. Neumeyer, *Juvenile Delinquency in Modern Society* [New York: D. Van Nostrand Co., 1949], p. 226); "[Sutherland's theory] . . . does not adequately explain why two or more children in the same home often respond differently to the situation of delinquent and criminal members of the family" (Milton L. Barron, *The Juvenile in Delinquent Society* [New York: A. A. Knopf, 1954], p. 147). We might also note the recurrent question by students: Why doesn't the prison guard become a criminal, since his association is primarily with criminals?

[16] Cf. "The opposition to 'differential association' as an explanation seems to be based on a misconception of a meaning of that process, as indicated by the sentence, 'Identification with a group of boys who stole was as important as contact with the differential association' " (Sutherland, *op. cit.*, n. 25, pp. 157–58; p. 138 in 4th ed.). In his posthumous revision of Sutherland, Cressey added to the above: "Differential identification is a clearly implied and congruous aspect of the differential association theory." The reformulation of "differential identification" set forth below supports everything in this added sentence except the word "clearly." Sutherland's theory has been very diversely interpreted.

quality of contacts with the two varieties of behavior problems. For example . . . a search for the differences in the typical vocabularies used by criminals and non-criminals in specific situations might reveal that it is the presence or absence of a specific, learned verbal label in a specific situation which determines the criminality or non-criminality of a particular person.[17]

These diverse comments suggest the need for a restatement of Sutherland's theory so as to make its behavioral referent less ambiguous.

A second criticism of Sutherland's theory consists of arguments for certain pluralistic criminality theories on the grounds that Sutherland's theory accounts for only one of several distinct types of criminality. The most common of these views evokes a dualistic image of criminality as manifesting either differential association or personality, or both.[18] It frequently ignores Sutherland's reference to personality as one of several factors determining patterns of differential association and therefore related to crime indirectly (cf. our n. 7). Usually it also involves the assumption that the major aspects of personality determining crime are relatively fixed from childhood on. A conception of personality reconcilable with Sutherland's theory would be as the sum total of a person's regular role patterns in a given period. This includes, as personality, aspects of roles which develop only in adulthood, such as class and occupational roles. Criminality itself would then be considered a component of personality, and the theory for explaining criminality presumably would be analogous with the theory for explaining other components of personality; it would go beyond descriptive designation of criminality as a component of the referent for the term "personality."

Some critics of Sutherland augment the dualism of personality and association by also calling for recognition of accidental and transitory situational causes of crime.[19] Such criticism, prompted by the premises of pluralistic theory, implies that Sutherland's theory either should be radically revised or should be applied to a much more limited range of criminality than he and his students believed. But neither of these changes is necessary if we reconceptualize Sutherland's theory in terms which we call "differential identification."

---

[17] Donald R. Cressey, "Application and Verification of the Differential Association Theory," *Journal of Criminal Law, Criminology, and Police Science*, XLIII (May–June, 1952), 43–52.

[18] Cf. Paul W. Tappan, *Juvenile Delinquency* (New York: McGraw-Hill Book Co., Inc., 1949), pp. 82 ff.; S. Kirson Weinberg, "Theories of Criminality and Problems of Prediction," *Journal of Criminal Law, Criminology, and Police Science*, XLV (November–December, 1954), 412–24.

[19] Cf. "The theory of differential association does not explain the incidental, the highly emotional, or the accidental crimes, but applies only to the confirmed types of criminality in which the offender accepts antisocial behavior as a suitable way of life" (Mabel A. Elliot, *Crime in Modern Society* [New York: Harper & Bros., 1952], p. 402).

Differential Identification as an
Integrative Criminality Theory

We describe identification somewhat unconventionally as "the choice of another, from whose perspective we view our own behavior." What we have called "differential identification" reconceptualizes Sutherland's theory in role-taking imagery, drawing heavily on Mead as well as on later refinements of role theory.[20] Most persons in our society are believed to identify themselves with both criminal and non-criminal persons in the course of their lives. Criminal identification may occur, for example, during direct experience in delinquent membership groups, through positive reference to criminal roles portrayed in mass media, or as a negative reaction to forces opposed to crime. The family probably is the principal non-criminal reference group, even for criminals. It is supplemented by many other groups of anticriminal "generalized others."

The theory of differential identification, in essence, is that *a person pursues criminal behavior to the extent that he identifies himself with real or imaginary persons from whose perspective his criminal behavior seems acceptable.* Such a theory focuses attention on the interaction in which choice of models occurs, including the individual's interaction with himself in rationalizing his conduct. This focus makes differential identification theory integrative, in that it provides a criterion of the relevance, for each individual case of criminality, of economic conditions, prior frustrations, learned moral creeds, group participation, or other features of an individual's life. These features are relevant to the extent that they can be shown to affect the choice of the other from whose perspective the individual views his own behavior. The explanation of criminal behavior on the basis of its imperfect correlation with any single variable of life-situations, if presented without specifying the intervening identification, evokes only a disconnected image of the relationship between the life-situation and the criminal behavior.

Sutherland supported the differential association theory by evidence that a major portion of criminality is learned through participation in criminal groups. Differential identification is a less disconnected explanation for such learning, and it also does not seem vulnerable to most of the objections to differential association. Because opposing and divisive roles frequently develop within groups, because our identification may be with remote reference groups or with imaginary or highly generalized others, and because identifications may shift rapidly with dialectical pro-

---

[20] Cf. D. Glaser, "A Reconsideration of Some Parole Prediction Factors," *American Sociological Review*, XIX (June, 1954), 335–41; G. H. Mead, *Mind, Self, and Society* (Chicago: University of Chicago Press, 1934), Foote, *op. cit.*; Mills, *op. cit.*; Shibutani, *op. cit.*

cesses of role change and rationalization during social interaction, differential association, as ordinarily conceived, is insufficient to account for all differential identification.

In practice, the use of differential identification to explain lone crimes the source of learning of which is not readily apparent (such as extremes of brutality or other abnormality in sex crimes) gives rise to speculation as to the "others" involved in the identification. The use of this theory to explain a gang member's participation in a professional crime against property presents fewer difficulties. In so far as the former types of offense are explained by psychiatrists without invoking instincts or other mystical forces, they usually are interpreted, on a necessarily speculative basis, in terms of the self-conception which the offender develops in supporting his behavior and the sources of that self-conception. Such differential identification, in the case of most unusual and compulsive crimes, offers a less disconnected explanation than explanations derived from the alternative theories.[21]

The one objection to the theory of differential association which cannot be met by differential identification is that it does not account for "accidental" crimes. Differential identification treats crime as a form of voluntary (i.e., anticipatory) behavior, rather than as an accident. Indeed, both legal and popular conceptions of "crime" exclude acts which are purely accidental, except for some legislation on felonious negligence, to which our discussion of criminality must be considered inapplicable. Even for the latter offenses, however, it is noteworthy that the consequences of accidentally committing a crime may be such as to foster identification with criminal-role models (whether one is apprehended for the accidental crime or not).

During any period, *prior identifications* and *present circumstances* dictate the selection of the persons with whom we identify ourselves. Prior identifications which have been pleasing tend to persist, but at any time the immediate circumstances affect the relative ease (or salience) of alternative identifications. That is why membership groups so frequently are the reference groups, although they need not be. That, too, is why those inclined to crime usually refrain from it in situations where they play satisfying conventional roles in which crime would threaten their acceptance. From the latter situations their identification with non-criminal others may eventually make them anticriminal. This is the essence of rehabilitation.[22]

---

[21] For an outstanding illustration of what becomes differential identification rather than the usual conception of differential association, applied to compulsive crimes, see Donald R. Cressey, "Differential Association and Compulsive Crimes," *Journal of Criminal Law, Criminology, and Police Science*, XLV (May–June, 1954), 29–40.

[22] Cf. Donald R. Cressey, "Contradictory Theories in Correctional Group Therapy Programs," *Federal Probation*, XVIII (June, 1954), 20–26.

There is evidence that, with the spread of urban secularism, social situations are becoming more and more deliberately rather than traditionally organized. Concurrently, roles are increasingly adjusted on the basis of the apparent authority or social pressure in each situation.[23] Our culture is said to give a common level of aspiration but different capacities of attainment according to socioeconomic class. At the same time, it is suggested, economic sources of status are becoming stronger while non-economic sources are becoming weaker. Therefore, when conventional occupational avenues of upward mobility are denied, people are more and more willing to seek the economic gains anticipated in crime, even at the risk of losing such non-economic sources of status as acceptance by non-criminal groups.[24] All these alleged features of urbanism suggest a considerable applicability of differential identification to "situational" and "incidental" crimes; focus on differential identification with alternative reference groups may reveal "situational imperatives" in individual life-histories.

Differential identification may be considered tautological, in that it may seem merely to make "crime" synonymous with "criminal identification." It is more than a tautology, however, if it directs one to observations beyond those necessary merely for the classification of behavior as criminal or non-criminal. It is a fruitful empirical theory leading one to proceed from the legalistic classification to the analysis of behavior as identification and role-playing.[25]

Implications

Three general hypotheses are derived from the assumption that the image of criminal behavior evoked by the theory of differential identification is more valid than those evoked by alternative formulations.

[23] This evidence has come most dramatically from recent studies of race relations. Cf. Joseph D. Lohman and Dietrich C. Reitzes, "Note on Race Relations in Mass Society," *American Journal of Sociology,* LVIII (November 1952), 240–46; Dietrich C. Reitzes, "The Role of Organizational Structures" *Journal of Social Issues,* IX, No. 1 (1953), 37–44; William C. Bradbury, "Evaluation of Research in Race Relations," *Inventory of Research in Racial and Cultural Relations,* V (winter–spring, 1953), 99–133.

[24] Cf. Merton, *op. cit.,* chap. iv. It may be noteworthy here that classification of Illinois parolees by status ratings of the jobs to which they were going was more predictive than classification by the status of their father's occupation or by whether their job was higher, lower, or equal status than their father's occupation. Regardless of their class background, the parolee's infractions seemed primarily to be a function of their failure to approach middle-class status (cf. Daniel Glaser, "A Reformation and Testing of Parole Prediction Factors" [unpublished Ph. D. dissertation, University of Chicago, 1954,] pp. 253–59).

[25] A number of examples of useful tautologies in social science are presented in Arnold Rose, *Theory and Method in the Social Sciences* (Minneapolis: University of Minnesota Press, 1954), pp. 328–38. In so far as a proposition is of heuristic use, however, one may question whether it is appropriately designated a "tautology."

The first hypothesis is that the imagery invoked by the theory of differential identification is the most adequate and parsimonious theoretical framework with which to account for the findings of criminology. We have shown the more disconnected imagery and the failure to comprehend major aspects of criminality inherent in theories which do not evoke an image of criminality as role-repressive activity. Parsimony of preconception is indicated by (1) its "integrative" function in interrelating the diverse phenomena which may be associated with crime through specifying intervening behavior; (2) its relating of criminal behavior to other behavior rather than to conceptually more distant phenomena; (3) its capacity to comprehend a tremendous diversity of criminal behavior. The theory of differential identification, by indicating the relevance of phenomena grossly correlated with crime, promotes continuity in research and theoretically should direct attention to phenomena having higher correlations with crime. Even more than differential association, as that theory is ordinarily conceived, differential identification should facilitate the recognition of "behavior systems" in crime.[26]

The second hypothesis is that differential identification orients one to evaluate soundly the rehabilitative effects of correctional techniques. Tests of this hypothesis will require more extensive and sophisticated research than that now applied to the appraisal of rehabilitative efforts.[27] However, some suggestive clues are available, for example, from studies of inmate social systems. These systems are seen as coercing each prison inmate into identification with fellow-inmates, and hampering, if not preventing, his identification with non-criminal persons. Many prison policies sometimes considered "progressive," such as housing men in large dormitories, facilitating freedom of contact between inmates, assigning prison social workers to cope with prisoners' grievance claims, and keeping relations between inmates and the rest of the institution staff highly formal, may be criticized from the standpoint of their effects upon identifications.[28]

The third hypothesis is that research workers of diverse background are converging on a differential identification type of theory. While the proposition can be tested only by time, illustrations of the trend can be provided from several areas.

1. Psychoanalysts are supplied by adult neurotic patients with a wealth of volunteered verbal data on which to speculate freely. When juve-

[26] Cf. Sutherland, *op. cit.*, chap. xiii.

[27] Cf. Daniel Glaser, "Testing Correctional Decisions," *Journal of Criminal Law, Criminology, and Police Science*, XLV (March–April, 1955), 679–84.

[28] A sophisticated analysis of the impact of inmate social systems on correctional programs is presented in Lloyd W. McCorkle and Richard Korn, "Resocialization within Walls," *Annals*, CXCIII (May, 1954), 88–98; see also Donald Clemmer, *The Prison Community* (Boston: Christopher Publishing House, 1940); Richard McCleary, "The Strange Journey," *University of North Carolina Extension Bulletin*, Vol. XXXII (March, 1953).

nile delinquents are referred to analysts, however, such cooperation is not always forthcoming. Milieu therapy, which developed in part to meet this contingency, requires that the analyst (a) live intimately with small groups of delinquents, (b) capture his data when manifested in their interaction, and (c) exert a therapeutic influence by counseling and manipulating the environment when strategic moments arise. It is interesting that milieu therapists increasingly seem to be forced by their data to interpret their observations and justify their treatment techniques by analysis of simple role expression. Their efforts to fit their data into traditional psychoanalytic frameworks then seem superfluous and the strain obvious. Aichhorn's pioneer discussion of the ego ideal in milieu therapy provides considerable analysis of differential identification in both group and individual delinquency. Redl and Wineman, who drop Aichhorn's postulation of instincts, are even more dependent on role analysis to interpret behavior and to justify therapeutic techniques. When superimposing Freudian conceptions on role analysis, they are forced to contradictory portrayals of the delinquent's reified ego as both weak and strong, depending on which chapter one reads. It is quite easy to reconceptualize their data as illustrating ambivalent and undefined roles in the case of the weak ego, highly organized learned delinquent roles in the case of delinquent egos and super-egos, and therapy as a shift of identification from delinquent to non-delinquent persons.[29]

2. The Gluecks once wrote: "It is the presence or absence of certain traits and characteristics in the constitution and early environment of the different offenders which determines . . . what such offenders will ultimately become and what will become of them."[30] This preconception is reflected in their choice of alternative possible explanations of their findings. For example, they have been criticized for dismissing their datum that gang membership was the feature most differentiating delinquents from non-delinquents.[31] It is interesting that, of three of the Glueck's delinquency prediction scales, two based on personality traits and one on early parent-child relationships ("Social Background Scale"), only the latter has been

---

[29] As another psychoanalytic milieu therapist has put it: "The basic requirement in all education [of delinquents] is that the adult place himself in relation to the child whereby the child accepts him and therefore accepts his social concepts and community values" (S. R. Slavson, *Re-educating the Delinquent through Group and Community Participation* [New York: Harper & Bros., 1954], p. 242, Cf. August Aichhorn, *Wayward Youth* [New York: Viking Press, 1935]; F. Redl and D. Wineman, *Children Who Hate* [Glencoe, Ill.: Free Press, 1951]; and Redl and Wineman, *Controls from Within* [Glencoe, Ill.: Free Press, 1952]).

[30] S. and E. Glueck, *Criminal Careers in Retrospect* (New York: Commonwealth Fund, 1943, p. 285 (original italicized).

[31] Cf. E. W. Burgess, review of Glueck's *Unravelling Juvenile Delinquency*, in *Federal Probation*, XV (March, 1951), 53–54; A. J. Reiss, Jr., "*Unravelling Juvenile Delinquency*. II. An Appraisal of the Research Methods," *American Journal of Sociology*, LVII (September, 1951), 115–20.

validated.[32] Warm and consistent relationships with parents are the basis for predicting non-delinquency by this scale, for, say the Gluecks, such relationships create personalities free of criminal tendencies. Yet there is no evidence that early personality classifications are as predictive of delinquency as classifications of the social relationships themselves. A more adequate explanation for the predictive value of the data on social relationships may be that warm relationships inside the family strengthen the identifications with it. These latter, which are predominantly non-criminal, compete with the identifications developing from delinquent and criminal contacts.

3. Psychologists studying delinquency have increasingly been forced by their data to focus on peer-group relations rather than on personality traits. Harris, in summarizing research findings, stated:

> It is interesting to note that Hart's factor analysis of 25 traits in 300 delinquent boys yielded six factors, at least four of which have a distinct group reference. . . .
> There is ample evidence that the delinquent is quite conversant with the wide social code, yet there are suggestions that on an absolute basis as well as on a relative basis his values are scaled somewhat differently than are similar values in the experience of non-delinquents. Much more research is needed, not only on the values that are accepted, but also on the process by which they become "interiorized."[33]

The differential identification theory, we suggest, offers a fruitful theoretical orientation for the fulfillment of the above-mentioned need.

Editors from diverse backgrounds in behavioral science have asserted: "The role concept provides the principal theoretical point of articulation between analyses of the behavior of groups by anthropologists and sociologists and analyses of individual motivation by psychologists and psychiatrists."[34] We have submitted differential identification as a frame of reference for fruitfully integrating criminality theory by giving that theory an image of behavior as role-playing.

[32] Cf. Richard E. Thompson, "A Validation of the Glueck Social Prediction Scale for Proneness to Delinquency," *Journal of Criminal Law, Criminology, and Police Science*, XLIII (November–December, 1952), 451–70; S. Axelrad and S. J. Glick, "Application of the Glueck Social Prediction Table to 100 Jewish Delinquent Boys," *Jewish Social Service Quarterly*, XXX (winter, 1953), 127–36.

[33] Dale B. Harris, "The Socialization of the Delinquent," *Child Development*, XIX (September, 1948), 1943–53.

[34] H. A. Murray, Clyde Kluckhohn, and D. M. Schneider, *Personality in Nature, Society, and Culture* (New York: A. A. Knopf, 1953), p. 361.

Becoming a Marihuana User

The use of marihuana is and has been the focus of a good deal of attention on the part of both scientists and laymen. One of the major problems students of the practice have addressed themselves to has been the identification of those individual psychological traits which differentiate marihuana users from nonusers and which are assumed to account for the use of the drug. That approach, common in the study of behavior categorized as deviant, is based on the premise that the presence of a given kind of behavior in an individual can best be explained as the result of some trait which predisposes or motivates him to engage in the behavior.[1]

This study is likewise concerned with accounting for the presence or absence of marihuana use in an individual's behavior. It starts, however, from a different premise: that the presence of a given kind of behavior is the result of a sequence of social experiences during which the person acquires a conception of the meaning of the behavior, and perceptions and judgments of objects and situations, all of which make the activity possible and desirable. Thus, the motivation or disposition to engage in the activity is built up in the course of learning to engage in it and does not antedate this learning process. For such a view it is not necessary to identify those "traits" which "cause" the behavior. Instead, the problem becomes one of describing the set of changes in the person's conception of the activity and of the experience it provides for him.[2]

This paper seeks to describe the sequence of changes in attitude and

Howard S. Becker, "Becoming a Marihuana User." Reprinted from *The American Journal of Sociology*, vol. 59 (November 1953), pp. 235–242, by permission of The University of Chicago Press. Copyright 1953 by the University of Chicago.

Paper read at the meetings of the Midwest Sociological Society in Omaha, Nebraska, April 25, 1953. The research on which this paper is based was done while I was a member of the staff of the Chicago Narcotics Survey, a study done by the Chicago Area Project, Inc., under a grant from the National Mental Health Institute. My thanks to Solomon Kobrin, Harold Finestone, Henry McKay, and Anselm Strauss, who read and discussed with me earlier versions of this paper.

[1] See, as examples of this approach, the following: Eli Marcovitz and Henry J. Meyers, "The Marihuana Addict in the Army," *War Medicine*, VI (December, 1944), 382–91; Herbert S. Gaskill, "Marihuana, an Intoxicant," *American Journal of Psychiatry*, CII (September, 1945), 202–4; Sol Charen and Luis Perelman, "Personality Studies of Marihuana Addicts," *American Journal of Psychiatry*, CII (March, 1946), 674–82.

[2] This approach stems from George Herbert Mead's discussion of objects in *Mind, Self, and Society* (Chicago: University of Chicago Press, 1934), pp. 277–80.

experience which lead to *the use of marihuana for pleasure*. Marihuana does not produce addiction, as do alcohol and the opiate drugs; there is no withdrawal sickness and no ineradicable craving for the drug.[3] The most frequent pattern of use might be termed "recreational." The drug is used occasionally for the pleasure the user finds in it, a relatively casual kind of behavior in comparison with that connected with the use of addicting drugs. The term "use for pleasure" is meant to emphasize the noncompulsive and casual character of the behavior. It is also meant to eliminate from consideration here those few cases in which marihuana is used for its prestige value only, as a symbol that one is a certain kind of person, with no pleasure at all being derived from its use.

The analysis presented here is conceived of as demonstrating the greater explanatory usefulness of the kind of theory outlined above as opposed to the predispositional theories now current. This may be seen in two ways: (1) predispositional theories cannot account for that group of users (whose existence is admitted)[4] who do not exhibit the trait or traits considered to cause the behavior and (2) such theories cannot account for the great variability over time of a given individual's behavior with reference to the drug. The same person will at one stage be unable to use the drug for pleasure, at a later stage be able and willing to do so, and still later, again be unable to use it in this way. These changes, difficult to explain from a predispositional or motivational theory, are readily understandable in terms of changes in the individual's conception of the drug as is the existence of "normal" users.

The study attempted to arrive at a general statement of the sequence of changes in individual attitude and experience which have always occurred when the individual has become willing and able to use marihuana for pleasure and which have not occurred or not been permanently maintained when this is not the case. This generalization is stated in universal terms in order that negative cases may be discovered and used to revise the explanatory hypothesis.[5]

Fifty interviews with marihuana users from a variety of social backgrounds and present positions in society constitute the data from which the generalization was constructed and against which it was tested.[6] The interviews focused on the history of the person's experience with the drug,

[3] Cf. Roger Adams, "Marihuana," *Bulletin of the New York Academy of Medicine*, XVIII (November, 1942), 705–30.

[4] Cf. Lawrence Kolb, "Marihuana," *Federal Probation*, II (July, 1938), 22–25; and Walter Bromberg, "Marihuana: A Psychiatric Study," *Journal of the American Medical Association*, CXIII (July 1, 1939), 11.

[5] The method used is that described by Alfred R. Lindesmith in his *Opiate Addiction* (Bloomington: Principia Press, 1947), chap. i. I would like also to acknowledge the important role Lindesmith's work played in shaping my thinking about the genesis of marihuana use.

[6] Most of the interviews were done by the author. I am grateful to Solomon Kobrin and Harold Finestone for allowing me to make use of interviews done by them.

seeking major changes in his attitude toward it and in his actual use of it, and the reasons for these changes. The final generalization is a statement of that sequence of changes in attitude which occurred in every case known to me in which the person came to use marihuana for pleasure. Until a negative case is found, it may be considered as an explanation of all cases of marihuana use for pleasure. In addition, changes from use to nonuse are shown to be related to similar changes in conception, and in each case it is possible to explain variations in the individual's behavior in these terms.

This paper covers only a portion of the natural history of an individual's use of marihuana,[7] starting with the person having arrived at the point of willingness to try marihuana. He knows that others use it to "get high," but he does not know what this means in concrete terms. He is curious about the experience, ignorant of what it may turn out to be, and afraid that it may be more than he has bargained for. The steps outlined below, if he undergoes them all and maintains the attitudes developed in them, leave him willing and able to use the drug for pleasure when the opportunity presents itself.

I

The novice does not ordinarily get high the first time he smokes marihuana, and several attempts are usually necessary to induce this state. One explanation of this may be that the drug is not smoked "properly," that is, in a way that insures sufficient dosage to produce real symptoms of intoxication. Most users agree that it cannot be smoked like tobacco if one is to get high:

> Take in a lot of air, you know, and . . . I don't know how to describe it, you don't smoke it like a cigarette, you draw in a lot of air and get it deep down in your system and then keep it there. Keep it there as long as you can.

Without the use of some such technique[8] the drug will produce no effects, and the user will be unable to get high:

> The trouble with people like that [who are not able to get high] is that they're just not smoking it right, that's all there is to it. Either they're not holding it down long enough, or they're getting too much air and not enough smoke, or the other way around or something like that. A lot of people just don't smoke it right, so naturally nothing's gonna happen.

[7] I hope to discuss elsewhere other stages in this natural history.

[8] A pharmacologist notes that this ritual is in fact an extremely efficient way of getting the drug into the blood stream (R. P. Walton, *Marihuana: America's New Drug Problem* [Philadelphia: J. B. Lippincott, 1938], p. 48).

If nothing happens, it is manifestly impossible for the user to develop a conception of the drug as an object which can be used for pleasure, and use will therefore not continue. The first step in the sequence of events that must occur if the person is to become a user is that he must learn to use the proper smoking technique in order that his use of the drug will produce some effects in terms of which his conception of it can change.

Such a change is, as might be expected, a result of the individual's participation in groups in which marihuana is used. In them the individual learns the proper way to smoke the drug. This may occur through direct teaching:

> I was smoking like I did an ordinary cigarette. He said, "No, don't do it like that." He said, "Suck it, you know, draw in and hold it in your lungs till you . . . for a period of time."
> I said, "Is there any limit of time to hold it?"
> He said, "No, just till you feel that you want to let it out, let it out." So I did that three or four times.

Many new users are ashamed to admit ignorance and, pretending to know already, must learn through the more indirect means of observation and imitation:

> I came on like I had turned on [smoked marihuana] many times before you know. I didn't want to seem like a punk to this cat. See, like I didn't know the first thing about it—how to smoke it, or what was going to happen, or what. I just watched him like a hawk–I didn't take my eyes off him for a second, because I wanted to do everything just as he did it. I watched how he held it, how he smoked it, and everything. Then when he gave it to me I just came on cool, as though I knew exactly what the score was. I held it like he did and took a poke just the way he did.

No person continued marihuana use for pleasure without learning a technique that supplied sufficient dosage for the effects of the drug to appear. Only when this was learned was it possible for a conception of the drug as an object which could be used for pleasure to emerge. Without such a conception marihuana use was considered meaningless and did not continue.

II

Even after he learns the proper smoking technique, the new user may not get high and thus not form a conception of the drug as something which can be used for pleasure. A remark made by a user suggested the reason for this difficulty in getting high and pointed to the next necessary step on the road to being a user:

I was told during an interview, "As a matter of fact, I've seen a guy who was high out of his mind and didn't know it."
I expressed disbelief: "How can that be, man?"
The interviewee said, "Well, it's pretty strange, I'll grant you that, but I've seen it. This guy got on with me, claiming that he'd never got high, one of those guys, and he got completely stoned. And he kept insisting that he wasn't high. So I had to prove to him that he was."

What does this mean? It suggests that being high consists of two elements: the presence of symptoms caused by marihuana use and the recognition of these symptoms and their connection by the user with his use of the drug. It is not enough, that is, that the effects be present; they alone do not automatically provide the experience of being high. The user must be able to point them out to himself and consciously connect them with his having smoked marihuana before he can have this experience. Otherwise, regardless of the actual effects produced, he considers that the drug has had no effect on him: "I figured it either had no effect on me or other people were exaggerating its effect on them, you know. I thought it was probably psychological, see." Such persons believe that the whole thing is an illusion and that the wish to be high leads the user to deceive himself into believing that something is happening when, in fact, nothing is. They do not continue marihuana use, feeling that "it does nothing" for them.

Typically, however, the novice has faith (developed from his observation of users who do get high) that the drug actually will produce some new experience and continues to experiment with it until it does. His failure to get high worries him, and he is likely to ask more experienced users or provoke comments from them about it. In such conversations he is made aware of specific details of his experience which he may not have noticed or may have noticed but failed to identify as symptoms of being high:

> I didn't get high the first time . . . I don't think I held it in long enough. I probably let it out, you know, you're a little afraid. The second time I wasn't sure, and he [smoking companion] told me, like I asked him for some of the symptoms or something, how would I know, you know. . . . So he told me to sit on a stool. I sat on—I think I sat on a bar stool—and he said, "Let your feet hang," and then when I got down my feet were real cold, you know.
> And I started feeling it, you know. That was the first time. And then about a week after that, sometime pretty close to it, I really got on. That was the first time I got on a big laughing kick, you know. Then I really knew I was on.

One symptom of being high is an intense hunger. In the next case the novice becomes aware of this and gets high for the first time:

> They were just laughing the hell out of me because like I was eating so much. I just scoffed [ate] so much food, and they were just laughing at me, you know. Sometimes I'd be looking at them, you know, wondering why

they're laughing, you know, not knowing what I was doing. [Well, did they tell you why they were laughing eventually?] Yeah, yeah, I come back, "Hey, man, what's happening?" Like, you know, like I'd ask, "What's happening?" and all of a sudden I feel weird, you know. "Man, you're on you know. You're on pot [high on marihuana]." I said, "No, am I?" Like I don't know what's happening.

The learning may occur in more indirect ways:

I heard little remarks that were made by other people. Somebody said, "My legs are rubbery," and I can't remember all the remarks that were made because I was very attentively listening for all these cues for what I was supposed to feel like.

The novice, then, eager to have this feeling, picks up from other users some concrete referents of the term "high" and applies these notions to his own experience. The new concepts make it possible for him to locate these symptoms among his own sensations and to point out to himself a "something different" in his experience that he connects with drug use. It is only when he can do this that he is high. In the next case, the contrast between two successive experiences of a user makes clear the crucial importance of the awareness of the symptoms in being high and re-emphasizes the important role of interaction with other users in acquiring the concepts that make this awareness possible:

[Did you get high the first time you turned on?] Yeah, sure. Although, come to think of it, I guess I really didn't. I mean, like that first time it was more or less of a mild drunk. I was happy, I guess, you know what I mean. But I didn't really know I was high, you know what I mean. It was only after the second time I got high that I realized I was high the first time. Then I knew that something different was happening.
[How did you know that?] How did I know? If what happened to me that night would of happened to you, you would've known, believe me. We played the first tune for almost two hours—one tune! Imagine, man! We got on the stand and played this one tune, we started at nine o'clock. When we got finished I looked at my watch, it's a quarter to eleven. Almost two hours on one tune. And it didn't seem like anything. I mean, you know, it does that to you. It's like you have much more time or something. Anyway, when I saw that, man, it was too much. I knew I must really be high or something if anything like that could happen. See, and then they explained to me that that's what it did to you, you had a different sense of time and everything. So I realized that that's what it was. I knew then. Like the first time, I probably felt that way, you know, but I didn't know what's happening.

It is only when the novice becomes able to get high in this sense that he will continue to use marihuana for pleasure. In every case in which use continued, the user had acquired the necessary concepts with which to express to himself the fact that he was experiencing new sensations caused by the drug. That is, for use to continue, it is necessary not only to use the drug so as to produce effects but also to learn to perceive these effects when they occur. In this way marihuana acquires meaning for the user as an object which can be used for pleasure.

With increasing experience the user develops a greater appreciation of the drug's effects; he continues to learn to get high. He examines succeeding experiences closely, looking for new effects, making sure the old ones are still there. Out of this there grows a stable set of categories for experiencing the drug's effects whose presence enables the user to get high with ease.

The ability to perceive the drug's effects must be maintained if use is to continue; if it is lost, marihuana use ceases. Two kinds of evidence support this statement. First, people who become heavy users of alcohol, barbiturates, or opiates do not continue to smoke marihuana, largely because they lose the ability to distinguish between its effects and those of the other drugs.[9] They no longer know whether the marihuana gets them high. Second, in those few cases in which an individual uses marihuana in such quantities that he is always high, he is apt to get this same feeling that the drug has no effect on him, since the essential element of a noticeable difference between feeling high and feeling normal is missing. In such a situation, use is likly to be given up completely, but temporarily, in order that the user may once again be able to perceive the difference.

III

One more step is necessary if the user who has now learned to get high is to continue use. He must learn to enjoy the effects he has just learned to experience. Marihuana-produced sensations are not automatically or necessarily pleasurable. The taste for such experience is a socially acquired one, not different in kind from acquired tastes for oysters or dry martinis. The user feels dizzy, thirsty; his scalp tingles; he misjudges time and distances; and so on. Are these things pleasurable? He isn't sure. If he is to continue marihuana use, he must decide that they are. Otherwise, getting high, while a real enough experience, will be an unpleasant one he would rather avoid.

The effects of the drug, when first perceived, may be physically unpleasant or at least ambiguous:

> It started taking effect, and I didn't know what was happening, you know, what it was, and I was very sick. I walked around the room, walking

[9] "Smokers have repeatedly stated that the consumption of whiskey while smoking negates the potency of the drug. They find it very difficult to get 'high' while drinking whiskey and because of that smokers will not drink while using the 'weed' " (cf. New York City Mayor's Committee on Marihuana, *The Marihuana Problem in the City of New York* [Lancaster, Pa.: Jacques Cattel Press, 1944], p. 13.)

around the room trying to get off, you know; it just scared me at first, you know. I wasn't used to that kind of feeling.

In addition, the novice's naive interpretation of what is happening to him may further confuse and frighten him, particularly if he decides, as many do, that he is going insane:

> I felt I was insane, you know. Everything people done to me just wigged me. I couldn't hold a conversation, and my mind would be wandering, and I was always thinking, oh, I don't know, weird things, like hearing music different. . . . I get the feeling that I can't talk to anyone. I'll goof completely.

Given these typically frightening and unpleasant first experiences, the beginner will not continue use unless he learns to redefine the sensations as pleasurable:

> It was offered to me, and I tried it. I'll tell you one thing. I never did enjoy it at all. I mean it was just nothing that I could enjoy. [Well, did you get high when you turned on?] Oh, yeah, I got definite feelings from it. But I didn't enjoy them. I mean I got plenty of reactions, but they were mostly reactions of fear. [You were frightened?] Yes, I didn't enjoy it. I couldn't seem to relax with it, you know. If you can't relax with a thing, you can't enjoy it, I don't think.

In other cases the first experiences were also definitely unpleasant, but the person did become a marihuana user. This occurred, however, only after a later experience enabled him to redefine the sensations as pleasurable:

> [This man's first experience was extremely unpleasant, involving distortion of spatial relationships and sounds, violent thirst, and panic produced by these symptoms.] After the first time I didn't turn on for about, I'd say, ten months to a year. . . . It wasn't a moral thing; it was because I'd gotten so frightened, bein' so high. An' I didn't want to go through that again, I mean, my reaction was, "Well, if this is what they call bein' high, I don't dig [like] it." . . . So I didn't turn on for a year almost, accounta that. . . .
> Well, my friends started, an' consequently I started again. But I didn't have any more, I didn't have that same initial reaction, after I started turning on again.
> [In interaction with his friends he became able to find pleasure in the effects of the drug and eventually became a regular user.]

In no case will use continue without such a redefinition of the effects as enjoyable.

This redefinition occurs, typically, in interaction with more experienced users who, in a number of ways, teach the novice to find pleasure in this experience which is at first so frightening.[10] They may reassure him as to the temporary character of the unpleasant sensations and minimize their seriousness, at the same time calling attention to the more enjoyable aspects. An experienced user describes how he handles newcomers to marihuana use:

> Well, they get pretty high sometimes. The average person isn't ready for that, and it is a little frightening to them sometimes. I mean, they've been high on lush [alcohol], and they get higher that way than they've ever been before, and they don't know what's happening to them. Because they think they're going to keep going up, up, up till they lose their minds or begin doing weird things or something. You have to like reassure them, explain to them that they're not really flipping or anything, that they're gonna be all right. You have to just talk them out of being afraid. Keep talking to them, reassuring, telling them it's all right. And come on with your own story, you know: "The same thing happened to me. You'll get to like that after awhile." Keep coming on like that; pretty soon you talk them out of being scared. And besides they see you doing it and nothing horrible is happening to you, so that gives them more confidence.

The more experienced user may also teach the novice to regulate the amount he smokes more carefully, so as to avoid any severely uncomfortable symptoms while retaining the pleasant ones. Finally, he teaches the new user that he can "get to like it after awhile." He teaches him to regard those ambiguous experiences formerly defined as unpleasant as enjoyable. The older user in the following incident is a person whose tastes have shifted in this way, and his remarks have the effect of helping others to make a similar redefinition:

> A new user had her first experience of the effects of marihuana and became frightened and hysterical. She "felt like she was half in and half out of the room" and experienced a number of alarming physical symptoms. One of the more experienced users present said, "She's dragged because she's high like that. I'd give anything to get that high myself. I haven't been that high in years."

In short, what was once frightening and distasteful becomes, after a taste for it is built up, pleasant, desired, and sought after. Enjoyment is introduced by the favorable definition of the experience that one acquires from others. Without this, use will not continue, for marihuana will not be for the user an object he can use for pleasure.

In addition to being a necessary step in becoming a user, the pleasure represents an important condition for continued use. It is quite common for experienced users suddenly to have an unpleasant or frightening experience, which they cannot defined as pleasurable, either because they have used a larger amount of marihuana than usual or because it turns out to be

[10] Charen and Perelman, *op. cit.*, p. 679.

a higher-quality marihuana than they expected. The user has sensations which go beyond any conception he has of what being high is and is in much the same situation as the novice, uncomfortable and frightened. He may blame it on an overdose and simply be more careful in the future. But he may make this the occasion for a rethinking of his attitude toward the drug and decide that it no longer can give him pleasure. When this occurs and is not followed by a redefinition of the drug as capable of producing pleasure, use will cease.

The likelihood of such a redefinition occurring depends on the degree of the individual's participation with other users. Where this participation is intensive, the individual is quickly talked out of his feeling against marihuana use. In the next case, on the other hand, the experience was very disturbing, and the aftermath of the incident cut the person's participation with other users to almost zero. Use stopped for three years and began again only when a combination of circumstances, important among which was a resumption of ties with users, made possible a redefinition of the nature of the drug:

> It was too much, like I only made about four pokes, and I couldn't even get it out of my mouth, I was so high, and I got real flipped. In the basement, you know, I just couldn't stay in there anymore. My heart was pounding real hard, you know, and I was going out of my mind; I thought I was losing my mind completely. So I cut out of this basement, and this other guy, he's out of his mind, told me, "Don't, don't leave me, man. Stay here." And I couldn't.
>
> I walked outside, and it was five below zero, and I thought I was dying, and I had my coat open; I was sweating. I was perspiring. My whole insides were all . . . , and I walked about two blocks away, and I fainted behind a bush. I don't know how long I laid there. I woke up, and I was feeling the worst, I can't describe it at all, so I made it to a bowling alley, man, and I was trying to act normal, I was trying to shoot pool, you know, trying to act real normal, and I couldn't lay and I couldn't stand up and I couldn't sit down, and I went up and laid down where some guys that spot pins lay down, and that didn't help me, and I went down to a doctor's office. I was going to go in there and tell the doctor to put me out of my misery . . . because my heart was pounding so hard, you know. . . . So then all weekend I started flipping, seeing things there and going through hell, you know, all kinds of abnormal things. . . . I just quit for a long time then. [He went to a doctor who defined the symptoms for him as those of a nervous breakdown caused by "nerves" and "worries." Although he was no longer using marihuana, he had some recurrences of the symptoms which led him to suspect that "it was all his nerves."] So I just stopped worrying, you know; so it was about thirty-six months later I started making it again. I'd just take a few pokes, you know. [He first resumed use in the company of the same user-friend with whom he had been involved in the original incident.]

A person, then, cannot begin to use marihuana for pleasure, or continue its use for pleasure, unless he learns to define its effects as enjoyable, unless it becomes and remains an object which he conceived of as capable of producing pleasure.

IV

In summary, an individual will be able to use marihuana for pleasure only when he goes through a process of learning to conceive of it as an object which can be used in this way. No one becomes a user without (1) learning to smoke the drug in a way which will produce real effects; (2) learning to recognize the effects and connect them with drug use (learning, in other words, to get high); and (3) learning to enjoy the sensations he perceives. In the course of this process he develops a disposition or motivation to use marihuana which was not and could not have been present when he began use, for it involves and depends on conceptions of the drug which could only grow out of the kind of actual experience detailed above. On completion of this process he is willing and able to use marihuana for pleasure.

He has learned, in short, to answer "Yes" to the question: "Is it fun?" The direction his further use of the drug takes depends on his being able to continue to answer "Yes" to this question and, in addition, on his being able to answer "Yes" to other questions which arise as he becomes aware of the implications of the fact that the society as a whole disapproves of the practice: "Is it expedient?" "Is it moral?" Once he has acquired the ability to get enjoyment out of the drug, use will continue to be possible for him. Considerations of morality and expediency, occasioned by the reactions of society, may interfere and inhibit use, but use continues to be a possibility in terms of his conception of the drug. The act becomes impossible only when the ability to enjoy the experience of being high is lost, through a change in the user's conception of the drug occasioned by certain kinds of experience with it.

In comparing this theory with those which ascribe marihuana use to motives or predispositions rooted deep in individual behavior, the evidence makes it clear that marihuana use for pleasure can occur only when the process described above is undergone and cannot occur without it. This is apparently so without reference to the nature of the individual's personal makeup, or psychic problems. Such theories assume that people have stable modes of response which predetermine the way they will act in relation to any particular situation or object and that, when they come in contact with the given object or situation, they act in the way in which their makeup predisposes them.

This analysis of the genesis of marihuana use shows that the individuals who come in contact with a given object may respond to it at first in a great variety of ways. If a stable form of new behavior toward the object is to emerge, a transformation of meanings must occur, in which the person develops a new conception of the nature of the object.[11] This happens in a series of communicative acts in which others point out new aspects of his experience to him, present him with new interpretations of events, and help him achieve a new conceptual organization of his world, without which the new behavior is not possible. Persons who do not achieve the proper kind of conceptualization are unable to engage in the given behavior and turn off in the direction of some other relationship to the object or activity.

This suggests that behavior of any kind might fruitfully be studied developmentally, in terms of changes in meanings and concepts, their organization and reorganization, and the way they channel behavior, making some acts possible while excluding others.

[11] Cf. Anselm Strauss, "The Development and Transformation of Monetary Meanings in the Child," *American Sociological Review*, XVII (June, 1952), 275–86.

43 WILLIAM R. ROSENGREN

The Self in the Emotionally Disturbed[1]

As George H. Mead has pointed out, human beings tend to act on the basis of their inferences about the probable behavior of others toward them.[2] Moreover, our feelings about ourselves are mediated by how we think others feel about us. This is to say that much of our behavior is guided by what we think others are thinking and by our confidence in what we judge to be the readiness of others to act upon what we think they impute to us. In brief, it is axiomatic in Mead's psychology that there are functional relationships between how we see ourselves, how we see others, and how we think others see us. Similarly, basic to Mead's theory is the idea that such relationships have important consequences in overt behavior and are also phenomena of interpersonal perception.

While it may be logically reasonable to set forth such principles, the occasion to validate them by means of operational procedures is less fre-

William R. Rosengren, "The Self in the Emotionally Disturbed." Reprinted from *The American Journal of Sociology*, vol. 66 (March 1961), pp. 454–462, by permission of The University of Chicago Press. Copyright 1961 by The University of Chicago.

[1] Part of a four-year project in social psychiatry under Grant OM-21 from the National Institute of Mental Health, United States Public Health Service.

[2] George Herbert Mead, *Mind, Self, and Society* (Chicago: University of Chicago Press, 1934).

quently at hand. For it seems implicit in Mead's theory that it is necessary to take temporal changes into account in order to demonstrate empirically functional relationships among the self processes. Ideally, changes in the self would occur over a relatively long period of time during which the individual moves sequentially through the stages of the play, the game, and the generalized other. Moreover, once having developed to that stage of socialization, most persons maintain a rather stable and continuing set of relationships among the functions of the self. In terms of the consequences in overt behavior, Sullivan has referred to such stability as "the repeated situations which characterize a human life."[3] Whatever the terminology, however, the behavior of persons becomes relatively stable and predictable insofar as there is some convergence between how they see themselves, how they see others, and how they think others see them.

In the case of persons undergoing intensive psychiatric treatment, however, basic changes in interpersonal behavior frequently occur very rapidly. Therefore, the study of emotionally disturbed persons may offer opportunities to put to the test some aspects of Mead's theory which, under normal circumstances, would require either many years to do or could be done only by clinical or retrospective analysis.

With the exception of clinical descriptions of distorted self-concepts of individual psychiatric patients, little empirical evidence is available about the processes of self-definition, inference, and imputation among persons who have been institutionalized for emotional disturbance.[4] The purpose of this paper is to report the findings of a study of interpersonal inference and imputation among a group of institutionalized emotionally disturbed children whose chief reason for hospitalization was inadequate reciprocity with others. A major aim is to demonstrate empirically changes in the functional relationships of the processes of the self, before and after long-term residential treatment, and to report their relationships to other indexes of changed behavior.

The subjects were ten boys, ranging in age from ten to twelve years, who were receiving long-term residential treatment in a private psychiatric hospital for children. The total patient population numbered fifty-six, of which the subjects constituted one of six units. They had all received clinical diagnoses of "Passive-Aggressive Personality—Aggressive Type" and were the only patients in the institution who were homogeneously grouped on the basis of diagnosis and symptomatology. Such patients are more commonly referred to as "acting-out"; their overt behavior is generally typified by spontaneous verbal and physical aggression, short attention

---

[3] Harry Stack Sullivan, *Conceptions of Modern Psychiatry* (Washington, D.C.: William Alanson White Psychiatric Foundation, 1947), p. vi.

[4] The most recent published attempt to put to test operational aspects of the social psychology of Mead is, perhaps, Carl J. Couch's "Self-attitudes and Degree of Agreement with Immediate Others," *American Journal of Sociology*, LXIII (1958), 491–96.

span, and inability to delay gratifications, and they tend to have histories of interpersonal difficulties with both adults and peers. At the time of the first testing, all of the boys had lived together twenty-four hours a day for at least one year, and some for as long as two years.

Procedures

INTERPERSONAL PERCEPTIONS

In September, 1958, an "inference-imputation" test was administered to the subjects along with tests of several other criteria. This "Self-definition Test" involved nineteen interpersonal qualities which were dichotomized into those which are "friendly-accepting" and those which are "hostile-reject-ing" in nature; these are shown in Table 1.

TABLE 1. Interpersonal qualities

Friendly-accepting	Hostile-rejecting
Generous	Selfish
Good	Bad
Nice	Mean
Smart	Dumb
Kind	Cruel
Brave	Afraid
Clean	Dirty
Well-liked	Ugly
Honest	
Strong	
Neat	

Two days prior to the individual testing sessions, each boy was asked the following "near-sociometric" questions: (1) "Which of the boys (in the unit) do you like best of all?" (2) "Which do you dislike the most?" (3) "Which do you think likes you the most?" and (4) "Which do you think dislikes you the most?"

For ease in administration, each quality was printed in India ink on a 5 x 7-inch card. Each boy then sorted the cards at least five times: (1) a description of himself (*self-definition*), (2) a description of the boy he had chosen as the one he liked best (*imputation*), (3) a description of the boy he had chosen as the most disliked (*imputation*), (4) a description of himself from the point of view of the boy whom he thought liked him (*inference*), and (5) a description of himself from the point of view of the boy whom he thought disliked him (*inference*). Those boys who had been chosen by

TABLE 2. Scale for behavior of rating "acting-out" patients

Symptomatic Behaviors	Non-symptomatic Behaviors
Irrelevant: Diffuse and random activity	*Relevant:* Goal-directed activity
Active: Mobile, labile, expressive behavior	*Passive:* Restrained, inexpressive, inactive behavior
Rejecting: Disassociates from others; rejects interactions	*Affiliative:* Associates with others; responds to and initiates interactions
Narcissistic: "Exclusive" interest in self	*Other-oriented:* Shows interest in others, positively or negatively
Dominant: Attempts to dominate, control, and direct	*Submissive:* Submits to domination, control, and direction by others
Succorant: Seeks help, assistance, support, and affection	*Nurturant:* Gives help, assistance, support, and affection
Aggressive: Attempts to destroy, humiliate, and degrade	*Blame avoidance:* Withdraws from or otherwise avoids aggression-eliciting situations
Immediacy: Seeks for immediate gratification	*Endurance:* Foregoes immediate satisfactions for future gratifications
Impulsive: Spontaneous and unreflectful behavior	*Deliberation:* Hesitant, cautious, and reflectful behavior
Non-verbal: Little talking of affiliative or rejecting type	*Verbal:* Much talking either of affiliative or rejecting type

others as either "I think he likes me" or "I think he dislikes me" were then asked to describe the individuals who had chosen them in those ways.

One year later, in September, 1959, the boys underwent the identical sociometric and inference-imputation procedures.

OBSERVATION

Over a six-month period—from October, 1958, to March, 1959,—the subjects were observed by a non-participant observer in a variety of situations for a total of sixty hours of direct observation. The overt behavior of the ten boys was rated on a "moreness-lessness" basis using the qualities of interaction listed in Table 2. Those on the left of the rating scale are symptomatic forms of behavior, while those on the right are non-symptomatic for this diagnostic category of patients. The methods, procedures, and findings of this part of the study are reported elsewhere.[5]

CONTROL-ELICITING BEHAVIOR

The behavior of patients of this type occasionally becomes so dangerous either to themselves or to others that, if some means of restraint were not used, severe physical harm would result. In such instances the acting-out

[5] See William R. Rosengren, "The Social Field in Relation to the Behavior of Emotionally Disturbed Children," *Sociometry* (in press).

patient is placed alone in a locked room until his behavior becomes physically tolerable. Accurate records are maintained of the use of this means of restraint in the institution. These data were accumulated for each of the ten subjects at the end of one year.

INSTITUTIONAL EXPECTATIONS

In both 1958 and 1959 the subjects responded to a test of "institutional expectations."[6] This consisted of ten story completions in which a boy was depicted as engaging in some moderately acting-out form of behavior in an institutional setting. The boys responded to each story by describing events which they expected would follow the incident which was presented. One, for example, read as follows: "Bob is supposed to take pills in the morning and in the afternoon. But he doesn't swallow them—he throws them out the window. One day the nurse found out about it and then. . . ." The subjects' responses were classified as involving either hostile or benign institutional responses. An example of a hostile expectation is, "She (the nurse) drags him to the room and gives him needles and he gets sicker." An example of a benign expectation is, "She tells him that the pills help him so he takes them." Typically, the more severely disturbed the patient, the more hostile are his expectations and, presumably, his anticipatory responses to them.

Treatment of Data

INTERPERSONAL PERCEPTIONS

Sums of "friendly-accepting" and "hostile-rejecting" choices were computed on the first (1958) and second (1959) series of self-definition tests on each of the dimensions—inference-imputation, definition-inference, and definition imputation. The study was chiefly concerned with changes in the similarity and dissimilarity in choices of qualities in the one year. Because the total number of choices was not the same for all the subjects on either the first or the second series, changes were measured in terms of proportions rather than raw choice scores. Comparing, for example, the similarity of self-definitions and inferences, a "similar" choice was regarded as one in which the subject defined himself as generous and expected (inferred) that others (either the liked or disliked person) would also define him as generous. There were two possibilities for "dissimilar" choices: (1) the subject defined himself as generous but felt that the referent person would not so define him; or (2) the subject did not ascribe the quality of generos-

---

[6] This was an adaption of a similar set of story completions reported in W. and J. McCord, *Psychopathy and Delinquency* (New York: Grune & Stratton, Inc., 1957).

ity to himself but felt that the referent person would define him as generous. Proportions of each similar inference-imputation, definition-inference, and definition-imputation dimension were computed in that fashion for each subject on the first and then on the second testing.

The significance of proportional change was computed through the use of the Wilcoxon Matched-Pairs Signed-Ranks Test, with probability levels derived directly from the value of T.[7] In all cases the one-tailed test was used because the direction of change was predicted.

The following classification was used for comparing the boys' patterns of interpersonal definition with the other indexes of change: Frequency distributions were made for the total quantity of proportional change under each perceptual relationship for each subject. Those whose total proportion of change in self functions was one standard deviation or more above the mean for the ten subjects were classified as "high self-changers." Those whose extent of change was one standard deviation or more below the mean are referred to as "low self-changers." In these terms there were three high and three low self-changers.

OTHER INDEXES OF CHANGE

At the end of the six-month period of observation, frequency distributions were made of the extent of change in overt behavior as indicated by the rating scale (Table 2). The extent of change was determined by the difference between the sums of scores on the left side of the scale during the first three months and the sum of scores on the left side during the second three months. Three of the boys had undergone significant changes from symptomatic to non-symptomatic behavior (one standard deviation or more above the mean), and three had experienced comparatively little change in behavior (one standard deviation or more below the mean).

Similar frequency distributions were made of the number of "isolations" which each boy had elicited by his physically intolerable behavior during the first six months as compared with the second. Finally, computations were made on both the first and second testings of the number of "benign" [and] the [number of] "hostile" expectations of the institution which each boy had expressed.

Some Expectations from Mead's Theory

Clinical knowledge concerning the disturbance syndrome of the patients as well as participant observation for a year and a half formed the chief basis of the general hypotheses; Mead's principles of the interrelatedness

---

[7] This statistic is described and probability tables presented in S. Siegel, *Nonparametric Statistics for the Behavioral Sciences* (New York: McGraw-Hill Book Co., 1956).

of self-definition, inferences of others, and imputations by others underlay each expectation.

It was expected that on the first test the boys would define themselves quite differently from the ways in which they thought others would define them, as compared with the second test. Moreover, it was anticipated that the inferences they made of others on the first test would be different from others' actual imputations, as compared with the second test. More specifically in Mead's terms, it was expected that after one year the subjects would tend to "call out in themselves the responses which they think they call out in others" and that they would "call out in others responses similar to those which they think they call out in others."

Furthermore, it was anticipated that inferences of others would be less contingent upon the "liked-disliked" distinction on the second test as compared with the first. More specifically, it was expected that the boys would infer *more* friendly-accepting qualities of disliked persons and *less* friendly-accepting qualities of liked persons on the second test as compared with the first. Both of these related hypotheses were intended to serve as a means of empirically demonstrating whether the boys would make inferences concerning the ways in which they thought others viewed them with regard to a generalized conception of others' points of view—what might be referred to as the "generalized others"—or would persist in making inferences with reference to specific others in the environment.

Third, it was expected that the boys would tend to make different inferences concerning liked and disliked persons on the first test and more similar inferences on the second. Specifically, it was anticipated that inferences concerning disliked persons' imputations would be less accurate on the first test as compared with the second. Moreover, it was expected that inferences concerning liked persons' imputations would also be less accurate on the first test than on the second, that is, that the boys would tend to "take the role of specific others" in regard to themselves in an inaccurate fashion on the first test and the "role of the generalized other" in a more accurate fashion on the second test.

Last, it was expected that the boys would tend to define themselves more similarly to the ways in which they thought others defined them on the second test as compared with the first. Specifically, the subjects would define themselves significantly more as they thought the disliked persons defined them. It was also anticipated that a similar change would take place with regard to the liked persons. These two propositions were designed to test the expectation that the subjects would tend to define themselves more in terms of a conception of a generalized other than in terms of a consideration of specific individuals about whom they had contrasting attitudes themselves.

In general, therefore, the data were analyzed with a view to determining the extent of convergence with some basic principles of Mead's social psychology.

TABLE 3. Similar self-definitions and inferences of others' imputations: signed ranks proportions for first and second tests

Inference	N*	T	Less Frequent Sign	p (One-tailed Test)
Liked and disliked persons	10	3	—	> .005
Disliked persons only	10	9	—	> .025
Liked persons only	10	8	—	> .025

*Refers to the elimination of tied proportions between pairs. Levels of significance for N's less than 25 are determined directly from the magnitude of T.

First, it was expected that on the first test the subjects would tend to define themselves differently from the ways in which they thought others defined them, while on the second test self-definitions and inferences of others' imputations would be more similar. This expectation was borne out with respect to disliked as well as liked persons (Table 3). There was significantly more similarity between how the boys defined themselves and how they thought both liked and disliked persons would define them on the second test as compared with the first.

Second, it was expected that a comparison of the responses on the first and second tests would reveal an increased tendency for the boys to define themselves more as others actually defined them. This expectation was also borne out with regard both to liked and disliked persons, although with somewhat greater confidence in relation to the liked persons (Table 4). In general, the data suggested that on the second test the subjects defined themselves more like the ways in which they thought others would define them. Moreover, there was a tendency for the "others" actually to impute those qualities which the boys thought would be imputed to them.

Furthermore, it was predicted that the subjects would be less likely to infer hostile-rejecting qualities of the disliked persons and friendly-accept-

TABLE 4. Similar inferences of others and imputations by others: signed-ranks proportions for first and second tests

Person Making Imputation by	N*	T	Less Frequent Sign	p (One-tailed Test)
Liked and disliked	10	2	—	> .01
Disliked only	10	8	—	> .025
Liked only	10	0	—	> .005

* See n. to Table 3.

TABLE 5. "Friendly-accepting" qualities inferred of specific others: signed-ranks proportions for first and second tests

Referent	N*	T	Less Frequent Sign	p (One-tailed Test)
Disliked person	10	1	—	> .005
Liked person	10	0	+	> .005

* See n. to Table 3.

ing qualities of the liked persons on the second test than they did a year earlier (Table 5). There was, in fact, a tendency for the boys to infer, proportionately, more friendly-accepting qualities of the persons whom they disliked and less hostile-rejecting qualities on the second test. Moreover, they also tended to expect proportionately less friendly-accepting imputations by liked persons on the second test. These findings may indicate that on the second test the subjects made inferences on the basis of a somewhat more generalized view of themselves rather than of a conception of specific persons' probable views of them.

The fourth general expectation was related to the issue of the subjects' accuracy in making inferences about other persons' imputations to them. Was there, in other words, a tendency for the boys increasingly to "call out from others the responses which they thought they called out in others?" The findings with regard to person referent—liked and disliked—and type of qualities inferred—friendly or hostile—are reported in Table 6.

As Table 6 indicates, the most discriminating differentiation was that in which the referent person involved as well as the distinction between

TABLE 6. Similar inferences and implications: signed-ranks proportions for first and second tests

Referent and Inference-Imputation	N*	T	Less Frequent Sign	p (One-tailed Test)
All persons, all qualities	10	2	—	> .01
All persons, "friendly"	10	1	—	> .005
All persons, "hostile"	10	1	—	> .005
Liked persons, all qualities	10	0	—	> .005
Liked persons, "friendly"	10	6	—	> .025
Disliked persons, all qualities	10	8	—	> .025
Disliked persons, "friendly"	9	1	—	> .005
Disliked persons, "hostile"	9	0	—	> .005
Liked persons, "hostile"	6	3	—	< .025

* See n. to Table 3.

friendly and hostile qualities were controlled. The most significant change between the first and second test was with respect to the disliked rather than the liked persons. Specifically, the subjects tended to infer qualities of disliked persons more similar to those which were actually imputed to them by disliked persons on the second test, as compared with the first. Furthermore, while there was increased similarity concerning inferences of friendly imputations by liked persons which was not statistically significant, the changes which did appear were in the predicted direction. With this qualification, the data do suggest two tentative conclusions. First, the boys were more accurate in inferring those qualities which others actually imputed to them. Second, this might indicate that on the first test the boys attempted to define themselves from the point of view of specific others, and to do this in a comparatively inaccurate way. On the second test, however, they seemed to define themselves from the point of view of a more generalized frame of reference which resulted, in fact, in considerably greater accuracy in inferring imputations by specific others.

Finally, it was anticipated that on the second test the boys would be more likely to define themselves in the same terms as they thought both the liked and disliked persons would define them. That is, greater similarity between self-definitions and inferences was expected. As can be seen in Table 7, significant changes could best be identified when the referent person and the type of interpersonal quality were controlled. Specifically, the boys did tend to define themselves somewhat more as they thought the disliked persons would define them, but only with regard to the hostile-rejecting qualities. Moreover, while the increased similarity in this regard relative to the liked persons was not beyond what could have been expected by chance alone, it was in the predicted direction. It might be concluded, therefore, that on the first test the boys defined themselves as they thought

TABLE 7. Similar self-definitions and inferences: signed-ranks proportions for first and second tests

Referent and Self-definition-Inference	N*	T	Less Frequent Sign	p (One-tailed Test)
All persons, "hostile"	9	0	—	> .005
Disliked persons, all qualities	10	5	—	> .01
Disliked persons, "hostile"	10	0	—	> .005
All persons, all qualities	9	10	—	< .025
All persons, "friendly"	10	22	+ = —	< .025
Liked persons, all qualities	10	14	—	< .025
Liked persons, "friendly"	10	10	—	< .025
Liked persons, "hostile"	9	8	—	< .025
Disliked persons, "friendly"	9	11	—	< .025

* See n. to Table 3.

both liked and disliked persons would do, but only with regard to friendly-accepting qualities. On the second test, however, they showed an increased inclination to include hostile-rejecting qualities in the similarities between how they defined themselves and how they thought significant others would define them.

When one contrasts the responses of the subjects on the first test with those on the second, several distinct patterns appear. On the *first* test they tended to define themselves dissimilar to the ways in which they thought others defined them. Second, both liked and disliked persons tended to impute to the subjects qualities dissimilar to those which the subjects expected would be imputed to them. Furthermore, the subjects tended to expect that liked persons would impute significantly more friendly-accepting qualities and that disliked persons would impute significantly more hostile-rejecting qualities. This is to say that their inferences about themselves appeared to be made with reference to particular persons in their immediate experience. Fourth, they were comparatively inaccurate in inferring what qualities others—both liked and disliked persons—would actually impute to them. Last, they tended to define themselves differently from the ways in which they thought both liked and disliked persons would define them with an accompanying tendency for them to be somewhat more sensitized to friendly-accepting than to hostile-rejecting attributes.

On the *second* test, on the other hand, they tended to define themselves more as they thought others defined them. Second, both the liked and the disliked persons tended to impute those qualities which the inferring subjects thought the others would. Third, the boys tended to expect that liked persons would impute significantly more hostile-rejecting qualities and that the disliked persons would impute more friendly-accepting qualities. Fourth, they were somewhat more accurate in inferring those qualities others actually imputed to them. Last, they tended to define themselves somewhat more as they thought both the liked and disliked persons would define them and were increasingly accurate in regard to hostile-rejecting qualities.

In terms of Mead's theory of the self, it would appear that on the first test the boys tended to (1) call out in themselves responses unlike those which they thought they called out in others, (2) call out in others responses unlike those which they thought they called out in others, (3) make inferences from the point of view of specific others rather than of a generalized other, and (4) define themselves in terms of specific other persons.

On the second test, on the other hand, they tended to (1) call out in themselves responses more like those which they thought they called out in others, (2) call out in others responses more like those which they thought they called out in others, (3) make inferences from the point of view of a generalized other rather than of specific others, and (4) define themselves in terms of a generalized other rather than of specific others.

Relationship to Other Indexes of Change

Although these findings may well suggest that both the functions and the content of the self changed significantly in the one year, it is of further interest to know to what extent and in what ways such patterns might be associated with other indexes of change.

First, the three "high self-changers" were also the three boys whose overt behavior changed most significantly from symptomatic to non-symptomatic during the six months in which observational ratings of behavior were made: the boys whose self functions more nearly approximated Mead's ideal were those who experienced increasingly fewer difficulties with both their peers and the adults working with them. Conversely, those whose self processes changed the least along lines of Mead's expectations were those who continued both to initiate symptomatic interactions and reacted to others in a significantly symptomatic fashion.

Second, with regard to highly disruptive behavior which necessitated isolation of the patient, the three high self-changers were also those who were significantly less often isolated in the one year than formerly. On the other hand, those boys whose self processes changed the least were also the ones who were isolated either significantly *more* often, or as often, in the one year.

Last, with regard to expectations of the institution, the three high self-changers were also the boys whose expectations of the institution's actions toward them changed most significantly from "hostile" at the beginning of the year to "benign" at the end. Conversely, the "low self-changers" continued comparatively often to expect hostile action and seldom to expect benign action in the one year.

On the basis of these findings it is concluded that, in the boys studied, changes in the functions and content of the self were associated with overt changes in behavior as well as with changes in a somewhat more basic orientation toward their immediate social environment.

Conclusions

This paper has reported an attempt to relate data from a test of interpersonal inferences, imputations, and self-definitions to some of the chief assertions of Mead's social psychology. The findings are tentative, and the conclusions and interpretations which have been made are best regarded as only suggestive. Because of the small number of subjects involved and the difficulties characteristic of studies of interpersonal perception,[8] both the findings and the conclusions are best regarded as a preliminary effort.

The concept of the self as used in the social psychology of Mead is one that continues to be an intriguing basis for much speculation and interpretation. It also continues, however, to present many difficulties for empirical investigation and validation. The limited field study reported in this paper is an attempt to put the concept of the self to empirical test with a view to further elaborating its importance in human behavior.

[8] See, e.g., L. J. Cronbach, "Proposal Leading to Analytic Treatment of Social Perception Scores," in R. Tagiuri and L. Petrullo (eds.), *Person, Perception and Interpersonal Behavior* (Stanford, Calif.: Stanford University Press, 1958), pp. 353–78.

**44   MICHAEL SCHWARTZ, GORDON F. N. FEARN, &
SHELDON STRYKER**

A Note on Self Conception
and the Emotionally Disturbed Role

Emotional disturbance among children may be conceived of as role-making behavior in the process of self-concept development. It is, as Cohen[1] has noted, reasonable to assume that the deviant finds, builds, tests, validates and expresses a self in the process of becoming deviant. The extension of this assumption to the "emotionally disturbed" child is not unreasonable.

We can postulate that human beings seek to create and to maintain a stable identity. Given rewards for disturbed behavior, that disturbed behavior may become integral to a role-making process out of which an identity as a disturbed child may be reinforced. Such reinforcement may, then, lead the child to form a coherent, stable identity as a disturbed child, and to value that identity positively. This in turn implies a high degree of commitment to a disturbed role.[2]

If this reasoning is valid, it suggests the following hypotheses: (1) children most committed to the disturbed role will (a) attribute positive

Michael Schwartz, Gordon F. N. Fearn, and Sheldon Stryker, "A Note on Self Conception and the Emotionally Disturbed Role," *Sociometry*, vol. 29 (September 1966), pp. 300–305. Reprinted by permission.
[1] Albert K. Cohen, "The Sociology of the Deviant Act: Anomie Theory and Beyond," *American Sociological Review*, 30 (February, 1965) pp. 5–14.
[2] Sheldon Stryker, "Identity Salience and Role Performance: the Relevance of Symbolic Interaction Theory for Family Research," paper delivered at meeting of the American Sociological Association, Chicago, Illinois, 1965.

self meanings to themselves, and (b) show low intra-individual variability in self meanings; while (2) children least committed to the disturbed role will (a) attribute negative self meanings to themselves, and (b) show high intra-individual variability in self meanings.

If what follows, we assume that those children most committed to a disturbed role will be viewed by therapists as having poor prognosis for recovery; and, conversely, those children least committed will be viewed by therapists as having a good prognosis. Not immediately related to the above hypotheses, but of considerable concern, is the issue of self meanings which the disturbed child attributes to himself and which he believes others to share with him. We are, therefore, interested in determining which of a number of possible significant others are seen by children as sharing self meanings with them. This concern is exploratory, and as we shall note later, the findings are extremely suggestive of lines of research into the nature of the disturbed role and the nature of the institutional setting in the therapy process.

Method

In the summer of 1965, seventy-eight emotionally disturbed in-patient children in two Canadian institutions were individually administered a twenty-scale semantic differential. The scales used were drawn from Osgood's thesaurus study: cruel-kind, honest-dishonest, bad-good, small-large, happy-sad, weak-strong, clean-dirty, beautiful-ugly, pleasant-unpleasant, fast-slow, heavy-light, unfriendly-friendly, gentle-violent, unimportant-important, unfair-fair, awful-nice, stupid-smart, hard-soft, girlish-boyish, and sick-healthy.

The children were asked to rate the following stimuli on each of the foregoing scales: "How do you feel about yourself"; "The way that you feel your mother sees you"; "The way that you feel your father sees you"; "The way that you feel your best friend sees you"; and "The way that you feel (the therapist) sees you." The therapists were asked to place each child for whom they were responsible into one of four prognosis categories: very good, good, poor, and very poor. The children in our sample were described primarily as "behavior (vs. personality) problems of an acting out, aggressive type." No autistic or other seriously psychotic children were included. The therapists were psychiatric social workers and institutionally trained child care workers, heavily grounded in Neo-Freudian milieu-oriented theory.

Once the children had been categorized by prognosis, we assessed the equivalence of the groups in terms of age, sex, length of time in therapy to date of testing, and percent who were wards of the institution. In no case were significant differences found. Average age in each group is 12.5 years, and the average length of time in therapy at the date of testing was twenty months. For purposes of analysis, it was necessary to collapse the poor and very poor prognosis groups. The distribution of cases in the three categories was: Very good = 38, Good = 31, Poor and Very Poor = 9.

An analysis of the twenty semantic differential items for each of the stimuli led us to retain ten of the original scales, since these correlated well with the total scores on all stimuli, while the remaining scales did not. The items retained were: cruel-kind, honest-dishonest, bad-good, clean-dirty, beautiful-ugly, pleasant-unpleasant, gentle-violent, unimportant-important, awful-nice, stupid-smart. Clearly, these are evaluative items. Taking every other item in the above list, and correlating the total score on those five items with the total score on the remaining five items, for each stimulus (e.g., "My mother thinks I am . . ."), produces reliability coefficients above .70 on all stimuli. Means are based on total scores across all the items. Intra-individual variability was assessed by calculating the standard deviation for each individual across the ten items on the self-description schedule, using the standard deviations as scores and calculating means for each prognosis category.

Results

Hypotheses 1a and 2a state that quality of meanings attributed to oneself should be best in the poor and very poor prognosis categories and worst in the very good prognosis category. The assumption is, again, that there is an ascending level of commitment to the disturbed role as one moves from the very good to the poor prognosis category. In order to test these hypotheses, we have compared the mean scores for the three prognosis groups on the stimulus "How you feel about yourself." The possible range of scores is from ten to seventy, where the lower the score the more positive the self meanings. Table 1 indicates that the mean scores are distributed in the pro-

TABLE 1. Mean self-concept scores for each prognosis category

Prognosis	N	Mean	S.D.
Very Good	31	25.52	10.8
Good	38	25.21	12.0
Poor and Very Poor	9	20.78	9.1

posed order. The hypotheses are not completely supported, however, for the indicated differences are not statistically significant. The trend of the data is in the appropriate direction and, to that extent, is encouraging.

Our next concern is with the level of intra-individual variability over the ten semantic differential scales. Hypotheses 1b and 2b proposed that on the average there would be less variability in the poor and very poor category than in the very good or good categories. Table 2 indicates that there is

TABLE 2. Mean intra-individual variability by three prognosis groups, with computed t-values

				t-tests	
Prognosis	*Mean*	*S.D.*	*N*	*Good*	*Poor/ Very Poor*
Very Good	2.02	1.69	31	1.93**	2.20*
Good	1.34	1.08	38	—	0.87
Poor/Very Poor	1.00	1.06	9	—	—

* p less than .05.
** p less than .06.

in fact less intra-individual variability in the poor and very poor prognosis category when compared to the very good category. The good category falls between these and differs significantly from the very good category but not from the poor and very poor category. Again, the trend is in accord with our hypothesis.

Thus far we have noted that those most committed to the disturbed role tend to have slightly more positive self-evaluations, and tend to have the most stable self-evaluations. Of interest is the extent to which the subjects' self meanings are shared with specific, relevant others. We have calculated the multiple correlation coefficients for each prognosis category, using the self-descriptions as dependent variables and the perceived perceptions of mother, father, best friend, and therapist as the independent variables. The partial correlations have also been computed. For the very good prognosis group and for the good prognosis group, Table 3 indicates that R is .52, while the R for the poor and very poor group is .98. When the partial correlations are examined for the very good and good prognosis categories, only the partial correlations between self-description and perceptions of best friends' descriptions are significant, these being .33 and .43 respectively.[3] The picture for the poor and very poor prognosis category is quite different; here the partial with best friend is − .79, and the partial with therapist is .97.

[3] The partial r of .33 for best friends' perceived evaluation and self evaluation holds constant the effect of perceived evaluation of mother, father, and therapist on self-evaluation. Similarly, the remaining partials were run holding each of the other perceived evaluations constant.

TABLE 3. Partial and multiple correlations between subjects' self descriptions and perceptions of others' descriptions of them

Prognosis (Dependent Variable)	Mean	S.D.	Partial R with Self-descriptions
Very Good (N = 31)			Multiple R = .52
Mother	21.25	21.32	.06
Father	18.39	19.53	.16
Best Friend	18.71	9.82	.33*
Therapist	16.90	12.34	.06
Good (N = 38)			Multiple R = .52
Mother	20.37	16.81	−.11
Father	14.63	13.69	.09
Best Friend	19.32	9.75	.43*
Therapist	19.74	10.85	.16
Poor/Very Poor (N = 9)			Multiple R = .98
Mother	21.22	17.70	.01
Father	17.89	15.28	.26
Best Friend	21.22	77.36	−.79*
Therapist	18.78	8.63	.97*

* p less than .01.

Discussion

From the point of view of our theoretical approach, these are most interesting findings. The relatively poorer self-meanings which the very good prognosis subjects attribute to themselves and the higher level of intra-person variability accompanying those meanings may be taken as an indication that these subjects have some anxiety about themselves. They are, because of that anxiety, good therapy risks since anxiety reduction can be used by therapists as reinforcement. At the same time, these subjects seem to have developed interpersonal relations with peers of significance and may be seeking through a variety of others a more efficacious self meaning. In short, they are not thoroughly committed to the disturbed role.

In some recent discussions with psychiatrists treating child in-patients, it was pointed out that among the good prognosis patients it was not uncommon for interpersonal friendships between patients and nurses' aides or janitors, etc., to spring up and develop. Such relations were said seldom to occur among poor prognosis patients. Because of his self-anxiety, the good prognosis patient is "tuned in" to a variety of people, and he accepts reflected self meanings from them. Our data indicate only that the good prognosis patients are tuned in to peers more than others, but had we tapped sources of reflection like janitors, etc., we may have found that the sources of self meanings were many and varied, each contributing fairly small amounts to the total variance.

The uncommitted, then, is the one who is still in the process of finding, validating, and building a self and is psychologically mobile among personal reference points. The multiple R's which explain only slightly more than 25% of the variance in self meanings of good prognosis patients make this point quite clear. Even though the therapist is not of great significance to these patients, a controlled environment providing a variety of possible significant others from whom to learn a non-disturbed self may be the best therapeutic device available. Those psychiatrists with whom we have spoken have concurred in this observation and have noted that the therapist is, in many cases, an over-rated aspect of the total therapeutic milieu. The availability of others in the hospital milieu who can serve as non-disturbed role models is of great use to the patient with anxiety about self, since he can reduce that anxiety by modeling non-disturbed roles and being rewarded for his modeling, either directly or vicariously.

Conversely, the subjects in our poor prognosis category have rejected the meanings which they believe their friends attribute to them, and describe themselves as true images of the meanings which they perceive their therapists to attribute to them. This may mean that their acceptance of the therapist as the only significant other is at the same time an unconditional definition of themselves in the disturbed role. The most significant other must be the one who knows the role best, finds the role player most predictable, and rewards the role player by giving support or by being permissive (as the worker-therapist tends to be). In measurement terms, it is not important that we failed to tap a larger sample of others for these poor and very poor prognosis cases: there is little room for them as sources in the subjects' self meanings.

We have interpreted these correlational data in a manner consistent with our theoretical position. In doing so, we have inferred causal relationships from the correlations. It is, of course, possible that the correlations are a function of a third variable, a possibility which could render these results invalid. Yet though our data are not as strongly supportive of the hypotheses as we might wish, if these results are repeated under properly extended and controlled conditions, their implications cannot be lightly dismissed. By being supportive of the behavior of the role player, the therapist engages in self-defeating activity. The support removes whatever little anxiety in self existed; because there is little if any anxiety, there is little or no possibility for rewards for alternative behavior which might normally be expected to reduce anxiety; and finding no way to alter the behavior, the therapist classifies the patient as a poor or very poor prognosis. The patient most committed to the role of disturbed child stands little chance of having his behavior altered if he perceives the only relevant other as reinforcing his present behavior.

Cohen has cogently argued the need to conceptualize the deviant as a role player in search of a social identity. This paper attempts to indicate the potentially great utility of his conceptualization for research in deviant behavior as well as other areas.

45   ERVING GOFFMAN

The Moral Career of the Mental Patient

Traditionally the term *career* has been reserved for those who expect to enjoy the rises laid out within a respectable profession. The term is coming to be used, however, in a broadened sense to refer to any social strand of any person's course through life. The perspective of natural history is taken: unique outcomes are neglected in favor of such changes over time as are basic and common to the members of a social category, although occurring independently to each of them. Such a career is not a thing that can be brilliant or disappointing; it can no more be a success than a failure. In this light, I want to consider the mental patient, drawing mainly upon data collected during a year's participant observation of patient social life in a public mental hospital,[1] wherein an attempt was made to take the patient's point of view.

One value of the concept of career is its two-sidedness. One side is linked to internal matters held dearly and closely, such as image of self and felt identity; the other side concerns official position, jural relations, and style of life, and is part of a publicly accessible institutional complex. The concept of career, then, allows one to move back and forth between the personal and the public, between the self and its significant society,

Erving Goffman, "The Moral Career of the Mental Patient," *Psychiatry: Journal for the Study of Interpersonal Processes,* vol. 22 (May 1959), pp. 123–142. Reprinted by permission.

[1] The study was conducted during 1955–56 under the auspices of the Laboratory of Socio-environmental Studies of the National Institute of Mental Health. I am grateful to the Laboratory Chief, John A. Clausen, and to Dr. Winfred Overholser, Superintendent, and the late Dr. Jay Hoffman, then First Assistant Physician of Saint Elizabeths Hospital, Washington, D.C., for the ideal cooperation they freely provided. A preliminary report is contained in Goffman, "Interpersonal Persuasion," pp. 117–193; in *Group Processes: Transactions of the Third Conference,* edited by Bertram Schaffner; New York, Josiah Macy, Jr. Foundation, 1957. A shorter version of this paper was presented at the Annual Meeting of the American Sociological Society, Washington, D.C., August, 1957.

without having overly to rely for data upon what the person says he thinks he imagines himself to be.

This paper, then, is an exercise in the institutional approach to the study of self. The main concern will be with the *moral* aspects of career— that is, the regular sequence of changes that career entails in the person's self and in his framework of imagery for judging himself and others.[2]

The category "mental patient" itself will be understood in one strictly sociological sense. In this perspective, the psychiatric view of a person becomes significant only in so far as this view itself alters his social fate—an alteration which seems to become fundamental in our society when, and only when, the person is put through the process of hospitalization.[3] I therefore exclude certain neighboring categories: the undiscovered candidates who would be judged "sick" by psychiatric standards but who never come to be viewed as such by themselves or others, although they may cause everyone a great deal of trouble;[4] the office patient whom a psychiatrist feels he can handle with drugs or shock on the outside; the mental client who engages in psychotherapeutic relationships. And I include anyone, however robust in temperament, who somehow gets caught up in the heavy machinery of mental hospital servicing. In this way the effects of being treated as a mental patient can be kept quite distinct from the effects upon a person's life of traits a clinician would view as psychopathological.[5] Persons who become mental hospital patients vary widely in the kind and degree of illness that a psychiatrist would impute to them, and in the at-

[2] Material on moral career can be found in early social anthropological work on ceremonies of status transition, and in classic social psychological descriptions of those spectacular changes in one's view of self that can accompany participation in social movements and sects. Recently new kinds of relevant data have been suggested by psychiatric interest in the problem of "identity" and sociological studies of work careers and "adult socialization."

[3] This point has recently been made by Elaine and John Cumming, *Closed Ranks;* Cambridge, Commonwealth Fund, Harvard Univ. Press, 1957; pp. 101–102. "Clinical experience supports the impression that many people define mental illness as 'That condition for which a person is treated in a mental hospital.' . . . Mental illness, it seems, is a condition which afflicts people who must go to a mental institution, but until they do almost anything they do is normal." Leila Deasy has pointed out to me the correspondence here with the situation in white collar crime. Of those who are detected in this activity, only the ones who do not manage to avoid going to prison find themselves accorded the social role of the criminal.

[4] Case records in mental hospitals are just now coming to be exploited to show the incredible amount of trouble a person may cause for himself and others before anyone begins to think about him psychiatrically, let alone take psychiatric action against him. See John A. Clausen and Marian Radke Yarrow, "Paths to the Mental Hospital," *J. Social Issues* (1955) 11:25–32; August B. Hollingshead and Fredrick C. Redlich, *Social Class and Mental Illness;* New York, Wiley, 1958; pp. 173–174.

[5] An illustration of how this perspective may be taken to all forms of deviancy may be found in Edwin Lemert, *Social Pathology;* New York, McGraw-Hill, 1951; see especially pp. 74–76. A specific application to mental defectives may be found in Stewart E. Perry, "Some Theoretic Problems of Mental Deficiency and Their Action Implications," *Psychiatry* (1954) 17:45–73; see especially p. 68.

tributes by which laymen would describe them. But once started on the way, they are confronted by some importantly similar circumstances and respond to these in some importantly similar ways. Since these similarities do not come from mental illness, they would seem to occur in spite of it. It is thus a tribute to the power of social forces that the uniform status of mental patient can not only assure an aggregate of persons a common fate and eventually, because of this, a common character, but that this social reworking can be done upon what is perhaps the most obstinate diversity of human materials that can be brought together by society. Here there lacks only the frequent forming of a protective group-life by ex-patients to illustrate in full the classic cycle of response by which deviant subgroupings are psychodynamically formed in society.

This general sociological perspective is heavily reinforced by one key finding of sociologically oriented students in mental hospital research. As has been repeatedly shown in the study of nonliterate societies, the awesomeness, distastefulness, and barbarity of a foreign culture can decrease in the degree that the student becomes familiar with the point of view to life that is taken by his subjects. Similarly, the student of mental hospitals can discover that the craziness or "sick behavior" claimed for the mental patient is by and large a product of the claimant's social distance from the situation that the patient is in, and is not primarily a product of mental illness. Whatever the refinements of the various patients' pyschiatric diagnoses, and whatever the special ways in which social life on the "inside" is unique, the researcher can find that he is participating in a community not significantly different from any other he has studied.[6] Of course, while restricting himself to the off-ward grounds community of paroled patients, he may feel, as some patients do, that life in the locked wards is bizarre; and while on a locked admissions or convalescent ward, he may feel that chronic "back" wards are socially crazy places. But he need only move his sphere of sympathetic participation to the "worst" ward in the hospital, and this too can come into social focus as a place with a livable and continuously meaningful social world. This in no way denies that he will find a minority in any ward or patient group that continues to seem quite beyond the capacity to follow rules of social organization, or that the orderly fulfilment of normative expectations in patient society is partly made possible by strategic measures that have somehow come to be institutionalized in mental hospitals.

The career of the mental patient falls popularly and naturalistically into three main phases: the period prior to entering the hospital, which I shall call the *prepatient phase;* the period in the hospital, the *inpatient phase;* the period after discharge from the hospital, should this occur,

[6] Conscientious objectors who voluntarily went to jail sometimes arrived at the same conclusion regarding criminal inmates. See, for example, Alfred Hassler, *Diary of a Self-made Convict;* Chicago, Regnery, 1954; p. 74.

namely, the *ex-patient phase*.[7] This paper will deal only with the first two phases.

The Prepatient Phase

A relatively small group of prepatients come into the mental hospital willingly, because of their own idea of what will be good for them, or because of wholehearted agreement with the relevant members of their family. Presumably these recruits have found themselves acting in a way which is evidence to them that they are losing their minds or losing control of themselves. This view of oneself would seem to be one of the most pervasively threatening things that can happen to the self in our society, especially since it is likely to occur at a time when the person is in any case sufficiently troubled to exhibit the kind of symptom which he himself can see. As Sullivan described it,

> What we discover in the self-system of a person undergoing schizophrenic changes or schizophrenic processes, is then, in its simplest form, an extremely fear-marked puzzlement, consisting of the use of rather generalized and anything but exquisitely refined referential processes in an attempt to cope with what is essentially a failure at being human—a failure at being anything that one could respect as worth being.[8]

Coupled with the person's disintegrative re-evaluation of himself will be the new, almost equally pervasive circumstance of attempting to conceal from others what he takes to be the new fundamental facts about himself, and attempting to discover whether others too have discovered them.[9] Here I want to stress that perception of losing one's mind is based on culturally derived and socially engrained stereotypes as to the significance of symptoms such as hearing voices, losing temporal and spatial orientation, and sensing that one is being followed, and that many of the most spectacular and convincing of these symptoms in some instances psychiatrically signify merely a temporary emotional upset in a stressful situation, however terrifying to the person at the time. Similarly, the anxiety consequent

---

[7] This simple picture is complicated by the somewhat special experience of roughly a third of ex-patients—namely, readmission to the hospital, this being the recidivist or "repatient" phase.

[8] Harry Stack Sullivan, *Clinical Studies in Psychiatry;* edited by Helen Swick Perry, Mary Ladd Gawel, and Martha Gibbon; New York, Norton, 1956; pp. 184–185.

[9] This moral experience can be contrasted with that of a person learning to become a marihuana addict, whose discovery that he can be 'high' and still 'op' effectively without being detected apparently leads to a new level of use. See Howard S. Becker, "Marihuana Use and Social Control," *Social Problems* (1955) 3:35–44; see especially pp. 40–41.

upon this perception of oneself, and the strategies devised to reduce this anxiety, are not a product of abnormal psychology, but would be exhibited by any person socialized into our culture who came to conceive of himself as someone losing his mind. Interestingly, subcultures in American society apparently differ in the amount of ready imagery and encouragement they supply for such self-views, leading to differential rates of *self*-referral; the capacity to take this distintegrative view of oneself without psychiatric prompting seems to be one of the questionable cultural privileges of the upper classes.[10]

For the person who has come to see himself—with whatever justification—as mentally unbalanced, entrance to the mental hospital can sometimes bring relief, perhaps in part because of the sudden transformation in the structure of his basic social situations; instead of being to himself a questionable person trying to maintain a role as a full one, he can become an officially questioned person known to himself to be not so questionable as that. In other cases, hospitalization can make matters worse for the willing patient, confirming by the objective situation what has theretofore been a matter of the private experience of self.

Once the willing prepatient enters the hospital, he may go through the same routine of experiences as do those who enter unwillingly. In any case, it is the latter that I mainly want to consider, since in America at present these are by far the more numerous kind.[11] Their approach to the institution takes one of three classic forms: they come because they have been implored by their family or threatened with the abrogation of family ties unless they go "willingly"; they come by force under police escort; they come under misapprehension purposely induced by others, this last restricted mainly to youthful prepatients.

The prepatient's career may be seen in terms of an extrusory model; he starts out with relationships and rights, and ends up, at the beginning of his hospital stay, with hardly any of either. The moral aspects of this career, then, typically begin with the experience of abandonment, disloyalty, and embitterment. This is the case even though to others it may be obvious that he was in need of treatment, and even though in the hospital he may soon come to agree.

The case histories of most mental patients document offense against some arrangement for face-to-face living—a domestic establishment, a work place, a semipublic organization such as a church or store, a public region such as a street or park. Often there is also a record of some *complainant*,

---

[10] See footnote 2; Hollingshead and Redlich, p. 187, Table 6, where relative frequency is given of self-referral by social class grouping.

[11] The distinction employed here between willing and unwilling patients cuts across the legal one, of voluntary and committed, since some persons who are glad to come to the mental hospital may be legally committed, and of those who come only because of strong familial pressure, some may sign themselves in as voluntary patients.

some figure who takes that action against the offender which eventually leads to his hospitalization. This may not be the person who makes the first move, but it is the person who makes what turns out to be the first effective move. Here is the *social* beginning of the patient's career, regardless of where one might locate the psychological beginning of his mental illness.

The kinds of offenses which lead to hospitalization are felt to differ in nature from those which lead to other extrusory consequences—to imprisonment, divorce, loss of job, disownment, regional exile, noninstitutional psychiatric treatment, and so forth. But little seems known about these differentiating factors; and when one studies actual commitments, alternate outcomes frequently appear to have been possible. It seems true, moreover, that for every offense that leads to an effective complaint, there are many psychiatrically similar ones that never do. No action is taken; or action is taken which leads to other extrusory outcomes; or ineffective action is taken, leading to the mere pacifying or putting off of the person who complains. Thus, as Clausen and Yarrow have nicely shown, even offenders who are eventually hospitalized are likely to have had a long series of ineffective actions taken against them.[12]

Separating those offenses which could have been used as grounds for hospitalizing the offender from those that are so used, one finds a vast number of what students of occupation call career contingencies.[13] Some of these contingencies in the mental patient's career have been suggested, if not explored, such as socio-economic status, visibility of the offense, proximity to a mental hospital, amount of treatment facilities available, community regard for the type of treatment given in available hospitals, and so on.[14] For information about other contingencies one must rely on atrocity tales: a psychotic man is tolerated by his wife until she finds herself a boy friend, or by his adult children until they move from a house to an apartment; an alcoholic is sent to a mental hospital because the jail is full, and a drug addict because he declines to avail himself of psychiatric treatment on the outside; a rebellious adolescent daughter can no longer be managed at home because she now threatens to have an open affair with an unsuitable companion; and so on. Correspondingly there is an equally important set of contingencies causing the person to by-pass this fate. And should the person enter the hospital, still another set of contingencies will help determine when he is to obtain a discharge—such as the desire of his family for his return, the availability of a "manageable" job, and so on. The

---

[12] Clausen and Yarrow; see footnote 4.

[13] An explicit application of this notion to the field of mental health may be found in Edwin M. Lemert, "Legal Commitment and Social Control," *Sociology and Social Research* (1946) 30:370–378.

[14] For example, Jerome K. Meyers and Leslie Schaffer, "Social Stratification and Psychiatric Practice: A Study of an Outpatient Clinic," *Amer. Sociological Rev.* (1954) 19:307–310. Lemert, see footnote 5, pp. 402–403. *Patients in Mental Institutions,* 1941; Washington, D.C., Department of Commerce, Bureau of the Census, 1941; p. 2.

society's official view is that inmates of mental hospitals are there primarily because they are suffering from mental illness. However, in the degree that the "mentally ill" outside hospitals numerically approach or surpass those inside hospitals, one could say that mental patients *distinctively* suffer not from mental illness, but from contingencies.

Career contingencies occur in conjunction with a second feature of the prepatient's career—the *circuit of agents*—and agencies—that participate fatefully in his passage from civilian to patient status.[15] Here is an instance of that increasingly important class of social system whose elements are agents and agencies, which are brought into systemic connection through having to take up and send on the same persons. Some of these agent-roles will be cited now, with the understanding that in any concrete circuit a role may be filled more than once, and a single person may fill more than one of them.

First is the *next-of-relation*—the person whom the prepatient sees as the most available of those upon whom he should be able to most depend in times of trouble; in this instance the last to doubt his sanity and the first to have done everything to save him from the fate which, it transpires, he has been approaching. The patient's next-of-relation is usually his next of kin; the special term is introduced because he need not be. Second is the *complainant*, the person who retrospectively appears to have started the person on his way to the hospital. Third are the *mediators*—the sequence of agents and agencies to which the prepatient is referred and through which he is relayed and processed on his way to the hospital. Here are included police, clergy, general medical practitioners, office psychiatrists, personnel in public clinics, lawyers, social service workers, school teachers, and so on. One of these agents will have the legal mandate to sanction commitment and will exercise it, and so those agents who precede him in the process will be involved in something whose outcome is not yet settled. When the mediators retire from the scene, the prepatient has become an inpatient, and the significant agent has become the hospital administrator.

While the complainant usually takes action in a lay capacity as a citizen, an employer, a neighbor, or a kinsman, mediators tend to be specialists and differ from those they serve in significant ways. They have experience in handling trouble, and some professional distance from what they handle. Except in the case of policemen, and perhaps some clergy, they tend to be more psychiatrically oriented than the lay public, and will see the need for treatment at times when the public does not.[16]

An interesting feature of these roles is the functional effects of their interdigitation. For example, the feelings of the patient will be influenced by

[15] For one circuit of agents and its bearing on career contingencies, see Oswald Hall, "The Stages of a Medical Career," *Amer. J. Sociology* (1948) 53:227–336.

[16] See Cumming, footnote 3; p. 92.

whether or not the person who fills the role of complainant also has the role of next-of-relation—an embarrassing combination more prevalent, apparently, in the higher classes than in the lower.[17] Some of these emergent effects will be considered now.[18]

In the prepatient's progress from home to the hospital he may participate as a third person in what he may come to experience as a kind of *alienative coalition*. His next-of-relation presses him into coming to "talk things over" with a medical practitioner, an office psychiatrist, or some other counselor. Disinclination on his part may be met by threatening him with desertion, disownment, or other legal action, or by stressing the joint and explorative nature of the interview. But typically the next-of-relation will have set the interview up, in the sense of selecting the professional, arranging for time, telling the professional something about the case, and so on. This move effectively tends to establish the next-of-relation as the responsible person to whom pertinent findings can be divulged, while effectively establishing the other as the patient. The prepatient often goes to the interview with the understanding that he is going as an equal of someone who is so bound together with him that a third person could not come between them in fundamental matters; this, after all, is one way in which close relationships are defined in our society. Upon arrival at the office the prepatient suddenly finds that he and his next-of-relation have not been accorded the same roles, and apparently that a prior understanding between the professional and the next-of-relation has been put in operation against him. In the extreme but common case the professional first sees the prepatient alone, in the role of examiner and diagnostician, and then sees the next-of-relation alone, in the role of advisor, while carefully avoiding talking things over seriously with them both together.[19] And even in those nonconsultative cases where public officials must forcibly extract a person from a family that wants to tolerate him, the next-of-relation is likely to be induced to "go along" with the official action, so that even here the prepatient may feel that an alienative coalition has been formed against him.

The moral experience of being third man in such a coalition is likely to embitter the prepatient, especially since his troubles have already probably led to some estrangement from his next-of-relation. After he enters the hos-

[17] Hollingshead and Redlich, footnote 4; p. 187.

[18] For an analysis of some of these circuit implications for the inpatient, see Leila C. Deasy and Olive W. Quinn, "The Wife of the Mental Patient and the Hospital Psychiatrist," *J. Social Issues* (1955) 11:49–60. An interesting illustration of this kind of analysis may also be found in Alan G. Gowman, "Blindness and the Role of Companion," *Social Problems* (1956) 4:68–75. A general statement may be found in Robert Merton, "The Role Set: Problems in Sociological Theory," *British J. Sociology* (1957) 8:106–120.

[19] I have one case record of a man who claims he thought *he* was taking his wife to see the psychiatrist, not realizing until too late that his wife had made the arrangements.

pital, continued visits by his next-of-relation can give the patient the "insight" that his own best interests were being served. But the initial visits may temporarily strengthen his feeling of abandonment; he is likely to beg his visitor to get him out or at least to get him more privileges and to sympathize with the monstrousness of his plight—to which the visitor ordinarily can respond only by trying to maintain a hopeful note, by not "hearing" the requests, or by assuring the patient that the medical authorities know about these things and are doing what is medically best. The visitor then nonchalantly goes back into a world that the patient has learned is incredibly thick with freedom and privileges, causing the patient to feel that his next-of-relation is merely adding a pious gloss to a clear case of traitorous desertion.

The depth to which the patient may feel betrayed by his next-of-relation seems to be increased by the fact that another witnesses his betrayal—a factor which is apparently significant in many three-party situations. An offended person may well act forbearantly and accommodatively toward an offender when the two are alone, choosing peace ahead of justice. The presence of a witness, however, seems to add something to the implications of the offense. For then it is beyond the power of the offended and offender to forget about, erase, or suppress what has happened; the offense has become a public social fact.[20] When the witness is a mental health commission, as is sometimes the case, the witnessed betrayal can verge on a "degradation ceremony."[21] In such circumstances, the offended patient may feel that some kind of extensive reparative action is required before witnesses, if his honor and social weight are to be restored.

Two other aspects of sensed betrayal should be mentioned. First, those who suggest the possibility of another's entering a mental hospital are not likely to provide a realistic picture of how in fact it may strike him when he arrives. Often he is told that he will get required medical treatment and a rest, and may well be out in a few months or so. In some cases they may thus be concealing what they know, but I think, in general, they will be telling what they see as the truth. For here there is a quite relevant difference between patients and mediating professionals; mediators, more so than the public at large, may conceive of mental hospitals as short-term medical establishments where required rest and attention can be voluntarily obtained, and not as places of coerced exile. When the prepatient finally arrives he is likely to learn quite quickly, quite differently. He then finds that the information given him about life in the hospital has had the effect of his having put up less resistance to entering than he now sees he would have put up had he known the facts. Whatever the intentions of

[20] A paraphrase from Kurt Riezler, "The Social Psychology of Shame," *Amer. J. Sociology* (1943) 48:458.
[21] See Harold Garfinkel, "Conditions of Successful Degradation Ceremonies," *Amer. J. Sociology* (1956) 61:420–424.

those who participated in his transition from person to patient, he may sense they have in effect "conned" him into his present predicament.

I am suggesting that the prepatient starts out with at least a portion of the rights, liberties, and satisfactions of the civilian and ends up on a psychiatric ward stripped of almost everything. The question here is *how* this stripping is managed. This is the second aspect of betrayal I want to consider.

As the prepatient may see it, the circuit of significant figures can function as a kind of *betrayal funnel*. Passage from person to patient may be effected through a series of linked stages, each managed by a different agent. While each stage tends to bring a sharp decrease in adult free status, each agent may try to maintain the fiction that no further decrease will occur. He may even manage to turn the prepatient over to the next agent while sustaining this note. Further, through words, cues, and gestures, the prepatient is implicitly asked by the current agent to join with him in sustaining a running line of polite small talk that tactfully avoids the administrative facts of the situation, becoming, with each stage, progressively more at odds with these facts. The spouse would rather not have to cry to get the prepatient to visit a psychiatrist; psychiatrists would rather not have a scene when the prepatient learns that he and his spouse are being seen separately and in different ways; the police infrequently bring a prepatient to the hospital in a strait jacket, finding it much easier all around to give him a cigarette, some kindly words, and freedom to relax in the back seat of the patrol car; and finally, the admitting psychiatrist finds he can do his work better in the relative quiet and luxury of the "admission suite" where, as an incidental consequence, the notion can survive that a mental hospital is indeed a comforting place. If the prepatient heeds all of these implied requests and is reasonably decent about the whole thing, he can travel the whole circuit from home to hospital without forcing anyone to look directly at what is happening or to deal with the raw emotion that his situation might well cause him to express. His showing consideration for those who are moving him toward the hospital allows them to show consideration for him, with the joint result that these interactions can be sustained with some of the protective harmony characteristic of ordinary face-to-face dealings. But should the new patient cast his mind back over the sequence of steps leading to hospitalization, he may feel that everyone's *current* comfort was being busily sustained while his long-range welfare was being undermined. This realization may constitute a moral experience that further separates him for the time from the people on the outside.[22]

[22] Concentration camp practices provide a good example of the function of the betrayal funnel in inducing cooperation and reducing struggle and fuss, although here the mediators could not be said to be acting in the best interests of the inmates. Police picking up persons from their homes would sometimes joke good-naturedly and offer to

I would now like to look at the circuit of career agents from the point of view of the agents themselves. Mediators in the person's transition from civil to patient status—as well as his keepers, once he is in the hospital—have an interest in establishing a responsible next-of-relation as the patient's deputy or *guardian;* should there be no obvious candidate for the role, someone may be sought out and pressed into it. Thus while a person is gradually being transformed into a patient, a next-of-relation is gradually being transformed into a guardian. With a guardian on the scene, the whole transition process can be kept tidy. He is likely to be familiar with the prepatient's civil involvements and business, and can tie up loose ends that might otherwise be left to entangle the hospital. Some of the prepatient's abrogated civil rights can be transferred to him, thus helping to sustain the legal fiction that while the prepatient does not actually have his rights he somehow actually has not lost them.

Inpatients commonly sense, at least for a time, that hospitalization is a massive unjust deprivation, and sometimes succeed in convincing a few persons on the outside that this is the case. It often turns out to be useful, then, for those identified with inflicting these deprivations, however justifiably, to be able to point to the cooperation and agreement of someone whose relationship to the patient places him above suspicion, firmly defining him as the person most likely to have the patient's personal interest at heart. If the guardian is satisfied with what is happening to the new inpatient, the world ought to be.[23]

Now it would seem that the greater the legitimate personal stake one party has in another, the better he can take the role of guardian to the other. But the structural arrangements in society which lead to the acknowledged merging of two persons' interests lead to additional consequences. For the person to whom the patient turns for help—for protection against such threats as involuntary commitment—is just the person to whom the mediators and hospital administrators logically turn for authorization. It is understandable, then, that some patients will come to sense, at least for a time, that the closeness of a relationship tells nothing of its trustworthiness.

There are still other functional effects emerging from this complement

---

wait while coffee was being served. Gas chambers were fitted out like delousing rooms, and victims taking off their clothes were told to note where they were leaving them. The sick, aged, weak, or insane who were selected for extermination were sometimes driven away in Red Cross ambulances to camps referred to by terms such as "observation hospital." See David Boder, *I Did Not Interview the Dead;* Urbana, Univ. of Illinois Press, 1949; p. 81; and Elie A. Cohen, *Human Behavior in the Concentration Camp;* London, Cape, 1954; pp. 32, 37, 107.

[23] Interviews collected by the Clausen group at NIMH suggest that when a wife comes to be a guardian, the responsibility may disrupt previous distance from in-laws, leading either to a new supportive coalition with them or to a marked withdrawal from them.

of roles. If and when the next-of-relation appeals to mediators for help in the trouble he is having with the prepatient, hospitalization may not, in fact, be in his mind. He may not even perceive the prepatient as mentally sick, or, if he does, he may not consistently hold to this view.[24] It is the circuit of mediators, with their greater psychiatric sophistication and their belief in the medical character of mental hospitals, that will often define the situation for the next-of-relation, assuring him that hospitalization is a possible solution and a good one, that it involves no betrayal, but is rather a medical action taken in the best interests of the prepatient. Here the next-of-relation may learn that doing his duty to the prepatient may cause the prepatient to distrust and even hate him for the time. But the fact that this course of action may have had to be pointed out and prescribed by professionals, and be defined by them as a moral duty, relieves the next-of-relation of some of the guilt he may feel.[25] It is a poignant fact that an adult son or daughter may be pressed into the role of mediator, so that the hostility that might otherwise be directed against the spouse is passed on to the child.[26]

Once the prepatient is in the hospital, the same guilt-carrying function may become a significant part of the staff's job in regard to the next-of-relation.[27] These reasons for feeling that he himself has not betrayed the patient, even though the patient may then think so, can later provide the next-of-relation with a defensible line to take when visiting the patient in the hospital and a basis for hoping that the relationship can be re-established after its hospital moratorium. And of course this position, when sensed by the patient, can provide him with excuses for the next-of-relation, when and if he comes to look for them.[28]

Thus while the next-of-relation can perform important functions for the mediators and hospital administrators, they in turn can perform important functions for him. One finds, then, an emergent unintended ex-

[24] For an analysis of these nonpsychiatric kinds of perception, see Marian Radke Yarrow, Charlotte Green Schwartz, Harriet S. Murphy, and Leila Calhoun Deasy, "The Psychological Meaning of Mental Illness in the Family," *J. Social Issues* (1955) 11:12–24; Charlotte Green Schwartz, "Perspectives on Deviance: Wives' Definitions of their Husbands' Mental Illness," *Psychiatry* (1957) 20:275–291.

[25] This guilt-carrying function is found, of course, in other role-complexes. Thus, when a middle-class couple engages in the process of legal separation or divorce, each of their lawyers usually takes the position that his job is to acquaint his client with all of the potential claims and rights, pressing his client into demanding these, in spite of any nicety of feelings about the rights and honorableness of the ex-partner. The client, in all good faith, can then say to self and to the ex-partner that the demands are being made only because the lawyer insists it is best to do so.

[26] Recorded in the Clausen data.

[27] This point is made by Cumming, see footnote 3; p. 129.

[28] There is an interesting contrast here with the moral career of the tuberculosis patient. I am told by Julius Roth that tuberculous patients are likely to come to the hospital willingly, agreeing with their next-of-relation about treatment. Later in their hospital career, when they learn how long they yet have to stay and how depriving and irrational some of the hospital rulings are, they may seek to leave, be advised against this by the staff and by relatives, and only then begin to feel betrayed.

change or reciprocation of functions, these functions themselves being often unintended.

The final point I want to consider about the prepatient's moral career is its peculiarly *retroactive* character. Until a person actually arrives at the hospital there usually seems no way of knowing for sure that he is destined to do so, given the determinative role of career contingencies. And until the point of hospitalization is reached, he or others may not conceive of him as a person who is becoming a mental patient. However, since he will be held against his will in the hospital, his next-of-relation and the hospital staff will be in great need of a rationale for the hardships they are sponsoring. The medical elements of the staff will also need evidence that they are still in the trade they were trained for. These problems are eased, no doubt unintentionally, by the case-history construction that is placed on the patient's past life, this having the effect of demonstrating that all along he had been becoming sick, that he finally became very sick, and that if he had not been hospitalized much worse things would have happened to him —all of which, of course, may be true. Incidentally, if the patient wants to make sense out of his stay in the hospital, and, as already suggested, keep alive the possibility of once again conceiving of his next-of-relation as a decent, well-meaning person, then he too will have reason to believe some of this psychiatric work-up of his past.

Here is a very ticklish point for the sociology of careers. An important aspect of every career is the view the person constructs when he looks backward over his progress; in a sense, however, the whole of the prepatient career derives from this reconstruction. The fact of having had a prepatient career, starting with an effective complaint, becomes an important part of the mental patient's orientation, but this part can begin to be played only after hospitalization proves that what he had been having, but no longer has, is a career as a prepatient.

The Inpatient Phase

The last step in the prepatient's career can involve his realization—justified or not—that he has been deserted by society and turned out of relationships by those closest to him. Interestingly enough, the patient, especially a first admission, may manage to keep himself from coming to the end of this trail, even though in fact he is now in a locked mental hospital ward. On entering the hospital, he may very strongly feel the desire not to be known to anyone as a person who could possibly be reduced to these present circumstances, or as a person who conducted himself in the way he did prior to commitment. Consequently, he may avoid talking to anyone, may stay by himself when possible, and may even be "out of contact" or "manic" so as to avoid ratifying any interaction that presses a politely reciprocal role upon him and opens him up to what he has become in the eyes of others. When the next-of-relation makes an effort to visit, he may be rejected by mutism, or by the patient's refusal to enter the visiting room, these strategies sometimes suggesting that the patient still clings to a remnant of relatedness to those who made up his past, and is protecting this remnant from the final destructiveness of dealing with the new people that they have become.[29]

Usually the patient comes to give up this taxing effort at anonymity, at not-hereness, and begins to present himself for conventional social interaction to the hospital community. Thereafter he withdraws only in special ways—by always using his nickname, by signing his contribution to the patient weekly with his initial only, or by using the innocuous "cover" address tactfully provided by some hospitals; or he withdraws only at special times, when, say, a flock of nursing students makes a passing tour of the ward, or when, paroled to the hospital grounds, he suddenly sees he is about to cross the path of a civilian he happens to know from home. Sometimes this making of oneself available is called "settling down" by the attendants. It marks a new stand openly taken and supported by the patient, and resembles the "coming out" process that occurs in other groupings.[30]

Once the prepatient begins to settle down, the main outlines of his fate tend to follow those of a whole class of segregated establishments— jails, concentration camps, monasteries, work camps, and so on—in which the inmate spends the whole round of life on the grounds, and marches through his regimented day in the immediate company of a group of persons of his own institutional status.[31]

[29] The inmate's initial strategy of holding himself aloof from ratifying contact may partly account for the relative lack of group-formation among inmates in public mental hospitals, a connection that has been suggested to me by William R. Smith. The desire to avoid personal bonds that would give license to the asking of biographical questions could also be a factor. In mental hospitals, of course, as in prisoner camps, the staff may consciously break up incipient group-formation in order to avoid collective rebellious action and other ward disturbances.

[30] A comparable coming out occurs in the homosexual world, when a person finally comes frankly to present himself to a "gay" gathering not as a tourist but as someone who is "available." See Evelyn Hooker, "A Preliminary Examination of Group Behavior of Homosexuals," *J. Psychology* (1956) 42:217–225; especially p. 221. A good fictionalized treatment may be found in James Baldwin's *Giovanni's Room*; New York, Dial, 1956; pp. 41–63. A familiar instance of the coming out process is no doubt to be found among prepubertal children at the moment one of these actors sidles *back* into a room that had been left in an angered huff and injured *amour-propre*. The phrase itself presumably derives from a *rite-de-passage* ceremony once arranged by upper-class mothers for their daughters. Interestingly enough, in large mental hospitals the patient sometimes symbolizes a complete coming out by his first active participation in the hospital-wide patient dance.

[31] See Goffman, "Characteristics of Total Institutions," pp. 43–84; in *Proceedings of the Symposium of Preventive and Social Psychiatry*; Washington, D.C., Walter Reed Army Institute of Research, 1959.

Like the neophyte in many of these "total institutions," the new inpatient finds himself cleanly stripped of many of his accustomed affirmations, satisfactions, and defenses, and is subjected to a rather full set of mortifying experiences: restriction of free movement; communal living; diffuse authority of a whole echelon of people; and so on. Here one begins to learn about the limited extent to which a conception of oneself can be sustained when the usual setting of supports for it are suddenly removed.

While undergoing these humbling moral experiences, the inpatient learns to orient himself in terms of the "ward system."[32] In public mental hospitals this usually consists of a series of graded living arrangements built around wards, administrative units called services, and parole statuses. The "worst" level involves often nothing but wooden benches to sit on, some quite indifferent food, and a small piece of room to sleep in. The "best" level may involve a room of one's own, ground and town privileges, contacts with staff that are relatively undamaging, and what is seen as good food and ample recreational facilities. For disobeying the pervasive house rules, the inmate will receive stringent punishments expressed in terms of loss of privileges; for obedience he will eventually be allowed to reacquire some of the minor satisfactions he took for granted on the outside.

The institutionalization of these radically different levels of living throws light on the implications for self of social settings. And this in turn affirms that the self arises not merely out of its possessor's interactions with significant others, but also out of the arrangements that are evolved in an organization for its members.

There are some settings which the person easily discounts as an expression or extension of him. When a tourist goes slumming, he may take pleasure in the situation not because it is a reflection of him but because it so assuredly is not. There are other settings, such as living rooms, which the person manages on his own and employs to influence in a favorable direction other persons' views of him. And there are still other settings, such as a work place, which express the employee's occupational status, but over which he has no final control, this being exerted, however tactfully, by his employer. Mental hospitals provide an extreme instance of this latter possibility. And this is due not merely to their uniquely degraded living levels, but also to the unique way in which significance for self is made explicit to the patient, piercingly, persistently, and thoroughly. Once lodged on a given ward, the patient is firmly instructed that the restrictions and deprivations he encounters are not due to such things as tradition or economy—and hence dissociable from self—but are intentional parts of his treatment, part of his need at the time, and therefore an expression of the

[32] A good description of the ward system may be found in Ivan Belknap, *Human Problems of a State Mental Hospital;* New York, McGraw-Hill, 1956; see especially p. 164.

state that his self has fallen to. Having every reason to initiate requests for better conditions, he is told that when the staff feels he is "able to manage" or will be "comfortable with" a higher ward level, then appropriate action will be taken. In short, assignment to a given ward is presented not as a reward or punishment, but as an expression of his general level of social functioning, his status as a person. Given the fact that the worst ward levels provide a round of life that inpatients with organic brain damage can easily manage, and that these quite limited human beings are present to prove it, one can appreciate some of the mirroring effects of the hospital.[33]

The ward system, then, is an extreme instance of how the physical facts of an establishment can be explicitly employed to frame the conception a person takes of himself. In addition, the official psychiatric mandate of mental hospitals gives rise to even more direct, even more blatant, attacks upon the inmate's view of himself. The more "medical" and the more progressive a mental hospital is—the more it attempts to be therapeutic and not merely custodial—the more he may be confronted by high-ranking staff arguing that his past has been a failure, that the cause of this has been within himself, that his attitude to life is wrong, and that if he wants to be a person he will have to change his way of dealing with people and his conceptions of himself. Often the moral value of these verbal assaults will be brought home to him by requiring him to practice taking this psychiatric view of himself in arranged confessional periods, whether in private sessions or group psychotherapy.

Now a general point may be made about the moral career of inpatients which has bearing on many moral careers. Given the stage that any person has reached in a career, one typically finds that he constructs an image of his life course—past, present, and future—which selects, abstracts, and distorts in such a way as to provide him with a view of himself that he can usefully expound in current situations. Quite generally, the person's line concerning self defensively brings him into appropriate alignment with the basic values of his society, and so may be called an *apologia*. If the person can manage to present a view of his current situation which shows the operation of favorable personal qualities in the past and a favorable destiny awaiting him, it may be called a *success story*. If the facts of a person's past and present are extremely dismal, then about the best he can do is to show that he is not responsible for what has become of him, and the term *sad tale* is appropriate. Interestingly enough, the more the person's past forces him out of apparent alignment with central moral values, the more often he seems compelled to tell his sad tale in any company in which

---

[33] Here is one way in which mental hospitals can be worse than concentration camps and prisons as places in which to "do" time; in the latter, self-insulation from the symbolic implications of the settings may be easier. In fact, self-insulation from hospital settings may be so difficult that patients have to employ devices for this which staff interpret as psychotic symptoms.

he finds himself. Perhaps he partly responds to the need he feels in others of not having their sense of proper life courses affronted. In any case, it is among convicts, 'wino's,' and prostitutes that one seems to obtain sad tales the most readily.[34] It is the vicissitudes of the mental patient's sad tale that I want to consider now.

In the mental hospital, the setting and the house rules press home to the patient that he is, after all, a mental case who has suffered some kind of social collapse on the outside, having failed in some over-all way, and that here he is of little social weight, being hardly capable of acting like a full-fledged person at all. These humiliations are likely to be most keenly felt by middle-class patients, since their previous condition of life little immunizes them against such affronts; but all patients feel some downgrading. Just as any normal member of his outside subculture would do, the patient often responds to this situation by attempting to assert a sad tale proving that he is not "sick," that the "little trouble" he did get into was really somebody else's fault, that his past life course had some honor and rectitude, and that the hospital is therefore unjust in forcing the status of mental patient upon him. This self-respecting tendency is heavily institutionalized within the patient society where opening social contacts typically involve the participants' volunteering information about their current ward location and length of stay so far, but not the reasons for their stay—such interaction being conducted in the manner of small talk on the outside.[35] With greater familiarity, each patient usually volunteers relatively acceptable reasons for his hospitalization, at the same time accepting without open

[34] In regard to convicts, see Anthony Heckstall-Smith, *Eighteen Months;* London, Wingate, 1954; pp. 52–53. For 'wino's' see the discussion in Howard G. Bain, "A Sociological Analysis of the Chicago Skid-Row Lifeway;" unpublished M.A. thesis, Dept. of Sociology, Univ. of Chicago, Sept., 1950; especially "The Rationale of the Skid-Row Drinking Group," pp. 141–146. Bain's neglected thesis is a useful source of material on moral careers.

Apparently one of the occupational hazards of prostitution is that clients and other professional contacts sometimes persist in expressing sympathy by asking for a defensible dramatic explanation for the fall from grace. In having to bother to have a sad tale ready, perhaps the prostitute is more to be pitied than damned. Good examples of prostitute sad tales may be found in Sir Henry Mayhew, "Those that Will Not Work," pp. 210–272; in his *London Labour and the London Poor*, Vol. 4; London, Griffin, Bohn, and Cox, 1862. For a contemporary source, see *Women of the Streets*, edited by C. H. Rolph; London, Zecker and Warburg, 1955; especially p. 6. "Almost always, however, after a few comments on the police, the girl would begin to explain how it was that she was in the life, usually in terms of self-justification." Lately, of course, the psychological expert has helped out the profession in the construction of wholly remarkable sad tales. See, for example, Harold Greenwald, *Call Girl*; New York, Ballantine, 1958.

[35] A similar self-protecting rule has been observed in prisons. Thus, Hassler, see footnote 6, in describing a conversation with a fellow-prisoner; "He didn't say much about why he was sentenced, and I didn't ask him, that being the accepted behavior in prison" (p. 76). A novelistic version for the mental hospital may be found in J. Kerkhoff, *How Thin the Veil: A Newspaperman's Story of His Own Mental Crack-up and Recovery;* New York, Greenberg, 1952; p. 27.

immediate question the lines offered by other patients. Such stories as the following are given and overtly accepted.

> I was going to night school to get a M.A. degree, and holding down a job in addition, and the load got too much for me.

> The others here are sick mentally but I'm suffering from a bad nervous system and that is what is giving me these phobias.

> I got here by mistake because of a diabetes diagnosis, and I'll leave in a couple of days. [The patient had been in seven weeks.]

> I failed as a child, and later with my wife I reached out for dependency.

> My trouble is that I can't work. That's what I'm in for. I had two jobs with a good home and all the money I wanted.[36]

The patient sometimes reinforces these stories by an optimistic definition of his occupational status: A man who managed to obtain an audition as a radio announcer styles himself a radio announcer; another who worked for some months as a copy boy and was then given a job as a reporter on a large trade journal, but fired after three weeks, defines himself as a reporter.

A whole social role in the patient community may be constructed on the basis of these reciprocally sustained fictions. For these face-to-face niceties tend to be qualified by behind-the-back gossip that comes only a degree closer to the "objective" facts. Here, of course, one can see a classic social function of informal networks of equals: they serve as one another's audience for self-supporting tales—tales that are somewhat more solid than pure fantasy and somewhat thinner than the facts.

But the patient's *apologia* is called forth in a unique setting, for few settings could be so destructive of self-stories except, of course, those stories already constructed along psychiatric lines. And this destructiveness rests on more than the official sheet of paper which attests that the patient is of unsound mind, a danger to himself and others—an attestation, incidentally, which seems to cut deeply into the patient's pride, and into the possibility of his having any.

Certainly the degrading conditions of the hospital setting belie many of the self-stories that are presented by patients; and the very fact of being in the mental hospital is evidence against these tales. And of course, there is not always sufficient patient solidarity to prevent patient discrediting patient, just as there is not always a sufficient number of "professionalized" attendants to prevent attendant discrediting patient. As one patient informant repeatedly suggested to a fellow patient:

> If you're so smart, how come you got your ass in here?

[36] From the writer's field notes of informal interaction with patients, transcribed as near verbatim as he was able.

The mental hospital setting, however, is more treacherous still. Staff has much to gain through discreditings of the patient's story—whatever the felt reason for such discreditings. If the custodial faction in the hospital is to succeed in managing his daily round without complaint or trouble from him, then it will prove useful to be able to point out to him that the claims about himself upon which he rationalizes his demands are false, that he is not what he is claiming to be, and that in fact he is a failure as a person. If the psychiatric faction is to impress upon him its views about his personal make-up, then they must be able to show in detail how their version of his past and their version of his character hold up much better than his own.[37] If both the custodial and psychiatric factions are to get him to cooperate in the various psychiatric treatments, then it will prove useful to disabuse him of *his* view of their purposes, and cause him to appreciate that they know what they are doing, and are doing what is best for him. In brief, the difficulties caused by a patient are closely tied to his version of what has been happening to him, and if cooperation is to be secured, it helps if this version is discredited. The patient must "insightfully" come to take, or affect to take, the hospital's view of himself.

The staff also has ideal means—in addition to the mirroring effect of the setting—for denying the inmate's rationalizations. Current psychiatric doctrine defines mental disorder as something that can have its roots in the patient's earliest years, show its signs throughout the course of his life, and invade almost every sector of his current activity. No segment of his past or present need to be defined, then, as beyond the jurisdiction and mandate of psychiatric assessment. Mental hospitals bureaucratically institutionalize this extremely wide mandate by formally basing their treatment of the patient upon his diagnosis and hence upon the psychiatric view of his past.

The case record is an important expression of this mandate. This dossier is apparently not regularly used, however, to record occasions when the patient showed capacity to cope honorably and effectively with difficult life situations. Nor is the case record typically used to provide a rough average or sampling of his past conduct. One of its purposes is to show the ways in which the patient is "sick" and the reasons why it was right to commit him and is right currrently to keep him committed; and this is done by extracting from his whole life course a list of those incidents that have

[37] The process of examining a person psychiatrically and then altering or reducing his status in consequence is known in hospital and prison parlance as *bugging*, the assumption being that once you come to the attention of the testers you either will automatically be labeled crazy or the process of testing itself will make you crazy. Thus psychiatric staff are sometimes seen not as *discovering* whether you are sick, but as *making* you sick; and "Don't bug me, man," can mean, "Don't pester me to the point where I'll get upset." Sheldon Messenger has suggested to me that this meaning of bugging is related to the other colloquial meaning, of wiring a room with a secret microphone to collect information usable for discrediting the speaker.

or might have had "symptomatic" significance.[38] The misadventures of his parents or siblings that might suggest a "taint" may be cited. Early acts in which the patient appeared to have shown bad judgment or emotional disturbance will be recorded. Occasions when he acted in a way which the layman would consider immoral, sexually perverted, weak-willed, childish, ill-considered, impulsive, and crazy may be described. Misbehaviors which someone saw as the last straw, as cause for immediate action, are likely to be reported in detail. In addition, the record will describe his state on arrival at the hospital—and this is not likely to be a time of tranquility and ease for him. The record may also report the false line taken by the patient in answering embarrassing questions, showing him as someone who makes claims that are obviously contrary to the facts:

> Claims she lives with oldest daughter or with sisters only when sick and in need of care; otherwise with husband, he himself says not for 12 years.
>
> Contrary to the reports from the personnel, he says he no longer bangs on the floor or cries in the morning.
>
> . . . conceals fact that she had her organs removed, claims she is still menstruating.
>
> At first she denied having had premarital sexual experience, but when asked about Jim she said she had forgotten about it 'cause it had been unpleasant.[39]

Where contrary facts are not known by the recorder, their presence is often left scrupulously an open question:

> The patient denied any heterosexual experiences nor could one trick her into admitting that she had ever been pregnant or into any kind of sexual indulgence, denying masturbation as well.
>
> Even with considerable pressure she was unwilling to engage in any projection of paranoid mechanisms.
>
> No psychotic content could be elicited at this time.[40]

And if in no more factual way, discrediting statements often appear in descriptions given of the patient's general social manner in the hospital:

[38] While many kinds of organization maintain records of their members, in almost all of these some socially significant attributes can only be included indirectly, being officially irrelevant. But since mental hospitals have a legitimate claim to deal with the 'whole' person, they need *officially* recognize no limits to what they consider relevant, a sociologically interesting license. It is an odd historical fact that persons concerned with promoting civil liberties in other areas of life tend to favor giving the psychiatrist complete discretionary power over the patient. Apparently it is felt that the more power possessed by medically qualified administrators and therapists, the better the interests of the patients will be served. Patients, to my knowledge, have not been polled on this matter.

[39] Verbatim transcriptions of hospital case record material.

[40] Verbatim transcriptions of hospital case record material.

When interviewed, he was bland, apparently self-assured, and sprinkles high-sounding generalizations freely throughout his verbal productions.

Armed with a rather neat appearance and natty little Hitlerian mustache, this 45 year old man, who has spent the last five or more years of his life in the hospital, is making a very successful hospital adjustment living within the role of a rather gay liver and jim-dandy type of fellow who is not only quite superior to his fellow patients in intellectual respects but who is also quite a man with women. His speech is sprayed with many multi-syllabled words which he generally uses in good context, but if he talks long enough on any subject it soon becomes apparent that he is so completely lost in this verbal diarrhea as to make what he says almost completely worthless.[41]

The events recorded in the case history are, then, just the sort that a layman would consider scandalous, defamatory, and discrediting. I think it is fair to say that all levels of mental hospital staff fail, in general, to deal with this material with the moral neutrality claimed for medical statements and psychiatric diagnosis, but instead participate, by intonation and gesture if by no other means, in the lay reaction to these acts. This will occur in staff-patient encounters as well as in staff encounters at which no patient is present.

In some mental hospitals, access to the case record is technically restricted to medical and higher nursing levels, but even here informal access or relayed information is often available to lower staff levels.[42] In addition, ward personnel are felt to have a right to know those aspects of the patient's past conduct which, embedded in the reputation he develops, purportedly make it possible to manage him with greater benefit to himself and less risk to others. Further, all staff levels typically have access to the nursing notes kept on the ward, which chart the daily course of each patient's disease, and hence his conduct, providing for the near-present the sort of information the case record supplies for his past.

I think that most of the information gathered in case records is quite true, although it might seem also to be true that almost anyone's life course could yield up enough denigrating facts to provide grounds for the record's justification of commitment. In any case, I am not concerned here with

[41] Verbatim transcriptions of hospital case record material.

[42] However, some mental hospitals do have a "hot file" of selected records which can be taken out only by special permission. These may be records of patients who work as administration-office messengers and might otherwise snatch glances at their own files; of inmates who had elite status in the environing community; and of inmates who may take legal action against the hospital and hence have a special reason to maneuver access to their records. Some hospitals even have a "hot-hot file," kept in the superintendent's office. In addition, the patient's professional title, especially if it is a medical one, is sometimes purposely omitted from his file card. All of these exceptions to the general rule for handling information show, of course, the institution's realization of some of the implications of keeping mental hospital records. For a further example, see Harold Taxel, "Authority Structure in a Mental Hospital Ward," unpublished M.A. thesis, Dept. of Sociology, Univ. of Chicago, 1953; pp. 11–12.

questioning the desirability of maintaining case records, or the motives of staff in keeping them. The point is that these facts about him being true, the patient is certainly not relieved from the normal cultural pressure to conceal them, and is perhaps all the more threatened by knowing that they are neatly available, and that he has no control over who gets to learn them.[43] A manly looking youth who responds to military induction by running away from the barracks and hiding himself in a hotel room clothes closet, to be found there, crying, by his mother; a woman who travels from Utah to Washington to warn the President of impending doom; a man who disrobes before three young girls; a boy who locks his sister out of the house, striking out two of her teeth when she tries to come back in through the window—each of these persons has done something he will have very obvious reason to conceal from others, and very good reason to tell lies about.

The formal and informal patterns of communication linking staff members tend to amplify the disclosive work done by the case record. A discreditable act that the patient performs during one part of the day's routine in one part of the hospital community is likely to be reported back to those who supervise other areas of his life, where he implicitly takes the stand that he is not the sort of person who could act that way.

Of significance here, as in some other social establishments, is the increasingly common practice of all-level staff conferences, where staff air their views of patients and develop collective agreement concerning the line that the patient is trying to take and the line that should be taken to him. A patient who develops a "personal" relation with an attendant, or manages to make an attendant anxious by eloquent and persistent accusations of malpractice can be put back into his place by means of the staff meeting, where the attendant is given warning or assurance that the patient is "sick." Since the differential image of himself that a person usually meets

---

[43] This is the problem of "information control" that many groups suffer from to varying degrees. See Goffman, "Discrepant Roles," Ch. 4, pp. 86–106; in *Presentation of Self in Everyday Life*; Monograph No. 2, Univ. of Edinburgh, Social Science Research Centre, 1956. A suggestion of this problem in relation to case records in prisons is given by James Peck in his story, "The Ship that Never Hit Port," in *Prison Etiquette*, edited by Holley Cantine and Dachine Rainer; Bearsville, N.Y., The Retort Press, 1950.

"The hacks of course hold all the aces in dealing with any prisoner because they can always write him up for inevitable punishment. Every infraction of the rules is noted in the prisoner's jacket, a folder which records all the details of the man's life before and during imprisonment. There are general reports written by the work detail screw, the cell block screw, or some other screw who may have overheard a conversation. Tales pumped from stool pigeons are also included.

"Any letter which interests the authorities goes into the jacket. The mail censor may make a photostatic copy of a prisoner's entire letter, or merely copy a passage. Or he may pass the letter on to the warden. Often an inmate called out by the warden or parole officer is confronted with something he wrote so long ago he had forgotten all about it. It might be about his personal life or his political views—a fragment of thought that the prison authorities felt was dangerous and filed for later use" (p. 66).

from those of various levels around him comes here to be unified behind the scenes into a common approach, the patient may find himself faced with a kind of collusion against him—albeit one sincerely thought to be for his own ultimate welfare.

In addition, the formal transfer of the patient from one ward or service to another is likely to be accompanied by an informal description of his characteristics, this being felt to facilitate the work of the employee who is newly responsible for him.

Finally, at the most informal of levels, the lunchtime and coffee-break small talk of staff often turns upon the latest doings of the patient, the gossip level of any social establishment being here intensified by the assumption that everything about him is in some way the proper business of the hospital employee. Theoretically there seems to be no reason why such gossip should not build up the subject instead of tear him down, unless one claims that talk about those not present will always tend to be critical in order to maintain the integrity and prestige of the circle in which the talking occurs. And so, even when the impulse of the speakers seems kindly and generous, the implication of their talk is typically that the patient is not a complete person. For example, a conscientious group therapist, sympathetic with patients, once admitted to his coffee companions:

> I've had about three group disrupters, one man in particular—a lawyer [sotto voce] James Wilson—very bright—who just made things miserable for me, but I would always tell him to get on the stage and do something. Well, I was getting desperate and then I bumped into his therapist, who said that right now behind the man's bluff and front he needed the group very much and that it probably meant more to him than anything else he was getting out of the hospital—he just needed the support. Well, that made me feel altogether different about him. He's out now.

In general, then, mental hospitals systematically provide for circulation about each patient the kind of information that the patient is likely to try to hide. And in various degrees of detail this information is used daily to puncture his claims. At the admission and diagnostic conferences, he will be asked questions to which he must give wrong answers in order to maintain his self-respect, and then the true answer may be shot back at him. An attendant whom he tells a version of his past and his reason for being in the hospital may smile disbelievingly, or say, "That's not the way I heard it," in line with the practical psychiatry of bringing the patient down to reality. When he accosts a physician or nurse on the ward and presents his claims for more privileges or for discharge, this may be countered by a question which he cannot answer truthfully without calling up a time in his past when he acted disgracefully. When he gives his view of his situation during group psychotherapy, the therapist, taking the role of interrogator, may attempt to disabuse him of his face-saving interpretations and encourage an interpretation suggesting that it is he himself who is to blame and who must change. When he claims to staff or fellow patients that he is well and has never been really sick, someone may give him graphic details of how, only one month ago, he was prancing around like a girl, or claiming that he was God, or declining to talk or eat, or putting gum in his hair.

Each time the staff deflates the patient's claims, his sense of what a person ought to be and the rules of peer-group social intercourse press him to reconstruct his stories; and each time he does this, the custodial and psychiatric interests of the staff may lead them to discredit these tales again.

Behind these verbally instigated ups and downs of the self, is an institutional base that rocks just as precariously. Contrary to popular opinion, the "ward system" insures a great amount of internal social mobility in mental hospitals, especially during the inmate's first year. During that time he is likely to have altered his service once, his ward three or four times, and his parole status several times; and he is likely to have experienced moves in bad as well as good directions. Each of these moves involves a very drastic alteration in level of living and in available materials out of which to build a self-confirming round of activities, an alteration equivalent in scope, say, to a move up or down a class in the wider class system. Moreover, fellow inmates with whom he has partially identified himself will similarly be moving, but in different directions and at different rates, thus reflecting feelings of social change to the person even when he does not experience them directly. As previously implied, the doctrines of psychiatry can reinforce the social fluctuations of the ward system. Thus there is a current psychiatric view that the ward system is a kind of social hothouse in which patients start as social infants and end up, within the year, on convalescent wards as resocialized adults. This view adds considerably to the weight and pride that staff can attach to their work, and necessitates a certain amount of blindness, especially at higher staff levels, to other ways of viewing the ward system, such as a method for disciplining unruly persons through punishment and reward. In any case, this resocialization perspective tends to overstress the extent to which those on the worst wards are incapable of socialized conduct and the extent to which those on the best wards are ready and willing to play the social game. Because the ward system is something more than a resocialization chamber, inmates find many reasons for "messing up" or getting into trouble, and many occasions, then, for demotion to less privileged ward positions. These demotions may be officially interpreted as psychiatric relapses or moral backsliding, thus protecting the resocialization view of the hospital, and these interpretations, by implication, translate a mere infraction of rules and consequent demotion into a fundamental expression of the status of the culprit's self. Correspondingly, promotions, which may come about because of ward population pressure, the need for a "working patient," or for other psychiatrically irrelevant reasons, may be built up into something claimed to be profoundly expressive of the patient's whole self. The patient himself may be expected by staff to make a personal effort to "get well," in something less than a year, and hence may be constantly reminded to think in terms of the self's success and failure.[44]

In such contexts inmates can discover that deflations in moral status are not so bad as they had imagined. After all, infractions which lead to these demotions cannot be accompanied by legal sanctions or by reduction to the status of mental patient, since these conditions already prevail. Further, no past or current delict seems to be horrendous enough in itself to excommunicate a patient from the patient community, and hence failures at right living lose some of their stigmatizing meaning.[45] And finally, in accepting the hospital's version of his fall from grace, the patient can set himself up in the business of "straightening up," and make claims of sympathy, privileges, and indulgence from the staff in order to foster this.

Learning to live under conditions of imminent exposure and wide fluctuation in regard, with little control over the granting or withholding of this regard, is an important step in the socialization of the patient, a step that tells something important about what it is like to be an inmate in a mental hospital. Having one's past mistakes and present progress under constant moral review seems to make for a special adaptation consisting of a less-than-moral attitude to ego-ideals. One's shortcomings and successes become too central and fluctuating an issue in life to allow the usual commitment of concern for other persons' views of them. It is not very practicable to try to sustain solid claims about oneself. The inmate tends to learn that degradations and reconstructions of the self need not be given too much weight, at the same time learning that staff and inmates are ready to view an inflation or deflation of a self with some indifference. He learns that a defensible picture of self can be seen as something outside oneself that can be constructed, lost, and rebuilt, all with great speed and some equanimity. He learns about the viability of taking up a standpoint—and hence a self—that is outside the one which the hospital can give and take away from him.

The setting, then, seems to engender a kind of cosmopolitan sophistication, a kind of civic apathy. In this unserious yet oddly exaggerated moral context, building up a self or having it destroyed becomes something of a shameless game, and learning to view this process as a game seems to make for some demoralization, the game being such a fundamental one. In the hospital, then, the inmate can learn that the self is not a fortress, but rather a small open city; he can become weary of having to show pleasure when

[44] For this and other suggestions, I am indebted to Charlotte Green Schwartz.

[45] In the hospital I studied there did not seem to be a kangaroo court, and so, for example, an engaging alcoholic, who managed to get two very well-liked student nurses sent home for drinking with him, did not apparently suffer much for his betrayal of the desires of the peer group.

held by troops of his own, and weary of having to show displeasure when held by the enemy. Once he learns what it is like to be defined by society as not having a viable self, this theatening definition—the threat that helps attach people to the self society accords them—is weakened. The patient seems to gain a new plateau when he learns that he can survive while acting in a way that society sees as destructive of him.

A few illustrations of this moral looseness and moral fatigue might be given. In state mental hospitals currently a kind of "marriage moratorium" appears to be accepted by patients and more or less condoned by staff. Some informal peer-group pressure may be brought against a patient who "plays around" with more than one hospital partner at a time, but little negative sanction seems to be attached to taking up, in a temporarily steady way, with a member of the opposite sex, even though both partners are known to be married, to have children, and even to be regularly visited by these outsiders. In short, there is license in mental hospitals to begin courting all over again, with the understanding, however, that nothing very permanent or serious can come of this. Like shipboard or vacation romances, these entanglements attest to the way in which the hospital is cut off from the outside community, becoming a world of its own, operated for the benefit of its own citizens. And certainly this moratorium is an expression of the alienation and hostility that patients feel for those on the outside to whom they were closely related. But in addition, one has evidence of the loosening effects of living in a world within a world, under conditions which make it difficult to give full seriousness to either of them.

The second illustration concerns the ward system. On the worst ward level, discreditings seem to occur the most frequently, in part because of lack of facilities, in part through the mockery and sarcasm that seem to be the occupational norm of social control for the attendants and nurses who administer these places. At the same time, the paucity of equipment and rights means that not much self can be built up. The patient finds himself constantly toppled, therefore, but with very little distance to fall. A kind of jaunty gallows humor seems to develop in some of these wards, with considerable freedom to stand up to the staff and return insult for insult. While these patients can be punished, they cannot, for example, be easily slighted, for they are accorded as a matter of course few of the niceties that people must enjoy before they can suffer subtle abuse. Like prostitutes in connection with sex, inmates on these wards have very little reputation or rights to lose and can therefore take certain liberties. As the person moves up the ward system, he can manage more and more to avoid incidents which discredit his claim to be a human being, and acquire more and more of the varied ingredients of self-respect; yet when eventually he does get toppled—and he does—there is a much further distance to fall. For instance, the privileged patient lives in a world wider than the ward, made up of recreation workers who, on request, can dole out cake, cards, table-tennis balls, tickets to the movies, and writing materials. But in absence of the social control of payment which is typically exerted by a recipient on the outside, the patient runs the risk that even a warm-hearted functionary may, on occasion, tell him to wait until she has finished an informal chat, or teasingly ask why he wants what he has asked for, or respond with a dead pause and a cold look of appraisal.

Moving up and down the ward system means, then, not only a shift in self-constructive equipment, a shift in reflected status, but also a change in the calculus of risks. Appreciation of risks to his self-conception is part of everyone's moral experience, but an appreciation that a given risk level is itself merely a social arrangement is a rarer kind of experience, and one that seems to help to disenchant the person who has it.

A third instance of moral loosening has to do with the conditions that are often associated with the release of the inpatient. Often he leaves under the supervision and jurisdiction of his next-of-relation or of a specially watchful employer. If he misbehaves while under their auspices, they can quickly obtain his readmission. He therefore finds himself under the special power of persons who ordinarily would not have this kind of power over him, and about whom, moreover, he may have had prior cause to feel quite bitter. In order to get out of the hospital, however, he may conceal his displeasure in this arrangement, and, at least until safely off the hospital rolls act out a willingness to accept this kind of custody. These discharge procedures, then, provide a built-in lesson in overtly taking a role without the usual covert commitments, and seem further to separate the person from the worlds that others take seriously.

The moral career of a person of a given social category involves a standard sequence of changes in his way of conceiving of selves, including, importantly, his own. These half-buried lines of development can be followed by studying his moral experiences—that is, happenings which mark a turning point in the way in which the person views the world—although the particularities of this view may be difficult to establish. And note can be taken of overt tacks or strategies—that is, stands that he effectively takes before specifiable others, whatever the hidden and variable nature of his inward attachment to these presentations. By taking note of moral experiences and overt personal stands, one can obtain a relatively objective tracing of relatively subjective matters.

Each moral career, and behind this, each self, occurs within the confines of an institutional system, whether a social establishment such as a mental hospital or a complex of personal and professional relationships. The self, then, can be seen as something that resides in the arrangements prevailing in a social system for its members. The self in this sense is not a property of the person to whom it is attributed, but dwells rather in the pattern of social control that is exerted in connection with the person by himself and those around him. This special kind of institutional arrangement does not so much support the self as constitute it.

In this paper, two of these institutional arrangements have been considered, by pointing to what happens to the person when these rulings are weakened. The first concerns the felt loyalty of his next-of-relation. The prepatient's self is described as a function of the way in which three roles are related, arising and declining in the kinds of affiliation that occur between the next-of-relation and the mediators. The second concerns the protection required by the person for the version of himself which he presents to others, and the way in which the withdrawal of this protection can form a systematic, if unintended, aspect of the working of an establishment. I want to stress that these are only two kinds of institutional rulings from which a self emerges for the participant; others, not considered in this paper, are equally important.

In the usual cycle of adult socialization one expects to find alienation and mortification followed by a new set of beliefs about the world and a new way of conceiving of selves. In the case of the mental hospital patient, this rebirth does sometimes occur, taking the form of a strong belief in the psychiatric perspective, or, briefly at least, a devotion to the social cause of better treatment for mental patients. The moral career of the mental patient has unique interest, however; it can illustrate the possibility that in casting off the raiments of the old self—or in having this cover torn away —the person need not seek a new robe and a new audience before which to cower. Instead he can learn, at least for a time, to practice before all groups the amoral arts of shamelessness.

46   ARLENE KAPLAN DANIELS

The Social Construction of Military Psychiatric Diagnoses[1]

Introduction

This paper analyzes the process of constructing psychiatric diagnoses in the military setting. The purpose of this case study is to examine the process of diagnosis in order to see how it contributes to the management of deviants. This particular method of deviance management is dependent upon the meaning of specific diagnostic categories in a variety of special contexts. The focus of this presentation is upon how restrictions in a specific setting affect the use of these diagnostic categories. In studying the process by which these categories become useful we may learn about both the application of deviant labels and the social construction of meanings.

This approach rests upon the theoretical perspective that Thomas P. Wilson has termed "the interpretive view of social interaction" or "radical symbolic interactionism." In this view definitions of situations and actions are never assumed to be settled once and for all by some literal application of traditional or previously established standards. Instead one always expects that the meanings of situations and actions are dependent upon particular interpretations that are influenced by both the context of particular occasions and the participants involved in that interaction. Accordingly meanings are always subject to reformulation on subsequent occasions.[2] Using this theoretical approach, then, it is not surprising that psychiatric diagnoses will not "hold still" but waver, change, and adjust to circumstances.

The diagnosis of mental illness is dependent not only upon the symtoms of the patient, but also upon the doctor's awareness of the consequences that a specific diagnostic label may have for the career of the patient. The doctor's use of this knowledge in his application of specific labels is what is meant when we speak of "the social construction of psychiatric diagnoses." Through an examination of the process of diagnosis in one context, we can discover some of the crucial social factors influencing or determining the nature of any psychiatric diagnoses.

Method

The data gathered for this study come from informants practicing military psychiatry. (All quotations in this paper are from verbatim transcripts of interviews that I personally conducted. Biophrasing, where used, is indicated by brackets.) Most of the informants were practicing in large military hospitals and had in-patient responsibilities. But many were also in what is called Mental Hygiene or Command Consultation at regular posts and bases. Generally the process of military psychiatric diagnosis begins here in the psychiatric dispensaries or field units. Routinely, Mental Hygiene will screen all potential psychiatric cases coming to official attention in an area of military jurisdiction. Those cases that are seen as serious or problematic are then sent to the major military medical centers for more specialized consideration.[3] Over two hundred interviews have been collected since 1964.[4] While most of them were conducted in Army settings, a few come from Air Force and Navy psychiatric services to ensure applicability of the analysis to any military psychiatry setting.

In the course of the interviews, information concerning diagnostic procedures in the military was obtained. Questions about these matters were couched in the military psychiatric language. Some examples of questions[5] specifically directed to residents in the military psychiatry training programs are:

1. What do you think of the diagnostic competency of the referral agencies?
2. Since all referrals are in-patients for relatively serious problems, how do you determine who returns to duty and who does not?
3. What percentage of the cases referred to you do you feel are simply referred for the purpose of administratively getting someone out of the way?
4. How often do you make direct contacts with unit commanders to help you in deciding final disposition?

These questions refer to some of the crucial decisions which military psychiatrists are asked to make in the services. Men whose future careers in the military are in any way problematic are ultimately reviewed or examined by the psychiatrist. His decision may be a major factor in the military decision to release or retain a man, to allow him special consideration or to withhold it. The psychiatrist is expected to use his professional judgment in evaluating each particular case. However the parameters of the psychiatric world—or the definition of where such professional judgments are appropriate—are set by the military regulations. They define what is to be considered mental illness and what is not; and then they indicate how the psychiatrist is to apply these interpretations. Military regulations also define the consequences which may befall any person who is certified as fitting within one or the other of these categories.

The military regulations about psychiatric diagnoses also provide a relatively neutral or middle ground for cases that are difficult to classify. And the consequences that may follow from this classification are similarly open for negotiation. So when the psychiatrist labels a man as: 1) mentally ill; 2) looking mentally ill at least for the moment; or 3) clearly not ill—even if showing bizarre or disturbing behavior, he becomes an important decision-maker in determining the fate of the patient at the hands of the military system. Thus, the psychiatrist has three major alternatives from which to choose in any specific diagnosis. These alternatives provide the labels and indicate the consequences that follow from their application.

The following three sections present the distinctions between mental illness and the other main diagnostic alternatives as they are understood within the military context. The remaining sections present a discussion of the application of these distinctions. The psychiatrist takes the consequences of each label into account when constructing a diagnosis. He has to consider what he hopes to accomplish for the patient—and then he applies the appropriate label which is likely to gain that end.

1. WHO IS MENTALLY ILL?

Military regulations use a very restrictive definition of mental illness. This definition includes only the psychoses (paranoia, schizophrenia, and chronic depression are examples within that category). Restrictive definitions of illness are common in the military for two reasons. First, the Armed Forces have the mission to "preserve the fighting strength." This usually means: retain men in the field. The psychiatrist, as other medical examiners, should try to select those men in service who can recover sufficiently to serve again.[6] Therefore one of the important functions of the psychiatrist is to *not* diagnose, for the mental illness diagnosis is likely to result in limited duty assignment or discharge from the service. A second reason for not diagnosing mental illness stems from the particular nature of the military organization's responsibility to its members. First, those mental illnesses that are recognized as diseases are considered medical disabilities equivalent to physical disabilities. Accordingly, the military offers compensation, particularly if disability occurred during, or was aggravated by, service activities "in the line of duty" (LOD, yes). In addition, the finding of illness usually outweighs other considerations for any soldier who is in disciplinary difficulties that may otherwise lead to legal action in the military court martial system: demotion, fines, or imprisonment. So while the mental-illness label does carry some stigma, it can offer advantages which may outweigh that disadvantage. From the standpoint of the military organization, the use of the disease label also offers benefits and liabilities. The organization benefits through removal of a problem; it demonstrates to the society at large that appropriate restitution has occurred. However it is expensive to offer such compensation. Thus it may be said that the mental-illness label offers both benefits and liabilities to all parties concerned.

There is an additional feature about mental-illness disability that makes application of this label even more restrictive than that for physical disability. Where accidents or illnesses have been clearly and physically disabling, the rationale for the whole procedure is much easier to grasp and more acceptable to everyone in the military than where the illness is "mental." Thus questions are not as likely to arise over these contractual responsibilities accepted by the military organization. Consequently, military psychiatrists must carefully consider the merits of the case to be made for illness, and the merits of the man to receive the mental-illness label. It is harder for a psychiatrist to convince a physical evaluation board (PEB) to accept an expensive decision than it is for other MD's to do so.

2. WHO APPEARS TO BE MENTALLY ILL BUT IS NOT

A second category of patients appearing before the psychiatrist are those who exhibit bizarre or symptomatic behavior that might look like mental illness but that does not fit the restrictive definitions of mental illness applicable in military settings. Such behavior is considered within two residual or borderline categories. One borderline diagnosis is meant to suggest that a particular behavior is interpreted as a reaction to a unique stress situation rather than a stable personality pattern. (These diagnoses include such categories as "situational stress" and variants like "a stress reaction," "adult situational reaction.") The other borderline category suggests that a behavior *looks* like mental illness (*e.g.*, schizoid-affective type) but is not *really* mental illness (*e.g.*, schizophrenia). They are not *officially* mental illness but they suggest it. They carry overtones of the mental illness categories without necessarily providing their range of benefits.[7] These diagnoses may be used with greater freedom than those designating mental illness since they make no clear diagnosis of mental illness and carry no attendant obligations upon the military organization for disability benefits. These diagnoses are useful because they provide the psychiatrist with the greatest leeway in that they are the least consequential in the initiation of further administrative action for or against the patient. The value of the diagnosis is that it shares with mental illness diagnoses the potential for excuse or mitigation. That is, it may be argued that the serviceman is not responsible for his behavior and so the military organization should not punish him for any misdeeds. However, this is not an automatic interpretation of the meaning of the diagnosis. When he makes this diagnosis, the psychiatrist is not determining the consequences for the man's service career. Higher administrative boards eventually decide this question— taking into account the particular manifestations of behavior and the outcome that is seen as most advantageous for the service and the man. Depending upon the decision of these boards, the man may leave without heavy penalty or remain in the service.

3. WHO IS DEFINITELY NOT MENTALLY ILL?

This category is the one most often used by military psychiatrists. It is applied to a variety of disruptive behaviors within the military context (constant quarreling, many absences without leave, minor but chronic disobedience are examples). It also includes such "social" problems as alcoholism and homosexuality. The label usually given is the "character and behavior" diagnosis, or rather quasidiagnosis, which carries no implication of mental illness within official military regulations. It also offers absolutely no exonerative connotations for those caught up in disciplinary proceedings.

The benefit for the serviceman is that no stigma of psychosis attaches to the label. The liability is that the diagnosis does not provide any excuse that the man so identified should not be considered responsible for his action.

Thus far we have considered the delimitations placed upon the psychiatrist's world by military definitions. Now let us consider how the psychiatrist comes to terms with these delimitations. When placing a label on an actual patient, the psychiatrist takes into account both the recognized consequences of the label within the military and the particular outcome he thinks most desirable and possible within the value system of the military. Given his understanding of how the label will be translated into legal and administrative terms, the psychiatrist evaluates each case that he sees. He has to decide what he wants to do and what he may do. What he may do depends upon social considerations not directly related to the diagnosis. Such considerations include the military view of the presenting symptom, the context in which it occurred, the amount of time already served in the military by the patient, the previous pattern of his career, and the nature of his relations with his commanding officers. Any or all of these considerations may have to be weighed in addition to those criteria involved in the definition of the diagnosis.

Social Conditions and Values Which Affect Diagnoses

In order to build an argument for one or another diagnosis, the psychiatrist raises such considerations as presenting symptom, context, and prior history of the patient. He weighs such considerations as "evidence" which suggests the feasibility of one or the other of these labels. Here is how one informant viewed the process.

> Phobic or conversion symptoms or genuine suicide attempt, the [service] is more tolerant of than the aggressor. If you see someone whose marriage is disrupted, and acts out—depending on how deviant, in a social sense—he can be labeled as "character and behavior" disorder, situational reaction, a neurotic [depressive] or schizophrenic [psychotic]. These are the labels. Then you worry about the manifestations. If depressed, suicidal, delusional and drinking—the crucial thing is: In what context? In what setting did he engage in the symptoms? Now we can . . . taking these into account . . . call him psychotic, and show we are worried about him [because this *is* a mental illness category]. We can say he is a situational reaction. In this case, we say the problem doesn't exist.

In making such distinctions, then, the psychiatrist places an evaluation upon the case in military terms and offers a method of dealing with the problem it presents. Within this context he understands that the amount of leeway available to him in using the disease diagnosis is most clearly affected by the military merit of the man and the length of his service.

These limitations reflect the values of the military system. They also reflect understandings about rules for retention of employees applicable in the larger society. One psychiatrist explained the rationale under which he worked in this way.

> . . . The military psychiatrist has to serve two masters, in a way—the service and the patient. . . . You want to [retain] a guy . . . who can (1) function adequately, and (2) probably not get into trouble again, who will not be a burden. . . . You also want to keep in mind that you may make a big difference to the individual in sending him back. . . . Suppose he had some kind of an associative reaction. A very brief kind of upset. . . . He was in a bar and suddenly he went crazy and started hitting people, and somebody said he was psychotic and sent him to you. You can help this person make a good adjustment if you feel that he has a good chance . . . if he has a good character structure underneath what problems there may be. . . . The ones we chose to send back to duty were those who were in for several years . . . made good progression in rank, and had done a good job.

If the man returns to duty, he loses the discharge benefit possibilities; but he also avoids the label of one who is seriously mentally ill. And he receives a second chance to "make good" in his military job.

> . . . How do we decide if the real psychotic patients stay or get out? If they have a long period of service, I consider them for going back to duty; if they don't, I think they ought to go out. . . . And this is sort of the directive we have had. If a person has a long period of service, and a year or two might make the difference for him; it might make all the difference to his pride and his self-image if he can complete twenty-year service and get out with an honorable discharge rather than a medical discharge with just as much disability—actually more—when you consider it is tax free. . . . He really wants to go back, then I go ahead and give him a chance. If you get these in-between people, they are under fifteen years and they are more than five, I think they ought to go out on a medical discharge.

Thus the doctor considers the problem of an employer's responsibility for his employees in addition to an absolute evaluation of the symptom. Military organizations thus shoulder some of the welfare responsibilities which most employing organizations today are expected to take. And, as is true for most employing organizations, the military responsibility for employees is less where the length of time in service is less. The psychiatrist provides the diagnosis which supports this generally valued position.

> . . . Psychotic (diagnoses) . . . a legitimate illness in our setting. But also a means of disposing. You could take someone with a full-blown psychotic picture and by soft pedaling or omission could bring in a diagnosis of "situational reaction" or neurosis—if time in service or value to service warrants. Or play it the other way—if—[we] felt [the condition existed prior to service] and so [we] could get rid of him easily [without paper work and expense connected with the medical discharge].

These considerations affect the recommendation the psychiatrist makes for the disposition (*i.e.*, separation from the service or return to duty) of anyone found to be mentally ill.

Thus, the seriousness of a psychiatric illness label—in terms of the responsibility of the military organization to the labeled—is considerably mitigated when the mentally ill person has been in the service a very short time. The illness label can be given; but social conditions suggest that the situation can be reasonably allowed to have occurred prior to service (EPTS [existed prior to service], LOD [line of duty], no) and therefore the types and amounts of disability benefits may be sharply curtailed. If the problem is seen by the psychiatrist as service-aggravated, *i.e.*, occurring during the line of duty (EPTS, LOD, yes), then he must build a strong case for this view in his diagnoses and explanation. The organizational tendency is to "expect" the psychiatrist to find the opposite (EPTS, LOD, no). Therefore, a somewhat stronger case must be built by the psychiatrist if he sees the former occurring rather than the latter. The psychiatrist has to build this argument in military terms, using arguments that are valid within that value system.

> I had one rather severe paranoid schizophrenic in the clinic. . . . This was a kind of . . . unusual situation because he was in intelligence. . . . The job he had when he had his psychotic break entailed sitting long, long hours in a dark room, bugging another room—hearing and seeing everything that went on in the room while he himself was sitting in the dark. And, it is a kind of psychotic existence; and we kind of pushed this point . . . to justify our "line of duty" estimation that the problem was service aggravated [even though the medical board decision was that the problem Existed Prior to Service].

In general, then, the problem for the psychiatrist may be to decide whether, in any particular situation, the medical discharge or return to duty is the most humane and reasonable alternative. Then he must decide how to present his evaluation in the most persuasive manner possible.

Another social condition delimiting the leeway of the military psychiatrist is the particular policy set by each post or hospital commander. The psychiatrist will then have to take these "guidelines" set by his commander into account as well. Some commanders are very lenient in their acceptance of psychiatric use of the mental illness diagnosis (*e.g.*, offer medical discharges easily and recommend partial disability even for short terms of service). Other commanders are less lenient about the matter of mental disability and suggest alternatives that are not likely to offer benefits (*e.g.*, use the medical discharge sparingly, but freely recommend the administrative discharge). Still other commanders demand a very strict interpretation of mental illness and are not at all lenient or permissive about those leaving service (*e.g.*, use neither type of discharge readily, leaving discharge decisions, if they arise, to other more punitive types of authorities). The military psychiatrist thus faces a number of varying and changing constraints, peculiar to this type of institutional setting, when searching for and diagnosing mental illness. And so he argues his cases with these contingencies in mind.[8]

Such diagnoses as "stress" and "schizoid reaction" or "borderline schizoid personality" can afford the psychiatrist some leeway in what exactly is meant. And they permit him to engage in evasive tactics. He may transfer a man from one jurisdiction to another by sending a patient to a distant hospital for further observation.

> A [psychiatrist] has been seeing a soldier who is going AWOL. He goes to the commander [and says, "this man is an] immature kid, impulse ridden, he acts out. I think you should administratively separate him." The C.O. says, "No . . . I'm not going to allow anybody to get away with that business" . . . and put[s] him in the stockade for court martial (proceedings as a prelude to a somewhat more punitive separation than that suggested by the psychiatrist). The patient then chooses another route of impulse . . . suicide gesture or threat. The [psychiatrist] is made very anxious by this, as are the (stockade authorities). They [informally indicate to the psychiatrist] if you want to call him sick and deal with him that way, you can have him. Otherwise, we are going to go ahead and court martial him. [The psychiatrist returns to the patient's] commander saying . . . "This guy may, you know, accidentally, just go ahead and kill himself." The commander is adamant. The [psychiatrist] feels that it is best for the whole situation to diagnose (the patient) . . . as a depressive reaction or something like that . . . and send him to the hospital.

The psychiatrist may intervene in these ways, in order to aid the proper functioning of the military organization as he sees it. He may also intervene, quite simply, for mercy. Labels of the situational or stress variety, and labels that suggest the possibility of psychosis but do not take full consequences for that type of label may be used by the psychiatrist when he feels that he ought to protect a man from punishment.

> We see a borderline schizoid personality kid who had gone AWOL. He had been gone for months . . . went back to the farm. He liked to talk to the cows. . . . He finally turned himself in because he began to feel guilty about [the absence]. The company wanted to boot him, and make an example of him because he had been gone for so long. I'm sure he's a better candidate than most to have a schizoid break. I really went to bat to get this man out. "A lot of other people you can make examples of. Let this poor boy go home." Spoke to a Colonel of Special Troops about it.

In the psychiatrist's view, his professional understanding of the patient's motivation is crucial in diagnosis. And therefore he may pit his own understanding of the motivation and capability of an individual against the view of some other military officer. By so doing, he exceeds his technical authority. But he does so with the techniques that he has been given by the organization (*e.g.*, diagnosis–transfer to hospital at a distant post). And so it may be said that this area of judgment is implicitly delegated to the psychiatrist by military authorities.

Value Judgments Involved in Finding No Diagnosis of Mental Illness

When the psychiatrist cannot find any reason for diagnosing mental illness or something like mental illness, he is in effect withholding his ability to negotiate on behalf of the patient. Within the military system, this often means that the initiation of some disciplinary action or some other action that the patient does not wish to occur, has no further impediment. The psychiatrist may simply report that no psychiatric disease or mental illness is present. (A notation of "NPD" [no psychiatric diagnosis] or "NMI" [no mental illness] will then be all that he will write about the case when he signs his name.) But he may also describe the patient—or diagnose him— in terms of the character and behavior disorder, or "c and b" as it is often called. This diagnosis is generally elicited when behavior by the person examined has been so disturbing, aggravating, or bizarre as to cause comment or trouble within the military system. Some justification that this person really is not mentally ill seems to be required. And so this diagnostic category is offered as a sort of explanation or rationale for why considerations surrounding mental illness diagnosis need not arise. In effect, the psychiatrist refuses to intervene on behalf of the patient; he may even implicitly or explicitly support the military organization's claim against the patient.

Thus the world which the psychiatrist constructs through his diagnoses bears many resemblances to the world of everyday life with its common-sense value judgments. The psychiatrist examines individual cases and assesses responsibility for behavior. In this activity he may see himself as a simple administrator or personnel manager making considered judgments about employment risks. If he takes this view, his diagnostic work merely expedites organizational procedures whereby men may be dismissed or "separated" from their jobs. Such men should be dismissed because, within the general "c and b" category, they are diagnosed as "emotionally unstable." "Instability" and "immaturity reactions" are also likely labels.

His past history was one of running away, delinquent behavior, distaste with the Army. His diagnosis was emotionally unstable personality, aggressive type, chronic moderate. Oh, he was one of these guys who was offered the Army or jail. . . . His history of running away, delinquent behavior and enuresis indicate a personality which is chronically unstable. He is not motivated to serve. It is very likely that retention on active duty will result in further immature and aggressive acts. And [so] I recommend that he be separated under [an administrative regulation].

In general, the diagnosis reflects the psychiatric acceptance of the idea that the military organization has "thrown up its hands," so to speak, and is ready to reject the man.

> This category tends to encompass the group that rocks the system. [The certificate recommending an administrative separation says] "No impairment," [so it is a] law enforcement rather than [a] psychiatric problem. [This type of separation allows for nice distinctions in the allotment of responsibility. The patient is either] unsuitable for our system [or] unfit for military service. . . . These people make waves, either [the] stormy AWOL way, or withdrawn or passive way. All of this behavior is kind of manipulative and disruptive. Military [authority] is less willing to keep these people than some of the sicker [in psychiatric terms, but who are not disruptive to the military system].

The implication is that, as far as psychiatry is concerned, punishment for such behavior may be just and deserved; however, it is not within the psychiatric province to consider the matter. Because the disorder is considered unappealing and untreatable, military psychiatrists are willing to diagnose but unwilling to give much attention to the "c and b."

> My rationalization for [facilitating] discharges through character and behavior disorder (diagnoses) is: I can't be of help. [The] line [commanders] can't hold them or they wouldn't get here.

And so an added implication suggested here is that the psychiatrist has no control in such matters, but he does possess evidence that such cases probably deserve the fate that befalls them. It is sometimes assumed that the whole referral and hospitalization system for the mentally ill really should not be put at the disposal of "c and b" cases who may really belong, quite simply, in jail.

> I feel that [Fort X] should keep its own character disorders, and take care of them down there. And a guy who is tearing up the place, and you think he is a character disorder, then you call the MP and have him thrown in the stockade. A person who is felt to be a character disorder, who is not . . . sick and has been seen by a competent psychiatrist, does not have to be sent to another hospital to control his behavior. There are plenty of jails where people who behave miserably are controlled.

A final assumption implicit within the use of this category is that sometimes psychiatrists will fully accept their part in judging such symptomatic behavior pejoratively and consider it right and proper to do so.

But often psychiatrists tend to feel harassed and disgruntled when forced to spend much time with such cases. They feel burdened when pressed by exigencies of military life to go beyond simple diagnosis.

> I regard a lot of the character and behavior disorders as a waste of time because, although they may be sick, I don't have the slightest idea what to do for them. And they're just making paper work for me. And they make lots of it. I've got a court martial coming up Monday that I have to testify at. . . . This is a young individual . . . exposed to a combat situation in Panama, and managed to get out of it by appearing to become hysterical or psychotic. . . . We sent him over to Medicine to have another disease worked up. He thought maybe they were using him for a guinea pig, so he got drunk, threatened suicide, and got back in our ward. After a couple of weeks, he bled all over me and I let him go out on pass. And he came back from pass drunk, a day late, pulled a gun on a nurse, demanded some Seconal—and from there on, the paper work really started to pile up. . . . And to me, it was just a total waste of time 'cause whatever his disorder is, it's not amenable to the type of psychiatry we're practicing right now.

Perhaps the implication here is that the psychiatrist really does not wish to enter into any extended negotiations about these cases once he has indicated his initial disinterest in them. However, the exigencies of military life sometimes restrict his leeway in these matters. And the reality that the psychiatrist constructs merely takes account of this restriction without much further comment.

To summarize, the use of the "c and b" label is applied by the psychiatrist to persons the psychiatrist accepts as disagreeable, aggravating, or otherwise unattractive to the military system. They have been given their chance for an evaluation to uncover some mental illness that might explain or excuse their behavior. If they had had a mental illness, an honorable "out" would have been provided. However, if a psychiatrist attests that they have no mental illness (but only a "quirk" or a "streak" of meanness, cowardice, depravity, hostility, or some other character flaw, as such are conceived in common-sense, lay evaluations) then they may take the consequences, as laid down in regulations, for whatever wrath they have incurred. The psychiatrist certifies that no moral, medical, or generally humanitarian considerations need mitigate the course of justice when he diagnoses "c and b."

In this area, then, there are many similarities between the psychiatric, the military, and the common-sense construction of judgments and the attribution of motives. But this general category of character and behavior disorder also includes some problems where these three perspectives are not so clearly parallel.

Such problems as alcoholism and homosexuality are usually categorized as "c and b." But there are a variety of special understandings to consider on behalf of such sufferers (or culprits—depending upon point of view). The exigencies which spur these considerations are peculiar to military settings and clearly illustrate the social pressures affecting a diagnosis. Accordingly, each of these problems is examined separately below.

ALCOHOLISM

Alcoholism is specifically exempted from the mental illness categories in the military psychiatric nosology. Thus alcoholics should be dismissed or "separated" from service. But in this case, the tendency informally encouraged by the military organization is to protect and excuse alcoholics rather than to use the full array of sanctions technically available. The view is embodied in the following expressions: "Give them another chance; try to rehabilitate them; suggest AA and other therapeutic devices to control the problem while the man remains on duty." Where these contradictions between regulation and informal policy exist, the negotiations over diagnoses can be seen most clearly. To facilitate opportunities for second chances, alcoholics or their intermediaries often request that the psychiatrist withhold the diagnosis of alcoholism in order to protect the offender from the formal requirement of prompt administrative separation. The argument for this exemption is usually made in terms of number of years the offender has already served. As in other types of diagnosis, length of service is an important consideration when formulating a diagnosis. But alcoholism may also be excused or ignored throughout the entire period of service.

> People don't want to get down and write "alcoholic" [on a man's record]. . . . The man's usually had 18 years experience. It is written all over his [medical] chart, but not . . . in black and white. It's inferred. They write all around and give you a diagnosis of [something else]. They don't want to ruin his career. Actually, they would probably do him a favor by saying it.

Sometimes the alcholics or their intermediaries who come to argue this point are high-ranking and powerful officers. Even when there are no such pressures, the possible injustice or hardship involved in "firing" a man, and so depriving him of an expected retirement pension, may weigh heavily with the psychiatrist.

> A major was hospitalized as a depressive. And the guy was a chronic alcoholic. . . . For ten years, on and off, he would get hospitalized every two or three years. . . . Once [he] got evacuated from Europe to Walter Reed. . . . All the time [for] depression, [and] the guy is an alcoholic—without question. He's also a very decorated soldier. . . . When sober, a very effective guy; when drunk, inadequate and couldn't stop. . . . And wouldn't show up for work. And people would cover up for him.
> . . . On the post . . . it became very obvious that the problem was alcohol and nothing else, (even though) alcohol never, never came up . . . on his records. And he denied it. The only reason I wondered about it was

that he showed up, the first time I saw him, . . . an hour late and drunk—and it was 9 or 10 o'clock in the morning. . . . I asked his commanding officer, "does this guy have a drinking problem?" [The colonel told me] "He drinks beer occasionally, but I've never seen him drunk." Nobody said he was an alcoholic. Well, the guy obviously was.

I don't think they knew, or they weren't willing to go that far in facing [the] alcoholic [question]. He admitted it himself. It got to the point. I hospitalized him twice: once for a short term, and saw him as an outpatient (afterward); put him on Antabuse, and I said, well this is a compromise. . . . The third hospitalization . . . I got him in AA.

But this time it came to post attention. The senior major and the colonel. . . . This was too much . . . too . . . many repeated instances of . . . not showing up for work. . . . I evacuated him to [a large military hospital], and I called [the hospital] and said, "Keep him and reassign him" . . . to save him from [the action that was beginning to start rolling on him]. I hospitalized him [with a diagnosis of] depression.

These considerations that the psychiatrist must weigh suggest that alcoholism may be associated with more "honorable" disabilities. And the alcoholic is more easily "managed" within the system than other deviants more abhorrent within the military framework (as the homosexual). The view that drinking is an important and manly pastime for a soldier is part of military culture. Thus, though the formal rules are similar in regard to both homosexuality and alcoholism, informal understandings require differing decisions or evaluations from the psychiatric practitioner.

HOMOSEXUALITY

A far greater bone of contention for many psychiatrists is created by the requirement that they diagnose homosexuality. Homosexuality is also specifically exempted from the mental illness or disease categories in the military regulations. If the psychiatrist makes this diagnosis, it is likely to result in a special punitive administrative separation (the Army regulations number is AR 635-89) which may then result in an undesirable discharge. Officially, then, the evaluation of homosexuality in the military is a pejorative judgment even though a medical doctor diagnoses it. Psychiatrists may refuse to use the diagnosis—or even to see the patient—until the CID (Criminal Investigation Department) men do their homework. In effect, they become the diagnostic agents. When finally diagnosed by the psychiatrist, the problem is to get the patient quickly out of the service. Separation rather than treatment is the military expectation whatever the personal or professional view of the psychiatrist who expedites this process.

A guy comes in here and says, "I'm queer." So I send in a report that says this guy tells me that he is queer. CID are the ones that do all this. They . . . get all the statements and take all the pictures. I personally think that, except for the obvious security risk involved, I don't see any reason why a homosexual can't be in the (service). Most of them . . . soldier fairly well.

However, less punitive types of administrative separations than the "89" may be arranged. In these situations, where the psychiatrist feels the military expectations contradict his own views of what is professionally appropriate, there are ways of managing cases so that diagnosis and disposition are more palatable to both doctor and patient. An often-mentioned technique in negotiating to escape the diagnosis of homosexuality is simply to withhold information. The CID may find itself in difficulty about producing evidence where homosexuality cannot be proven. The psychiatrist may refuse to keep notes so there is nothing to subpoena; or he may destroy any notes that have incriminating evidence. Another alternative is that he may keep records in such vague and ambiguous language that no evidence is provided by them. Particularly when evaluating referrals who have fears about potential homosexuality, the psychiatrist has the greatest leeway to influence disposition through his diagnosis. Here he is only limited in his discretion by the discretion of the referral. Here are examples of policy in this matter from an Army and then a Navy psychiatrist.

> . . . we specifically recommend [one of the other administrative discharges] and fought for no "89" [separations] unless a guy confessed [homosexuality] and [put it] in black and white, and there was no choice. . . . If a company commander has it in for a guy, and has a guy cold [on grounds of homosexuality], you don't go down the line for someone who has been nailed cold. Don't try to change reality, but use it [your discretion to be less punitive] when you have a chance of succeeding.

> A young sailor comes in and says—I think with a tremendous amount of pain—that he's a homosexual. You have got to decide whether he's homosexual and in a panic, or manipulating the decision [*i.e.*, trying to get out of the service on that pretext]. One way [to decide] is to indicate the dangers of this diagnosis and what's going to happen to him. Maybe a BCD [Bad Conduct Discharge] or DD [Dishonorable Discharge] if you confess, or if you dispute [the charge] and they find you guilty. I never said homosexual [made the diagnosis] unless he had already told someone. My first question always was: "Who else have you told?" When I went to my chief officer, *his* first question was: "Who else have you told?" [If the homosexual suspect had not told anyone] we would put him on the hospital ward for some length of time, and write up some sort of character disorder, EPTS [Existing Prior to Service] to get him out.

The power of the psychiatrist to effect the outcome through diagnosis is also enhanced by his own judgment about how to "stretch" an evaluation in cases which come to trial. By judicious commission of his speculations to the record, a psychiatrist can influence the outcome in the direction he desires. An ex-Air Force psychiatrist described his tactics in the following manner.

> A man in delivering cargo overseas got drunk and made a definite homo-
> sexual advance toward a member of his crew. I was called to give expert
> testimony. They wanted to know whether or not he was a homosexual. In
> my heart, I thought he was; but didn't take that position . . . what I did
> say was impossible to attack. I pointed out the vast quantity of alcohol the
> man had consumed. Enough to knock a man flat. I pointed out that a man
> coming out of anesthesia behaves in a way not regular [or usual]. [And I
> managed to get him off.]

Sometimes, to attain what he considers the appropriate end, the psychiatrist
will enter in direct private negotiation with the patient. Keeping a wary
eye on what incriminating evidence may already have been collected, what
antagonisms have already been provoked, and what chances yet remain for
the man to "make it" in the service, the psychiatrist offers the best "deal"
that he can.

> I haven't given anybody an "89." I have had two candidates for it, and I
> have talked to both of them and told them: "You have trouble. If you get
> caught, they will anchor you with this for life. You can get out on an ad-
> ministrative separation right now. Why don't you take it?" They always
> jump at it.

Conclusions

The preceding discussions of the management of specific types of deviance
suggest how deviant categories are socially constructed. Special social contexts, like that provided by the military setting, show very clearly that the
psychiatrist keeps well in mind a variety of contingencies that must be
taken into account in formulating a diagnosis. The diagnosis may become
the tangible representation of the way in which the psychiatrist negotiates
with or for the patient. The psychiatrist may use his diagnostic power to
negotiate *for* the patient with the system—buying time, opening the way
for leniency in the management of a case, suggesting a way out of some
difficulty. On the other hand, it cannot be forgotten that the psychiatrist is
also negotiating on behalf of the system, taking into account its coercive
and regulatory powers over both the patient and himself. The powers of
that system, the margins or boundaries to its regulations which cannot be
transgressed, the rulings that must be supported—these are all realities
that the psychiatrist translates into concrete, practical suggestions or recommendations when he signs certificates and presents diagnoses.

In this system, problems of diagnosis are inextricably mixed with
questions about appropriate disposition. This confusion of area arises
because psychiatry has always faced problems of circular reasoning in its
explanations of human behavior.[9] In situations where diagnostic procedures
carry clear consequences for disposition of cases, the principle seems to be:

Tell me what is feasible or reasonable to do with this person and I will give you a diagnosis which can explain, justify, or in some cases, modify that disposition.

These principles are by no means limited to the military setting. Circumscriptions also exist in courts of law where psychiatrists for the defense and the prosecution each have a vested interest in a type of diagnosis that either does or does not permit further legal action against an accused. And diagnoses have just such meaning in these settings. Such problems also exist in prison psychiatry where the amount of leniency that can be introduced by psychiatrists through the range of diagnoses is quite curtailed.[10] (Powelson and Bendix, 1955.) In these settings the predominance of punitive and custodial values makes it difficult to present diagnoses which suggest lenient dispositions. This pattern is found in military prisons as well. The effect of the prison or custodial establishment is to encourage the psychiatrist to diagnose in certain directions only. As one psychiatrist serving in a military prison explained the situation, the psychiatrist can only diagnose punitively.

> They [command authorities] give us the kiss of death for negative recommendations [to their policies]. . . . They use the psychiatrist for their own purpose—so he gets blamed [if the decision should later come up for unfavorable review on an appeal]. To hell with the psychiatrist when he goes against their wishes. . . .

The categories that the psychiatrist uses do not exist in a vacuum. They are not independent of the circumstances in which they arise. And the more circumscribed the system in which he operates, the more influenced he is in the direction taken by his evaluations of the behavior he examines. Thus one can anticipate that the bureaucratic expectations of prison or prisonlike total institutions will be reflected in certain tendencies or trends of psychiatric diagnoses and dispositions. These comparisons in settings for practice suggest, of course, that psychiatry may be adaptable, that new methods and theories may be developed out of adversity. However, they also suggest that the construction of psychiatric reality may be almost entirely social. The actual disease base or the actual significance of the presentation of symptoms may be of such slight importance in the formulation of diagnoses as to warrant our rephrasing of Marx's dicta once again. Being determines consciousness, and social pressures determine psychiatric nosology.

Notes

1. I would like to thank Rachel Kahn-Hut for help in editing this paper.
2. T. P. Wilson, "Conceptions of Interaction and Forms of Sociological Explanation," presented at the American Sociological Association Annual Meeting, San Francisco, September, 1969.

3. A. K. Daniels, "Military Psychiatry: The Emergence of a Sub-specialty," in E. Freidson and J. Lorber (eds.), *Reader in Medical Sociology* (New York: Atherton Press, 1970).

4. The research of which this study is a part has been conducted under various auspices: The U.S. Army Research and Development Command (No. DA-MD-49-193-66-G9209 & 2212), the National Institute of Child Health and Human Development (No. RO1 HD02776-01 BS), and an NIMH post-doctoral fellowship to study the relationship between military psychiatry and military legal procedures, 1F3-8885-01.

5. I would like to thank Colonel Roy E. Clausen, Jr., M.C. for his assistance in constructing the interview schedule.

6. A. K. Daniels, *op. cit.*

7. Of course, it must be understood that no psychiatric label or diagnosis is totally without consequences in the military organization, and any statement from a psychiatrist can ultimately be used by some official as a basis for requesting that a referral receive some kind of administrative action.

8. A. K. Daniels, "The Captive Professional: Bureaucratic Limitations in the Practice of Military Psychiatry," *Journal of Health and Social Behavior*, Vol. 10, No. 4, December 1969.

9. See T. S. Szasz, *The Myth of Mental Illness* (New York: Hoeber-Harper, 1961), and N. Zinberg, "Psychiatry: A Professional Dilemma" in K. Lynn (ed.), *The Professions in America* (Cambridge: Houghton Mifflin Company, 1965), pp. 154–169.

10. See H. Powelson and R. Bendix, "Psychiatry in Prisons" in A. Rose (ed.) *Mental Health and Mental Disease* (New York: W. W. Norton, 1955), pp. 459–481.

Selected Bibliography V

Becker, Howard S. *The Outsiders.* Glencoe, Illinois: The Free Press, 1963, pp. 1–18. Shows how responses to deviation shape deviant behavior. This reference should be compared with the one by Lemert, below.

Brookover, Wilbur B., Shailer Thomas, and Ann Paterson. "Self-Concept of Ability and School Achievement." *Sociology of Education,* vol. 37 (Spring 1964), pp. 271–278. Research relating self and role theory to classroom performance.

Cohen, Albert K. "The Sociology of the Deviant Act." *American Sociological Review,* vol. 30 (February 1965), pp. 5–14. An effort to integrate anomie theory with Mead's role theory.

Deutscher, Irwin. "Words and Deeds: Social Science and Social Policy." *Social Problems,* vol. 13 (Winter 1966), pp. 235–254. A careful consideration of the implications of research findings on inconsistencies between verbalized attitudes and overt behavior. Applies the perspective of symbolic interactionism in explaining the findings.

Elkin, Frederick. *The Child and Society.* New York: Random House, 1960, pp. 25–30. Describes the role of significant others in early socialization.

Faris, Ellsworth. "The Retrospective Act and Education." *Journal of Educational Sociology,* vol. 14 (October 1940), pp. 79–91. A contemporary of Mead's at the University of Chicago analyzes some educational implications of a common form of human behavior: viewing one's own past behavior.

Goffman, Erving. *Stigma: Notes on the Management of Spoiled Identity.* Englewood Cliffs, New Jersey: Prentice-Hall, Inc., 1963. Analyzes feelings toward self and others of such "discredited and discreditable" persons as the physically deformed, the ex-mental patient, the drug addict, the prostitute, and the ugly.

Haskell, Martin R. "Toward a Reference Group Theory of Juvenile Delinquency." *Social Problems,* vol. 8 (Winter 1960–1961), pp. 220–230. Exemplifies a growing tendency to incorporate symbolic interactionism into theories of delinquent and criminal behavior.

Lemert, Edwin M. *Social Pathology.* New York: McGraw-Hill Book Company, 1951, pp. 75–78. Introduces the concept "secondary deviation" to describe how the reactions of others reinforce the individual's deviance.

Lindesmith, Alfred R. "Problems in the Social Psychology of Addiction." In D. M. Wilner and G. G. Kassebaum (eds.) *Narcotics.* New York: McGraw-Hill Book Company, 1965. The author is a prominent student of drug addiction, which he views from the perspective of symbolic interactionism.

Lofland, John. *Deviance and Identity.* Englewood Cliffs, New Jersey: Prentice-Hall, Inc., 1969. A symbolic interactionist approach to the subject.

McPartland, Thomas S., John H. Cumming, and Wynona S. Garretson. "Self-Conception and Ward Behavior in Two Psychiatric Hospitals." *Sociometry,* vol. 24 (June 1961), pp. 111–124. Categorizing responses to the TST in an unusual way, the authors find support for certain basic propositions of symbolic interactionism.

Simmons, L. J. *Deviants.* Berkeley: The Glendessary Press, 1969. An elementary exposition of the labeling approach to the analysis of deviance.

Spitzer, Stephan P., and Norman K. Denzin (eds.) *The Mental Patient: Studies in the Sociology of Deviance.* New York: McGraw-Hill Book Company, 1968. Emphasizes the symbolic interactionist tradition.

Stewart, Robert L., and Glenn M. Vernon. "Four Correlates of Empathy in the Dating Situation." *Sociology and Social Research,* vol. 43 (March–April 1959), pp. 279–285. A processual conception of empathy is tested on 52 dating couples.

Turner, Ralph H. "Self and Other in Moral Judgment." *American Sociological Review,* vol. 19 (June 1954), pp. 249–259. Responses of 88 individuals and their friends toward the respondent's hypothetical involvement in a theft.

Vercors (Jean Bruller). *You Shall Know Them.* New York: Pocket Books, Inc., 1955. A novel that raises the question: What are the attributes which most clearly distinguish man from other living forms?

Waisanen, Fred B. "Self-Attitudes and Performance Expectations." *Sociological Quarterly,* vol. 3 (July 1962), pp. 208–219. Replication of a study on the relationship between self-attitudes and aspirations.

Conclusion

A brief summary and assessment of symbolic interactionism may help tie things together. Listed below are the basic theoretical propositions of the symbolic interactionist which have been presented, explicitly and implicitly, at various points in this book:

1. Mind, self, and society are most usefully viewed as processes of human and interhuman conduct.
2. Language is the mechanism for the rise of mind and self.
3. Mind is an importation of the social process—that is, of interaction—within the individual.
4. Human beings construct their behavior in the course of its execution, rather than responding mechanically to either external stimuli or such internal forces as drives, needs, or motives.
5. Human conduct is carried on primarily by the defining of situations in which one acts.
6. Socialization of a human being both enmeshes him in society and frees him from society. The individual with a self is not passive but can employ his self in interactions which may result in behavior divergent from group definitions.

Among the major adverse criticisms leveled at symbolic interaction theory have been (1) the indeterminism of many of its exponents, (2) its presumed inapplicability to broad, societal phenomena, (3) its neglect of the emotional dimension in human conduct, (4) its failure to come to grips with the unconscious, and (5) the limited researchability of some of its concepts.

1. Viewing human behavior in terms of the interaction between the "I" and the "Me" aspects of self, Mead's closest followers built into such

behavior an unpredictable, indeterminate dimension. For some, this interaction is the fundamental source of innovation in society. Exponents of the Iowa School, however, reject the "I" (indeterminism in human conduct) and the explanation of social innovation on the basis of the emergent, creative element in "I"–"Me" interaction.

2. In the running debate between advocates of symbolic interactionism and those of structural-functionalism, each side refers to the putative shortcomings of the other relative to level or scope of analysis. Thus, the former perspective is held to be limited to such microsociological phenomena as intra- and interpersonal relations, while the latter is presumed to apply only to such macrosociological phenomena as institutional and societal patterns. At the same time, adherents of each theory reject the restrictions in scope placed upon their theory by their opposite numbers.[1] Like so many other controversies in sociology and social psychology, this one still awaits a crucial test and resolution.

3. Mead's major ideas overlooked the role of emotional elements in human behavior and interaction. Modern symbolic interactionists have not significantly remedied this omission. The affective aspects of the self and of personal relationships are so thoroughly ignored, by all but a few writers, as to suggest an unacceptable image of man as purely rational.

4. Closely related to the preceding stricture is another that similarly concerns scanting of the irrational aspect in man. It is difficult to find a considered discussion of the "unconscious" in the writings of symbolic interactionists. The few references tend to renounce the concept without substituting adequate explanations.

5. It is with regard to its heuristic value that most critics of symbolic interactionism believe themselves to be on firmest ground.[2] The paucity of significant research generated by the theory is especially reflected in Part II and Part IV in this book. Contributing to this deficiency is the vague, "intuitive" character of various concepts of Mead's, some of which have not yet been revised or discarded. "Impulse," "meaning," the "I," "objects," "images," and other ambiguous and inconsistently used concepts persist in substantially the same non-operationalized form in which Mead used them.

The considerable number of researches in this book, and the many more that are left out, attest to the researchability of this perspective. Yet it must be admitted that such researches are still comparatively sparse—and difficult. This may be accounted for, in part, by the shortcomings enumerated above.

---

[1] See Helmut R. Wagner, "Displacement of Scope: A Problem of the Relationships between Small-Scale and Large-Scale Sociological Theories," *American Journal of Sociology*, vol. 69 (May 1964), pp. 571–584.

[2] For a recent example of such criticism, see Robert F. Bales, "Comment on Herbert Blumer's Paper," *American Journal of Sociology*, vol. 71 (March 1966), pp. 545–547.

Also influential is the symbolic interactionist injunction to "respect the nature of the empirical world and organize a methodological stance to reflect that respect."[3] The view of man as constructing his own behavior, and of human society as a *process* of interacting people, has appeared to be beyond the research capabilities of many social psychologists.

In face of the criticisms of symbolic interactionism, why has this frame of reference commended itself to most sociologically oriented social psychologists? The answer probably lies in the fact that symbolic interactionism clearly represents the most sociological of social psychologies. Adopting a distinctly sociological perspective, it directs attention to the social derivation of man's unique attributes; it presents mind and self as society in microcosm; it describes how the members of any human group develop and form a common world; it illuminates the character of human interaction by showing that human beings share one another's behavior instead of merely responding to each other's overt behavior; and, in numerous other ways, it implicates the individual with society and society with the individual.

The perspective of symbolic interactionism is not a finished product. A comparison of this volume with its earlier edition demonstrates some of the more recent changes. Among those we have already noted are the diffusion of its basic outlook from a few universities to many, the substantial increase in empirical studies, the ties with phenomenology and ethnomethodology, and the attention to deviant behavior.

The theory of symbolic interactionism affords us an explanation of its own development. Like other theories, symbolic interactionism undergoes continual construction, rather than expounding a received set of truths. Like other theories, it will be criticized and modified. Our hope is that the present volume will facilitate its testing and revision.

---

[3] Herbert Blumer, *Symbolic Interactionism: Perspective and Method* (Englewood Cliffs, New Jersey: Prentice-Hall, Inc., 1969), p. 60.

Index

F

family, 144, 156, 304, 332
  as non-criminal reference group, 492
  research, 433, 435-47
  and role perceptions, 464
  role specialization in, 284-9
  and role-taking, 474-9
Faris, C., 21, 29, 42
Faris, Ellsworth, 57, 58, 62, 63, 145, 173, 177, 185, 572
Faris, R. E. L., 59, 74
Fearn, Gordon, 434
  on self-conception and the emotionally disturbed role, 521-27
Fenichel, O., 42
Ferri, Enrico, 489
Fiedler, Fred E., 74
Foote, Nelson, 67, 74, 341, 342, 351-53, 354, 430, 435, 445, 447, 481
formal theory, 87, 89, 91, 245*n*.
formalized theory, 245-52
Frake, C. A., 126
French, J. R. P., 481
Frenkel-Brunswik, E., 36, 42
Freud, Sigmund, 2, 68
  Mead compared with, 23-43
  problems of, 27
Fromm, Erich, 36, 37, 42
functionalism, 28-31, 39-41
  and intra-psychic events, 32-9
functional analysis, 143
functional theory, 88-9

G

Gage, N. L., 481
Gallagher, Ruth, 66
Garfinkle, Harold, 3, 131, 132, 135, 136, 140, 144, 213, 214, 226, 319-20
  on common sense knowledge of social structures, 356-78
  on conditions of successful degradation ceremonies, 201-8
Garretson, Wynona Smutz, 66, 74, 572
Geer, Blanche, 3, 73
  comparison of participant observation and interviewing, 102-12
generalized other, 20, 148, 164, 169, 173, 441, 510
  and attitudes, 256-7
  and biological phenomena, 257-9

and criminality, 492-3
  in emotionally disturbed, 515
  internalization of, 272-4
  and particular others, 276
  and self-concept, 280-3
  and societal control, 397
generic relations, 95
Gerth, Hans, 74, 144, 343, 354
  on institutions and persons, 197-201
gesture, 324, 326
  conversation of, 17, 19, 53, 172, 438, 453
  definition of, 6
  emotional, 199
  and infrahuman communication, 6-7
  and internalization of roles, 199*n*.
  and meaning, 172
  meaning of, 7-8, 438, 442
  response to, 7-8
  and self, 9
  as sign, 438
  symbolic, 7, 79
Getzels, J. W., 74
Ghuryne, Govind S., 302
Gist, N. P., 302
Glaser, Barney G., 354, 433
  on awareness contexts and social interaction, 447-62
Glaser, Daniel, 70, 74, 434
  on criminality theories and behavioral images, 482-97
Glueck, E., 485, 496, 497
Glueck, S., 485, 496, 497
Goethe, 163
Goffman, Erving, 56, 67, 68, 74, 86, 87, 89, 91, 180, 226, 230, 358, 434, 453, 455-57, 572
  on presentation of self to others, 234-44
  on the moral career of the mental patient, 527-54
Goldhammer, H., 74
Goldstein, Kurt, 320
  on speech and thinking, 385-93
Goodenough, W., 126, 127
Gorden, R. L., 337, 354
Gough, H. G., 74
Gouldner, Alvin, 462
grand theory, 89, 91
gratification, 33-6, 40
  limited by environment, 41
Gross, E., 214, 226
Gross, Neal, 62, 74
group identification, 175
Grummon, Donald L., 73